Perspectives from *Historical Archaeology*:

The Archaeology of Native American-European Culture Contact

Compiled by
Timothy K. Perttula

No. 3

SOCIETY *for* HISTORICAL ARCHAEOLOGY

Compiled by: Timothy K. Perttula

Contact Information:
Timothy K. Perttula
Archeological & Environmental Consultants, LLC
10101 Woodhaven Dr.
Austin, TX 78753

Cover: Bellin, Jacques-Nicolas. *Carte De La Louisiane et Pays Voisins.* 1757.

Perspectives from Historical Archaeology is a reader series providing collected articles from the journal of the Society for Historical Archaeology (SHA). Published since 1967, Historical Archaeology is the oldest North American scholarly publication on the archaeology of sites and materials from the historic past, and one of the world's premier publications on this subject. Each volume in the *Perspectives* series is developed on either a subject or regional basis by a compiler, who selects the articles for inclusion and their order. The compilers also provide an introduction that presents an overview of the substantive work on that topic. *Perspectives* volumes offer non-archaeologists a convenient source for important publications on a subject or a region; an excellent resource for students interested in developing a specialization in a specific topic or area; as well as a convenient reference for archaeologists with an interest in the material.

The *Perspectives* series is managed by the SHA's Journal Editor and Co-Publications Editor and is published through the SHA's Print-On-Demand Press. Individuals interested in compiling a volume for publication through this series are encouraged to contact the Series Editors:

J. W. Joseph, PhD, RPA
Journal Editor, SHA
New South Associates, Inc.
6150 East Ponce de Leon Avenue
Stone Mountain, GA 30083
jwjoseph@newsouthassoc.com

Annalies Corbin, PhD
Co-Publications Editor, SHA
The PAST Foundation
1929 Kenny Road, Suite 200
Columbus, OH 43210
annalies@pastfoundation.org

Formed in 1967, the SHA is the largest scholarly group concerned with the archaeology of the modern world (A.D. 1400-present). The main focus of the society is the era since the beginning of European exploration. SHA promotes scholarly research and the dissemination of knowledge concerning historical archaeology. The society is specifically concerned with the identification, excavation, interpretation, and conservation of sites and materials on land and underwater. Geographically the society emphasizes the New World, but also includes European exploration and settlement in Africa, Asia, and Oceania. To learn more about the SHA and historical archaeology, visit www.sha.org.

Part I: Introduction

1. *Perspectives on Native American-European Culture Contact*
     Timothy K. Perttula...1

Part II: Colonial Perspectives

2. *Colonial Origins and Colonial Transformations in Spanish America*
     Kathleen Deagan (HA 2003 37(4):3-14).................................15

3. *An Encounter in the Baroque Age: French and Amerindians in North America*
     Marcel Moussette (HA 2003 37(4):29-39) 26

Part III: The Effects of Introduced Epidemic Diseases

4. *Correlates of Contact: Epidemic Disease in Archaeological Context*
     Dale R. Hutchinson and Jeffrey M. Mitchem (HA 2001 35(2):58-72)..........37

5. *Contact and Contagion: The Roanoke Colony and Influenza*
     Peter B. Mires (HA 1994 28(3):30-38)............................52

Part IV: Case Studies in North America

6. *Continuity and Change: De Soto and the Apalachee*
     Charles R. Ewen (HA 1996 30(2):41-53) 61

7. *Evidence of Early Spanish Contact on the Georgia Coast*
     Charles Pearson (HA 1977 11:74-83) 74

8. *San Luis de Talimali: The Archaeology of Spanish-Indian Relations at a French Mission*
     Bonnie G. McEwan (HA 1991 25(3):36-60) 84

9. *Native Americans and French Cultural Dynamics on the Gulf Coast*
     Diane E. Silvia (HA 2002 36(1):26-35)........................109

10. *Nativism, Resistance, and Ethnogenesis of the Florida Seminole Indian Identity*
     Brent R. Weisman (HA 2007 41(4):198-212)................119

11. *Presidio Los Adaes: Spanish, French, and Caddoan Interaction on the Northern Frontier*
    H. F. Gregory, George Avery, Aubra L. Lee, and Jay C. Blaine
    (HA 2004 38(3):65-77) 134

12. *Material Culture of the Koasati Indians of Texas*
    Timothy K. Perttula (HA 1994 28(1):65-77) 147

13. *Summer Island III: An Early Historic Site in the Upper Great Lakes*
    David S. Brose (HA 1970 4:3-33)...160

14. *"True Portraitures of the Indians, and of Their Own Peculiar Conceits of Dress":*
Discourses of Dress and Identity
    Rob Mann (HA 2007 41(1):37-52) 191

15. *Missions, Indians, and Cultural Continuity*
    Paul Farnsworth (HA 1992 26(1):22-36).......................................207

16. *Social Differentiation and Exchange among the Kumeyaay Indians during the*
Historic Period in California
    Lynn H. Gamble and Irma Carmen Zepeda (HA 2002 36(2):71-91).............222

17. *Chinookan Survival and Persistence on the Lower Columbia: The View*
from Kathlamet Village
    Rick Minor and Laurie E. Burgess (HA 2009 43(4):97-114) 243

18. *Representing Colonizers: An Archaeology of Creolization, Ethnogenesis,*
and Indigenous Material Culture among the Haida
    Paul R. Mullins and Robert Paynter (HA 2000 34(3):73-84) 261

19. *Russian Colonization: The Implications of Mercantile Colonial Practices in the*
North Pacific
    Kent G. Lightfoot (HA 2003 37(4):14-28) 273

20. *Russian Exploitation of Aleuts and Fur Seals: The Archaeology of Eighteenth*
and Early-Nineteenth Century Settlements in the Pribilof Islands, Alaska
    Douglas W. Veltre and Allen P. McCartney (HA 2002 36(3):8-17)...............288

Timothy K. Perttula

Perspectives on Native American-European Culture Contact

ABSTRACT

The introduction to this volume provides a perspective on archaeological studies of Native American-European culture contact in North America, as well as an overview of the contents of the selected articles included in this reader volume.

Introduction to the Volume

Archaeological research on Native American-European culture contact in North America has a long and distinguished history, one that can be traced back to the foundations of the discipline (Cusick 1998a; Silliman 2005a, 2005b; Loren 2008), that was brought into modern times by acculturation studies (cf. Cusick 1998b; see also Linton 1940; Quimby and Spoehr 1951) and classic publications such as Cycles of Conquest (Spicer 1962) and Europe and the People Without History (Wolf 1982). Other notable published studies on Native American-European contact over the past few decades, in a variety of contact settings, particularly across North America, include works by Fitzhugh (1985), Ramenofsky (1987), Smith (1987), Thomas (1989, 1990, 1991), Rogers (1990), Hudson and Tesser (1994), Cusick (1998a); Deagan (1998), Larsen (2001), Rubertone (2001), Wesson and Rees (2002), Rothschild (2003), Hutchinson (2006), Lightfoot (2005a, 2005b), Silliman (2005a), Kelton (2007), Gamble (2008), Loren (2008), Wade (2008), Ferris (2009), and Ethridge and Shuck-Hall (2009). Broader, comparative perspectives (e.g., Wilson and Rogers 1993; Gosden 2004; Stein 2005) concerning recent archaeological studies of colonial encounters are relevant to the field, as are archaeological studies in Australia (cf. Colley 2002; Harrison and Williamson 2004) and Africa (DeCorse 2001; Kelly 2002).

The interest in Native American-European culture contact is flourishing anew in part because of the 1990s focus on the Columbian Quincentenary which considered the "social, demographic, ecological, ideological, and human repercussions of European-Native American encounters" (Thomas 1991:xv).

Essentially, the archaeological interest in cultural change and continuity among Native American peoples beginning from their colonization of the New World more than 13,000 years is turned on its head in culture contact studies through focusing on the processes of profound cultural, demographic, environmental, and technological changes that were initiated a little more than 500 years ago through contacts, encounters, and colonial enterprises among vastly different cultures and peoples: Native Americans and Europeans, Africans, and people of mixed-blood (see Deagan 1998:35).

Mindful of Silliman's (2005b:58-59, 69) concerns regarding the use, and conflation, of terms such as culture contact and colonialism in archaeological studies of "the complete process of entanglement in all of post-Columbian North America" between Europeans and Native American peoples, culture contact from the perspective of this reader (especially the case studies in Part IV of this volume) explicitly emphasizes the Native American side of complex Native-European encounters and interactions, rather than solely the impact of European expansion on Native Americans or the rest of the world. In this sense, however, cultural contact is more than simply an account of "first contacts" between these different groups, but also concerns these Native American groups "struggling with power, domination, and economic transformation" (Silliman 2005b:69) in the colonial worlds they found themselves in. The articles in this reader deal with the theme of culture contact through their consideration of short- and long-term processes of many Native American entanglements with the European colonial world (cf. Silliman 2005b:59), and their incorporation within it. In other words, as Loren (2008:2) nicely put it, "culture contact was not a one-time European affair, but in fact characterized many small-scale and large-scale historical encounters and cultural entanglements of different groups of people with each other" (italics in the original).

The study of Native American-European culture contact in North America is foremost an opportunity to delve into the complex and diverse archaeological and historical records relating to both initial and sustained contact, as well as the consequences of these contacts—such as the introduction of diseases and declines in population, new social practices and social relations, and the forging of new identities—for the indigenous peoples of North America. Careful archaeological and historical study of European-Native American political and economic relationships in the colonial era, the types of interactions and encounters Native Americans had with Europeans at different times, the material evidence of those interactions, the effects of colonization and colonial practices on native societies, and the timing of disease and its demographic effects, have led to better understandings of the native histories of North America's indigenous peoples (e.g., Rogers 1990; Usner 1992; Rubertone 2001; Wesson and Rees 2002; Calloway 2003; Rothschild 2003; Silliman 2004, 2009; Lightfoot 2005a, 2005b; Tveskov 2007; Gamble 2008; Loren 2008; Ferris 2009).

The Society for Historical Archaeology (SHA) has devoted several issues of Historical Archaeology to topics of colonialism; creolization; French, Spanish, and Mexican colonial archaeology; and the archaeology of presidios that are concerned to varying degrees with different aspects of how Native American-European culture contact proceeded in North America. These include "The Archaeology of the Spanish Colonial and Mexican Republican Periods" (Farnsworth and Williams 1992a), "Creolization" (Dawdy 2000a), "French Colonial Archaeology At Old Mobile: Selected Studies" (Waselkov 2002a), "Colonial Origins: The Archaeology of Colonialism in the Americas" (McEwan and Waselkov 2003), and "Presidios of the North American Spanish Borderlands" (Bense 2004a). None of these Historical Archaeology thematic issues, however, has been explicitly assembled to focus directly on the archaeology of Native American-European culture contact, particularly a focus that emphasizes the Native American side of complex Native-European encounters and interactions. To date, SHA has not published a thematic issue that deals with Native American-European contact and interaction.

It is important, nevertheless, in this introduction to the volume to review the scope of these thematic issues because their content forms the foundational core of SHA's contributions to the study of Native American-European culture contact. First, the special volume edited by Farnsworth and Williams (1992a) was designed to call attention to research archaeological research concerning sites "that developed as part of Spanish America between 1492 and 1850" (Farnsworth and Williams 1992b:1) with contributions from Spain, North Africa, Mexico, the Caribbean, Spanish Florida, and northern New Spain. The various articles shared a particular focus on "the effects of Indian-Spanish interaction, or the impacts of changing economic relations throughout the Spanish empire, or both" (Farnsworth and Williams 1992b:1). The concern with "creolization" and the study of Native American-European culture contact comes from the use of the term to mean "a form of cultural interaction, culture contact, acculturation, transculturation, ethnogenesis, identity negotiation, the result of intermarriage, or the blending and transplantation of different traditions in material culture" (Dawdy 2000b:1). Each of these aspects of the creolization process are explored in the articles in this special volume of Historical Archaeology, several of which deals with Native Americans as part of multi-ethnic communities (Groover 2000; Loren 2000), with a particular focus on "localized cultural products of European colonialism: intensive human interaction, struggles for power, and the constructions of group/political identities" (Ferguson 2000:5). Loren (2005) further examines the process of creolization in the French and Spanish colonies in the Southeastern U.S.

In the case of the Old Mobile volume edited by Waselkov (2002a), one of the many research themes under archaeological investigation at this early capitol (1702-1711) of the Louisiana colony is the impact of European—specifically French—colonization efforts on the many Native American societies living on the northern Gulf Coast (McEwan 2002; Waselkov 2002b:6, 10-11). Papers in that volume also addressed other archaeological concerns regarding "the French presence in North America" (Moussette 2002:143).

The series of papers in McEwan and Waselkov (2003:1) were presented at a plenary session of the Society for Historical Archaeology at its 35th annual meeting (January 2002) in Mobile, Alabama. The presentations dealt with the archaeology of colonialism in the Americas, specifically Spanish, French, Russian, and British colonialism (see Parts II and IV, below), with a particular focus on what has been learned about "the social and intercultural complexities of individual colonies through time and of developing theoretical models that permit meaningful comparisons to be drawn" through the archaeological study of colonialism (McEwan and Waselkov 2003:1).

Bense's (2004b:5) consideration of presidios on the North American Spanish Borderlands emphasizes the distinctive type of frontier settlement in this part of the continent, and the effects of Native American-European contact at those specific contact locales. In particular, the study of presidios leads to the conclusion that "their residents were the frontline of culture contact and change. Cultural and biological hybrids developed at frontier presidios" (Bense 2004b:5).

Colonial Perspectives

Part II includes two articles that provide broad perspectives on the character of Spanish and French colonial enterprises in North America (see Bitterli [1989]; Gosden [2004]; as well as the volume edited by Stein [2005] for comparative studies of colonial encounters in various parts of the world). Kathleen Deagan's chapter (Chapter 2) on Spain's colonial expansion into the Americas in the 16th century makes clear that it was "an invasion, a colonization effort, a social experiment, a religious crusade, and a highly structured economic enterprise" (Deagan 2003:3). How these patterns and practices—among them the conversion of Native Americans to Catholicism, the control of land and labor, life in towns versus life on the frontier, and ethnogenesis through intermarriage and consensual relationships (Deagan 2003:4-8)—were formed, transformed, and crystallized across Spanish colonial America because of culture contact led to the creation of multiple, distinctive, and new cultural identities, influences, and experiences across the Americas (see also Deagan 1988, 1996, 1998; McEwan 2001).

In Chapter 3, Marcel Moussette takes a different angle in his consideration of French and Native American encounters in North America, one that deemphasizes in this particular context the economic efforts of the French colonies, in particular the economic realities of the fur trade (see Loren 2008:38-42). Moussette is particularly interested in the specific nature of the encounters between the French and native peoples, leading as they did to cultural metissage and political alliances. He proposes that contact led to a "deepening of the relationships among the peoples involved" (Moussette 2003:30), and suggests that this contact progressed from an encounter to sustained contact, then exchange (primarily in economic terms), and finally metissage, or the

mixing of cultures. Mousette (2003:31) believes that the underlying character of French-Native American encounters can be attributed to "a certain compatibility with one another... in the structure of mental universes, with all the ensuing consequences this may have for the world vision of each, the relation to the Other, and the negotiation of each one's own identity." A bipartite or dual ideology and system of representation shared by Native peoples and the French led to accommodations between both groups, and created the conditions for cultural metissages (Mousette 2003:36).

The Effects of Introduced Epidemic Diseases

Part III of this reader has two articles that address the effects of European introduced diseases among Native American populations in two different areas of North America: Virginia and Florida. The concerted study of European epidemic diseases in the New World by historians, ethnohistorians, and archaeologists has led to the near universal conclusion that the introduction of these diseases had catastrophic effects on Native American population—leading eventually to population declines among Native groups at their nadir to as much as 90 percent after European contact—as well as significant social and cultural effects (e.g. Crosby 1972; Ramenofsky 1987, 1990, 1993; Dobyns 1983; Smith 1987; Thornton 1987; Watts 1997; Thomas 1989, 1990, 1991; Cook 1998; Alchon 2003; Kelton 2007; Loren 2008; Warrick 2008). But even with the recognition that European-introduced diseases led to the massive decline of native populations in the Americas over the long-term, recent studies have focused less on the possibility of a uniform and continental demographic collapse among Native American peoples immediately following first contact. Rather, it seems more likely that the effects of epidemic diseases on Native peoples were "highly variable and regionally specific" (Silliman 2005a:276), and were dependent on a host of factors, among them when contact first took place and how sustained it was; the types of diseases that may have been introduced by Europeans; the consequences of warfare, famine, and resettlement brought on by many, if not most, European incursions; as well as the demographic and settlement character (i.e. nucleated vs. dispersed, sedentary vs. mobile) of Native communities during and after first contact. To place demographic changes among Native American peoples in a broader context, it is important to "examine the entire suite of dynamic interactions that shaped and altered the ecological and social landscape of the colonies. Epidemiological studies of modern populations support the view that broad-scale disease epidemics likely occurred after the establishment of permanent colonial centers, when the combined effects of resettlement and reorganization of native lifeways inaugurated changes that facilitated acute infectious disease" (Hutchinson 2006:173).

Dale L. Hutchinson and Jeffrey M. Mitchem (Chapter 4) consider the bioarchaeological evidence from the ca. A.D. 1525-1550 burial component at the Tatham Mound in central Florida to evaluate the possibility that European-introduced diseases may have played a primary role in possible early catastrophic demographic collapse among Southeastern U.S. aboriginal groups (Hutchinson and Mitchem 2001:67; see also Larsen 2005; Hutchinson 2006). At Tatham Mound, an aboriginal mound site likely situated along the route of the de Soto expedition, the large bioarchaeological sample (187 individuals from primary and secondary burials) had no skeletal evidence of infectious diseases (but acute infectious diseases rarely leave skeletal evidence), but two skeletal elements had evidence for sword cuts; these burials may be from a large contemporary death event, but distinctive mortuary behaviors could also account for the large number of contemporaneous burials. In any case, there does not appear to have been any change in mortuary ritual from pre- to post-contact burials at the Tatham Mound (Hutchinson 2006:169). Their consideration of the literature on the introduction and effects of epidemic diseases on Native American societies leads Hutchinson and Mitchem to conclude that there was no immediate and universal demographic collapse at or immediately after the initial contacts with European explorers. Instead, they conclude that the "timing, speed, and magnitude" of cultural changes to Native Americans from a variety of long-term social, political, economic, and biological factors "varied from population to population and region to region, just as the composition and size of native populations themselves varied, and the type of contact varied" (Hutchinson and Mitchem 2001:67).

Chapter 5 by Peter B. Mires examines the devastating effects of the introduction of influenza among the Powhatan on Virginia's Atlantic shore by the establishment of the Roanoke colony in 1585-1586. Mires suggests that the "Roanoke colonists themselves were the vectors of death" (Mires 1994:33). Mires concludes that at least one aboriginal village was abandoned as a direct result of rapid depopulation caused by a European disease, although he cautions that detailed archaeological evidence in this case is needed to determine whether demographic change arising from initial Native American-European contact "occurred swiftly over large regions, or can be characterized by more temporal and spatial complexity" (Mires 1994:35).

Case Studies in North America

The majority of chapters in Part IV of this book provide a good sampling of the range of archaeological case studies of Native American-European culture contact in North America that have been published in *Historical Archaeology*. These archaeological studies included herein range in time from the early 16th century to the late 19th century, and concern Native American groups living in the southeastern United States (the Apalachee, Mobile, and Seminole), northwestern Louisiana (the Caddo) and eastern Texas (the Koasati), the upper Great Lakes (possibly the Potawatomi or Huron, although no specific ethnic identity was offered by Brose [1970:27-28]), the Mid-continent (the Potawatomi and Miami Indians), California (Kumeyaay, Coastal Miwok, and Pomo), Oregon (Chinook), British Columbia (Haida), and Alaska (the Aleuts Alutiiq, and Chugach), and consider a diverse range of contact situations and the different geo-political realities of contact with Spanish, French, British, American, and Russian explorers, colonists, missionaries, traders, mercantilists, and military forces. The social, economic, and demographic results of a changing world for Native American groups after initial contact with Europeans led to an incredible diversity of adaptations in an increasingly hostile and marginalized colonial world, as demonstrated in archaeological, ethnohistorical, and historical/archival research (cf. Lightfoot 1995). The diversity in contact and geo-political settings in these different parts of North America had and continues to have consequent effects on the adaptive possibilities of Native groups over time, the establishment and maintenance of cultural traditions (see essays in Pauketat [2001]), as well as the character of the archaeological and historical records available for culture contact studies.

Charles R. Ewen, in Chapter 6, tackles the consequences of Native American-European contact directly by summarizing relevant material evidence obtained in the archaeological investigation of the Governor Martin site in northern Florida. This site is an Apalachee village that was occupied by Hernando de Soto and his army for five months in 1539-1540 (Ewen 1996; see also Ewen and Hann 1998). Ewen expected that the long-term consequences of European contact, particularly change caused by disease-introduced catastrophic change, would be evident in the archaeological record from this important village in the Apalachee province because "contact occurred early and more directly in Apalachee than in the interior chiefdoms of the Southeast" (Ewen 1996:42). What the material evidence from the Apalachee village showed, however, was that although there were changes in the archaeological record at this village, including the adoption and use of European goods, there were no substantial changes in native ceramic or lithic technologies nor radical changes in settlement patterns or regional population densities. From these disparate lines of evidence, Ewen (1996:51) suggest that, "the impact of European diseases upon the New World, although considerable, was probably highly variable." Bioarchaeological studies of Native American groups in Florida (although not including the Governor Martin site, as only two burials were excavated there), and elsewhere in the Spanish borderlands, have clearly shown that the effects of European contact on health, population/demography, and adaptations were complex and diverse through time and across Native American space (e.g. Baker and Kealhofer 1996; Larsen 2001, 2005; Stojanowski 2005).

In Chapter 7, Charles Pearson (1977) discusses the archaeological discovery of ca. A.D. 1540-1560 European goods (Nueva Cadiz glass beads, copper Spanish coins, iron axes, an iron awl, an iron knife, and iron spikes) from aboriginal burials in the Taylor Mound on St. Simons Island on the Georgia coast. Although these materials represent the very early aboriginal use of European goods by a Native American group along the Georgia coast, Pearson (1977:82) suggests these goods were likely obtained through aboriginal exchange networks rather than being a product of "actual Spanish occupation." In this area, Spanish missions were not established until ca. A.D. 1580 (see Thomas 1987, 2008).

Bonnie G. McEwan's contribution in Chapter 8 is a detailed study of the archaeology of the San Luis de Talimali village and mission (1656-1704) established by the Spanish in the Apalachee province of present-day northwestern Florida. The mission system established by the Spanish among the Apalachee represent "the frontier of cultural exchange between relatively isolated Spanish and local native populations" (McEwan 1991:36). The Apalachee were expected to provide labor and goods to the missionaries, as part of the Spanish attempts to "civilize" them (see also McEwan 2001), and the Spanish authorities attempted to establish new forms of social and political control, allegiances, and obligations between themselves and the Apalachee.

Extensive archaeological investigations at San Luis de Talimali identified a massive (36 m in diameter) Apalachee council house that sat across the plaza from the Spanish mission church complex. The character of its construction, and the material goods recovered in the council house make clear that "the Spanish exerted little influence over the ways by which the Apalachee organized their ritual and civic ceremonies" (McEwan 1991:43). The same may be said for Apalachee material culture (especially the technology and form of weaponry and native ceramics), although some ceramic Colono-ware (cf. Cordell 2002) reflects the manufacture by native potters of certain vessel forms intended for European use in the village. In some cases, Apalachee women played significant roles in Spanish households at San Luis de Talimali. Archaeological investigations in the Spanish part of the village also indicate that Hispanic traditions of architecture, use of certain material goods, and diet were maintained, although cultivated plants grown by the Apalachee remained the dietary staple of both native and Spanish groups. Changes in burial practices suggest there may have been some religious conversions among the Apalachee during the mission occupation, but it appears more likely that these practices reflect a considerable degree of Spanish-Indian accommodation and "cultural tolerance" (McEwan 1991:58).

Archaeological investigations in the Old Mobile area of the Alabama Gulf Coast has provided important insights into the effects of contact between

French colonists at Old Mobile (1702-1711) and local Native American groups (the Mobile and Tomes), as well as Apalachees and Chatos that had left Spanish missions in Florida. Diane Silvia's chapter (Chapter 9) demonstrates that there was "intense interaction between French and Indians throughout the 18th century, and a lengthy dependence on aboriginal wares by the colonists" (Silvia 2002:31). The occurrence of colono-wares at sites in the Old Mobile area is seen as evidence of material assimilation by Native Americans, more specifically by Apalachee Indian settlers in the area, who made colono-wares that are similar to vessel forms they had made in their Florida homeland. In other material terms, French trade goods were abundant in Native American contexts, as were aboriginal ceramics and lithic artifacts. Native American and French structures could be differentiated by "location, orientation, building technique, size and shape" (Silvia 2002:32), as well as by the composition and proportion of both European and Native American goods in their associated artifact assemblages. Overall, contact between Native Americans and the French in the Old Mobile area was based on close social interaction and stable reciprocal relationships in food ways and material exchanges.

Brent R. Weisman (Chapter 10) employs material evidence recovered from ca. 1835-1842 Seminole sites in Florida to make the case that the ethnogenesis of the Seminole can be traced to military conflict (the Second Seminole War) with the U.S. army. Weisman argues that Seminole ethnogenesis is "seen largely as a nativistic phenomenon influenced strongly by resistance to American domination" (Weisman 2007:198; see also Weisman 2000). Processes that were important in leading to this ethnogenesis or new ethnic identity included the active rejection of American cultural influences (i.e., rejecting American cultural ways in favor of traditional technologies and lifeways), the equalizing of power relations between Americans and Seminole through the display of trophy clothing, and gift giving as a way to strengthen clan ties. The archaeological expression of these processes on Seminole sites are seen in the continued use of a native ceramic tradition, the absence of European-American ceramics, the appearance of military buttons on these sites—indicating that Seminole warriors were wearing captured U.S. military uniforms—and the strengthening of clan ties

as seen in new burial practices. The combination of traditional behaviors, when allied with new adaptive responses brought on by external political and military conflicts, led to the survival of the Seminole peoples even in the face of intense cultural contacts with a hostile American government.

The archaeological record at Presidio Los Adaes, the capitol of Texas between 1721-1773, preserves in material evidence the development and maintenance of a long-standing and mutually respectful relationship between the local Native American population (the Adaes tribe) in Caddo lands (Barr 2007; Wade 2008); the Spanish soldiers and missionaries (from the nearby mission San Miguel de Cuellar de los Adaes); and French colonists living less than 20 miles away at the Natchitoches trading post and civil settlement (see also Loren 2001, 2008). Gregory et al. (2004) (Chapter 11) attribute the unique and symbiotic character of the contact situation at Los Adaes to its remoteness on the Spanish Texas frontier, the absence of French missionary efforts, the willingness of the French population to intermarry with both the Spanish and Caddo groups, unrestricted French trade, and the political/economic savvy of the Caddo (Gregory et al. 2004:65): "The Caddo Indians viewed the Spanish [at Los Adaes] more as a source for material goods rather than spiritual edification." The material culture found in excavations at Los Adaes is dominated by sherds from Caddo ceramic vessels, indicating their use by Spanish soldiers and the governor of Texas, along with a wide variety of Spanish and French goods, including tin-enameled ceramics, French wine bottles, lead seals from bolts of cloth, knives and gun parts, as well as Spanish horse gear and weaponry as well as metates and manos brought from Mexico.

Perttula's contribution to this volume (Chapter 12) concerns the Koasati or Coushatta Indians who had moved into Spanish Texas in the 1790s (Perttula 1994:65-77). Their diaspora from what is now Alabama was a result of their choice not to associate with the British and American traders and settlers who had moved into Creek Indian territory after the French and Indian War and the American Revolution (Shuck-Hall 2008). The study of the material culture of the Koasati Indians living in Texas illustrates the extent and character of cultural contacts between the Koasati themselves, Euro-Americans, and Texans, particularly through the lens of the deer hide trade; the Koasati were also successful herders and agriculturists. By the time the Koasati had resettled in Texas, they, along with their Creek Indian brethren (e.g., Knight 1985; Waselkov 1992) were experienced consumers of European trade goods as such goods had become increasingly available to individual households (see Wesson 2008). The range and diversity in the types of European goods used by the Koasati included ornaments, metal containers, tools, dishes, and guns. However, Perttula's study also documented the continued importance of native culinary traditions as seen by the use of Koasati-made ceramic vessels for the cooking, processing, and storage of foodstuffs.

The late 17th century occupation at the Summer Island site on Lake Michigan in the Upper Great Lakes represents an aboriginal encampment of a small number of extended families of uncertain ethnic identity whose focus, David S. Brose (Chapter 13) argued, was on the hunting of deer and other hide and fur-bearing animals for the burgeoning French and British fur trade (Brose 1970:27). The Native American participation in the fur trade at this early date was seen as the best means to obtain European trade goods upon which they eventually became dependent, and this apparently led to the collapse of pre-contact exchange networks between farmers, fishermen, and hunters living in the Upper Great Lakes. The majority of European trade goods at the Summer Island site were items of personal adornment or jewelry, as well as iron tools (awls, fish hooks, knives, and a needle), lead balls, and a gunflint, while aboriginal chipped stone tools and ceramic vessels remained important. On that basis, Brose (1970:23) suggested that the material culture of the aboriginal group encamped at Summer Island "had not been too greatly altered by the contact with European trade."

The ethnogenesis of a multi-ethnic fur trade society in the Wabash Valley, in the Great Lakes region between ca. 1830-1850, is the subject of Rob Mann's contribution (Chapter 14). This society was comprised of Native American groups like the Potawatomi and Miami, French Canadiens, and Métis individuals (Mann 2007:38). Mann's concern is with their mode of dress and styles of personal ornamentation, as adduced from contemporary paintings and archaeological findings of dress-related artifacts from the Cicott Trading Post, as "a constitutive component of" fur trade society ethnogenesis (Mann 2007:46). He concludes that the members of this Great Lakes fur trade society actively were creating a new social grouping and unique identity through a variety of seemingly mundane practices, among them new styles of dress and personal ornamentation that employed Anglo-American goods in inventive combinations.

Paul Farnsworth's contribution (Chapter 15) to this volume is a study of archaeological assemblages from late 18th to early 19th century Mission Nuestra Senora de la Soledad, Mission San Antonio de Padua, and Mission La Purisima Concepcion in Alta California (see also Deetz's [1963] earlier pioneering study of Mission La Purisima). His purpose is to devise through material culture analysis a means to explicitly measure "the rate and degree of culture change represented in archaeological assemblages from the California Missions" (Farnsworth 1992:22). Farnsworth created several categories and indices based on material that he felt measured culture change, including measurements of "continuity of traditional culture, continuity of new culture, intensity of cultural exchange, availability of imported goods, and degree to which new culture is supplying unchanged traditional culture" (Farnsworth 1992:Table 4). The results of these analyses indicated that California Indians in the missions maintained much of their traditional culture while living at the missions, although "the longer the Indians were in the missions, the more acculturated they became" (Farnsworth 1992:33). Cultural changes experienced by the California Indians in the missions also appear to be closely linked with changes in the development, intensification, and character of the Spanish colonial economic structure in Alta California.

In Chapter 16, Lynn H. Gamble and Irma Carmen Zepeda consider the effects of European contact (missionization, the occurrence of epidemic diseases, and the seizure of California Indian lands) on the Kumeyaay Indians of the San Diego area during the period from A.D. 1769-1850 through the archaeological findings from the Amat Inuk site. They accomplish this by examining two distinctive characteristics of Kumeyaay society: long distance exchange of shell beads with other Native American societies, particularly the Chumash (see Gamble 2008), and sociopolitical complexity as adduced from mortuary analysis. Their findings are that a complex but traditional exchange network of shell beads remained intact long after the establishment of Mission San Diego de Alcala, and that grave good associations (of both native and non-native goods) indicate the existence of status differentiation by individuals and certain family groups (Gamble and Zepeda 2002:86-87). That traditional exchange networks established by the Kumeyaay and other native California societies persisted more than 80 years after Spanish colonization is notable "given the attempt by the Spaniards to destroy the traditional life of California Indians" (Gamble and Zepeda 2002:87).

Rick Minor and Laurie Burgess (Chapter 17) compare the accounts of the Chinookan Kathlamet on the lower Columbia River as reported by Lewis and Clark and other explorers with archaeological materials from the Kathlamet Village site. The Kathlamet Village site was located on the south shore of the Columbia River on a point now known as Aldrich Point. The settlement was observed by Meriwether Lewis and Willam Clark during their expedition, in 1805 and 1806, and Minor and Burgess (2009:97) note that "William Clark referred to Indians 'of a nation who reside above and on the opposit [sic] Side who call themselves Calt-har-ma.'" Lewis and Clark commented at length on the canoes of the Kathlamet and of their ability as navigators and paddlers, and described the Kathlamet as middlemen in trade along the Columbia. However, early ethnographic research along the Columbia by Verne Ray (1938) and others stated that the Kathlamet were devastated by European-introduced diseases and had abandoned their village by 1810 and joined with the Wahkakum as elements of the Upper Chinookan. Minor and Burgess' analysis of artifacts recovered from the Kathlamet Village site indicated that the village survived until the mid 19th century. They thus urge caution in the consideration of ethnographic surveys on cultural identities, and state "that little is gained, and much is lost, by lumping distinct local groups of Chinookans like the Kathlamet into 'ethnic units' based on their disasterous experiences in the post-contact world (Minor and Burgess 2009:111).

Paul Mullins and Robert Paynter (Chapter 18) look at the archaeology of creolization and ethnogenesis through a consideration of specific aspects of the material culture of the Haida Indians of the Queen Charlotte Islands in British Columbia, namely the 19th century manufacture of carved argillite pipes of different styles and representational art produced for the European trade. According to Mullins and Paynter (2000:81), the continued manufacture of these trade goods by the Haida "were a constant production whose stylistic shifts confronted, mediated, or evaded the material and social dynamism of colonization in the Queen Charlotte Islands." In other words, Haida material culture as seen from the perspective of argillite pipe styles represents "an active negotiation of colonial power relations," one that draws its significance from both native and colonial power relationships, inequality, conflict and conflict resolution, and mediation. How the Haida chose to represent Europeans in their material culture was a reaffirmation of their own cultural traditions and their view of the place of their European colonizers.

In Chapter 19, Kent G. Lightfoot discusses Russian colonization in North America, which was specifically based on the development of an extensive maritime fur trade (sea otter and fur seal) between ca. 1740 and 1867. A key component of the Russian colonization effort was the forced resettlement of native and creole workers to colonies in Alaska, Russia, Hawaii, and California, which "had significant consequences for the composition of multiethnic communities and the kinds of colonial encounters that took place with indigenous communities" (Lightfoot 2003:15; see also Lightfoot 2005a, 2005b; Lightfoot et al. 1998). For the Russian colonists, native peoples living in the North Pacific were primarily important as sources of cheap labor, as they "were dependent on native producers to provide them with pelts" (Lightfoot 2003:21), and they developed practices such as resettlement/relocation, tribute (iasak), and hostage taking to insure that the labor of native and multi-ethnic workers was available. Russian colonization left a significant legacy of cultural impacts to native populations, but the archaeological evidence from Russian colonial sites points to "the strong persistence of native cultural beliefs and practices" (Lightfoot 2003:23). Lightfoot (2003:24) attributes this to the efforts of local indigenous peoples to actively create and re-create native identities when confronted with Russian colonial practices.

The final chapter in Part IV of this reader is a 2002 article by Douglas W. Veltre and Allen P. McCartney on what the late 18th and early 19th century (ca. 1786-1820) archaeological record from the Pribilof Islands, Alaska, contributes to the study of Native Alaska cultural change following the

Russian colonization of Alaska. Russian colonization practices and relationships with Native groups "were determined by the desirability of continuous, uninterrupted trade" (Black 2004:xiii).

As part of fur hunting enterprises, the Russian-American Company's exploitation of Alaskan natives was based on their compelling "Aleut men to work for them, often taking them away from their families an villages for long periods" (Veltre and McCartney 2002:9). On the Pribilof Islands, the Russians established work camps with male Aleut laborers. European diseases and violent conflicts led to an estimated 80 percent decline in Aleut populations within 50 years of the first Russian contact, and there were changes in native settlement patterning, house forms, religious practices, and social organization. The material culture evidence from the Aleut work camps is a combination of both native artifacts, such as stone projectile points and whale bone harpoon pieces, and Russian-traded goods, among them glass beads and metal tools.

Future Prospects

As this volume illustrates, there have been a number of articles in past issues of Historical Archaeology, especially since the 1990s, that have been concerned with the study of Native American-European culture contact, in its broadest sense and in eras of progressive mercantilism, colonialism, and globalization (Earle 2008:199), These studies have examined various first encounters in different colonial settings in North America. The archaeological study of culture contact in the early 21st century in North America is one where acculturative models (e.g., Quimby and Spoehr 1951) and simple dichotomous models of culture contact and change are being replaced by approaches that examine agency, individual choices, social memory, and practices/traditions among different Native American groups in culture contact and colonial entanglements (see Rubertone 1989; Thomas 1989, 1990, 1991; Wilson and Rogers 1993; Lightfoot 2005b; Worth 2006; Loren 2008; Silliman 2009:213). Such a multi-varied perspective, when viewed in an historical dimension, should lead to a more nuanced consideration of material culture evidence and other aspects of the archaeological and historical records of culture contact to understand strategies and responses—some successful, some not—by Native

American groups that are not necessarily apparent from either just archaeological, historical, or oral historical records, but that are synthetic in perspective (Silliman 2009). In these respects, the archaeological study of cultural contact and colonialism, at least from the perspective of their effects on Native American individuals, communities, and populations, is becoming more about recognizing through material culture and archaeological context identity negotiation, tactics, and context/historical and social situations in the archaeological sites occupied in the post-Columbian North American world.

The study of the material culture evidence found on Native American sites occupied in post-Columbian times is fundamental to understandings reached about Native American responses to their multi-faceted encounters with Europeans, as well as the consequences of those encounters (Kelly 2005:1125). Depending on the time and context, European goods on Native American sites may be many times more revealing about gift exchanges and Native social relationships (within a Native community and between different Native groups) than they are about participation in European colonial or market economies or as evidence of the adoption of functionally mundane commodities that may have "replaced" traditional material culture goods. It is important in culture contact studies to look beyond the obvious (i.e., the presence of European goods on Native American sites) to concentrate on what those European goods may reveal about Native American practices and strategies through a native-centric perspective. Such a perspective emphasizes local actions and the beliefs and traditions of individuals, communities, and populations—from both short- and long-term diachronic measures—of Native American peoples for their explanatory power. It is in how these material culture items were produced, used, and/or modified by Native Americans that the archaeologist needs to be cognizant of when studying the material products of European-Native American culture contact in colonial settings.

Archaeologists and bio-archaeologists are currently focused on the complexity of "landscapes of contact" (Silliman 2005a), and such research holds great promise to "illuminate the Native American side of colonialism and culture contact and the material aspects of everyday life" (Silliman 2005a:292). This focus leads to the recognition that the continued detailed study of culture contact and colonial entanglements between Native Americans and Europeans, from case studies such as the ones published over the years in Historical Archaeology as well as in a plethora of books and journal articles published in North America and Europe by other institutions and research facilities, represent a unique opportunity to advance the archaeological understanding of Native American life both before and after Europeans came to America's shores.

REFERENCES

ALCHON, SUZANNE AUSTIN
2003   *A Pest in the Land: New World Epidemics in a Global Perspective.* University of New Mexico Press, Albuquerque, NM.

BAKER, BRENDA J. AND LISA KEALHOFER (EDITORS)
1996   *Bioarchaeology of Native American Adaptation in the Spanish Borderlands.* University Press of Florida, Gainesville, FL.

BARR, JULIANA
2007   *Peace came in the Form of a Woman: Indians and Spaniards in the Texas Borderlands.* University of North Carolina Press, Chapel Hill, NC.

BENSE, JUDITH A.
2004a   (Editor) Presidios of the North American Spanish Borderlands. *Historical Archaeology* 38(3):1-153.
2004b   Introduction: Presidios of the North American Spanish Borderlands. *Historical Archaeology* 38(3):1-5.

BITTERLI, URS
1989   *Cultures in Conflict: Encounters Between Europeans and Non-European Cultures, 1492-1800.* Stanford University Press, Stanford, CA.

BLACK, LYDIA T.
2004   *Russians in Alaska, 1732-1867.* University of Alaska Press, Fairbanks, AK.

BROSE, DAVID S.
1970   Summer Island III: An Early Historic Site in the Upper Great Lakes. *Historical Archaeology* 4:3-33.

CALLOWAY, COLIN G.
2003   *One Vast Winter Count: The Native American West before Lewis and Clark.* University of Nebraska Press, Lincoln, NA.

COLLEY, SARAH
2002   *Uncovering Australia: Archaeology, Indigenous people and the Public.* Smithsonian Institution Press, Washington, D.C.

COOK, NOBLE DAVID
1998   *Born to Die: Disease and New World Conquest, 1492-1650.* Cambridge University Press, Cambridge, UK.

CORDELL, ANN S.
2002   Continuity and Change in Apalachee Pottery Manufacture. *Historical Archaeology 36(1):36-54.*

CROSBY, ALFRED W., JR.
1972   *The Columbian Exchange: Biological and Cultural Consequences of 1492.* Greenwood Press, Westport, CT.

CUSICK, JAMES G.
1998a   (Editor) *Studies in Culture Contact: Interaction, Culture Change, and Archaeology.* Occasional Paper No. 25. Center for Archaeological Investigations, Southern Illinois University, Carbondale, IL.
1998b   Historiography of Acculturation: An Evaluation of Concepts and Their Application in Archaeology. In *Studies in Culture Contact: Interaction, Culture Change, and Archaeology,* edited by James G. Cusick, pp. 126-145. Occasional Paper No. 25. Center for Archaeological Investigations, Southern Illinois University, Carbondale, IL.

DAWDY, SHANNON LEE
2000a   (Editor) Creolization. *Historical Archaeology* 34(3):1-133.
2000b   Preface. *Historical Archaeology* 34(3):1-4.

DEAGAN, KATHLEEN
1988   The Archaeology of the Spanish Contact Period in the Caribbean. *Journal of World Prehistory* 2(2):187-233.
1996   Colonial Transformations: Euro-American Cultural Genesis in the Early Spanish-American Colonies. *Journal of Anthropological Research* 52(2):135-160.
1998   Transculturation and Spanish American Ethnogenesis: The Archaeological Legacy of the Quincentenary. In *Studies in Culture Contact: Interaction, Culture Change, and Archaeology,* edited by James G. Cusick, pp. 23-43. Occasional Paper No. 25. Center for Archaeological Investigations, Southern Illinois University, Carbondale, IL.
2003   Colonial Origins and Colonial Transformations in Spanish America. *Historical Archaeology* 37(4):3-13.

DECORSE, CHRISTOPHER R.
2001   *An Archaeology of Elmina: Africans and Europeans on the Gold Coast, 1400-1900.* Smithsonian Institution Press, Washington, D.C.

DEETZ, JAMES
1963   Archaeological investigations at La Purisima Mission. In *UCLA Archaeological Survey Annual Report 1962-1963,* pp. 163-208. University of California, Los Angeles. CA.

DOBYNS, HENRY F.
1983   *Their Numbers Became Thinned: Native American Population Dynamics in Eastern North America.* University of Tennessee Press, Knoxville, TN.

EARLE, TIMOTHY
2008   Cultural Anthropology and Archaeology: Theoretical Dialogues. In *Handbook of Archaeological Theories,* edited by R. Alexander Bentley, Herbert D. G. Maschner, and Christopher Chippindale, pp. 187-202. AltaMira Press, Lanham, MD.

ETHRIDGE, ROBBIE and SHERI M. SHUCK-HALL (EDITORS)
2009   *Mapping the Mississippian Shatter Zone: The Colonial Indian Slave Trade and Regional Instability in the American South.* University of Nebraska Press, Lincoln, NE.

EWEN, CHARLES R.
1996   Continuity and Change: De Soto and the Apalachee. *Historical Archaeology* 30(2):41-53.

EWEN, CHARLES R. AND JOHN H. HANN
1998   *Hernando de Soto Among the Apalachee: The Archaeology of the First Winter Encampment.* University Press of Florida, Gainesville, FL.

FARNSWORTH, PAUL
1992   Missions, Indians, and Cultural Continuity. *Historical Archaeology* 26(1):22-36.

FARNSWORTH, PAUL AND JACK S. WILLIAMS
1992a   (Editors) The Archaeology of the Spanish Colonial and Mexican Republican Periods. *Historical Archaeology* 26(1):1-147.
1992b   The Archaeology of the Spanish Colonial and Mexican Republican Periods: Introduction. *Historical Archaeology* 26(1):1-6.

FERGUSON, LELAND
2000   Introduction. *Historical Archaeology* 34(3):5-9.

FERRIS, NEAL
2009   *The Archaeology of Native-Lived Colonialism: Challenging History in the Great Lakes.* University of Arizona Press, Tucson, AZ.

FITZHUGH, WILLIAM W. (EDITOR)
1985   *Cultures in Contact: The European Impact on Native Cultural Institutions in Eastern North America, A.D. 1000-1800.* Smithsonian Institution Press, Washington, D.C.

GAMBLE, LYNN H.
2008   *The Chumash World at European Contact: Power, Trade, and Feasting among Complex Hunter-Gatherers.* University of California Press, Berkeley, CA.

GAMBLE, LYNN H. AND IRMA CARMEN ZEPEDA
2002   Social Differentiation and Exchange among the Kumeyaay Indians during the Historic Period in California. *Historical Archaeology* 36(2):71-91.

GOSDEN, CHRIS
2004   *Archaeology and Colonialism: Cultural contact from 5000 BC to the present.* Cambridge University Press, Cambridge, UK.

GREGORY, H. F., GEORGE AVERY, AUBRA L. LEE, AND JAY C. BLAINE
2004   Presidio Los Adaes: Spanish, French, and Caddoan Interaction on the Northern Frontier. *Historical Archaeology* 38(3):65-77.

GROOVER, MARK D.
2000   Creolization and the Archaeology of Multiethnic Households in the American South. *Historical Archaeology* 34(3):99-106.

HARRISON, RODNEY AND CHRISTINE WILLIAMSON (EDITORS)
2004   *After Captain Cook: The Archaeology of the Recent Indigenous Past in Australia.* AltaMira Press, Walnut Creek, CA.

HUDSON, CHARLES AND CARMEN CHAVES TESSER (EDITORS)
1994   *The Forgotten Centuries: Indians and Europeans in the American South, 1521-1704.* The University of Georgia Press, Athens, GA.

HUTCHINSON, DALE L.
2006   *Tatham Mound and the Bioarchaeology of European Contact: Disease and Depopulation in Central Gulf Coast Florida.* University Press of Florida, Gainesville, FL.

HUTCHINSON, DALE L. AND JEFFREY M. MITCHEM
2001   Correlates of Contact: Epidemic Disease in Archaeological Context. *Historical Archaeology* 35(2):58-72.

KELLY, KENNETH G.
2002   Indigenous Responses to Colonial Encounters on the West African Coast: Hueda and Dahomey from the 17th through 19th Centuries. In *The Archaeology of Colonialism,* edited by Claire L. Lyons and John Papadopoulos. Getty Research Institute, Los Angeles, CA.
2005   Historical Archaeology. In *Handbook of Archaeological Methods,* edited by Herbert D. G. Maschner and Christopher Chippindale, pp. 1108-1137. 2 Vols. AltaMira Press, Lanham, MD.

KELTON, PAUL
2007   *Epidemics & Enslavement: Biological Catastrophe in the Native Southeast, 1492-1715.* University of Nebraska Press, Lincoln, NE.

KNIGHT, VERNON J.
    1985   *Tukabatchee: Archaeological Investigations at an Historic Creek Town, Elmore County, Alabama, 1984.* Report of Investigations No. 45. Office of Archaeological Research, Alabama State Museum of Natural History, University of Alabama, Tuscaloosa, AL.

LARSEN, CLARK S.
    2001   *Bioarchaeology of Spanish Florida: The Impact of Colonialism.* University Press of Florida, Gainesville, FL.
    2005   Bioarchaeology of the Spanish Missions. In *Unlocking the Past: Celebrating Historical Archaeology in North America,* edited by Lu Ann De Cunzo and John H. Jameson, Jr., pp. 25-29. University Press of Florida, Gainesville, FL.

LIGHTFOOT, KENT G.
    1995   Culture Contact Studies: Redefining the Relationship between Prehistoric and Historic Archaeology. *American Antiquity* 60(2):199-217.
    2003   Russian Colonization: The Implications of Mercantile Colonial Practices in the North Pacific. *Historical Archaeology* 37(4):14-28.
    2005a   *Indians, Missionaries, and Merchants: The Legacy of Colonial Encounters on the California Frontier.* University of California Press, Berkeley.
    2005b   The Archaeology of Colonization: California in Cross-Cultural Perspective. In *The Archaeology of Colonial Encounters: Comparative Perspectives,* edited by Gil J. Stein, pp. 207-235. School of American Research Press, Santa Fe.

LIGHTFOOT, KENT G., ANTOINETTE MARTINEZ, AND ANN SCHIFF
    1998   Daily Practice and Material Culture in Pluralistic Social Settings: An Archaeological Study of Culture Change and Persistence from Fort Ross, California. *American Antiquity* 63(2):199-222.

LINTON, RALPH (EDITOR)
    1940   *Acculturation in Seven American Indian Tribes.* D. Appleton-Century, New York, NY.

LOREN, DIANA DIPAOLO
    2000   The Intersections of Colonial Policy and Colonial Practice: Creolization on the Eighteenth-Century Louisiana/Texas Frontier. *Historical Archaeology* 34(3):85-98.
    2001   Manipulating Bodies and Emerging Traditions at the Los Adaes Presidio. In *The Archaeology of Traditions: Agency and History Before and After Columbus,* edited by Timothy R. Pauketat, pp. 58-76. University Press of Florida, Gainesville, FL.
    2005   Creolization in the French and Spanish Colonies. In *North American Archaeology,* edited by Timothy R. Pauketat and Diana DiPaolo Loren, pp. 297-318. Blackwell Publishing, Malden, MA.

    2008   *In Contact: Bodies and Spaces in the Sixteenth- and Seventeenth-Century Eastern Woodlands.* AltaMira Press, Lanham, MD.

MANN, ROB
    2007   "True Portraitures of the Indians, and of Their Own Peculiar Conceits of Dress": Discourses of Dress and Identity. *Historical Archaeology* 41(1):37-52.

MCEWAN, BONNIE G.
    1991   San Luis de Talimali: The Archaeology of Spanish-Indian Relations at a French Mission. *Historical Archaeology* 25(3):36-60.
    2001   The Spiritual conquest of Florida. *American Anthropologist* 103(3):633-644.
    2002   Preface. *Historical Archaeology* 36(1):1-2.

MCEWAN, BONNIE G. AND GREGORY A. WASELKOV
    2003   Colonial Origins: The Archaeology of Colonialism in the Americas. *Historical Archaeology* 37(4):1-2.

MINOR, RICK AND LAURIE E. BURGESS
    2009   Chinookan Survival and Persistence on the Lower Columbia: The View from the Kathlamet Village. *Historical Archaeology* 43(4):97-114.

MIRES, PETER B.
    1994   Contact and Contagion: The Roanoke Colony and Influenza. *Historical Archaeology* 28(3):30-38.

MOUSSETTE, MARCEL
    2002   Discussion: Towards an Archaeology of the French in America. *Historical Archaeology* 36(1):143-148.
    2003   An Encounter in the Baroque Age: French and Amerindians in North America. *Historical Archaeology* 37(4):29-39.

MULLINS, PAUL R. AND ROBERT PAYNTER
    2000   Representing Colonizers: An Archaeology of Creolization, Ethnogenesis, and Indigenous Material Culture among the Haida. *Historical Archaeology* 34(3):73-84.

PAUKETAT, TIMOTHY R. (EDITOR)
    2001   *The Archaeology of Traditions: Agency and History Before and After Columbus.* University Press of Florida, Gainesville, FL.

PEARSON, CHARLES
    1977   Evidence of Early Spanish Contact on the Georgia Coast. *Historical Archaeology* 11:74-83.

PERTTULA, TIMOTHY K.
    1994   Material Culture of the Koasati Indians of Texas. *Historical Archaeology* 28(1):65-77.

QUIMBY, GEORGE L. AND ALEXANDER SPOEHR
    1951   Acculturation and Material Culture. *Fieldiana: Anthropology* 36(6):107-147. Field Museum of Natural History, Chicago.

RAMENOFSKY, ANN F.
    1987   *Vectors of Death: The Archaeology of European Contact.* University of New Mexico Press, Albuquerque, NM.

    1990   Loss of Innocence: Explanations of Differential Persistence in the Sixteenth-Century Southeast. In *Columbian Consequences, Volume 2, Archaeological and Historical Perspectives on the Spanish Borderlands East*, edited by David Hurst Thomas, pp. 31-48. Smithsonian Institution Press, Washington, D.C.

    1993   Diseases of the Americas, 1492-1700. In *The Cambridge World History of Human Disease*, edited by K. Kiple, pp. 317-327. Cambridge University Press, Cambridge, UK.

RAY, VERNE F.
    1938   Lower Chinook Ethnographic Notes. University of Washington Publications in Anthropology Vol. 7, No. 2, Seattle, WA.

ROGERS, J. DANIEL
    1990   *Objects of Change: The Archaeology and History of Arikara Contact with Europeans.* Smithsonian Institution Press, Washington, D.C.

ROTHSCHILD, NAN A.
    2003   *Colonial Encounters in a Native American Landscape: The Spanish and Dutch in North America.* Smithsonian Books, Washington, D.C.

RUBERTONE, PATRICIA E.
    1989   Archaeology, Colonialism, and 17th-century Native America: Towards an Alternative Interpretation. In *Conflict in the Archaeology of Living Traditions*, edited by Robert Layton, pp. 32-45. Unwin Hyman, London.

    2001   *Grave Undertakings: An Archaeology of Roger Williams and the Narragansett Indians.* Smithsonian Institution Press, Washington, D.C.

SHUCK-HALL, SHERI M.
    2008   *Journey to the West: The Alabama and Coushatta Indians.* University of Oklahoma Press, Norman, OK.

SILLIMAN, STEPHEN W.
    2004   *Lost Laborers in Colonial California: Native Americans and the Archaeology of Rancho Petaluma.* University of Arizona Press, Tucson, AZ.

    2005a   Social and Physical Landscapes of Contact. In *North American Archaeology*, edited by Timothy R. Pauketat and Diana DiPaolo Loren, pp. 273-296. Blackwell Publishing, Malden, MA.

    2005b   Culture Contact or Colonialism? Challenges in the Archaeology of Native North America. *American Antiquity* 70(1):55-74.

    2009   Change and Continuity, Practice and Memory: Native American Persistence in Colonial New England. *American Antiquity* 74(2):211-230.

SILVIA, DIANE E.
    2002   Native Americans and French Cultural Dynamics on the Gulf Coast. *Historical Archaeology* 36(1):26-35.

SMITH, MARVIN T.
    1987   *Archaeology of Aboriginal Culture Change in the Interior Southeast.* University of Florida Press, Gainesville, FL.

SPICER, EDWARD H.
    1962   *Cycles of Conquest: The impact of Spain, Mexico, and the United States on the Indians of the Southwest, 1533-1960.* The University of Arizona Press, Tucson, AZ.

STEIN, GIL J.
    2005   *The Archaeology of Colonial Encounters: Comparative Perspectives.* School of American Research Press, Santa Fe, NM.

STOJANOWSKI, CHRISTOPHER M.
    2005   *Biocultural Histories in La Florida: A Bioarchaeological Perspective.* University of Alabama Press, Tuscaloosa, AL.

THOMAS, DAVID HURST
    1987   *The Archaeology of Mission Santa Catalina de Guale: 1. Search and Discovery.* Anthropological Papers No. 63(2). American Museum of Natural History, New York, NY.

    2008   *Native American Landscapes of St. Catherines Island, Georgia, Parts I-III.* Anthropological Papers No. 88. American Museum of Natural History, New York, NY.

THOMAS, DAVID HURST (EDITOR)
    1989   *Columbian Consequences, Volume 1: Archaeological and Historical Perspectives on the Spanish Borderlands West.* Smithsonian Institution Press, Washington, D.C.

    1990   *Columbian Consequences, Volume 2: Archaeological and Historical Perspectives on the Spanish Borderlands East.* Smithsonian Institution Press, Washington, D.C.

    1991   *Columbian Consequences, Volume 3: The Spanish Borderlands in Pan-American Perspective.* Smithsonian Institution Press, Washington, D.C.

THORNTON, RUSSELL
    1987   *American Indian Holocaust and Survival: A Population History Since 1492.* University of Oklahoma Press, Norman, OK.

TVESKOV, MARK
    2007   Social Identity and Culture Change on the Southern Northwest Coast. *American Anthropologist* 109(3):431-441.

USNER, DANIEL H., JR.
1992   *Indians, Settlers, & Slaves in a Frontier Exchange Economy: The Lower Mississippi Valley before 1783.* University of North Carolina Press, Chapel Hill, NC

VELTRE, DOUGLAS W. AND ALLEN P. MCCARTNEY
2002   Russian Exploitation of Aleuts and Fur Seals: The Archaeology of Eighteenth and Early-Nineteenth Century Settlements in the Pribilof Islands, Alaska. *Historical Archaeology* 36(3):8-17.

WADE, MARIAH F.
2008   *Missions, Missionaries, and Native Americans: Long-Term Processes and Daily Practices.* University Press of Florida, Gainesville, FL.

WARRICK, GARY
2008   *A Population History of the Huron-Petun, A.D. 500-1650.* Cambridge University Press, Cambridge, UK.

WASELKOV, GREGORY A.
1992   French Colonial Trade in the Upper Creek Country. In *Calumet and Fleur-de-Lys: Archaeology of Indian and French Contact in the Midcontinent*, edited by John A. Walthall and Thomas E. Emerson, pp. 35-53. Smithsonian Institution Press, Washington, D.C.
2002a   (editor) French Colonial Archaeology At Old Mobile: Selected Studies. *Historical Archaeology* 36(1):1-148.
2002b   French Colonial Archaeology at Old Mobile: An Introduction. *Historical Archaeology* 36(1):3-12.

WATTS, SHELDON
1997   *Epidemics and History: Disease, Power and Imperialism.* Yale University Press, New Haven, CT.

WEISMAN, BRENT R.
2000   Archaeological Perspectives on Florida Seminole Ethnogenesis. In *Indians of the Greater Southeast: Historical Archaeology and Ethnohistory*, edited by Bonnie G. McEwan, pp. 299-318. University Press of Florida, Gainesville, FL.
2007   Nativism, Resistance, and Ethnogenesis of the Florida Seminole Indian Identity. *Historical Archaeology* 41(4):198-212.

WESSON, CAMERON B.
2008   *Households and Hegemony: Early Creek Prestige Goods, Symbolic Capital, and Social Power.* University of Nebraska Press, Lincoln, NE.

WESSON, CAMERON B. AND MARK A. REES (EDITORS)
2002   *Between Contacts and Colonies: Archaeological Perspectives on the Protohistoric Southeast.* University of Alabama Press, Tuscaloosa, AL.

WILSON, SAMUEL M. AND J. DANIEL ROGERS (EDITORS)
1993   *Ethnohistory and Archaeology: Approaches to Postcontact Change in the Americas.* Plenum Press, New York, NY.

WOLF, ERIC R.
1982   *Europe and the People Without History.* University of California Press, Berkeley, CA.

WORTH, JOHN E.
2006   Bridging Prehistory and History in the Southeast: Evaluating the Utility of the Acculturation Concept. In *Light on the Path: The Anthropology and History of the Southeastern Indians*, edited by Thomas J. Pluckhahn and Robbie Ethridge, pp. 196-206. University of Alabama Press, Tuscaloosa, AL.

TIMOTHY K. PERTTULA
ARCHEOLOGICAL & ENVIRONMENTAL
CONSULTANTS, LLC
10101 WOODHAVEN DRIVE
AUSTIN, TX 78753

Kathleen Deagan

Colonial Origins and Colonial Transformations in Spanish America

ABSTRACT

Archaeological data have been critical in articulating the manner by which system-wide structuring elements of Europe's colonial projects in America were adjusted or transformed in local settings. This paper explores the ways in which certain of these structuring elements in Spanish colonial America were played out in a variety of households and communities, with the ultimate goal of approaching an archaeologically informed, comparative study of American colonialism. Several parameters are offered as examples of potentially fruitful points of comparison among colonial systems through which researchers might assess local agency at both intra- and inter-colonial scales. These include varieties of economic and governmental centrality, forms of labor organization, varieties of religious experience, gender relations, idealized social identities, and frontier-urban dichotomies.

Introduction

Some general observations are offered about the economic, socio-political, and ideological structures that shaped Spain's colonization of America, with the caveat that literally dozens of historians and archaeologists in North America, Mexico, the Caribbean, and South America have already devoted their careers to this same effort. That work will be drawn from extensively.

The observation of the 1992 Columbian quincentenary stimulated a tremendous surge of historical archaeological research in areas of Spanish colonization over the past two decades. That work has been crucially important in gaining a more balanced understanding of the complexity, diversity, and range of human experience in the Spanish colonial past as well as in understanding the personal and institutional power negotiations that conditioned local cultural practices. Less inquiry, however, has been oriented toward a better-informed understanding of the larger, aggregate cultural structures within which local traditions are embedded and which suggest commonalities shared by members of social groups

on a broader scale. The mandate of The Society for Historical Archaeology session from which this article is derived offers us an opportunity to engage in a newly informed and, perhaps, even neo-processual conversation about American colonization in which questions of structure and agency can articulate and inform one another in a dynamic way. It is this interscalar dialectic that offers us a potentially productive focus for the comparative study of the American colonial project through historical archaeology.

Spain in America

Spain's imperial expansion into the 16th-century Americas was simultaneously an invasion, a colonization effort, a social experiment, a religious crusade, and a highly structured economic enterprise. Unlike most earlier or later colonial ventures, it was both sudden and unexpected, involving two parts of the world that had no prior idea of the other's existence. The Spanish colonial empire in the Americas of the 16th century was the largest ever known in the Western hemisphere, incorporating an extraordinarily diverse array of societies, ethnic groups, geographic landscapes, and polities (including at least two American empires), and it endured as a colonial entity for more than three centuries (for English-language overviews of historical-archaeological studies of Spanish imperial expansion and its consequences, see Deagan 1988; Milanich and Milbrath 1989; Thomas 1989, 1990, 1991; Dillehay and Deagan 1992; Farnsworth and Williams 1992; Bray 1993).

The Spanish colonies were also marked by certain consistent political, religious, and social patterns that cut across and conditioned the local experiences of people in all of these diverse settings. Among the most pervasive of these were the centralization of government and economy under Crown control, monolithic Catholicism, an emphasis on life in towns, and formalized notions of class and race. These elements will be the focus of the following discussion—to consider how they structured colonial life and how they were adjusted by colonial experience. These concepts are also inextricably interrelated in the Spanish colonial arena, and it must be noted that it is probably both impossible and inappropriate to fully segregate them as analytical units.

Colonial Origins

That said, it is necessary to briefly divert to pre-Columbian Spain, since the Spanish colonial empire in the Americas can only be understood against the backdrop of more than 2,000 years of invasion, colonization, and multiculturalism in the Iberian Peninsula itself. From the 8th century B.C., Iberia was colonized by Greeks, Phoenicians, Carthaginians, Romans, Visigoths, and, finally, in the 8th century A.D. by Muslim Arabs and Berbers.

Under the subsequent eight centuries of Muslim rule, a richly diverse society developed, blending elements of Roman, Iberian, and Arab cultures, in which Muslims, Christians, and Jews coexisted and intermarried (Mann et al. 1992; Vernet 1992). Nevertheless, Christian rulers began efforts almost immediately after A.D. 711 to recapture Spain from its Muslim overlords, and in 1492 the last Moorish stronghold of Santa Fe de Granada fell to the Catholic monarchs, Ferdinand and Isabela. The fall of Granada not only united Spain under Christian rule but also ushered in a new era of religious fervor, intolerance, and intense proselytizing promoted by Queen Isabela. It was in this context that Columbus returned from his first voyage of exploration with news of the New World, and the invasion of America by Spain began.

The initial Spanish colonial effort was very different from the system that ultimately prevailed in the Americas. The Columbian project was an economic partnership between the Crown and Columbus's private interests, self-consciously modeled on the Portuguese *feitoria* system. It was specifically organized as a moneymaking trading venture in which largely self-contained European communities would establish profitable trading alliances with American natives and share the profits with the Crown. Once in America, however, this economic vision did not remain compelling to either the Spanish colonists or the colonized people of America. Local needs and expectations were simply not met by the institutional model of the *feitoria*. Resistance, rebellion, and individual enterprise among both American Indians and nonelite Spaniards quickly recast the original imperial project from one of a

private-monarchical mercantile partnership to the territorially based and centrally controlled pattern of political and economic domination that came to characterize the Spanish empire from the 16th century onward (for expanded discussions of these themes, see Pérez de Tudela Bueso 1954, 1955; Stevens-Arroyo 1993; Deagan and Cruxent 2002:15–18).

The shift that occurred after 1500 (and after Christopher Columbus) in Spain's colonial strategy was a return, in a sense, to an earlier medieval pattern and a rejection of the economic modernity that persisted in the Portuguese colonies. The second mode of Spanish expansion into the Americas followed a pattern that had been translated from the Iberian *reconquista* to the Spanish conquest and colonization of the Canary Islands, which took place between about 1477 and 1497. Crown-licensed *adelantados* (expedition leaders) led largely self-supported expeditions of conquest during which successful conquistadors were rewarded with allocations of land and the servitude of the native people who occupied it.

Although the conquered populations were obligated to contribute labor as a token of their submission to Spain; nevertheless, they were theoretically granted the privileges of Castilian subjects as long as they adopted Christianity and accepted the sovereignty of Spain. The status and privileges of their chiefs were formally recognized. However, those new subjects who continued resistance (and the conquistadors defined the concept of resistance in very broad terms) were considered appropriate candidates for enslavement and despoliation (for detailed discussions of the structure and policy of early contact in the Canary Islands see Gibson 1966, 1987; Sauer 1966; Aznar Vallejo 1983; Lockhart and Schwartz 1983:59–86; McAlister 1984:63–65; and Tejera Gaspar and Aznar Vallejo 1992; and in America see McAlister 1984; Moya Pons 1986; Elliott 1987).

American Encounter and Dominion

American colonization was also (at least from the point of view of the Spanish Crown) a compelling religious mission in which the conversion of conquered peoples to Catholicism was a paramount goal equal to that of economic exploitation. The revelation that uncounted numbers of souls in need of Christian conversion were waiting in the New World intensified the religious motive for this enterprise. The justification for colonization itself was explicitly religious, codified in 1493 by the Bulls of Donation, issued by Pope Alexander VI (a Spaniard), which assigned Spain "a just title" to American lands. The colonizers were obliged to evangelize the inhabitants and make them Christians. Officially, this was the sole authority and justification for the Spanish empire in America.

The encounter with indigenous Americans provoked intense discussion, debate, and soul-searching in late-15th and early-16th-century Spain about the nature of these people and their potential capacity to live like Christian Spaniards (for synthetic and contrasting discussions of these see Hanke 1949; Brading 1991:79–101; Pagden 1992). From the very beginning, the official position of the dominant colonial institutional powers—the Crown and the Church—was in conflict with the practical position of the Spanish colonists and indigenous peoples who lived in the Americas. The Crown, vigorously encouraged by the Catholic Church, asserted that the Indians were their legal subjects and merited both rights and protection, while the colonists asserted that the Indians were subhuman and were best suited as a resource of labor. After it was formally determined in 1500 that they were, in fact, human beings by virtue of possessing souls, the Spanish Crown was careful to legally ensure that indigenous Americans could not be officially enslaved, and it issued a series of edicts to protect the American Indians (the Laws of Burgos) in 1512 (Hussey 1932). Much social and economic institutional development in America after that time was designed to ensure that the "free" Indians would be, nevertheless, a ready and reliable source of labor.

The problem of observing the Church and Crown's mandates to protect and respect the rights of the Indians while at the same time ensuring a reliable source of labor was initially resolved by a uniquely American interpretation of *encomienda*, implemented in Hispaniola in 1503 (for discussions of this institution see Lockhart and Schwartz 1983:64–72; McAlister 1984: 157–166; Elliott 1987; Gibson 1987). Those Indians associated with a particular allocation of land to an *adelantado* or conquistador were

obliged to exchange their labor for instruction in Christianity and civilization. In order to make this more efficient, the Indians were regularly relocated and consolidated at centralized town locations convenient for Spanish labor exploitation and conversion. This process, known as *reducción*, figured centrally in the transformation of the American social landscape under colonization, leading in many cases to both a breakdown of traditional cultural patterns among many American Indian groups after contact and the spread of epidemic disease.

Epidemics provoked a rapid demographic decline in the native populations of the earliest Spanish-American colonies (Crosby 1972; Dobyns 1983; Henige 1986; Ramenofsky 1987; Bray 1993; Cook 1998), and this led in turn to a desperate (perceived) need by the Spanish colonists for alternate sources of labor. Their solution spelled doom for the hundreds of thousands of African people brought unwillingly to the Americas as slaves and introduced another social and population element into the colonial arena after 1520.

The enslavement of African peoples was justified by reference to the same religious-legal arguments that prohibited the enslavement of Indians, the Bulls of Donation issued by Alexander VI in 1493, which implied no obligation to evangelize and convert Africans since Spain held no territorial presence there. Furthermore, Africa was tainted by the hint of Islamic influence, which was sufficient justification for slavery. Curiously, once African slaves reached the American colonies, they were subjected to the ministrations of the Church, including evangelization and conversion. Conversion, however, did not bring liberation (Klein 1967:88–89). At the same time, we should note that a number of black Christian Spaniards (*ladinos*), both free and unfree, participated in the conquest and colonization of America as conquistadors and *encomenderos* (Landers 1990).

Race did not structure social interactions with conquered peoples in the Spanish empire in the same way that it appears to have in other European colonial arenas. In many ways, class and religion (although certainly an issue) overrode considerations of race. The labor requirements imposed on American Indians by *encomienda* and *reducción*, for example, applied principally to nonelite individuals. From the beginning of imperial expansion in both the Canary Islands and in the Americas, official policy stressed respect for and recognition of the political importance of the *caciques* (paramount leaders). Elite accommodation was a cornerstone of initial Spanish policy toward the American Indians, based on the recognition, at least in principle, of a legitimate "Republic of Indians" and the political authority of its leaders (Hanke 1949:27; McAlister 1984:180; Gibson 1987:377; Bushnell 1989). These policies were formalized in 1512 by the Laws of Burgos and came to characterize Spanish-American interaction in those areas of the Americas with strongly differentiated chiefs and stratified societies.

In its own way, the accommodation of elites helped mitigate the tension between Crown policies to protect Indians as free subjects and colonists' desires to exploit Indian labor. By securing the alliance of the *caciques*, it was expected that they would impose conversion, labor requirements, and tribute on their vassals (Hanke 1949; Gibson 1987:377). This alliance came to be an especially important mechanism in frontier areas where there were few Spaniards and fewer towns.

In the earliest years of contact, the accommodation of elite American Indians included intermarriage between Spanish conquistadors or soldiers and Indian *caciquas* and noblewomen (Morner 1967:37; Floyd 1973:59–61; Lyon 1976: 148; Deagan 1985:304–305). Such marriages were intended to legitimize Spanish claims to land and labor, although in some cases, such as Spanish Florida, the marriages were entered into mistakenly through a misunderstanding of matrilineal descent rules.

Economy and Identity

The need to control land and labor was critical to elite Spaniards. Such control was essential to gain access to American resources and raw materials (such as metals, cattle, and sugar), which were the primary sources of wealth in the context of Spain's mercantile colonial economic system. Control of labor and land was also necessary to maintain the elite social identity of *hidalguía*, being identified as a *hidalgo* (a person with claims to elite lineage, an *hijo de algo*). *Hidalguía* depended on a visibly Spanish lifestyle, the acquisition of wealth in the form of rewards for service to God and country, and the avoidance of labor (Wolf 1963:55–59; Lockhart and Schwartz 1983:61–63; Elliott 1987:1–10). To sustain *hidalguía*, it was essential, therefore, to control American resources that could be translated into wealth in the highly regulated colonial economy.

Spanish trade with the American colonies operated under a mercantilist policy, that is, the colonies were permitted to import from and export to Spain alone. To implement the policy and control commerce, a system of annual trade fleets known as the *Carrera de Indias* was implemented in 1503 (for detailed discussions of the *Carrera* and its impacts see Haring 1947; Parry 1966; Lynch 1969; Phillips 1990; Morales Padrón 1992; Avery 1997). The *Carrera* was controlled by a government institution known as the *Casa de la Contratación*, which was located in Seville. Through the *Casa*, Seville came to establish a monopoly on the control of Spanish-American shipping, and throughout most of the colonial period the mechanisms for the distribution of goods were designed to work to the advantage of the powerful Sevillian merchants who, in turn, made strategic trading alliances with land- and labor-owning colonists.

European manufactured goods were exchanged for such American materials as bullion, spices, cattle hides, sugar, and dyewood at annual and highly regulated trade fairs. This is not to say that the European goods arriving in Spanish America were of exclusively Sevillian or even Spanish origin. Archaeological assemblages (as well as shipping records from various archives) show an immediate and sustained international character in Spanish colonial material life in all parts of the Spanish Americas; German, French, Portuguese, Chinese, Dutch, Italian, English, and Spanish goods passed through Seville and made their way to the colonies (Deagan 2002a: 24–27; 2002b).

The *Carrera* system primarily benefited those who controlled resources on both sides of the Atlantic, but it proved to be inefficient and unable to meet the needs of the majority of Spanish-American colonists. Irregular scheduling, pirate attacks, hurricanes, shipwrecks, and a multitude of taxes and duties on shipped goods all contributed to the inadequacy of the Sevillian system as the exclusive mechanism for colonial trade. These problems provoked widespread dissatisfaction in the colonies and contributed to the colonists' willingness to engage in *rescate* (illicit, non-Spanish sources of trade). The Crown authorities were simply unable to control their subjects' *rescate*, and, in fact, the control of *rescate* came to be a very lucrative monopoly for many colonial officials. In some instances, such as in western Hispaniola, Spain was forced to relinquish its colonial territorial claims in order to impede smuggling activities (Hernández Tápia 1970; Hamilton and Hodges 1995).

Colonists also responded to the inadequacy of the exclusionary trade system by initiating the production of European-style goods in the Americas. Craft guilds (*gremios*) were established in New Spain during the first half of the 16th century to regulate the commercial production of a wide variety of commodities (Santiago Cruz 1960; Deagan 2002b:31–33). To archaeologists, among the most interesting have been the ceramics industries studied by Florence Lister, Patricia Fournier, Thomas Charlton, and others (Lister and Lister 1987; Charlton and Fournier 1993; Fournier 1998). Such production was not encouraged by the authorities who were "chronically suspicious of the commercial activities of its colonial subjects. If they traded with one another they could not easily be prevented from trading with foreigners" (Parry 1964:317). By the early decades of the 17th century, Spain had prohibited (although apparently could not prevent) all intercolonial trade in those commodities that were important Spanish exports, including wine, raisins, olives, almonds, silk, metals, and china goods.

Excavations in home sites throughout the Spanish empire reveal the extent to which these prohibitions failed. During the 17th century, for example, Mexican majolicas overwhelmingly dominated the assemblages of Spanish colonial households in Central and South America as well as in Florida, the Caribbean, and the American West. Ceramics produced in Spain are rare after 1600 in nearly all contexts but American-bound shipwrecks (Deagan 2002b:xvi–xvii).

Life in Towns

The establishment of settled towns for both Spaniards and Indians was central to the Spanish imperial strategy for asserting social, political, and economic control in the Americas, and towns were the idealized setting for "civilized"

life. The creation of Spanish towns in the Americas was a closely regulated and centrally controlled undertaking, both in the physical and the administrative organization of these settlements. The regulations governing town planning and organization were developed through the 16th century and formally codified in 1573. They provide a remarkable statement about Spanish intentions and ideals concerning "civilized" life and address not only spatial patterning but also environmental concerns, health, civic authority and organization, relations with Indians, religious matters, status, economy, commerce, and urban aesthetics (these are largely translated and reproduced in Crouch et al. 1982 and discussed by McAlister 1984:134–139). Nearly all Spanish-American municipalities established after 1500, whether urban centers or borderland *presidios*, show an overwhelming adherence to the general spatial patterns established in these ordinances (Foster 1960; Jones 1978:5–11; Chueco Goitia and Torres Bálbas 1981; Crouch et al. 1982; Deagan 1982).

However Spanish cultural practice was not sustained with such zeal within the households of these Spanish colonial towns. Archaeologists throughout the Spanish Americas have revealed striking adjustments to traditional Spanish practices in the domain of women in Spanish colonial households. Excavations at 16th- through 18th-century home sites in the Caribbean, Florida, Mexico, Panamá, Venezuela, and the Rio de la Plata region consistently reveal that domestic, female-associated aspects of those households are represented predominantly by American elements or mixed European-American-African elements, regardless of their documentary-based ethnic or racial identification. These include cooking technology (*manos, metates*, griddles, pots), ceramic technology, foodstuffs, and household management (such as the use of American Indian-style smudge pits in Spanish homes) (Deagan 1983: 108, 1995; Domínguez 1984; McEwan 1988, 1992; Ewen 1991; Charlton and Fournier 1993; Reitz and McEwan 1995; Senatore 1995). In contrast to this, as has been argued elsewhere (Deagan 1983, 1996; Ewen 1991), both traditionally "male" categories and socially visible categories of the material world (e.g., architecture, religious items, clothing) remained Spanish or European in form from the 15th through the 18th centuries.

This pattern of carefully maintaining the ideal of Spanish identification in socially visible areas while adapting to the local circumstances of the colonial setting in private and domestic life developed very rapidly as a mechanism for social integration in the towns of the Spanish empire. It suggests adherence to a highly structured set of pre-existing precepts—embodied in this case by the centralized church and government controls and the ideal of Spanish identification but implemented simultaneously with a high degree of flexibility and accommodation to local, indigenous conditions. Non-European women were a potent force in this process. Whether as wives, concubines, or servants, they were the brokers for European, Indian, and African exchanges within Spanish-American households and communities.

Mestizaje and Cultural Genesis

Intermarriage and consensual relationships among Spaniards (mostly men) and Indians and Africans (mostly women) formed a crucial dynamic in creating, transforming, and stabilizing the social milieus of the Spanish-American colonies (Morner 1967; Nash 1980; Esteva-Fabregát 1995). Alliances between European and non-European partners accounted for between one-quarter and one-half of all marriages in some parts of the Spanish colonies during the 16th and 17th centuries (Arranz Márquez 1991). This was not a simple function of gender ratios since the proportion of Spanish women to Spanish men in the first 50 years of colonization was about the same as English gender proportions in the first decades of the Anglo-American colonization (Konetzke 1945; Deagan 1996). It was, rather, the influence of both the Catholic Church and, probably, the centuries-long traditions of *convivencia* and intermarriage in Spain itself.

While canonical law considered different religions to be an obstacle to marriage, it did not consider race an obstacle as long as both parties were Catholic (Konetzke 1946; Morner 1967:26, 36). Queen Isabela, for example, instructed the governor of Santo Domingo in 1503 to see to it that "some Christians marry some Indian women and some Christian women marry some Indian men, so that both parties can communicate and teach each other, and the Indians become men and women of reason" (Morner 1967:26). A large number of Spanish men also lived in *concubinage*

with Indian and African women, and the Church tried vigorously to make them marry.

These unions led to a bewildering array of genetic (and social) admixture among European, Indian, and African populations, to which Spanish imperial ideology responded in characteristic fashion by the formal institutionalization of race mixture into more than 25 categories (which were explicitly illustrated in more than 1,000 colonial Mexican "Casta" paintings, best seen in García Saíz 1989). Although these categories reflected a commitment to social hierarchy and racial prejudice; nevertheless, they provided a formal means of integrating and legitimizing virtually any combination of racial attributes in a recognized institutional structure. Furthermore, they were used very flexibly in social practice. In 18th-century Mexico, for example, individuals often identified themselves at different times as belonging to different racial categories depending on the relative advantages of a category in a specific situation (Boyer 1997). Regardless of imperial legal categories and distinctions, people in the Americas apparently regarded their racial identity "not so much as an indicator of group membership or even as a badge of self definition within a static and rigid system, but rather as a component of (his) personal identity that could be manipulated and often changed" (Chance 1978:130–131).

The Frontier

The goals of establishing civilized Christian life as dictated by the Church and the Crown were apparently adjusted most strikingly (and perhaps even largely ignored) in rural and frontier areas of the empire. There was little social integration of colonized people in these areas into the empire beyond the symbolic acknowledgment of imperial and Catholic dominion. In fact, there is some indication that the Spaniards who lived in these communities made far greater adjustments to the American mode of life than vice versa (Deagan 1985:300–304; Fowler 1991; Smith 1991; Thomas 1991; Charlton and Fournier 1993; Gasco 1993; Loucks 1993; Ruhl and Hoffman 1997). One historian of the Spanish frontier in New Mexico characterizes "Spanish colonists" as "anyone living in a manner more Spanish than Indian" (Kessell 1997:50).

The Catholic Church, however, was as profoundly influential on the colonial frontier as it was in town settings. Missions evolved along the frontiers of the Spanish empire not only as centers of Christianity but also of Spanish political presence, economic production, labor organization, and defense. Both the institution of the mission and the concept of peaceful evangelization were features found exclusively in Spain's overseas holdings, evolving in response to local conditions. The idealized goal of empire—the creation of a Catholic state—had been achieved in Spain itself exclusively by force: warfare, forced conversions, expulsion, and the Inquisition. It was only in the isolated territories of the overseas empire that the greatly outnumbered Spaniards developed the principle and quite often the process of peaceful proselytizing and conversion.

Catholicism in America of A.D. 1500 was faced with a situation that recalled the original spread of doctrine more than a thousand years earlier—the accommodation of Catholic doctrine and practice to deeply held pagan beliefs and practice. The Spanish missionaries were, for the most part, flexible in recognizing that the acceptance of Catholicism was a highly variable and selective process for most American Indians, both materially and spiritually (McEwan 2001). Historical and archaeological research in Spanish-American missions documents the many ways in which elements of Catholic ritual were selected, rejected, and transformed by various groups from the Maya to the peoples of the United States southwest and southeast (Clendinnen 1987; Thomas 1990:357–397; Gutiérrez 1991:82–91; Weber 1992:105–121; McEwan 1993, 2001).

Archaeology has also begun to suggest that the Spanish missionaries themselves may have actively negotiated the adjustment of church ritual at the missions. Excavations have documented, for example, the inclusion of native and European grave goods with Christian Indian burials inside mission churches as well as the incorporation of charnel-house remains into Christian contexts (Thomas 1988:120–122; Milanich 1999:139; Larsen et al. 2001). And one of the most dramatic expressions of missionaries' accommodation to native patterns can be seen at the 17th-century site of San Luis de Talimali in Florida. There the massive Apalachee council house, symbolically and ritually important in native terms, looms over and faces the Catholic Church across the town plaza where the traditional ritual ball game was played (Hann and McEwan 1998:75–77).

This accommodation of non-Christian practices and Catholic ritual can still be seen today throughout Spanish America in such things as the correlation of the Virgin of Guadalupe (Patroness of America) with the Aztec Maize goddess Tonantzín and the incorporation of native music, dance, and images into celebrations of the Mass and other rituals.

Conclusion

There is no more relevant issue for historical archaeology than the European expansion and colonization after 1500, which was arguably the most influential historical process shaping the world in which most of us live and do archaeology today. Engaging in a comparative, archaeologically informed study of colonial systems in the Americas is something that we as archaeologists often talk about but rarely do. This undoubtedly has to do with the complexity of such a project, which not only requires investigation at a variety of distinct and explicit scales of inquiry (ranging from individual household experience to the colonial "system" itself) but also requires maintaining a continuous, vertical conversation among those scales.

The preceding assessment, admittedly selective and heavily condensed, of Spanish colonial practice and origins has tried to suggest some potential parameters along which such a comparative study of American colonization might be approached. They include the degrees and varieties of economic and governmental centrality, forms of labor organization, varieties of religious experience, gender relations, idealized social identities, and frontier-urban dichotomies. The aspects of such a comparison to which archaeological research can be particularly vital lie in understanding how these parameters, once defined, are played out in communities and how they shaped—through resistance, innovation, or incorporation of the "other"—the evolution of the colonial project itself.

REFERENCES

Arranz Márquez, Luis
  1991 *Repartimiento y encomienda en la isla Española.* Fundación García Arévalo, Santo Domingo, Dominican Republic.

AVERY, GEORGE
1997 *Pots As Packaging: The Spanish Olive Jar and Andalucian Transatlantic Commercial Activity, 16th–18th Centuries.* Doctoral dissertation, Department of Anthropology, University of Florida, Gainesville. University Microfilms International, Ann Arbor, MI.

AZNAR VALLEJO, EDUARDO
1983 *La integraciín de las Islas Canarias en la Corona de Castilla (1487–1526). Aspectos administrativos, sociales y económicos.* Ediciones Universidad de Sevilla, Seville, Spain.

BOYER, RICHARD
1997 Negotiating *Calidad*: The Everyday Struggle for Status in Mexico. In *Diversity and Social Identity in Colonial Spanish America: Native American, African and Hispanic Communities during the Middle Period,* Donna L. Ruhl and Kathleen Hoffman, editors, pp. 64–73. *Historical Archaeology,* 31(1):1–103.

BRADING, D. A.
1991 *The First America.* Cambridge University Press, Cambridge.

BRAY, WARWICK (EDITOR)
1993 The Meeting of Two Worlds: Europe and the Americas 1492-1650. *Proceedings of the British Academy,* 81. Oxford University Press, Oxford.

BUSHNELL, AMY TURNER
1989 Ruling the "Republic of Indians" in Seventeenth-Century Florida. In *Powhatan's Mantle: Indians in the Colonial Southeast,* Peter Wood, Gregory Waselkov, and M. Thomas Hatley, editors, pp. 134–150. University of Nebraska Press, Lincoln.

CHANCE, JOHN K.
1978 *Race and Class in Colonial Oaxaca.* Stanford University Press, Stanford, CA.

CHARLTON, THOMAS, AND PATRICIA G. FOURNIER
1993 Urban and Rural Dimensions of the Contact Period: Central Mexico 1521-1620. In *Ethnohistory and Archaeology: Approaches to Post-Contact Change in the Americas,* J. Daniel Rogers and Samuel Wilson, editors, pp. 201–222. Plenum Press, New York.

CHUECO GOITIA, FERNANDO, AND LEOPOLDO TORRES BÁLBAS
1981 *Planos de ciudades Ibéroamericanos y Filipinas, Vol. 1, Láminas.* Instituto de Estudios en Administración Local, Madrid, Spain.

CLENDINNEN, INGA
1987 *Ambivalent Conquests. Maya and Spaniard in Yucatan, 1517–1570.* Cambridge University Press, Cambridge, Great Britain.

COOK, NOBLE DAVID
1998 *Born to Die: Disease and New World Conquest, 1492–1650.* Cambridge University Press, Cambridge, Great Britain.

CROSBY, ALFRED
1972 *The Columbian Exchange.* Greenwood, Westport, CT.

CROUCH, DORA P., DANIEL J. GARR, AND AXEL I. MUNDIGO
1982 *Spanish City Planning in North America.* MIT Press, Cambridge, MA.

DEAGAN, KATHLEEN
1982 St. Augustine: America's First Urban Enclave. *North American Archaeologist,* 3(3):183–205.
1983 *Spanish St. Augustine: The Archaeology of a Colonial Creole Community.* Academic Press, New York.
1985 Spanish-Indian Interaction in Sixteenth-Century Florida and Hispaniola. In *Cultures in Contact,* W. Fitzhugh, editor, pp. 281–318. Smithsonian Institution Press and the Anthropological Society of Washington, Washington, DC.
1988 The Archaeology of the Spanish Contact Period in the Caribbean. *Journal of World Prehistory,* 2(2): 187–233.
1996 Colonial Transformations: Euro-American Cultural Genesis in the Early Spanish-American Colonies. *Journal of Anthropological Research,* 52(2):135–160.
2002a *Artifacts of the Spanish Colonies of Florida and the Caribbean, 1500–1800, Volume 2, Portable Personal Possessions.* Smithsonian Institution Press, Washington, DC.
2002b *Artifacts of the Spanish Colonies of Florida and the Caribbean, 1500-1800, Volume 1, Ceramics, Glassware, and Beads,* updated from 1987 edition. Smithsonian Institution Press, Washington, DC.

DEAGAN, KATHLEEN (EDITOR)
1995 *Puerto Real: The Archaeology of a Sixteenth-Century Spanish Town in Hispaniola.* University Press of Florida, Gainesville.

DEAGAN, KATHLEEN, AND JOSÉ M. CRUXENT
2002 *Columbus's Outpost among the Taínos: Spain and America at La Isabela, 1493–1498.* Yale University Press, New Haven, CT.

DILLEHAY, THOMAS, AND KATHLEEN DEAGAN (EDITORS)
1992 The Spanish Quest for Empire. *Antiquity,* 66 (250): 115–242. Oxford, Great Britain.

DOBYNS, HENRY
1983 *Their Number Become Thinned: Native American Population Dynamics in Eastern North America.* University of Tennessee Press, Knoxville.

DOMÍNGUEZ, LOURDES
1984 *Arqueología Colonial Cubana. Dos estudios.* Editorial de Ciencias Sociales, Havana, Cuba.

ELLIOT, J. H.
1987 The Spanish Conquest. In *Colonial Spanish America,* L. Bethell, editor, pp. 1–58. Cambridge University Press, Cambridge, Great Britain.

ESTEVA-FABREGÁT, CLAUDIO
1995 *Mestizaje in Ibero-America*, John Wheat, translator. University of Arizona Press, Tucson.

EWEN, CHARLES R.
1991 *From Spaniard to Creole: The Archaeology of Hispanic American Cultural Formation at Puerto Real, Haiti.* University of Alabama Press, Tuscaloosa.

FARNSWORTH, PAUL, AND JACK S. WILLIAMS (EDITORS)
1992 The Archaeology of the Spanish Colonial and Mexican Republican Periods. *Historical Archaeology*, 26(1): 1–147.

FLOYD, TROY
1973 *The Columbus Dynasty in the Caribbean 1492–1526.* University of New Mexico Press, Albuquerque.

FOSTER, GEORGE
1960 Culture and Conquest: America's Spanish Heritage. *Viking Fund Publications in Anthropology*, 27. Wenner Gren Foundation, New York.

FOURNIER, PATRICIA
1998 La cerámica colonial del templo mayor. *Arqueologia Mexicana*, 6 (31):52–59.

FOWLER, WILLIAM J.
1991 The Political Economy of Indian Survival in Sixteenth-Century Izalco, El Salvador. In *Columbian Consequences, Vol. 3, The Spanish Borderlands in Pan-American Perspective*, D. H. Thomas, editor, pp. 187–204. Smithsonian Institution Press, Washington, DC.

GARCÍA SAÍZ, MARÍA CONCEPCIÓN
1989 *Las castas (The Mexican Castes).* Olivetti, Mexico City.

GASCO, JANINE
1993 Socioeconomic Change within Native Society in Colonial Sononusco, New Spain. In *Ethnohistory and Archaeology: Approaches to Post-Contact Change in the Americas*, J. Daniel Rogers and Samuel Wilson, editors, pp. 163–180. Plenum Press, New York.

GIBSON, CHARLES
1966 *Spain in America.* Harper and Row, New York.
1987 Indian Society under Spanish Rule. In *Colonial Spanish America*, L. Bethell, editor, pp. 361–399. Cambridge University Press, Cambridge, Great Britain.

GUTIÉRREZ, RAMÓN A.
1991 *When Jesus Came, the Corn Mothers Went Away: Marriage, Sexuality, and Power in New Mexico, 1500–1846.* Stanford University Press, Palo Alto, CA.

HAMILTON, JENNIFER, AND WILLIAM HODGES
1995 The Aftermath of Puerto Real: Archeology at Bayahá. In *Puerto Real: The Archaeology of a Sixteenth-Century Spanish Town in Hispaniola*, K. Deagan, editor, pp. 377–418. University Press of Florida, Gainesville.

HANKE, LEWIS
1949 *The Spanish Struggle for Justice in the Conquest of America.* Little, Brown and Co., Boston, MA.

HANN, JOHN, AND BONNIE G. McEWAN
1998 *The Apalachee Indians and Mission San Luis.* University Press of Florida, Gainesville.

HENIGE, DAVID
1986 Primary Source by Primary Source? On the Role of Epidemics in New World Population. *Ethnohistory*, 33:293–312.

HERNÁNDEZ TÁPIA, CONCEPCIÓN
1970 Despoblaciones de la isla de Santo Domingo en el siglo XVII. *Anuário de Estudios Americanos*, 27:281–320. Madrid, Spain.

HUSSEY, RAYMOND
1932 Text of the Laws of Burgos Concerning the Treatment of the Indians. *Hispanic American Historical Review*, 12:301–326.

JONES, GRANT
1978 The Ethnohistory of the Guale Coast through 1684. In *The Anthropology of St. Catherines Island: 1. Natural and Cultural History*, D. H. Thomas, editor. *American Museum of Natural History Anthropological Papers*, 52(22).

HARING, CLARENCE H.
1947 *The Spanish Empire in America.* Harcourt, Brace and Jovanovitch, New York.

KESSELL, JOHN L.
1997 Restoring Seventeenth-Century New Mexico, Then and Now. *Historical Archaeology*, 31(1): 46–54.

KLEIN, HERBERT S.
1967 *Slavery in the Americas*, reprinted in 1989 by Elephant Paperbacks, Chicago, IL.

KONETZKE, RICHARD
1945 La emigración de mujeres españolas a America durante la época colonial. *Revista Internacional de Sociologia*, III (9):125–150. Madrid, Spain.
1946 El mestizaje y su importancia en el desarrollo de la población hispanoamericana durante la época colonial. *Revista de Indias*, 25:581–586. Madrid, Spain.

LANDERS, JANE G.
1990 African Presence in Early Spanish Colonization of the Caribbean and Southeastern Borderlands. In *Columbian Consequences, Vol. 2, Archaeological and Historical Perspectives on the Spanish Borderlands East*, D. H. Thomas, editor, pp. 315–328. Smithsonian Institution Press, Washington, DC.

LARSEN, CLARK, MARK C. GRIFFIN, DALE L. HUTCHINSON, VIVIAN E. NOBLE, LYNETTE NORR, ROBERT F. PASTOR, CHRISTOPHER B. RUFF, KATHERINE F. RUSSELL, MARGARET J. SCHOENINGER, MICHAEL SCHULTZ, SCOTT W. SIMPSON, AND MARK F. TEAFORD
    2001   Frontiers of Contact: Bioarchaeology of Spanish Florida. *Journal of World Prehistory*, 15(1):69–123.

LISTER, FLORENCE, AND ROBERT LISTER
    1987   *Andalucian Ceramics in Spain and New Spain*. University of New Mexico Press, Albuquerque.

LOCKHART, JAMES, AND STUART B. SCHWARTZ
    1983   Early Latin America. *Cambridge Latin American Studies,* 46. Cambridge University Press, Cambridge, Great Britain.

LOUCKS, L. JILL
    1993   Spanish-Indian Interaction in the Florida Missions: The Archaeology of Baptizing Springs. In *The Spanish Missions of La Florida*, B. G. McEwan, editor, pp. 193–216. University Press of Florida, Gainesville.

LYNCH, JOHN
    1969   *Spain under the Hapsburgs*. New York University Press, New York.

LYON, EUGENE
    1976   *The Enterprise of Florida*. University Press of Florida, Gainesville.

MANN, VIVIAN, THOMAS GLICK, AND JERRILYNN DODD (EDITORS)
    1992   *Convivencia: Jews, Muslims, and Christians in Medieval Spain*. George Braziller and the Jewish Museum, New York.

MCALISTER, LYLE
    1984   *Spain and Portugal in the New World*. University of Minnesota Press, Minneapolis.

MCEWAN, BONNIE G.
    1988   *An Archaeological Perspective on Sixteenth Century Spanish Life in the Old World and the Americas*. Doctoral dissertation, Department of Anthropology, University of Florida, Gainesville. University Microfilms International, Ann Arbor, MI.
    1992   The Role of Ceramics in Spain and Spanish America during the 16th Century. *Historical Archaeology*, 26(1): 92–108.
    2001   The Spiritual Conquest of La Florida. *American Anthropologist*, 103(3):633–644.

MCEWAN, BONNIE G. (EDITOR)
    1993   *The Spanish Missions of La Florida*. University Press of Florida, Gainesville.

MILANICH, JERALD T.
    1999   *Laboring in the Fields of the Lord: Spanish Missions and Southeastern Indians*. Smithsonian Institution Press, Washington, DC.

MILANICH, JERALD T., AND SUSAN MILBRATH (EDITORS)
    1989   *First Encounters, Spanish Explorations in the Caribbean and the United States, 1492–1570*. University Press of Florida, Gainesville.

MORALES PADRÓN, FRANCISCO
    1992   *Andalucía y América*. Editorial MAPFRE, Madrid, Spain..

MORNER, MAGNUS
    1967   *Race Mixture in the History of Latin America*. Little, Brown and Co., Boston, MA.

MOYA PONS, FRANK
    1986   *Después de Colón: Trabajo, sociedad y política en la economía de oro*. Alianza Editorial, Madrid, Spain.

NASH, JUNE
    1980   Aztec Women: The Transition from Status to Class in Empire and Colony. In *Women and Colonization: Anthropological Perspectives*, Mona Etienne and Eleanor Leacock, editors, pp. 134–148. Praeger Publishers, New York.

PAGDEN, ANTHONY
    1992   Fabricating Identity in Spanish America. *History Today*, (42):44–50.

PARRY, JOHN H.
    1964   *The Age of Reconnaissance*. Mentor Books, New York.
    1966   *The Spanish Seaborne Empire*, reprinted in 1990 by University of California Press, Berkeley.

PÉREZ DE TUDELA BUESO, JUAN
    1954   La Negociación Colombina de las Indias. *Revista de Indias*, 57-58:289–357. Madrid, Spain.
    1955   La quiebra de la factoría y el nuevo poblamiento de la Española. *Revista de Indias*, 60(15):208–210.

PHILLIPS, CARLA RAHN
    1990   The Growth and Composition of Trade in the Iberian Empires, 1450–1750. In *The Rise of Merchant Empires*, James D. Tracey, editor, pp. 34–101. Cambridge University Press, Cambridge, Great Britain.

RAMENOFSKY, ANN F.
    1987   *Vectors of Death: The Archaeology of European Contact*. University of New Mexico Press, Albuquerque.

REITZ, ELIZABETH J., AND BONNIE G. MCEWAN
    1995   Animals and the Environment at Puerto Real. In *Puerto Real: The Archaeology of a Sixteenth-Century Spanish Town in Hispaniola*, K. Deagan, editor, pp. 287–334. University Press of Florida, Gainesville.

RUHL, DONNA L., AND KATHLEEN HOFFMAN (EDITORS)
    1997   Diversity and Social Identity in Colonial Spanish America: Native American, African, and Hispanic Communities during the Middle Period. *Historical Archaeology*, 31(1):1–103.

SANTIAGO CRUZ, FRANCISCO
   1960   *Las artes y los grémios en la Nueva España.* Editorial Jus, Mexico City, Mexico.

SAUER, CARL O.
   1966   *The Early Spanish Main.* University of California Press, Berkeley.

SENATORE, MARÍA XIMENEZ
   1995   Tecnologías Nativas y Estratégias de Ocupación Española en la Región del Rio de la Plata. *Historical Archaeology in Latin America,* 11. Institute for Archaeology and Anthropology, Columbia, SC.

SMITH, GREG C.
   1991   *Heard It through the Grapevine: Andean and European Contributions to Spanish Colonial Culture and Viticulture in Moquegua, Peru.* Doctoral dissertation, Department of Anthropology, University of Florida, Gainesville. University Microfilms International, Ann Arbor, MI.

STEVENS-ARROYO, ANTHONY
   1993   The Inter-Atlantic Paradigm: The Failure of Spanish Medieval Colonization in the Canary and Caribbean Islands. *Comparative Studies in Society and History,* 35(3):515–543.

TEJERA GASPAR, ANTONIO, AND EDUARDO AZNAR VALLEJO
   1992   Lesson from the Canaries: First Contact between Europeans and Canarians, ca. 1312–1477. *Antiquity,* 66(250):120–129.

THOMAS, DAVID HURST
   1988   Saints and Soldiers at Santa Catalina: Hispanic Designs for Colonial America. In *The Recovery of Meaning,* Mark Leone and Parker Potter, editors, pp. 73–140. Smithsonian Institution Press, Washington, DC.

THOMAS, DAVID H. (EDITOR)
   1989   *Columbian Consequences, Volume 1, Archaeological and Historical Perspectives in the Spanish Borderlands West.* Smithsonian Institution Press, Washington, DC.
   1990   *Columbian Consequences, Volume 2, Archaeological and Historical Perspectives in the Spanish Borderlands East.* Smithsonian Institution Press, Washington, DC.
   1991   *Columbian Consequences, Volume 3, The Spanish Borderlands in Pan-American Perspective.* Smithsonian Institution Press, Washington, DC.

VERNET, JUAN
   1992   The Legacy of Islam in Spain. In *Al Andalus: The Art of Islamic Spain,* Jerrilyn Dodd, editor, pp. 173–187. Metropolitan Museum of Art, New York.

WEBER, DAVID
   1992   *The Spanish Frontier in North America.* Yale University Press, New Haven, CT.

WOLF, ERIC
   1963   *Sons of the Shaking Earth.* University of Chicago Press, Chicago, IL.

KATHLEEN DEAGAN
FLORIDA MUSEUM OF NATURAL HISTORY
BOX 117800
UNIVERSITY OF FLORIDA
GAINESVILLE, FL 32611

Marcel Moussette

An Encounter in the Baroque Age: French and Amerindians in North America

ABSTRACT

European colonization of North America had its origins in the expansion of European capitalism. But, on the ground, what occurred during the 16th and 17th centuries was the encountering of certain European nations by certain native peoples. Our present field of interest is the particular nature of the encounter between Amerindians and the French, expressed in cultural *métissage* (mixture or hybridity) and political alliances, since this interaction contains all the ingredients that would lend distinctive colors to the new colonial societies. Exploration of European-Amerindian contacts on the part of archaeologists has already resulted in numerous studies focused on the economy, particularly with respect to the fur trade, or on the newcomers' adaptations to a different environment. For the past few years, however, the author has attempted to approach the issue from another angle, that of representations. It is hoped that this approach will lead to a better understanding of the encounter and shed light on the elusive perceptions of that encounter deep in the minds of the actors involved. The thesis presented here is that a true compatibility existed between representations of the world by the French and by the Amerindians, that this compatibility explains the special nature of the relation between the two groups, and, finally, that the archaeological remains left behind by the two groups lend support to the argument for compatibility, enabling the author to make an original contribution to the comprehension of this encounter. The problem of colonial origins in New France may be approached within a dynamic framework whose main stages are linked one to another in time and space, from Europe to North America: the departure, the passage, the encounter, the contact, the exchange, and the *métissage*.

Departure and Passage

Departure from the homeland and trans-Atlantic passage took place mainly in the second half of the 17th century at a time when, following the Spaniards, greater numbers of the French became involved in far-away travels. "Modernity is the first unity of the world, the terrestrial globe caught up in a common adventure, however fragile that community life might be ... a world that tends towards unity," writes Fernand Braudel (1997:301). For the great French historian, this period was marked by the expansion of European capitalism on other continents: Africa, Asia, and America. Initially this incipient capitalism was mercantile and distant, and used bills of exchange (Braudel 1997:328). However, this definition of capitalism is not accepted unanimously. Eric Wolf (1982:78–87) has contrasted the capitalist mode of production, which he linked mainly to the Industrial Revolution of the 18th and 19th centuries, to a tributary mode of production "in which the primary producer, whether cultivator or herdsman, is allowed access to the means of production, while tribute is exacted from him by political or military means" (Wolf 1982: 79–80). For Wolf, the tributary mode of production includes Braudel's incipient capitalism with merchants conducting their business within a feudal system. Yet, regarding an activity such as the fur trade, in which Amerindians indebted to traders had to pledge the results of their future trapping, Wolf (1982:87) agreed that what was happening was close to capitalism, though not yet governed by capitalistic types of relations. Immanuel Wallerstein best reconciles the diverse authors' ideas on the nature of what he calls the capitalist "rupture." He sees it as a three-step phenomenon marked by three important dates—

around 1500, 1650, and 1800; three (or more) theories of history: 1800, with an emphasis on industrialism as the crucial change; 1650, with an emphasis either on the moment when the first "capitalist" states (Britain and the Netherlands) emerged or on the emergence of the presumably key "modern" ideas of Descartes, Leibnitz, Spinoza, Newton, and Locke; and 1500, with an emphasis on the creation of a capitalist *world*-system, as distinct from other forms of economies. It follows that the answer one gives to the query, "crisis of the seventeenth century?" is a function of one's presuppositions about the modern world. The term *crisis* ought not to be debased into a mere synonym for *cyclical shift*. It should be reserved for times of dramatic tension that are more than a conjuncture and that indicate a turning point in structures of *longue durée* (Wallerstein 1980:7).

For the topic under study, it is the earliest and particularly the second epochs of capitalism that are most interesting. In the 17th century, France was still feudal, and Braudel has presented it as a large country kept on the sidelines of the world economy by its economic backwardness. In fact, Braudel (1979:287) distinguished two Frances; one that is Atlantic, the "France of the margins," rich and trading; and the other, the "France of the interior," agrarian and underdeveloped. In this he agreed with Edward Fox who drew a distinction between a maritime France and a landowning France, thus contrasting a more modern France, open to the sea and commerce, with a backward France, tangled in its old ways (Fox 1971; Braudel 1979:292). It is from the ports of the Atlantic France that ships set off westward on their way to the "pays de Canada," the "Terres Neuves," "Labrador," the "Grand Baye," and "Norembègue," following the maritime route already traced by cod fishermen and whale hunters by the end of the 15th century. The motivations—or pretexts—underlying these expeditions were numerous: the search for a passage to China, the lure of precious metals or diamonds, the wish to add new territories to the Kingdom of France, the mission of converting the indigenous peoples, etc. But, aside from fish, it was the furs taken back from this part of the New World that generated the most profit and continued to dominate the economy of New France and then Canada during the 17th and 18th centuries.

The Encounter, Contact, Exchange, and *Métissage*

This sequence is unidirectional and necessarily progresses towards a deepening of the relationships among the peoples involved in its trajectory. An encounter often has the meaning of a fortuitous or unplanned event between two or more persons. The first glance (at the Other) exchanged between Europeans and the Amerindians of the Northeast has been very well described by James Axtell (1988) in his book, *After Columbus: Essays in the Ethnohistory of Colonial North America*. As for *contact*, it may be defined literally as being the state of things or peoples touching each other. Being "in contact," for the purposes of this study, thus signifies that the encountering parties have a certain interest in each other and that they are ready to spend some time communicating. From a thorough encounter, contact results. From sustained contact, the exchange that leads to *métissages* results. The final stage of

the sequence, characterized by *métissages* (the mixture or hybridity) (Davis 2001) occurring among the actors of this encounter (that is to say, the French and the Amerindians of the Northeast during the 17th and 18th centuries), interests us since this outcome marks one of the most important aspects of colonialism.

Wolf (1982:286–387) has written, "the encounter of different modes (of production) spells contradictions and conflicts for the populations they encompass." In the 17th and 18th centuries, precisely this type of encounter took place between the French and the Amerindians, with the French participating in a tributary or feudal mode of production and the Amerindians engaged in a mode of production based on kinship relations. Denys Delâge (1985:126) has studied the exchange between the French and Dutch on the one hand and the Amerindian horticulturalists on the other. According to Delâge, modes of production played a crucial role in establishing the dynamics of relations among these different groups. It was because of this that France, still bogged down in its feudal system and economically disadvantaged, was to base its action in good part on the missionaries' evangelization, while Holland with Amsterdam at the center of the world economy would favor capitalist-type relationships. In any case, these encounters between European modes of production, capitalist or tributary (according to the point of view of different authors), and Amerindian modes of production (based on blood ties) were bound to end in conflict, which Delâge has called the unequal exchange—a situation that has endured with all its negative effects to this day.

> The more deeply the Amerindian societies became involved in the exchange, the more they increased their working time, in spite of the acquisition of more efficient tools. Since the development of the forces of production did not enable the Amerindians to reproduce the European goods on their own, subordination to the Europeans constituted the framework on which commercial relations were woven (Delâge 1985:339).

An interpretation of the relations between Europeans and Amerindians in terms of exchange, that is, in economic terms, concurs with the model of capitalism proposed by Immanuel Wallerstein (1980), based on the subjection of the periphery by the center. This explains the tragic destiny experienced by the Amerindian population of North America. However, the strong polarization posited by this recognition of the inequality of the exchange between the French and the Amerindians may color interpretations of the protagonists' behaviors. For example, whereas Delâge (1985:177–178) simply saw in the display and magnificence of church decorations and religious offices a means for missionaries to persuade Amerindians to convert (which was no doubt to a great degree the case), Victor Tapié (1957: 134–136) regarded the opulent European Baroque churches as places where common peoples were admitted to admire the richness of the sanctuaries and to participate in the joy of the Roman Catholic Church's celebrations. These sumptuous architectural and religious productions belong to the Counter-Reformation in the Baroque age, and they cannot be entirely explained in terms of inferiority and superiority.

Beyond the exchange stage comes the stage corresponding to *métissages*; for only after intensive, diversified, and well-assimilated exchanges can there arise conditions propitious to the mixing of cultures. In this line of thought, how the pomp and ceremony of Baroque religious art gave birth to a hybrid peculiar to the autochthonous societies of Iberian America should be recalled, where native art

> blended into the ocean of Mannerist and Baroque forms that eventually inundated town and countryside, contributing its prodigious inventivity and exuberance to a style that very soon became a civilization. The magnification of the image by the Catholic Church and the indigenous tradition, the shared taste for spectacle, recourse to sensual pleasure, and triumph of the senses, of color, of light gave an impulse to Baroque America, the mirror of all the *métissages*, past and present (Gruzinski 1991:222).

Inferiority of the Amerindians? Superiority of the Europeans? The issue cannot be approached in these terms; new identities had been negotiated and were expressed through new mixed forms, both among the natives and among the *métis* and Creoles of the colony. To go back to the initial question, that of the colonial origins of New France, it is clear that *métissages* offer a very important lead since it is through them that the deep effects of mutual connections can be identified but also understood better with respect to mental universes.

The Baroque

Most basic anthropology textbooks discuss the mechanisms of rejection or acceptance of cultural elements from one cultural system to another. One condition for the acceptance of a cultural element is that the host system must be able to integrate the element into its functioning or its structure by making a place for it—a place that does not necessarily correspond to what it was intended for at its conception. This is equally true for cultural elements invented inside a cultural system and for those transferred from one system to another. When we consider a cultural complex, for example, a system of beliefs, a mode of exploiting the environment, or even representations of the world through decorative arts, the same principles still apply but with an incomparably higher degree of complexity. Thus, for a transfer of cultural elements or complexes to be effected from a transmitting group to a receiving group (and in the case of North America where the roles of transmitter and receiver were shared by each of the groups), there must exist favorable conditions for such cultural transfers and the changes that necessarily come with them. These conditions are three in number. First, each group must have a motive or a basic motivation that colors its undertakings. For the French, this motivation can be summed up in three words: commerce, evangelization, and power. For the Amerindians, it is clear that such motives included commerce and power linked to the acquisition of European goods and technologies. Second, the encounters, contacts, and exchanges must create a certain instability, indeed even a state of crisis, between the two groups involved so that the cultural systems become more flexible and more open to change. And third, the two communicating cultural systems must show a certain compatibility with one another, a compatibility expressed less in the content than in the structure of mental universes, with all the ensuing consequences this may have for the world vision of each, the relation to the Other, and the negotiation of each one's own identity.

It is the third condition, the compatibility of the mental universes of the actors involved, that is favored here as a research path. In order to evaluate this compatibility or noncompatibility, it is first necessary to describe mentalities, define their main characteristics, and establish their general outlines.

At the end of the 15th century and during the first half of the 16th century, the Indians of the Caribbean and Mexico met and were conquered by the Spaniards who were, in fact, men of the Renaissance, still caught up in the spirit of their combats against the Moors. One hundred years later, the Amerindians of northeastern North America had to deal with French people who were experiencing the jolts of capitalist expansion and the tensions accompanying the Protestant Reformation and the Catholic Counter-Reformation. The French-Amerindian meeting took place at the height of the Baroque age, described by historian Johan Huizinga as a vast complex of ideas that, while not necessarily well defined, cumulatively expressed the essence of civilization in the 17th century.

> Now painting, poetry, literature, even politics and theology, in short, every field of skill and learning in the 17th century, have to measure up to some preconceived idea of "the Baroque." Some apply the term to the beginning of the epoch, when men delighted in colourful and exuberant imagination; others to a later period of sombre stateliness and solemn dignity. But, taken by and large, it evokes visions of conscious exaggeration, of something imposing, overawing, colossal, avowedly unreal. Baroque forms are, in the fullest sense of the word, art-forms (Huizinga 1971:208).

The Baroque paradigm, born in reaction to the Protestant Reformation, had at its center an obsession with reconciling the human with the divine. For Roman Catholics, God was present on Earth in a perceptible way, while for Protestants he could be reached only through his Word. Consequently, the spirit of Roman Catholicism was strongly characterized by the reconciliation of contraries, the absorption of difference, and the resolution of the tensions between reality and appearance. To express this fundamental tension between two poles, the Baroque offered a performance of the world, often exuberant and sometimes outrageous, in which theatricality and rhetorical figures sought to persuade the spectator through a sensation of being engulfed or of stupefaction. As expressed by Claude-Gilbert Dubois (1995:15), the "fundamental principle of Baroque imagination is the search for unity through the irrepressible duality related to the human condition."

In France the Baroque evolved in opposition to Classicism. However, the two art styles were so intertwined that, at the level of stylistic typology, modern authors no longer agree on what was Baroque and what was Classical, to the point that Tapié (1957:238) has spoken of "Classicism on a Baroque background," and Robert Muchembled (1995) of the "Baroque temptation." C-G Dubois's proposal on this subject appears most valuable to the line of thought pursued here, since he brings together under the Baroque label both baroquism and classicism, considering them "as internal movements, oscillatory and indissociable, which are nourished by one another, through conjunction or reaction, depending on the period and the country" (Dubois 1995:15). This debate need not concern us since it was the segments of society nearest to the Baroque spirit, according to Muchembled (1995:145–147), who formed substantial ingredients of the colonial society that emerged in New France—the Jesuits, the military, and the hired hands among the lower classes. In fact, a migrant stream emanated largely from the "France of the margins," open to the Atlantic space, trading and adventurous, described by Braudel.

The Baroque in New France

With respect to the history of New France, the term "Baroque" has been used almost exclusively by art historians and then only sparingly until recently; the expression "French Classical style" is much more prevalent. Although hesitant yet to talk about a "Baroque New France," the few studies carried out so far on some of the material stored in the basement of the King's Stores in Québec City during the first half of the 18th century seem to lead towards such an interpretation. The study of a collection of 21 brass religious medallions of three different types from that site (Figure 1), along with those already studied by Charles Rinehart (1990) for the Great Lakes region and the Mississippi Valley and some others from the St. Lawrence Valley, has revealed unequivocal affinities between Counter-Reformation spirituality, Baroque representations, and the Amerindian world view (Moussette 2002). The result is a collection of 84 medallions dug from more than 15 different sites, most of them made of coppery metals much appreciated by the Amerindians. The nature of these sites and

TYPE I

TYPE II

TYPE III

⊏⊐ 1 cm

FIGURE 1. The three types of religious medallions found on the site of the Intendant's Palace in Québec City. (*A*) Type I: obverse, Christ; reverse, the Virgin Mary. (*B*) Type II: obverse, Immaculate Conception; reverse, two angels holding a monstrance. (*C*) Type III: obverse, St. Bruno; reverse, St. Rosalina offering a rose to the Virgin Mary and the Christ child. (Photo by Lise Jodoin; computer graphics by Andrée Héroux.)

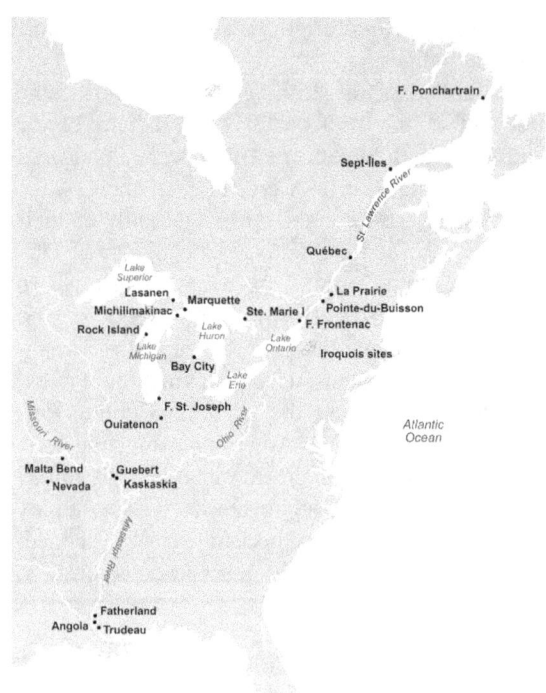

FIGURE 2. Sites of the French Regime where religious medallions and trade gun parts have been excavated. (Drawing by Andrée Héroux.)

their very wide distribution (Figure 2) demonstrate that from the medallions' point of arrival in New France (at the site of the Intendant's Palace in Québec City), they were transported, in some cases via a portage trail (Pointe-du-Buisson), towards French settlements (Ouiatenon), Amerindian villages (Guebert), and some fur trade posts (Frontenac, St. Joseph, Michilimackinac) as well as missions (St. Marie I, La Prairie, Marquette). The medallions might accompany deceased Amerindians on their final journey, since some of the medallions have been found in burials (Rock Island, Lasanen).

Counter-Reformation spirituality is shown in three main ways through the motifs molded on the obverse and reverse of these medallions. First, there is the fundamental theme of Christ's incarnation and his true presence on Earth, which is represented by the adoration of the Holy Sacrament (Figure 1*B*, two angels holding a Monstrance); the head and shoulder of Christ viewed in profile, often accompanied on the reverse by his mother shown in the same way (Figure 1*A*); and by certain aspects of Jesus Christ's life or by persons of his entourage (the Holy Family, Mary Magdalen, the apostles, etc.). A second set of representations is mostly characterized by Baroque theatricality, either related to the rapture of ecstasy (Figure 1*C*, St. Bruno; Figure 3, St. Theresa of Avila) or to physical pain (the descent from the Cross and the martyrs Venantius, Agatha, Barbara, and Lucia). Third, certain obverse and reverse images represent to the Amerindian, whether baptized or about to be converted, the devotions

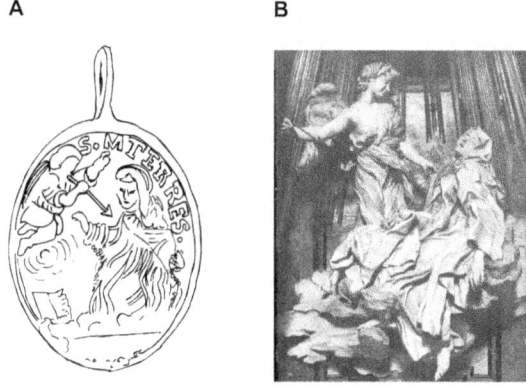

A   B

FIGURE 3. The ecstasy of St. Theresa of Avila: (A) medallion from Michilimackinac (drawing by Marcel Moussette); (B) sculpture by Bernini (Santa Maria della Vittoria, Rome).

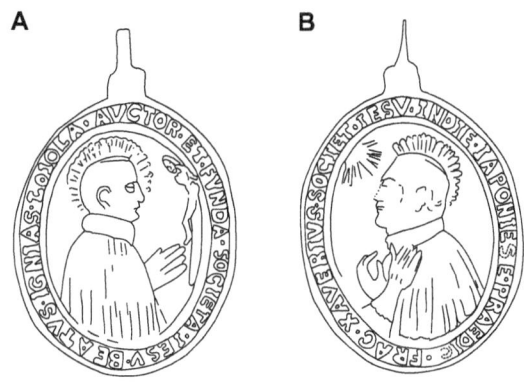

A   B

FIGURE 4. New saints of the Counter-Reformation: (A) Ignatius of Loyola; (B) Francis Xavier. Obverse and reverse of a medallion found on the site of St. Marie among the Hurons. (Drawing by Marcel Moussette.)

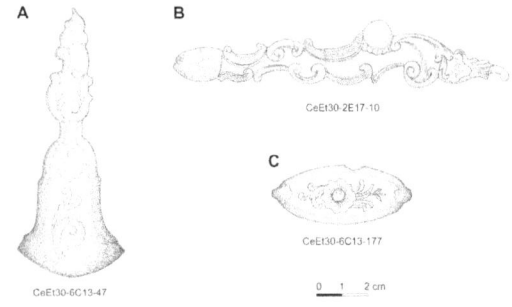

A   B

FIGURE 5. Brass trade gun parts from the site of the Intendant's Palace in Québec City decorated in the Rococo style: (A) buttplate finial (CeEt-30-6C13-47); (B) sideplate (CeEt-30-2E17-10); (C) trigger guard (CeEt-30-6C13-177). (Drawing by Alain Delisle; computer graphics by Andrée Héroux.)

of the Counter-Reformation (the Sacred Hearts and, Figure 1B, the Immaculate Conception); and the new saints of the Church, many of them linked to the Jesuit order: Bruno, Ignatius of Loyola, Francis of Sales, John Capistrano, John of the Cross, Francis Xavier, John Francis Regis, Theresa of Avila, and Rosa of Lima (Figure 4).

Comparable results have been obtained from a collection of more than 2,000 iron and brass trade gun parts—trigger guards, butt plates, side plates, and ramrod holders (Figure 5) with incised decorations in the purest Rococo style. These gun parts were uncovered in Québec City from the rubble of the King's Stores, destroyed during the battle of the spring of 1760 (Moussette 2001). The Rococo style was used to decorate firearms made between 1735 and 1790 (Gusler and Lavin 1977:2) and may be considered the ultimate stage of the Baroque style. It is characterized by a subtle and lively grace that materializes in the asymmetry of flowing scrolls and the interlacing of vegetal and shell motifs, producing forms in constant metamorphosis. Generally, this ornamental style is found on the very fine guns of European aristocrats, on "the most beautiful firearms of that period" (Venner 1979:72–73; Gaier and Sabatti 1998). In regard to the collection from the site of the Intendant's Palace, the decorations are incised in brass or iron instead of being embossed or embellished with gold or silver damascening, so these are certainly more common objects, acquired for a cheaper price. But the fact remains that the work of the gunsmiths is of good quality; firearms that bore such parts could very well be considered "fine guns." An important fact revealed by the study of this collection is the vast distribution of gun parts decorated in the Rococo style on sites occupied by Amerindians and the French, from the North Shore of the Gulf of St. Lawrence to the Great Lakes to the Mississippi Valley (Figure 2). Apart from Québec City, most of the sites where such gun parts have been recovered are Amerindian sites (Old Kaskaskia, Angola Farm, Malta Bend, Nevada, and Trudeau), or fur trade posts (Michilimackinac, St. Joseph, Pontchartrain, Sept-Îles), as well as one undetermined site, Bay City (Moussette 2001:69–70). Consequently, it is plausible to think that these objects were intended for exchange in the fur trade, as ornaments on the "trade guns" used by the Amerindians that are mentioned in archival documents,

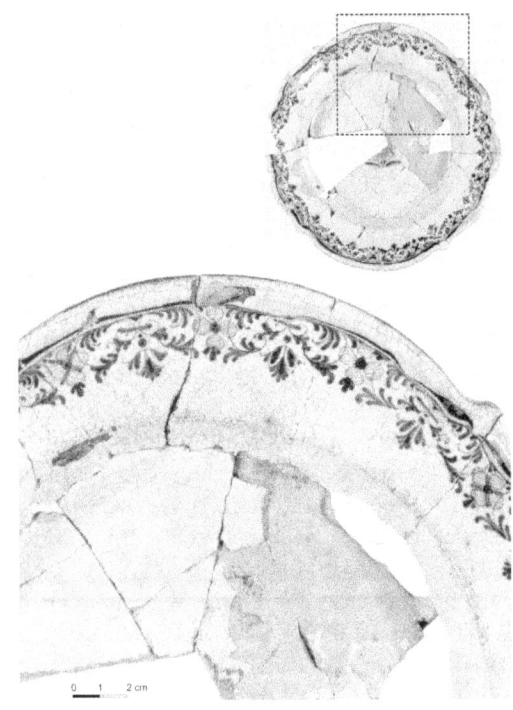

FIGURE 6. Moustiers style faïence platter (CeEt-30-27D82-1) from the site of the Intendant's Palace, Québec City. (Photo by Lise Jodoin; computer graphics by Andrée Héroux.)

without ever being described precisely by French merchants or administrators.

The presence of the Baroque has been attested to in many other cultural elements of New France. Music had an important place in the work of evangelization by the missionaries, and Baroque music was certainly known to the Amerindians of New France, as demonstrated by the recent discovery of a manuscript score of Baroque inspiration to which words in the Abnaki language were added (Pacquier 1996; P-A Dubois 1997). Religious paintings and prints were part of the propaganda used by Counter-Reformation agents seeking to "civilize" the Amerindians and persuade them to convert to the Catholic faith. Different categories of pottery decorated in the Baroque and Rococo styles, especially the faïence of Moustiers and Rouen (Figure 6) as well as the gray German stonewares, have been unearthed on Amerindian sites and French advanced posts (Neitzel 1965; Brain 1979; Walthall 1991; Genêt 1996; Gaimster 1997). Carved wooden statues and altar screens were often gilded with gold leaf in the workshops of the Ursuline and Augustine

nuns in Québec City and Montréal (Porter 1975). The nuns, who embroidered altar cloths and sacerdotal vestments with silk, silver, and gold threads in the Baroque style, also taught their craft to Indian girls (as well as taking care of sick Amerindians). Wrought-iron work in this style is best exemplified by Lozeau's crosses (Figure 7) with the double-curve motif, one of which stood above the chapel of the Chicoutimi Indian mission. In fact, this artistic and decorative production was used as an instrument of Baroque theatricality, laid out before the eyes of the Amerindians to impress them and convince them of the superiority of French civilization. All these elements were demonstrations of power, albeit on a smaller scale but not all that different from the fantastic gilded Baroque decorations of tall galleys (such as the *Grande Reale de France*), which transported persons of royal rank (Musée du Québec et Musée national de la Marine 2001), or the great Baroque festivities given by the Sun King and other monarchs of European courts (Alewyn 1964).

The Bipartite Ideology of the Amerindians

Turning to the Amerindians, what characterized their systems of representation at the time of their contacts with the French? Some fundamental elements in the answer to this question are found in one of Claude Lévi-Strauss's (1991) most recent books, *Histoire de Lynx*. In this general study of Amerindian myths of the Pacific Northwest Coast, Lévi-Strauss recounted a myth concerning the origin of wind and mist, the first represented by Coyote and the second by Lynx. Through the intrigues of this mis-

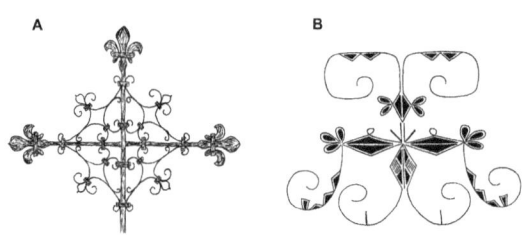

FIGURE 7. (*A*) Iron cross at the Ursuline convent in Québec City made by Jean-Baptiste Lozeau (drawing by Marcel Moussette); (*B*) Penobscot double-curve design (Speck 1914: figure 5a). (Computer graphics by Andrée Héroux.)

matched couple or pair, Lévi-Strauss recognizes, as he has elsewhere as well, the impossible or paradoxical twinness that serves as a basis for the bipartite ideology of the Amerindians. Indeed, from the imbalance and the disparity that govern the pair's relationship, there arise dynamics of difference, of opening up to the Other and to the World, which characterize the mental universe of the Amerindians. It is thus, according to the author, an unstable dualism, one from which there "always results another unstable dualism" (Lévi-Strauss 1991:306) or "a dualism in perpetual imbalance, the successive states of which fit into each other" (Lévi-Strauss 1991:316).

But the structures generated by the bipartite ideology are not only found in mythology. They also have been recognized in an ancient ornamental tradition of bilateral symmetry, which Franz Boas (1955:32, 223–244) identified among the Amerindians of the Northwest Coast of Canada and which, according to Rémi Savard (1969), is spread all over America and in many other regions of the world. From this ornamental tradition of bilateral symmetry, the botanist-ethnologist Jacques Rousseau (1956) derived the double-curve motif (Figure 8) that had been studied by Franck G. Speck (1914). This motif, based on the principle that "one half maintains with the other a mirrored relation" (Savard 1977:29–30), has its main expression among the Algonkians of the Northeast. In spite of the fact that no example of this style has been found so far on objects dating from the prehistoric period, some historians and anthropologists (Guy 1969; Savard 1969, 1977; Dickason 1974; Phillips 1987:61; Whitehead 1987:42) have seen in it an ancient indigenous ornamental tradition. In this, they were no doubt influenced by Speck (1914) who established the vast distribution of this motif, which spread from the Northeast to the Iroquoians of the East, to the nations of the Northwest, as well to the Algonkians of the central and upper Mississippi Valley regions. In fact, Camil Guy (1969:18) and Olive Dickason (1974:38) thought that the double-curve style, because of its formal poly-valence, could have constituted a link between the ancient geometric style and the vegetal style introduced by the Europeans. Actually, it cannot be concluded with certainty that the double-curve ornamentation existed before the arrival of the Europeans. It is known that this motif was used on European-made objects in the 17th and 18th centuries in conjunction with floral ornamenta-tion. However, for our purposes, what is impor-tant is not to determine if the double-curve motif is of Amerindian or European origin but, rather, what its use by both peoples tells us about their bipartite representation of the world.

To return to the original question, it could, at this stage in our reflection, be proposed that the duality characterizing the mental universes of both the French and the Amerindians of the Northeast created a fertile middle ground for cultural *métissages* and transfers between the two groups. In this way the French and Amerindians, caught in the meshes of the net set by the capitalist world system, had to adapt to the conditions created by unequal exchange and accommodate their cultural systems, one to the other. These processes of accommodation and of adaptation, so well analyzed by Richard White (1991:10), of mixing and blending, are at the origin of all cultural *métissages*.

Conclusion

In conclusion, a few cases of such *métissages* will be outlined. The double-curve motif and the vegetal ornamentation that replaced it were orna-mental motifs appropriated by Amerindians who reproduced them in paintings and as embroider-ies made with glass beads or porcupine quills on clothes or other ordinary objects. But they are

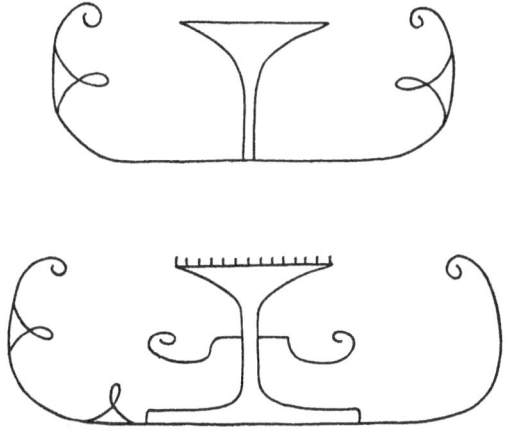

FIGURE 8. Micmac double-curve motif (Speck 1914: figure 9).

also found in the repertory of Baroque decoration, on embroidered altar screens, faïence plates and stoneware containers, gun parts, and even wrought-iron crosses. This should not come as too much of a surprise, since Euro-American and European folk art traditions also show a binary structure very much akin to the Amerindian bilateral symmetry.

> Through the utilization of different patterns in a single artifact, a complex, over-all design can be accomplished, but the thinking in the design of folk ornamentation (or in the performance of folksong or tale) does not often go beyond repetition, with bilateral symmetry being a special case of repetition. And it does not often go beyond variation in terms of the number two, with three being a special case of two, when two of the three elements form a pair (Glassie 1972:272).

For example, it is interesting to compare the complex execution of the double-curve motif in two different objects—the cross that surmounted the Québec Ursulines chapel in 1724 (Dupont 1979:90) and the collar-cape worn by a Penobscot chief during a funerary ceremony (Figure 7). While the iron cross shows a perfect symmetry in all directions, the Penobscot motif, also cruciform, is symmetrical only bilaterally, showing a clear asymmetry from top to bottom. From a symbolic viewpoint, the Ursulines' cross with its stylized fleur-de-lys proclaims the Gallic character of the institution, while the motif on the Penobscot collar-cape signifies the central place for mourning the deceased chief. Finally, in spite of their strong geometrical compositions, the two motifs show vegetal elements: the fleur-de-lys in the case of the Ursulines' cross, and leaves and boughs in the case of the Penobscot collar-cape. The mingling of these elements clearly exemplifies how the morphology of the double-curve ornamentation fitted very naturally between the geometrical and the floral or vegetal stylistic traditions. Another example of the same sort is a Pottawatomi glass-bead and porcupine-quill embroidery decoration, whose central motif is a flower flanked by symmetrical boughs bearing flowers and leaves (Figure 9). A similar composition is found engraved on a brass trigger guard from the 1760 destruction context of the King's Stores in Québec City (Moussette 2001), with a central motif consisting of a Rococo shell with one leafy bough on each side (Figure 9). Could this not be seen

as expressing the construction of a renewed identity resulting from exchanges and alliances with the Europeans? The same question might be asked about Amerindian stories and myths incorporating traditional French-Canadian tales in which the hero "Ti-Jean" (Little John), the famous trickster, is associated with Coyote, another great trickster, paired with Lynx (Lévi-Strauss 1991; Jacquin 1996). In the same vein, a recent article by the ethnologist Jean-Pierre Pichette (1995) demonstrates how the tale entitled "Le Lynx et le Renard" (The Lynx and the Fox), now incorporated in the oral tradition of the Ojibways of northern Ontario, is in fact a French-Canadian tale coming from a more ancient French oral tradition.

The French of New France also had to rethink and renegotiate their identity. By the end of the 17th century, they were already referring to themselves as *Canadiens*. The study of French colonial sites in light of this question of construction of identity and of *métissages* has barely begun. However, Hélène Côté (2001), who has done such a study for one of the sites dug under the author's supervision on Île aux Oies, has already been able to point out a few identity markers, such as stone pipes decorated in the Amerindian fashion but made locally by *Canadien* settlers as well as a preference for game over the meat of domestic animals. Also, very recently, on the site of the Jesuit's mission of La Prairie de la Magdeleine, some archaeological contexts have been discovered that are culturally so mixed that so far it can not be decided if they were French or Amerindian. The hunch is that they are hybrid.

These avenues of research seem promising enough and certainly deserve to be pursued using

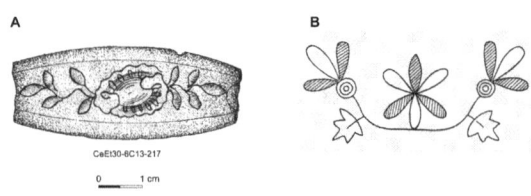

FIGURE 9. (*A*) Brass trigger guard (CeEt-30-6C13-217) found on the site of the Intendant's Palace in Québec City (drawing by Alain Delisle); (*B*) Pottawatomi double-curve design (Speck 1914: figure 23). (Computer graphics by Andrée Héroux.)

the conceptual framework just outlined. How-ever, it must be confessed that the scope and complexity of such a research project present quite an overwhelming challenge. For any suc-cess in reaching a solution to the problem will depend on an eclectic marshalling of extremely diverse resources from the history of art, social history, the history of mentalities, anthropology, and refined archaeometric analyses, in addition to classic archaeological approaches linked to spa-tial, chronological, and typological analysis.

ACKNOWLEDGMENTS

I am very grateful to the persons who were involved in one way or another in the production of this article: Bonnie G. McEwan and Gregory A. Waselkov, who invited me to participate in the plenary session at the 2002 Society for Historical Archaeology Conference in Mobile, where a first version of this article was read; Jane Macaulay, who revised my sometime laborious English; Lise Jodoin, who photographed some of the artifacts; Alain Delisle, who drew the gun parts; Andrée Héroux, who created the computer graphics; and Clara Marceau, who typed the text. This research was financed in part by the City of Québec and Laval University through an agreement with the Ministère de la Culture et des Communications du Québec. I should also mention the important role played by Célat (Centre d'études sur la langue, les arts et la tradition), which provided me with a favorable and creative intellectual environment.

REFERENCES

ALEWYN, RICHARD
    1964 *L'univers du baroque.* Éditions Gonthier, Geneva, Switzerland.

AXTELL, JAMES
    1988 *After Columbus: Essays in the Ethnohistory of Colonial North America.* Oxford University Press, New York.

BOAS, FRANZ
    1955 *Primitive Art.* Dover Publications, New York.

BRAIN, JEFFREY P.
    1979 Tunica Treasure. *Papers of the Peabody Museum of Archaeology and Ethnology, 71.* Harvard University, Cambridge, MA.

BRAUDEL, FERNAND
    1979 *Le temps du monde: Civilisation matérielle, économie et capitalisme, vol. 3.* Armand Collin, Paris, France.
    1997 Expansion européenne et capitalisme (1450–1650). In *Les ambitions de l'histoire: Les écrits de Fernand Braudel, vol. 2,* Roselyne de Ayala and Paule Braudel, editors, pp. 299–345. Éditions de Fallois, Paris, France.

CÔTÉ, HÉLÈNE
    2001 Le site de la Nouvelle Ferme à l'Île aux Oies. Doctoral dissertation (Archéologie), Département d'histoire, Université Laval, Québec, PQ.

DAVIS, NATALIE ZEMON
    2001 Polarities, Hybridities: What Strategies for Decentering? In *Decentering the Renaissance: Canada and Europe in Multidisciplinary Perspective, 1500–1700,* G. Warkentin and C. Podruchny, editors, pp. 19–32. University of Toronto Press, Toronto, ON.

DELÂGE, DENYS
    1985 *Le pays renversé.* Boréal Express, Montréal, PQ.

DICKASON, OLIVE P.
    1974 *Indian Arts in Canada.* Indian and Northern Affairs, Ottawa, ON.

DUBOIS, CLAUDE-GILBERT
    1995 *Le baroque en Europe et en France.* Presses universitaires de France, Paris, France.

DUBOIS, PAUL-ANDRÉ
    1997 Naissance du cantique en langue vernaculaire dans les missions de la Nouvelle-France et conquête des langues amérindiennes. *Recherches amérindiennes au Québec,* 27 (2):19–31.

DUPONT, JEAN-CLAUDE
    1979 *L'artisan forgeron.* Les Presses de l'Université Laval, Québec, PQ.

FOX, EDWARD WHITING
    1971 *History in a Geographic Perspective: The Other France.* Norton, New York.

GAIER, CLAUDE, AND DE PIETRO SABATTI
    1998 *Les plus belles gravures d'armes de chasse.* Hatier, Paris, France.

GAIMSTER, DAVID
    1997 *German Stoneware, 1200–1900.* British Museum Press, London, UK.

GENÊT, NICOLE
    1996 La faïence de Place Royale. *Collection patrimoine, dossier 45.* Ministère de la Culture et des Communications, Québec, PQ.

GLASSIE, HENRY
    1972 Folk Art. In *Folklore and Folklife: An Introduction,* Richard M. Dordson, editor, pp. 253–280. University of Chicago Press, Chicago, IL.

GRUZINSKI, SERGE
    1991 *L'Amérique de la conquête peinte par les Indiens du Mexique.* Flammarion, Paris, France.

GUSLER, WALLACE B., AND JAMES D. LAVIN
    1977 *Decorated Fire Arms, 1540–1870, from the Collections of Clay P. Bedford.* Colonial Williamsburg Foundation, Williamsburg, VA.

GUY, CAMIL
    1969   L'Art décoratif des Indiens de l'Est. *Culture vivante*, 14:9–18.

HUIZINGA, JOHAN
    1971   *Homo Ludens*. Paladin, London, UK.

JACQUIN, PHILIPPE
    1996   *Les Indiens blancs*. Libre Expression, Montréal, PQ.

LÉVI-STRAUSS, CLAUDE
    1991   *Histoire de Lynx*. Plon, Paris, France.

MOUSSETTE, MARCEL
    2001   Les garnitures de fusils de traite des magasins du roi à Québec: un autre chemin de l'univers baroque en Amérique du Nord. *Archéologiques*, 14:50–78.
    2002   Les médailles religieuses, une forme de l'imagerie baroque en Nouvelle-France. *Les Cahiers des Dix*, 55:295–329.

MUCHEMBLED, ROBERT
    1995   *Culture et société en France du début du XVIe siècle au milieu du XVIIe siècle*. Sedes, Paris, France.

MUSÉE DU QUÉBEC ET MUSÉE NATIONAL DE LA MARINE
    2001   *Les génies de la mer*. Musée du Québec, Québec, PQ, and Musée National de la Marine, Paris, France.

NEITZEL, ROBERT S.
    1965   Archaeology of the Fatherland Site: The Grand Village of the Natchez. *Anthropological Papers of the American Museum of Natural History*, 51(1).

PACQUIER, ALAIN
    1996   *Les chemins du baroque dans le Nouveau Monde*. Fayard, Paris, France.

PHILLIPS, RUTH B.
    1987   Like a Star I Shine: Northern Woodland Artistic Traditions. In *The Spirit Sings*, Glenbow-Alberta Institute, editor, pp. 51–92. McCelland and Stewart, Toronto, ON.

PICHETTE, JEAN-PIERRE
    1995   Le Lynx et le Renard: Un relais déroutant dans la transmission du conte populaire français en Ontario. *Cahiers Charlevoix*, 6:169–240.

PORTER, JOHN A.
    1975   *L'art de la dorure au Québec du XVIIe siècle à nos jours*. Éditions Garneau, Québec, PQ.

RINEHART, CHARLES J.
    1990   Crucifixes and Medallions: Their Role at Fort Michilimackinac. *Volumes in Historical Archaeology*, 11. South Carolina Institute of Archaeology and Anthropology, University of South Carolina, Columbia.

ROUSSEAU, JACQUES
    1956   L'origine du motif de la double courbe dans l'art algonkin. *Anthropologica*, (2):218–221.

SAVARD, RÉMI
    1969   Les Indiens de l'Est du Canada et leur art. In *Chefs-d'oeuvre des arts indiens et esquimaux du Canada*, n.p. Société des amis du Musée de l'Homme, Paris, France.
    1977   *Destins d'Amérique, les autochtones et nous*. L'hexagone, Montréal, PQ.

SPECK, FRANK G.
    1914   The Double-Curve Motive in Northeastern Algonkian Art. In *Geological Survey of Canada, Memoir 42 (No. 1 of the Anthropological Series)*. Department of Mines, Ottawa, ON.

TAPIÉ, VICTOR L.
    1957   *Baroque et classicisme*. Plon, Paris, France.

VENNER, DOMINIQUE
    1979   *Les armes à feu françaises*. Jacques Grancher, Paris, France.

WALLERSTEIN, IMMANUEL
    1980   *The Modern World-System II: Mercantilism and the Consolidation of the European World-Economy, 1600–1750*. Academic Press, New York.

WALTHALL, JOHN A.
    1991   French Colonial Fort Massac: Architecture and Ceramic Patterning. In *French Colonial Archaeology: The Illinois Country and the Western Great Lakes*. John A. Walthall, editor, pp. 42–64. University of Illinois Press, Urbana.

WHITE, RICHARD
    1991   *The Middle Ground: Indians, Empires, and Republics in the Great Lakes Region, 1650–1815*. Cambridge University Press, Cambridge, UK.

WHITEHEAD, RUTH H.
    1987   I Have Lived Here Since the World Began: Atlantic Coast Artistic Traditions. In *The Spirit Sings*, Glenbow-Alberta Institute editor, p. 17–49. McClelland and Stewart, Toronto, ON.

WOLF, ERIC
    1982   *Europe and the People without History*. University of California Press, Berkeley.

MARCEL MOUSSETTE
CÉLAT, DÉPARTEMENT D'HISTOIRE
UNIVERSITÉ LAVAL
QUÉBEC, QUÉBEC, CANADA
G1K 7P4

Correlates of Contact: Epidemic Disease in Archaeological Context

Dale L. Hutchinson
Jeffrey M. Mitchem

ABSTRACT

Over the past several decades, historians, geographers, demographers, anthropologists and others interested in the demographic effects of contact between Europeans and Native Americans have emphasized epidemic diseases as a major factor in declining native populations. Little progress, however, has been made toward developing a method and theory for testing hypotheses regarding epidemic diseases and depopulation in the archaeological record. Tatham Mound, an early contact period mortuary locality in Florida serves as a useful example of the difficulties encountered when testing propositions regarding epidemic disease in archaeological context.

Introduction

> The crucial factor is not the disease's severity, its incidence, or its duration. What matters is whether the disease acted as an independent and identifiable force in pushing power toward certain groups or institutions. Diseases such as tuberculosis in the nineteenth century or syphilis in Europe in the sixteenth century decimated populations, but their effects were so general that whether they had any political, cultural, or ethnogenetic importance is impossible to determine, human disasters though they were (Robins 1981:155).

The issue of culture contact and colonialism is one of widespread contemporary discussion. Fueled partially by the Columbian quincentennial, New World encounters between Native Americans and Europeans have dominated much of the recent literature on colonialism and culture contact. Of particular interest has been recovering and deciphering the evidence regarding the role of European-introduced diseases in the demise of Native American populations during the first two centuries of European colonization. A central problem facing researchers studying early diseases concerns the historic record; documentation is scant, spotty, and frequently inconsistent. Termed "the forgotten centuries" by Hudson and Tesser (1994), the protohistoric or initial contact period is of immense importance for understanding the depopulation that occurred among Native American populations throughout the continent.

Most would agree that epidemic diseases were an important variable in depopulation, but the timing of epidemics and the universal effects of epidemic diseases are issues of debate. Two main models of epidemic disease predominate in the discussions. The "disease impact" model emphasizes the rather immediate effects of new epidemic diseases introduced by Europeans which swept through native populations like a scythe reaping high percentages among the non-immune. While not a universal viewpoint, it clearly permeates many discussions of European colonization of the New World and it incorporates an early and rather complete demographic collapse (Crosby 1972, 1976; Borah 1976; Cook 1976; Dobyns 1983; Ramenofsky 1987; Smith 1987). An alternative "combined effects" model emphasizes disease as one component of a prolonged, multi-component colonial process with a more delayed and steady demographic impact (Kroeber 1939; Thornton 1987, 1997; Baker and Kealhofer 1996).

One other interpretation is that the early contact experience included cycling epidemics in restricted geographic ranges (Trigger 1976, 1985; Ramenofsky 1987). As Ramenofsky (1987) proposed, not all settlement locations or settlement types are susceptible to the same types of disease exposure or disease experience. In her model of differential persistence, she proposed that some settlement types, such as sedentary settlement types located on watersheds, might have a higher disease transmission than mobile dispersed settlement types. Cycling epidemics of smallpox are well documented for the Northeast following 1632 (Trigger 1976, 1985).

A central problem with addressing any of these models of epidemic disease and demographic collapse is the paucity of documentary evidence. Unlike the Old World with its well-recorded documentary records for the plague years in the 15th century, there are few historic records for disease epidemics in the New World during this early 200 year period, and no written records which can be used for comparative purposes from the period prior to contact. Archaeological and osteological data offer the only possible sources for assessing the effects of epidemic diseases during this time period. Consequently, a variety of scholars including biologists, anthropologists, historians, demographers, and others interested in the early contact period have directed their attention toward the problem of reconstructing the events that transpired during the early contact period using archaeological remains and historical documents.

In the past 20 years, attention to alternate sources of data, the application of new technologies, and revised approaches to detecting and reconstructing the events that occurred during the first two centuries of European contact have resulted in major adjustments in hypotheses of early contact disease effects. As emphasized recently by several researchers (Anderson 1994, 1996; Johnson and Lehman 1996), native populations at the time of contact were not arranged in a homogeneous landscape. Settlement location, settlement density, settlement type, mobility patterns, sociopolitical organization, subsistence regimes, and many other factors fluctuated continuously in late prehistory. All would have been influential in the outcome of disease epidemics. Ramenofsky (1987, 1990, 1993), by providing excellent discussions on types of disease and disease transmission, has applied an epidemiological approach to these considerations of settlement variability. Ramenofsky (1993) and others (Trimble 1985; Wolforth 1997) remind us that each disease has specific epidemiological requirements that depend on specific agent, host, and environmental characteristics. Finally, numerous osteological studies of contact period populations have resulted in a database of observations on health and disease that can be used to assess shifting patterns from prehistoric to historic populations (Larsen 1990, 1994; Hutchinson 1991, 1993; Verano and Ubelaker 1992; Hutchinson and Norr 1994; Larsen and Milner, 1994; Baker and Kealhofer 1996; Hutchinson and Mitchem 1996).

One result of these studies is a more tempered approach to the study of European-introduced diseases. This approach stresses accommodation and adaptation rather than universal and immediate devastation, but also recognizes the importance of introduced diseases in the eventual depopulation of Native American groups. It also emphasizes that disease episodes may have been discontinuous, gradual, and localized. Archaeologists have, however, made few advances in recognizing these epidemic events within the confines of archaeological space and time. In some ways archaeologists have avoided the problem of delineating epidemic disease and its effects, but continued to use the epidemic hypothesis as an integral part of our reconstructions.

There remain two primary issues that need to be addressed: 1) determining what evidence is useful for recognizing disease epidemics, and 2) reconstructing the demographic and sociopolitical effects of those diseases for native populations. The purpose of this paper is to review many of the propositions that lie behind the disease model, and then present an example of the difficulties encountered when making interpretations of early contact mortuary behaviors.

The Vague and Thin Line: Assessing the Impact

The primary problem in delineating large-scale disease epidemics among Native American populations, or any population for that matter, is that often the evidence is indirect. There has been only limited success at isolating direct evidence of diseases, most notably when it has been possible to obtain particular disease pathogens from soft tissue specimens, such as *Mycobacterium tuberculosis* located in Chilean mummies dating to A.D. 700 (Allison et al. 1973; Salo et al. 1994). Although immunological information has been derived from human skeletal remains (Ortner et al. 1992), knowledge of an immune reaction to a particular antigen only provides information regarding exposure and is not necessarily useful for assessing morbidity or mortality. As well, interpreting skeletal lesions can be difficult. Although smallpox has been offered as one acute epidemic disease which might produce recognizable skeletal lesions (Jackes 1983), in many cases skeletal responses to infectious disease can be variable or lack pathognomic lesions which allow differential diagnosis for particular diseases.

Indirect evidence takes several forms. The primary type of evidence that has been used is demographic, both historical and archaeological. Historical records, sometimes combined with ethnographic observations (Ubelaker 1976), have long formed a basis for aboriginal population estimates. See Borah (1976) for a thorough review. The second type of indirect evidence is historical descriptions of epidemic diseases and disease epidemics.

A point often debated in the discussions about protohistoric aboriginal population size generated from ethnohistoric observations is the reliability of those observations for constructing demographic estimates. On the one hand, Cook (1976), Borah (1976), Borah and Cook (1960, 1963), and Sauer (1966) argue that various documents such as church records, state tax or labor censuses, observations by the Spanish *conquistadors*, and native estimates accurately reflect the population size. On the other, Helm (1980), Kroeber (1934, 1939), Rosenblat (1976), and Sanders (1976) challenge the reliability of ethnohistoric documentation in reconstructing early contact period population size. Population estimates derived from ethnohistoric records are therefore often subject to adjustments because of assumptions of either under or over enumeration in the original counts.

Mooney (1928), for instance, published estimates for North America that were derived from ethnohistoric records, sometimes separated in date by as much as 250 years (Ubelaker 1976), and estimates based upon colleagues' ethnographic observations. Kroeber (1939) presented some of the lowest estimates, derived from Mooney (1928), but replaced Mooney's estimates for California by lower estimates of his own. He admitted that they were based on little other than his own decisions about the data, and that only more careful regional analyses would lead to better estimates. Others have argued that contemporary ethnohistoric accounts reflect native populations that have already undergone severe depopulation. Borah (1976) and Dobyns (1963, 1966, 1983), for instance, stress the importance of including calculated population loss due to disease epidemics into population estimates for periods prior to reliable historical accounts.

The problems with historic accounts of epidemic diseases are (1) they are often not very useful for identifying specific diseases, (2) the diseases may have changed (evolved), and therefore might not be familiar despite very accurate descriptions, (3) the accounts are often vague and rarely present any quantitative figures, (4) they tend to record the most obvious and striking aspects of epidemics, while not necessarily recording the breadth of the epidemic, and 5) related to the previous point, they often are dependent on the presence of some literate figure, such as a Jesuit priest. Records, thus, tend to be sparse for areas remote from European settlements.

On the larger scale, the individual recording the information is generally accessing only certain sources, often informants. These may be accurate for areas as small as a particular village or mission complex and as large as a region. In a regional discussion, more information is likely secondary, and for a regional epidemic it might be unclear what percentage of villages are impacted, which villages are impacted, or other details. Consider, for example, this often-cited passage from the Gentlemen of Elvas about the southeastern United States:

"About the town within the compass of a league and a half league were large uninhabited towns, choked with vegetation, which looked as though no people had inhabited them for some time. The Indians said that two years ago there had been a plague in that land and they had moved to other towns" (Gentleman of Elvas 1993:83).

Although the report indicates an epidemic, many questions remain to be answered such as the geographic extent of the epidemic, the type of disease, other contributing factors such as nutrition or famine, the length of the epidemic, and morbidity and mortality effects.

Another indirect source of information is human remains interred at mortuary localities. Mortuary localities are probably one of the better sources of data but they are complicated, accretional features which preserve a combination of biological and social aspects of human environment, behavior, and organization. Furthermore, until recently human burials dating to the early contact period have largely been analyzed for their artifactual contents (Smith 1956; Brain 1979; Smith 1987). Examination of mortuary facilities for other correlates of European contact has occurred only recently, and at present there is no established "marker" of change in mortuary contexts and little established method and theory for conducting analysis of human burial space in order to delineate abrupt change.

For evidence of an epidemic, aberrant mortuary patterns are a potential marker and would perhaps be apparent. Among the most often cited deviations from "normal" mortuary behavior are mass burials, high proportions of cremations, disproportionate age or sex profiles, and burials placed within specially constructed mortuary facilities. Unfortunately, none of these is solely dependent on epidemic diseases and each has been documented in non-epidemic situations. Furthermore, few examples of these conditions exist, and the examples we have, were derived from either older and less precise methods of excavation and analysis or through investigations with research designs not specifically oriented to investigating changes in mortuary behavior. Consequently, each example of deviation has limitations in its potential for application to the epidemic disease situation.

Mass burials are difficult to interpret because they can arise from a number of circumstances that include natural disaster, warfare, sacrifice, or epidemic disease. Although there are a few examples of mass burials with documentation of warfare or violent death (Mant 1987), they were generally conducted with other research designs and the results are of no use in examining infectious disease. One promising new development is the exhumation of mass graves in several global locations such as Haiti (McDonald 1995; Skolnick 1995), Guatemala (Gibbons 1992), Rwanda (Vidal 1995), and Bosnia/Croatia (Stover 1997). Unsettling as these investigations are, they provide data that can be applied to the epidemic disease situation. Few historical or archaeological data have been recovered which can be used to address these issues; no data are present from plague cemeteries because few have been excavated, however, see Leonetti et al. (1997).

Another approach that can be taken is looking for unique circumstances regarding the mortuary pattern. Often the problem with this approach is that there is insufficient regional data to allow enough comparison in order to derive deviations from a normal mortuary pattern. Even when there is sufficient regional data, any number of cultural or behavioral factors can result in abnormal burial situations. Consequently, it is important to understand traditional cycles of aboriginal mortuary ritual in order to enable the recognition of aberrant mortuary situations.

Any disruption in these behavioral and organizational principles should be reflected in the use of mortuary space (O'Shea 1984). Changes in mortuary ritual, however, are likely to be complex and subtle. The Iroquois, for instance, continued to retrieve the bones of their dead after burning off their flesh between 1634 and 1637 when smallpox epidemics raged through their territory (Trigger 1976). If markedly increased mortality were taking place, one would expect the degradation of traditional mortuary ritual; however, discerning those changes in the archaeological record might be difficult. Non-western mortuary rituals (including those of prehistoric populations) often encompass several phases following death. There might be a period prior to interment where burials are placed in trees, scaffolds, or charnel structures; or a temporary interment, followed by a communal ritual during which the community dead were either interred, or as in contemporary Bali, cremated. These final events occur only periodically with substantial periods of time between them.

Preliminary storage of the dead with the intent of later reburial is well-documented in the ethnographic and ethnohistoric literature pertaining to North America. Ethnohistoric accounts of late prehistoric populations in the southeastern United States indicate that the mortuary program often included storage in an above-ground structure generally referred to as a charnel house (Oviedo 1944[10]:272-273; Le Page du Pratz 1947; Romans 1962). Excavations at Angel (Black 1967), Fatherland (Neitzel 1965), Irene (Caldwell and McCann 1941), and Parrish Mound 2 (Willey 1982) provide archaeological support that such structures were present.

This ritual cycle in the burial of the dead was not a new idea in the Southeast. Crypts associated with the Hopewell Middle Woodland (100 B.C.-A.D. 400) sites of Liverpool Mound (Cole and Deuel 1937), Weaver Mound (Wray and MacNeish 1961), Albany Mounds (Herold 1971), and others (Brown 1979) were utilized in a similar manner. Burials placed in these facilities were covered, often with a stone cover and earth, allowed to decompose, and then pushed to the periphery or buried outside the crypt. The last individuals interred in any particular round of ritual are found in extended, often supine positions inside the facility. This pattern appears to have continued as late as the Mississippian Mouse Creek Phase in Tennessee (A.D. 1400-1600) (Peters-Sullivan 1986:309).

A further complication when interpreting mortuary evidence is the problem of establishing the chronological use of a mortuary locality and of demonstrating culture contact. At the eve of European contact, a necessary prerequisite to establishing European contact is placing a site within the correct temporal range, a task often accomplished by European artifacts. The presence of European artifacts, however, does not indicate direct contact. Equally problematic is that the absence of European artifacts does not necessarily disprove contact nor is direct European and native interaction an essential component of disease transmission.

Difficult Interpretations: A Case Example from Tatham Mound

The primary example of demographic collapse provided by Dobyns (1983) in his classic *Their Number Become Thinned* is the Timucua of northern Florida. Based on ethnographic and archaeological evidence, Dobyns estimates that the Timucuan population declined from 722,000 in 1515 to 72,900 by 1596, a 90% reduction in eight decades. The extreme reduction is even more impressive when one considers that the Spaniards established their first settlement in St. Augustine in 1565. Ubelaker (1988) examined the evidence for depopulation from several areas of the United States and concluded as well that the Southeast suffered a rather immediate and steady decline in native population beginning in the 16th century.

Very few early contact period sites have been documented and excavated which provide evidence relevant to the proposed Timucuan demographic collapse. Although several sites have produced items of European manufacture which are known to have been traded, the mechanisms of trade are unclear, and there is little other evidence which can be used to document the nature of European and native interactions (Smith 1956; Mitchem et al. 1985; Mitchem and Leader 1988; Ewen 1989, 1996; Mitchem 1989a; Mitchem and Hutchinson 2000).

Probably the most complete and well-documented artifactual and skeletal assemblage which can be used to address the issue of European introduced diseases was excavated at Tatham Mound in west-central Florida between 1985 and 1986 (Mitchem 1989a, 1989b; Hutchinson 1991; Mitchem and Hutchinson 2000) (Figure 1). Tatham was a completely undisturbed burial mound comprised of two burial components, a contact period component dating to A.D. 1525-1550 and a precontact component dating between A.D. 1200 and 1400. These two components were separated by a lens of thick black sand. A ramp on the east side of the mound had been constructed and an intrusive pit was located roughly in the center. No other grave pits were noted in the stratigraphy. The contact component contained hundreds of European artifacts including glass and metal beads, silver objects, a brigandine armor plate, and chain mail. Most of these materials were directly associated with the 339 primary and secondary human burials recovered from the site. Over a 10 year period, efforts were concentrated on the analysis and interpretation of the archaeological and skeletal evidence recovered from Tatham Mound in an attempt to define and reconstruct the sequence of events that occurred there (Mitchem 1989a; Hutchinson 1991, 1996; Mitchem and Hutchinson 2000).

Figure 1. Location of Tatham Mound, Citrus County, Florida.

Soon after excavations began at Tatham Mound, it became apparent that several hundred individuals were interred there, varying in degree of preparation and length of curation prior to burial. The burial types included primary burials of single individuals, secondary discrete bundle burials of single individuals, and discrete bone areas of usually more than one individual. Among and between articulated individuals and discrete bone areas were skeletal elements that could not be associated with particular burials.

A primary effort was directed at defining the type of contact that transpired, direct or indirect. Although the large quantity of European artifacts suggested direct contact, some items were less likely to have been traded and suggest possible recovery from shipwrecks and ensuing trade among the indigenous populations of the peninsula. The two primary items of this latter nature were a silver ingot fashioned into a pendant and a brigandine armor plate clutched in the hand of an elderly woman, and from which a smaller piece had been cut. The cut piece was rolled into a bead and was located around her neck. It is worth noting that Gentleman of Elvas (1993:67) in his account of the de Soto expedition mentions that Luis de Moscoso buried some iron and other things at the village of Cale before proceeding north, and this could be the origin of the brigandine plate. In a footnote to the Robertson translation of the account, however, Hann (Gentleman of Elvas 1993:67) notes that the Portuguese *ferragem* is best translated as "hardware" or "iron fittings" and especially "horseshoes" as it means "things made of iron" rather than "iron" per se which is *ferro*. The sheer volume of trade beads, however, supports direct trade or presentation, and the material assemblage can be dated to a period between A.D. 1525 and 1550 (Smith 1976, Smith and Good 1982; Deagan 1987; Mitchem and Leader 1988; 1983, 1987; Mitchem 1989a). Reconstructed routes of the two major expeditionary forces that passed through the region in the early 16th century including those of Pánfilo de Narváez and Hernando de Soto, place the De Soto route directly on the path of Tatham Mound (Milanich and Hudson 1993; Hudson and Tesser 1994).

Although it is impossible to determine with certainty which expedition was in direct contact with the Tatham population, several factors argue for the de Soto expedition rather than Narváez. In chapter five of the account of the 1528 Narváez expedition, Álvar Núñez Cabeza de Vaca described traveling from Tampa Bay to the Withlacoochee River: "In all this time we did not encounter any Indian at all, nor did we see a settlement or house" (Hann 1987). The expedition also stayed near the coast in an ultimately unsuccessful attempt to stay in contact with their supply ships. Tatham Mound is located south of the Withlacoochee River some 30 km (19 mi.) inland from the coast.

The de Soto expedition, which landed near Tampa Bay in 1539, first passed through the area in July of that year (Rangel 1993:259). In contrast to the Narváez expedition, the de Soto party encountered several groups of aboriginal people, and were involved in some skirmishes (Rangel 1993:261). When the main force reached the Apalachee area of northwest Florida, they decided to remain there for the winter. A small company of soldiers was sent south, traveling on the same route they had taken north, to contact the supply ships anchored at Tampa Bay. They relayed instructions for the ships to travel north and offload supplies at a bay near Anhaica Apalache. After sending the ships north, some of the soldiers then traveled north on foot to rejoin the main force, passing through the Tatham Mound region a third time (Hernández de Biedma 1993:227; Gentleman of Elvas 1993:72; Rangel 1993:268). Some additional skirmishes were reported on the final northern trek through the region (Gentleman of Elvas 1993:72). It is safe to assume that other undocumented incidents of contact (both violent and peaceful) occurred during these travels.

The Narváez expedition stayed near the coast and reported seeing no natives or villages, thus the de Soto expedition is a more likely source of contact. Additional support is provided by examining the similarity of glass beads between Tatham Mound and the Governor Martin site in Tallahassee, arguably the best candidate for the location of de Soto's 1539-1540 winter encampment at Anhaica (Mitchem and Leader 1988; Ewen and Hann 1998). The specific varieties of faceted chevron beads and the single Nueva Cadiz bead from Governor Martin are identical to specimens excavated from Tatham Mound. The Governor Martin site also has many other Spanish artifacts, including coins, Olive Jar sherds, chain mail links, and a crossbow bolt tip (Ewen and Hann 1998:59-98). While at first glance this would seem to argue against contact by the same expedition at the sites, it is important to remember that the entire expedition army stayed at Anhaica for nearly five months in the winter of 1539-1540, while contact with the Tatham population was much more fleeting.

Supporting a hypothesis of direct contact between the Spanish expeditionary forces and the native inhabitants interred at Tatham Mound is the skeletal evidence. In a detailed analysis of several skeletal elements, Hutchinson (1991, 1996) determined that at least two elements exhibited evidence of sharp edge trauma from wedge-shaped metal weapons, probably swords. The location of the cuts suggests that they were made by people with experience using these types of weapons and not by the untrained indigenous inhabitants. Unfortunately, the skeletal elements were isolated and were not associated with complete burials.

Despite the probability of direct contact, however, several other issues remain unresolved. The number of contacts, their duration, and the number of people involved are difficult to obtain from the archaeological record. The historic documents, however, are of some use. Hernando de Soto's personal secretary, Rodrigo Rangel, kept a diary of their travels. Although the original has been lost, an account generally credited to come directly from the original is included in Oviedo's monumental history of the Caribbean region (Rangel 1993).

Rangel reports that shortly after the arrival of the expeditionary forces in late May, 1539, DeSoto began dispatching segments of his forces north and east to search for resources. On 15 July, de Soto departed from his Tampa Bay base camp leaving a small force behind to guard the supplies and caravels. De Soto was searching for Ocale, a large town now thought to have been located north of Lake Tsala Apopka. On 24 July they reached a village called Tocaste on a large lake. Milanich and Hudson (1993:86) believe the lake to be Lake Tsala Apopka, with a probable location for Tocaste on Duval Island (8Ci5). As de Soto moved north with a smaller party, several messengers traversed the distance between the current location of the small party and Tocaste where the larger camp had been established. One of these trips was to report

a skirmish with the natives in which several of de Soto's men had been wounded and a horse killed.

At present, then, the evidence points toward direct contact between at least some of those interred at Tatham Mound and the Spaniards who accompanied Hernando de Soto across Florida. There was at least one episode of conflict resulting in injury, and likely death. Other skeletal evidence of the consequences of contact between the two groups, however, is lacking. For the population interred at Tatham Mound, analysis has provided information regarding diet (Hutchinson and Norr 1994; Hutchinson et al. 1998, 2000) and some pathological conditions (Hutchinson 1991, 1996; Mitchem and Hutchinson 2000), but no information on infectious disease in epidemic proportions.

The burials and associated mortuary objects were examined to delineate any patterns regarding changing mortuary behavior. Unlike most reported Safety Harbor burial mounds, the large number of primary burials interred at Tatham suggests some deviation from previous mortuary behaviors. Characteristic of Safety Harbor period mounds is a predominance of secondary burials (Mitchem 1989a:589). Ninety-four burials at Tatham were primary interments as indicated by the articulation of most skeletal elements at the time of burial (Table 1; Figure 2). Some burial positions generally occur at the perimeter of the mound, such as flexed burials on the right side. Those are so few in number, however, that the only clear pattern that emerged during analysis is for a predominance of males buried in this position.

Two primary burial positions did continue to stand out during analysis–those in supine positions with their legs tightly flexed over the chest ("tightly flexed") and those who were supine and extended with the tibiae and fibulae tightly flexed under the femora ("flexed leg"). The tightly flexed position is interesting only due to its predominance over other positions in the mound. It occurs as a predominant position also at the Blue Rock cemetery in Pennsylvania, where European artifacts were used to date the time of use between A.D. 1580 and 1590 (Heisey and Witmer 1962). The flexed leg position has only rarely been reported, and always in low frequencies. Stewart encountered eight skeletons in the same position, with "the lower

TABLE 1
PRIMARY BURIAL POSITION BY SEX

	Male	Female	Indeter-minate	Row Total
Supine, legs extended	1	1	0	2
Flexed, right side	4	0	2	6
Supine, legs tightly flexed over chest	13	20	10	43
Supine, lower leg flexed under upper	4	9	1	14
Indeterminate	7	5	17	29
Column Total	29	35	30	94

*One cremation of indeterminate sex not tabulated

legs unnaturally arranged" at the early contact mortuary site of Patawomeke (44St2) located on the Potomac river in Virginia (Stewart 1992). At the precontact period Bay Pines site in Florida, 2 individuals (1 male, 1 female) were interred in this position out of 10 primary and 14 secondary interments (Gallagher and Warren 1975). Another such interment was found at the bottom of the Juhle ossuary in Maryland (Ubelaker 1974). It is clear that individuals buried in this position were interred relatively recently after death, because the articulations would not remain for more than a few months (Morse et al. 1983).

The flexed leg position remains anomalous in other respects as well. Placement of the flexed leg burials occurs in the center of the mound (Figure 2). Burials in this position are predominantly female, and European artifacts are more consistently associated with burials in this position than any other–36% as compared to 16% for tightly flexed burials. Figure 2 illustrates the horizontal pattern of European and aboriginal artifact placement with primary burials by burial form. The pattern confirms that the majority of individuals interred in flexed leg positions are located in a relatively circumscribed area between grid points 499 and 506 east, and 517 and 522 north. Additionally, they are confined within the two excavation levels (2 and 3) that contain the most European artifacts.

Examination of the distribution of European artifacts with primary burials confirms a pattern of distribution that is predominant for females of the flexed leg position (Table 2). The three positions most consistently buried with European artifacts are presented in Table 3 after being

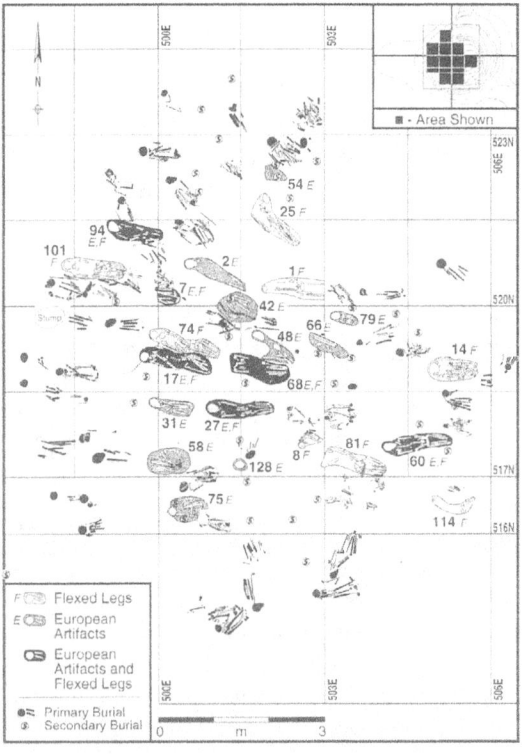

Figure 2. Primary burials showing burial position, sex, and associated artifacts.

TABLE 2
DISTRIBUTION OF ARTIFACTS BY SEX AND PRIMARY BURIAL POSITION

	European Male	Aboriginal Female	Indet.	Male	Female	Indet.	Totals
Supine, legs extended	0	1	0	0	0	0	1
Flexed, right side	0	0	1	0	0	0	1
Supine, legs tightly flexed over chest	1	5	1*	4	4	1	16
Supine, lower leg flexed under upper	1	4	0	2	2	0	9
Indeterminate	0	1	2*	2	0	2	7
Totals	2	11	4	8	6	3	34

*Juveniles

subjected to median polish. Median polish is a technique for exploring the relationship between cells of tabular data (Hartwig and Dearing 1979; Velleman and Hoaglin 1981). It uses an additive model which takes into account a row effect, a column effect, and a response. Much like the slope obtained in a regression line, a common value is used to describe data values in the table as a whole. Once the table has been polished, residuals are left in the cells, and the fitted values which explain row and column effects are left in the margin. The median polished table shows a strong positive relationship for females interred with European artifacts. Aboriginal artifacts are more evenly distributed between females and males.

Discussion

Critics of the epidemic hypothesis often cite the absence of evidence as a validation of the unimportance of early epidemic diseases. Two major arguments, however, can be made against such interpretations. First, the absence of "plague cemeteries" in the New World does not disprove epidemic diseases. Very few plague cemeteries have been excavated or reported in the literature for Europe, however, see Leonetti et al. (1997), yet few would question the validity of the plague or its effects on 15th century Europe. Second, because there has been little investigation of such "special purpose" cemeteries, we have very little understanding of how such a mortuary site would appear if we encountered one in the archaeological record. Extend this to a set of mortuary behaviors that we are reconstructing without any historical documentation, and it becomes even more difficult.

Tatham Mound is a good example of the problems encountered in mortuary contexts dating to the time of the earliest contacts between Native Americans and Europeans in the New World. Some interpretations have been facilitated by the abundance and clarity of the evidence, such as the chronological assignment and the

TABLE 3
DISTRIBUTION OF ARTIFACTS BY SEX AND PRIMARY BURIAL POSITION AFTER MEDIAN POLISH

	European Male	Aboriginal Female	Indet.	Male	Female	Indet.	Totals
Supine, legs tightly flexed over chest	0	0	0	1	1	0	1
Supine, lower leg flexed under upper	1	0	0	0	0	0	0
Indeterminate	0	-3	2	0	-2	2	0
Totals	-1	3	-1	1	1	-1	0

sharp weapon trauma. Other interpretations have been extremely difficult to make, and remain inconclusive. The large number of primary burials, presumably contemporary, and the association between European artifacts, females, and the flexed leg burial position fall into the latter category.

Earlier, five possible explanations were proposed (Mitchem and Hutchinson 1986) to account for the large number of primary interments as compared to secondary interments within a single stratum and it is difficult to improve on those:

Normal charnel house mortuary storage for several years with a larger contemporary death event such as an epidemic;

A large mortality event of some duration, with secondary burials representing individuals whose bodies had decomposed due to disruption of normal mortuary activities, assuming that primary burials represent those later victims of an extended disease epidemic;

A large contemporary mortuary event, with some corpses defleshed prior to interment and others not defleshed–the reasons could be cultural or due to circumstances resulting from an abnormally large number of contemporary deaths;

Dispersed settlement patterns, with primary burials representing those who lived in the near vicinity of the mound and secondary burials representing those who lived farther away;

Normal charnel house mortuary activity over a long time period with no large, contemporaneous death event.

Obviously, the hypotheses reflect a tendency toward interpreting the evidence from Tatham as indicative of a large contemporary death event. The European artifacts accompanying the burials might support such a hypothesis given their restricted chronological range. Interpreting the distribution of the objects, however, remains an issue. The clear predominance of European artifacts with females and children could signal changing mortuary rituals that indicate increased mortality. In the Northeast, burials of early contact date show a clear pattern of European artifacts with children (Wray et al. 1987, 1991), and mixed patterns of male and female association, but this pattern may be as much due to cultural responses to contact as to increased morbidity and mortality. During the period of

occupation of the Adams and Culbertson sites in New York (A.D. 1560-1575), mortuary behaviors were dramatically changing as reflected by increased frequency of multiple burials, increased depth of grave pits, changing orientation of burials, techniques of grave preparation, and especially a dramatic increase in the inclusion of material items in graves (Wray et al. 1987, 1991). We know from the Jesuit accounts (Thwaites 1896-1901) that epidemics of smallpox and perhaps other diseases cycled through the area after 1632 (Trigger 1976). Wray and coworkers (1987, 1991) cautiously suggest that increased mortality may play a role in the changing mortuary behaviors. Tantalizing as the evidence is from both the Northeast and Southeast, we know as well that mortuary behaviors are among the most complicated to understand and interpret, especially when the conditions of morbidity and mortality are deviating from normal circumstances.

Native communities in the New World all shared a rapid and somewhat interruptive culture change that began with the arrival of Europeans into the New World. The timing, speed, and magnitude of those changes, however, varied from population to population and region to region, just as the composition and size of native populations themselves varied, and the type of contact varied. It goes without saying the ultimate impact of the colonial process was the complete demographic collapse of native populations and disintegration of native cultural systems.

Clearly, the evidence presented from Tatham Mound can be interpreted in multiple ways. It is not the "smoking gun" that we hope will demonstrate unequivocally that epidemic disease can be demonstrated in the archaeological record. We have endeavored in our analyses to be cautious in constructing our hypotheses and to address the available evidence with scrutiny. Some evidence, such as the cut bones, we can interpret with confidence given the available comparative database. The available comparative mortuary evidence for epidemic diseases is scant, and derived from several sources that each consist of distinct types of disease, cultural interment patterns, and time period.

Recognizing special events of short duration within the archaeological context of cumulative time and material remains will always be difficult. When events exhibit a wide cultural variance, such as mortuary behavior, interpretation is even more difficult. Nonetheless, if we are to improve our ability to decipher the remains that are recovered archaeologically we must begin to construct a method and theory for investigating the challenging contexts. Ironically, as archaeologists move toward understanding how to interpret social and historical processes using data recovered from human skeletal remains, the remains are becoming more restricted and sensitive data sources. Certainly, recognizing disease epidemics in the archaeological record is one of the more challenging tasks, and before we completely withdraw from the epidemic hypothesis citing "lack of evidence" perhaps we should discuss what material remains or features would comprise that evidence.

ACKNOWLEDGMENTS

Over the years, we have benefited immensely from discussions of the issues addressed in this paper with Lorraine Aragon, Deborah Bakken, Charles R. Ewen, Eugene Giles, David Grove, Kristin Hedman, Clark Spencer Larsen, Linda Klepinger, Laura Kozuch, Donald Lathrap, R. Barry Lewis, Jacqueline McDowell, Bonnie McEwan, Kevin McGowan, Jerald Milanich, George Milner, Ann Ramenofsky, Katherine Russell, Demitri Shimkin, and Lynne Wolforth. For editing and comments of this manuscript, we thank Lorraine Aragon, Clark Spencer Larsen, R. Barry Lewis, Bonnie McEwan, George Milner, and the anonymous reviewers. Susan Brannock-Gaul did the artwork for Figure 2.

REFERENCES

ALLISON, MARVIN J., D. MENDOZA, AND A. PEZZIA
1973 Documentation of a Case of Tuberculosis in Precolumbian America. *American Review of Respiratory Disease,* 107:985-991.

ANDERSON, DAVID G.
1994 *The Savannah River Chiefdoms: Political Change in the Late Prehistoric Southeast.* University of Alabama Press, Tuscaloosa.
1996 Fluctuations Between Simple and Complex Chiefdoms: Cycling in the Late Prehistoric Southeast. In *Political Structure and Change in the Prehistoric Southeastern United States,* John F. Scarry, editor, pp. 231-252. University of Florida Press, Gainesville.

BAKER, BRENDA J., AND LISA KEALHOFER (EDITORS)
1996 *Bioarchaeology of Native American Adaptation in the Spanish Borderlands.* University of Florida Press, Gainesville.

BLACK, G. A.
1967 *The Angel Site.* Indiana Historical Society, Indianapolis.

BORAH, WOODROW
1976 The Historical Demography of Aboriginal and Colonial America: An Attempt at Perspective. In *The Native Population of the Americas in 1492,* William M. Denevan, editor, pp. 13-34. University of Wisconsin Press, Madison.

BORAH, WOODROW, AND SHERBOURNE F. COOK.
1960 The Population of Central Mexico in 1548. *Ibero-Americana,* 43. Berkeley.
1963 The Aboriginal Population of Central Mexico on the Eve of Spanish Conquest. *Ibero-Americana,* 45. Berkeley.

BRAIN, JEFFREY P. (EDITOR)
1979 Tunica Treasure. *Papers of the Peabody Museum of Archaeology and Ethnology,* No. 71. Cambridge, MA.

BROWN, JAMES A.
1979 Charnel Houses and Mortuary Crypts: Disposal of the Dead in the Middle Woodland Period. In *Hopewell Archaeology, The Chillicothe Conference,* David Brose and N'omi Greber, editors, pp. 211-219. Kent State University Press, Kent, OH.

CALDWELL, JOSEPH, AND CATHERINE McCANN.
1941 *Irene Mound Site, Chatham County, Georgia.* University of Georgia Press, Athens.

COLE, F. C., AND T. DEUEL.
1937 *Rediscovering Illinois.* University of Chicago Press, Chicago, IL.

COOK, SHERBOURNE F.
1976 *The Conflict Between the California Indian and White Civilization.* University of California Press, Berkeley.

CROSBY, ALFRED W., JR.
1972 *The Columbian Exchange: Biological and Cultural Consequences of 1492.* Greenwood Press, Westport, CN.
1976 Virgin Soil Epidemics as a Factor in the Aboriginal Depopulation in America. *William and Mary Quarterly,* 33(2):289-299.

DEAGAN, KATHLEEN A.
1987 *Artifacts of the Spanish Colonies of Florida and the Caribbean 1500-1800, Volume 1: Ceramics, Glassware, and Beads.* Smithsonian Institution Press, Washington, DC.

DOBYNS, HENRY F.
1963 An Outline of Andean Epidemic History to 1720. *Bulletin of the History of Medicine,* 37(6):493-515.
1966 An Appraisal of Techniques for Estimating Aboriginal American Population with a New Historical Estimate. *Current Anthropology,* 7(4):395-416.

1983   *Their Number Become Thinned: Native American Population Dynamics in Eastern North America.* University of Tennessee Press, Knoxville.

EWEN, CHARLES R.
1989   Anhaica: Discovery of Hernando de Soto's 1539-1540 Winter Camp. In *First Encounters: Spanish Explorations in the Caribbean and the United States, 1492-1570,* Jerald T. Milanich and Susan Milbrath, editors, pp. 110-118. Ripley P. Bullen Monographs in Anthropology and History, No. 9. University of Florida Press, Gainesville.
1996   Continuity and Change: De Soto and the Apalachee. *Historical Archaeology,* 30:41-53.

EWEN, CHARLES R., AND JOHN H. HANN
1998   *Hernando De Soto Among the Apalachee: The Archaeology of the First Winter Encampment.* University Presses of Florida, Gainesville.

GALLAGHER, JOHN C., AND LYMAN O. WARREN
1975   The Bay Pines Site, Pinellas County, Florida. *The Florida Anthropologist,* 28(3):96-117.

GENTLEMAN OF ELVAS
1993   True Relation of the Hardhips Suffered by Governor Hernando de Soto & Certain Portuguese Gentlemen During the Discovery of the Province of Florida. In *The De Soto Chronicles: The Expedition of Hernando de Soto to North America in 1539-1543, Volume I,* Lawrence A. Clayton, Vernon James Knight, Jr., and Edward C. Moore, editors, pp. 18-219. University of Alabama Press, Tuscaloosa.

GIBBONS, ANN
1992   Scientists Search for "The Disappeared" in Guatemala. *Science,* 257:479.

HANN, JOHN H.
1987   Translations of the Accounts of the Pánfilo de Narváez Expedition's Experiences in Florida. Manuscript translation, Bureau of Archaeological Research, Florida Department of State, Tallahassee.

HARTWIG, FREDERICK, AND BRIAN E. DEARING
1979   Exploratory Data Analysis. *Quantitative Applications in the Social Sciences,* No. 16. Sage University Press, Beverly Hills, CA.

HEISEY, H. W., AND J. P. WITMER
1962   Of Historic Susquehannock Cemeteries. *Pennsylvania Archaeologist,* 32(3-4):99-130.

HELM, JUNE
1980   Female Infanticide, European Diseases and Population Levels Among the McKenzie Dene. *American Ethnologist,* 7(2):259-285.

HERNÁNDEZ DE BIEDMA, LUYS
1993   Relation of the Island of Florida. In *The De Soto Chronicles: The Expedition of Hernando de Soto to North America in 1539-1543, Volume I,* Lawrence A. Clayton, Vernon James Knight, Jr., and Edward C. Moore, editors, pp. 221-246. University of Alabama Press, Tuscaloosa.

HEROLD, ELAINE B. (EDITOR)
1971   The Indian Mounds at Albany Illinois. *Davenport Museum Anthropological Papers,* No. 1. Davenport Museum, Davenport, IA.

HUDSON, CHARLES M., AND CARMEN TESSER (EDITORS)
1994   *The Forgotten Centuries.* University of Georgia Press, Athens.

HUTCHINSON, DALE L.
1991   *Postcontact Native American Health and Adaptation: Assessing the Impact of Introduced Diseases in Sixteenth-Century Gulf Coast Florida.* Ph.D. dissertation, Department of Anthropology, University of Illinois, Champaign-Urbana. University Microfilms International, Ann Arbor, MI.
1993   Treponematosis in Regional and Chronological Perspective from Central Gulf Coast Florida. *American Journal of Physical Anthropology,* 92(2):249-261.
1996   Brief Encounters: Tatham Mound and the Evidence for Spanish and Native American Confrontation. *International Journal of Osteoarchaeology,* 6(1):51-65.

HUTCHINSON, DALE L., AND JEFFREY M. MITCHEM
1996   The Weeki Wachee Mound, An Early Contact Period Mortuary Locality in Hernando County, West-Central Florida. *Southeastern Archaeology,* 15(1):47-65.

HUTCHINSON, DALE L., AND LYNETTE NORR
1994   Late Prehistoric and Early Historic Diet in Gulf Coast Florida. In *In the Wake of Contact: Biological Responses to Conquest,* Clark Spencer Larsen and George R. Milner, editors, pp. 9-20. Wiley-Liss, New York, NY.

HUTCHINSON, DALE L., CLARK SPENCER LARSEN, LYNETTE NORR, AND MARGARET J. SCHOENINGER
2000   Agricultural Melodies and Alternative Harmonies in Florida and Georgia. In *Life During the Age of Agriculture,* Patricia M. Lambert, editor, in press.

HUTCHINSON, DALE L., CLARK SPENCER, LARSEN, MARGARET J. SCHOENINGER, AND LYNETTE NORR
1998   Regional Variation in the Pattern of Maize Adoption and Use in Florida and Georgia. *American Antiquity,* 63:397-416.

JACKES, M. K.
1983   Osteological Evidence for Smallpox: A Possible Case from Seventeenth Century Ontario. *American Journal of Physical Anthropology,* 60(1):75-81.

JOHNSON, JAY K., AND GEOFFREY R. LEHMANN
1996 Sociopolitical Devolution in Northeast Mississippi and the Timing of the de Soto Entrada. In *Bioarcaheology of Native American Adaptation in the Spanish Borderlands,* B. J. Baker and L. Kealhofer, editors, pp. 38-55. University of Florida Press, Gainesville.

KROEBER, ALFRED L.
1934 Native American Population. *American Anthropologist,* 36(1):1-25.
1939 Cultural and Natural Areas of Native North America. *University of California Publications in American Archaeology and Ethnology,* No. 38. Berkeley.

LARSEN, CLARK SPENCER (EDITOR)
1990 The Archaeology of Mission Santa Catalina de Guale: 2. Biocultural Interpretations of a Population in Transition. *Anthropological Papers of the American Museum of Natural History,* 68. New York, NY.

LARSEN, CLARK SPENCER
1994 In the Wake of Columbus: Native Population Biology in the Postcontact Americas. *Yearbook of Physical Anthropology,* 37:109-154.

LARSEN, CLARK SPENCER, AND GEORGE R. MILNER (EDITORS)
1994 *In the Wake of Contact: Biological Responses to Conquest.* Wiley-Liss, New York, NY.

LEONETTI, G., M. SIGNOLI, A. L. PELISSIER, P. CHAMPSAUR, I. HERSHKOVITZ, C. BRUNET, AND O. DUTOUR.
1997 Evidence of Pin Implantation as a Means of Verifying Death During the Great Plague of Marseilles (1722). *Journal of Forensic Science,* 42(4):744-748.

LE PAGE DU PRATZ, A. S.
1947 *The History of Louisiana or of the Western Parts of Virginia and Carolina.* J. S. W. Hamilton, New Orleans, LA.

MANT, A. K.
1987 Knowledge Acquired from Post-war Exhumations. In *Death, Decay, and Reconstruction: Approaches to Archaeology and Forensic Science,* A. Boddington, A. N. Garland, and R. C. Janaway, editors, pp. 67-78. Manchester University Press, Manchester, England.

MCDONALD, K. A.
1995 Unearthing the Sins of the Past. *Chronicle of Higher Education,* 42(6):12-20.

MILANICH, JERALD T., AND CHARLES M. HUDSON
1993 *Hernando de Soto and the Indians of Florida.* University of Florida Press, Gainesville.

MITCHEM, JEFFREY M.
1989a *Redefining Safety Harbor: Late Prehistoric/ Protohistoric Archaeology in West Peninsular Florida.* Ph.D. dissertation, Department of Anthropology, University of Florida, Gainesville. University Microfilms International, Ann Arbor, MI.

1989b Some Alternative Interpretations of Safety Harbor Burial Mounds. *Florida Scientist,* 51(2):100-107.

MITCHEM, JEFFREY M., AND DALE L. HUTCHINSON
1986 Interim Report on Excavations at the Tatham Mound, Citrus County, Florida: Season II. Department of Anthropology, Florida State Museum, *Miscellaneous Project Report Series,* No. 28. Gainesville.
2000 Tatham Mound: Spanish Explorers and Native Americans in West Central Florida. University of Florida Press, Gainesville. Manuscript.

MITCHEM, JEFFREY M., AND JONATHON M. LEADER
1988 Early Sixteenth Century Beads from the Tatham Mound, Citrus County, Florida: Data and Interpretations. *Florida Anthropologist,* 41(1):42-60.

MITCHEM, JEFFREY M., MARVIN T. SMITH, ALBERT C. GOODYEAR, AND ROBERT R. ALLEN
1985 Early Spanish Contact on the Florida Gulf Coast: The Weeki Wachee and Ruth Smith Mounds. In Indians, Colonists, and Slaves: Essays in Memory of Charles H. Fairbanks; Kenneth W. Johnson, Jonathan M. Leader, and Robert C. Wilson, editors, pp. 179-219. *Florida Journal of Anthropology Special Publication,* No. 4. Gainesville.

MOONEY, JAMES
1928 The Aboriginal Population of America North of Mexico. *Smithsonian Miscellaneous Collections,* 80:1-40. Washington, DC.

MORSE, DAN, J. DUNCAN, AND J. STOUTAMIRE (EDITORS)
1983 *Handbook of Forensic Archaeology and Anthropology.* Bill's Book Store, Tallahassee, FL.

NEITZEL, ROBERT S.
1965 Archaeology of the Fatherland Site: The Grand Village of the Natchez. *Anthropological Papers of the American Museum of Natural History,* 51:1-108. New York, NY.

O'SHEA, JOHN M.
1984 *Mortuary Variability: An Archaeological Investigation.* Academic Press, New York, NY.

ORTNER, DONALD J., NOREEN TUROSS, AND ALIX STIX
1992 New Approaches to the Study of Disease in Archaeological New World Populations. *Human Biology,* 64(3):337-360.

OVIEDO, GONZALO FERNANDO DE
1944 *Historia General y Natural de las Indias: Islas y Tierra-Firme del Mar Oceano.* Editorial Guarania, Asuncion del Paraguay.

PETERS-SULLIVAN, LYNNE A.
1986 *The Late Mississippian Village: Community and Society of the Mouse Creek Phase in Southeastern Tennessee.* Ph.D. dissertation, Department of Anthropology, University of Wisconsin, Milwaukee. University Microfilms International, Ann Arbor, MI.

RAMENOFSKY, ANN F.

1987　*Vectors of Death: The Archaeology of European Contact.* University of New Mexico Press, Albuquerque.

1990　Loss of Innocence: Explanations of Differential Persistence in the Sixteenth-Century Southeast. In *Columbian Consequences, Volume 2: Archaeological and Historical Perspectives on the Spanish Borderlands East*, David Hurst Thomas, editor, pp. 31-48. Smithsonian Institution Press, Washington, DC.

1993　Diseases of the Americas, 1492-1700. In *The Cambridge World History of Human Disease*, K. Kiple, editor, pp. 317-327. Cambridge University Press, Cambridge, England.

RANGEL, RODRIGO

1993　Account of the Northern Conquest and Discovery of Hernando de Soto. In *The De Soto Chronicles: The Expedition of Hernando de Soto to North America in 1539-1543, Volume I*, Lawrence A. Clayton, Vernon James Knight, Jr., and Edward C. Moore, editors, pp. 247-306. University of Alabama Press, Tuscaloosa.

ROBINS, ROBERT S.

1981　Disease, Political Events, and Populations. In *Biocultural Aspects of Disease*, Henry Rothschild, editor, pp. 153-175. Academic Press, New York, NY.

ROMANS, BERNARD

1962　*A Concise Natural History of East and West Florida.* University of Florida Press, Gainesville. Reprint of 1775 edition, Printed for the Author, New York, NY.

ROSENBLAT, A.

1976　The Population of Hispaniola at the Time of Columbus. In *The Native Population of the Americas in 1492*, William H. Denevan, editor, pp. 43-66. University of Wisconsin Press, Madison.

SALO, W. L., ARTHUR C. AUFDERHEIDE, JANE BUIKSTRA, AND T. A. HOLCOMB

1994　Identification of *Mycobacterium tuberculosis* DNA in a pre-Columbian Peruvian mummy. *Proceedings of the National Academy of Sciences*, 91(6):2091-2094.

SANDERS, WILLIAM T.

1976　The Population of the Central Mexican Symbiotic Region, the Basin of Mexico, and the Teotihuacán Valley in the Sixteenth Century. In *The Native Population of the Americas in 1492*, William M. Denevan, editor, pp. 85-150. University of Wisconsin Press, Madison.

SAUER, CARL O.

1966　*The Early Spanish Main.* University of California Press, Berkeley.

SKOLNICK, A. A.

1995　Forensic Scientists Helping Haiti Heal. *Journal of the American Medical Association*, 274:1181-1182.

SMITH, HALE G.

1956　The European and the Indian. *Florida Anthropological Society Publications*, No. 4. Gainesville.

SMITH, MARVIN T.

1976　The Route of De Soto through Tennessee, Georgia, and Alabama: The Evidence from Material Culture. *Early Georgia*, 4(1&2):27-48.

1983　Chronology from Glass Beads: The Spanish Period in the Southeast, 1513-1670. In Proceedings of the 1982 Glass Bead Conference, Charles Hayes, editor, pp. 147-158. *Rochester Museum Research Records*, No. 16. Rochester, NY.

1987　*Archaeology of Aboriginal Culture Change in the Interior Southeast.* Ripley P. Bullen Monographs in Anthropology and History, No. 6. University of Florida Press, Gainesville.

SMITH, MARVIN T., AND M. ELIZABETH GOOD

1982　*Early Sixteenth-century Glass Beads in the Spanish Colonial Trade.* Cottonlandia Museum, Greenwood, MS.

STEWART, T. DALE

1992　Archeological Exploration of Patawomeke: The Indian Town Site (44St2) Ancestral to the One (44St1) Visited in 1608 by Captain John Smith. *Smithsonian Contributions to Anthropology*, No. 36. Washington, DC.

STOVER, ERIC

1997　The Grave at Vukovar. *Smithsonian Magazine*, March:40-51.

THORNTON, RUSSELL

1987　*American Indian Holocaust and Survival: A Population History Since 1492.* University of Oklahoma Press, Norman.

1997　Aboriginal North American Population and Rates of Decline, ca. A.D. 1500-1900. *Current Anthropology*, 38:310-315.

THWAITES, RUEBEN GOLD (EDITOR)

1896-1901　*The Jesuit Relations and Allied Documents: Travels and Explorations of the Jesuit Missionaries in New France 1610-1791.* Burrows Brothers, Cleveland, OH.

TRIGGER, BRUCE G.

1976　*The Children of Aataentsic II: A History of the Huron People to 1660.* McGill-Queen's University Press, Montreal, Quebec.

1985　*Natives and Newcomers: Canada's "Heroic Age" Reconsidered.* McGill-Queen's University Press, Montreal, Quebec.

TRIMBLE, MICHAEL K.

1985　*Epidemiology on the Northern Plains: A Cultural Perspective.* Ph.D. dissertation, Department of Anthropology, University of Missouri, Columbia. University Microfilms International, Ann Arbor, MI.

UBELAKER, DOUGLAS H.
  1974 Reconstruction of Demographic Profiles from Ossuary
        Skeletal Samples: A Case Study from the Tidewater
        Potomac. *Smithsonian Contributions to Anthropology*,
        No. 18. Washington, DC.
  1976 The Sources and Methodology for Mooney's Estimates
        of North American Indian Populations. In *The
        Native Population of the Americas in 1492,* William
        M. Denevan, editor, pp. 243-288. University of
        Wisconsin Press, Madison.
  1988 North American Indian Population Size, A.D. 1500 to
        1985. *American Journal of Physical Anthropology,*
        77(3):289-294.

VELLEMAN, PAUL F., AND D. C. HOAGLIN.
  1981 *Applications, Basics, and Computing of Exploratory
        Data Analysis.* Duxbury Press, Boston, MA.

VERANO, JOHN W., AND DOUGLAS H. UBELAKER (EDITORS)
  1992 *Disease and Demography in the Americas.* Smithsonian
        Institution Press, Washington, DC.

VIDAL, J.
  1995 Emerging from Hell: Rwandans Slowly Rebuild Their
        War-Shattered Country. *McLean's,* 3 April:32-33.

WILLEY, GORDON R.
  1982 *Archeology of the Florida Gulf Coast.* Florida Book
        Store, Gainesville. Reprint of 1949, *Smithsonian
        Miscellaneous Collections*, Vol. 113, Washington,
        DC.

WOLFORTH, LYNNE M.
  1997 *Smallpox Diffusion Between Small and Dispersed
        Historic Native American Populations*. Ph.D.
        dissertation, Department of Anthropology, University
        of Illinois, Champaign-Urbana. University Microfilms
        International, Ann Arbor, MI.

WRAY, D. E., AND RICHARD S. MACNEISH
  1961 The Hopewellian and Weaver Occupations at the
        Weaver Site, Fulton County, Illinois. *Illinois State
        Museum Scientific Papers,* 1949, 7(2). Springfield.

WRAY, CHARLES F., MARTHA L. SEMPOWSKI, AND LORRAINE
P. SAUNDERS
  1991 Tram and Cameron: Two Early Contact Era Seneca
        Sites. *Rochester Museum and Science Center Research
        Records,* No. 21. Rochester, NY.

WRAY, CHARLES F., MARTHA L. SEMPOWSKI, LORRAINE P.
SAUNDERS, AND G. C. CERVONE
  1987 The Adams and Culbertson Sites. *Rochester Museum
        and Science Center Research Records,* No. 19.
        Rochester, NY.

DALE L. HUTCHINSON
DEPARTMENTS OF ANTHROPOLOGY AND BIOLOGY
EAST CAROLINA UNIVERSITY
GREENVILLE, NC 27858-4353

JEFFREY M. MITCHEM
ARKANSAS ARCHAEOLOGICAL SURVEY
P.O. BOX 241
PARKIN, AR 72773-0241

PETER B. MIRES

Contact and Contagion: The Roanoke Colony and Influenza

ABSTRACT

A comparison of the writings of Thomas Hariot, leader of the ill-fated Roanoke colony, and John Smith, founder of the first successful British settlement in North America, reveals that the Roanoke colonists were the vectors of epidemic disease. The disease was probably influenza, and it was especially lethal to the American Indians whom the Roanoke colonists contacted. Thomas Hariot recorded direct observations of the progress of the epidemic, including symptoms, mode of transmission, and virulence. John Smith, upon his arrival in the Chesapeake Bay region, heard stories of a devastating epidemic that had ravaged the Accomac, one of the groups visited by the Roanoke colonists during the winter of 1585/86. This article critically assesses the historical evidence surrounding this epidemic and proposes influenza as the probable pathogen. Depopulation of American Indians in the vicinity of the Roanoke colony, specifically the Accomac, is placed within the wider context of European epidemic disease in the New World. One implication of this historical record is the identification of Virginia's Eastern Shore as an area likely to contain archaeological resources relevant to the research problem of American Indian demographic change during the Contact period.

Introduction

Something happened to the American Indian population of Virginia's Eastern Shore between the visits of the English Roanoke settlers during the winter of 1585/86 and John Smith's exploration of the Chesapeake Bay in the summer of 1608. A comparison of observations made by these two groups, separated in time by 22 years, indicates that the American Indians who inhabited what is now Virginia's Eastern Shore succumbed to a European epidemic disease and experienced devastating depopulation. Heretofore, at least one researcher has implicated smallpox (McCary 1957: 84), but a closer examination of the evidence suggests that influenza was the probable pathogen.

The earlier group, part of whom were members of the ill-fated first attempt at British colonization in the New World, did not stay (Quinn 1955; Meinig 1986; Mitchell 1990). They were merely on a reconnaissance of the territory to the north of their proposed colony on Roanoke Island, which was located in the protected waters between Pamlico and Albemarle sounds along the coast of what is now the state of North Carolina (Figure 1). The colony did not survive, and, as all students of American history know, permanent British settlement on these shores did not become a reality until 1607 (Arber 1884; Barbour 1969). In the late summer of that year, the Jamestown colony, led by the energetic John Smith, achieved a tenuous foothold in Tidewater Virginia among a chiefdom of American Indians known collectively as the Powhatan (Mooney 1907a; Garrow 1974; Feest 1978a).

Two groups belonging to the Powhatan chiefdom, the Accomac and Accohanock (Mooney 1907b), lived across the Chesapeake Bay at the tip of what is today the Delmarva Peninsula (Figure 1). John Smith, eager to know his new neighbors in the Chesapeake Bay region, sought out the "Werowance," or tribal leader, of the Accomac in June of 1608. During this initial contact, Smith was told of "a strange mortalitie" which affected "a great part of his people . . . and but few escaped" (Arber 1884:413). The Werowance of Accomac had described an epidemic disease which was "strange" and new, and therefore, one which the population had never experienced. And, the disease apparently had an extremely high case fatality rate. The horror of epidemic disease, in all probability of Old World origin, had clearly visited the Accomac. For reasons described below, that visit seems likely to have occurred during the winter of 1585/86.

European Epidemic Disease in the New World

Although scholars continue to debate the temporal and spatial parameters, it appears that American Indian populations declined drastically after even cursory contact with Europeans, not to mention during initial colonization and subsequent settlement (Quaife 1930; Dobyns 1966; Crosby 1972,

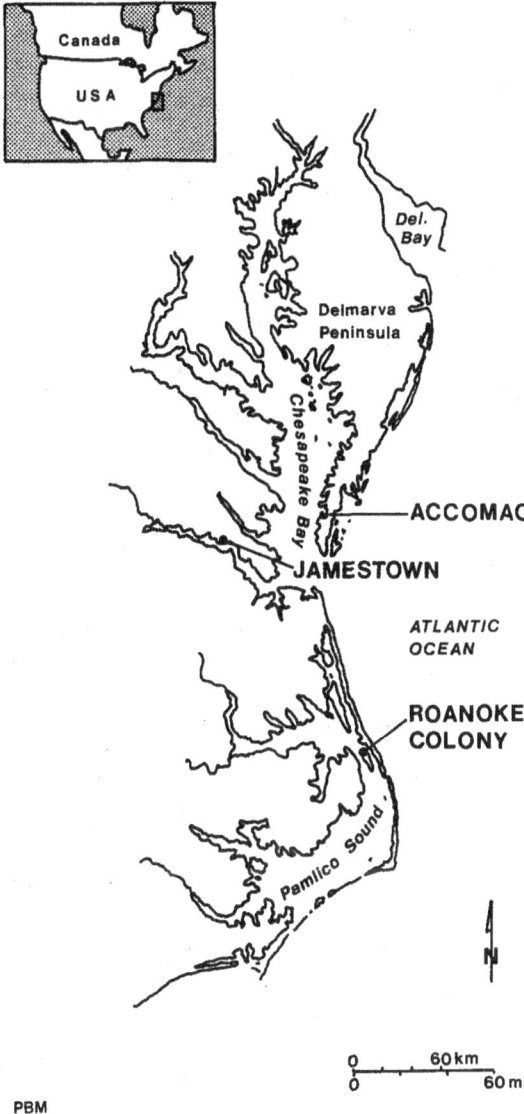

FIGURE 1. Location of the land of the Accomac, James-town, and the Roanoke Colony.

PBM

New World populations by Old World pathogens constituted one of the world's greatest biological cataclysms.''

Diseases such as influenza, smallpox, measles, typhus fever, yellow fever, malaria, and plague have all been identified as contributing to dramatic reductions of New World populations in the wake of European contact. A number of studies in the historical demography of American Indians have reached the conclusion that populations frequently declined from 50 to 90 percent following a century of European contact (Dobyns 1976). Certainly warfare and the collapse of a way of life were important considerations in the near extinction of many American Indian groups, but on a hemispheric scale disease was the primary causal factor in depopulation.

Many researchers (e.g., Crosby 1972, 1986; Jennings 1975; Dobyns 1976, 1983) implicate smallpox as the ''single most lethal disease Europeans carried to the New World'' (Dobyns 1976:1–2). Its devastating impact upon American Indians, especially in Spanish America, is well documented (Lovell 1992). As Francis Jennings (1975:22) has so aptly put it, ''Not even the most brutally depraved of the conquistadors was able purposely to slaughter Indians on the scale that the gentle priest unwittingly accomplished by going from his sickbed ministrations to lay his hands in blessing on his Indian converts.''

The social implications of swift and massive depopulation due to American Indian contact with pathogens for which they had no natural immunity are several. There can be no doubt that disease facilitated European colonization. For example, Cortez took Tenochtitlán only after disease had severely debilitated its resident population (Borah and Cook 1969), and the Massachusetts Bay colony survived by cultivating fields vacated by victims of the documented 1616–1619 epidemic (Cook 1973). Depopulation also gave rise to American ''Manifest Destiny'' based on a perception that North America was a virgin land. North America, however, was actually more of a ''widowed land'' (Jennings 1975:15). Among other social consequences of hemispheric depopulation is the institution of the African slave trade to supply labor for tropical and subtropical colonial planta-

1986; Jacobs 1974; Jennings 1975; Thomas 1989; Lovell 1992; Ramenofsky 1992; Verano and Ubelaker 1992). Chronicles from the conquest and colonization of the New World are replete with accounts of catastrophic depopulation. The major cause of such rapid depopulation was the American Indian's susceptibility to Old World diseases. In Dobyns's (1976:21–22) words, ''the invasion of

FIGURE 2. Portrait of Thomas Hariot. (Courtesy of the President and Fellows of Trinity College, Oxford, England.)

Within a few dayes after our departure from everies such townes, that people began to die very fast, and many in short space; in some townes about twentie, in some fourtie, in some sixtie, & in one six score, which in trueth was very manie in respect to their numbers. . . . The disease also was so strange that they neither knew what it was, nor how to cure it; the like by report of the oldest men in the countrey never happened before, time out of mind (Quinn 1955:378).

The similarities which exist between Hariot's account and what had been told to John Smith by the Werowance of Accomac are striking. A "strange," extremely contagious epidemic disease with a high case fatality rate was experienced by Carolina Algonquians and Eastern Shore Virginia inhabitants alike.

Furthermore, the Roanoke settlers must have only been mildly affected by the disease. Their individual immunity permitted them to walk freely among the American Indians who were dropping like flies around them. This characteristic puzzled both the English and the American Indian, a curious fact that did not go unrecorded in Hariot's journal:

This maruelous accident in all the countrie wrought so strange opinions of vs, that some people could not tel whether to thinke vs gods or men, and the rather because that all the space of their sicknesse, there was no man of ours knowne to die, or that was specially sicke (Quinn 1955: 379).

It is significant that the Roanoke settlers failed to identify the disease. Such intelligent and observant men as Thomas Hariot, Ralph Lane, and especially the talented artist John White (see Lorant 1946) must surely have had some familiarity with European epidemics and their symptoms. But, in this case, they were apparently as puzzled as the American Indian victims. Hariot revealed his bewilderment by his choice of words; he referred to the epidemic as "rare and strange." One may assume that although he recognized high morbidity and mortality among the American Indians, he was unable to identify the specific contagion.

tions. In the Caribbean, for example, the demography of the whole region can be explained, in large measure, by the substitution of one population for another. Historical archaeologists, like other social scientists, are wary of simple cause-and-effect relationships, but the role of nonindigenous disease in the history of European colonization and settlement of the Western Hemisphere cannot be ignored.

The Roanoke Colony

Thomas Hariot (Figure 2), Sir Walter Raleigh's hand-picked leader of the Roanoke colony, noticed that there was a direct correlation between their visits to neighboring American Indian villages and the outbreak of epidemic disease:

The Symptoms and Possible Disease Suspects

To assist in the identification of symptoms and the determination of disease suspects one must rely on the observations made by Thomas Hariot and John Smith. One man observed firsthand the epidemic in progress; the other, 22 years later, recorded a chilling tale as told to him by a tribal leader. By piecing this information together it is possible to eliminate some disease suspects and assess the probability of others.

One question that immediately presents itself is, What diseases would have been recognized by English people of the late 16th or early 17th centuries? They would have undoubtedly identified smallpox. This notoriously virulent disease could, in Crosby's (1972:56) words, "transform a healthy man into a pustuled, oozing horror, whom his closest relatives can barely recognize." And, according to Cook (1973:488), "English colonists were thoroughly familiar with the symptoms and appearance of small pox, and could diagnose the disease without hesitation." In fact, with the exception of influenza, the diseases of smallpox, measles, typhus fever, yellow fever, malaria, and plague, mentioned above, all have outward and visible symptoms such as pox (typical of eruptive fevers), jaundice, hemorrhages, persistent vomiting, and black vomit that would not have escaped the attention of Hariot and others. No doubt these symptoms would have been commented on even if an incorrect diagnosis were made.

If the Roanoke colonists were unclear as to the actual cause of the epidemic, they were certain of the mechanism by which it was transmitted. Hariot wrote, "This happened in no place that wee coulde learne but where we had bene . . . a thing specially observed by vs, as also by the naturall inhabitants themselues" (Quinn 1955:378). It appears that the Roanoke colonists themselves were the vectors of death.

The disease in question was also typified by a short duration of illness in which mortality occurred quickly. To quote Hariot again, "The people began to die very fast, and many in short space" (Quinn 1955:378). The Werowance of Accomac was also particularly emphatic on this point. He also added that there were no obvious signs of outward or disfiguring symptoms. The first victims to die in the Accomac epidemic were described as having "such delightful countenances, as though

they had regained their vital spirits" (Arber 1884: 413).

An important clue that assists one in eliminating some of the possible disease suspects is the timing of both outbreaks with respect to season. The epidemic outbreak among the coastal Carolina Algonquians took place in the fall of the year (Quinn 1955), and the Accomac outbreak probably occurred sometime during the winter as the Roanoke colony reconnaissance party wintered in the lower Chesapeake Bay region (Quinn 1955). The obvious significance of this fact is that it eliminates yellow fever and malaria as suspects because the vector of both diseases—the mosquito—begins to die off with the onset of cool weather. Its tolerance to cool temperatures, in fact, seems to be around 16°C (Carter 1931). By the same token, a disease such as influenza becomes more virulent during the winter because of the additional complications of viral and bacterial pneumonia (Kilborne 1975).

Two lines of evidence make the serious consideration of malaria or yellow fever a moot point. First, it seemed clear to Hariot and others that the Europeans themselves were transmitting the disease, not a swarm of mosquitos. Second, historians of disease in the New World are in apparent consensus that the first positively identified outbreak of yellow fever "did not occur until well into the seventeenth century" (Duffy 1953:140). Malaria, on the other hand, seems to have a longer history in the New World and cannot be so easily dismissed on the grounds of probable date of importation (Rutman and Rutman 1976).

Measles seems unlikely because of its lower case fatality rate among non-resistant populations as reported by Burnet and White (1972), Panum (1939), Carter (1931), and Dobyns (1966). Also, Europeans have known about measles and smallpox since at least 1347 (Winslow and Duran-Reynals 1948). Although measles would have been less diagnostic, it seems certain that its symptoms would have been noted.

Typhus fever should not be considered a suspect because this body-louse-borne disease would have claimed European victims as well as American Indian (Duffy 1953). The symptoms of typhus fever—jaundice, black vomit, prostration, and a characteristic skin eruption—stood a good chance of being commented on by European and American Indian alike. The high mortality figures with which researchers are dealing would also have been less likely with typhus fever.

Lastly, plague can be ruled out on the grounds that Europeans would have recognized it, would not have had such an apparent immunity to it, and the bubonic form of plague is not transmitted human to human, but via the flea vector. An outbreak of bubonic plague with high mortality occurring "within a few dayes" after the initial introduction of the vector seems incredulous. Pneumonic plague, in which a human is the carrier, seems impossible given the evidence because that would mean that the Roanoke colonists had the plague. Besides, the epidemiologist Henry R. Carter (1931: 57) felt confident that "quite certainly there was never plague in America before 1898." And even though Cook (1973:489) implicated plague as the contagion responsible for the 1616–1619 epidemic among New England Indians, he admits that "there is little solid evidence . . . that the epidemic of 1616–1619 was some type of bubonic or pneumonic plague."

There are various reasons for suspecting influenza as the contagion in question. They all fit neatly with the information given by Thomas Hariot and John Smith regarding circumstances and characteristics associated with the outbreak. Researchers know that the disease was not endemic to the American Indian population which, according to all reports, had never seen anything like it in the past. The illness was of short duration in which death occurred quickly—a high case fatality rate is suggested. The disease seems to have been transmitted by the English Roanoke colonists, yet they were unable to recognize it by outward or disfiguring symptoms, and they did not report any illness among themselves. They were apparently carriers and not victims. Finally, the outbreaks took place in the fall and winter of the year.

The virulence of influenza and its associated complication, pneumonia, among an immunologically deficient population could have been extremely high. Modern medical historians examining case histories from identifiable influenza epidemics have demonstrated a case fatality rate as great as 75–100 percent (Carter 1931; McBryde 1940). The characteristic of a short duration of illness with mortality occurring quickly is typical of other influenza epidemics among non-resistant populations: "In overt community epidemics, the disease is easily recognized by its explosive nature" (Kilborne 1975:495).

That the Roanoke colonists would have had a "herd immunity" to the disease and would have been only mildly affected, yet capable of transmission, is highly probable. The disease was transmitted via human vector, and, as Thomas Hariot (Quinn 1955) noted, outbreaks did not occur in villages where the English had not visited. According to Kilborne (1975:495), "dependent as influenza is upon direct dissemination from man to man, the rapidity of its spread cannot exceed the speed of human travel and communication." Although some of the other diseases discussed above could conceivably fit this description of probable transmission, it seems especially suited to the spread of influenza.

As mentioned earlier, influenza is probably the only epidemic disease among the possible suspects that could have killed so quickly and violently without any diagnostic symptoms. In fact, according to Dobyns (1983:18), "the historic role of influenza is probably significantly underestimated in records of its extent because its symptoms do not include readily perceived red rash or similar marker." Even the sensitive artist John White, who was meticulous in detail and acutely observant when recording on canvas the land and life of the North Carolina Algonquians (Figure 3), would have been quick to make note of unusual physical symptoms typical of all the other contagions, but with influenza there would have been none to record.

The timing of the disease is important. The English colonists made extensive contacts with both the French and Spanish while in the Caribbean prior to sailing up the coast to Pamlico Sound. It is postulated here that the influenza virus was picked up at this time. That influenza was endemic to the Caribbean in the 1580s has been documented (McBryde 1940). Furthermore, modern research has

FIGURE 3. De Bry engraving of a Roanoke chief (ca. 1586). (Courtesy of the William L. Clements Library, University of Michigan, Ann Arbor.)

established that influenza infections are present in the general population on a continuous basis, and that "epidemics" are simply statistically significant peaks in the number of reported cases. It seems entirely plausible that the English colonists came into contact with the disease while in the Caribbean in May and June of 1585. The month of July occupied the colonists in regrouping lost ships—four of the original nine had been lost (one had possibly taken a layover in Jamaica). These others did not rejoin the group at Pamlico Sound until the 27th of that month. Although initial contact was made with the native inhabitants sometime during the middle of July, regular interaction did not occur until August and September. Indeed, the American Indians seemed standoffish at first,

and according to Quinn (1955:384), the colonists complained of "some slowness in organizing Indian supplies to the settlers at the beginning of the settlement in August and September." The outbreak among the coastal Algonquians occurred in the first week of October!

Archaeological Implications

This article has focused on the historical and epidemiological evidence suggesting severe depopulation among the Accomac of the 17th century without benefit of corroborating archaeological evidence. Unfortunately, the paucity of known Contact-period sites on the lower Delmarva Peninsula, a situation resulting from limited archaeological reconnaissance, forces one to employ analogy in lieu of firm archaeological data (Feest 1973; Turner 1973; Custer 1989:337). Several recent studies, however, have attempted to define eastern North American Indian depopulation through the examination of the archaeological record (Ramenofsky 1987; Smith 1987; Blakely and Detweiler-Blakely 1989; Ward and Davis 1991). Although there is general agreement that earlier estimates of American Indian population at the ethnographic present (e. g., Kroeber 1939) failed to appreciate the magnitude of depopulation due to epidemic disease, the cultural and biological mechanisms, as well as hypothesized archaeological manifestations, are topics of considerable professional debate (Ward and Davis 1991:171). Whether protohistoric demographic change occurred swiftly over large regions, or can be characterized by more temporal and spatial complexity, is a question whose resolution requires additional hard evidence. Archaeological evidence for a known example of protohistoric depopulation may well exist on what is now Virginia's Eastern Shore.

One potentially productive avenue of inquiry suggested by extant documents would be the implementation of systematic archaeological survey of selected drainages along the Chesapeake Bay side of Northampton County. Cartographic evidence suggests that the Roanoke settlers visited three villages on the Eastern Shore, two of which are identified as *Combec* (Accomac) and *Mashawatoc* (Quinn 1955, 1:map 7; Feest 1973:74, 1978b:248). The third village was probably Accohanock. John Smith's famous map of the Chesapeake Bay and its environs (Paullin and Wright 1932), however, only identifies two villages, *Accawmack* (Accomac) and *Acohanock* (Barbour 1969:344–359; Feest 1978b:248); it appears that the village of *Mashawatoc* had disappeared in the intervening 22 years. Smith obviously charted Nassawadox Creek, where the village of *Mashawatoc* should have been, but found nothing. In fact, according to Smith's journal, after leaving Accomac he sailed north, "Passing along the coast, searching every inlet, and Bay, fit for harbours and habitations" (Arber 1884:413). One has to conclude, therefore, that only the villages of Accomac and Accohanock were in existence by 1608.

Of course, a variety of equally plausible explanations could be offered to account for the disappearance of *Mashawatoc*. Regional adjustments in settlement pattern, however, are not an uncommon cultural response to demographically devastating events such as an epidemic with a high case fatality rate. It is suggested that the archaeological record of any of the three villages mentioned above should contain direct or indirect evidence supportive of sudden depopulation.

Conclusions

It is evident that the Roanoke colonists were transmitting influenza to neighboring Indian groups during the fall and winter of 1585/86. Hariot knew that the English settlers were the vectors of something extremely lethal to most American Indians with whom they had contact. He had no idea as to the contagion. John Smith recorded the aftermath of this epidemic among the Accomac of Virginia's Eastern Shore according to the testimony of a tribal leader. Smith estimated that their tribal area, which later became known as Northampton County, Virginia, contained some 400 individuals at the time of his 1608 visit (Arber 1884). But, these were people struggling to rebound from the demographically devastating effects of epidemic disease, the death rate of which could easily have been in the neighborhood of 70–90 percent.

Although potentially informative archaeological evidence is currently unavailable, the documentary record suggests that the Roanoke colonists visited three villages on the Eastern Shore, one of which, *Mashawatoc*, may have been abandoned as a result of depopulation. Archaeologists whose research interests include American Indian demographic change during the Contact period have lamented the difficulty of locating and identifying archaeological evidence that can shed light on this fascinating but elusive topic. As outlined in this article, Virginia's Eastern Shore is a likely candidate for the productive combination of necessary historical and archaeological data.

A careful reading of the writings of Thomas Hariot and John Smith has yielded a plethora of "clues" to what amounts to a colonial murder mystery. The suspected killer is identified as influenza. The identity of the Accomac victims, however, will remain shrouded in anonymity. Despite the human misery that accompanies a massive death toll during an especially virulent epidemic, the Accomac survivors and their descendants were described by the newly arrived Jamestown colonists in glowing terms. John Smith referred to the Accomac as "very kind," John Pory called them "the most ciuill and tractable people we have met with," and their tribal leaders were known to all as "the laughing kings of Accomac" (Arber 1884).

ACKNOWLEDGMENTS

I would like to thank Darrett B. Rutman for stimulating my interest in the Contact period of the Eastern Seaboard. Others who were influential in molding the views expressed in this article include: Stanley E. Aschenbrenner, Arthur Aufderheide, Michael P. Hoffman, Ann Marie Wagner Mires, the late Milton B. Newton, Jr., Ann F. Ramenofsky, and Jerome C. Rose. I would also like to thank the three anonymous reviewers for their cogent remarks. The author, however, is solely responsible for any inaccuracies contained herein.

REFERENCES

ARBER, EDWARD (EDITOR)
1884   *Captain John Smith's Works.* English Scholars Library, Birmingham, England.

BARBOUR, PHILIP L.
1969   *The Jamestown Voyages under the First Charter, 1606–1609: Documents Relating to the Foundation of Jamestown.* Published for the Hakluyt Society. Cambridge University Press, London.

BLAKELY, ROBERT L., AND BETTINA DETWEILER-BLAKELY
1989   The Impact of European Diseases in the Sixteenth-Century Southeast: A Case Study. *Midcontinental Journal of Archaeology* 14:62–89.

BORAH, WOODROW W., AND SHERBURNE F. COOK
1969   Conquest and Population: A Demographic Approach to Mexican History. *Proceedings of the American Philosophical Society* 113:117–183.

BURNET, SIR MACFARLANE, AND DAVID O. WHITE
1972   *Natural History of Infectious Disease.* Cambridge University Press, London.

CARTER, HENRY R.
1931   *The Early History of Yellow Fever.* Williams and Wilkins, Baltimore, Maryland.

COOK, SHERBURNE F.
1973   The Significance of Disease in the Extinction of the New England Indians. *Human Biology* 45:485–508.

CROSBY, ALFRED W.
1972   *The Columbian Exchange: Biological and Cultural Consequences of 1492.* Greenwood, Westport, Connecticut.

1986   *Ecological Imperialism: The Biological Expansion of Europe, 900–1900.* Cambridge University Press, New York.

CUSTER, JAY F.
1989   *Prehistoric Cultures of the Delmarva Peninsula: An Archaeological Study.* University of Delaware Press, Newark.

DOBYNS, HENRY F.
1966   Estimating Aboriginal American Population: An Appraisal of Techniques with a New Hemispheric Estimate. *Current Anthropology* 7:395–416.

1976   *Native American Historical Demography: A Critical Bibliography.* Indiana University Press, Bloomington.

1983   *Their Numbers Become Thinned: Native American Population Dynamics in Eastern North America.* University of Tennessee Press, Knoxville.

DUFFY, JOHN
1953   *Epidemics in Colonial America.* Louisiana State University Press, Baton Rouge.

FEEST, CHRISTIAN F.
1973   Seventeenth-Century Virginia Algonquian Population Estimates. *Quarterly Bulletin of the Archeological Society of Virginia* 28(2):66–79.

1978a   Virginia Algonquians. In *Handbook of North American Indians,* edited by William Sturtevant. Vol. 15, *Northeast,* edited by Bruce G. Trigger, pp. 253–270. Smithsonian Institution, U.S. Government Printing Office, Washington, D.C.

1978b   Nanticoke and Neighboring Tribes. In *Handbook of North American Indians,* edited by William Sturtevant. Vol. 15, *Northeast,* edited by Bruce G. Trigger, pp. 240–252. Smithsonian Institution, U.S. Government Printing Office, Washington, D.C.

GARROW, PATRICK H.
1974   An Ethnohistorical Study of the Powhatan Tribes. *The Chesopiean* 12(1–2). The Chesopiean Archaeological Association, Norfolk, Virginia.

JACOBS, WILBUR R.
1974   The Tip of an Iceberg: Pre-Columbian Indian Demography and Some Implications for Revisionism. *William and Mary Quarterly,* third series, 31:123–132.

JENNINGS, FRANCIS
1975   *The Invasion of America: Indians, Colonialism, and the Cant of Conquest.* University of North Carolina Press, Chapel Hill.

KILBORNE, EDWIN D.
1975   *The Influenza Virus and Influenza.* Academic Press, New York.

KROEBER, ALFRED L.
1939   Cultural and Natural Areas of Native North America. *University of California Publications in American Archaeology and Ethnology* 38. Berkeley.

LORANT, STEFAN (EDITOR)
1946   *The New World: The First Pictures of America.* Duell, Sloan and Pearce, New York.

LOVELL, W. GEORGE
1992   "Heavy Shadows and Black Night": Disease and Depopulation in Colonial Spanish America. *Annals of the Association of American Geographers* 82(3):426–443.

McBRYDE, WEBSTER F.
1940   Influenza in America During the Sixteenth Century. *Bulletin of the History of Medicine* 8:296–302.

McCARY, BEN C.
1957   Indians in Seventeenth-Century Virginia. *The Jamestown 350th Anniversary Historical Booklets* No. 18. Garrett and Massie, Richmond, Virginia.

MEINIG, DONALD W.
1986   *The Shaping of America: A Geographical Perspec-*

tive on 500 Years of History. Vol. 1, *Atlantic America, 1492–1800.* Yale University Press, New Haven, Connecticut.

MITCHELL, ROBERT D.
1990   The Colonial Origins of Anglo-America. In *North America: The Historical Geography of a Changing Continent,* edited by R. D. Mitchell and P. A. Groves, pp. 93–120. Rowman and Littlefield, Savage, Maryland.

MOONEY, JAMES
1907a The Powhatan Confederacy, Past and Present. *American Anthropologist* 9(1):129–152.
1907b Accomac. In Handbook of American Indians North of Mexico, Vol. 1, edited by F. W. Hodge. *Bureau of American Ethnology Bulletin* 30:3. Washington, D.C.

PANUM, PETER L.
1939   Observations Made During the Epidemic of Measles on the Faroe Islands in the Year 1856. *Medical Classics* 3(9). Williams and Wilkins, Baltimore, Maryland.

PAULLIN, CHARLES O., AND JOHN K. WRIGHT
1932   *Atlas of the Historical Geography of the United States.* Carnegie Institution, Washington, D.C.

QUAIFE, MILO M. (EDITOR)
1930   The Smallpox Epidemic on the Upper Missouri. *Mississippi Valley Historical Review* 17:278–279.

QUINN, DAVID B. (EDITOR)
1955   *The Roanoke Voyages, 1584–1590.* Two vols. Published for the Hakluyt Society. Cambridge University Press, London.

RAMENOFSKY, ANN F.
1987   *Vectors of Death: The Archaeology of European Contact.* University of New Mexico Press, Albuquerque.
1992   Death by Disease. *Archaeology* 45(2):47–49.

RUTMAN, DARRETT B., AND ANITA H. RUTMAN
1976   Of Agues and Fevers: Malaria in the Early Chesapeake. *William and Mary Quarterly,* third series, 33(1):31–60.

SMITH, MARVIN T.
1987   *Archaeology of Aboriginal Culture Change in the Interior Southeast: Depopulation During the Early Historic Period.* University of Florida Press and the Florida State Museum, Gainesville.

THOMAS, DAVID HURST
1989   *Columbian Consequences.* Three volumes. Smithsonian Institution Press, Washington, D.C.

TURNER, RANDOLPH
1973   A New Population Estimate for the Powhatan Chiefdom of the Coastal Plain of Virginia. *Quarterly Bulletin of the Archeological Society of Virginia* 28(2): 57–65.

VERANO, JOHN W., AND DOUGLAS H. UBELAKER (EDITORS)
1992   *Disease and Demography in the Americas.* Smithsonian Institution Press, Washington, D.C.

WARD, H. TRAWICK, AND R. P. STEPHEN DAVIS, JR.
1991   The Impact of Old World Diseases on the Native Inhabitants of the North Carolina Piedmont. *Archaeology of Eastern North America* 19:171–181.

WINSLOW, C.-E. A., AND M. R. DURAN-REYNALS
1948   Jacme d'Agramont and the First of the Plague Tractates. *Bulletin of the History of Medicine* 22:747.

PETER B. MIRES
DEPARTMENT OF GEOGRAPHY
UNIVERSITY OF MINNESOTA
DULUTH, MINNESOTA 55812

CHARLES R. EWEN

Continuity and Change: De Soto and the Apalachee

ABSTRACT

The expedition of Hernando de Soto has been touted as one of the primary factors of the demise of the native societies in the Southeast. European steel and infectious disease were the reputed agents of their destruction. While the de Soto entrada battled many of the native polities it encountered, recent studies suggest that the consequences were less disruptive in some places than previously thought. Indeed, changes were already in progress when the Europeans arrived. Evidence from the excavation of the Governor Martin site in northern Florida indicates that the Apalachee who received Franciscan missionaries in the 17th century were little different from those encountered by de Soto in 1540. The impact of European diseases on the native cultures was clearly significant; however, it would be imprudent to invoke monocausal explanations without exploring other factors that could have contributed to the social and demographic changes experienced by these societies.

Introduction

The interaction between different cultures is an enduring subject of research in anthropology. The nature of the archaeological research on this topic and interpretations thereof have evolved over the past century, usually reflecting the sympathies of the times in which they were written (Trigger 1989: 1). The prevailing sentiments concerning the consequences of European contact are characterized in the following quote:

Just as we today believe in and support our way of life, so did the northwest Florida Mississippian peoples maintain their societies through their beliefs and actions. Into this well-ordered world the Spanish in the early sixteenth century brought their diseases, leading to a rapid decrease in aboriginal populations. By the time of the establishment of the Spanish missions in the Fort Walton region in 1633 (then known as the territory of the Apalachee Indians), the most complex of the aboriginal cultures in Florida and the most

dense aboriginal society had been decimated. The Indian cultures of the historic period are only a reflection of those which had evolved prior to the "discovery" of the New World by Europeans (Milanich and Fairbanks 1980:204).

This scenario, though written about northern Florida, seems generally to reflect archaeological thought pertaining to the contact period.

The two decades leading up to the Columbian Quincentennial saw a tremendous increase in archaeological investigations of the contact period. The excavations at the Governor Martin site, the alleged de Soto winter encampment in Tallahassee, Florida, are a typical example of this kind research. The prevailing wisdom has been that European contact, specifically with their diseases, rapidly and radically changed the native societies they encountered—and often the change was believed to have been initiated even before actual face-to-face contact. Thus, scholars have tended to discount any other factors that might account for the demographic and social changes noted in the archaeological record. Did these changes occur only at contact? Were the Spanish conquistadors and the diseases they carried solely responsible for the disruption of the native culture, and if so, how rapidly was their presence felt? An examination of the data recovered from the Governor Martin and other contact-period sites is beginning to reveal the complexity of these processes.

The contact period is a somewhat ambiguous designation because contact between Europeans and the indigenous cultures of the Western Hemisphere occurred at different times in different places. Often the contact period is considered to include the time when European materials and ideas reached the natives before the Europeans themselves were encountered, i.e., the protohistoric period. For this discussion of north Florida, the contact period will refer to the 16th century.

The presumed consequences of European contact are cataclysmic: depopulation and cultural upheaval. Henry Dobyns (1983:342–343) states that "the ethnohistorical approach clearly shows that historical archaeology of Native Americans is—and because of depopulation and its sequelae must be—the study of rapid cultural change and abrupt cultural discontinuities. This act poses a very great challenge to archaeologists, who have for the most part thought in terms of (and searched for) static cultures and continuities in cultural traditions." It is instructive to examine the basis for these "cultural discontinuities."

The changes in the archaeological record that prompted the search for some causal explanation are varied. Changes in pottery styles and technology are often attributed to European influence; abandonment of sites and shifts in settlement patterns are also seen as the result of depopulation due to European contact, i.e., disease (Smith 1994). Virtually every difference in the pre- and postcontact material assemblage is attributed either directly or indirectly to European contact.

The primary agent of change has been attributed to European epidemic diseases such as typhus, smallpox, and even malaria, for which the indigenous people had little immunity. Again, according to Dobyns (1983:248), perhaps the most liberal theorist concerning the effects of European diseases on the native population, "... the Native American peoples of Florida suffered perhaps eight major epidemic episodes during the protohistoric half century from A.D. 1512 to 1562. Native American numbers did not merely become thinned; biological disaster struck the inhabitants of the peninsula." Many archaeologists studying the contact period have embraced the biological genocide hypothesis to the extent that it is no longer being tested, but accepted as fact.

This is not to say alternative explanations have been completely ignored. For example, Smith (1987:84–85), who supports the biological imperative, states, "It must be conceded that population curves suggestive of epidemics could be the result of famine or other causes. . . . But certainly other events [than epidemics] may account for population displacements, among them ecological disasters or warfare." Whereas alternative explanations are at least paid lip service in the scholarly literature, this is certainly not true of the popular literature (e.g., Sale 1990). The popular view that the Native Americans were the subject of biological warfare, albeit inadvertent, has tended to hinder the serious examination of alternative explanations.

The Apalachee: A Case Study

Apalachee Province in the north Florida panhandle has been the subject of archaeological investigation for over 50 years. A summary is provided in Milanich (1994, 1995). Sites spanning the entire period of human occupation are well documented, particularly during the Mississippian and succeeding historic period. Contact occurred early and more directly in Apalachee than in the interior chiefdoms of the Southeast; thus changes due to contact should be most readily apparent in this region. The Governor Martin site (8LE853b) is a particularly good locus for the study of the consequences of contact. The excavations conducted there revealed a multicomponent occupation with the primary component being a late Ft. Walton occupation (Ewen 1989). Its identification with the five-month winter encampment of Hernando de Soto in 1539–1540 provides evidence of direct, sustained contact with Europeans. Regional surveys (Tesar 1980; Marrinan and Bryne 1986; Smith and Scarry 1987) and synthetic studies (Scarry 1990, 1994a, 1994b) permit it a regional perspective with a complete chronology for the province. Finally, an extensive body of documentary materials pertains to the 16th- and 17th-century Apalachee (Hann 1988, 1994) to complement the archaeological data.

To understand the impact of European contact on the Apalachee, it is first necessary to examine their society prior to that contact. Apalachee Province was located in the north–central part of Florida at the juncture of the panhandle and peninsular portions of the state (Figure 1). The province was bounded by the Ochlockonee River to the west, the Aucilla River to the east, and the Gulf of Mexico to the south, and went north approximately to the Georgia state line. The most notable topographic feature in this area is the Cody Scarp. This landform divides the province into two distinct areas: the Tallahassee Red Hills to the north—red-clay fertile uplands, and the southern Coastal Lowlands—flat and sandy with pine scrub forests. The fertility of the Tallahassee Red Hills has made it an important agricultural region since at least A.D. 1000.

Prior to the development of agriculture as the chief means of subsistence, the Tallahassee Red

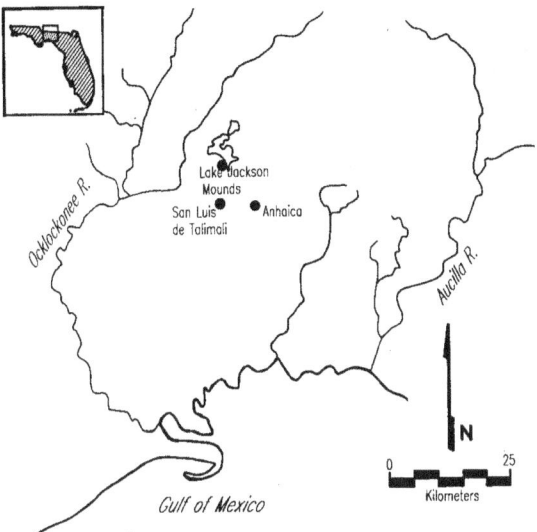

FIGURE 1. Location of Anhaica, the Governor Martin site, in Apalachee Province.

Hills were only sparsely inhabited. Most of the pre-Mississippian population in the region followed a coastal adaptation, and numerous sites have been reported in the Coastal Lowlands (Smith and Scarry 1987). During the Weeden Island period (A.D. 400–900), the domestication of plants became an important part of the population's adaptive strategy, which seems to have initiated a movement north to better agricultural soils. This period has been divided into several subphases (Percy and Brose 1974) which Tesar (1980:113) believes is indicative of rapid culture change. The final Weeden Island phase, the Wakulla phase (A.D. 750–950), has been characterized as a period of social instability that gave rise to the Ft. Walton culture (Milanich 1994: 197).

The Weeden Island period was replaced by the Ft. Walton period around A.D. 1000. The Ft. Walton period in Florida can be roughly equated with the Mississippian period in the eastern United States. It also, at least in the area between the Ochlockonee and Aucilla rivers, corresponds to the florescence of the Apalachee chiefdom. Curiously, while the Apalachee chiefdom itself is well documented both historically and archaeologically, its origins are not

well understood. It is possible that this chiefdom is the product of an evolving Weeden Island society adapting to an agrarian lifestyle (Brose 1984:188–189). Weeden Island sites, though present, are not abundant in the Tallahassee Red Hills. They are common along the adjacent Gulf Coast, and their relatively low numbers in the Red Hills may be due to the lack of systematic surveys performed in the area. Scarry (1984:381–387), however, believes that the Apalachee chiefdom was the result of a division of the Apalachicola-Chattahoochee River polity to the west. Thus, Ft. Walton in Apalachee Province is the result of migration rather than in situ development. Whether the changes were brought about by invasion or development, the Ft. Walton culture had much in common with the preceding Weeden Island population.

Like the Weeden Island period, the Fort Walton period can be subdivided into shorter phases. Scarry (1994b) identifies three phases for the Fort Walton in the Tallahassee Red Hills: Lake Jackson (A.D. 1100–1500), Velda (A.D. 1500–1633), and San Luis (A.D. 1633–1704). The San Luis phase has also been called the mission period. The transitions between phases are marked by technological and stylistic changes in the ceramic assemblages and by presumed periods of sociopolitical change and instability.

The Lake Jackson phase (A.D. 1100–1500) is the prehistoric phase of the Fort Walton period in the Apalachee territory. The phase name is derived from the Lake Jackson site, a ceremonial mound center that served as the paramount Apalachee village during this first phase. Mississippian in character, the Lake Jackson phase has been characterized as

> the earliest recognizable Apalachee polity. There is no evidence of contact between Lake Jackson-phase Apalachee and Europeans. . . . The late Lake Jackson-phase polity was a complex chiefdom with two administrative levels above the local community. There are four classes of Lake Jackson-phase settlements—homestead, hamlet, single mound center, and multimound centers. . . . And status differentiation and political (or religious) offices are evident in mortuary patterning (Scarry 1994b:162).

Maize agriculture probably formed the basis of the Apalachee subsistence during the Lake Jackson phase, though hunting and gathering of wild plants were, no doubt, still important.

It is significant that even before European contact the Apalachee are thought to have undergone major changes. According to Smith and Scarry (1987), the beginning of the Velda phase (A.D. 1500–1633) was a period of significant demographic shifts. The major mound center at Lake Jackson was abandoned and the paramount center shifted to Anhaica Apalachee, the Martin site. Mound building, in general, was discontinued, and vessel forms and decorative motifs that previously had linked the Apalachee with other Mississippian polities to the north and west declined in abundance (Scarry 1994b:170). The impetus for these changes is not known, but it seems unlikely that European influences were wholly responsible.

Spaniards are not recorded as having set foot on the continent until 1513, and no direct contact was made in northwest Florida until 1528. However, some scholars contend that Europeans were preceded by their diseases on the mainland by many years (cf. Dobyns 1983). Scarry (1994b:170) feels the changes described above "reflect a change in the ruling line, perhaps with new symbols of chiefly authority, perhaps with a diminution of sacra associated with the old line, and perhaps with new external links." Apalachee society, however, remained a complex chiefdom with social stratification and a hierarchically arranged settlement pattern. The subsistence base also remained unchanged.

It was during the Velda phase that contact with Europeans first occurred. Nearly a century passed after the expeditions of Pánfilo de Narváez and Hernando de Soto before the Spaniards ventured once more into Apalachee Province, this time at the request of the Apalachee themselves. Though the Spaniards began placing missions in *La Florida* during the latter part of the 1560s, it was not until 1633 that the first mission was established in the Apalachee province.

One of the first and certainly the most important of perhaps as many as 15 missions in north Florida was the mission of San Luis (Hann 1988; McEwan 1991, 1993). It supported a garrison of soldiers and served as the western anchor for the north Florida

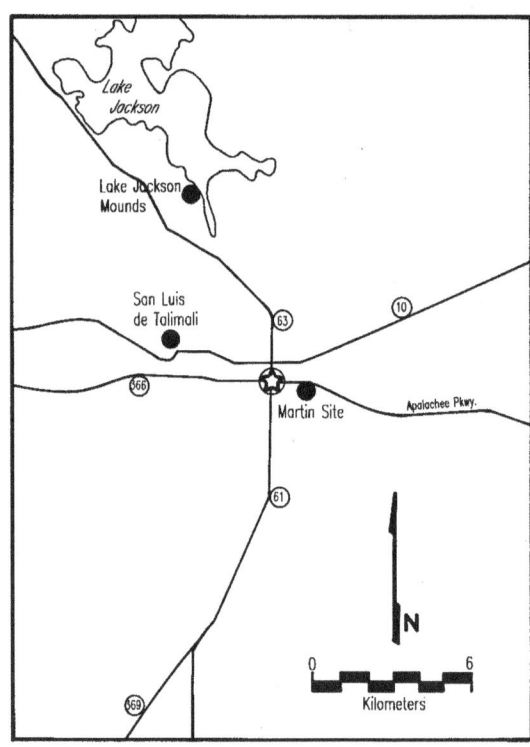

FIGURE 2. Location of San Luis de Talimali and the Governor Martin site.

chain of missions. Founded shortly after 1633, the mission moved once before being abandoned in 1704 (Figure 2). According to Hann,

the site to which San Luis relocated in 1656 is evidently the one currently identified with that mission which is being explored under the auspices of Florida's Bureau of Archaeological Research under the direction of the Secretary of State. Comparison of data from the 1655 mission list with that from the two 1675 sources for the location of the missions vis-à-vis one another indicates that prior to 1656 San Luis was one league [2.6 mi.] east–southeast of today's San Luis. Tallahassee's Capitol hill or the de Soto encampment [Governor Martin] site are likely candidates for the earlier site of the mission (Hann 1988:79).

Very little mission-period material was uncovered at the Governor Martin site proper. However, the results of a survey of adjacent properties (Ewen 1989) suggest that the first location of the San Luis mission, known as San Luis de Xinyaca (Anhaica), is along the eastern edge of the nearby Capitol City

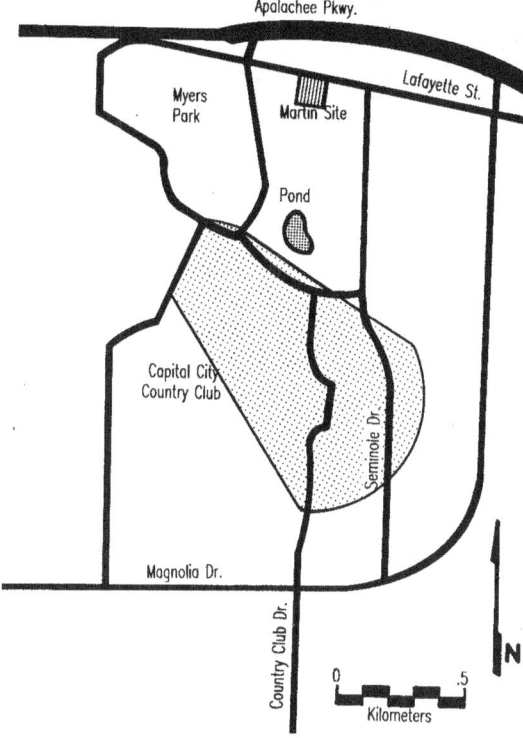

FIGURE 3. Hypothesized location of San Luis de Xinyaca, based on the distribution of mission-period ceramics.

Country Club golf course (Figure 3). The mission period in Apalachee Province effectively ended in 1704 after a series of British-instigated raids. By July 1704, all of the missions were destroyed or abandoned. For the most part, those Apalachee that were not killed or captured left the province for safer havens.

The Governor Martin site was a native settlement that appears to have been occupied by de Soto and his army for five months and abandoned by the Apalachee shortly after the establishment of the mission of San Luis. It is here that the consequences of contact should be most apparent.

The Governor Martin Site

The Martin tract is situated on top of a ridge in the fertile Tallahassee Red Hills amidst abundant water sources. It is located on Old St. Augustine

Road, which was formerly part of the mission trail between St. Augustine and San Luis. This trail, in turn, followed previously existing native trails in the area. Given its location close to arable land, fresh water, and a major transportation route, the Governor Martin site has been prime real estate for centuries.

There is evidence for a Late Archaic component to the site. The presence of Kirk serrated points and fiber tempered pottery suggest a pre-Apalachee presence, although the nature of this limited occupation could not be determined. However, Swift Creek and Weeden Island ceramics are noticeably absent from the material assemblage, which implies a considerable hiatus in occupation.

The first major occupation of the site occurred immediately after the Lake Jackson phase of the Fort Walton period, ca. A.D. 1500. Scarry (1994b: 170) has suggested that when the Lake Jackson site was abandoned, the capital moved to the Governor Martin site. The ceramic assemblage places the major occupation of the Governor Martin site during the Velda phase of the Fort Walton period. It was during this period that de Soto made his camp at Anhaica as the village was called.

The site of Hernando de Soto's first winter encampment has been sought by cartographers, historians, and archaeologists for many years. Since the pioneering attempts of Guillaume de l'Isle in 1718, researchers have pursued a variety of alternative routes. The evidence, however, has been very meager with very little agreement between scholars on any position along the de Soto trail. John R. Swanton chaired the first United States de Soto Expedition Commission, which produced the first systematic study of the route in 1939. Based on geographic descriptions of de Soto's chroniclers and the distances that they reported traveling from place to place, Swanton placed the location of Anhaica in the Tallahassee area:

> The position of Iniahica [Anhaica] is fixed with reasonable accuracy by estimating the distance from the Aucilla River probably covered in two days' march. We should expect this to be not less than 20 nor more than 40 miles, and the distance from the Aucilla River to Tallahassee is, in fact, about 31 miles, which is not much greater than the distance in leagues given by Garcilaso, about 11 leagues or 28.6 miles. The country around Tallahassee is indicated clearly though the

exact spot may have been on the site of Tallahassee itself, at the site of the later mission of San Luis de Talimali slightly west of Tallahassee or the mound group on Lake Jackson somewhat to the north. Judging by the distance to the sea . . . one of the first two sites is the most likely, and Tallahassee has more remains of the aborigines while the location of San Luis suggests that it was selected by the Spaniards with an eye to its defense (Swanton 1985[1959]:158).

Despite the predictions by all researchers that the first winter encampment must be located in Tallahassee, no trace of the site was recognized, even after a century of development and land clearing.

An important clue to the search neglected by previous researchers was a description of how the site of Anhaica should appear in the archaeological record. Tesar presumed, based on the documentary record, that

> division of the village into identifiable sections is characteristic of large Apalachee villages. . . . In this respect, it is noted that the results of the Leon County Survey indicated that possible simultaneous occupation of several adjacent finger ridges [occurred] in the Tallahassee Red Clay Hills area in the northern half of the county. If such an interpretation is correct, then the dwelling sites on these ridges should be considered as part of a single dispersed village with each ridge serving to divide the whole into apparent parts (Tesar 1980:303).

This distinction is important since separate, but adjacent, ridgetops are usually assigned separate site numbers. Such assignments would have made the delineation of a large site such as Anhaica difficult.

Jeffrey Brain noted optimistically that although the site had not yet been found, the chances for discovery were good. He stated,

> the possibilities are fairly well circumscribed and within the scope of a realistic program of archaeological research. Furthermore, the stay was a lengthy one by the entire army, and many buildings and fortifications were constructed that should be manifest in architectural features contrasting with native constructions. Finally, only in its first year, the army was still well accoutered and recently resupplied from its base camp at the landing. It might be expected that discarded artifacts would be relatively abundant compared to subsequent stages of the journey (Brain in Swanton 1985[1959]: xxiii).

Such was the state of the search for Anhaica in the mid-1980s. The parameters of the search were well-defined as well as the criteria against which all claimants would be judged.

The Governor Martin site was fortuitously discovered when B. Calvin Jones, an archaeologist with the Florida Bureau of Archaeological Research, investigated an area in downtown Tallahassee being converted into an office complex. The recovery of 16th-century artifacts gave a clue to the site's identity and prompted a full-scale excavation. The working hypothesis was that the Governor Martin site was the first winter encampment of de Soto's army. To test this hypothesis it was necessary to define what evidence would be needed.

Artifacts are an important category of evidence that must be used judiciously. The presence of a 16th-century Spanish artifact on a site does not necessarily mean that de Soto slept there. Beads, coins, tools, and so on, are very portable items that could easily have been carried far from their original point of deposition. A good indication of a Spanish encampment would be large numbers of 16th-century artifacts in contexts that suggest loss or disposal rather than ritualistic burial of a prized item. The artifacts must have a tightly dated terminus post quem or be peculiar to the de Soto expedition. The artifact assemblage should also be predominantly aboriginal in composition and these aboriginal artifacts should date to the early 16th century. The Spaniards spent less than six months in this populous Apalachee village, so it is unlikely that their impact on the total artifact assemblage would have been very great. Finally there is the site itself, which is described as a large village of over 250 houses which the Spaniards took for themselves (de la Vega 1993:197). The Governor Martin site would have to be a part of a large Apalachee village to qualify as the site of Anhaica.

The Material Evidence

Aboriginal artifacts account for 90 percent of the material assemblage recovered from the Governor Martin site. The majority of the ceramics recovered are late Fort Walton types (A.D. 1450–1633) including: Lake Jackson plain, several varieties of

TABLE 1
ABORIGINAL CERAMICS

Period	Ceramic Type	Weight (g)	Percentage	Group %
Late Archaic	Fiber-tempered	31.1	0.18	0.18
Weeden Island	Wakulla check stamped	122.2	0.71	0.79
	Wakulla check stamped var. Wakulla	13.3	0.08	
Fort Walton	Cool Branch incised	43.3	0.25	60.01
	Cool Branch incised var. Cool Branch	21.7	0.13	
	Cool Branch incised var. Ft. Gaines	22.1	0.13	
	Ft. Walton incised	3,465.9	20.10	
	Ft. Walton incised var. Blalock	54.0	0.31	
	Ft. Walton incised var. Cayson	8.9	0.05	
	Ft. Walton incised var. Crowder	103.3	0.60	
	Ft. Walton incised var. Englewood	19.5	0.11	
	Ft. Walton incised var. Ft. Walton	176.7	1.02	
	Ft. Walton incised var. Safety Harbor	20.0	0.12	
	Lake Jackson incised	253.9	1.47	
	Carabelle punctate var. Meginnis	6,159.3	35.72	
Transitional	Lamar bold incised	29.3	0.17	20.96
	Lamar complicated stamped var. Early	265.7	1.54	
	Leon check stamped	3,040.9	17.63	
	Marsh Island incised	32.7	0.19	
	Marsh Island incised var. Columbia	20.4	0.12	
	Marsh Island incised var. Marsh Island	4.1	0.02	
	Point Washington incised	191.3	1.11	
	Point Washington incised var. Nunnaly	30.6	0.18	
Mission	Lamar complicated stamped	14.6	0.08	0.57
	Lamar complicated stamped var. Curvilinear	41.5	0.24	
	Lamar complicated stamped var. Jefferson	3.8	0.02	
	Lamar complicated stamped var. Rectilinear	17.5	0.10	
	Ocmulgee Fields incised	5.4	0.03	
	Copy wares	14.8	0.09	
Other	Alachua cob-marked	50.7	0.29	17.50
	Chattahoochee brushed	2,966.9	17.20	
Total		17,245.4	100.00	100.00

Fort Walton incised, and Carrabelle punctate var. Meginnis, the most common decorated ceramic at the site (Table 1). In other words, the aboriginal ceramic assemblage is consistent with the interpretation of the site as being part of a Velda phase Apalachee settlement, presumably Anhaica.

Spanish ceramics at the site (Table 2) consist mainly of olive jar fragments. Ubiquitous to Spanish sites in Florida and the Caribbean, the utilitarian olive jar can be distinguished chronologically on the basis of rim type and vessel form. Identifiable rim fragments from the Governor Martin site can be classified as the early type with date ranges of A.D. 1490–1650. Also recovered were such 16th-century majolica types as Columbia plain (A.D. 1492–1650), including a pre-1550 green variant, and Caparra Blue (A.D. 1492–1600).

Beads of European manufacture have been one of the primary tools for tracking the route of de Soto through the Southeast. A faceted amber bead, a dozen faceted chevron beads, and a single Nueva Cadiz bead recovered at the Governor Martin site are good 16th-century marker artifacts. All of the above-mentioned bead types have been found at

TABLE 2
SPANISH CERAMICS

Category	Ceramic Type	Count (N)	Weight (g)	% by Weight
Majolica	Columbia plain, green variant	8	6.7	0.09
	Columbia plain	4	5.0	0.07
	Caparra Blue	4	2.6	0.03
	Aranama polychrome	3	1.7	0.02
	Blue on White majolica	5	3.1	0.04
	Polychrome majolica	49	51.1	0.67
	Plain majolica	34	26.9	0.35
Utilitarian	Olive jar, glazed	412	1,859.1	24.48
	Olive jar, unglazed	1,952	5,513.3	72.60
	Bisque	1	2.3	0.03
	Lead-glazed coarse earthenware	55	92.7	1.22
	Unglazed coarse earthenware	6	10.4	0.14
Tablewares	Cologne stoneware	1	4.0	0.05
	Melado	5	15.0	0.20
	Black lead-glazed coarse earthenware	1	0.1	0.00
Total		2,540	7,594.0	100.00

other sites thought to be associated with the de Soto expedition. Dozens of wrought nails of various sizes and types are present in the material assemblage. One unusual type has also been reported from a site in New Mexico possibly associated with the Coronado expedition exploring the Southwest at the same time that de Soto was exploring the Southeast (Vierra 1989:132). A crossbow quarrel is the only example of 16th-century weaponry recovered. The 4-cm-long iron point has a circular, socketed base which tapers to a pyramidal head. It can be classified as an armor-piercing short bodkin point (Arnold et al. 1995:16). Similar points have been reported from excavations at Santa Elena (South et al. 1988:103–107). The crossbow was the principal weapon of de Soto's army, but had become obsolete when Spain returned to the panhandle in the 17th century. Other examples of the military nature of the expedition were the many pieces of chain mail armor. Over 2,000 links of iron mail were recovered, as well as 20 links of brass mail.

The most notable artifacts in terms of popular appeal and chronological value were five copper coins. These were found scattered across the site and appear to have been deposited as a result of loss.

The first coin is a four-maravedi minted in Burgos, Spain, expressly for use in the New World, and it dates between 1505 and 1517. The other Spanish coin is a one-maravedi dating to the same period. The other three coins are badly corroded but appear to be Portuguese ceitils dating to the late 15th or early 16th century.

All of these items place the site in the early 16th century but cannot distinguish between the expedition of Pánfilo de Narváez in 1528 and that of Hernando de Soto 11 years later. True, the documents associated with the expeditions place Narváez closer to the coast than Tallahassee (Cabeza de Vaca 1988; de la Vega 1993) but these descriptions are sketchy at best. Fortunately, just before the close of the 1987 field season a shattered maxilla of a domestic pig (*Sus scrofa*) was unearthed during the excavation in a good 16th-century context, including Ft. Walton ceramics and a Nueva Cadiz bead. This is significant because it is recorded that a herd of swine accompanied the de Soto expedition. There is no record of pigs on the earlier Narváez expedition, which was eventually reduced to eating their horses (Cabeza de Vaca 1988:18). Hogs (*Sus scrofa*) are not native to the Southeast.

The chronicles associated with the expedition describe the site of the first winter encampment as being in the principal Apalachee village of Anhaica. Given the hierarchical settlement pattern of the Apalachee, one would expect large villages to be widely spaced geographically with intervening areas occupied by smaller hamlets or individual farmsteads (Scarry 1994b:162–163). A survey of properties surrounding the Governor Martin site confirms that it is part of a large Late Fort Walton Indian village (Ewen 1989). There are no other recorded sites that qualify as far as size, location, and chronological placement for identification as Anhaica.

After de Soto and his men left Anhaica and Apalachee Province, the Apalachee appear to have reoccupied their village. They were still there when the Spanish returned to the Florida panhandle in 1633. While there is only scant evidence of any 17th-century material at the Governor Martin site proper, a survey conducted of adjacent properties turned up mission-period artifacts on the nearby Capitol City Country Club. As mentioned earlier, it is tempting to call this evidence of the first location of the San Luis mission, San Luis de Xinyaca (Anhaica). Given the close proximity and continuous distribution of aboriginal artifacts, the Governor Martin site and the material on the Capitol City Country Club are considered part of the same site, the principal village of Anhaica.

In 1656 the village moved to the present location of San Luis de Talimali in order to be closer to the garrison of soldiers (Hann 1990:486). It appears, based on the absence of late mission-period ceramics, that the Governor Martin site was more or less abandoned at this time. All of Apalachee Province was vacated after the devastating raids by the British and their Creek allies in 1704.

Discussion

The Apalachee at Anhaica were in sustained, direct contact with the de Soto expedition for five months, October 1539–March 1540. Should the catastrophic model of contact be true, changes should be readily apparent in the archaeological record. There are a number of ways that these changes

would be manifest. Smith (1987:67–68) and Ramenofsky (1987) note that in the wake of the diseases brought about at initial contact, populations would be expected to decline rapidly. Sites established during this period by people fleeing disease areas would probably be much smaller and, for at least a limited time, should continue to decline in size. When town populations reach a certain low limit, regrouping of populations could be expected to take place. Milner (1980:47) has noted that long-term effects of European epidemic disease and ensuing famine would be an insufficient labor force, including specialists, necessitating the reorganization of society and the coalescence of formerly discrete groups in order to remain viable social and economic entities. Thus, there should be an archaeologically detectable population movement accompanied by a decrease in the number of sites through time. Smith (1987:89) considers several factors in the demise of chiefdoms, including the end of public works such as mounds and palisades, the loss of a settlement hierarchy or at least its simplification, the breakdown of status systems as reflected in grave goods, and the breakdown in organized, part-time craft specialization.

It appears, at least in north Florida, that there was more continuity than change in the Apalachee province following 16th-century Spanish contact. Although change did occur as a result of the invasion by de Soto's army, it was not the disease-induced, catastrophic change proposed by some scholars (e.g., Dobyns 1983; Crosby 1994; Smith 1994). Those changes came about a century later as part of the rise and fall of the north Florida mission system. To confirm this hypothesis, it is easier to test the null hypothesis—that is, that drastic change did occur as a result of contact.

The preceding discussion provides a list of test implications for the drastic change hypothesis. At the regional level one would expect the size of sites to decrease precipitously, followed by a decrease in the number of sites as depleted populations coalesced into post-plague villages. The catastrophic population loss would seriously undermine the political stability of the chiefdom which would be signaled by the end of the construction of public works—i.e., mounds, village palisades—and the reduction of exotic grave goods in burials as trade relations and craft production decreased. Changes in the ceramic tradition have often been used by archaeologists to discern changes in populations or technological innovation. The exact nature of this change would depend upon the nature of the population change, i.e., degradation due to loss of skilled craftspeople, replacement by or increased trade with another population, and so on. Finally, demographic changes in burial populations and practices would be definitive evidence for disease-related population loss.

Most of these changes did, in fact, occur in Apalachee Province. However, they occurred either earlier or later than the contact period. The Velda phase, which initiated prior to European contact, was characterized by a cessation of mound building, changes in the ceramic assemblage, and a shift of the principal village from Lake Jackson to the Governor Martin site. Ceramic changes occurred both before, during, and after the contact period. The role of the Spaniards in these later changes is unclear. The bioarchaeological evidence from the contact period is almost completely lacking. Only two burials were discovered at the Governor Martin site, an adult cremation and a subadult burial so poorly preserved that only the burial pit and tooth enamel remained. Most of the other burials uncovered in Apalachee province date to the later mission period.

What could account for the changes that do occur in the Apalachee chiefdom? Is disease the only or even the primary factor? In a discussion of a model of complex chiefdoms proposed by Henry Wright, Scarry characterizes chiefdoms as politically volatile, claiming that

> there will be brief periods of breakdown every generation or so; successional disputes, minor rebellions, and small wars. Region-wide rebellions, civil wars, and the replacement of one chiefly line by another will occur less frequently. . . . These major breakdowns should be evident in the destruction or abandonment of great centers or by changes in traditional chiefly symbolism (Scarry 1990:178).

The causes of these breakdowns, the weakening of chiefly authority, could certainly be exacerbated by population decimation. Lake Jackson, however, appears to have been abandoned before the Spaniards ever came to the New World, let alone Florida.

Conclusion

There can be little doubt that the de Soto expedition had an immediate effect on Apalachee Province. The population of Anhaica had been forced to flee their village and food stores which was subsequently co-opted by de Soto's army. This prompted a series of guerrilla actions with the inevitable reprisals, as recorded by Rodrigo Rangel (1993:267), de Soto's secretary: ''they [the Apalachee] set fire to the town twice, and with many ambushes they killed many Christians at other times, and although the Spaniards pursued and them and burned them, never did they wish to come in peace.'' The impacts of the occupation were especially apparent at the departure of the army:

> On Wednesday, the third of March 1540, the governor left Anhaica Apalachee in search of Yupaha [a province said to have much gold]. He ordered all his men to provide themselves with maize for a journey of sixty leagues through uninhabited land. Those of horse carried their maize on their horses and those on foot on their backs; for most of the Indians whom they had to serve them, being naked and in chains, had died of the hard life they suffered during that winter (Elvas 1993:174).

Clearly the Apalachee of Anhaica, and of the province in general, suffered at the hands of the Spaniards. But what were the long-term consequences of the encounter?

The appearance of a foreign, unbeatable army in their midst must have had a profound effect on the Apalachee psyche. The inhabitants of Anhaica were able to acquire some items of a foreign technology that the Spaniards had lost, discarded, or had stolen from them. But these were not many and probably of negligible impact. No, the most insidious aftereffect of the encounter is usually assumed to be disease. As I, myself, once wrote elsewhere:

> The impact of the Spaniards' passing, particularly in a biological sense, was tremendous. Widespread losses to the aboriginal population due to disease introduced by de Soto's party resulted in demographic shifts and social upheaval. Later, during the seventeenth century, Spanish soldiers and missionaries in Apalachee Province described an aboriginal culture that must have been greatly changed from that encountered by the de Soto expedition (Ewen 1990:89).

Perspectives from *Historical Archaeology:*

But where is the evidence for these devastating epidemics? To date there have been no discoveries of plague cemeteries in Apalachee Province, although documentary sources state that a plague swept San Luis in 1703 (Hann 1988:167). Settlement patterns do not appear to have been radically affected by the European presence until the British dispersed the population in 1704. In fact, an archaeological survey surrounding the Governor Martin site indicates that the first mission established in the area, San Luis de Xinyaca, was probably at the original village of Anhaica, hardly what one would expect of a plague-devastated town.

This is not to say that European-introduced disease was not a factor in the cultural transformation of native societies in the Southeast or even in Apalachee Province, only that it may be one of several factors, some having little to do with European contact. As can be shown in Apalachee Province, some changes were already underway prior to contact. Some social changes were engendered by the political response to the presence of the Europeans. Rather than using disease as a *deus ex machina* for explaining these changes, other alternatives should be explored. In short, the disease hypothesis needs to be tested, not accepted as a given.

Recently some scholars have begun to consider alternative explanations for demographic shifts other than the disease scenario. Northeastern Arkansas, a thriving center of Mississippian culture when de Soto passed through in 1541 was a sparsely populated wilderness when Marquette and Joliet visited the area in 1673. The disappearance of these populous villages is commonly attributed to European diseases (Ramenofsky 1987; Morse and Morse 1990). However, research involving dendrochronological data suggests that due to deteriorating environmental conditions the population may have moved out rather than died out. This study claims that

> abandonment of northeast Arkansas and the depopulation of east–central Arkansas cannot be associated with any single factor. The evidence strongly suggests that the de Soto entrada did not bring epidemics with it. The major depopulation of this area occurred afterward and may have been initiated by a significant environmental disaster, the drought between 1549 and 1577, and later accelerated by further intrusions of Europeans and their diseases (Burnett and Murray 1993: 236).

Again, disease is not discounted as a later, contributing factor. Rather, it is removed from its monocausal role.

One of the most compelling pieces of evidence concerning European-introduced plagues in the southeastern United States involves a passage from the Gentleman of Elvas's narrative of the de Soto expedition. As the expedition approached the town of Cofitachequi, they noticed that "about the town within the compass of a league and a half a league were large inhabited towns, choked with vegetation, which looked as though no people had inhabited them for some time. The Indians said that two years ago there had been a plague in that land and they had moved to other towns" (Elvas 1993:83). This account is reiterated by Garcilaso de la Vega (1993: 285–307), citing Alonso de Carmona, a member of the expedition who witnessed the vacant villages as well as houses full of corpses of plague victims. Yet, there are disturbing contradictions that beg at least a reconsideration of these 16th-century interpretations.

Chester DePratter (1994:216–218), in a reexamination of the historical and archaeological data, finds it curious that the main town of Cofitechequi was spared the ravages of the plague while surrounding towns were decimated. He suggests instead that the "recently abandoned" villages were long abandoned mound centers and that the structures containing plague victims may have been charnel houses for the nobility like those illustrated by John White in 1580 North Carolina. Historical documents pertaining to the contact period, like archaeological data, are subject to variable interpretation. This can be due to the vagueness of the passage, an erroneous translation, or even a misconception on the part of the original author.

The impact of European diseases upon the New World, although considerable, was probably highly variable. Some populations may have been virtually wiped out, while others were left unscathed. Before assigning an a priori consequence of contact to a native polity, it is best to take a holistic approach as opposed to invoking monocausal explanations. In his investigation of the contact-period Southeast,

Smith (1987:147) intended to stimulate more research into the processes of the decline of the New World chiefdoms brought about by the European conquest. He called for the collection of more data, particularly skeletal-demographic, using a regional approach. This emphasis has since occurred at the Governor Martin site and other sites in the Southeast. In addition to collecting new data, it is important that archaeologists reconsider the data already available. The importance of these reinterpretations, to paraphrase DePratter (1994:217), is if there were no epidemics, how would that difference affect the interpretation of the later history of these indigenous peoples?

ACKNOWLEDGMENTS

The research at the Governor Martin site was funded primarily by the National Endowment for the Humanities, the State of Florida, and numerous donations by private individuals and organizations. The excavations were administered by the Florida Department of State, Bureau of Archaeological Research, with the assistance of the Institute for Early Contact Period Studies, University of Florida. Although many people assisted with the administration and execution of this research, I am especially grateful to state archaeologist Jim Miller, University of Florida professors Jerald Milanich and Michael Gannon, and archaeologist B. Calvin Jones. I am also grateful to Linda Wolfe and East Carolina University for granting me the time and resources to pursue my research. Special thanks to Bonnie McEwan and Dale Hutchison for their helpful comments on an earlier draft of this manuscript. The comments and advice of dozens of individuals have affected this work, both directly and indirectly. However, I assume responsibility for any errors and interpretations contained herein.

REFERENCES

ARNOLD, J. BARTO III, DAVID R. WATSON, AND DONALD KEITH
   1995   The Padre Island Crossbows. *Historical Archaeology* 29(2):4–19.

BROSE, DAVID S.
   1984   Mississippian Period Cultures in Northwestern Florida. In *Perspectives on Gulf Coast Prehistory*, edited by Dave D. Davis, pp. 165–197. University Presses of Florida, Gainesville.

BURNETT, BARBARA, AND KATHERINE MURRAY
   1993   Death, Drought, and de Soto: The Bioarchaeology of Depopulation. In *The Expedition of Hernando de Soto West of the Mississippi, 1541–1543*, edited by Gloria Young and Michael P. Hoffman, pp. 227–236. University of Arkansas Press, Fayetteville.

CABEZA DE VACA, ALVAR NUÑEZ
   1988   The Florida Section of the Alvar Nuñez Cabeza de Vaca Accounts of the 1528 Trek from South Florida to the Apalachee Led by Pánfilo de Narváez, translated by John Hann. Manuscript on file, Florida Bureau of Archaeological Research, Tallahassee.

CROSBY, ALFRED W.
   1994   *Germs, Seeds, and Animals: Studies in Ecological History*. M. E. Sharpe, Armonk, New York.

DE LA VEGA, GARCILASO
   1993   La Florida, edited by D. Bost, translated by C. Shelby. In *The De Soto Chronicles*, Vol. 2, edited by Lawrence Clayton, Vernon J. Knight, and Edward Moore, pp. 1–560. University of Alabama Press, Tuscaloosa.

DEPRATTER, CHESTER B.
   1994   The Chiefdom of Cofitachequi. In *The Forgotten Centuries*, edited by Charles Hudson and Carmen Chavez Tesser, pp. 197–226. University of Georgia Press, Athens.

DOBYNS, HENRY F.
   1983   *Their Number Become Thinned*. University of Tennessee Press, Knoxville.

ELVAS, GENTLEMAN FROM
   1993   The Account of the Gentleman from Elvas, translated by J. Robertson and J. Hann. In *The De Soto Chronicles*, Vol. 1, edited by Lawrence Clayton, Vernon J. Knight, and Edward Moore, pp. 19–220. University of Alabama Press, Tuscaloosa.

EWEN, CHARLES R.
   1989   The Search for Hernando de Soto's First Winter Camp: Excavations at the Martin Site. Manuscript on file, Florida Bureau of Archaeological Research, Tallahassee.
   1990   Soldier of Fortune: Hernando de Soto in the Territory of the Apalachee, 1539–1540. In *Columbian Consequences*, Vol. 2, edited by David H. Thomas, pp. 83–92. Smithsonian Institution Press, Washington, D.C.

HANN, JOHN H.
   1988   *Apalachee: The Land between the Rivers*. University Presses of Florida, Gainesville.
   1990   Summary Guide to the Spanish Florida Missions and Visitas with Churches in the Sixteenth and Seventeenth Centuries. *The Americas* 46(4):417–513.
   1994   The Apalachee of the Historic Era. In *The Forgotten Centuries*, edited by Charles Hudson and Carmen Chavez Tesser, pp. 327–354. University of Georgia Press, Athens.

MARRINAN, ROCHELLE, AND STEVEN BRYNE
1986   Apalachee-Mission Archaeological Survey Final Report, Vol 1. Manuscript on file, Department of Anthropology, Florida State University, Tallahassee.

MCEWAN, BONNIE G.
1991   San Luis de Talimali: The Archaeology of Spanish–Indian Relations at a Florida Mission. *Historical Archaeology* 25(3):36–60.

MCEWAN, BONNIE G. (EDITOR)
1993   *The Spanish Missions of La Florida*. University Press of Florida, Gainesville.

MILANICH, JERALD T.
1994   *Archaeology of Precolumbian Florida*. University Press of Florida, Gainesville.
1995   *Florida Indians and the Invasion from Europe*. University Press of Florida, Gainesville.

MILANICH, JERALD T., AND CHARLES H. FAIRBANKS
1980   *Florida Archaeology*. Academic Press, New York.

MILNER, GEORGE
1980   Epidemic Disease in the Postcontact Southeast: A Reappraisal. *Midcontinental Journal of Archaeology* 5:39–56.

MORSE, DAN, AND PHYLLIS MORSE
1990   The Spanish Exploration of Arkansas. In *Columbian Consequences*, Vol. 2, edited by David H. Thomas, pp. 197–210. Smithsonian Institution Press, Washington D.C.

PERCY, GEORGE W., AND DAVID BROSE
1974   Weeden Island Ecology, Subsistence, and Village Life in Northwest Florida. Paper presented at the 39th Annual Meeting of the Society for American Archaeology, Washington, D.C.

RAMENOFSKY, ANN F.
1987   *Vectors of Death: The Archaeology of European Contact*. University of New Mexico Press, Albuquerque.

RANGEL, RODRIGO
1993   Account of the Northern Conquest and Discovery of Hernando de Soto, translated by J. Worth. In *The De Soto Chronicles*, Vol. 1, edited by Lawrence Clayton, Vernon J. Knight, and Edward Moore, pp. 247–306. University of Alabama Press, Tuscaloosa.

SALE, KIRKPATRICK
1990   *The Conquest of Paradise*. Alfred A. Knopf, New York.

SCARRY, JOHN F.
1984   Fort Walton Development: Mississippian Chiefdoms in the Lower Southeast. Unpublished Ph.D. dissertation, Department of Anthropology, Case Western Reserve University, Cleveland, Ohio.

1990   The Rise, Transformation, and Fall of the Apalachee. In *Lamar Archaeology*, edited by M. Williams and G. Shapiro, pp. 175–186. University of Alabama Press, Tuscaloosa.
1994a   The Late Prehistoric Southeast. In *The Forgotten Centuries*, edited by Charles Hudson and Carmen Chavez Tesser, pp. 17–35. University of Georgia Press, Athens.
1994b   The Apalachee Chiefdom: A Mississippian Society on the Fringe of the Mississippian World. In *The Forgotten Centuries*, edited by Charles Hudson and Carmen Chavez Tesser, pp. 156–178. University of Georgia Press, Athens.

SMITH, MARION F., AND JOHN F. SCARRY
1987   Apalachee Settlement Distribution: The View from the Master Site File, 1987. Paper presented at the Annual Meeting of the Southeastern Archaeological Conference, Charleston, South Carolina.

SMITH, MARVIN T.
1987   *Aboriginal Culture Change in the Interior Southeast*. University Presses of Florida, Gainesville.
1994   Aboriginal Depopulation in the Postcontact Southeast. In *The Forgotten Centuries*, edited by Charles Hudson and Carmen Chavez Tesser, pp. 257–275. University of Georgia Press, Athens.

SOUTH, STANLEY, RUSSELL K. SKOWRONEK, AND RICHARD E. JOHNSON
1988   Spanish Artifacts from Santa Elena. *Anthropological Studies* 7. South Carolina Institute of Archaeology and Anthropology, Columbia.

SWANTON, JOHN R.
1985   *Final Report of the United States De Soto Expedition Commission*. Reprint of 1959 edition. Smithsonian Institution Press, Washington D.C.

TESAR, LOUIS
1980   *The Leon County Bicentennial Survey Report: An Archaeological Survey of Selected Portions of Leon County*. Florida Bureau of Historic Sites and Properties, Tallahassee.

TRIGGER, BRUCE
1989   *A History of Archaeological Thought*. Cambridge University Press, Cambridge.

VIERRA, BRADLEY
1989   A Sixteenth-Century Spanish Campsite in the Tiguex Province. *Laboratory of Anthropology Notes* 475. Museum of New Mexico, Santa Fe.

CHARLES R. EWEN
DEPARTMENT OF ANTHROPOLOGY
EAST CAROLINA UNIVERSITY
GREENVILLE, NORTH CAROLINA 27858

CHARLES PEARSON

Evidence of Early Spanish Contact on the Georgia Coast

ABSTRACT

Excavations at the Taylor Mound, a late Savannah phase burial mound on St. Simons Island, Georgia, resulted in the discovery of several intrusive burials containing material of European origin. These artifacts produce specific 16th Century dates and represent what are among the earliest historic remains recovered from coastal Georgia.

The Taylor Mound

The Taylor Mound (9GN 55) is located on northeastern St. Simons Island, Georgia, on a tract of land known as Lawrence Plantation (Figure 1). The site is situated on sloping ground at the head of a shallow fresh water slough which drains into the salt marsh about 150 m to the southeast. The areas to the north, west, and south of the mound have been under cultivation for a considerable period of time and are presently in pasture. The mound itself

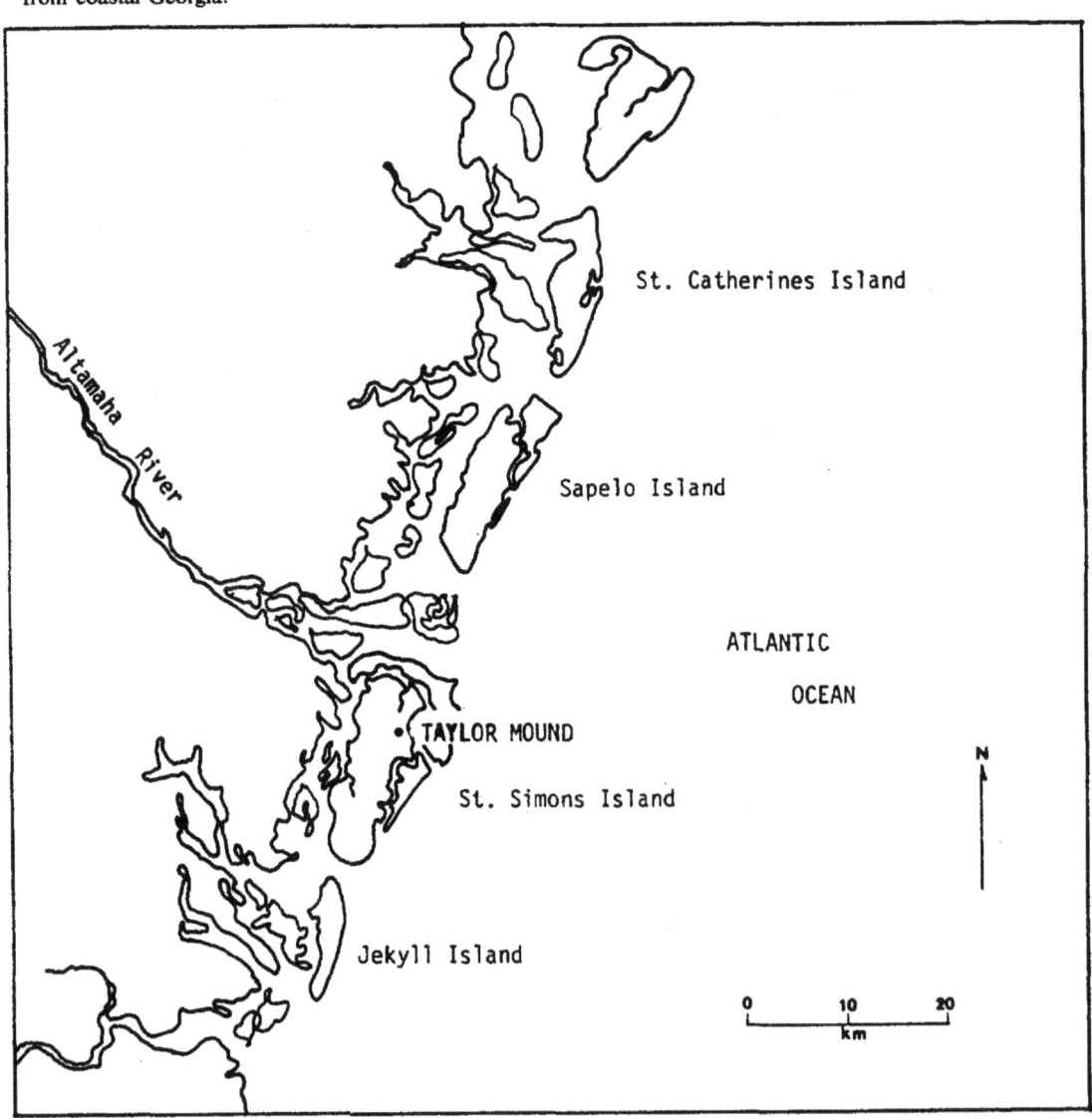

FIGURE 1. Coastal region of Georgia and location of Taylor Mound.

lies in a grove of live oaks (*Quercus virginiana*) and has apparently never been plowed.

Surface indications of prehistoric occupation in the fields around the mound include scattered shell midden deposits and aboriginal ceramics. On the bank of Lawrence Creek, about 900 m northeast of the mound, is an area of extensive shell middens 150 m wide, 500 m long, and up to 1 m in depth. Excavation into this shell deposit to obtain material for road construction has produced ceramics representing every coastal archaeological phase from the late Archaic St. Simons phase (ca. 2000 B.C.) to the late prehistoric Irene phase (ca. A.D. 1500).

The Taylor Mound is a low circular mound 18 m in diameter (Figure 2). Since the mound lies on sloping ground, the maximum height from the northeast ground surface is 45 cm while the height measured from the southeast is 85 cm. Just south of the mound is a shallow depression which may be a barrow pit.

During the summer of 1971 partial excavation of the mound was undertaken to determine its relationship with other burial mounds in the area (Cook and Pearson 1972). Excavations into the mound indicated that it consisted of a central shell core covered and flanked by yellow sand (Figure 2). The shell core was square in shape measuring 7 m on a side and 0.6 m thick. This central shell core was composed primarily of oyster shell (*Crassostrea virginica*) with smaller amounts of clam (*Mercenaria mercenaria*), whelk (*Busycon* sp.), and Atlantic ribbed mussel (*Modiolus demissus*). Although sand sur-

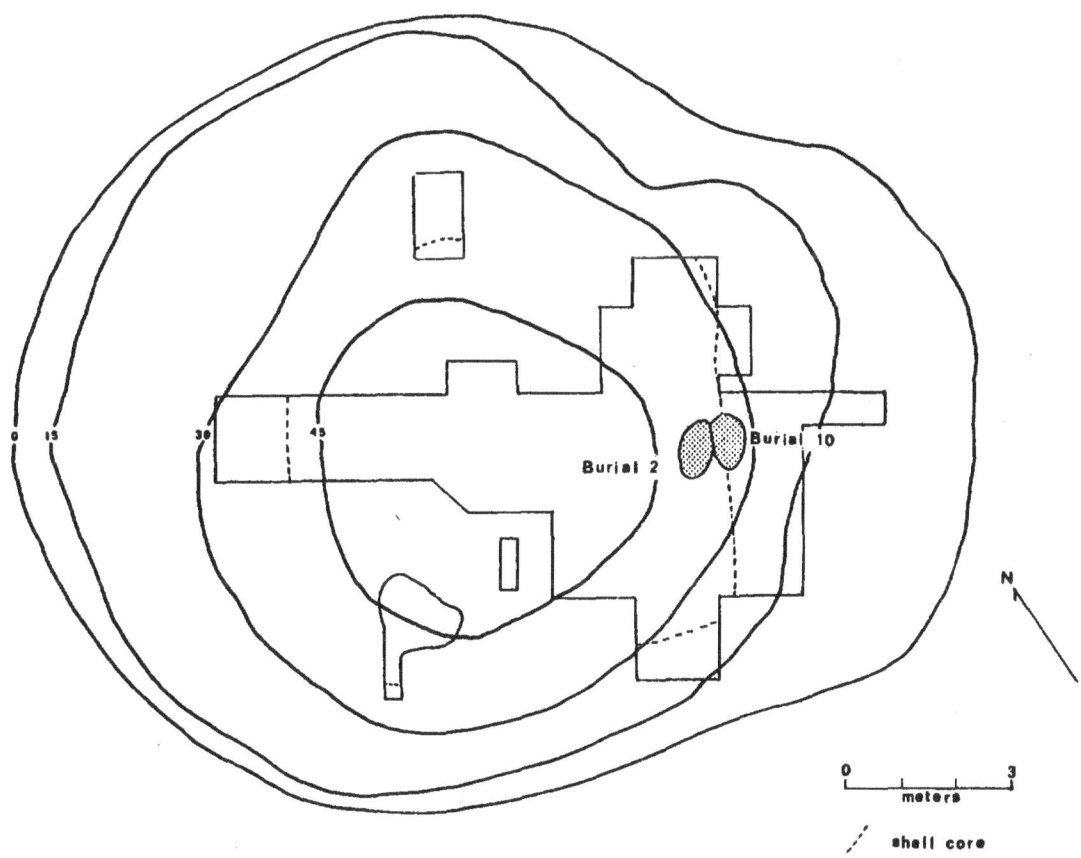

FIGURE 2. Taylor Mound, showing area excavated.

rounded all of the shell core, it was most extensive on the eastern side. Much of this eastern flanking sand may represent a later addition.

Approximately 30% of the mound was excavated and 13 burials were recovered. All of the burials were intrusive into the flanking sand on the eastern side of the mound or into the shell core. Types of inhumation represented were flexed, cremation, and bundle burials. Prehistoric artifacts were associated with eight of the burials and included shell beads, shell earpins, and stone celts. Historic artifacts were found in association with three burials, all located on the eastern margin of the shell core.

Few cultural remains were recovered in the mound fill. A total of 74 sherds were found, with the majority of these coming from the shell core. The types of pottery recovered are identified as: Savannah Check Stamped, Savannah Complicated Stamped, and Savannah Burnished Plain (Caldwell and Waring 1939).

The ceramics, the mode of burial, the artifactual content of the prehistoric burials and the type of mound construction are most similar to those described for the Savannah II phase (A.D. 1150–A.D. 1300) of the north and central Georgia coast (Caldwell and McCann 1941; Caldwell and Waring 1939; Cook 1971; Cook and Pearson 1972; Larson 1957). The major portion of the mound appears to have been constructed and used during the Savannah II phase. The three burials containing historic artifacts are assumed to have been placed into the mound after its initial Savannah II phase period of use.

The Historic Burials

Burial 2 (the burial numbers employed herein are those given in the report on the Taylor Mound excavations, Cook and Pearson 1972) was placed in a shallow pit scooped out of the shell core near its eastern margin (Figure 2). The burial was encountered 2 cm below the mound surface and the grave pit had a depth of 12 cm. The skeleton, that of an adult male, lay

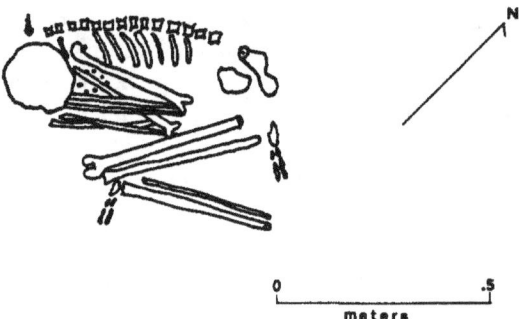

FIGURE 3. Burial 2.

on its right side in a flexed position (Figure 3). The body was oriented with the head to the south and the face to the east. The left half of the skull had been destroyed, probably by surface disturbances due to the shallowness of the burial. The left femur was missing and the lower left leg was inverted with the foot in the knee position. Some metatarsals and metacarpals were missing. This disarrangement and the missing bones could be the result of partial decomposition before burial resulting from charnal house activity which is known to have been practiced in the Southeast during the early historic period (Swanton 1922). Burial 2 had been made directly over an earlier prehistoric burial (Burial 3) and had partially intruded into the burial disturbing the burial pit but not the skeleton itself.

A small shell ear pin made from the columella of a species of Busycon lay under the skull (Figure 5). Ten perforated pearls, 22 discoidal shell beads measuring 3–10 mm in diameter, and 6 tubular glass beads were found scattered under the skull and in front of the chest.

Three of the glass beads have been identified as Nueva Cadiz Plain and three as Nueva Cadiz Twisted (Charles Fairbanks 1967). All of these beads are constructed of three layers of glass. The inner layer is translucent black, the middle layer is opaque white, and the outer layer is translucent turquoise. On several of the beads the outer layer has a cracked surface possibly due to weathering. The beads are square in cross section and

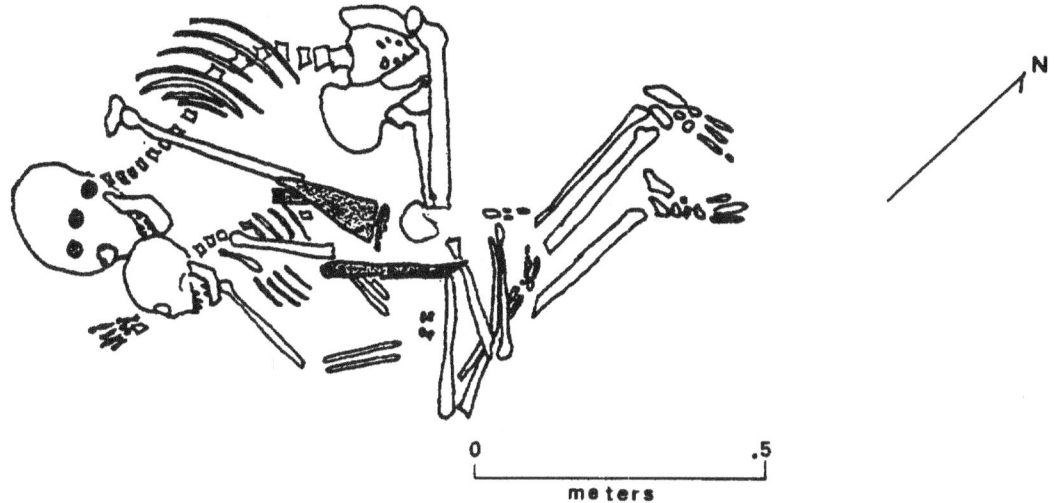

FIGURE 4. Burial 10.

have irregularly ground or worn ends. The end grinding is at oblique angles to expose the alternating layers of glass. Bead widths range from 5 to 6 mm and lengths from 13 to 21 mm. Nueva Cadiz Plain and Nueva Cadiz Twisted are usually quite long beads, ranging in length from 40 to 60 mm (Fairbanks 1967). It is likely that the Taylor Mound beads represent 2 or 3 complete beads that have been broken.

Beads of this type have been found in several Circum-Carribean sites and can be accurately dated to the 16th century, with only rare occurrences after 1600 (Fairbanks 1967). Although most commonly found in Central and South America, a few specimens of Nueva Cadiz beads have been reported from the Southeastern United States. A single specimen is known from Ogiltree Island, Alabama (Morrell 1964). Fairbanks, in his discussion of Nueva Cadiz beads, mentions four sites in Florida where these beads have been found (Fairbanks 1967). These are the Grantham Mound, the Ortona Mound, one of the mounds on Murphy Island excavated by C. B. Moore (Moore 1896b), and a mound at Lake Butler. All of these mounds have been assigned 16th century dates.

The two other burials with associated historic artifacts were found in a single circular burial pit dug into the eastern margin of the shell core (Figure 2). Both individuals in this pit were designated with a single number, Burial 10, in the original report (Cook and Pearson 1972).

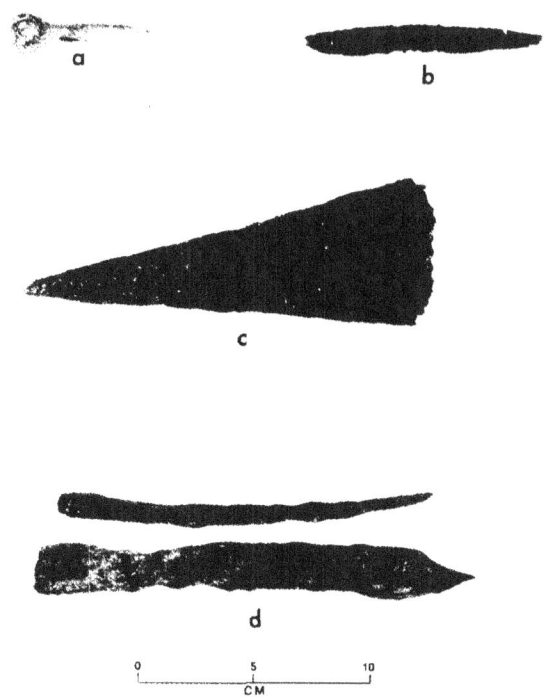

FIGURE 5. a, shell ear pin, Burial 2; b, iron awl, Burial 10; c, iron celt, Burial 10; d, iron spikes.

This burial pit had been dug partially into the shell core and partially into the flanking sand. The base of the pit was 50 cm below the mound surface, a depth corresponding to the base of the shell core. The pit outline could be easily discerned in the shell but was difficult to follow in the sand. The digging of this pit had disturbed a portion of an earlier burial, Burial 3. The left humerus and the left femur of Burial 3 had been broken and the distal end of the broken femur was found in the fill of the historic burial pit.

The two individuals buried in the pit were an adult male and a child aged 10 to 12 years (Figure 4). Skeletal preservation was excellent for both individuals. The adult male lay in a flexed position on its right side with the head oriented to the south and the face to the east. The child had been placed immediately in front of and slightly above the adult. The child was flexed and oriented exactly as the adult. An organic stain and a few organic (wood?) fragments were found along the western side of the pit, on the pelvis and feet of the adult, and in the sand immediately below the child. This stain appears to be the remains of a burial covering or lining of some sort. The pit fill consisted of yellow sand containing a scattering of oyster shell.

A large variety of historic artifacts were found in association with both the adult and the child. Nine copper coins were located on and around the skull of the adult. Five of these coins were *in situ* and lay flat against the skull, spaced across the forehead and down the temporal bones. Twenty-four small olivella shell (*Olivella* sp.) beads were scattered between the coins. The position of the coins and the shell beads suggests that they formed part of a headband or a cap of some sort.

A hole had been punched through the center of each coin and several nodes had been punched around the margin of each to produce a simple circular beaded repoussé design (Figure 6). All of the coins have a slightly concavo-convex shape, probably due to the hammering and punching of the central hole.

The coins are all extremely worn and only four retain any traces of lettering. Only one coin has enough detail to allow tentative identification. This coin appears to be an early issue copper maravedies of the reign of Charles I of Spain (Charles V of the Holy Roman Empire) and his mother Johanna (Nesmith 1944; 1955: 6,127). Robert Nesmith (1955: 40) states that copper coins of this type are often referred to as the "Santo Domingo type," though he argues that no mint was ever estab-

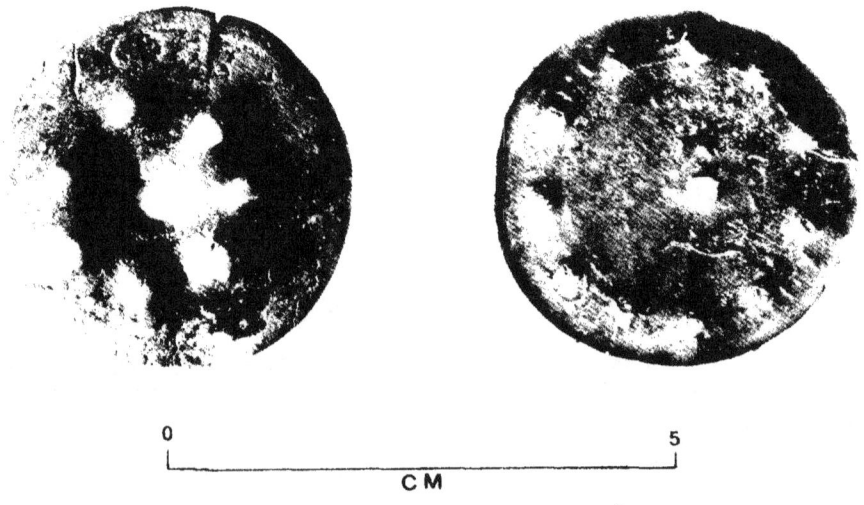

0   5
└───┘
                    C M

FIGURE 6. Copper maravedes, Burial 10.

lished in Santo Domingo in the 16th century and that all of these coins were minted in Spain at either Burgos or Seville. Copper coins of the Santo Domingo type were made "by the million at the Sevilla mint, or at any mint that the conassionaire Lope Perez de Maldonado saw fit to employ. Records show that as early as 1506, the Sevilla mint was sending silver and copper currency to Santo Domingo (Nesmith 1944: 98)."

The Santo Domingo type maravedies was first authorized by Ferdinand in 1505 and again by Johanna in 1531. Apparently the design of these coins was changed in 1517 at the ascension to the throne by Charles and Johanna to include the inscription CAROLVS ET IHOANA REGES or variations thereon. A crowned Y (Ysabel) appears on the reverse and on the obverse the crowned pillars of Hercules (see Nesmith 1955: 127 for an illustration of this type of coin). The Santo Domingo type is known only in the four maravedies (cuarto) demonination. It appears that in 1531 or 1532 the design of the copper coinage was again changed to include a castle or a variation of the Spanish coat of arms on the reverse instead of the crowned Y.

The Taylor Mound coin is most similar to those coins minted between 1517 and the early 1530s (Figure 6). One side of the coin appears to contain the crowned pillars of Hercules with possibly an S to its right and portions of the inscription CAROLVS ET IHOANA REGES. The S suggests that the coin was minted in Seville. This coin is approximately the same size (28 mm diameter) as the Santo Domingo type shown by Nesmith (1955: 127) and weighs 5.9 gm.

Copper coins were also minted in the New World in the 16th century. The Mexico City mint produced copper coins between 1542 and 1552 (Nesmith 1955: 41–42). Copper coins were officially outlawed in 1556 because of Indian resistance to their use and not until 1814 were copper coins again minted in Mexico (Olds 1976: 116). The copper coins produced at the Mexico City mint differed from the earlier Santo Domingo type minted in

Spain in many respects; however, the design of the lettering was similar for some issues. A slight possibility exists that the Taylor Mound coin was minted in Mexico. If so, based on the letter style, it is an "Early series" coin. These were produced only in 1542, and the only denomination known is the four maravedies (Nesmith 1955: 41; Olds 1976).

Some authorities argue that a mint operated in Santo Domingo between 1532 and 1557 (Lazarus 1965) or between 1542 and 1552 (Burzio 1958). Coins supposedly minted in Santo Domingo are notorious for their poor quality, misspelled words, upside down letters, etc. The S on the Taylor Mound coin is on the right side of the pillars of Hercules while the S on the supposedly Santo Domingo coins is on the left (Olds 1976: 108). The lack of consistency in the Santo Domingo coins suggests that the S on the Taylor Mound coin may simply have been stamped on the wrong side of the coin. If, by chance, this coin was minted in Santo Domingo, it would probably have been struck in 1542 or earlier since the letter punches were changed in 1542 (Nesmith 1955).

The wear and treatment of this Taylor Mound coin prevents positive identification. The evidence which is available, however, strongly suggests that the coin is of four maravedies denomination, minted in Spain (Seville) probably between 1517 and the early 1530s. There is only a slight possibility that the coin was minted in Santo Domingo between 1532 and 1542 or in Mexico City in 1542.

Five of the other coins recovered are approximately the same size and weight as the tentatively identified coin, averaging 28 mm in diameter and 5.8 gm in weight. It is suggested that these six coins are of a similar date and of the same denomination. The remaining three coins are slightly larger, averaging 8.2 gm in weight and 32 mm in diameter. None of these larger coins contain any discernible lettering; however, their size corresponds to the four maravedies produced in Mexico City between 1542 and 1552 as shown in Nesmith (1955). These coins likely date to this period although it is impossible to determine whether they were minted in Spain or the New World.

In the area around the adult's wrists were found 677 small discoidal shell beads and 4 perforated pearls. The beads average 2 mm in length and 4 mm in diameter. These beads lay directly under the child's neck and head and may have been associated with the child rather than with the adult.

On the chest and midsection of the child lay a tapered celt-form iron axe, a rectangular celt-form iron axe, an iron awl or punch, and an iron knife (Figure 4). All of these items were heavily encrusted with rust.

The tapered celt-form axe measures 18.7 cm in length and has a cutting blade 6.9 cm wide (Figure 5). Portions of wood were preserved at the poll end of the axe and probably represent the remains of a handle. Under the poll end of the axe lay a rectangular piece of iron which also appears to be a celt-like axe. This axe measures 13.7 cm in length, 3.1 cm wide, and 1.6 cm thick. One end has been ground or hammered to a cutting edge.

The iron awl lay at the blade end of the tapered axe. The awl consists of a tapered piece of iron inserted into a wooden handle, fragments of which have been preserved (Figure 5). The awl is badly corroded but appears to have been round in cross section. The awl tip has been broken off.

An iron sheath knife lay in the stomach area of the child. The blade has a "hunting knife" shape with an angular point. Portions of a two piece wooden handle with three brass rivets are preserved. Total length of the knife is 23 cm; blade length is 15 cm.

A small amount of fibrous material was preserved under the celts and may represent the remains of a bag or container for the iron objects.

Two iron spikes were found in the sand fill of the mound 1 m southeast of Burial pit 10. These spikes were not associated with any burials. The larger spike is 19 cm long, circular in cross-section with a diameter of 2.4 cm (Figure 5). The other spike is square in cross-section and measures 17.8 cm in length and is 1.2 cm wide at the head (Figure 5). Both of these spikes appear to be hand forged.

Discussion

The rather precise dating for the coins and the Nueva Cadiz beads indicates the possibility of a pre-1600 date for the burials. Although the iron items from the Taylor Mound do not lend themselves to such precise dating, there is considerable historical and archaeological evidence indicating that similar items were in use in the Southeast during the middle and late 1500s (Smith 1956).

During the early 1500s the majority of European goods in Florida and Georgia were likely salvaged from shipwrecks rather than obtained through direct contact with Europeans (Smith 1956: 10–11). The Spanish were sailing along the Georgia and east Florida coast by the 1520s and shipwrecks frequently occurred. Although St. Simons Island lies north of the area where most wrecks are known to have occurred, European items could have been obtained indirectly from shipwrecks by way of aboriginal exchange networks. The most common types of tools traded or in use during this early contact period appear to have been the celt-form axe, hafted axes, hunting knives, iron chisels, iron spikes, and iron fish spears (Smith 1956).

One of the earliest accounts indicating the presence of iron tools among Indians of the Southeast occurred in A.D. 1540 at the town of Cofitachique, presumably on the Savannah River in the vicinity of Augusta, Georgia, where DeSoto's party found buried "two wood axes of Castillian make, a rosary of jet beads, and some false pearls, such as are taken from this country to traffic with the Indians, all of which were supposed they got in exchange made with those who followed the Licentiate Ayllon (Smith 1968: 240)." Ayllon, in A.D. 1526, had unsuccessfully attempted to establish a colony on the South Carolina coast. His expedition would have been one of the earliest sources of European items in the Georgia coastal area.

A review of archaeological sites in the Southeast which have produced early contact material reveals a number of items similar to those from the Taylor Mound. Two celt-form iron axes are reported from the Goodnow Mound in south-central Florida along with a large number of other historic artifacts (Griffin and Smith 1948). These included three "copper discs" which had central perforations. These discs resemble the copper coins from the Taylor Mound, but the authors do not indicate if the discs may, in fact, be worn or hammered copper coins. An iron knife was also found in this mound. The Goodnow Mound has been assigned a date of mid to late 1500s.

At the Phillip Mound in Polk County, Florida, Carl Benson (1967) reports finding an iron knife, a celt-form iron axe and several copper beads apparently made from hammered copper coins. Benson estimates the date of the mound as 1600 to 1700, though Karklins (1974) suggests a 16th century date.

From the Picnic Mound near Tampa Bay, Ripley Bullen (1952: 69) reports an "iron celtiform axe" and glass beads. These items were found in historic burials which were intrusive into an earlier Weeden Island period mound.

At the Spruce Creek Mound, three copper and silver "discs" with central perforations and a slight concavo-convex shape were found in association with several crania (Smith 1956: 20). The Spruce Creek material has been assigned a 16th century date (Smith 1956: 20).

Clarence B. Moore's extensive work on Florida burial mounds yielded a number of historic items resembling those from the Taylor Mound. Several iron tools were recovered from a mound on Murphy Island in northeast Florida. These consisted of an iron knife, 2 narrow bladed iron axes, 2 "chisels," a "triangular chisel or tomahawk," and several other unidentified iron objects (Moore 1896b: 513–514). Moore (1896a: 534) found an iron spike and an iron hunting knife at a mound near Fort Mason, Florida. The knife blade was 22.5 cm in length. In the Thursby Mound, on the St. Johns River, he found an iron axe and several iron celts (Moore 1894a, 1894b). At the Raulerson Mound, in the same area, were found an iron knife blade, 2 iron chisels, 3 iron fish spears, a chisel of metal with a curved edge, an iron spike, and fragments of iron tools (Moore 1894: 94). Two iron axes and 2 "cold chisels" were found at the Dunn's Creek Mound on the St. Johns River (Moore 1894a: 11).

Hale G. Smith (1956) has reviewed the historical material from the mounds excavated by Moore and assigns them to the 16th or early 17th centuries. It is interesting to note that in all of these mounds the burials containing historic artifacts appear to be intrusive into earlier prehistoric mounds.

At the King site on the Coosa River in north Georgia, several iron objects have been found in association with burials in what appears to be an early historic context (Smith 1975). These items are: 3 celt-form iron axes, 2 iron knife blades, an iron spike, an iron rod with a flattened "chisel-like" end, and an iron "wedge" (Smith 1975: 63–64). No other items of European manufacture were found at the site, and it appears that the burials have a date prior to the massive influx of trade items in the mid 1600s. A possible pre-1600 date is suggested for the material (Smith 1975).

Iron celts have been found at several other sites in the upper Coosa River area of north Georgia. These celts occur alone or with iron spikes or kinves and are assumed to date in the mid to late 16th century (Marvin Smith 1976, pers. comm.).

The only other site on the Georgia coast which has produced items similar to those from the Taylor Mound is the Kent Mound located on the south end of St. Simons Island (Cook n.d.). Historic items recovered consist of one chevron bead and an iron knife similar to the one from the Taylor Mound. This knife was found in association with several protohistoric San Marcos ware vessels and probably dates circa 1600.

Summary

Archaeological and documentary evidence indicates that all of the historic items from the

Taylor Mound had been in use or occurred as trade items during the period from A.D. 1500 to A.D. 1600. Even though these particular items were also in use after A.D. 1600, several lines of evidence would seem to indicate a pre-1600 date. It is suggested that the number and similarity of the coins and beads weighs against heirlooming and that the material was likely buried soon after acquisition, before the items could be lost, broken, or dispersed. The variety of glass beads commonly found at 17th century sites is lacking at the Taylor Mound, suggesting that the burials were made before such items came into the area.

The lack of European ceramics at the mound is also seen as indicative of a date prior to the period of actual Spanish occupation. Spanish ceramics (majolica and olive jars), which occur frequently along the Georgia coast (Caldwell 1971; Goggin 1968; Larson 1958), were not found at the mound. These ceramics were unlikely to have been important as early trade items and probably did not appear in any quantity on the Georgia coast until after substantial Spanish mission establishment in the late 1500s and early 1600s (Lanning 1935). Also indicative of an early contact date is the lack of San Marcos or Altahama ceramics which were the aboriginal wares in use on the Georgia coast during the period of Spanish occupation (ca. A.D. 1600–1700).

Conclusions

The historic items from the Taylor Mound have been shown to have been of a type available to and in use among Southeastern Indians during the very earliest period of European contact. The lack of certain other types of trade items which appeared during the 17th century is interpreted as being indicative of a pre-1600 date for the Taylor Mound burials. The data would indicate that a date of around A.D. 1540–1560 is reasonable for the burials. This date represents what appears to be the earliest evidence of the use of European items yet recorded for the Georgia cost.

ACKNOWLEDGEMENTS

I wish to thank Fred C. Cook, who served as my co-worker at the Taylor Mound, and Marvin T. Smith who has provided valuable comments and suggestions concerning this paper. Special thanks are extended to my grandmother, Mrs. Reginald A. Taylor Sr. of St. Simons Island, for her permission to excavate on her property and for her interest in the project.

REFERENCES

BENSON, CARL A.
1967 The Phillip Mound: a historic site. *Florida Anthropologist* 20(3 and 4): 118–32.

BULLEN, RIPLEY
1952 Eleven archaeological sites in Hillsborough County, Florida. *Report of Investigations 8.* Florida Geological Survey, Tallahasee.

BURZIO, H. F.
1958 *Diccionaria de la Moneda Hispanaoamericano.* Fondo Historico y Bibliografico Jose Toribio Medina. Peuser, Buenos Aies.

CALDWELL, JOSEPH R.
1971 Excavations on St. Catherines Island, Georgia. Department of Anthropology. University of Georgia, Athens. Mimeograph.

CALDWELL, JOSEPH R. AND CATHERINE MCCANN
1941 *Irene Mound Site, Chatham County, Georgia.* University of Georgia Press, Athens.

CALDWELL, JOSEPH R. AND ANTONIO WARING
1939 Some Chatham County pottery types. *Southeastern Archaeological Conference Newsletter 5 and 6.*

COOK, FRED C.
1971 Excavation at the Lewis Creek Site, McIntosh County, Georgia. Department of Anthropology, University of Georgia, Athens. Mimeograph.
n.d. Excavations at the Kent Mound, St. Simons Island, Georgia. Manuscript in preparation.

COOK, FRED C. AND CHARLES PEARSON
1972 Three late Savannah burial mounds in Glynn County, Georgia. Department of Anthropology, University of Georgia, Athens. Mimeograph.

FAIRBANKS, CHARLES
1967 Early Spanish colonial beads. *The Conference on Historic Site Archaeology Papers* 2(1): 3–21.

GOGGIN, JOHN M.
1968 Spanish majolica in the New World. *Yale University Publications in Anthropology 72.* Yale University, New Haven.

GRIFFIN, JOHN W. AND H. G. SMITH
1948 The Goodnow Mound Highlands County, Flor-

ida *Contributions to the Archaeology of Florida 1*. Florida Park Service, Tallahassee.

KARKLINS, KARLIS
1974 Seventeenth Century Dutch Beads. *Historical Archaeology* 8: 64–82.

LANNING, JOHN TATE
1935 *The Spanish missions of Georgia*. University of North Carolina Press. Chapel Hill.

LARSON, LEWIS
1957 The Norman Mound, McIntosh County, Georgia. *Florida Anthropologist* 10(1): 37–53.
1958 Cultural relationships between the northern St. Johns area and the Georgia coast. *Florida Anthropologist* 11: 11–22.

LAZARUS, W. C.
1965 Coin dating in the Fort Walton Period. *Florida Anthropologist* 18: 221–24.

MOORE, CLARENCE B.
1894a Certain sand mounds of the St. Johns River, Florida. *Journal of the Academy of Natural Sciences* 10(1).
1894b Certain sand mounds of the St. Johns River, Florida. *Journal of the Academy of Natural Sciences* 10(2).
1896a Certain river mounds of Duval County, Florida. *Journal of the Academy of Natural Sciences* 10(6).
1896b Two sand mounds on Murphy Island, Florida. *Journal of the Academy of Natural Sciences* 10(7).

MORRELL, L. ROSS
1964 Two historic sites in the Coosa River. *Florida Anthropologist* 17(2): 75–76.

NESMITH, ROBERT
1944 The coinage of Charles and Johanna for Spanish Colonial America 1536–1556. *The Coin Collectors Journal* 11: 95–98.
1955 The coinage of the first mint of the Americas at Mexico City 1536–1572. The American Numismatic Society, *Numismatic Notes and Monographs 131*.

OLDS, DORRIS L.
1976 Texas legacy from the Gulf: a report on sixteenth century shipwreck materials recovered from the Texas tidelands. Texas Memorial Museum, *Miscellaneous Papers 5*.

SMITH, BUCKINGHAM (TRANSLATOR)
1968 *Narratives of DeSoto in the conquest of Florida*. Palmetto Books, Gainesville.

SMITH, HALE G.
1956 The European and the Indian. *Florida Anthropological Society Publication 1*.

SMITH, MARVIN
1975 European materials from the King site. *Southeastern Archaeological Conference Bulletin*. 18: 63–66.

SWANTON, JOHN R.
1922 Early history of the Creek Indians and their neighbours. *Bureau of American Ethnology Bulletin 73*. Washington, D.C.

CHARLES PEARSON
DEPARTMENT OF ANTHROPOLOGY
UNIVERSITY OF GEORGIA
ATHENS, GEORGIA 30601

BONNIE G. McEWAN

San Luis de Talimali: The Archaeology of Spanish-Indian Relations at a Florida Mission

ABSTRACT

Despite a historical propensity to characterize the Spanish treatment of Native Americans as brutal, archaeological and historic data gathered since 1984 from religious, civic, and domestic contexts at San Luis have revealed otherwise. It appears that both Spanish and Apalachee residents maintained a strong sense of their respective cultural identities and material life, and demonstrated a marked degree of accommodation.

Introduction

Almost immediately after Columbus's voyages of discovery, Spaniards were forced to make controversial decisions about the treatment of native inhabitants living within their New World dominion. One contingent, supported primarily by colonists who wanted jurisdiction over the native labor force and by Aristotelian theologians such as Juan Ginés de Sepúlveda, believed that Indians could be justifiably enslaved because of their inherent inferiority (Elliott 1963:71–72). However, there was also a benevolent faction, championed by Bartolomé de las Casas, who argued that Indians were legal subjects of the Spanish Crown and, as such, should enjoy the same rights as Spaniards (Hanke 1951). The repercussions of Las Casas's efforts were two-fold. On the one hand, his detailed accounts of atrocities against New World natives fueled anti-Spanish propaganda among northern Protestants and led to *La Leyenda Negra,* or Black Legend, of Spanish cruelty and inhumanity (Gibson 1971; Maltby 1971; Steele 1975). On the other hand, Las Casas's eloquent arguments to the Spanish government prevailed, and in 1542 the *encomienda* system which had permitted the virtual enslavement of Indians was legally abolished

through the New Laws (Haring 1963 [1947]:50–52; Simpson 1966:123–144; McAlister 1984:162–163). The "Laws and Ordinances Newly Made by His Majesty for the Government of the Indies and the Good Treatment and Preservation of the Indians" outlawed the enslavement of Indians and demanded freedom for those who had been taken illegally (McAlister 1984:162).

The mission system was a direct outgrowth of this legislative reform and provided an alternative means of subjugation. It was the most important institution in *La Florida* for effecting large-scale religious conversion among the Southeastern Indians, exploiting natural and cultural resources, and establishing a Spanish presence in the hinterlands as a deterrent against foreign incursions (Bolton 1917; Geiger 1937). As such, missions are an invaluable source of information about the nascent stages of Hispanic-American culture since they represent the frontier of cultural exchange between relatively isolated Spaniards and local native populations.

The History of San Luis

The mission period, or San Luis Phase (Scarry 1987), can be assigned finite dates based on the beginning (1633) and end (1704) of the Franciscan mission system in Apalachee Province. However, some level of cultural disintegration must have been occurring among the Apalachee long before 1633 since they began requesting friars as early as 1607, an occurrence that Scarry (1988) has suggested is evidence of upheaval among the native ruling elite.

It is believed that during the Mississippian Lake Jackson period (A.D. 1100–1500), and presumably through the protohistoric and mission periods, the Apalachee paramount was both the head-priest and cacique (Scarry 1989a:4). There is little doubt that chiefly power began to wane with the first European contacts. By the beginning of the 17th century, technologically superior European powers were rapidly encroaching and, more importantly, disease was taking a devastating toll on the native population. Although bioanthropological data are

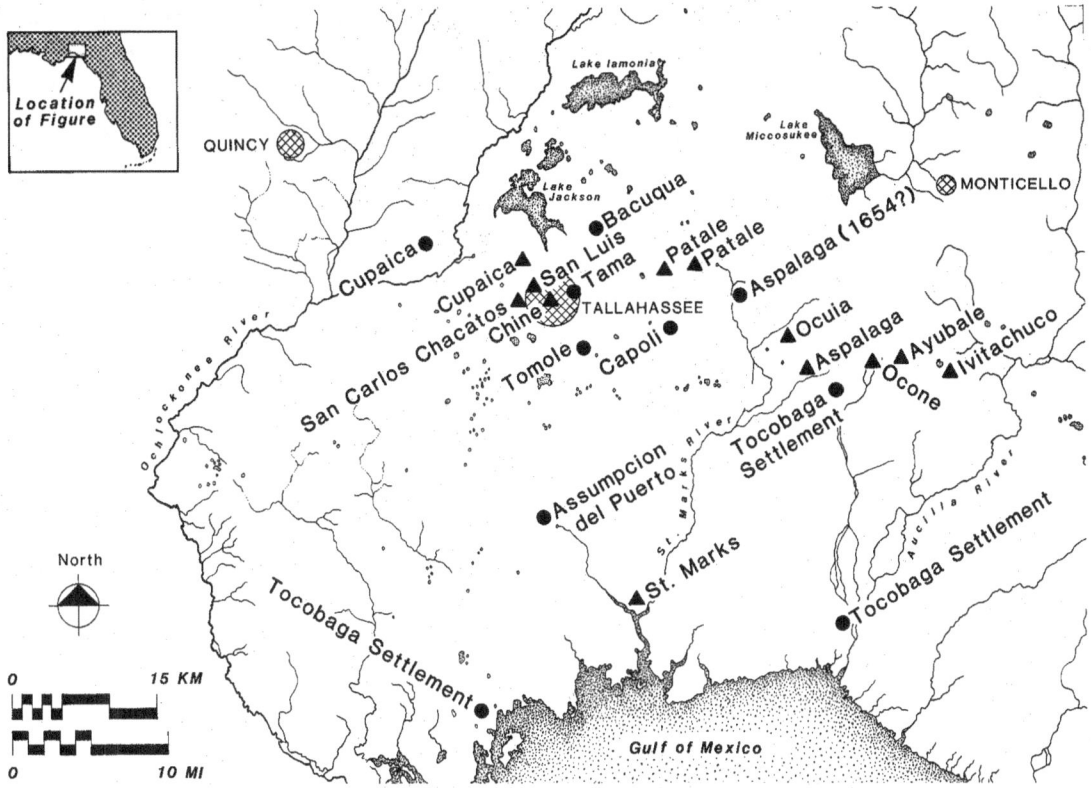

FIGURE 1. Location of San Luis in relation to other Apalachee missions.

not available, an evaluation of census records indicates that the population of Apalachee plummeted from about 30,000 in 1608 to around 10,520 by 1675 (Hann 1988:164–166). Once traditional religious and political practices were no longer effective against external pressures, the paramount cacique/priest and lesser chiefs lost power over their people which, in turn, resulted in a loss of cultural vitality and continuity. This is supported by comments made by friars prior to the establishment of missions in Apalachee who remarked that "the [Apalachee] chiefs would like to gain control over their Indians with the aid of Spanish authorities" (Hann 1989:13).

The first Franciscans intent on establishing a permanent presence arrived in Apalachee Province in October 1633, followed shortly thereafter by the first soldiers in 1638. San Luis de Jinayca was probably one of the first missions established, given the importance of the village and the fact that it was home to one of the most powerful Apalachee chiefs. It was probably the same corporate entity as Anhayca (also referred to as Iniahico) where Hernando de Soto spent the winter of 1539–1540 (Ewen 1990).

In 1656 the chief of San Luis de Jinayca moved his village to a new location where he offered to build housing for the Spanish garrison. It is this village, established in 1656, that is recognized today as San Luis (Figure 1). From 1675 onward, San Luis was never again referred to in the documents as San Luis de Jinayca, but rather as San Luis de Talimali.

As the religious, military, and administrative

capital of the Spanish mission chain in western Florida from 1656–1704, San Luis was the most populous mission in Apalachee Province. Over 1,400 individuals fell under the *doctrina's* (mission with a resident priest) jurisdiction, including several nearby satellite villages (Hann 1988:174). Despite a short-lived revolt in 1647, there were between 8,000 and 9,000 Indian converts in Apalachee by 1672 and the region was described as being "thoroughly Christianized" (Hann 1989: 24).

By the turn of the 18th century, the Spanish missions were under constant threat of attack from the north by Carolinian raiders and their Creek allies. In 1703 the provincial mission of San Joseph de Ocuya was destroyed, followed by Ayubale, Patale, Aspalaga, and Escambe in 1704 (Hann 1987:143). Although San Luis itself was never under siege, the failure to plant crops in the spring of 1704 suggests that the residents saw the end in sight (Hann 1988:212). San Luis was burned and abandoned by the Spaniards and their native allies on July 31, 1704, two days prior to the arrival of an attack force.

Demography of San Luis

Most of the residents of San Luis were Christianized Indians. A 1689 census indicates that 300 families lived at San Luis (Hann 1988:Table 7.2), although the composition and division of labor within many of the households may have been somewhat unstable under missionization. In order to fill *repartimiento* quotas (requisite tribute in the form of labor and goods), men were regularly sent from Apalachee Province to serve as laborers in St. Augustine. Alternatively, some chose to work for wages at ranches, often far from their own villages. As a result, there were regular complaints from native wives whose lives were disrupted by the absence of their husbands for extended periods of time (Hann 1988:146–147).

The number of Spanish soldiers stationed at San Luis varied over time from 12 to 45 (Hann 1988:200). There may also have been a number of *reformados*, or inactive military men, who received partial pay and remained on call (Hann 1989, pers. comm.). When not engaged in military activities, these men are presumed to have worked at various occupations such as farming and crafts to supplement their incomes.

In 1675 Governor Hita Salazar made a number of land grants that encouraged civilians to populate the fertile areas in the vicinity of San Luis. These *rancherias* were successful in a number of agricultural endeavors including wheat farming and cattle ranching. Although records provide no exact count of the number of ranches, the tax rolls for 1698 and 1699 indicate that there were nine Spanish cattle ranches in Apalachee at that time (Arnade 1965:9).

There was usually only one friar living at San Luis at any given time, but there were exceptions. In 1690 three friars were in residence at the mission (Quiroga y Losada 1690). While the Church always had a relatively small numerical representation, members of its clergy wielded a disproportionate amount of power and influence over their congregations. As institutions supported by the State and the Church, missions had a function that extended well beyond religious conversion. Adherence to Christian principles in the broadest sense demanded that the native population become "civilized." Friars actively worked with their charges by encouraging rigid moral standards, developing new social and political allegiances, and revising systems of obligation and tribute (Milanich and Sturtevant 1972; Deagan 1985:302–303; Marrinan 1985).

Because church and military records have provided the primary sources of documentary data pertaining to San Luis, knowledge is heavily biased toward men and their activities. However, ample evidence exists from elsewhere in the New World to suggest that the disproportionate number of Spanish men led to Spanish-Indian miscegenation in Apalachee Province (Deagan 1973, 1974, 1985; McEwan 1990). This would have been particularly true for the San Luis mission since, in addition to friars, its Hispanic population included a military garrison and civilians. As the Apalachee adopted Catholic mores, intermarriage between Spanish men and native women was probably a regular occurrence. John Hann (1988:170) has suggested that the repeated proscriptions against concubinage made by official visitors must have been precipitated by the frequency of such consensual relationships.

In addition to the large number of native women who probably were assimilated into the community, researchers know that a small number of Spanish women resided at San Luis. The most notorious of these was Juana Caterina de Florencia, who was married to Deputy Governor Jacinto Roque Pérez. Juana Catarina

> gave two slaps in the face to a cacique of [the Indians of] San Luis, because he had not brought her fish on Friday, and obliged the village to furnish six Indian women for the grinding every day without payment for their work; and although this was [contrary to] an order of the inspector, it is not observed, and not withstanding, [they] continue doing it. As also that she be given an Indian to go and come every day with a pitcher of milk for the house of the said deputy (Boyd et al. 1951:25).

In fact, several generations of the Florencia women lived in Apalachee, as indicated by a document describing Juana Caterina and her mother accompanying Captain Jacinto Roque to free imprisoned Indian leaders (Matheo Chuba 1687:folio 31).

The Physical Appearance of San Luis

The mission complex is known to have consisted of a fort with a blockhouse, fortified country house, church, *convento,* cemetery, central plaza, council house, public granary, and village. One year after San Luis's abandonment in 1704, a Spanish reconnaissance party was led by Admiral Antonio de Landeche into Apalachee Province. Upon returning to Havana, he noted in a letter of 11 August 1705 to the Viceroy of New Spain:

> We arrived at that locality on the 10th [1705], notwithstanding the mired roads due to the rains which never ceased, as it was the time for them. No trails of people or of cattle were found in the entire region; the blockhouse was demolished in such a manner that there remained only some portions of the stockade, which, from the scarcity of rosin, the flames that consumed the rest did not reach. It was, according to our reconnaissance, a very regular fortress, capable of any defense, as Your Excellency will recognize from the plan

> which I ordered made, and which I will transmit to Your Excellency as soon as I arrive at the port of San Juan de Ulúa (translated in Boyd et al. 1951:82–85).

In addition to the map made by Landeche's party (Figure 2), there is another, slightly different, set of dimensions of the San Luis fort palisade and blockhouse described in an 1823 letter by J. L. Williams (Boyd et al. 1951:Plate II caption). One other description of the fort is available from a 1700 document (Zúñiga y Zerda 1700).

Archaeology at San Luis

The first professional archaeological activity at San Luis was a surface collection made in 1940 by Gordon Willey (1949:285–286), although Willey made reference to the fact that amateur historian Mark Boyd had already conducted archaeological tests at the site. Systematic excavations were first conducted at the San Luis fort in 1948 by John Griffin (Griffin 1951:139–160) and later by Hale Smith in 1950. In 1956 and 1957 Charles Fairbanks continued excavations in the fort area and, most important for the current program, drafted a map tying Griffin's and Smith's excavations into his grid. Their investigations successfully determined the location of the fort's blockhouse and moat, although many architectural details remain unknown. These early excavations recovered large amounts of Spanish materials including bottles, ceramics, hardware, and weaponry. To date, the fort at San Luis remains the most exclusively Spanish structure in regard to its construction and associated artifacts.

Recent Archaeology at San Luis

In 1983, about 50 acres (20 hectares) of the former mission of San Luis de Talimali were purchased by the State of Florida. The San Luis Archaeological and Historic Site has since maintained a full-time staff of archaeologists, a project historian, and education specialists. Other than the Landeche map, historic descriptions, and previous

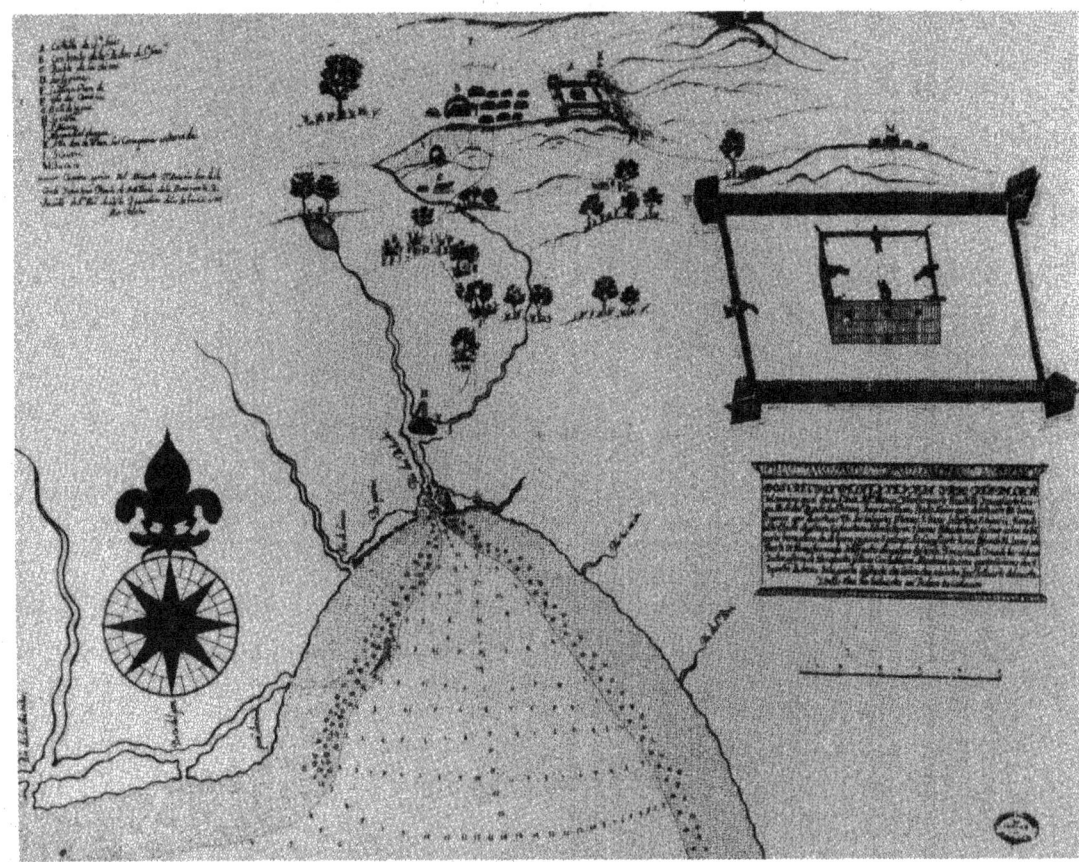

FIGURE 2. 1705 Landeche map depicting the San Luis fort and associated features.

excavations that focused exclusively on the fort, virtually nothing was known about the 17th-century community of San Luis.

Under the direction of Gary Shapiro (1987), broad-scale remote sensing, topographic, and subsurface surveys were conducted at the site in 1984. The resistivity survey at San Luis proved disappointing, presumably because the subsurface remains at the site are not as conducive to electronic detection as those from other Spanish colonial contexts (Shapiro 1984; Thomas 1987:126–134). During the topographic mapping of the site, elevations were taken at 2-m intervals, which provided the detailed data necessary to generate high resolution maps of the site. An auger survey was also conducted during the same year by digging 8-in. diameter holes every 10 m to sterile soil (usually

30–80 cm below surface) and screening the materials through 1/4-in. mesh. The results of the auger survey were plotted on distribution maps. Taken together, the topographic maps and auger survey results provided important clues about the overall layout of the mission complex and the possible locations of various structures.

The most revealing result of the topographic survey was the recognition of subtle, yet distinct, features that had not been identified with the naked eye (Figure 3). A large circular area encompassed by a low earthen embankment was recognized as a likely location for the central plaza. This interpretation was supported by the auger survey which yielded very small amounts of the materials from the area, suggesting that it was swept regularly (Figure 4).

Perspectives from *Historical Archaeology:*

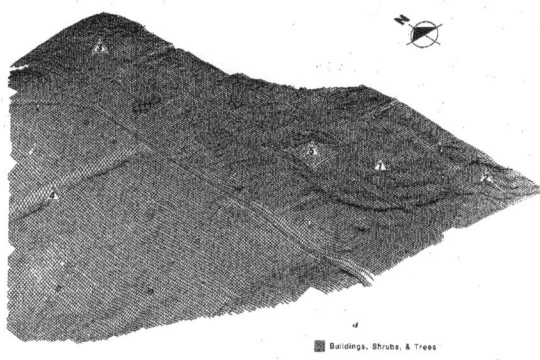

Buildings, Shrubs, & Trees

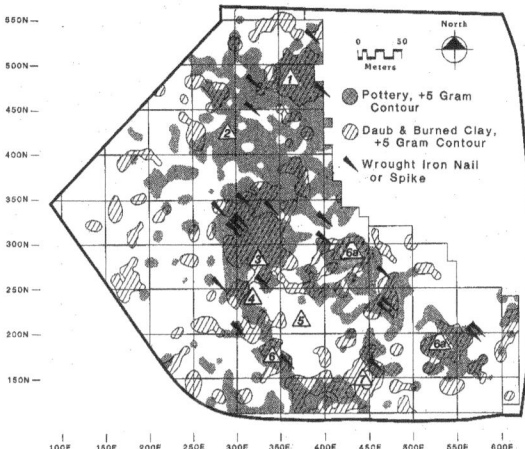

North

0   50
Meters

⬤ Pottery, +5 Gram
   Contour

◖ Daub & Burned Clay,
   +5 Gram Contour

◥ Wrought Iron Nail
   or Spike

FIGURE 4. Distribution of materials at San Luis based on the auger survey results: *1*, fort; *2*, activity area; *3*, church; *4*, cemetery; *5*, central plaza; *6*, Apalachee village; *6a*, Spanish village; *7*, council house.

San Luis de Talimali

FIGURE 5. Speculative view of San Luis de Talimali from the north.

At the southeast corner of the central plaza was a slightly elevated, circular platform. The auger survey turned up some burned clay, but few artifacts. Although several alternative hypotheses were offered for this feature—including an outlying fortification, the house site of a high-ranking Spaniard or Indian, or the location of the church—Shapiro speculated from the beginning that it was the location of the Apalachee council house (Shapiro 1985:5).

Determination of the probable location of the church complex was based on the recovery of large amounts of daub and European hardware from a structure on the north-northwest end of the plaza. Similarly, Spanish and Apalachee residential areas were identified based on structural remains in conjunction with large amounts of aboriginal materials (west of the plaza) and Spanish artifacts (east of the plaza), respectively.

The final phase of the broad-scale survey consisted of excavating eight judgmentally placed 2-×-2-m test pits in areas of high pottery or burned clay concentrations. These data lent further support to the hypothesized town plan. Based on these preliminary findings, a speculative rendering of San Luis was prepared by Ed Jonas of the Museum of Florida History (Figure 5). Six subsequent years of excavation have served to confirm this original interpretation.

The Apalachee Council House

The suspected Apalachee council house was the focus of the first two years of intensive excavation at the site in 1985–1986 (Shapiro and McEwan

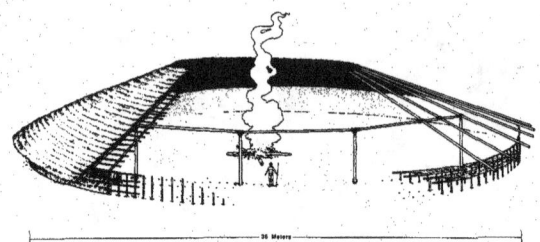

FIGURE 7. Conjectural view of the Apalachee council house.

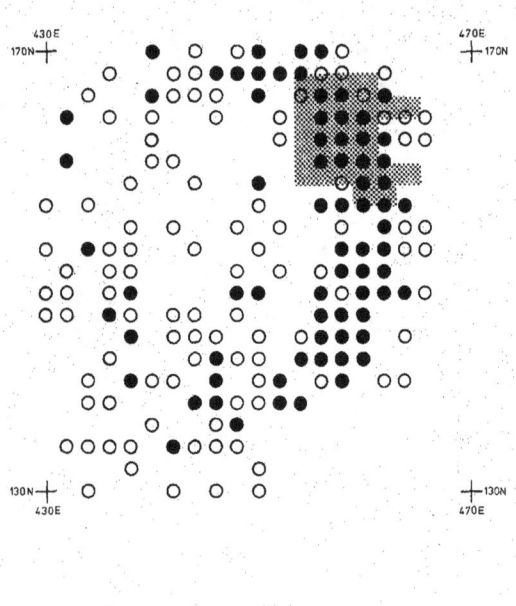

● Encountered solid burned clay
○ Encountered traces of burned clay

FIGURE 6. Distribution of burned clay across the council house floor at San Luis, as revealed by 1-in. diameter soil cores taken at 2-m intervals.

1991). Southeastern council houses traditionally were used for dances, ceremonies, civic meetings, and as a lodge for guests (Shapiro and Hann 1990). Investigations revealed that the council house at San Luis was constructed on a natural platform that was leveled off on the eastern side by a clay cap ranging from 10–20 cm in thickness (Figure 6). Several borrow pits adjacent to the eastern edge of the council house were a likely source for this clay. The structure was approximately 36 m in diameter, and is one of the largest historic-period aboriginal structures known in the southeastern United States. The council house at San Luis is also about three times larger than the other two council houses that have been excavated in Apalachee Province. Council houses from both the Borrow Pit site and from the mission of San Pedro y San Pable de Patale were about 12 m in diameter (B.

Calvin Jones 1989, pers. comm.; Rochelle Marrinan 1989, pers. comm.).

C. Margaret Scarry (1991) has determined that the council house was constructed from pine posts. Areas between the posts were probably filled with thatch. All of the burned clay recovered from the structure had smooth surfaces, suggesting that it was from the prepared clay cap rather than from wattle-and-daub construction (clay plastered over a wooden framework).

The council house had a large roof opening, or skylight, that could have been as wide as 15 m or about 40 percent of the building's diameter (Figure 7). The interior walls were lined with two concentric rows of benches, under which smudge pits, fueled with corn cobs, were used to keep insects away. Located within the interior row of benches were eight massive central support posts, each about 50 cm in diameter (Figure 8). At the center of the council house was a large, shallow hearth which provided light and heat. Hearth fires were fueled primarily by pine wood and hickory nutshells. The recovery of *Ilex vomitoria* seeds from the hearth (probably brought in inadvertently with leaves), suggests that the council house continued to serve as a ritual center where ceremonial black drink was prepared. A variety of other plant remains, including two European cultigens—wheat and watermelon, were probably refuse from meals served to visitors, indicating that the council house also maintained its function as a lodge for guests staying at the mission (C.M. Scarry 1991).

In addition to its markedly aboriginal style of architecture, the council house yielded artifacts that are almost exclusively Indian in origin (Table 1). Most of these were concentrated in the hearth

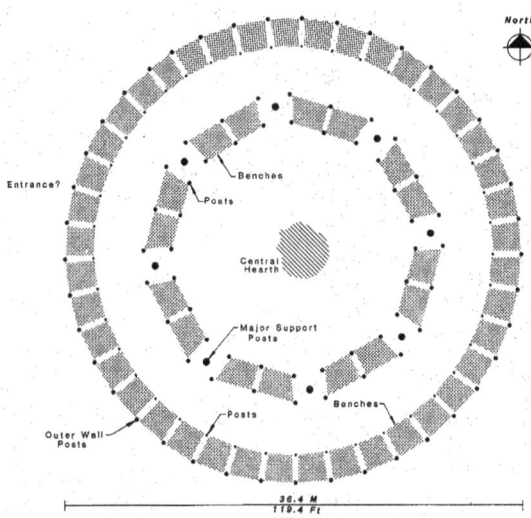

FIGURE 8. Interior features of the council house.

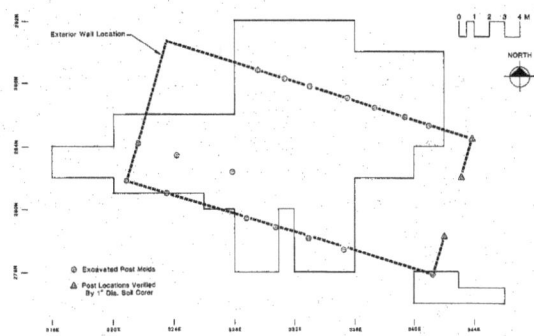

FIGURE 9. Plan view of the *convento* at San Luis.

and under benches where trash was apparently swept at regular intervals. The floor itself was kept very clean. A few sherds of Spanish pottery, lead shot, glass beads and pendants (Smith 1990), gunflints, and a religious medallion were among the small number of European artifacts found. However, large amounts of Indian pottery and thousands of chert flakes were recovered. The substantial number of whole and partial projectile points, along with a vast quantity of debitage, suggest that arrowhead production was among the activities performed inside the council house.

The excavation of the Apalachee council house at San Luis has revealed a strong degree of resistance to Spanish influence with regard to architecture, technology, and at least some ritual activities, including the consumption of black drink. Although the Apalachee were thoroughly familiar with European construction techniques, the San Luis council house provides evidence of equally sophisticated native architecture. With the exception of a few European cultigens, traditional plant remains dominated the botanical assemblage. Furthermore, Apalachee material life from this public context exhibited little change as a result of sustained European contact.

Although it is well documented that the friars took exception to some native activities associated with the council house, such as the ball game and certain dances (Hann 1989:23), the very traditional council house at San Luis suggests that the Spaniards exerted little influence over the ways by which the Apalachee organized their ritual and civic activities.

The Church Complex

After the excavation of the Indian council house, three field seasons were spent on the hypothesized church complex at San Luis (Vernon and McEwan 1990). Based primarily on excavations conducted by B. Calvin Jones, a model was developed for Apalachee church complexes (Jones and Shapiro 1990). Most church complexes included a wattle-and-daub church, a *convento* or friary, and a cemetery. Using data from nine Apalachee mission sites, it was concluded that churches were generally rectangular and ranged from 17.8 to 26.0 m in length and from 11 to 12.6 m in width (Jones and Shapiro 1990:504). The suspected church at San Luis was a wattle-and-daub structure measuring approximately 9 by 21 m with a clay floor 5–10 cm thick (Figure 9). The walls of the building were probably quite massive based on the nearly three tons of daub recovered. Many of these daub fragments had smooth sides with successive layers of whitewash (Vernon and McEwan 1990:28), while others retained impressions of planks or split logs rather than unfinished poles, lending evidence that Spanish tools were used in the construction of the building. Posts preserved through carbonization were square in cross section, and the building's timbers were held together with wrought iron nails and spikes.

Based on the spacing of the wall posts, the location of the building's door and facade is thought to have been in the east wall facing onto the plaza. The number of artifacts from the building was fairly sparse (Table 2). Daub and wrought nails were by far the most common materials recovered, although 32 glass beads were also found within the structure (Mitchem 1990).

Two problems remained with the identification of the wattle-and-daub structure as the church. Ethnobotanical analysis of the floor deposits revealed concentrations of hundreds of beans and maize kernels (C. Scarry 1991). If this structure was the church, only sacramental foodstuffs such as wheat would be expected. Also, because San Luis was the capital of Apalachee Province, it was anticipated that all of the public structures would be significantly larger than others in the province. Clearly this was the case with the council house which was three times the size of other council houses. As noted above, the hypothesized church was approximately 9 by 21 m, well within the range of the average Apalachee mission church.

Verification of the church complex required locating and limited testing of the cemetery. The cemetery was located 35 m southwest of the presumed church structure (Vernon and McEwan 1990:25). Although only one excavation unit was opened, about 20 separate superimposed burial pits, oriented approximately 75 degrees west of north, were identified within the unit (Figure 10). Only subadult teeth and skull fragments were recovered, all from individuals under 10 years of age (Larsen 1990). Despite the limited amount of excavation in the cemetery, 845 glass beads (Mitchem 1990), 21 turquoise glass pendants, an amber bead, a quartzite fragment, conch columella beads, and a sheet copper projectile point with the tip of a cane arrow shaft inside were recovered (Figure 11). Only one clearly religious object was found—a copper alloy cross. Due to time limitations, a coring survey of the surrounding area was conducted to determine the extent of the cemetery. The coring results suggested that the cemetery was approximately 25 by 15 m, the long axis of which was oriented 75 degrees west of north (Vernon and McEwan 1990:25).

UNIT 244N 304E

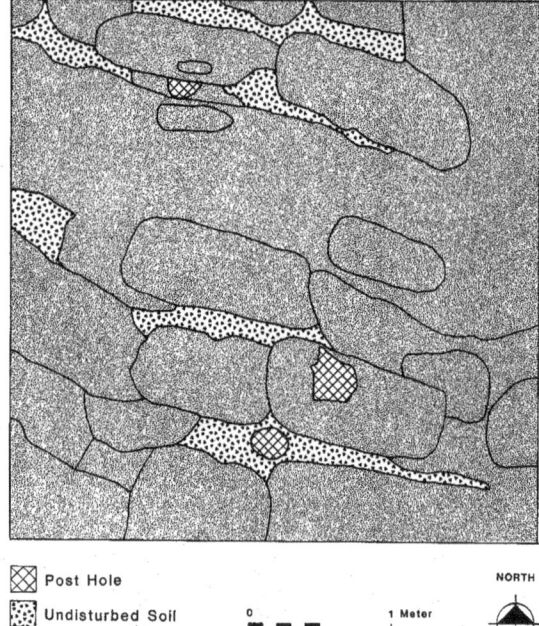

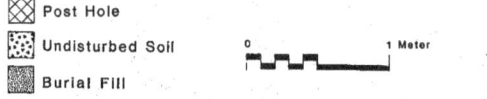

⊠ Post Hole
▦ Undisturbed Soil
▦ Burial Fill

NORTH

0   1 Meter

FIGURE 10. Floor plan of the cemetery excavation at 70 cm below surface.

One possible post was identified during the cemetery excavations which suggested the possibility that the burials were actually interred within a structure. If this were the case, the building containing the burials would most logically have been the church. Placing burials beneath the floors of churches was a common practice in Europe and is known from other missions in Spanish Florida such as Santa Catalina de Guale on St. Catherines Island (Thomas 1988:111) and at San Pedro y San Pablo de Patale in Apalachee Province (Jones et al. 1991).

Taken together, the recovery of large amounts of foodstuffs from floor deposits, the relatively modest size, and the possibility of a structure directly associated with the cemetery suggested that the original interpretation of the wattle-and-daub structure as the mission church was incorrect. However, additional testing was necessary to determine if the burials were actually interred beneath the floor of the church.

Excavations were recently (1990) conducted in

TABLE 1
ARTIFACTS FROM THE COUNCIL HOUSE

Artifact Class	N	%
Aboriginal Ceramics		
Plain Aboriginal	5,476	84.83
Other Aboriginal	2	0.03
UID Aboriginal	256	3.97
Ft. Walton Incised	11	0.17
Lake Jackson Incised	1	0.02
Lake Jackson Incised var. Lake Lafayette	1	0.02
Marsh Island Incised	5	0.08
Marsh Island Incised var. Marsh Island	1	0.02
Ocmulgee Fields Incised	28	0.43
Ocmulgee Fields Incised var. Ocmulgee	11	0.17
Pt. Washington Incised	3	0.05
Pt. Washington Incised var. Pt. Washington	6	0.09
Pt. Washington Incised var. Pedro	2	0.03
UID Incised	111	1.72
Lamar Complicated Stamped	47	0.73
Lamar Complicated Stamped var. Curlee	20	0.31
Lamar Complicated Stamped var. Early	19	0.29
Lamar Complicated Stamped var. Jefferson	25	0.39
Leon Check Stamped	21	0.33
Cross/Simple Stamped	1	0.02
Wakulla Check Stamped	9	0.14
UID Stamped	156	2.42
UID Complicated Stamped	136	2.11
UID Simple Stamped	2	0.03
Alachua Cob Marked	4	0.06
Chattahoochee Brushed	2	0.03
UID Impressed	1	0.02
UID Pinched/Punctated	2	0.03
Mission Red Filmed	96	1.49
Total	6,455	100.03
Imported Ceramics		
UID Coarse Earthenware	2	1.89
UID Glazed Coarse Earthenware	3	2.83
Unglazed Olive Jar	30	28.30
Glazed Olive Jar	7	6.60
Santo Domingo Blue on White	1	0.94
San Luis Blue on White	6	5.66
Fig Springs Polychrome	1	0.94
Aucilla Polychrome	3	2.83
Puebla Polychrome	9	8.49
San Luis Polychrome	1	0.94
Castillo Polychrome	3	2.83
Puebla Blue on White	1	0.94
San Agustín Blue on White	1	0.94
UID Polychrome Majolica	14	13.21
UID White Majolica	6	5.66
UID Blue on White Majolica	7	6.60

(*continued*)

TABLE 1 (Continued)

Artifact Class	N	%
Ming Porcelain	1	0.94
Blue on White Oriental Porcelain	10	9.43
Total	106	99.97
Kitchen		
Case Bottle	5	4.81
UID Bottle Fragment	35	33.65
UID Glass Fragment	62	59.62
UID Glass Lump	2	1.92
Total	104	100.00
Personal		
Glass Pendant	2	1.16
UID Wire-Wound Bead	13	7.51
Faceted Crystal Bead	1	0.58
UID Cane Bead	149	86.13
Small Brass Bell Fragments	5	2.89
Copper Tube Bead	3	1.73
Total	173	100.00
Weaponry		
Chipped Glass Biface	1	1.82
Pellet Shot (<.22 caliber)	15	27.27
Lead Shot (≥.22 caliber)	5	9.09
Prism Gunflint	1	1.82
Local Gunflint	4	7.27
Quartz Biface	1	1.82
Chert Biface	26	47.27
Coral Biface	1	1.82
Kaskaskia Point (copper alloy)	1	1.82
Total	55	100.00
Structural Hardware		
UID Nail	2	3.28
Wrought Nail	8	13.11
Wrought Spike	3	4.92
Iron Staple	2	3.28
UID Nail Fragment	24	39.34
Wrought Nail Fragment	19	31.15
Wrought Spike Fragment	3	4.92
Total	61	100.00
Sewing and Clothing		
Iron Button	1	100.00
Religious Objects		
Copper Alloy Medallion	1	100.00
Activities		
Kaolin Pipestem (5/64)	1	10.00
Kaolin Pipestem (6/64)	3	30.00
Slag	6	90.00
Total	10	100.00

TABLE 1 (Continued)

Artifact Class	N	%
Miscellaneous Lithic Objects		
Chert Core with Cortex	2	0.12
Chert Flake with Cortex	110	6.76
Chert Flake without Cortex	1,417	87.09
Used Chert Flake with Cortex	3	0.18
Used Chert Flake without Cortex	14	0.86
Chert Unifacial Tool	1	0.06
Chert Shatter	27	1.66
Cortex Fragment	7	0.43
Coral Flake with Cortex	14	0.86
Coral Flake without Cortex	12	0.74
Used Coral Flake with Cortex	2	0.12
Used Coral Flake without Cortex	2	0.12
Coral Shatter	12	0.74
Quartz Flake without Cortex	1	0.06
UID Flake without Cortex	2	0.12
Used UID Flake without Cortex	1	0.06
Total	1,627	99.98
Construction Materials, Weight in grams		
UID Brick	1.6 gm	<.01
Daub	2,514.2 gm	1.00
Burned Clay	221,738.4 gm	87.94
Burned Clay, Flat	27,736.0 gm	11.00
Whitewashed Burned Clay, Flat	163.3 gm	0.06
Total	252,153.5 gm	100.00

Note. Table does not include miscellaneous materials (i.e., pebbles, fauna, etc.).

the northwest corner of the cemetery to determine if the burials were, in fact, situated inside a structure. At the edge of the cemetery, a 4- × -4-m unit was opened where the corner of the building would logically be located if a structure were present. Two massive burnt posts were found in the unit. One postmold (PM 12) (Figure 12) was 42 cm in diameter and extended 1.49 m below ground surface, while the other (PM 13) (Figure 13) was approximately 40 cm in diameter and extended 1.48 m below ground surface. Both posts combined contained over 50 wrought iron spikes and nails suggesting that they were major support posts for a large wooden structure. Furthermore, PM 13 contained large amounts of thick plaster with a smoothed surface suggesting that at least some of the structure's walls were plastered.

These recent findings have required a reevaluation of earlier interpretations of the church complex. Contrary to the original idea that the cemetery was adjacent to a modest wattle-and-daub church, it is the current hypothesis that the San Luis cemetery is located beneath the floor of the church. The church was a large wooden structure (at least 15 by 25 m), oriented 75 degrees west of north, with some plastered walls. The altar was presumably at the west end, while the door faced directly onto the central plaza at the east end of the building. Although European churches traditionally faced west with their altars or sanctuaries at the east end, a great deal of variation on this pattern has been documented (Kubler 1940:23).

The modest wattle-and-daub building was probably the *convento* or friary. It was located 35 m

TABLE 2
ARTIFACTS FROM THE *CONVENTO* AT SAN LUIS

Artifact Class	N	%
Aboriginal Ceramics		
Plain Aboriginal	519	85.22
Unidentified Aboriginal	33	5.42
Fort Walton Incised	10	1.64
Lake Jackson Incised	1	0.16
Lake Jackson Incised var. Blountstown	1	0.16
Ocmulgee Fields Incised	2	0.33
Lamar Complicated Stamped	8	1.31
Lamar Complicated Stamped var. Rectilinear	2	0.33
Leon Checked Stamped	6	0.99
Mission Red Filmed	6	0.99
Chattahoochee Brushed	8	1.31
Unidentified Incised	8	1.31
Unidentified Stamped	1	0.16
Unidentified Pinched/Punctated	2	0.33
Marsh Island Incised var. Columbia	2	0.33
Total	609	99.99
Imported Ceramics		
San Luis Blue on White	1	4.76
Puebla Polychrome	1	4.76
Castillo Polychrome	1	4.76
Unidentified Polychrome Majolica	1	4.76
Unidentified White Majolica	2	9.52
Olive Jar, Unglazed	14	66.66
Storage Jar, Glazed	1	4.76
Total	21	99.98
Kitchen		
UID Bottle Fragment	1	100.00
Personal		
UID Tube Bead	1	100.00
Weaponry		
Lead Pellet	3	60.00
Lead Shot	2	40.00
Total	5	100.00
Structural Hardware		
Wrought Nail	13	15.29
Wrought Spike	1	1.18
Wrought Tack	1	1.18
UID Nail Fragment	16	18.82
Wrought Nail Fragment	54	63.53
Total	85	100.00
Miscellaneous Lithic Objects		
Chert Bifacial Tool	4	9.30
Used Chert Flake without Cortex	1	2.33
Chert Flake with Cortex	6	13.95
Chert Flake without Cortex	27	62.79

Perspectives from *Historical Archaeology:*

TABLE 2 (Continued)

Artifact Class	N	%
Chert Shatter	4	9.30
Ground Sandstone	1	2.33
Total	43	100.00
Construction Materials, Weight in grams		
Daub with Impressions	18,939.8 gms	11.35
Burned Clay	140,200.1 gm	84.04
Burned Clay with Flat Surface	7,023.9 gm	4.21
Whitewashed Clay with Flat Surface	654.3 gm	0.39
Total	166,818.1 gm	99.99

Note. Table does not include miscellaneous materials (i.e., pebbles, fauna, etc.)

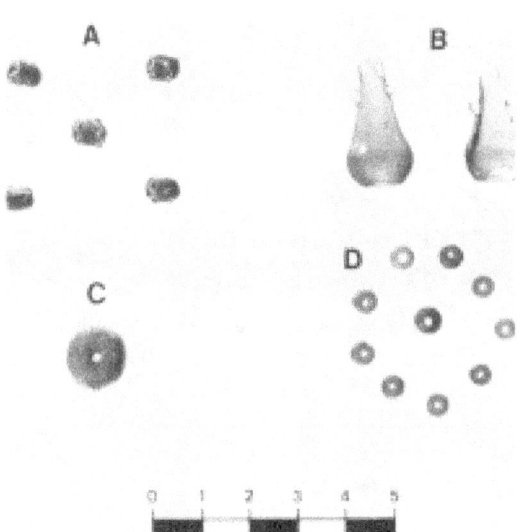

FIGURE 11. Beads and pendants from the cemetery. A. gilded, applique beads. B. Punta Rassa pendants. C. faceted amber bead. D. plain drawn beads.

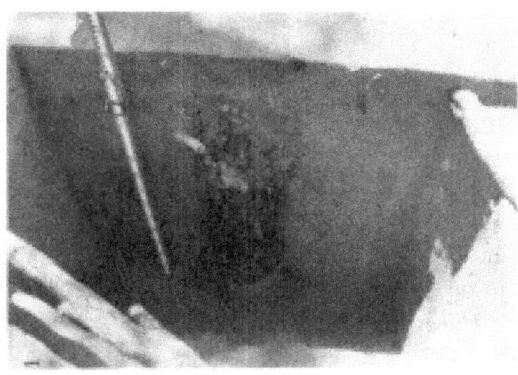

FIGURE 12. Major support post (PM 12) from the church burned in situ.

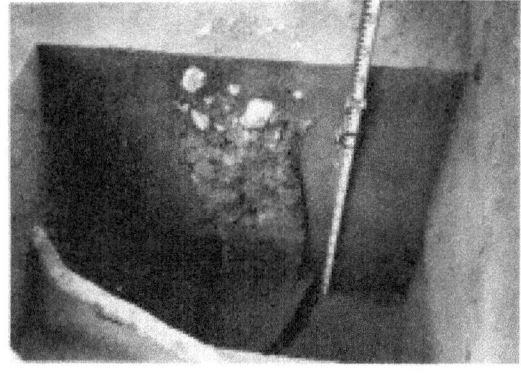

FIGURE 13. Major support post (PM13) from the church filled with wall plaster.

northeast of the church, oriented on approximately the same axis as the church (73 degrees west of north), and contained stored foodstuffs. Although the paucity of artifacts recovered from the *convento* might be explained by the vows of poverty taken by the friars, they did receive the same salary as soldiers and undoubtedly purchased some goods, particularly books such as breviaries and spiritual readings (John Hann 1990, pers. comm.). Book clasps have been identified from other Florida missions such as Santa Catalina de Santa Maria

on Amelia Island and the Franciscan headquarters in St. Augustine, Nuestra Señora de la Concepción (Hoffman 1990:131). The absence of personal objects, as well as other valued possessions, from the San Luis *convento* is most logically explained by the planned abandonment of the site in 1704 when goods were transported to St. Augustine (Hann 1986).

Over 60 percent of the imported ceramics identified from the *convento* consisted of olive jars, typically associated with the shipping and storage of European staples such as olive oil and wine. The most abundant type of material recovered from the *convento* was aboriginal ceramics. It is highly probable that some of these vessels contained tribute, in the form of foodstuffs, that was provided to the resident friar. It is also likely that the friar had native servants who performed household tasks such as cooking.

The Spanish Village

Since 1988, the research program at San Luis has been devoted to Spanish domestic sites in order better to understand the adaptations made by Spaniards living among the Apalachee within a mission setting. Despite an exceptional data base of Spanish domestic site archaeology from the capital of St. Augustine (for example, Deagan 1983), the adaptations made by Spaniards on the "frontier of the frontier" remained uninvestigated.

Although excavations and analysis are still in progress, two building episodes have been identified in the Spanish village, each one exhibiting distinct construction techniques (Figure 14). The earliest structure was identified by wall trenches oriented 30 degrees west of north. These wall trenches held split logs that served as foundations and supported sills. This small building (3.75 by 6 m) was probably a two-celled "common plan" Spanish house (Manucy 1978:49–50) with vertical board walls and a thatch roof (Albert Manucy 1989, pers. comm.), as illustrated in Figure 15. It was similar in size, construction methods, and design to contemporaneous houses in other Spanish colonies such as St. Augustine.

A third wall trench to the south may have been the remnant of a detached kitchen, henhouse, or storage building. Although no wood samples were

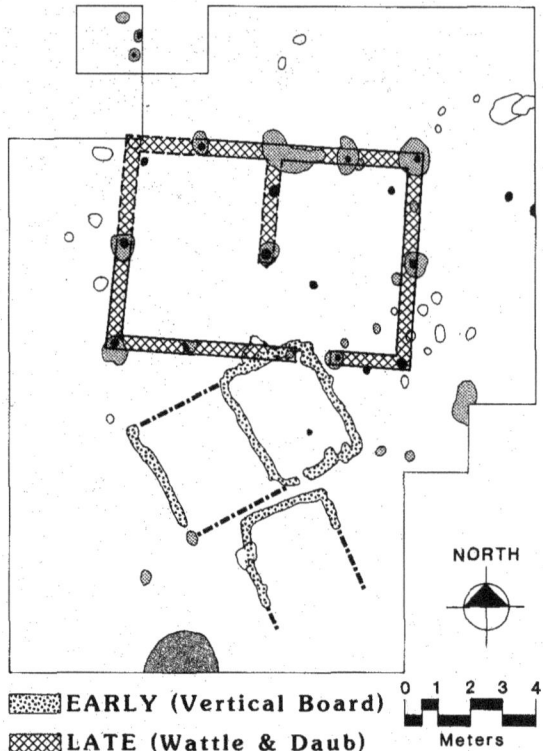

EARLY (Vertical Board)
LATE (Wattle & Daub)

0 1 2 3 4
Meters

FIGURE 14. Structures identified from the Spanish village.

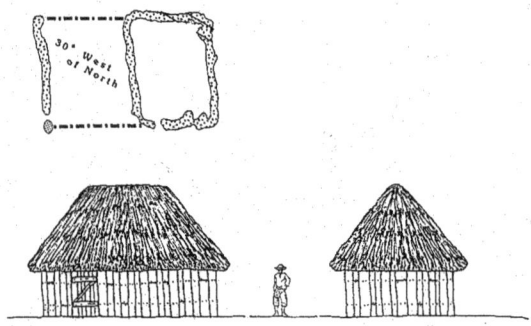

FIGURE 15. Conjectural view of early plank and thatch structure in the Spanish village.

recovered from the trenches, Albert Manucy (1989, pers. comm.) has noted that building foundations in Spanish Florida were typically either of the Pondcypress variety of Baldcypress (*Taxodium ascendens*) or of Southern Redcedar (*Juniperus silicicola*) since both species are straight, massive, and rot resistant in the ground.

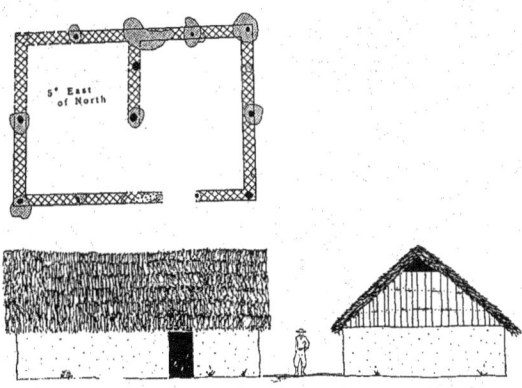

FIGURE 16. Conjectural view of late wattle-and-daub structure in the Spanish village.

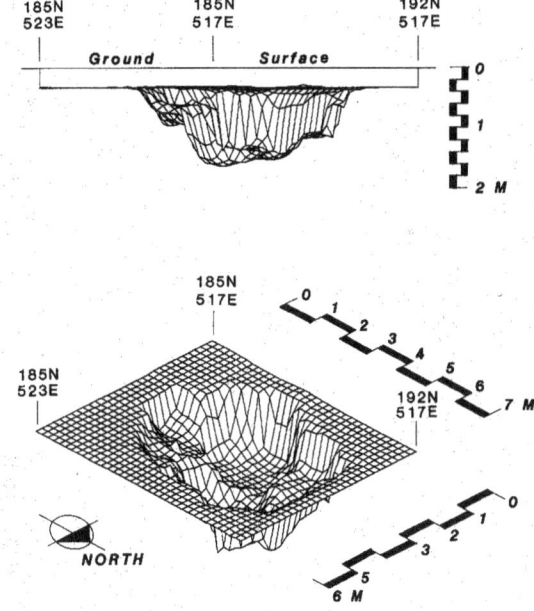

FIGURE 17. Computer-generated views of the trash pit in the Spanish village.

Very few artifacts were found in or around the structure, suggesting that the house was probably the residence of a Spaniard, possibly a soldier, based on its modest size and architecture. The identification of this building is also of interest to understanding of the formation of the archaeological record of San Luis since these "early" structures were not detectable from the auger survey, which identified buildings based on the recovery of daub and hardware.

The later building was oriented 5 degrees east of north and intruded into a wall trench from the early plank and thatch residence. It was a large (6 by 9 m) wattle-and-daub structure with a central partition running approximately halfway down the middle (Figure 16). Two posts located off-center on the south side of the structure were probably the remains of the doorway. Wattle-and-daub construction was not frequently found in local native settlements. Although there are a few exceptions to this (Ewen 1990; Claudine Payne 1990, pers. comm.), documentary and archaeological research suggests that Apalachee houses were typically circular post and thatch structures (Scarry 1989b). However, the wattle-and-daub house identified in the San Luis village probably looked similar to many wood and plaster dwellings commonly found in rural Spain for many centuries (Manucy 1985).

A few meters away, an extremely large trash pit (5.5 m wide by 1.6 m deep) was uncovered (Figure 17). Given its size, the presence of several discrete

basins in the bottom, and the lack of any architectural evidence such as postmolds, it is assumed that this pit originally was a clay mine or borrow pit that was subsequently filled with refuse. The trash recovered from the pit was probably associated with the later wattle-and-daub house, based on its *terminus post quem* (1680–1700), which suggests that it was deposited late in San Luis's occupation (Table 3). Although the quantity of exotic goods from the trash pit was limited, the range of imported materials was exceptional for mission sites as a whole. Artifacts recovered included a silver spoon, a brass weight, and the most concentrated deposit of Spanish pottery and Oriental porcelain from the site. These objects suggest that this trash was probably the refuse of a high-ranking Spaniard. Additionally, copper alloy ring settings, silver sequins, jet *higas* or protective amulets (Muller 1972:68–69), large quantities of beads, and faceted jet rings were found (Figure 18). Although it is speculative, the amount of jewelry identified from this single context suggests that a Spanish or *mestiza* woman may have lived in the

TABLE 3
ARTIFACTS FROM THE SPANISH VILLAGE

Artifact Class	N	%
Aboriginal Ceramics		
Plain Aboriginal	13,145	76.88
Unidentified Aboriginal	814	4.76
Fort Walton Incised	3	0.02
Fort Walton Incised var. Englewood	10	0.06
Lake Jackson Incised	2	0.01
Lake Jackson Incised var. Blountstown	3	0.02
Marsh Island Incised	12	0.07
Marsh Island Incised var. Marsh Island	23	0.13
Marsh Island Incised var. Columbia	9	0.05
Ocmulgee Fields Incised	24	0.14
Ocmulgee Fields Incised var. Ocmulgee	6	0.04
Ocmulgee Fields Incised var. Aucilla	10	0.06
Point Washington Incised	39	0.23
Point Washington Incised var. Pt. Washington	28	0.16
Point Washington Incised var. Chambliss	18	0.11
Point Washington Incised var. Pedro	7	0.04
Unidentified Incised	406	2.37
Unidentified Punctate	2	0.01
Keith Incised	12	0.07
Lamar Complicated Stamped	319	1.87
Lamar Complicated Stamped var. Curlee	112	0.66
Lamar Complicated Stamped var. Early	13	0.08
Lamar Complicated Stamped var. Jefferson	64	0.37
Lamar Complicated Stamped var. Pine Tuft	1	0.01
Lamar Complicated Stamped var. Curvilinear	149	0.87
Lamar Complicated Stamped var. Rectilinear	518	3.03
Leon Check Stamped	155	0.91
Cross Simple Stamped	1	0.01
Wakulla Check Stamped	5	0.03
Unidentified Stamped	285	1.67
Unidentified Complicated Stamped	14	0.08
Unidentified Simple Stamped	1	0.01
Chattahoochee Brushed	5	0.03
Unidentified Impressed	16	0.09
Unidentified Pinched/Punctated	2	0.01
Mission Red Filmed	863	5.05
Unidentified Incised and Red Filmed	1	0.01
Unidentified Filmed	1	0.01
Total	17,098	100.03
Imported Ceramics		
Unidentified Bisque	31	1.65
Unidentified Unglazed Coarse Earthenware	3	0.16
Unidentified Lead Glazed Coarse Earthenware	1	0.05
Unidentified Tin Enamelled Ware	9	0.48
Olive Jar, Unglazed	1,141	60.76
Storage Jar	3	0.16
Olive Jar, Glazed	17	0.91
Guadalajara Polychrome	14	0.75
San Luis Blue on White	27	1.44
Ichtucknee Blue on White	2	0.11

TABLE 3 (Continued)

Artifact Class	N	%
Aucilla Polychrome	15	0.80
Abó Polychrome	49	2.61
Puebla Polychrome	68	3.62
San Luis Polychrome	19	1.01
Castillo Polychrome	27	1.44
San Agustín Blue on White	14	0.75
Unidentified Polychrome Majolica	254	13.53
Unidentified White Majolica	114	6.07
Unidentified Blue on White Majolica	37	1.97
Unidentified Majolica	1	0.05
Ming Porcelain	2	0.11
Blue on White Oriental Porcelain	5	0.27
Plain Oriental Porcelain	25	1.33
Total	1,878	100.03
Kitchen Artifacts		
Case Bottle	3	1.31
Glass Bottle	7	3.06
UID Blown Bottle	4	1.75
Ornamental Glass Elements	13	5.68
Drinking Glass	1	0.44
UID Glass Fragment	198	86.46
UID Glass Lump	1	0.44
Iron Knife Blade	1	0.44
Silver Spoon	1	0.44
Total	229	100.02
Personal Objects		
Ceramic Bead	1	0.07
Mirror Glass	1	0.07
Glass Pendant	8	0.55
UID Wire Wound Bead	22	1.51
UID Tube Bead	1,210	83.05
Jet Finger Ring	2	0.14
Gooseberry Bead	1	0.07
Cornaline d'Aleppo Bead	176	12.08
Blown Bead	5	0.34
Copper Tube Bead	2	0.14
Brass Finger Ring	1	0.07
Copper Commemorative Coin	1	0.07
Brass Hawksbells (Flushloop)	4	0.27
Pewter Stickpin	1	0.07
Silver Thread	6	0.41
Silver Sequins	7	0.48
Jet Higa Pendant	7	0.48
Quartz Crystal Pendant	2	0.14
Total	1,457	100.01
Weaponry		
Brass Projectile Point	1	2.27

(continued)

TABLE 3 (Continued)

Artifact Class	N	%
Lead Pellet	13	29.55
Lead Shot	3	6.82
Lead Puddle	3	6.82
Lead Splatter	9	20.45
European Gunflint Spall	1	2.27
Locally Manufactured Gunflint	6	13.64
Chert Projectile Point	7	15.91
Coral Projectile Point	1	2.27
Total	44	100.00
Structural Hardware		
UID Whole Iron Nail	1	1.14
Wrought Nail	6	6.82
Wrought Spike	2	2.27
Wrought Tack	3	3.41
UID Nail Fragments	20	22.73
Wrought Nail Fragment	52	59.09
Wrought Spike Fragment	3	3.41
Iron Tack Fragment	1	1.14
Total	88	100.01
Sewing and Clothing		
Iron Sewing Needle	5	26.32
Iron Straight Pin	9	47.37
Brass Straight Pin	2	10.53
Brass Aglet	1	5.26
UID Brass Button	1	5.26
Brass Rivet	1	5.26
Total	19	100.00
Activities		
Kaolin Pipestem (5/64)	1	2.13
Kaolin Pipestem (7/64)	1	2.13
Aboriginal Ceramic Pipe	2	4.26
Iron Chain	1	2.13
Iron Wire	34	72.34
Iron Slag	7	14.89
Brass Nested Counter Weight	1	2.13
Total	47	100.01
Construction Materials, Weight in grams		
Spanish Brick	12.2 gm	0.02
Daub with Impressions	4,321.6 gm	5.38
Burned Clay	54,860.7 gm	68.35
Burned Clay, Flat Surface	20,870.5 gm	26.00
Whitewashed Burned Clay, Flat Surface	197.7 gm	0.25
Mortar	0.3 gm	<.01
Total	80,263.0 gm	100.00

Note. Table does not include miscellaneous materials (i.e., pebbles, fauna, etc.).

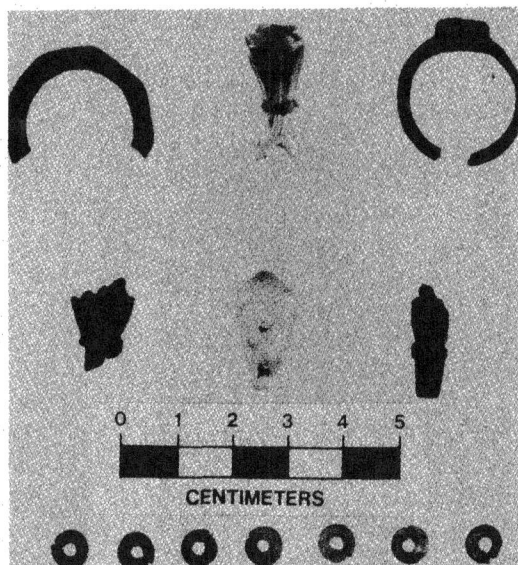

FIGURE 18. Artifacts possibly associated with a Spanish or *mestiza* woman from San Luis: *top,* faceted jet ring, turquoise glass pendant, and a brass ring setting; *middle,* two jet *higas* and a faceted quartz pendant; *bottom,* silver sequins.

associated wattle-and-daub structure, which is further supported by the recovery of Hispanic-tradition toys from the trash pit. Several *juquetes* or small, clay figurines, similar to the Spanish clay dolls found throughout Latin America were found in the refuse (Robert Lister 1990, pers. comm.).

Despite the relatively high proportion of exotic goods from the trash pit, the vast majority of materials consisted of locally made aboriginal-style ceramics and "Colono-ware," vessels manufactured using aboriginal technology in European forms (Vernon 1988). This suggests that although a Hispanic woman may have been in residence at the associated house, native women played an active role in food preparation as well as other domestic activities.

The first good bone preservation from San Luis—and from Apalachee Province for that matter—has also come from this trash pit. Cow, pig, horse, deer, mullet, freshwater bass and catfish, turkey, chicken, and pond turtle remains have been identified from the deposit (Reitz 1990). The vertebrate remains from the San Luis village contain the highest proportion of domestic fauna from any mission complex in Spanish Florida analyzed to date (Reitz 1990). A variety of both indigenous and introduced plant species was also recovered including grape, peach, and maize.

Although some native elements were being incorporated into Spanish households, excavations in the Spanish village at San Luis have demonstrated that Spaniards were able to maintain traditional patterns of architecture, diet, and, to a slightly lesser degree, material life. Despite its remote location, the unique conditions of Apalachee Province resulted in a distinct pattern unknown from other Florida mission settlements. The natural fertility, successful agricultural endeavors, surplus economy, and active shipping from Apalachee afforded at least some of the Spanish residents of San Luis economic affluence and access to an exceptional range of imported materials.

Discussion

The community of San Luis provides a unique set of parameters for investigating Spanish-Indian relations since the settlement was designed and constructed with full knowledge that both Spaniards and Indians would cohabit the site. The Apalachee's decision to request Spaniards was motivated by their desire to restore chiefly power and cultural vitality. The Spaniards, on the other hand, were determined to establish a strong alliance with the native leadership and maintain a foothold in the fertile and densely populated region to meet their needs for food and labor, and to effect large-scale religious conversion.

Viewed in this light, it is not surprising that the results of archaeological research at San Luis do not suggest a clear-cut pattern of a dominant and a recipient culture, but rather one of accommodation and interdependence. While the site selection conforms more closely to Spanish preferences, the location of the buildings across the site reveals the emergence of a new strategy for town plan, guided by both native and Spanish traditions. Based on 18th-century illustrations of historic Creek villages (Bartram 1976 [1853]), circular council houses typically faced onto the plaza. Similarly, the 1573 ordinances issued by Philip II dictated that Spanish towns were to be build on a grid with all public buildings, such as the church, located on the central plaza (Crouch et al. 1982:15–16, Ordinance 126). At San Luis, the Indian council house and the Franciscan church complex were situated at opposite ends of the plaza. The buildings themselves also maintained traditional designs and construction techniques, and the associated materials suggest that activities carried on within them were not altered significantly. This indicates a separation of both traditional Apalachee and traditional Spanish patterns within the public areas of the mission settlement.

There has been little archaeological evidence from any area at San Luis that either Spanish or Apalachee technology changed dramatically as a consequence of sustained contact. In fact, copper alloy and glass projectile points recovered from the council house provide examples of ways in which introduced European materials were modified by the Apalachee to fit preexisting categories of material life. And although the presence of European-style structures such as the fort, church, and houses demonstrate that the Apalachee were forced to alter their construction techniques when working on Spanish buildings (including the preparation and use of hewn and squared timbers, iron hardware, and perhaps even wattle-and-daub walls), there is no indication that they adopted these techniques or materials on native ceremonial or public structures.

There was also little evidence of change in aboriginal technology with regard to weaponry. European firearms were coveted by the native population; however, according to documentary evidence, their distribution was restricted to the ruling elite. Although future excavations in the Apalachee village may prove otherwise, the evidence of active projectile point production in the council house suggests that the majority of Apalachee continued to use bows and arrows throughout the mission period.

The emergence of "Colono-ware" represents one of the few material changes made by Spaniards and Indians. However, the production and use of this new ceramic type presumably did not require marked behavioral changes for either cultural group. Petrographic analyses are currently underway to determine whether Colono-ware used at San Luis was manufactured nearby (Ann Cordell 1990, pers. comm.), although presumably it was being produced by local, native women for use by Europeans. This is based on the recovery of these ceramics primarily from European contexts. Again, future excavations in the Apalachee village may reveal that Colono-ware also was being used by some members of the native population as well.

The large proportion of native ceramics recovered from the *convento* and Spanish village does suggest that native women were incorporated into Hispanic households. Traditional female activities included cooking, cleaning, sewing, and childrearing. The full extent of native female influence within individual homes undoubtedly depended on whether or not a Spanish woman was in residence and, if not, the nature of the Indian woman's relationship with the male head of household. Spanish colonial studies have repeatedly demonstrated that Indian women were the primary agents of acculturation among the largely male colonial populations, and San Luis was undoubtedly no exception (Burkett 1978; Deagan 1985; McEwan 1990).

Investigations in the Spanish village have led to the tentative conclusion that Spaniards living at San Luis were able to maintain many Hispanic traditions and revealed little evidence of acculturation. Houses incorporated Spanish design elements and were constructed using European hardware. Imported luxury items appear to have been available through documented direct shipping routes to St. Augustine and the Caribbean entrepôt of Havana. As a result, exotic forms of material culture such as European and Oriental serving dishes and jewelry remained predominantly Hispanic in nature. Even Spanish diet at San Luis consisted primarily of introduced European animals, although these staples were augmented with locally available foodstuffs.

The success of introduced European plants and animals may have been one of the most far-reaching changes to the native population brought about by the Spanish presence in Apalachee Province. It is apparent from subsistence remains, as well as documentary evidence, that the success of domestic agriculture in conjunction with the establishment of numerous ranches impacted Apalachee subsistence patterns, the native labor pool, and the local economy. Although maize remained the staple crop, traditional Apalachee subsistence was probably supplemented with a variety of non-indigenous fruits, vegetables, and grains. Similarly, while deer, wild turkey, small mammals, fish, and turtles were still actively procured, domestic fauna provided a controlled source of dairy products, meat, animal by-products, and export commodities. The prosperity of Apalachee's export business is well documented. Between 1675 and 1681 the number of hides exported to Havana rose from 150 to 700, and the pounds of tallow exported increased from 3,800 to 5,070 (Boniface 1971:200). Other exports from Apalachee include corn, beans, lard, chickens, and hams (Boniface 1971: 201). Hog-raising became so successful that "by 1670 an Apalachee hog could be purchased in St. Augustine for about four pesos, the cost of a poncho or middling woolen blanket" (Hann 1988: 136).

The native population provided the labor force for herd management, slaughtering activities, processing animal by-products, and transporting goods. Many of the agriculture-related tasks took place at outlying *rancherias* that kept men away for extended periods of time and disrupted family life. European agriculture undoubtedly impacted even those natives who lived in and around San Luis since they were encouraged by the governor to raise livestock (Boyd et al. 1951:31).

The limited excavations in the cemetery revealed perhaps the most concrete evidence of Apalachee acculturation as a result of religious conversion. The discovery of glass, lapidary, and shell beads and pendants, as well as metal objects, in association with Indian burials provides evidence of the ritual significance which these objects were given by the aboriginal population. Furthermore, since the native population traditionally buried its dead with grave goods in large mounds while the Catholic Church maintained a strict pol-

icy of burial practices which forbade grave offerings, the very occurrence of grave offerings with otherwise Christian-style burials is suggestive of a form of Spanish-Indian accommodation (Thomas 1988:120–123). Future excavations in the cemetery may also provide evidence of the demographic consequences of sustained contact—perhaps the most profound result of Spanish-Indian interaction at San Luis.

Summary

Although many aspects of pre-mission Apalachee life were irrevocably altered as a result of interaction with Spaniards, the archaeology at San Luis has been able to demonstrate a marked degree of accommodation. Despite the fact that the Apalachee voluntarily accepted Christianity and Spanish military protection, the council house— the traditional center of native ritual and political life—was the largest of all public structures at San Luis. Furthermore, remains from the council house provide very little evidence that Spanish goods were integrated into traditional activities.

The council house was counterbalanced at the other end of the central plaza by the church complex. Remains from the *convento* or friary suggest that the friars received tribute in the form of indigenous foodstuffs and that native women probably performed domestic tasks for them. Burials were located beneath the church floor and indicate that, despite the Catholic church's strict religious policies and procedures, Indian interments incorporated both Spanish and Indian burial traditions.

Investigations in the Spanish village suggest that Spaniards were able to maintain a highly traditional material life in this frontier setting. However, both archaeological and historical evidence indicate that Indian women played an active role in Spanish households as domestic servants, concubines, and wives.

The findings of the first six years of research at San Luis stand in direct contradiction to the brutal and insensitive attitudes perpetuated in *La Leyenda Negra* of Spanish aggression. Rather, they reflect a relationship characterized by a remarkable degree of cultural tolerance within this frontier community.

ACKNOWLEDGMENTS

The San Luis Archaeological and Historic Site is maintained by the State of Florida's Conservation and Recreation Lands (CARL) Trust Fund and the Florida Legislature. Portions of the excavations in the church complex and Spanish village were also supported by the National Endowment for the Humanities (Grant RO-21395-87). I will always be deeply indebted to Gary Shapiro for laying a solid foundation of exemplary research as San Luis's first director. I thank John Hann for his never-ending contributions as our project historian and for reading and commenting on this manuscript. Richard Vernon has served as the field supervisor at San Luis for the past five years and continues to be an invaluable asset to the project. Charles Poe has ably handled our logistical needs and has kept everyone in line. We have been most fortunate in attracting extremely competent and dedicated crew members. I thank all of them for their contributions to our archaeology program over the years. Charles Poe, Bill Celander, Ed Jonas, and Roy Lett are gratefully acknowledged for the figures and artifact photographs used in this article. I would also like to thank George Percy, John Girvin, and Jim Miller for their constant support and for making archaeology at San Luis possible. I am also grateful to Jeffrey M. Mitchem of the Arkansas Archaeological Survey, KC Smith of the Museum of Florida History, and the *Historical Archaeology* reviewers for making thoughtful suggestions about the manuscript. Finally, I would like to acknowledge my debt to Kathleen Deagan and my other fellow researchers working on southeastern missions who have been exceedingly generous with their thoughts and data.

REFERENCES

ARNADE, CHARLES W.
1965 Cattle Raising in Spanish Florida, 1513–1763. Reprint of 1961 publication. *St. Augustine Historical Society Publication* No. 21. St. Augustine, Florida.

BARTRAM, WILLIAM
1976 Observations of the Creek and Cherokee Indians. *Transactions of the American Ethnological Society* 3(1):11–81. Reprint of 1853 publication. Kraus, Millwood, New York.

BOLTON, HERBERT E.
1917 The Mission as a Frontier Institution in the Spanish American Colonies. *American Historical Review* 23: 42–61.

BONIFACE, BRIAN GEORGE
1971 A Historical Geography of Spanish Florida, circa 1700. Unpublished M.A. thesis, Department of History, University of Georgia, Athens.

BOYD, MARK F., HALE G. SMITH, AND JOHN W. GRIFFIN
1951 *Here They Once Stood.* University of Florida Press, Gainesville.

BURKETT, ELINOR C.
1978 Indian Women and White Society: The Case of Sixteenth-Century Peru. In *Latin American Women,* edited by Asunción Lavrin, pp. 101–128. Greenwood Press, Westport, Connecticut.

CHUBA, MATHEO
1687 Testimony by, San Luis de Talimali, 29 May 1687. In Alonso Solana 1687, Autos and Inquiry Made Concerning the Impossibility that Exists for Achieving the Exploration of the Coast of the Bay of Concepción, Which is Called of the Holy Spirit, that Is Planned to be Made from Apalachee. Archivo General de Indias, Escribania de Cámara legajo, 156, Cuaderno E, folio 31. Stetson Collection, P. K. Yonge Library of Florida History, University of Florida, Gainesville.

CROUCH, DORA, DANIEL GARR, AND AXEL MUNDIGO
1982 *Spanish City Planning in North America.* MIT Press, Cambridge, Massachusetts.

DEAGAN, KATHLEEN
1973 *Mestizaje* in Colonial St. Augustine. *Ethnohistory* 20(1):53–65.
1974 Sex, Status and Role in the Mestizaje of Spanish Colonial Florida. Ph.D. dissertation, Department of Anthropology, University of Florida, Gainesville.
1983 *Spanish St. Augustine: The Archaeology of a Colonial Creole Community.* Academic Press, New York.
1985 Spanish-Indian Interaction in Sixteenth-Century Florida and Hispaniola. In *Cultures in Contact,* edited by William Fitzhugh, pp. 281–318. Smithsonian Institution Press, Washington, D.C.

ELLIOTT, JOHN H.
1963 *Imperial Spain 1469–1716.* St. Martin's Press, New York.

EWEN, CHARLES R.
1990 Soldier of Fortune: Hernando de Soto in the Territory of the Apalachee, 1539–1540. In *Columbian Consequences: Archaeological and Historical Perspectives on the Spanish Borderlands East,* edited by David Hurst Thomas, pp. 77–84. Smithsonian Institution Press, Washington, D.C.

GEIGER, MAYNARD J.
1937 The Franciscan Conquest of Florida (1573–1618). *Studies in Hispanic-American History*, Vol. 1. Catholic University, Washington, D.C.

GIBSON, CHARLES (EDITOR)
1971 *The Black Legend: Anti-Spanish Attitudes in the Old World and in the New*. Alfred Knopf, New York.

GRIFFIN, JOHN W.
1951 Excavations at the Site of San Luis. In *Here They Once Stood*, by Mark F. Boyd, Hale G. Smith, and John W. Griffin, pp. 139–160. University of Florida Press, Gainesville.

HANKE, LEWIS
1951 *Bartolomé de las Casas: An Interpretation of His Life and Writings*. M. Nijhoff, The Hague.

HANN, JOHN H.
1986 Church Furnishings, Sacred Vessels and Vestments Held by the Missions of Florida: Translation of Two Inventories. *Florida Archaeology* 2:147–164. Florida Bureau of Archaeological Research, Tallahassee.
1987 Chronology for San Luis: The Spanish Period. *Florida Archaeology* 3:137–141. Florida Bureau of Archaeological Research, Tallahassee.
1988 *Apalachee: Land Between the Rivers*. University Presses of Florida, Gainesville.
1989 The Apalachee of the Historic Era. Paper Presented at National Endowment for the Humanities Summer Institute, "Spanish Explorers and Indian Chiefdoms: The Southeastern United States in the Sixteenth and Seventeenth Centuries." University of Georgia, Athens.

HARING, CLARENCE H.
1963 *The Spanish Empire in America*. Reprint of 1947 edition. Harbinger, New York.

HOFFMAN, KATHLEEN
1990 Archaeological Excavations at the Florida National Guard Headquarters, St. Augustine, Florida. Report on file, Florida Museum of Natural History, Gainesville.

JONES, B. CALVIN, JOHN HANN, AND JOHN SCARRY
1991 San Pedro y San Pablo de Patale: A Seventeenth-Century Mission in Leon County, Florida. *Florida Archaeology* 5. Bureau of Archaeological Research, Tallahassee.

JONES, B. CALVIN, AND GARY SHAPIRO
1990 Nine Mission Sites in Apalachee. In *Columbian Consequences: Archaeological and Historical Perspectives on the Spanish Borderlands East*, edited by David Hurst Thomas, pp. 491–509. Smithsonian Institution Press, Washington, D.C.

KUBLER, GEORGE
1940 *The Religious Architecture of New Mexico in the Colonial Period and Since the American Occupation*. The Taylor Museum, Colorado Springs.

LARSEN, CLARK SPENCER
1990 A Bioarchaeological Investigation of San Luis de Talimali. *Florida Archaeology* 6, Part II, Appendix 1. Florida Bureau of Archaeological Research, Tallahassee.

MALTBY, WILLIAM S.
1971 *The Black Legend in England*. Duke University Press, Durham, North Carolina.

MANUCY, ALBERT
1978 *The Houses of St. Augustine*. St. Augustine Historical Society, St. Augustine, Florida.
1985 The Physical Setting of Sixteenth-Century St. Augustine *Florida Anthropologist* 38(1–2):34–53.

MARRINAN, ROCHELLE
1985 The Archaeology of the Spanish Missions of Florida: 1565–1704. In Indians, Colonists, and Slaves, edited by K. W. Johnson, J. M. Leader, and R. C. Wilson. *Florida Journal of Anthropology Special Publication* 4:241–252. University of Florida, Gainesville.

McALISTER, LYLE N.
1984 *Spain and Portugal in the New World, 1492–1700*. University of Minnesota Press, Minneapolis.

McEWAN, BONNIE
1990 The Archaeological Evidence of Women on Spanish Sites. Paper Presented at the Annual Meeting of the Society for Historical Archaeology Conference on Historical and Underwater Archaeology, Tucson, Arizona.

MILANICH, JERALD T., AND WILLIAM C. STURTEVANT
1972 *Francisco Pareja's 1613 Confessionario: A Documentary Source for Timucuan Ethnography*. Division of Archives, History, and Records Management, Tallahassee.

MITCHEM, JEFFREY M.
1990 Glass and Lapidary Beads and Pendants from San Luis de Talimali. *Florida Archaeology* 6, Part II, Appendix 2. Florida Bureau of Archaeological Research, Tallahassee.

MULLER, PRISCILLA E.
1972 *Jewels in Spain, 1500–1800*. The Hispanic Society of America, New York.

QUIROGA Y LOSADA, GOVERNOR DIEGO DE
1690 Letter to the King, 31 August 1690. Archivo General de Indias, Santo Domingo, 228. Stetson Collection, P.K. Yonge Library of Florida History, University of Florida, Gainesville.

REITZ, ELIZABETH J.
1990 Vertebrate Fauna from the Spanish Village at San Luis de Talimali, Feature 6. Ms. on file, Florida Bureau of Archaeological Research, Tallahassee.

SCARRY, C. MARGARET
1991 Plant Remains from the San Luis Council House. *Florida Archaeology* 6, Part 1, Appendix 6. Florida Bureau of Archaeological Research, Tallahassee.

SCARRY, JOHN F.
1987 A Provisional Sequence for Apalachee Province. Ms. on file, Florida Bureau of Archaeological Research, Tallahassee.
1988 Stability and Change in the Apalachee Chiefdom: Centralization, Decentralization, and Social Reproduction. Ms. on file, Florida Bureau of Archaeological Research, Tallahassee.
1989a The Apalachee Chiefdom: A Mississippian Chiefdom on the Fringe of the Mississippian World. Paper Presented at National Endowment for the Humanities Summer Institute, "Spanish Explorers and Indian Chiefdoms: The Southeastern United States in the Sixteenth and Seventeenth Centuries." University of Georgia, Athens.
1989b Apalachee Homesteads: Examining the Basal Social and Economic Units of a Mississippian Chiefdom. Paper Presented at the 54th Annual Meeting of the Society for American Archaeology, Atlanta, Georgia.

SHAPIRO, GARRY
1984 A Soil Resistivity Survey of 16th-Century Puerto Real, Haiti. *Journal of Field Archaeology* 11:101–110.
1985 The Apalachee Council House at Seventeenth-Century San Luis. Paper Presented at the Southeastern Archaeological Conference, Birmingham, Alabama.
1987 Archaeology at San Luis: Broad Scale Testing, 1984–85. *Florida Archaeology* 3. Florida Bureau of Archaeological Research, Tallahassee.

SHAPIRO, GARY, AND JOHN HANN
1990 Documentary Image of the Council Houses of Spanish Florida Tested by Excavations at the San Luis de Talimali Mission. In *Columbian Consequences: Archaeological and Historical Perspectives on the Spanish Borderlands East,* edited by David Hurst Thomas, pp. 477–491. Smithsonian Institution Press, Washington, D.C.

SHAPIRO, GARY, AND BONNIE MCEWAN
1991 Archaeology at San Luis: The Apalachee Council House. *Florida Archaeology* 6. Florida Bureau of Archaeological Research, Tallahassee.

SIMPSON, LESLEY BYRD
1966 *The Encomienda in New Spain.* Second edition. University of California Press, Berkeley and Los Angeles.

SMITH, MARVIN T.
1990 Glass Beads from the Council House at San Luis. *Florida Archaeology* 6, Part I, Appendix 4. Florida Bureau of Archaeological Research, Tallahassee.

STEELE, COLIN
1975 *English Interpreters of the Iberian New World from Purchas to Steven.* Dolphin, Oxford.

THOMAS, DAVID HURST
1987 The Archaeology of Mission Santa Catalina de Guale: 1. Search and Discovery. *Anthropological Papers of the American Museum of Natural History* 63:Part 2. New York.
1988 Saints and Soldiers at Santa Catalina: Hispanic Designs for Colonial America. In *The Recovery of Meaning in Historical Archaeology,* edited by Mark P. Leone and Parker B. Potter, Jr., pp. 73–140. Smithsonian Institution Press, Washington, D.C.

VERNON, RICHARD
1988 17th Century Colono-Ware as a Reflection of Demography, Economics, and Acculturation. *Historical Archaeology* 22(1):76–82.

VERNON, RICHARD, AND BONNIE MCEWAN
1990 Investigations in the Church Complex and Spanish Village at San Luis. *Florida Archaeological Reports* 18. Florida Bureau of Archaeological Research, Tallahassee.

WILLEY, GORDON R.
1949 Archaeology of the Florida Gulf Coast. *Smithsonian Miscellaneous Collections* 113. Washington, D.C.

ZÚÑIGA Y ZERDA, GOVERNOR DON JOSEPH DE
1700 *Residencia* for Governor Laureano de Torres y Ayala, 16 November 1700. Archivo General de Indias, Escribania de Cámara, legajo 157A, Microfilm roll 27-p. Stetson Collection, P.K. Yonge Library of Florida History, University of Florida, Gainesville. Microfilm.

BONNIE G. MCEWAN
SAN LUIS ARCHAEOLOGICAL SITE
2020 MISSION ROAD
TALLAHASSEE, FLORIDA 32304

Diane E. Silvia

Native American and French Cultural Dynamics on the Gulf Coast

ABSTRACT

Archaeological investigations at Old Mobile and Port Dauphin, and at the later sites of Bienville Square, Fort Condé Village, Bottle Creek, and Dog River, document the evolution of a relatively reciprocal and stable relationship between colonists and native peoples spanning the entire French colonial period, from 1699 to 1763. The nature of French-Indian interaction on the Gulf Coast contrasts with other areas of eastern North America at that time, such as the Mississippi Valley and the Northeast, where relations often were more fragile and alliances went with the best offer.

Introduction

Recent archaeological investigations in southwestern Alabama have included the first detailed examinations of early historic Indian and French colonial sites in the region. Ongoing excavations at the site of Old Mobile (1MB94) provide an excellent starting point and framework for exploring how initial and subsequent French contact affected Native American life.

French colonization along the Gulf Coast, beginning at the turn of the 18th century, was integrally linked with the indigenous and immigrant Native American societies encountered there. Until recently, however, archaeological investigation of the region's colonial era has focused primarily on sites occupied by colonists, to the neglect of contemporary Indian sites. Among the most important French colonial sites are Old Mobile (1MB94), dating from 1702 to 1711 (Waselkov 1991, 1999); Port Dauphin (1MB61), occupied primarily between 1711 and 1725 (Stowe 1977; Shorter 1995); Bienville Square (1MB32), 1711–1763 (Silvia 1989); the Mobile County Courthouse Annex (1MB156), 1711–1763 (Sheldon and Cottier 1983); Fort Condé Village (1MB132), 1711–1763 (Silvia and Waselkov 1993); and the Rochon plantation site on Dog River (1MB161), ca. 1725–1763

(Barnes Smith 1995; Waselkov and Silvia 1995; Waselkov and Gums 2000). On the other hand, only three excavations have occurred at historic Native American sites: 1MB147, which is contemporaneous with and adjacent to Old Mobile (Silvia 2000); a component on Mound L at the Bottle Creek site (1BA2), ca. 1740s (Silvia 2000); and a Chato occupation area at the Rochon plantation site on Dog River, ca. 1725–1740 (Waselkov and Gums 2000).

Marvin Smith's review of the historic and archaeological records indicates that the introduction of Old World diseases led to depopulation, migration, political and social reorganization, and loss of cultural elements in the Southeast, a trend that was well underway prior to French attempts at colonization (Smith 1987:60). With the founding of Mobile, local Indian groups, as well as Apalachees and Chatos from Spanish missions in Florida, saw the French colony as a refuge from English-inspired slave raids where some of their material and spiritual wants and needs could be satisfied.

A sparse population, in terms of Europeans as well as Indians, is one factor that distinguishes the colonial situation around Mobile Bay from that of the British along the Atlantic seaboard or later French settlements in the lower Mississippi Valley. The population density of Native Americans in the Mobile-Tensaw delta was low, when compared with Choctaw or Creek territories of the interior Southeast. Early in the century Iberville had received word that, while the nearby Tomés and Mobilians had a total of 600 warriors, Choctaw warriors to the northwest numbered over 6000 (Galloway 1995:190). On the European side of the population ledger, in 1704 the colonial settlements contained about 255 souls, including 11 enslaved Indian children (Rowland and Sanders 1929:19). In ensuing decades, the local Indian population dropped precipitously, due to disease mortality, while the colonists' numbers continued to hover around 300 in the Mobile area (Wood 1989). With both societies struggling to maintain viable population levels, colonists and Native Americans found common interest in cooperation.

From historic records we know that, despite official sanctions against French-Indian intermarriage, many enslaved Indian women were taken as wives by the French colonists (Miller Surrey 1916:226–230). The archaeology at Old Mobile certainly attests to the multi-ethnic nature of that settlement, and, together with other excavated sites, suggests that many Native Americans lived in French households throughout the French colonial period.

At another scale, the French hoped for geo-political advantage in establishing their town of Mobile at a strategic location near Indian villages on the Mobile River, to ward off British encroachment and to keep a wary eye on the nearby Spanish settlement of Pensacola (Galloway 1995:192; Shorter 1995:1). They endeavored to accomplish these goals by cultivating a paternal relationship toward neighboring Indians, offering sanctuary for refugees fleeing British aggression, fostering distrust of the British, encouraging peace between tribes, officially discouraging enslavement of allied Indians, and giving gifts (Galloway 1995:184–185).

Since supplies seldom arrived in a timely fashion from France at the beginning of the 18th century, Old Mobile became heavily dependent on interaction with nearby Indian groups, who supplied maize, venison, furs, deerskins, and pottery in exchange for glass beads, catlinite pipes, and metal implements, such as guns, knives, and nails. Many of the items the Indians provided were perishable plant and animal resources (Clute and Waselkov, this volume; Gremillion, this volume). Of these, some maize remains have been recovered at Old Mobile and the Rochon plantation from traditional "Indian-style" smudge pits. At Old Mobile, the aboriginal ceramic assemblage suggests that the town had trade connections with several different native groups, including the Mobilians, Tomés and Naniabas, Chatos, and Apalachees. Vessels made by Tomé and Mobilian potters are shown in Figure 1 (Fuller 1991:12–13). The Apalachees appear to be the best represented group in terms of ceramics at Old Mobile (Cordell, this volume).

All of the French sites in southwest Alabama have yielded tremendous quantities of Indian goods, especially pottery, from French domestic contexts. This demonstrates close social interaction as well as French use of aboriginally-made

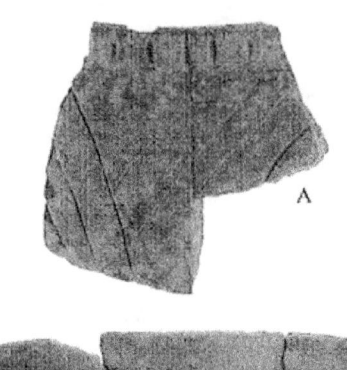

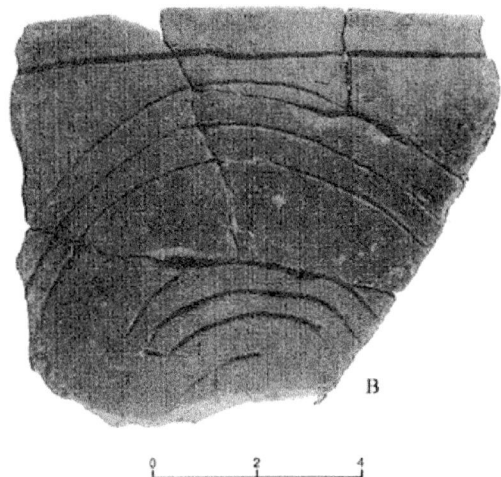

FIGURE 1. Historic aboriginal pottery types: A, Doctor Lake Incised, a Tomé type (1MB94, Structure 3, Vessel 6); B, Port Dauphin Incised, a Mobilian type (1MB94, Structure 3, Vessel 8).

wares throughout the 18th century. The diversity of aboriginal wares at each household does, however, indicate that pottery was acquired from multiple sources and seldom, if ever, was produced by members of French households for their own use. The aboriginal ceramic assemblage at Old Mobile also demonstrates that inter-group contact weakened both local and non-local pottery making traditions during this time. For instance, several complicated stamped, globular jars recovered from Old Mobile and Dog River were executed in traditional Apalachee and Chato fashion with folded and pinched or punctated rims, but constructed of coarse lamellar or angular shell-tempered paste instead of the grog-tempered and sand-tempered pastes typical of the Apalachees and Chatos in Florida (Figure 2) (Silvia 2000; Waselkov and Gums 2000:130).

FIGURE 2. Possible Apalachee decoration and surface treatment on a coarse shell-tempered ware; rectilinear complicated stamped surface treatment with punctated rim fold (1MB161, Vessel 2).

sample, which she attributes to the ready availability of European ceramics at the warehouse. Evidently, although French colonists' dependency on Native American potters decreased through time, European-Indian interaction and exchange remained strong and continued into the British colonial period.

Since aboriginal ceramics are rarely mentioned in French inventories, the nature of their acquisition is uncertain. The majority probably were produced nearby in Native American villages at the level of a "household industry," (made in the home on a small scale for use beyond the household), as opposed to "household production" (ceramics made and used by the individual household), or a "workshop industry" (ceramic specialists working on a large scale) (Sinopoli 1991:98–99). The presence of ceramic household industries is suggested by the range of ethnic

Most telling is the comparison of aboriginal to European vessels in different assemblages. Aboriginal pottery vessels comprise 64% of Old Mobile's Structure 1 ceramic assemblage and 73% of the Dauphin Island stockade assemblage. The slightly later Port Dauphin assemblage (ca. 1715–1725) contains 41% aboriginal pottery (Shorter, this volume). Excavation of French colonial contexts at Dog River has yielded substantially less Native American ceramics than found at earlier sites, demonstrating better access to European French goods by the middle of the 18th century (Barnes Smith 1995:53–56, 94; Waselkov and Gums 2000:125, 152). This is supported by Hammersten's (1990:50–54) results at the site of a French warehouse on Ship Island (1717–1750s), off the coast of Mississippi, where aboriginal wares constitute less than 50% of the

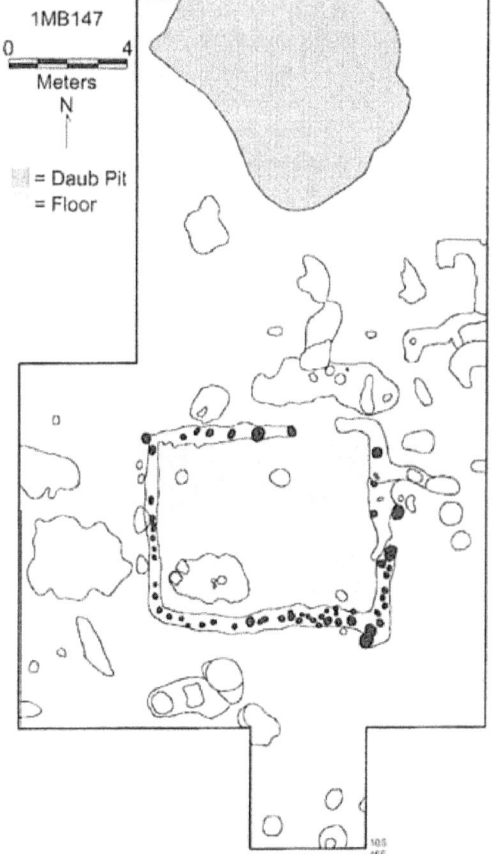

FIGURE 3. Structure plan view at 1MB147.

diversity represented in the ceramic assemblages at Old Mobile. Aboriginal ceramics were probably traded for European goods, although their value must have been low since no transactions were recorded in historical documents. Other items, such as aboriginal clay pipes and locally-made gunflints, projectile points, and other lithic tools have also been recovered at the French structures. The nature of these exchanges certainly ranged all along Marshall Sahlins' (1960:39–236) continuum of generalized, balanced, and negative reciprocity.

Aboriginal and French Sites: An Intersite Comparison

A sample of four structures has been selected for comparative purposes. From the early 18th century, a French structure at Old Mobile and an aboriginal structure (1MB147) on the town's periphery, are compared with examples dating from the middle of the century, including a French-style structure at Dog River and an aboriginal one at Bottle Creek (Waselkov 1997).

Structure 1 at Old Mobile was selected for this comparison because it has been intensively studied and was constructed similarly to most of the other French structures investigated there (Waselkov 1991; Gums, this volume, Figure 4). This three-room structure measured 11.4 m (37.4 ft.) northwest to southeast by 5.4 m (17.7 ft.) northeast to southwest, and was built using the *poteaux sur sole* technique, with the exception of a portion of one wall corner repaired by *pieux en terre*. A raised clay floor was at least partially covered with wood planks, and the walls were plastered with *bousillage* (Waselkov 1991:43–44, 180). The artifact assemblage is rich and diverse, including Spanish colonial and French tin-glazed earthenwares, English and German stonewares, and Chinese porcelain. Aboriginal ceramics, such as Fatherland Incised, Doctor Lake Incised, Lamar Complicated Stamped, and Old Town Red, attest to contact with several Native American groups, including the Apalachees, Tomés, and Mobilians. Numerous handwrought iron nails, roof tile and brick fragments, kaolin pipe fragments, gunflints, red pipestone worked into unfinished smoking pipes, glass beads, bottle glass, brass buttons, coins,

0   2
CM

FIGURE 4. Ceramic smoking pipe bowl, calumet form (1MB147, FS 80).

and many more categories of artifacts were also recovered.

When shovel testing beyond the northwest boundary of Old Mobile yielded an isolated cluster of artifacts, recorded as site 1MB147, unusual proportions of familiar artifact types suggested that perhaps this was an Indian structure occupied contemporaneously with Old Mobile. Excavations in 1996 confirmed that this was an Indian house and, in fact, it is the only aboriginal structure known from archaeology in southwest Alabama that dates to the period of initial French contact (Silvia 2000). The structure was quite small, measuring about 3.2 m (10.5 ft.) north-south by 4.2 m (13.8 ft.) east-west (Figure 3). The shallow wall trenches contained closely-spaced postmolds that were extremely difficult to detect during excavation. Clay subsoil had been obtained from a spot about 3.5 m (11.5 ft.) north of the structure for the construction of the daub walls, resulting in a borrow pit more than 3 m (10 ft.) in diameter that fortuitously provided drainage for the structure. The borrow pit yielded abundant artifacts within water-sorted soils that accumulated during the house's occupation.

Artifacts recovered from 1MB147 include glass trade beads, a jet rosary bead, a number of red pipestone fragments, white clay pipe fragments, a brass bead and tinkler, gunflints, iron nails, aboriginal and European ceramics, and abundant lithics knapped mainly from a local material known as Tallahatta sandstone. Portions of several iron clasp knives and a pistol barrel were also found. Among the most interesting finds was a red-filmed clay pipe (Figure 4), fashioned exactly after a red pipestone calumet form recovered from French structures at Old Mobile (Waselkov 1991:94–96), with the same octagonal-shaped bowl and pierced holes along the base of the stem for the insertion of feathers. In addition the pipe maker created striations along both sides of the bowl, as if to imitate the appearance of cut stone.

One archaeological feature that set this structure apart from any investigated to date at Old Mobile was a pit, filled with shells of the marsh clam (*Rangia cuneata*), located just west of the structure. *Rangia* spp. clams rarely occur at Old Mobile, but are abundant at nearby prehistoric sites. Analysis of the faunal assemblage from 1MB147 has shown that all of the identifiable specimens are from wild species, as opposed to faunal remains from the Old Mobile structures that include bones of domestic pig and chicken (Clute and Waselkov, this volume).

Another obvious difference between the two structures is their orientation. While the walls of 1MB147 squarely face the cardinal directions, all of the French structures at Old Mobile are oriented along the town grid that runs about 40° west of north. The paucity of ceramic tiles at 1MB147 contrasts dramatically with their abundance at contemporaneous French house sites, where they were used in roof construction. So common are they, in fact, that their recovery in shovel tests is an excellent indicator of structure locations at Old Mobile. While nearly 3,000 g (6 lb. 10 oz.) of tile fragments were recovered from a single 2.0 x 2.0 m (6.6 x 6.6 ft.) unit at Structure 1 (Waselkov 1991:67), the entire excavation at 1MB147 yielded only two fragments (weighing 56 g [2 oz.]) found in the nearby borrow pit. One of these tile frag-

ments has an abraded surface, perhaps resulting from use as a whetstone.

The aboriginal ceramic collection from 1MB147 includes the types Doctor Lake Incised, Port Dauphin Incised, and Lamar Complicated Stamped, all indicating direct or indirect contact with (or even the presence of) Tomés, Mobilians, and Apalachees, respectively. Common forms include globular jars, simple open bowls, and Colono types such as brimmed bowls, ring based plates, and pitchers with loop handles. Both shell-tempered and grog-tempered wares are present, as they are from the structures excavated at Old Mobile. The presence of both local and Apalachee ceramics makes it difficult to determine the identity of the structure's native inhabitants. The high percentage of grog-tempered vessels (57% at 1MB147 versus 47% at Old Mobile's Structure 1) and the large proportion of vessels attributable to Apalachee potters (73%, based on complicated stamped surface treatment and pinched rim decorations) suggests that a female occupant of 1MB147 may have been Apalachee. On the other hand, the house does not resemble traditional Apalachee architecture in plan or construction—they were thatch-walled, circular, posthole structures—and is, instead, most similar to the early historic aboriginal structure discovered at the Bottle Creek site. Perhaps the adult male occupant of 1MB147 was Mobilian.

French and aboriginal structures from the middle of the 18th century show only minor differences from their earlier counterparts. Excavations by the University of Alabama on the summit of Mound L at the Bottle Creek site (1BA2), a major Mississippian center located on an island in the heart of the Mobile-Tensaw delta, revealed a series of structures dating from Mississippian through early historic times (Brown and Fuller 1993; Silvia 2000). Since a number of structures were superimposed, it has been very difficult to interpret the 689 features found within an excavated area only 6 x 8 m (20 x 26 ft.) in size, with little deposition creating separation. The most recent structure is historic aboriginal, measuring about 3.5 m (11.5 ft.) east-northeast to west-southwest by 5 m (16 ft.) north-northwest to south-southeast.

Historic Indian pottery types such as Fatherland Incised, Old Town Red, Mission Red

Filmed, Pensacola Red Filmed, Port Dauphin Incised, and Mississippi Plain, *var. Douglas* were recovered, indicating the presence of Mobilians. While few artifacts of European origin were found, the small assemblage was diverse, including several glass beads, olive-green glass bottle fragments, a large iron spike intentionally bent to form a hook, three handwrought nails, an iron bail from a copper kettle, a brass French military button, an iron clasp knife blade, and a lock plate from a French gun. The absence of European-made ceramics is puzzling. Particularly interesting is a tabular piece of hematitic sandstone with striations left from sawing. Three sides are ground flat while one is rounded. It resembles the prow of a calumet and may represent a failed attempt to produce such a pipe. These artifacts suggest that the structure dates to around the middle of the 18th century.

Julie Barnes Smith (1995) excavated a French-style structure at the Rochon plantation site (1MB161), located at the mouth of Dog River overlooking Mobile Bay. This multi-component site spans most of the historic period, from ca. 1725 to 1848. Structure 2, which apparently was built in the 1770s, during the British colonial period, was constructed in the French-colonial *poteaux en terre* style (Figure 5). Judging from the few postmolds detected in the trenches, the structure evidently was dismantled (Barnes Smith 1995:46–49). Evidently, the two-room structure was oriented west-northwest by east-southeast and measured approximately 5 x 10 m (16 x 33 ft.), with an attached fenced enclosure (Barnes Smith 1995:46–49; Waselkov 2000:189–190). An array of artifacts dating to the mid-18th century was recovered from this area, such as tin-glazed ceramics, stoneware, white clay pipe bowl and stem fragments, nails, glass beads, and historic aboriginal pottery types such as Port Dauphin Incised, Chickachae Combed, and Old Town Red (Silvia 1995).

Cultural Patterning

The two historic Native American structures described above, at Bottle Creek and site 1MB147, are the only ones excavated in southwest Alabama. Although other French-style structures have been excavated, just two are discussed here to simplify this comparison. All of these investigations have involved similar

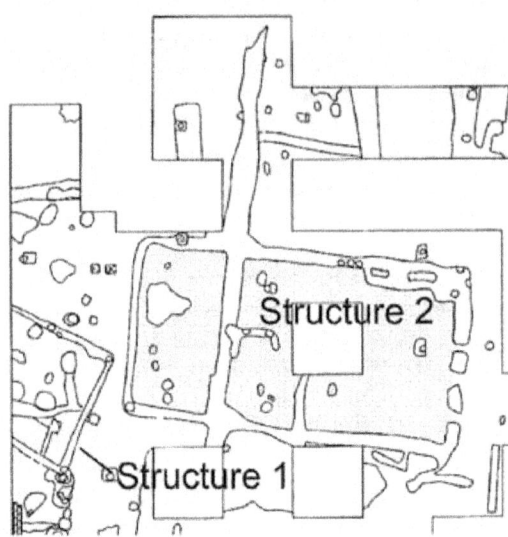

FIGURE 5. Structure 2 plan view at 1MB161, the Rochon plantation at Dog River.

methods of excavation and artifact analysis. Of course, no two sites are exactly comparable, since location, structure size and use, length and nature of occupation, artifact assemblages, and area excavated are all quite variable. In addition, the sample of excavated structures is still very small.

Overall, though, assemblages from aboriginal structures have fewer artifacts and contain very different proportions of artifact classes in comparison to their French counterparts. For example, while 8 gunflints were found at 1MB147, Structure 1 at Old Mobile contained 38 (Waselkov 1991:84–85; Silvia 2000). Likewise, more than 2000 iron nails and nail fragments were recovered from Structure 1 (Waselkov 1991:64), while excavations yielded 419 from 1MB147 and 3 from the Bottle Creek structure.

The two French structures were both associated with abundant quantities of aboriginal and European ceramics, demonstrating intense interaction between French and Indians throughout the 18th century, and a lengthy dependence on aboriginal wares by the colonists. In contrast, at 1MB147 the percentage of European wares in the ceramic assemblage is markedly lower, with a European-to-aboriginal vessel ratio of about 1:4, compared to a European-to-aboriginal vessel ratio of about 1:2 at Old Mobile's Structure 1.

European ceramics were entirely absent from the Bottle Creek structure, despite the presence of other European goods. This structure may have been used as a hunting camp, rather than for year-around habitation (Silvia 2000).

It is interesting to note that the European tin-glazed ceramic assemblage at Old Mobile's Structure 1 contains as much Spanish colonial majolica as French faience. This, together with the very large aboriginal ceramic collection, is strong archaeological evidence for a shortage of goods reaching the colony from France, as well as a commentary on relations between the French and their Spanish rivals. The Rochon plantation structure yielded substantially lower percentages of Native American and Spanish colonial ceramics than its earlier counterpart, demonstrating better access to French goods with time (Barnes Smith 1995:53–56, 94).

One might surmise that the presence of Colono ware at Old Mobile's Structure 1 was also a response to shortages of French ceramics, but the situation seems much more complex. For instance, most of the Colono vessels found at Old Mobile seem to be Apalachee-made. Research in the Florida homeland of the Apalachees indicates that they developed Colono plate and pitcher forms there, well before their migration to the Mobile area (Vernon and Cordell 1993). Furthermore, the presence and use of Colono wares at Native American structures is evidence of assimilation, and certainly not a response to French market demand.

The pattern emerging from this comparison suggests that while close interaction between French and Indians resulted in considerable material assimilation by both groups, French and Indian structures remained differentiated and can be distinguished archaeologically by location, orientation, building technique, size and shape, length of occupation, and proportions of artifact classes. The Bottle Creek structure is similar to the aboriginal structure at 1MB147; both were constructed of small posts set in shallow trenches, and their width-to-length ratios are very similar at 0.70 and 0.76, respectively. These differ markedly from the ratios of French buildings, 0.46 for Old Mobile's Structure 1 and 0.50 for Structure 2 at the Rochon plantation. There were no internal partitions within the Native American structures indicating functionally specific rooms.

Both aboriginal structures were small, reflecting a continuity in Native lifeways from the late prehistoric to colonial periods, with much household activity occurring outside and around the buildings. Both aboriginal structures discussed here were built in isolated locations with some thought to minimize the effects of flooding. The 1MB147 structure sat at the edge of a seasonal swamp but was drained by a large borrow pit situated downslope, and the Bottle Creek structure sat atop a Mississippian mound.

Three of the structures considered here were built of posts set in trenches and the exception, Structure 1 at Old Mobile, was repaired with a short section of wall trench. Trench widths range from 25 to 40 cm (10 to 16 in.), though neither Native Americans nor French colonists seem to have been very precise in their construction. The aboriginal wall trenches were very shallow, between 5 and 12 cm (2 and 5 in.) in depth. At Structure 1, the repair trench ranged from 17 to 28 cm (7 to 11 in.) deep (Waselkov 1991:37–42), and similar trench depths were found at Rochon's Structure 2 (Barnes Smith 1995:46). Clay *bousillage* or daub was used to finish the walls of both French and Native American structures in the same way daub had been used prehistorically throughout the Southeast. Similar conservatism existed at the Canadian mission site of Saint-Louis-des-Hurons, where native house construction "seems to have represented a last stronghold of traditional life, in resistance to the European-style dwellings of the Jesuit missionaries" (Moussette 1997; also Jury and Jury 1955:45–46).

All of the Mobile-area sites with ethnic French components post-dating the abandonment of Old Mobile in 1711—Port Dauphin, Bienville Square, Fort Condé Village, the Mobile County Courthouse Annex, and Rochon plantation at Dog River—show a high level of interaction with native peoples continuing throughout the 18th century. For example, at Dog River the presence of numerous historic aboriginal sherds and clay pipes, projectile points, and *Rangia* spp. clam shell features reflect a Chato Indian occupation immediately south of the plantation during the French colonial period. The early influence of Indian women, as wives and slaves of the first colonists, had a lasting impact on food preparation, cooking, serving, and storage practices in Louisiana. Long after improved supply lines to France brought the colonists ready access to European ceramics, Indian-made jars and bowls—particularly bowls—continued in great demand in the colony until the early 19th century.

The Mobilian Trade Language

The origin of the Mobilian trade language (technically known to linguists as a pidgin), which was used as a lingua franca between tribes and with Europeans, remains in question. James Mooney long ago described the language as "spoken and understood among all the tribes of the Gulf states . . . it was called Mobilienne by the French, from Mobile, the Great trading center of the Gulf region" (Mooney 1900:187). The trade language consisted of selected elements of Choctaw, Creek, Chickasaw, Natchez, and Apalachee and incorporated a few French and Spanish words (Haas 1975:257–261). Emanuel Drechsel (1994:25–43) convincingly argues that Mobilian existed prior to European contact, perhaps originating in late Mississippian times.

Generally the language of an encroaching, colonizing group is adopted or pidginized for inter-group communication. The possible existence of a specialized language for inter-group communication along the Gulf Coast prior to French contact is suggested by archaeological and historical evidence for an ethnically complex situation created by the influx of immigrant societies from elsewhere in the Southeast during the late 16th and 17th centuries. By 1699, ethnically distinct native groups like the Mobilians, Tomés, Pensacolas, and Pascagoulas had interacted intensely within a confined area for a long period of time. If the French were simply incorporated into an already established system of trade and diplomacy, they may have adopted the Mobilian trade language for communication with native groups for practical reasons (Drechsel 1994:25–43). They also might not have seen themselves, initially, as the most powerful group in the region. The French needed Native Americans for their geographical knowledge, food, goods, and labor, and it was to their advantage to be accommodating.

An aspect of Speech Accommodation theory, as it pertains to linguistics, suggests that the group with something to gain shows good-will by accommodating to the speech of the other (Bonvillain 1993:318). Patricia Galloway has pointed out that advantages of the French approach to native cultures can be seen historically in French maps from the period that incorporate a good deal of Native American knowledge, as opposed to maps of the Spanish and British (Galloway 1995:262). She also suggests that the diplomatic role assumed by Bienville as a father figure eased relations with the Choctaws, who saw the French as "kind and generous, but they had no authority" (Galloway 1989:273).

Conclusions

Although the Mobile area is one of the richest archaeological and historical regions in southeastern North America, it has, until recently, been one of the least studied. As archaeological research in this region proceeds at an accelerated pace, we are beginning to understand better the effects of initial French colonization on Native American life and the degree to which each of these groups underwent assimilation.

In summary, while the French soon adapted to local environmental conditions, some of their cultural norms were maintained. They built larger homes and divided them into separate rooms, used roof tiles, and built fences to enclose domestic animals and gardens. Structures at Old Mobile and Rochon plantation provide clear evidence of attached fenced enclosures. None of these elements was incorporated in the aboriginal structures, which remained small and constructed of traditional materials.

French influence is more clearly seen in other aspects of Native American material culture. As aboriginal ceramics often form the bulk of artifact collections, they receive much attention and, as David and Hennig (1972:1) have written, are seen as "a vehicle for the expression of cultural patterning." Aboriginal ceramics with Colono-ware attributes are present at all of these sites, and their use at Native American structures is evidence of assimilation, rather than merely a response to French market demand. The aboriginal ceramic assemblages differ between French and aboriginal structures, more in the proportions of vessels rather than types, throughout the French colonial period. Their continued importance at ethnic French households reflects the strong influence of native cultures on Louisiana colonial foodways.

ACKNOWLEDGMENTS

This article is based on a number of excavations I had the privilege to work on from 1990 to 1995. I thank the many outstanding co-workers and students I met along the way for their hard work and dedication in the field and lab. Their efforts made this analysis possible. As always, it was an honor and pleasure to work with Ian Brown (Principal Investigator) and Rick Fuller at the Bottle Creek site. Greg Waselkov was Principal Investigator for the excavations at Old Mobile, the Indian house near Old Mobile (1MB147), and the Dog River site. Many thanks, Greg, for giving me this opportunity and for supporting my dissertation research in so many ways over the years.

REFERENCES

BARNES SMITH, JULIE
   1995   Archaeological Investigations of Site 1MB161, Dog River, Mobile County, Alabama. *University of Alabama Museums, Office of Archaeological Services, Report of Investigations*, No. 73. Moundville.

BONVILLAIN, NANCY
   1993   *Language, Culture, and Communication: The Meaning of Messages*. Prentice Hall, Englewood Cliffs, NJ.

BROWN IAN W., AND RICHARD S. FULLER (EDITORS)
   1993   Bottle Creek Research: Working Papers on the Bottle Creek Site (1Ba2), Baldwin County, Alabama. *Journal of Alabama Archaeology*, 40(1–2):1–169.

DAVID, NICHOLAS, AND HILKE HENNIG
   1972   The Ethnography of Pottery: A Fulani Case Seen in Archaeological Perspective. *McCaleb Module in Anthropology*, No. 21. Addison Wesley, Reading, MA.

DRECHSEL, EMANUEL J.
   1994   Mobilian Jargon in the "Prehistory" of Southeastern North America. In *Perspectives on the Southeast*, Patricia B. Kwachka, editor, pp. 25–43. University of Georgia Press, Athens.

FULLER, RICHARD S.
   1991   A Ceramic Lingua Franca? The Origins, Attributes, and Dimensions of Historic Period Indian Pottery Tradition on the Northern Gulf Coastal Plain. Manuscript, Alabama Museum of Natural History, University of Alabama, Tuscaloosa.

GALLOWAY, PATRICIA
   1989   "The Chief Who is Your Father:" Choctaw and French Views of the Diplomatic Relation. In *Powhatan's Mantle: Indians in the Colonial Southeast*, Peter

H. Wood, Gregory A. Waselkov, and M. Thomas Hatley, editors, pp. 254–278. University of Nebraska Press, Lincoln.
   1995   *Choctaw Genesis, 1500–1700*. University of Nebraska Press, Lincoln.

HAAS, MARY R.
   1975   What is Mobilian? In *Studies in Southeastern Indian Languages*, James M. Crawford, editor, pp. 257–263. University of Georgia Press, Athens.

HAMMERSTEN, SUSAN
   1990   *Archeological Investigations at the French Warehouse Site, East Ship Island, Mississippi Gulf Islands National Seashore*. Southeast Archeological Center, National Park Service, Tallahassee, FL.

JURY, WILFRID, AND ELSIE McLEOD JURY
   1955   Saint Louis: Huron Indian Village and Jesuit Mission Site. Museum of Indian Archaeology, University of Western Ontario, *Museum Bulletin*, No. 10. London, ON.

MILLER SURREY, N. M.
   1916   The Commerce of Louisiana During the French Regime, 1699–1763. *Columbia University, Studies in the Social Sciences*, No. 167. New York, NY.

MOONEY, JAMES
   1900   Myths of the Cherokee. *Nineteenth Annual Report of the Bureau of American Ethnology*, Part 1. Washington, DC.

MOUSSETTE, MARCEL
   1997   French Colonial Mobile (1702–1711) Discussion. Paper presented at the 30th Annual Conference on Historical and Underwater Archaeology, Corpus Christi, TX.

ROWLAND, DUNBAR, AND ALBERT G. SANDERS (EDITORS)
   1929   *Mississippi Provincial Archives, French Dominion, Vol. 2, 1701–1729*. Mississippi Department of Archives and History, Jackson.

SAHLINS, MARSHALL D.
   1960   The Origin of Society. *Scientific American*, 203(3):86.

SHELDON, CRAIG T., JR., AND JOHN W. COTTIER
   1983   Origins of Mobile: Archaeological Excavations at the Courthouse Site, Mobile, Alabama. *Auburn University, Archaeological Monograph*, No. 5. Montgomery, AL.

SHORTER, GEORGE W., JR.
   1995   The Archaeological Site of Port Dauphin (1MB61): Its Role in the French Colony on Mobile Bay. Master's thesis, Department of Geography and Anthropology, Louisiana State University, Baton Rouge.

SILVIA, DIANE E.
   1989   Archaeological Test Excavations at Bienville Square, A Public Park in Downtown Mobile, Alabama. *Journal*

of Alabama Archaeology, 35(1):1–16.

1995 Aboriginal Ceramics. In *Archaeological Investigations of Site 1MB161, Dog River, Mobile County, Alabama*, by Julie Barnes Smith, pp. 84–91. *University of Alabama Museums, Office of Archaeological Services, Report of Investigations*, No. 73. Moundville.

2000 *Indian and French Interaction in Colonial Louisiana during the Early Eighteenth Century.* Doctoral dissertation, Department of Anthropology, Tulane University, New Orleans, LA. University Microfilms International, Ann Arbor, MI.

SILVIA, DIANE E., AND GREGORY A. WASELKOV

1993 *Roads to the Past: Phase II Archaeological Research and Testing Prior to Interstate 10 Revisions in Mobile, Alabama (Virginia Street Interchange to West Tunnel Interchange).* Center for Archaeological Studies, University of South Alabama, Mobile.

SILVIA MUELLER, DIANE E.

1995 See Silvia, Diane E.

SINOPOLI, CARLA M.

1991 *Approaches to Archaeological Ceramics.* Plenum, New York.

SMITH, MARVIN T.

1987 *Archaeology of Aboriginal Culture Change in the Interior Southeast: Depopulation During the Early Historic Period.* University Press of Florida, Gainesville.

STOWE, NOEL READ

1977 Archaeological Excavations at Port Dauphin. University of South Alabama, *Archaeological Research Series*, No. 1. Mobile.

VERNON, RICHARD, AND ANN S. CORDELL

1993 A Distributional and Technological Study of Apalachee Colono-Ware from San Luis de Talimali. In *The Spanish Missions of La Florida*, Bonnie G. McEwan, editor, pp. 418–441. University Press of Florida, Gainesville.

WASELKOV, GREGORY A.

1991 Archaeology at the French Colonial Site of Old Mobile (Phase I: 1989–1991). *University of South Alabama, Anthropological Monograph*, No. 1. Mobile.

1997 French and Indian Structures Revealed. University of South Alabama, *The Old Mobile Project Newsletter*, 14(Winter):1–2. Mobile.

1999 Old Mobile Archaeology. *University of South Alabama, Center for Archaeological Studies, Archaeology Booklet*, No. 1. Mobile.

WASELKOV, GREGORY A., AND BONNIE L. GUMS

2000 Plantation Archaeology at Rivière aux Chiens, ca. 1725–1848. *University of South Alabama, Center for Archaeological Studies, Archaeological Monograph*, No. 7. Mobile.

WASELKOV, GREGORY A., AND DIANE E. SILVIA

1995 *Final (Phase IIA) Archaeological Data Recovery at the Dog River Site, 1MB161 (ALDOT Project BRS-BRM-7500(10)), Mobile County, Alabama.* Center for Archaeological Studies, University of South Alabama, Mobile.

WOOD, PETER H.

1989 The Changing Population of the Colonial South: An Overview by Race and Region, 1685–1790. In *Powhatan's Mantle: Indians in the Colonial Southeast*, Peter H. Wood, Gregory A. Waselkov, and M. Thomas Hatley, editors, pp. 34–103. University of Nebraska Press, Lincoln.

DIANE E. SILVIA
19812 DATE PALM DRIVE
SUGARLOAF KEYS, FL 33042

Brent R. Weisman

Nativism, Resistance, and Ethnogenesis of the Florida Seminole Indian Identity

ABSTRACT

The Seminole Indians of Florida call themselves the "unconquered people," referring to the years of the Second Seminole War (1835–1842) when the U.S. Army failed to remove them to Indian Territory. Although the Seminoles have diverse origins and a deep cultural foundation in the prehistoric Southeast, their modern identity can be traced to this era of military conflict. Nativistic resistance movements aided by a strengthening of clan ties formed an adaptive response to the threat of cultural extinction and fueled the process of Seminole ethnogenesis. Using the archaeological record in conjunction with historical and anthropological sources brings a new perspective to the study of ethnogenesis by identifying material dimensions of Seminole resistance and unity. Specifically, the presence and absence of aboriginal versus European American pottery, the presence of military buttons at Seminole sites, and evidence for the ceremonial exchange of wealth by clans are examined as material evidence for the process of identity formation.

Introduction

Historical archaeology of Florida Seminole ethnogenesis in the 19th century provides an excellent opportunity to examine the complex processes of identity formation in an indigenous population of the relatively recent past by integrating method and theory from anthropology, archaeology, and history. Ethnogenesis is a cultural process in which sets of people create a new, shared group identity, distinct from other self-defined groups (Moore 1993; Hill 1996: 1,2; Whitten 1996:194). Seminole ethnogenesis, as presented here, is seen largely as a nativistic phenomenon influenced strongly by resistance to American domination. This research explicitly identifies nativism and resistance movements as potential ethnogenetic catalysts and suggests ways in which nativism can be observed in the archaeological record. The view presented here is heavily historical and microethnogenetic in scale and brings a new perspective to "rhizotic" models of ethnogenesis in which ethnic boundaries are seen as fluid, breakable, and capable of being reformed (Moore 1993:13). Resistance as an ethnogenetic process is given distinct treatment because it can be recognized archaeologically, specifically by the recovery of traditional native pottery at Second Seminole War period sites (ca. 1836) and the absence of imported European ceramics (Nabokov 1996: 43–44 for examples of Plains Indian and native Californian material culture used as elements of resistance).

This approach complements rather than challenges previous approaches to Seminole ethnogenesis (Sturtevant 1971; Sattler 1996) and adds an explicit material culture dimension as revealed by the archaeological record. Further, when placed near the end of the historical and cultural sequence of pan-Indian movements in eastern North America beginning in the 1760s (Dowd 1992:36,99; Starkey 1998:140,141), Seminole ethnogenesis is seen as a specific nativistic response to the threat of cultural extinction at the hands of a dominant power. Given the isolated geographical and cultural position of the Seminoles in Florida by the 1830s (Starkey 1998:163), their ethnogenesis was the last gasp of a pan-Indian impulse played out on a local level where unity was sought between distinct bands or towns rather than between various nations. Like other native peoples in postcontact North America whose political and ethnic identities reflect contact with an intrusive society (Moore 1987; Utley 1988:163; Hickerson 1996), the Seminoles had pluralistic cultural and biological origins (Stojanowski 2005) and were composed of groups speaking different languages and with distinct histories.

The period of the Second Seminole War (1835–1842) is proposed as the catalyst for Seminole ethnogenesis. This was a war of Indian removal undertaken by the U.S. government with the ultimate objectives of opening up Florida for white American settlement (Prucha

1988) and returning escaped black slaves who had sought refuge with the Seminoles to their southern plantation owners (Sprague 1848; Mahon 1967, 1988). In the organized resistance to the removal effort, the Seminole identity was given birth as a "creative adaptation" to violent change (Hill 1996:1). Even today, the Florida Seminoles proudly proclaim themselves to be the "unconquered people," referring to the fact that they are descended from a group of 200 or less who would not be moved despite the military's best efforts to subdue them. To the degree that modern Seminoles embrace their unconquered status, Seminole ethnogenesis is still underway and clearly demonstrates the "historical self-consciousness" (Hill 1996:2) that is part of the ethnogenetic process and was surely present among the Seminoles of the 1830s.

At some level, Seminole identity today is managed to keep outsiders away and to control and define contacts with the non-Seminole world. The identity of "unconquered people" has become part of what the outside world expects the Seminoles to be and has provided a set of symbols and dramatic historical tableaus of resistance (as expressed in battle re-enactments, for instance) that the Seminoles stage in part for the benefit of cultural tourism. This identity has also been deeply internalized and truly forms a basis for action (Whitten 1996:194) and the core of who they are as a people.

Cultural and Historical Background

The people popularly known as the Seminoles are divided between three federally recognized tribes. Because of this, they have distinct political identities. The Seminole Tribe of Florida has about 2,600 members, most of them living on the three largest reservations at Hollywood, Big Cypress, or Brighton, located in the Lake Okeechobee and Everglades regions of south Florida. The 500 or so members of the Miccosukee Tribe live on the Tamiami Reservation on the "40-mile bend" of the Tamiami Trail (U.S. 41) west of Miami in the Everglades. Descendants of the Florida Seminoles deported from Florida during the Seminole wars era today form the 12,000 member Seminole Nation of Oklahoma, centered in the Wewoka area of Seminole County (Howard and Lena 1984:18). There is also a small group in Florida known

as the Independents who have resisted federal recognition and pride themselves on maintaining a traditional identity and staying away from modern society.

Two related but mutually unintelligible native languages were spoken by these people and are still regularly used by people over the age of 60. The Miccosukee and most of the Seminoles speak Mikasuki, a language derived from the ancestral Hitchiti of the lower Southeast. The Brighton group of the Seminole tribe speaks Muskogee, or Creek Seminole, reflecting their origin in the Upper Creek region of central Alabama. The division between the Seminole and Miccosukee tribes reflects differing responses by groups of related people to the federal tribal recognition process rather than deep-seated differences in cultural or historical origins. Seminole people who were pressing for formal ties with the federal government officially organized themselves as the Seminole Tribe of Florida in 1957. Others formed a second group and held out for their own terms, officially forming the Miccosukee Tribe in 1962. There is no known credible evidence that these contemporary political divisions are continuous with distinct political entities of the 19th century, although the historic sources are laced with the term "Mikasuki" (various spellings) in referring to people from foundational towns around the Lake Miccosukee area east of present-day Tallahassee. Scholars simply do not know if the Mikasukis of history are the ancestors of today's Miccosukees exclusively and not also of the Mikasuki-speaking Seminoles. In this paper the term Seminole will be used to cover those people ancestral to both the contemporary Seminoles and Miccosukees.

Although political identities are important in understanding the complexities of who the Seminoles are in the contemporary world, politics alone is not nearly sufficient to gain an inside view of how these people think of themselves. Even today, Seminoles first reference their clan, with membership determined through the mother's line. Over the years, some clans have split to form new clans or have simply dissolved. The famed war leader Osceola was said to have belonged to the Eagle clan (Cory 1896), which no longer exists. Chicago ornithologist Charles Cory spent time with the Seminoles in the 1890s and noted the following clans: Rattlesnake, Alligator, Panther, Big Blue Heron, Little Black Snake, Bear, Wind, Otter, Little Yellow Bird, Wolf, Frog, Little Blackbird, Wildcat, and Deer (Cory 1896:preface). In 2003, eight clans existed among the Florida Seminoles: Panther, Snake, Bear, Wind, Otter, Bird, Deer, and Big Town. Traditionally among native people of the southeast, clan membership fixed the individual within a network of social expectations and obligations (Swanton 1928), although in recent years clans were most important in determining eligible marriage partners among the Seminoles (Garbarino 1972:75–78).

Beginning in the mid-18th century and continuing through the early-19th century, Creek towns mostly from the so-called Lower Creek region of central and southwest Georgia moved into Florida and established themselves in new economic and political networks with the Spanish and British overlords of Florida. The earliest migrations can be tied to direct Spanish invitation, in part arising from the colony's need to place yet another human buffer between St. Augustine's backdoor and the ever-encroaching English (Fairbanks 1974, 1978). Indian fear of British retaliatory attacks on their Georgia towns following the failed Yamasee War provided additional motivation to cross national borders and move within the shadow of St. Augustine (Swanton 1922:398).

By the 1760s, the Lower Creeks in Florida were being called Seminoles, a word derived from the Spanish *cimarron* and usually translated as "wild one" or "runaway." The term *cimarron* had also been used by the Spanish authorities in 17th-century Florida in referring to aboriginal refugee or fugitive groups of native Florida people deliberately avoiding Spanish contact (Worth 1998:2,44,121). In the context of the times it is likely that the term Seminole (the native pronunciation of *cimarron*) came to mean people who were living beyond the boundaries of established political control, apart from direct participation in the Creek Confederacy (Swan 1855) and free from obligatory and potentially dangerous political alliances with either the Spanish or British. The term Seminole is used with increasing frequency through the late-18th and early-19th centuries as a term of convenience for all native groups living in peninsular Florida. The American victory in the Creek War of 1813–1814 sent a major

exodus of Upper Creeks into Florida. For U.S. governmental purposes after 1821, these groups too became subsumed under the term Seminole (Figure 1).

Ancestral Creek Pattern

The early Seminoles were bearers of the Ancestral Creek Pattern (Weisman 1989:24–36) that they transplanted largely intact to their new settlements on the rim of the great Alachua savanna (Goggin et al. 1949), to the steep banks of the Suwannee River in its middle "big bend" region (Gluckman and Peebles 1974), and to the Red Hill uplands around the eastern panhandle east of present-day Tallahassee, centered on the large lake now known as Lake Miccosukee. The Ancestral Creek Pattern was a way of life based on (1) the community created by the relationship between associated matrilineal households and a central squareground town, together known as *talwa*; (2) a mixed farming and hunting-foraging subsistence; and (3) a complex of religious beliefs rooted in prehistoric Mississippian chiefdoms prescribing purity, balance, and order, but also almost certainly reflecting transformation and change resulting from European contact and demographic transition. Material correlates of the ancestral Creek pattern include settlement patterns emphasizing access to agriculturally productive soils, open range or prairie suitable for livestock grazing and connection to major transportation routes, and a pottery assemblage containing diverse vessel forms and styles, indicative of settled village life (Goggin 1964; Gluckman and Peebles 1974).

In part, the search for the origins of the Seminoles takes us to transformations in the ancestral Creek pattern, as geographical and political distance from the Creek heartland and proximity to the seat of colonial rule in St. Augustine bring new adaptive pressures to bear on the ancestral Creek pattern, de-emphasizing elements that had traditionally been important (the social and religious integration provided by the squareground, for example) and causing other elements to take on new importance or new contexts of meaning (the integrative importance of the *busk* ground, for instance, in the absence of the squareground town and apart from the camps or villages). The transition

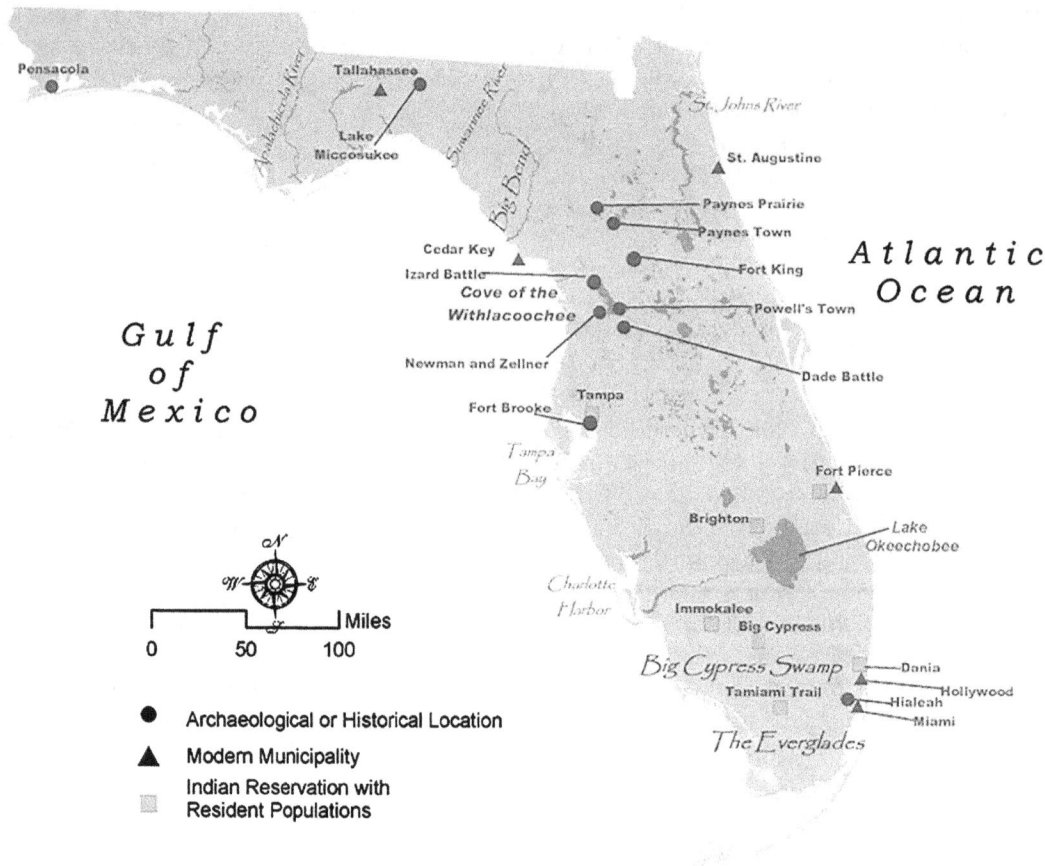

FIGURE 1. Second Seminole War sites and locations in Florida. (Map by Brent R. Weisman and Lori D. Collins, 2005.)

from Creek to Seminole began as soon as the first Creeks moved into Florida, but this should not imply that the process was gradual, slowly cumulative, or inevitably the result of cultural adaptations to new environments or to new economic opportunities such as herding cattle abandoned by the failed Spanish ranchos in the Alachua savanna (Paynes Prairie).

Seminole ethnicity has been seen as the result of political separation by the Florida bands from both the Creek Confederacy and Spanish and British colonial administrations. Treaties and trading policies were the primary catalysts for the cultural change that led to the emergence of a Seminole identity (Fairbanks 1974, 1978; Weisman 1989:5). A second perspective places Seminole ethnogenesis in an ecological adaptation model (Craig and Peebles 1974) in which selection pressures exerted on Seminole culture as it moved south into subtropical

niches forced the transition from Creek to Seminole. Others argue for strong cultural continuity between Creek and Seminole and suggest that the interactions between Seminole clans through the formation of busk groups associated with the Green Corn Dance after the Seminole wars in the 19th century contributed to Seminole ethnicity (Sturtevant 1971). In this view, Seminole ethnicity is defined by both persistence and change—persistence in the basic elements of southeastern cosmology, change in the expression of those beliefs through the group maintenance of a medicine bundle under the direction of a medicine man. A generalized and ahistorical structuralist variant of this approach sees the modern Seminoles as incarnate versions of archetypal southeastern Indians whose entire cultural repertoire is embedded in the Mississippian moundbuilding culture (Wickman 1999).

Perspectives from *Historical Archaeology:*

The view of Seminole ethnogenesis proposed here incorporates elements of all of these perspectives and acknowledges that ethnicity reflects a dynamic process unlikely to reveal itself archaeologically by the appearance of single traits or static artifact complexes. Archaeologists working with an archaeological record also claimed by modern descendant groups must be aware of the relationship between the material record and various forms of group self-identification. Archaeological research of ethnogenesis can be informed by ethnographic contexts, by first understanding in what ways groups of modern people feel themselves to be distinctive. On the other hand, archaeological research can independently yield the recognition of patterns in the archaeological record that can be linked to and tested against processes of ethnogenesis. Used in this way, archaeology can contribute original perspectives on ethnic formation, working from evidence that is largely lost to other fields of anthropological inquiry and beyond the immediate experience of living people. The extent to which living people can learn about who they are through the results of archaeological research is one measure of archaeology's value in the contemporary world (McDonald et al. 1991). Further, archaeological approaches to the study of Seminole ethnogenesis demonstrate the value of archaeology's contribution to the integrated study of the Seminole people and to the method and theory of anthropology.

A Stress Model of Seminole Ethnogenesis

Three processes were set into motion in Seminole society as cultural responses to the stresses of the Second Seminole War. These processes are fundamental to the genesis of the contemporary Seminole cultural identity. The archaeological correlates of these processes reveal ways in which archaeology can uniquely contribute to an understanding of Seminole ethnogenesis. These processes include (1) a rejection of European American cultural influences through the creation of a nativistic movement, (2) attempted equalization of power relations through the symbolic display of trophy clothing, and (3) strengthening of clan ties through ritual gift giving to the deceased.

Ethnogenesis as a transformative process does not take place in a human void or in the abstract. Cultural generation depends on people interacting with one another and communicating shared values about the symbolic meaning of the material world. Communication needs to be frequent enough and predictable so that people can pool their energies to form a common basis for action. Communication nodes can become formalized through communal ceremonial activities and through the regular use of routes of travel, such as roads, trails, or waterways leading to locations of trade. By maintaining trade relationships and participation in annual ceremonial events, dispersed bands of Seminoles were able to keep in contact with one another and build bonds of common identity. Evidence presented later will indicate the existence of viable communication networks during the Second Seminole War, the use of which accelerated and facilitated the process of identity formation during this period.

Archaeological Evidence of a Nativistic Movement

Nativistic movements among American Indian cultures as a response to rapid and dramatic acculturation are well discussed in the literature (Linton 1943; Wallace 1956; Mooney 1991). In the Southeast, the policies of Indian Agent Benjamin Hawkins in the early-19th century are often held responsible for stimulating the Creek nativistic movement (Nunez 1958:3–5), but less well-documented nativism almost certainly dates to the early years of the Spanish missions and may have had some role in fomenting mission revolts (Milanich 1978:65). The impacts of Tecumseh, the Shawnee Prophet, and the Prophet Francis on the development of a nativistic core to the Creek Red Stick movement are implicated in the literature (Wright 1986:161–179; Martin 1991) as precipitating influences on the Creek Civil War of 1814 (Starkey 1998). Tecumseh most likely did not visit Florida, but his message was brought to the Seminoles by leaders who attended his 1811 address at Tukabatchee (Saunt 1999:235) The influence on the early Seminole resistance movement of the Red Stick Creeks who survived the Creek War is also well known, principally through the actions of the legendary Osceola, himself of Red Stick ancestry and leader of a small group of Red Sticks within the Seminoles.

Direct documentary evidence of actual prophets among the Seminoles is largely restricted to mentions of Otulke-thloco, a Creek who migrated to south Florida's Big Cypress region in 1836 to take up his teachings of "witches and prophets" with the Seminoles (Covington 1993:100–101). Otulke-thloco, also known as the Prophet or the Big Wind, sharpened his spiritual abilities and his control over the Seminole leadership through great attention to ritual detail and his special knowledge of herbal cures (Sprague 1848:295,296,318). Osceola, although never described as a prophet, was believed by his followers at least for a time to have extraordinary spiritual power, which, in the case of the assassination of the Indian Agent Wiley Thompson, was said to have been responsible for drawing out Thompson's spirit to make him vulnerable to Osceola's bullets. It is known from the teaching of Tecumseh that the desired return to the old ways meant rejecting the ways of the white man in favor of traditional technologies and lifeways. Cast aside the plow and loom, cried Tecumseh, and return to wearing the skin of beasts (Nunez 1958:7).

The success of a nativistic movement's message depends on the ability of a people to recognize and respond to symbolic meanings of material culture. In Ralph Linton's classic words (1943:231), "what really happens in all nativistic movements is that certain current or remembered elements of culture are selected for emphasis and given symbolic value." Because the medium is the message, so to speak, and exists materially, researchers can reasonably expect that some aspects of nativistic movements can have archaeological correlates. The challenge is in identifying what specific categories of material culture are being symbolically manipulated because of the meanings given them within the dynamic of the acculturation process. This relies on in-depth analyses of both the archaeological and historical contexts in which the objects functioned. In southeastern Indian societies of the 18th and 19th centuries, European ceramics fit the criterion of a category of objects given meaning as symbolic expressions of the nature of the interaction between native and European American societies. The overall use of ceramics for social display has been amply documented in a variety of contexts, and, particularly as embedded in consumerism, is one of the main reasons that historical archaeologists are interested in ceramics (Deetz 1977:85–86; Majewski and Schiffer 2001).

The famed Philadelphia-born naturalist William Bartram spent nearly five years on the eve of the American Revolution among the southeastern Indians on a vast botanical collecting trip financed by plant enthusiast Dr. John Fothergill of London. Called Puc Puggy, the Flower Hunter, by the Seminoles, Bartram later went on to publish on Indian life as he saw it and provided a crucial benchmark for ethnographic studies of the Seminole, Creek, and Cherokee peoples (Bartram 1853, 1955; Waselkov and Braund 1995). When visiting a Creek chief by the name of Bosten, "young negro slaves" served him coffee in "china ware" cups (Bartram 1853:38) as one of many signs of wealth described in his later account. Bartram wrote at length about the "honors and distinctions" shown him by this man of "excellent character" to convince those with a prejudice against the Creeks (and presumably, other Indians) that they could in fact "be brought over to our modes of civil society" (Bartram 1853:38,39). Archaeological evidence from the Upper Creek Tukabatchee area of central Alabama indicates that by the 19th century "any native family would have possessed pearlware or whiteware plates, platters, saucers, serving bowls, and even teacups" (Knight 1985:180).

In Florida, similar evidence is found from Seminole sites dating from the last quarter of the 18th century through the first several decades of the 1800s. In this latter position is the site of Paynestown, attributed to the chief Payne (most likely Cowkeeper's nephew, and after whom Payne's Prairie State Preserve is named), with a date of abandonment around 1812. English and nonnative ceramics marking the site include banded and transfer-print pearlwares, salt-glazed stoneware, and lead-glazed earthenware, in addition to the familiar scatter of Chattahoochee Brushed sherds (Mykel 1962; Mullins 1978:78; Weisman 1989:77–78). Many sites throughout the sand ridge uplands of central Florida show this same pattern (Weisman 1989:69–77; Weik 2002).

Given the dominance of European ceramics in Creek-Seminole archaeological assemblages, it is striking to find a series of sites dating to the 1830s completely lacking in them but containing

FIGURE 2. Second Seminole War period Seminole pottery jar from the Cove of the Withlacoochee (Photo by author.)

plentiful native ceramics (Figure 2). These sites, which the author interprets as loosely aggregated clan camps, are located in the "Cove of the Withlacoochee," a freshwater wetland formed by the Withlacoochee River that sheltered the core of the Seminole resistance movement in the early years of the Second Seminole War. Military uniform buttons of types in service during the 1835–1842 period of the war provide dating (Weisman 1989:112–123). Based on military accounts, the abandonment of the villages most likely occurred after the first failed army invasions of the cove from January to March 1836 but prior to the more sustained penetration by troops in November. Initial occupation began perhaps before 1820 but was certainly well established before the outbreak of the war in December 1835. Archaeological surveys and excavations of these sites, among them Osceola's camp (known as Powell's Town), reveal a material culture based on native ceramics, glass bottles, iron tools and utensils, and firearms but lacking in the expected occurrence of European or American ceramics (Weisman 1989:121) (Figure 3).

At Powell's Town (8CI198), 96 sherds of Seminole pottery and 2 glass bottle fragments were recovered from Seminole archaeological contexts across about 1,200 sq. m of site area.

At the single component Newman's Garden site (8CI206), 564 Seminole sherds were recovered but no European American ceramics from an area of 36 sq. m. From the four discrete site clusters of the Zellner Grove site (8CI215), covering some 40,000 sq. m, 172 Seminole sherds were found, with European American sherds completely absent (Weisman 1989: 115,119,140).

Due to the constraints of war, it is possible that the supply of ceramics simply dried up, but documentary evidence indicates to the contrary, suggesting that the black market was kept very much alive by traders and entrepreneurs hedging their bets on the war's outcome. It is also unlikely that what must have been a vast ceramic repertoire across a number of sites was depleted at the same time and is absent in the archaeological record because it could not be restocked. The absence of European American ceramics from the Withlacoochee sites is best accounted for by proposing the existence of an undocumented nativistic movement among the Seminoles, a movement formed in direct response to the need to mobilize fervor for a difficult struggle and centered around one

FIGURE 3. Seminole War-era U.S. military buttons from Seminole sites in the Cove of the Withlacoochee: (top) "great-coat" brass button from Zellner Grove; (bottom) plain brass button from Newman's Garden. (Weisman 1989:118.)

of the more ostensible symbols of the white man's ways. It is further suggested that the sparse material inventory of Osceola's village at Powell's Town reflects Osceola's rejection of the trappings of white society. In the words of a captured Seminole, Osceola was "the most gentlemanly Indian in the nation—he don't take white folks things" (Laumer 1998:75). It is also significant that the Seminole speaker used the term "nation" in referring to the larger body of native people in Florida then at war with the United States, indicating the perception of some degree of unity (Moore 1987:12–14).

Glimpses of native behaviors recorded in military accounts provide further support for a nativistic movement in the early phase of the war, such as soldiers' scalps hanging on scalp poles (Rowles 1841), the importance of the black drink and other ceremonies (Rowles 1841; Sprague 1848), and one report (7 October 1836) by a "friendly" Creek brought in to negotiate with the Seminoles that "their prophets and witches had said that the Great Spirit was on their side" (Laumer 1998:60). Nativism was the first plank in the platform of Seminole ethnicity and is expressed in the archaeological record.

It is also important to ask if the ethnogenesis of the so-called Black Seminoles will be evidenced in the archaeological record in the same way as it is for the Seminoles. The Black Seminoles, escaped plantation slaves mostly from Georgia and Carolina, sought refuge after the American Revolution and the War of 1812 within the protection of the Seminoles deep in Spanish Florida beyond the reach of slave catchers (Wright 1986). Living in their own towns throughout central Florida, the Black Seminoles participated in a tributary relationship with the Seminoles, exchanging crops from their fields for a measure of security and material well being (Weisman 2000). Although the Seminole claim to them as property became a major flashpoint for the Second Seminole War, the Black Seminoles developed their own identity distinct from the Seminoles. The term Black Seminole itself has become highly contentious and has multiple meanings, depending on who is using it. At the core of the debate is the precise relationship between the blacks and the Seminoles. Were the Black Seminoles simply African versions of the Seminoles, seeking freedom and opportunity in Spanish Florida as the Seminoles had done (Noah 1995)? Were they essentially Seminoles, having been integrated into Seminole society by virtue of marriage and clan membership? In the political reality of the modern world, there are vested interests in the outcome of these questions. History provides no ready answers.

It is likely that the specific process of identity formation for the Seminoles and Black Seminoles would be distinct. Given the overall theoretical framework of ethnogenesis, each group of people would be activating its own symbols and giving them meaning within specific historical contexts. That each group would define itself partly in relation to the other is not so remarkable, given their mutual subdominant status in relation to the Americans and the mutualism of their own relationship. Different means for assembling identity should be expected, as Rebecca Bateman (2002) demonstrates in her examination of Black Seminole naming practices. The situation does become complex, owing in part to the interrelationship between the Africans and Seminoles and the transference of material culture. European American ceramics may have been given value as symbolic of the exchange between Africans and Seminoles and might have quite a different meaning to the Black Seminoles in the symbolic context of ethnogenesis. European ceramics might well be present at Black Seminole villages (Weik 2002) and absent at the contemporary Seminole villages such as those in the Cove of the Withlacoochee. Both groups might value the persistence of native-made pottery—the Seminoles because it reinforces traditional female roles, the Black Seminoles because it evinces some connection to or integration in Seminole society.

Symbolic Display of Trophy Clothing

Even as the Seminoles were eschewing pearlwares in their rejection of European American culture, Seminole warriors on the battlefield began dressing in captured U.S. military uniforms. Given their first message of nativism, this second message also makes sense to the Seminoles who believed they had not only gathered strength by returning to their roots, but they had the power to defeat whites on their own terms. Wearing army uniforms by Seminole warriors had tactical benefit by adding confusion to tangled battled lines on heavily forested battlefields (as recorded, for example, in the Battle of Camp Izard on 3 March 1836, [Laumer 1998:20]). The archaeological record further indicates that military buttons are found only in Seminole sites associated with Second Seminole War contexts. These include two village sites in the Cove of the Withlacoochee: the cemetery at the military post at Fort Brooke, where numerous Seminoles who died awaiting deportation were buried (Piper and Piper 1982); and the apparent burial of a Seminole warrior by his fellows in the top of a prehistoric midden at the eastern edge of the Everglades (Laxson 1954). The buttons, which include plain brass and General Service types and white metal, are from U.S. army and state militia uniforms.

The most direct explanation for the archaeological occurrence of the buttons is that the Seminoles present at the various sites were wearing the jackets to which the buttons were attached, rather than the buttons themselves being trade items for example. At the Fort Brooke cemetery, all of the military buttons (25 total) were found with adult burials, including that of a woman (Piper and Piper 1982: 144,132–198). Further, dead soldiers buried in temporary graves on or near battlefields were at times later discovered by burial parties to have been disinterred presumably by the Seminoles (Laumer 1998:15), suggesting one source of the jackets. Some of the men of Major Dade's doomed command, including Dade himself, were stripped of their clothing after the fatal ambush of 28 December 1835. Seminoles left them dead on the ground and exposed to the elements until late March 1836 (Laumer 1998:12–13). Military buttons or any evidence of military uniforms are extremely rare in aboriginal southeastern burial contexts, despite 100 years or more of contact between uniformed military of various colonial powers across the region by the early-19th century. A recent summary of 17 comparative burial contexts in the southeast from 1650 to 1850 found only one recorded case other than Fort Brooke and Hialeah of the inclusion of a military uniform with a burial (Fitts 2001: 187–192,189), this from a French-influenced burial in the Fort Toulouse vicinity in Alabama dating to 1700–1750 (Heldman and Ray 1975). The overall distributional pattern supports the conclusion that military buttons in Seminole

graves reflect the specific definition of symbolic power operating between the Seminoles and the U.S. military.

The Seminoles have a long tradition of wearing their wealth, continuing up through the elaborate patchwork clothing of the present day. Bartram (1955:214) observed that in the 1770s "predatory bands" of young warriors were plaguing the Florida frontier, dressed with "singular elegance, richly ornamented with silver plates, chains, and after the Seminole mode, with waving plumes of feathers on their crests" (Bartram 1955:206).

The archaeological record suggests that army jackets functioned in two contexts. When worn on the battlefield, they packed a double punch of tactical trickery and defiance. As personal possessions, they had trophy value—as a record of victory in battle and as a symbol of power. The cultural antecedent of this behavior may reside in the warrior trophy complex of the native Southeast in which scalps, heads, or other body parts were displayed as trophies by the victor (for reference to the historic Creeks in 1791, Swan 1855:280). The scalping part of the complex was still in existence during at least the early years of the Second Seminole War, and scalping poles adorned with freshly obtained soldiers' scalps were discovered by soldiers in several abandoned villages (Rowles 1841:116; Welch 1977). Another function of displaying enemy scalps may have been to placate the wrath of their ghosts (Swanton 1928:419,424).

It is probably the case that the symbolic importance of the trophy jackets was reinforced by a larger complex of cultural beliefs pertaining to protocols of war and warrior status. The core of these beliefs may have had considerable time depth in the prehistoric Southeast but were stimulated by the conflict of the Second Seminole War and perhaps took on slightly new forms and meanings. The process through which an ancient symbolic complex was revived, reinvented, and given new specific meaning in response to the demands of pressing conflict can be seen as one of the key elements in Seminole ethnogenesis. Clearly, the archaeological record alone is not sufficient to support this premise, consisting as it does of fewer than 50 military buttons recovered from several different contexts. When the archaeologist seeks to place the military buttons found at Seminole domestic sites and burials within a larger context of meaning, however, the archaeological record can be productively joined with historical and ethnographic evidence to yield new anthropological interpretation.

Material Evidence for the Strengthening of Clan Ties

Looking again at the Fort Brooke site (beneath the city streets of present-day Tampa, Piper and Piper 1982; Piper et al. 1982), associations of grave goods and personal possessions with groups of burials are seen that indicate the presence of patterned group behaviors on the part of the living. Analysis of the placement of the burials within the cemetery suggests that 21 of the identified 37 Seminole burials can be divided into at least 5 contemporaneous burial groups, the core of each being the burial of children (15 of the 21 burials were of children) (Weisman 1989:90–91). Three of the five groups contained burials of children under the age of seven, four of whom were buried with perforated coins, most likely strung on necklaces. Additional perforated coins were found with child burials outside of the defined groups, but no perforated coins were found with burials of people over the age of seven. Further, with the exception of one bodice piece found with an adult male, all iron cups, knives, spoons, other bodice pieces, and metal crescent gorgets were found exclusively with child burials.

The archaeologists who worked at the site, Harry Piper and Jacqueline Piper, saw the pattern of wealth disposal among the subadults as evidence of ceremonial exchange engaged in by a society under stress (Piper and Piper 1982:325; Piper et al. 1982). The original site report (Piper and Piper 1982:325–326) states,

> A system of ceremonial exchange which evolved among North American aborigines over hundreds of years whereby clan members donated grave offerings reflecting the status of an infant would normally help maintain social cohesion. A clan element that had previously made ceremonial donations to other groups may well expect an even greater repayment. A larger symbolic display would thus require the involvement of more clan elements thereby strengthening their obligatory responsibilities. By involving more members of society in a funeral and exchange network, social cohesion is enhanced. This social cohesion of larger groups would have been important at this stressful time in Seminole

society even though it was an obvious disposal of valuable and useful items.

This process of social cohesion has implications for the emergence of identity in those Seminoles deported to Indian Territory and for those remaining in Florida. Given the major importance of the clan as the dominant means of social, political, and ceremonial organization in later documented Seminole culture (and indeed up to the present day), that the burial groups were in fact clan groups and the burial behavior an expression of clan relationships also seem highly likely. The role of clan membership and the relationships between clans in southeastern Indian society long predated the Second Seminole War. The need to maintain the annual ritual of the Green Corn Dance among the Seminoles even during times of war also required the maintenance of the clan structure on which the ceremony was predicated. Using the tragic opportunity provided by the death of young children as a means for reactivating and strengthening the clan network might well have been one cultural response to this period of stress (Piper et al. 1982) and as such was an important contributor to the formation of Seminole identity.

Building Communication Networks

If the notion is accepted that ethnogenesis moved forward as a set of behaviors based on ideas in the minds of individual Seminoles, the circumstances that favored groups of Seminoles getting together to share and reinforce their bonds of common interest and identity should be examined. Certainly battlefields are important places where this can happen, especially given the premise that Seminole ethnicity emerged as a response to the conditions of war. The communication networks that would later serve the Seminoles so well took shape during the Second Seminole War as a tactical requirement for moving large groups of dispersed warriors to and from battlefields and in the coordinated movements of women and children away from existing village locations and into the swamps where approaching armies would be unlikely to (and rarely did) discover them.

Recent research on the historical archaeology of Seminole war battlefields calls into question long-held stereotypes about the guerilla nature of the war, fought opportunistically with few fixed battles and a lack of centralized leadership (Weisman 1999). In fact, the battles can be organized into classes of engagement that shared formal properties, among them selection of battle locations by the Seminoles that show consistent concern with the placement of their battle positions relative to the natural protections of forests and bodies of water, means of communication between battle positions on the front line, and identification of secure means of retreat (Butler 2001). On the Seminole side, combat behavior suggests both tactical execution and stability. At the siege of Camp Izard, for example, in March 1836, Seminole front lines were constantly reinforced from the rear. Recent archaeology suggests that stable Seminole battle positions can be identified at this battlefield (Ellis et al. 1997), and future work will be directed at identifying the archaeological battlefield signatures of the Second Seminole War. Seminole success in combat depended on the coordinated movements of bands of warriors under different (and equal) leadership, communicating with each other under adverse conditions across the vast interior spaces of peninsular Florida.

Locations where trade and exchange occurred provide another venue for communication. Evidence from various military documents suggests that goods and supplies taken in Seminole raids on towns, plantations, and from military sources moved across the Florida peninsula overland or through inland waterways and along the Gulf Coast in exchange networks among Seminole bands (Sprague 1848: 236,252,317–318; Sturtevant 1953:46–53; Carrier 2004). The military hoped to intercept large concentrations of Seminoles at suspected trade locations but rarely did. One gets the impression from the documents (many of which record the testimony of captured Seminoles) that Seminoles moved with relative ease between locations across central Florida from the Withlacoochee River east to the St. Johns River via Jumper Creek and the mid-Florida lakes, and from central Florida south to the Everglades and Big Cypress Swamp by routes east and west of Lake Okeechobee. In the words of one observer "constant intercourse was had between the bands living in these secluded spots, traversing from one to the other, as convenience and comfort required, without leaving a track behind" (Sprague 1848:252). These secluded spots also became sanctuaries for the annual Green Corn Dance, which was maintained throughout the war years (Sprague 1848:252,260,276,281,350, 397). The Suwannee River in north peninsular Florida also served as a conduit for commerce and communication from the Gulf of Mexico as far inland as the Okefenokee Swamp in what is now south Georgia (Sprague 1848: 224–225,412–413).

Dispersed groups of Seminoles could and did gather together during the course of the war, to form battle lines, to cleanse in the Green Corn Dance, to develop strategy and plot tactics, and to grieve their dead. This means that there were opportunities for social interactions above the family level, therefore providing the level of group energy needed to sustain a social movement.

Conclusion

Those Seminoles surviving in Florida after the war era (those people ancestral to today's Seminoles and Miccosukees), although physically dispersed into groups of small camps, continued to be held together by the threads of communication and interaction so vital to their cultural survival during the war years. The ethnogenesis of the contemporary Seminole and Miccosukee people involved a complex process of interaction between traditional cultural behaviors and stresses forcing cultural extinction. Traditional behaviors formed a repertoire for the creation of adaptive responses, resulting in the emergence of a new ethnic identity, subsequently reinforced from within and by external political and social developments. Historical archaeology of the Second Seminole War has an innovative role to play in discerning the integrated processes of Seminole Indian ethnogenesis because of its focus on the materiality of a cultural phenomenon.

All forms of evidence converge to implicate the Second Seminole War as the cultural watershed of the Seminole people (for published accounts of relevant Seminole oral traditions, Sturtevant 1954a and 1954b). This is not the same thing as saying that the Seminoles themselves unanimously credit the Second Seminole War for their ethnic origins, but their self-referral as "unconquered people" clearly reflects their pride in resisting military efforts to subdue and exterminate them. The Seminoles of today recognize that part of their identity in the popular mind comes from their reputation as warriors during the Second Seminole War and are now popularizing that image (Seminole Tribe of Florida 2003).

The origins of modern Seminole cultural identity are almost certainly more complex than is now understood, but the archaeological record contains at least traces of physical evidence of some of the processes involved. Examining the archaeological record by itself or any part of it in isolation would not sufficiently yield conclusions about Seminole ethnogenesis. On the other hand, a view of Seminole ethnogenesis as presented here has not come independently from historians, anthropologists, or from the Seminoles themselves. An integrated approach using history, anthropology, archaeology, and some knowledge of contemporary Seminole culture provides a more comprehensive understanding of how the Seminoles came to be Seminole than might otherwise be forthcoming.

References

BARTRAM, WILLIAM
 1853 Observations on the Creek and Cherokee Indians, 1789. *Transactions of the American Ethnological Society* 3:1–81.
 1955 *The Travels of William Bartram*, edited by Mark van Doren. Dover Publications, New York, NY. Originally published in 1791 by James and Johnson, Philadelphia, PA.

BATEMAN, REBECCA B.
 2002 Naming Patterns in Black Seminole Ethnogenesis. *Ethnohistory* 49(2):227–257.

BUTLER, DAVID
 2001 An Archaeological Model of Seminole Combat Behavior. Master's thesis, Department of Anthropology, University of South Florida, Tampa.

CARRIER, TONI
 2004 Trade and Plunder Networks During the Second Seminole War. Master's thesis, Department of Anthropology, University of South Florida, Tampa.

CORY, CHARLES B.
 1896 *Hunting and Fishing in Florida*. Estes and Lauriat, Boston, MA.

COVINGTON, JAMES W.
 1993 *The Seminoles of Florida*. University Press of Florida, Gainesville.

CRAIG, ALAN K., AND CHRISTOPHER PEEBLES
 1974 Ethnoecologic Change among the Seminoles, 1740–1840. *Geoscience and Man* 5:83–96.

DEETZ, JAMES
 1977 *In Small Things Forgotten: The Archaeology of Early American Life*. Anchor Books, Garden City, NY.

DOWD, GREGORY EVANS
 1992 *A Spirited Resistance: The North American Struggle for Unity, 1745–1815*. Johns Hopkins University Press, Baltimore, MD.

ELLIS, GARY D., R. L. DENSON, R. A. DORSEY, J. R. JONES III, AND J. E. ELLIS
 1997 The Archaeological Study of the Camp Izard Tract, Marion County, Florida. Manuscript, Gulf Archaeological Research Institute. Lecanto, FL.

FAIRBANKS, CHARLES H.
 1974 *Ethnohistorical Report of the Florida Indians*. Garland Publishing, New York, NY.
 1978 The Ethno-Archeology of the Florida Seminole. In *Tacachale: Essays on the Indians of Florida and Southeast Georgia during the Historic Period*, Jerald T. Milanich and Samuel Proctor, editors, pp. 163–193. University Press of Florida, Gainesville.

FITTS, MARY ELIZABETH
 2001 Two Eighteenth-Century Seminole Burials from Alachua County, Florida. Master's thesis, Department of Anthropology, University of South Florida, Tampa.

GARBARINO, MERWYN S.
 1972 Big Cypress: A Changing Seminole Community. Holt, Rinehart and Winston, New York, NY.

GLUCKMAN, STEPHEN J., AND CHRISTOPHER PEEBLES
 1974 Oven Hill (Di-15), A Refuse Site in the Suwannee River. *The Florida Anthropologist* 27(1):21–31.

GOGGIN, JOHN M.
 1964 Seminole Pottery. In *Indian and Spanish Selected Writings* by John M. Goggin; Charles H. Fairbanks, Irving Rouse, and William C. Sturtevant, editors, pp. 180–213. University of Miami Press, Coral Gables, FL.

GOGGIN, JOHN M., MARY E. GODWIN, EARL HESTER, DAVID PRANGE, AND ROBERT SPANGENBERG
 1949 A Historic Indian Burial, Alachua County, Florida. *The Florida Anthropologist* 2(1–2):10–24.

HELDMAN, DONALD P., AND R. CRAIG RAY
 1975 A Late Historic Burial in Montgomery County, Alabama. *Journal of Alabama Archeology* 21(1):80–87.

HICKERSON, NANCY P.
1996 Ethnogenesis in the South Plains: Jumano to Kiowa? In *History, Power, and Identity: Ethnogenesis in the Americas, 1492–1992*, Jonathan D. Hill, editor, pp. 70–89. University of Iowa Press, Iowa City.

HILL, JONATHAN D.
1996 Introduction. In *History, Power, and Identity: Ethnogenesis in the Americas, 1492–1992*, Jonathan D. Hill, editor, pp. 1–19. University of Iowa Press, Iowa City.

HOWARD, JAMES H., AND WILLIE LENA
1984 *Oklahoma Seminoles: Medicines, Magic, and Religion*. University of Oklahoma Press, Norman.

KNIGHT, VERNON J.
1985 *Tukabatchee: Archaeological Investigations at an Historic Creek Town, Elmore County, Alabama, 1984*. Report of Investigations, No. 45, Office of Archaeological Research, University of Alabama, Alabama State Museum of Natural History, Tuscaloosa.

LAUMER, FRANK (EDITOR)
1998 *Amidst a Storm of Bullets: The Diary of Lt. Henry Prince in Florida*. University of Tampa Press, Tampa, FL.

LAXSON, D. D.
1954 An Historic Seminole Indian Burial in a Hialeah Midden. *The Florida Anthropologist* 7(4):111–118.

LINTON, RALPH
1943 Nativistic Movements. *American Anthropologist* 45(2):230–240.

MAHON, JOHN K.
1967 *History of the Second Seminole War*. University Press of Florida, Gainesville.
1988 Indian-United States Military Situation, 1775–1848. In *Handbook of North American Indians, Vol. 4, History of Indian-White Relations*, Wilcomb E. Washburn, editor, pp. 144–162. Smithsonian Institution, Washington, DC.

MAJEWSKI, TERESITA, AND MICHAEL BRIAN SCHIFFER
2001 Beyond Consumption: Toward an Archaeology of Consumerism. In *Archaeologies of the Contemporary Past*, Victor Buchli and Gavin Lucas, editors, pp. 26–50. Routledge, New York, NY.

MARTIN, JOEL W.
1991 *Sacred Revolt*. Beacon Press, Boston, MA.

MCDONALD, J. DOUGLAS, LARRY J. ZIMMERMAN, A. L. MCDONALD, WILLIAM TALL BULL, AND TED RISING SUN
1991 The Northern Cheyenne Outbreak of 1879: Using Oral History and Archaeology as Tools of Resistance. In *The Archaeology of Inequality*, Robert Paynter and Randall H. McGuire, editors, pp. 64–78. Basil Blackwell, Oxford, England.

MILANICH, JERALD T.
1978 The Western Timucua: Patterns of Acculturation and Change. In *Tacachale: Essays on the Indians of Florida and Southeastern Georgia during the Historic Period*, Jerald T. Milanich and Samuel Proctor, editors, pp. 59–88. University Press of Florida, Gainesville.

MOONEY, JAMES
1991 *The Ghost-Dance Religion and the Sioux Outbreak of 1890*. University of Nebraska Press, Lincoln. Originally published in 1897 as Part 2 of the *Fourteenth Annual Report of the Bureau of Ethnology to the Secretary of the Smithsonian Institution, 1892–93*, by J. W. Powell, director, Bureau of Ethnology, pp. 641–1110. Smithsonian Institution, Washington, DC.

MOORE, JOHN H.
1987 *The Cheyenne Nation*. University of Nebraska Press, Lincoln.
1993 Ethnogenetic Theory. *National Geographic Research and Exploration* 10(1):10–23.

MULLINS, SUE ANN
1978 Archaeological Survey and Excavations in the Payne's Prairie State Preserve. Master's thesis, Department of Anthropology, University of Florida, Gainesville.

MYKEL, NANCY
1962 Seminole Sites in Alachua County. Manuscript, Florida Museum of Natural History, Gainesville, and copy in author's possession.

NABOKOV, PETER
1996 Native Views of History. In *The Cambridge History of the Native Peoples of the Americas, Vol. 1, North America*, Bruce G. Trigger and Wilcomb E. Washburn, editors, pp. 1–59. Cambridge University Press, Cambridge, England.

NOAH, BELINDA
1995 *Black Seminoles*. Noah Productions, Tallahassee, FL.

NUNEZ, THERON
1958 Creek Nativism and the Creek War of 1813–1814. *Ethnohistory* 5(3):1–47,131–175,292–301.

PIPER, HARRY M., KENNETH W. HARDIN, AND JACQUELYN G. PIPER
1982 Cultural Responses to Stress: Patterns Observed in American Indian Burials of the Second Seminole War. *Southeastern Archaeology* 1(2):122–137.

PIPER, HARRY M., AND JACQUELYN G. PIPER
1982 Archaeological Excavations at the Quad Block Site, 8Hi998. Manuscript, Piper Archaeological Research, St. Petersburg, FL.

PRUCHA, FRANCIS PAUL
1988 United States Indian Policies, 1815–1860. In *Handbook of North American Indians, Vol. 4, History of Indian-White Relations*, Wilcomb E. Washburn, editor, pp. 40–65. Smithsonian Institution, Washington, DC.

ROWLES, W. P.

1841   Incidents and Observations in Florida in 1836. *Southron*, p. 54ff. Manuscript, P. K. Yonge Library of Florida History, Special Collections, University of Florida Libraries, Gainesville.

SATTLER, RICHARD A.

1996   Remnants, Renegades, and Runaways: Seminole Ethnogenesis Reconsidered. In *History, Power, and Identity: Ethnogenesis in the Americas, 1492–1992*, Jonathan D. Hill, editor, pp. 36–69. University of Iowa Press, Iowa City.

SAUNT, CLAUDIO

1999   *A New Order of Things*. Cambridge University Press, Cambridge, England.

SEMINOLE TRIBE OF FLORIDA

2003   Guns Blaze at Fifth Annual Kissimmee Slough Shootout. *News from the Ah-Tah-Thi-Ki Museum of the Seminole Tribe of Florida*, Winter 2003:1.

SPRAGUE, JOHN T.

1848   *The Origin, Progress, and Conclusion of the Florida War*. D. Appleton and Company, New York, NY.

STARKEY, ARMSTRONG

1998   *European and Native American Warfare, 1675–1815*. University of Oklahoma Press, Norman.

STOJANOWSKI, CHRISTOPHER M.

2005   Unhappy Trails. *Natural History* 114(6):38–44.

STURTEVANT, WILLIAM C.

1953   Chakaika and the "Spanish Indians": Documentary Sources Compared with Seminole Tradition. *Tequesta* 13:35–73.

1954a   The Medicine Bundles and Busks of the Florida Seminole. *The Florida Anthropologist* 7(2):31–70.

1954b   The Mikasuki Seminole: Medical Beliefs and Practices. Doctoral dissertation, Department of Anthropology, Yale University, New Haven, CT.

1971   Creek into Seminole. In *North American Indians in Historical Perspective*, Eleanor Burke Leacock and Nancy Oestreich Lurie, editors, pp. 92–128. Random House, New York, NY.

SWAN, CALEB

1855   Position and State of Manners and Arts in the Creek, or Muscogee Nation in 1791. In *Information Respecting the History, Condition, and Prospects of the Indian Tribes of the United States*, Vol. 5, by Henry Rowe Schoolcraft, pp. 251–283. Lippincott and Grambo, Philadelphia, PA.

SWANTON, JOHN R.

1922   Early History of the Creek Indians and Their Neighbors. *Bureau of American Ethnology Bulletin*, No. 73, Smithsonian Institution. Washington, DC.

1928   Social Organization and Social Usages of the Indians of the Creek Confederacy. *Forty-Second Annual Report of the Bureau of American Ethnology to the Secretary of the Smithsonian Institution*, 1924–25, by F. W. Fewkes, pp. 23–472. Smithsonian Institution, Washington, DC.

UTLEY, ROBERT M.

1988   Indian-United States Military Situation, 1848–1891. In *Handbook of North American Indians*, Vol. 4, *History of Indian-White Relations*, Wilcomb E. Washburn, editor, pp. 163–184. Smithsonian Institution, Washington, DC.

WALLACE, ANTHONY F. C.

1956   Revitalization Movements. *American Anthropologist* 58:264–281.

WASELKOV, GREGORY A., AND KATHRYN E. HOLLAND BRAUND (EDITORS)

1995   *William Bartram and the Southeastern Indians*. University of Nebraska Press, Lincoln.

WEIK, TERRANCE M.

2002   A Historical Archeology of Black Seminole Maroons in Florida: Ethnogenesis and Culture Contact at Pilaklikaha. Doctoral dissertation, Department of Anthropology, University of Florida, Gainesville.

WEISMAN, BRENT R.

1989   *Like Beads on a String: A Culture History of the Seminole Indians in North Peninsular Florida*. University of Alabama Press, Tuscaloosa.

1999   Archaeological Perspectives on Seminole Indian Ethnogenesis. *In Indians of the Greater Southeast: Historical Archaeology and Ethnohistory*, Bonnie G. McEwan, editor, pp. 299–317. University Press of Florida, Gainesville.

2000   The Plantation System of the Florida Seminole Indians and Black Seminoles during the Colonial Era. In *Colonial Plantations and Economy in Florida*, Jane G. Landers, editor, pp. 136–149. University Press of Florida, Gainesville.

WELCH, ANDREW

1977   *A Narrative of the Early Days and Remembrances of Oceola Nikkanochee, Prince of Econchatti*. University Press of Florida, Gainesville. Originally published in 1841 by Hatchard and Son, London, England.

WHITTEN, NORMAN E., JR.

1996   The Ecuadorian Levantamiento Indigena of 1990 and the Epitomizing Symbol of 1992: Reflections on Nationalism, Ethnic-Bloc Formation, and Racist Ideologies, in *History, Power, and Identity, Ethnogenesis in the Americas 1492–1992*, Jonathan D. Hill, editor, pp. 193–218. University of Iowa Press, Iowa City.

WICKMAN, PATRICIA RILES

1999   *The Tree That Bends: Discourse, Power, and Survival of the Maskoki People*. University of Alabama Press, Tuscaloosa.

WORTH, JOHN E.
 1998 *Timucuan Chiefdoms of Spanish Florida*, Vol. 1, *Assimilation*. University Press of Florida, Gainesville.

WRIGHT, J. LEITCH
 1986 *Creeks and Seminoles*. University of Nebraska Press, Lincoln.

BRENT R. WEISMAN
DEPARTMENT OF ANTHROPOLOGY
UNIVERSITY OF SOUTH FLORIDA
SOC107, 4202 E. FOWLER AVENUE
TAMPA, FL 33620

H. F. Gregory
George Avery
Aubra L. Lee
Jay C. Blaine

Presidio Los Adaes: Spanish, French, and Caddoan Interaction on the Northern Frontier

ABSTRACT

Presidio Los Adaes was the capital of the Spanish Province of Texas for much of the 18th century. Named after the local Adaes Indians, a Caddoan group, Los Adaes was built in reaction to the French presence at Natchitoches, less than 20 miles to the east. The remoteness of Los Adaes, the lack of a French missionary effort, the willingness of the French to intermarry with both the Caddoan peoples and the Spanish, and the political/economic savvy of the Caddoan peoples were all factors that contributed to a Spanish, French, and Caddoan interaction characterized by cooperation, accommodation, and mutual support.

Introduction

Presidio Los Adaes (16NA16) is located in present-day northwest Louisiana, where it was occupied between 1721 and 1773. Named after the Adaes Indians, a Caddoan group, the site of Los Adaes is defined by a presidio, a mission, settlers' houses, agricultural fields, and roads. Much of the site is now owned by the State of Louisiana and is operated as a state historical site by the Louisiana Office of State Parks. Los Adaes is on the National Register of Historic Places and has also been named a National Historic Landmark. The presidio was called Nuestra Señora del Pilar de los Adaes, and the mission was called San Miguel de Cuellar de los Adaes. Historians and archaeologists follow the shorthand observed in 18th-century documents and refer to the fort, mission, and settlement as simply Los Adaes. Los Adaes was located about 20 miles west of Fort St. Jean Baptiste, a French post established among the Natchitoches Indians, another Caddoan group.

Presidio Los Adaes was hardly an exemplary military post (one inspection revealed only two operable muskets for 60 soldiers), and the mission had no living converts (the only baptisms of neophytes were *in articulo mortis*, or, at the hour of death) (Gregory and McCorkle 1981; Avery 1999). The French were more interested in trading than acquiring territory, and the Caddo Indians viewed the Spanish more as a source for material goods rather than spiritual edification. As a result, Los Adaes functioned more as a trading post and settlement than as a fortification and mission. When Los Adaes was abandoned in 1773, the settlement had a population between 300 to 500 people (Gregory and McCorkle 1981; McCorkle 1981, 1996; Perttula 1992; Avery 1999).

Archaeological investigations conducted at Los Adaes by H. F. "Pete" Gregory of Northwestern State University in Natchitoches, Louisiana, have yielded much information about the interaction between the Spanish, French, and Caddoan peoples in northwest Louisiana (Gregory 1973, 1980, 1982, 1984, 1985). In contrast to the exploitation and domination that characterized many of the earlier examples of prolonged contact between Spanish and Native American populations, the 18th century at Los Adaes witnessed a Spanish, French, and Caddoan relationship based, for the most part, on cooperation, accommodation, and mutual support. A key factor in understanding the interaction among the Spanish, French, and Caddoan peoples is the military strength of the Caddoan people. The Caddoans, who numbered upwards of 10,000 people (Swanton 1996:22–23), were allied with the Wichita, who, in turn, were allied with the Comanche (Barr 2002). The Caddo, therefore, did not need the protection of either the Spanish or French, and, in fact, it is very likely that the Caddoan people could have forcibly removed both the French and Spanish from their land. The Caddoan people invited the Spanish and French into their territory (Carter 1995), and as long as these European visitors behaved themselves, they were allowed to stay (Gregory and McCorkle 1981; McCorkle 1981, 1996; Smith 1995; Avery 1999).

The French set the tone of the European intrusion by establishing economic and social relationships with both the Caddoan groups and the Spanish. The French practice of unrestricted trade and intermarriage with both the Caddoan groups and the Spanish, and the lack of a French missionary effort, created a situation where each cultural group could freely adopt or reject traits of the other groups, without fear of reprisals. The Spanish had little choice but to follow the example set by the French, even though the Spanish would not trade firearms or alcohol to the Caddoan people. The Spanish, French, and Caddoan interaction was a cultural symbiosis whereby three ethnic groups were able to maintain their distinct identities while adopting certain elements of the other groups (Gregory 1973). This interrelationship is quite clear in the archaeological assemblage from Los Adaes. The large percentage of French and Caddoan artifacts recovered from Los Adaes clearly indicates strong economic ties among the Spanish, French, and Caddoan peoples.

Historical Background

Ever since the 16th century, Spain was unable to produce all the merchandise required by her colonies, and, therefore, the Spanish Crown would buy goods from France and other countries and then sell them in the Spanish colonies at a sizable profit. But in order to maximize their profit, the Spanish Crown would not allow the French to trade directly with the Spanish colonies. The early leaders of French Louisiana tried to establish trade relations with New Spain at Vera Cruz in 1710 but were rebuffed. Father Hidalgo, a Spanish priest working near the Rio Grande, wrote two letters to the French governor of Louisiana in 1711 that offered to introduce the French to potential Spanish trading partners with the understanding that the French would support the Spanish missionary efforts in this area. The Louisiana governor instructed Louis Juchereau de St. Denis to establish a trading post among the Natchitoches Indians on the Red River and then to go find Father Hidalgo near the northernmost presidio in New Spain—Presidio San Juan Bautista (Figure 1). In essence, the French had failed to establish trade relations with New Spain through the "front door" at Vera Cruz, and so St. Denis's task was to try the "back door," at Presidio San Juan Bautista (Avery 1999).

St. Denis left his post at Natchitoches in 1714 and within the same year encountered commandant Diego Ramón at Presidio San Juan Bautista (Figure 1). St. Denis's passport made reference to Father Hidalgo's letter, but it has also been suggested that the St. Denis and Ramón families were not complete strangers—it appears that they also had economic ties in Europe (Lemée 1998). Strangers or not, it was still against Spanish law for the French to trade directly with the Spanish colonies, and so St. Denis was placed under house arrest, held literally in the house of Diego Ramón. Within two years he had married the step-granddaughter of Ramón and was hired to guide the expedition to set up Spanish presidios and missions in response to his own trading post at Natchitoches. Diego Ramón's son, Domingo Ramón, who was the uncle of St. Denis's new wife, led the expedition (Gregory and McCorkle 1981; McCorkle 1981, 1996; Avery 1999).

The Ramón expedition set up two presidios (Dolores and La Bahía) and six missions (Purísima Concepción, Guadalupe, San José de los Nazonis, Espíritu Santo de Zúñiga, Dolores de los Ais, and San Miguel de Los Adaes). The mission for the Adaes Indians was located near modern-day Robeline, Louisiana. St.

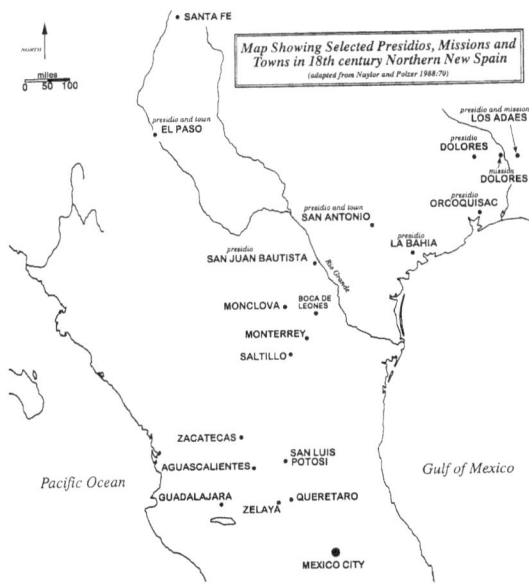

Figure 1. Map of 18th-century New Spain showing location of presidios mentioned in text.

Denis returned to his trading post among the Natchitoches, and Domingo Ramón became commandant of Presidio Dolores in modern-day northeast Texas. So at the onset, Mission Los Adaes was located between a Spanish presidio and French trading post whose leaders were related by marriage. This set of familial circumstances set the tone of Spanish-French relations for much of the 18th century (Gregory and McCorkle 1981; Avery 1999).

The only military conflict between the Spanish and French in eastern Spanish Texas came in 1719 when France and Spain were at war, and the French in Louisiana attacked the Spanish on both eastern and western fronts. On the eastern front, Spanish Pensacola was attacked with upwards of 1,200 men, but on the western front, six French soldiers led by Lieutenant Blondel marched out of Natchitoches and entered the Spanish mission for the Adaes. The priest and one of the soldiers were off visiting at Mission Dolores, which left a lay brother and one soldier at Mission Los Adaes. The soldier was asleep and was easily captured, but the chickens did not submit so readily to the French and made such a racket that Lieutenant Blondel was thrown from his horse. The lay brother escaped, and the French lieutenant made prisoners of the Spanish soldier and the chickens and returned with them to Natchitoches. Historians refer to this event as the "Chicken War" (Gregory and McCorkle 1981; Chipman 1992; Avery 1999).

In 1720, there was peace again between France and Spain, but the new governor of Spanish Texas, the Marqués de San Miguel de Aguayo, had already assembled an expedition to drive the French from east Texas. Rather than re-establish Mission Los Adaes at its original location, Aguayo chose to locate the new mission closer to Natchitoches, about one and a half miles east of the former location (Foster 1995). In addition, a presidio was built. The shape of Presidio Los Adaes is unique among colonial fortifications of the northern frontier. Most of the Spanish forts of the northern frontier were square or block shaped, while Presidio Los Adaes was hexagonal. Presidio La Bahia, built at the same time as Los Adaes, also deviated from the block shape, and was a 16-pointed star shape. The location at the Spanish/French border may account for the more elaborate design of Presidios Los Adaes and La Bahía

(Moorhead 1975:161–165). The architect's 1720 plan of the presidio at Los Adaes designates the dwellings for the governor, priests, soldiers, and officers (Figure 2a). The church is clearly shown; the warehouses are designated; and the streets and the defensive ditches in front of the stockade are labeled.

Aguayo's plans for a mission and presidio at Los Adaes reflected a clear understanding of the social dynamics necessary for a successful settlement. The two short-lived east Texas missions established in 1690 (Habig 1990:152–153) caused difficulties with the local Native American groups. Part of the problem was attributed to wandering Spanish livestock (John 1975), but mostly it was viewed as a result of the "evil conduct of the soldiers" stationed at the missions (Barker 1929:28). The Spanish soldiers were unmarried men, and they created problems with the Caddoan women. Aguayo realized that more of a family atmosphere was needed to establish successful settlements, and he therefore focused his efforts on recruiting married men—many of whom were in jail at the time, but those who had committed less serious crimes were favored over the more serious criminals (Yoakum 1855:74–76; Buckley 1911). Of the 100 soldiers who were stationed at Presidio Los Adaes by Aguayo in 1721, 31 had families (Foster 1995:155). It is estimated that by the 18th century, 25% of the population of New Spain was of mixed heritage as a result of intermarriage between Spanish, Native American, and African peoples (Moorhead 1975). A document from 1731 that describes the *casta* or (roughly) ethnicity of the soldiers at Los Adaes indicates that 50% were of mixed Spanish, Native American, and African heritage (Avery 1997).

By 1727, it was clear that the French had no intention of attacking Los Adaes, and a military inspector recommended reducing troop strength from 100 to 60. The inspector stated that even if there were 200 soldiers at Los Adaes, they still would not be able to defend against an attack from the French. The French at Natchitoches numbered less than 40 soldiers, but they could rely on upwards of 1,000 Native American allies, while the Spanish apparently were not counting on any Native American support. Los Adaes officially became the capital of the province of Texas in 1729, and many of the

A **1720 Architect's plan
for Presidio Los Adaes**

B **Portions of Joseph Urrutia map
of Los Adaes, drawn in 1767**

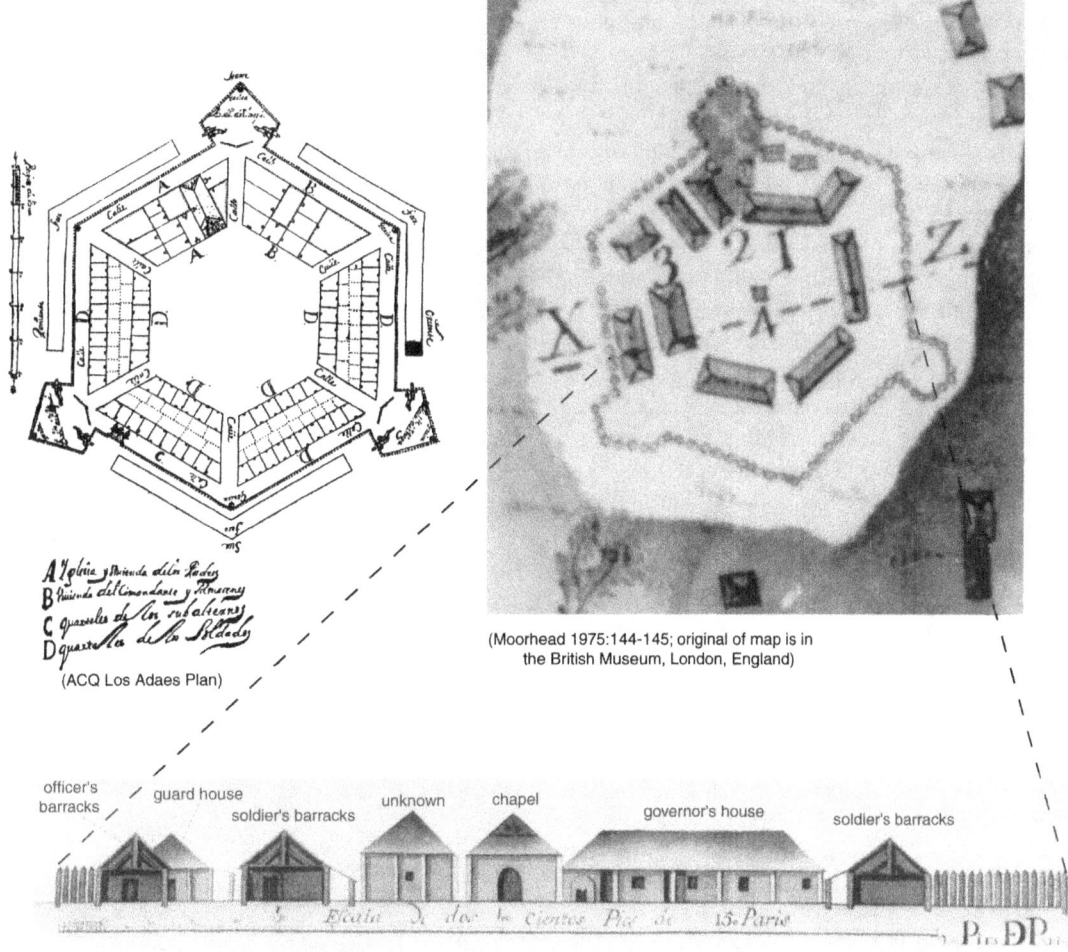

A *Yglesia y vivienda delos Padres*
B *Vivienda del Comandante y Almazen*
C *quarteles de los subalternos*
D *quartel.a de los Soldados*

(ACQ Los Adaes Plan)

(Moorhead 1975:144-145; original of map is in
the British Museum, London, England)

officer's
barracks   guard house
                    soldier's barracks   unknown   chapel   governor's house   soldier's barracks

Figure 2. Comparison of 1720 architect's plan (A) with portions of Urrutia's 1767 map of Presidio Los Adaes.

Texas governors were involved in illegal trade with the French. The historical documents tell of political, social, and spiritual interaction as well. Priests at Los Adaes would say Mass at the French post before permanent clergy were present, and troops from Los Adaes, accompanied by Caddoan Indians, went to the aid of the French when Natchez Indians attacked the post at Natchitoches in 1731 (Gregory and McCorkle 1981; Weber 1992:172–177; Avery 1999).

In 1762, near the end of the French and Indian War, France ceded all its holdings west of the Mississippi River to Spain, so that they would not fall into the hands of the British. Therefore,

the French fort at Natchitoches became a Spanish fort. In 1767, an inspection of the Texas forts was conducted to determine which forts should remain open now that the so-called French "threat" had disappeared. The inspection of Los Adaes resulted in a map of the fort, mission, associated buildings, agricultural fields, and roads. This map, drawn by Joseph Urrutia, is incredibly detailed and identifies the governor's house, chapel, guardhouse, and powder house inside the fort as buildings 1, 2, 3, and 4, respectively (Figure 2*b*). Profile and frontal views of these buildings are also part of the Urrutia map, and the architectural style is revealed as being more

French than Spanish (Figure 2b). The presidio buildings appear to represent examples of French *poteau en terre*, or post-in-ground construction with slats wedged between the posts and filled with *bousillage*—a mixture of mud and moss or deer hair (Gregory 1983:14). The gabled, shingled roofs show in profile the detail of king-post construction, a Norman tradition. This is a clear contrast to the flat-roofed adobe structures found at the other Spanish presidios of Texas (cf. Moorhead 1975).

The inspections of Los Adaes found that there was no longer a need to maintain the fort and mission, and an order was issued in 1772 to close Los Adaes. In 1773, the fort and mission were closed, and roughly 300 to 500 people left Los Adaes for San Antonio. Many of the people from Los Adaes, or Adaeseños, were not happy in San Antonio, and they left to form a settlement initially at Bucareli and later in 1779 at Nacogdoches, Texas. Adaeseños also were returning to Louisiana. By 1814 a village called Adaes was established within 2 miles of the abandoned Presidio Los Adaes (Gregory 1973, 1983; Gregory and McCorkle 1981; Pleasant and Pleasant 1990).

Archaeology at Los Adaes—Overview

The fort and mission of Los Adaes are located on hill spurs separated by an intermit-tent, spring-fed branch. The mission area has seen limited testing, and most of the archaeological work at Los Adaes has focused on the presidio and adjacent structures. Initial excavations at the site focused on site validation. Later excavations were conducted to determine content and extent of the site. Excavations in the area of the presidio include portions of the palisade wall and two bastions of the fort, portions of the governor's house, and three structures outside the fort (Gregory 1973, 1980, 1982, 1984, 1985) (Figure 3). Figure 4 shows the rough locations of excavated areas on the Urrutia map. These excavations led to the site validation for the National Register of Historic Places, a necessary step for acquisition by the Louisiana Office of State Parks. Most archaeological investigations at Los Adaes have been related to management concerns such as land purchase, development, and salvage, such as the recent excavation of stumps of storm-damaged trees in the area of the presidio (Avery 1995, 1996, 1997, 2001).

Variation in both status and ethnicity has been identified among the structures excavated at Los Adaes. Higher status ceramics such as Chinese porcelain, German stoneware, and decorated

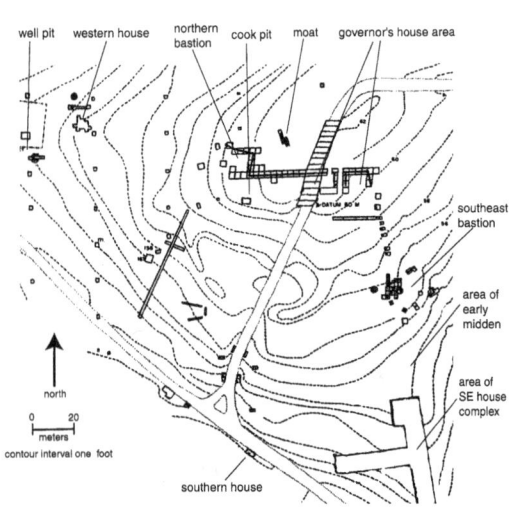

FIGURE 3. Archaeological excavations in the vicinity of Presidio Los Adaes.

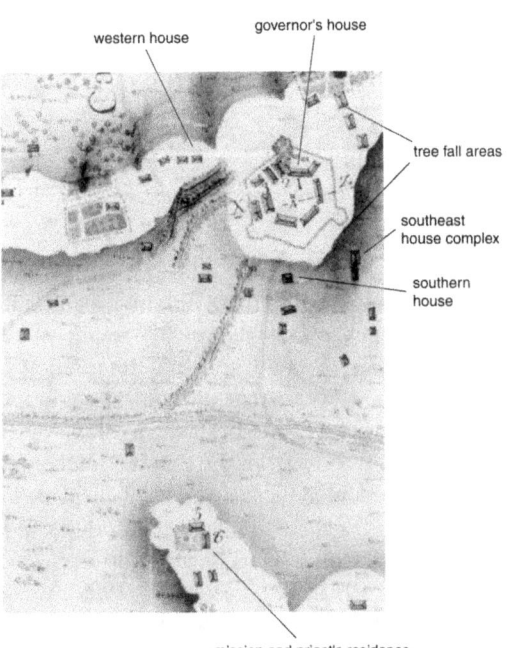

Figure 4. Excavation areas plotted on Joseph Urrutia's 1767 map of Los Adaes.

Perspectives from *Historical Archaeology:*

Caddoan wares are concentrated around the governor's house. The high proportion of French faience from one structure outside the fort suggests the presence of a French trader. Several activity areas have also been identified. They include a kitchen area, associated with evidence for gun repair and shot production just outside the northern palisade, and a probable blacksmith area, indicated by concentrations of slag in the southwest part of the fort or possibly just outside the fort (the location of the palisade line in this area has not been precisely determined).

The cooperative nature of the relationship between the Spanish, French, and Caddoan groups at Los Adaes is abundantly clear in the archaeological assemblage. There are roughly equal amounts of tin-enameled wares from France and Spanish colonial Puebla, located in present-day Mexico. Fragments of French wine bottles are well represented at Los Adaes, and most of the lead cloth seals are French. French trade knives and French and British firearm fragments occur with less frequency. British goods, including tin-enameled sherds, salt-glazed ceramics, and pipestem fragments occur in small amounts, as do German (stoneware) and Asian (porcelain) goods. Hispanic traditions are represented by Spanish horse gear, Spanish weaponry, basalt *metates* and *manos*, Spanish holy medals, a cloth seal from the Spanish port of Cádiz, and *higas* to combat the *mal de ojo*, or evil eye. The most dramatic non-Spanish artifact is the overwhelming presence of Native American pottery at Los Adaes. Caddoan pottery, represented by more than 30,000 sherds, dominates the Los Adaes ceramic assemblage. Faunal remains, mostly domesticates (cattle, pigs, horse, etc.), represent by bulk more than 60% of the Los Adaes collections (Lee 1986; Pavao-Zuckerman 1999). Analysis of floral remains indicates the presence of maize and beans and a variety of hardwoods and pine, along with peach tree and watermelon (Dering 2001).

Archaeology of the Presidio

Comparison of the architect's plan and the 1776 inspection reveal that construction of the presidio generally followed the architect's plan (Figure 2). Two notable differences between the plan and the Urrutia map include the powder house (not shown on the plan but depicted in the middle of the presidio on the Urrutia map) and the defensive ditch, which is shown on the plan but not depicted on the Urrutia map. Excavations of two bastions and the connecting palisade wall have verified the general accuracy of the Urrutia map, although the angle at the northeastern corner of the palisade is less than that shown on Urrutia's map (compare Figures 2b and 3).

Excavations of the palisade between the northern and southeastern bastions revealed a trench (50 cm wide, 40 cm deep), with post molds spaced no closer than 20 cm. The post molds ranged from 8 to 15 cm in diameter. Test excavations failed to locate the western palisade or southwestern bastion. Excavations of the defensive ditch just north of the northern palisade (Figure 3) revealed a ditch (6 m wide, 1.1 m deep) filled with cultural debris and capped with a layer of clay. It appears that the defensive ditch was indeed excavated with the initial construction of the presidio but was subsequently filled in with refuse and capped with a layer of clay before 1767, the date of the military inspection that produced the Urrutia map. It is not yet determined if all the ditches were excavated or if only portions were completed, then filled and capped.

Several activity areas have also been identified in association with the presidio. A possible kitchen area associated with evidence for gun repair and lead shot production was identified just outside the northern palisade, and a probable blacksmith area defined by concentrations of slag was identified in the area where the southwest bastion would have been located. A cook pit with large reconstructible portions of five Native American pots (Figure 3) was located near the governor's house and the northwest bastion, and a well was excavated within the southeast bastion. Another well with a lift or *noria* was excavated outside the western palisade area. A well and a small jacal (hut) were excavated adjacent to the southwest palisade, likely well outside the presidial walls. At least two other wells were located.

Excavations in the area of the governor's house were related to salvage along a 20th-century road (1930s) that cut through the presidio (Figure 3). Architectural remains were observed, including areas of burned beams and burned clay. One interesting observation relating to the structural remains of the governor's house was the presence of snipe hinges (Gregory 1973:100). This reflects a Spanish practice, and although Urrutia's 1767 drawing of the governor's house clearly indicates a French style *bousillage* construction (Figure 2*b*), it is possible that these French influences came later, and that the initial construction was more similar to the Spanish pattern (Gregory 1973:100). German stoneware, decorated Caddoan wares, and French tin-enameled polychromes were found in greater proportions at the governor's house than in other areas of the site and suggest that these items may have been higher status goods.

The area immediately west of the presidio was tested to locate the western palisade and other cultural features. Sixty-three excavation units (1 x1 m) were excavated at 12 m intervals along north-south transects spaced 20 m apart in a 4.6 acre area, including and adjacent to the hypothesized western palisade. Three trash pits and two wells were investigated, and another two wells were observed but not excavated. The western palisade was not located. Unfortunately, this area had been clear-cut just prior to acquisition by the Louisiana Office of State Parks, and it is possible that any remnants of the western palisade were destroyed; however, it seems more likely that the excavation strategy was too limited to find this section.

Excavation of Jacal Structures Adjacent to the Presidio

A French visitor to Los Adaes in 1763 described the structures in the area surrounding the presidio as "about 40 miserable houses constructed with stakes driven into the ground" (Pagès 1801). This French visitor appears to be describing jacal-type structures. Three structures that have been interpreted as jacal-type structures have been excavated at Los Adaes, and are located within 50 m of the presidio.

The first structure excavated just south of the southern wall of the presidio consisted of a shallow pit with a clay cap (Figure 3) (Gregory 1973:83–86). This shallow pit is located in the vicinity of a structure depicted south of the presidio on the Urrutia map (Figure 4). Similar pits have been observed at the Gilbert Site, an 18th-century *Norteño* site along the Sabine River in Texas (Jelks 1966). No post molds or hearths were observed, but the predominance of Native American ceramics and the presence of Virginia deer and freshwater mussel suggested a

temporary Native American structural depression (Gregory 1973:86).

Another structure associated with pit features was excavated near the southeastern bastion of the presidio (Figure 5). This structure appears to have two components. It is possible that

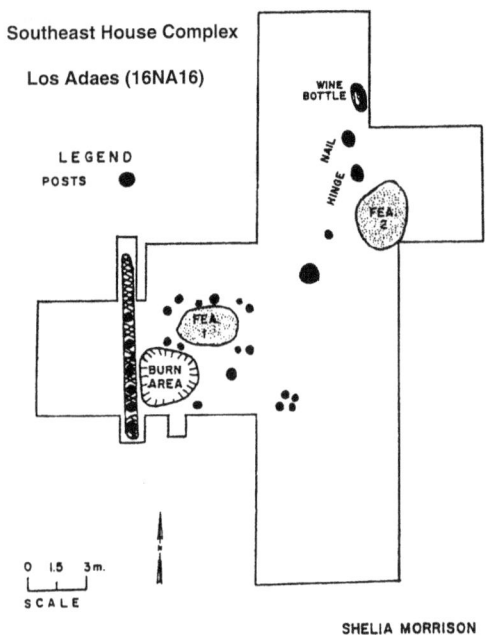

FIGURE 5. Southeast house complex, Los Adaes (16N16).

this structure may correspond to the rectangular house with an adjoining structure depicted on the 1767 Urrutia map near the bastion (see Figure 4). A high proportion of French tin-enameled sherds were recovered from an associated pit feature (Feature 2), and Indian pottery from Mexico was concentrated in this area of the site. It is suggested that this house might have been the residence of a French trader (Gregory 1984). This structure was originally interpreted as a jacal, apsidal in shape, oriented northwest/southeast, with a hearth encircled by posts located in the northeast corner of the structure (Figure 5). Clay had been placed within the interior of the structure along the west wall to mitigate the deep sand present at the location. Architectural items such as nails were present, although they were thinly scattered across the footprint of the building and not directly associated with any remnant structural elements. The complete absence of hinges, pintles, and *bousillage* suggests that the jacal was open-ended. The hearth, size of the structure, and artifact content suggested that the building was a detached kitchen combining Native American and European construction techniques (Gregory 1984:12–19, figure 3).

Another interpretation of this structure differs from the former in that the building is rectangular in shape, oriented east/west, and the hearth placed in the center of the building. The original interpretation of the west wall remains unchanged; however, a cluster of four small posts is believed to form the southeast corner of the jacal, while a single, large post denotes the northeast corner. Rather than a circle of posts around the hearth, the building plan suggests that pairs of posts were placed at each end of the hearth. These post sets, along with the central post placed in the hearth, served as interior roof supports for the jacal. A door or entrance to the jacal may have existed between the west wall and a small post located just south of the burned area.

Walls of the structure were open to allow heat to escape from the hearth during the hot season between April and October. The *poteau en terre* west wall protected the hearth from prevailing southwesterly winds and rain crossing the region during spring, summer, and early fall. It is suggested that some type of temporary covering and/or combinations of coverings was placed on the walls during late fall, winter, and early spring to protect the interior of the structure from inclement weather entering the region primarily from the north and northwest. Location of the suspected entrance on the south side of the structure would allow ingress/egress during the cold season without exposing the interior to inclement weather.

The third structure excavated at Los Adaes was located west of the presidio, and also appears to be depicted on the Urrutia map (figures 3 and 4). This structure also consists of a shallow depression surrounded by intermittent post molds, a central hearth, and contains post-1740 trash, including the French tin-enameled ware Rouen Polychrome, which dates after 1770 (Gregory 1985). Archival documents state that three French traders and their wives remained at Los Adaes after the presidio was abandoned (Avery 1998), and this structure may contain material from this post-1773 occupation. This structure clearly was a small jacal-type structure, even though it may have had French occupants.

Tree-Fall Excavations

In spring 1993, a severe storm possibly associated with a tornado knocked down close to 100 trees at Los Adaes. Some of the larger trees ripped up large portions of earth when they fell, many of them exposing 18th-century deposits. The excavations of the stumps of storm-damaged trees revealed that tree-falls with high artifact densities were located in the vicinity of structures depicted on the 1767 Urrutia map (Figure 4). The tree-fall associated with the structure adjacent to the road trace just north of the palisade had a higher proportion of glass trade beads and French wine bottle glass and seems to indicate commercial activity. The tree-fall located just south of the southeast bastion revealed a 25 cm deep midden dating to an early occupation of the presidio (Figure 4). Puebla Polychrome and Abó Polychrome were present, and the absence of Aranama Polychrome suggests a pre-1750 date (Deagan 1987:79–82,87). Native American ceramics again dominate, but very few French artifacts are present, suggesting that the early years at Los Adaes saw more Spanish interaction with local Caddoan peoples than with the French (Avery 2001).

Artifact Discussion: Ceramics

The ceramics are dominated by Native American wares, which number over 30,000 sherds and comprise almost 85% of the total sherd collection. Most of the Native American wares are plain; only 15% of the sherds show any form of decoration. Vessel forms include bowls, jars, and rarely bottles. Some bowls and jars were clearly for cooking (as evidenced by sooting and associations with cook pits). There are some Native American forms that show European influences. These include shallow, brimmed bowls and pitchers. Less than 1% of the Native American pottery is non-Caddoan. These non-Caddoan wares include Natchez and Choctaw sherds as well as lead-glazed sherds, presumably from northern Mexico or Texas.

Roughly equal amounts of Spanish, and French and British and/or Dutch tin-enameled wares are present. The Spanish tin-enameled wares are all from New Spain and include Puebla Polychrome (blue variety), Puebla Blue-on-White, San Agustín Blue-on-White, Huejotzingo Blue-on-White, Abó Polychrome, Aranama Polychrome, and San Elizario Polychrome. Guadalajara Polychrome and other unidentified slipped wares are present in small amounts. Spanish olive jars are represented by only one rim sherd and less than 50 body sherds. The French tin-enameled wares include Brittany Blue-on-White, Provence Blue-on-White, Provence Yellow-on-White, Normandy Blue-on-White, Normandy Polychrome, Moustiers Blue-on-White, Moustiers Yellow-on-White, La Rochelle Polychrome, Rouen Polychrome, and St. Cloud Polychrome. The less-expensive French lead-glazed wares are present only in small amounts at Los Adaes. There appears to have been a preference for the more-expensive tin-enameled wares. There are also small amounts of British or Dutch tin-enameled sherds. Hard-paste ceramics, including British stoneware, pearlware, and creamware, have also been recovered from Los Adaes and may be associated with French traders who remained at the presidio after it was closed.

The ratios of Native American to European wares for the western house (8.3 to 1), the area of the southeastern house complex (8.2 to 1), and the governor's house (9.9 to 1) are very similar; Native American ceramics are less at the southern house (2.0 to 1) and substantially more in the early midden area (24.7 to 1). The southeastern house complex is notable for the predominance of French (n=273) over Spanish (n=153) tin-enameled ware sherds.

Artifact Discussion: Glass

Bottles, drinking glasses, and stemmed ware are ubiquitous at Los Adaes. French wine bottles seem to predominate. Each of the soldiers at Los Adaes were supposed to have six horses and a mule. When one military inspection revealed that soldiers had much less than this number, the governor explained that his soldiers liked French wine and would trade one horse for one bottle of wine (Avery 1997).

Glass "sets" from buckles, earrings, and rings are also present. At least one "neck" bead from a rosary was found. Glass beads suggest the presence of the Indian trade and the advent of sewn beadwork at the site. Seed beads of several varieties were common. Large compound and simple construction "necklace" beads were found. These seem to include both Venetian and "Dutch" beads. Mulberry beads (in three colors) and large press-faceted and wire-wound beads seem related to necklaces. Seed beads from tiny to medium in size, included several sizes of Corneline d'Aleppo red beads; various tubular (mostly blue) beads round out the sample. The beads recovered from Los Adaes encompass all the variation seen on local Native American Sites (Gregory and Webb 1965).

Artifact Discussion: Metal

A wide variety of metal artifacts have been recovered from Los Adaes. Space limitations prevent discussion of all metal artifact categories; therefore, the following discussion is necessarily selective. A detailed description of all metal artifacts by Jay C. Blaine is currently in progress. Before discussing the metal artifacts, it is important to relate a management concern regarding the metal artifacts from Los Adaes. The marked deterioration of metal artifacts recovered from Los Adaes since the mid 1960s has been observed and attributed to variation in rainfall acidity by Blaine (1993). Metal artifacts, particularly iron, will oxidize until equilibrium is reached with the surrounding soil. If this equilibrium is changed, the artifact will oxidize to reach a new equilibrium. It is hypothesized that regular variation in soil pH can result in overall degradation and eventual destruction of buried metal artifacts (Blaine 1993). Measurement of rainfall acidity at Los Adaes since 1996 has demonstrated higher acidity rates during the summer and winter months, possibly caused by increased emissions from nearby power plants burning coal to produce more electricity during these months (Avery 2001). Studies of the effect of variation in rainfall acidity have generally focused on aboveground artifacts such as buildings and sculpture (NCPTT 1999). The effect of rainfall acidity variation on buried artifacts is largely unstudied.

Los Adaes was ostensibly a Spanish military post, but Spanish gun parts are not common on the site, and most came from a large trash pit/cook pit just outside the palisade. French gun parts are even less common, with an "MNI" of two, that is, while it cannot be said that all the French gun parts come from the *same* two weapons, they only represent the component parts of *two different* weapons. A single English firearm part has been identified. Spanish military buckles have been recovered, but only one Spanish military button has been recovered from excavations at Los Adaes; the rest are French. French cloth was much in demand in New Spain, and lead seals from bolts of cloth of French origin have been recovered from Los Adaes. One Spanish customs lead seal has been recovered, but most of the other lead seals recovered from Los Adaes are French; one is British. Only two French trade knives have been identified at Los Adaes; the Spanish seemed to have preferred their own knives, which had a straight cutting edge and curved back. The Spanish also preferred their own horse gear; all the horse gear from Los Adaes is distinctly Spanish. A caveat must be inserted here in that there are few, if any, recorded finds of specifically identified French horse gear from any colonial site in Louisiana. It may be identical to Spanish gear in many respects. Certainly the primary source of livestock and horses for French Louisiana was Spanish Texas (Blaine 1982, 1984, 1985).

Los Adaes Station Archaeology Program

Consolidating the Los Adaes collections and summarizing the excavations of Gregory's excavations, as well as compiling archival material related to Los Adaes, have been part of the activities of the Los Adaes Station Archaeology program. The collections and archival material are currently available to researchers. Aubra Lee's (1986) master's thesis analyzed the faunal remains from a large trash pit in the southeastern bastion and noted exotic wild fauna as well as corn, beans, and peach pits. His analysis suggests the population was well nourished. The analysis of the faunal material from the *jacal* structure near the western palisade area revealed an assemblage dominated by deer, unlike the faunal assemblages from the other excavated structures within and adjacent to the presidio (Gregory 1985). Shawn Carlson's (1994) dissertation, which included a study of ceramics from the Texas missions, included Los Adaes. Diana Loren's (1999) dissertation focused on the social order at Los Adaes, and Raymond Berthelot (2001) has recently completed his master's thesis that compared material culture recorded in the documents to artifacts recovered in the excavations. Barnet Pavao-Zuckerman (1999) of the University of Georgia analyzed faunal material recovered from Gregory's excavations of the presidial area and found no statistical difference between faunal remains recovered from the governor's house and the jacal structures located near the southeast bastion and southern palisade. Gregory Waselkov (n.d.) very graciously helped with identifying some of the French, British, and Dutch tin-enameled ware sherds in the Los Adaes collections.

Concluding Remarks

Los Adaes offers a wonderful opportunity for the study of culture contact in a frontier situation. The site is one of the best-preserved examples of Spanish, French, and Caddoan interaction in the area. Past archaeological investigations have been prudent, and although much has been learned already, there is still potential for addressing a myriad of research questions related to culture contact. The story of Los Adaes does not stop with the closing of the presidio in 1773, as descendents of the people of Los Adaes still live in northwest Louisiana and northeast Texas. The park facility at Los Adaes is currently in the planning stage for future development, and part of this process has required identifying and understanding the legacy of Los Adaes. Presidio Los Adaes will not be remembered for any military prowess, but, rather, the legacy of Los Adaes is the new economic and social order that was created during the colonial period, and which still exists today.

ACKNOWLEDGMENTS

The Daughters of the American Colonists, with the assistance of avocational historian J. Fair Hardin, facilitated the establishment of Los Adaes as a parish historical park in 1933. Robert Welch and Dottie Cooper were instrumental in starting the Los Adaes Foundation in 1972. Natchitoches Parish Police Juror Younger Stewart established a parish ordinance prohibiting unauthorized excavations at Los Adaes in the mid 1970s. Most of the archaeological investigations at Los Adaes from 1966 to 1979 were conducted as part of Northwestern State University field schools in archaeology, directed by H. F. Gregory. Members of the Texas Archeological Society also assisted during this time and include R. King Harris, Jay C. Blaine, and Jerrylee M. Blaine. Members of the Los Adaes Foundation are acknowledged for their tireless efforts to place Los Adaes on the National Register of Historic Places in 1978. In 1979, the parish donated the Los Adaes historical park property to the State of Louisiana and the Louisiana Office of State Parks. From 1979 to 1985, archaeological investigations at Los Adaes have been funded by the State of Louisiana through the Louisiana Office of State Parks. In 1986, the efforts of the Los Adaes Foundation, H. F. Gregory's archaeological investigations, and the Louisiana Office of State Parks culminated in the naming of Los Adaes as a National Historic Landmark. Beginning in 1995, the Los Adaes Station Archaeology Program was funded by the National Park Service and the State of Louisiana through the Louisiana Division of Archaeology, in cooperation with the Louisiana Office of State Parks and Northwestern State University. After 1996, the Los Adaes Station Archaeology Program has been funded solely by the State of Louisiana through the Louisiana Division of Archaeology.

REFERENCES

ARCHIVO COLEGIO QUERÉTERO (ACQ)
  1721 Concerning the Transfer of Missions from the Río San Marcos to the area of the Río San Antonio. Includes plans of the Presidio de los Adaes. ACQ reel 9, frames 1639-1647, at The Old Spanish Missions Historical Research Library, Our Lady of the Lake University, San Antonio, TX. Document original from Archivo Colegio Querétero, Mexico.

AVERY, GEORGE
  1995 *1995 Annual Report for the Los Adaes Station Archaeology Program.* Dept. of Social Sciences, Northwestern State University, Natchitoches, LA.
  1996 Archival investigations of the people of Los Adaes. *Southern Studies,* 7(1):65–88.
  1997 *1997 Annual Report for the Los Adaes Station Archaeology Program.* Dept. of Social Sciences, Northwestern State University, Natchitoches, LA.
  1998 *1998 Annual Report for the Los Adaes Station Archaeology Program.* Dept. of Social Sciences, Northwestern State University, Natchitoches, LA.
  1999 *1999 Annual Report for the Los Adaes Station Archaeology Program.* Dept. of Social Sciences, Northwestern State University, Natchitoches, LA.
  2001 *2001 Annual Report for the Los Adaes Station Archaeology Program.* Dept. of Social Sciences, Northwestern State University, Natchitoches, LA.

BARKER, EUGENE (EDITOR)
  1929 *Texas History for High Schools and Colleges.* The Southwest Press, Dallas, TX.

BARR, JULIANA
  2002 Beyond Their Control, Spaniards in Native Texas. Paper presented at the conference, "Social Control on Spain's North American Frontiers: Choice, Persuasion, and Coercion," sponsored by the William P. Clements Center for Southwest Studies, Southern Methodist University, Dallas, TX.

BERTHELOT, RAYMOND OCTAVE
  2001 A Comparison of the Archaeological and Documentary Evidence Relating to the Material Culture from Nuestra Señora del Pilar de los Adaes, an Eighteenth-Century Spanish Colonial Frontier Presidio. Master's thesis, Department of History, Louisiana State University, Baton Rouge.

BLAINE, JAY C.
  1982 Appendix 1. Analysis and Description of Armaments and Associated Items. In *Excavations 1981–82, Presidio de Nuestra Señora del Pilar de los Adaes,* H. F. Gregory, editor, pp. 110–144. Williamson Museum, Northwestern State University, Natchitoches, LA.
  1984 Los Adaes 16NA16 Inventory. *In Excavations, Presidio de Nuestra Señora del Pilar de los Adaes,* H. F. Gregory, editor, pp. 106–144. Williamson Museum, Northwestern State University, Natchitoches, LA.
  1985 Metal Artifacts. In *Excavations Unit 227, Presidio de Nuestra Señora del Pilar de los Adaes,* H. F. Gregory, editor, pp. 35–39. Williamson Museum, Northwestern State University, Natchitoches, LA.
  1993 Problems in the preservation and study of archaeological metals in East Texas. *Notes on Northeast Texas Archaeology,* 1:10–12.

BUCKLEY, ELEANOR CLAIRE
  1911 The Aguayo Expedition into Texas and Louisiana, 1719–1722. *The Quarterly of the Texas State Historical Association,* 15(1):1–65.

CARLSON, SHAWN BONATH
  1994 Texas beyond the Periphery: An Archaeological Study of the Spanish Missions during the Eighteenth Century. Doctoral dissertation, Department of Anthropology, Texas A&M University, College Station.

CARTER, CECILE ELKINS
  1995 *Caddo Indians. Where We Come From.* University of Oklahoma Press, Norman.

CHIPMAN, DONALD E.
  1992 *Spanish Texas, 1519–1821.* University of Texas Press, Austin.

DEAGAN, KATHLEEN A.
  1987 *Artifacts of the Spanish Colonies of Florida and the Caribbean, 1500–1800: Ceramics, Glassware, and Beads.* Smithsonian Institution Press, Washington, DC.

DERING, PHILLIP
2001 Los Adaes Botanical Analysis, 2000–2001 Project Year. In *2001 Annual Report for the Los Adaes Station Archaeology Program*, by George Avery, pp. 142–148. Department of Social Sciences, Northwestern State University, Natchitoches, LA.

FOSTER, WILLIAM C.
1995 *Spanish Expeditions into Texas: 1689–1768*. University of Texas Press, Austin.

GREGORY, H. F.
1973 *Eighteenth Century Caddoan Archaeology: A Study in Models and Interpretation*. Doctoral dissertation, Department of Anthropology, Southern Methodist University, Dallas TX. University Microfilms, Ann Arbor, MI.
1983 Los Adaes, the Archaeology of an Ethnic Enclave. In *Historical Archaeology of the Eastern United States*, Robert W. Neuman, editor, pp. 63–68. School of Geoscience, Louisiana State University, Baton Rouge.

GREGORY, H. F. (EDITOR)
1980 *Excavations: 1979—Presidio de Nuestra Señora del Pilar de Los Adaes Report*. Williamson Museum, Northwestern State University, Natchitoches, LA.
1982 *Excavations 1981–82, Presidio de Nuestra Señora del Pilar de los Adaes*. Williamson Museum, Northwestern State University, Natchitoches, LA.
1984 *Excavations: Presidio de Nuestra Señora del Pilar de los Adaes*. Williamson Museum, Northwestern State University, Natchitoches, LA.
1985 *Excavations, Unit 227, Presidio Nuestra Señora del Pilar de los Adaes (16Na16)*. Williamson Museum, Northwestern State University, Natchitoches, LA.

GREGORY, H. F., AND JAMES MCCORKLE
1981 *Los Adaes, Historical and Archaeological Background*. Williamson Museum, Northwestern State University, Natchitoches, LA.

GREGORY, H. F., AND CLARENCE H. WEBB
1965 European Trade Beads from Six Sites in Natchitoches Parish, Louisiana. *The Florida Anthropologist*, 18(3): 15–44.

HABIG, MARION A.
1990 *Spanish Texas Pilgrimage. The Old Franciscan Missions and Other Spanish Settlements of Texas 1632–1821*. Franciscan Herald Press, Chicago, IL.

JELKS, EDWARD B. (EDITOR)
1966 The Gilbert Site. A Norteño Focus Site in Northeastern Texas. *Bulletin of the Texas Archeological Society*, 37: 1–248.

JOHN, ELIZABETH A. H.
1975 *Storms Brewed in Other Men's Worlds: The Confrontation of Indians, Spanish, and French in the Southwest, 1540–1795*. University of Nebraska Press, Lincoln.

LEE, AUBRA LANE
1986 Floral and Faunal Analyses of House Remains at Los Adaes, Natchitoches Parish, Louisiana. Master's thesis, Northwestern State University of Louisiana, Natchitoches.

LEMÉE, PATRICIA R.
1998 *Tíos* and *Tantes:* Familial and Political Relationships of Natchitoches and the Spanish Colonial Frontier. *Southwestern Historical Quarterly*, 101(3):341–350.

LOREN, DIANA DI PAOLO
1999 Creating Social Distinction: Articulating Colonial Policies and Practices along the 18th-Century Louisiana/ Texas Frontier. Doctoral dissertation, Department of Anthropology, SUNY, Binghamton, NY.

MCCORKLE, JAMES
1981 Los Adaes: Outpost of New Spain. *Journal North Louisiana Historical Association*, 12(4):113–122.
1996 Los Adaes. In *The New Handbook of Texas*, Vol. 4. The Texas State Historical Association, Austin.

MOORHEAD, MAX L.
1975 *The Presidio. Bastion of the Spanish Borderlands*. University of Oklahoma Press, Norman.

NCPTT (NATIONAL CENTER FOR PRESERVATION TECHNOLOGY AND TRAINING)
1999 *Acid Rain and Beyond*. Compact disc. Explore the Materials Research Program, PTT Publications, No. 1999-15. National Center for Preservation Technology and Training, Natchitoches, LA.

PAGÈS, PIERRE MARIE FRANCOIS DE
1801 *Travels Round the World, Performed by Sea and Land, in the Years 1767, 1768, 1769, 1770, and 1771*. Translated from the French. J. Murray, London, UK.

PAVAO-ZUCKERMAN, BARNET
1999 Subsistence at Los Adaes (16NA16), Features 1, 2, and 3. In *1999 Annual Report for the Los Adaes Station Archaeology Program*, by George Avery, pp. 107–172. Dept. of Social Sciences, Northwestern State University, Natchitoches, LA.

PERTTULA, TIMOTHY K.
1992 "*The Caddo Nation*": *Archaeological and Ethnohistoric Perspectives*. University of Texas Press, Austin.

PLEASANT, RANDALL L., AND DARRYL O. PLEASANT
1990 The Adaes Village: A Nineteenth-Century Mestizo Village in Northwest Louisiana. Paper presented at the 1990 Caddo Archaeological Conference, Northwestern State University, Natchitoches, LA.

SMITH, F. TODD
1995 *The Caddo Indians: Tribes at the Convergence of Empires, 1542–1854*. Texas A&M University Press, College Station.

SWANTON, JOHN R.
    1996 *Source Material on the History and Ethnology of the Caddo Indians.* University of Oklahoma Press, Norman.

WASELKOV, GREGORY
    n.d. Identifications of selected French, British, and Dutch Tin-Enameled Ware Sherds in the Los Adaes Collections. Manuscript, Los Adaes Station Archaeology Program, Northwestern State University of Louisiana, Natchitoches.

WEBER, DAVID J.
    1992 *The Spanish Frontier in North America.* Yale University Press, New Haven, CT.

YOAKUM, H.
    1856 *History of Texas from Its First Settlement in 1685 to Its Annexation to the United States in 1846.* J. S. Redfield, New York, NY.

H. F. GREGORY
DEPARTMENT OF SOCIAL SCIENCES
NORTHWESTERN STATE UNIVERSITY
NATCHIDOCHES, LA 71497

GEORGE AVERY
DEPARTMENT OF SOCIAL SCIENCES
NORTHWESTERN STATE UNIVERSITY
NATCHIDOCHES, LA 71497

AUBRA L. LEE
EARTH SEARCH, INC.
PO BOX 770336
NEW ORLEANS, LA 7017785-0336

JAY C. BLAINE
TEXAS VOLUNTEER ARCHAEOLOGICAL STEWARD
1609 CLEARBROOK
ALLEN, TX 75002

TIMOTHY K. PERTTULA

Material Culture of the Koasati Indians of Texas

ABSTRACT

This article discusses the types of European trade goods and materials found at 19th-century Koasati (or Coushatta) Indian sites in Texas, particularly those from the Carl Matthews site (41PK2) in the Trinity River basin in southeast Texas. Discovered by an archaeologist from the University of Texas in 1933, the Carl Matthews site appears to have been occupied ca. 1820–1835 by the Koasati Indians, immigrants from Alabama and Georgia who had first moved into the Spanish province of Texas around 1800. Carl Matthews may be the Upper Village of the Koasati visited in 1831 by Jose Francisco y Madero, a land commissioner for the Mexican province of Coahuila y Tejas.

Introduction

When Mirabeau Buonaparte Lamar became the President of the Republic of Texas on 10 December 1838, he instituted the Republic's policy of Indian removal. Indeed, as Sam Houston, previous governor of the Republic of Texas stated, "the peace policy was the policy of Houston. 'We will kill off Houston's d____d pet Indians.' That was the new policy" (Williams and Barker 1938–1943, 3:451).

The implementation of this policy over the next 20 years precipitated many pitched battles between the Republic and Indian groups within its boundaries, either those native to the Republic (such as the Hasinai Caddo) or comparative newcomers (such as the Cherokee and Kickapoo), driving them out of east Texas by 1840 and then completely out of Texas by 1860 (Murry 1992). The Alibamu (or Alabama) and Koasati (Coushatta) tribes, who had moved into Spanish Texas as early as the 1790s to settle, were the only east Texas Indian tribe permitted to remain in the Republic and, later, State of Texas. Following a considerable struggle after 1840 for land rights, the Alibamu and Koasati now live on a 4,351-acre reservation in Polk County, Texas (Martin 1974).

While Lamar's presidency was characterized by a general intolerance towards Native Americans in Texas, he held the Koasati and Alibamu in high regard, opposing their removal. In a 12 November 1839 message to the Fourth Congress of the Republic of Texas, Lamar stated:

> To the Coshattis and Alabamas, who seem to have some equitable claims upon the country for the protection of their property and persons, the hand of friendship has been extended, with a promise that they shall not be interrupted in the peaceful enjoyment of their possessions, so long as they continue the same amicable relations towards the Govt. which they have hitherto preserved (Smither 1931, 1:11–12).

Gelo and Morales (1992:i), Martin (1967:40, 44), and Smither (1932:95–96), among others, discuss the unique circumstances that contributed towards why the Alibamu and Koasati were not removed from Texas when all other Native Americans were forced to move. All agree that their physical and social isolation in the Big Thicket of southeast Texas was important in limiting contact with Anglo-American Texans, as it was in maintaining their language and kinship systems or other aspects of their traditional culture. Certainly, these characteristics should be reflected in the early 19th-century archaeology of the Koasati and Alibamu.

Of equal importance was the strong tribal leadership between the 1830s and 1850s of chiefs such as Long King, Colita, and Antone during this crucial period in their history. Martin (1967:40) aptly points out how the tribes "refused to use force against the white settlers." Rather, they exercised considerable diplomacy, after the fashion of the Texan government, in vigilantly writing petitions and memorials to Presidents Sam Houston and Mirabeau Lamar, and to various governors of Texas, requesting lands for reservations. In 1854, with the support of local Anglo-American residents, the State of Texas purchased 1,280 acres for the Alibamu and Koasati (Smither 1932:98).

Perspective on Native History

Studying the 19th-century archaeology and ethnohistory of the Koasati and Alibamu provides an excellent opportunity to document their heritage in

Texas. Furthermore, to examine certain dimensions of native history of these Native American groups that have been overlooked or unmentioned in standard histories of Texas (e.g., such as the role of Native Americans in the development of political and economic relationships in the Province and Republic of Texas) is a pathway to a fuller understanding of the diverse cultural, economic, social, and political lifeways of Native Americans, Euroamericans (principally the Spanish and French of colonial Texas), and Anglo-Americans in the late 18th and early 19th centuries in the state (e.g., Murry 1992; Perttula 1993a). The European trade goods discussed here, from an early 19th-century Koasati site in Polk County, Texas, illustrate the extent of cultural contacts between Euroamericans, Texans, and the Alibamu-Koasati from an archaeological perspective.

Cultural Context

From at least the early 1700s the Alibamu and Koasati had lived along the Alabama River and its main tributaries, the Coosa and Tallapoosa rivers, in east-central Alabama. They were important members of the Creek Indian confederacy, but maintained their separate ethnic, linguistic, and social identity while part of the confederacy (Martin 1974; Wright 1990). Their support for the French and Spanish led many of the more traditional members of the Alibamu and Koasati to choose resettlement in Louisiana, and then Texas, rather than to associate with the British and American traders and settlers who moved into Creek territory after the French and Indian War, which ended in 1763, and the American Revolution (Green 1982:28–33; Kniffen et al. 1987).

The area was not totally unknown to the two tribes. Creek Indian Agency letters indicate that movements beyond the Mississippi River were common in the late 18th century, but intensified after the Creek Wars of 1813–1814 (Wright 1990). For example, Alexander McGillivray, a Koasati of the Wind Clan, who became the most prominent Creek tribal leader between 1783 and 1793, and his brother-in-law, Le Clerc de Milfort, supposedly had visited the upper Red River in Louisiana as early as 1781 as part of a seasonal hunting foray (Flores 1977; Wright 1990:283–284).

The decision to move was not an easy one to make, for it meant having to decide between associating with the Americans, or as the Creek Oche Haujo commented in 1804, associating with "the wild beasts of the forests, and in the latter case we must fly our country and go to the wilds of the west" (Hawkins 1916:477). Most of the Creeks in the confederacy chose to remain in Alabama and Georgia, where they stayed until the 1830s when they were removed to Indian Territory by the federal government under President Andrew Jackson (Green 1982).

Between ca. 1803 and 1810 Alibamu and Koasati villages and paths had been established on the Red River in Louisiana, and throughout the lower Sabine, Neches, and Trinity river valleys in Texas (Abel 1907:95–96). By the 1820s the main settlements of the Koasati and Alibamu had moved into the Big Thicket country on the Neches and Trinity rivers (Martin 1974; Flores 1977).

In 1831, Jose Francisco y Madero, a land commissioner for the Mexican province of Coahuila y Tejas, visited the Alibamu and Koasati villages on the Trinity and Neches rivers some distance below the El Camino Real crossing of those streams (Bexar Archives 1831). He was to gather information for the Mexican government on the Alibamu and Koasati petition for permanent lands in the province. Contemporary maps, such as Stephen F. Austin's 1822 map (Figure 1), and descriptions of the locations of the villages place the Upper Village (or Long King's village) of the Koasati in the same area as the Carl Matthews archaeological site in Polk County, Texas (Martin 1967:Map 2). This location is on a tributary to the Trinity River where Battise's, Colita's, and Long Tom's traces intersected with Long King's trace; Martin (1967:Map 2) ground-truthed the modern locations of these 19th-century Alibamu and Koasati trails. Long King's trace was one of the main Alibamu and Koasati trails from the important trading post at Nacogdoches to San Felipe de Austin or Washington-on-the-Brazos, the early capital of the Republic of Texas on the Brazos River.

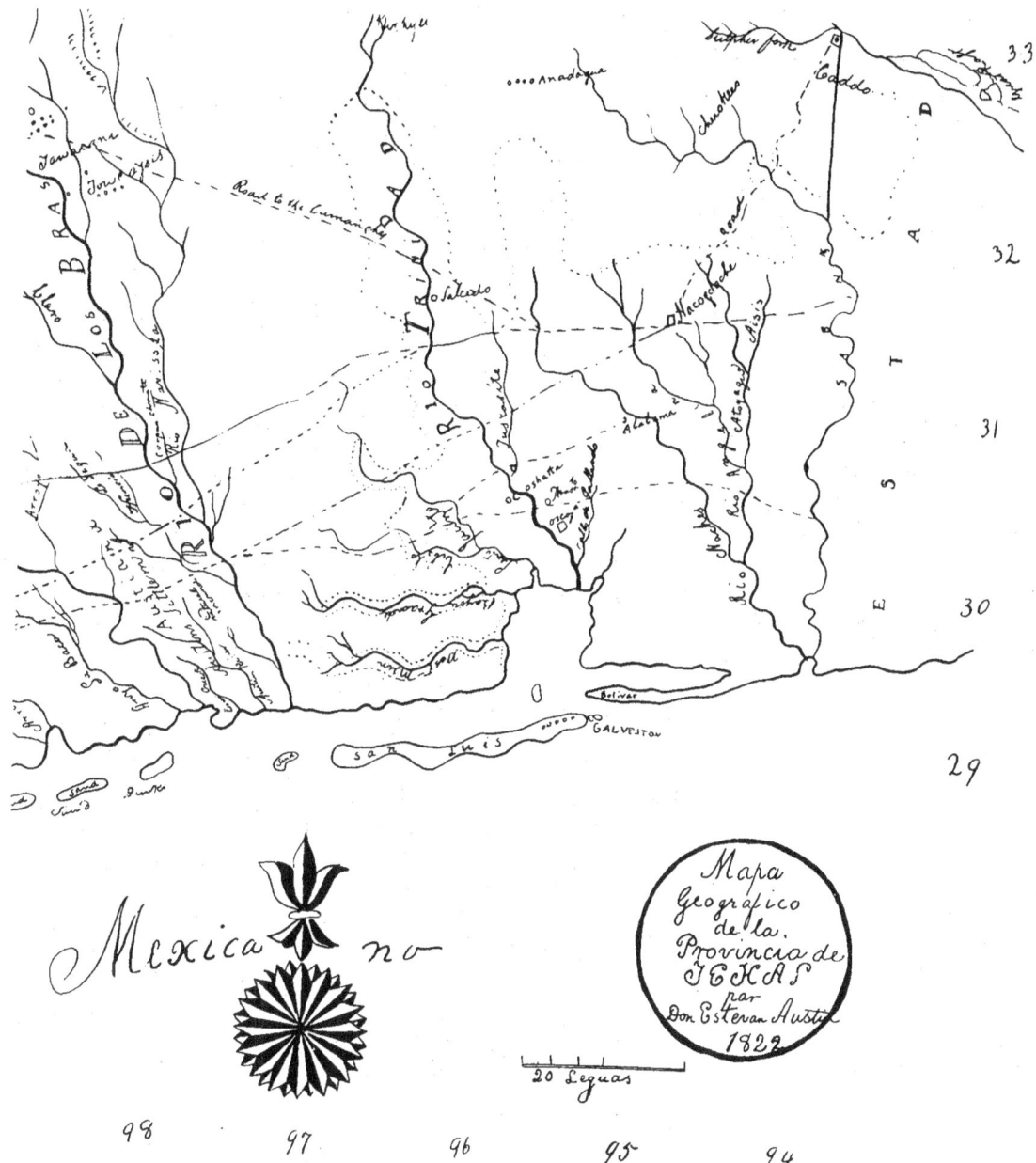

FIGURE 1. Detail of *Mapa Geografico de la Provincia de Tehas par Estevan Austin*, 1822. (Courtesy of Barker Texas History Center, University of Texas, E. C. Barker Collection.)

According to Madero (Bexar Archives 1831), the Koasati lived in two nearby villages on the east bank of the Trinity River. Long King was their principal chief or *mico*, along with Nekimapa and Keleite (known to the Texas Republic as the respected Koasati chief Colita), and lived in the Upper Village. Madero's census listed 120 families in the two villages, along with 82 single men and 104 single women. They had 25 solidly constructed houses while the rest were described by him as "of inferior construction." The Upper Village also had a "large house destined to religious cult"; this was undoubtedly the Koasati temple used for religious ceremonies such as the *posketa* or *bosketa,* the celebration of the first-fruits or Green Corn harvests.

The three Alibamu villages (Peachtree, Fenced-in, and Cane's Island) were not far apart on the west bank of the Neches River. Under *micos* Talustah and Oppaya, the villages had 103 families, 100 single men, and 64 unmarried women living in 69 wood or log houses and other "inferior" structures. Among the Alibamu villages were two large wood houses or temples.

The types of houses built by the Alibamu and Koasati in the 19th century included: rectangular log cabins fashioned from cypress or cedar frames, with mud-cat chimneys, that were used in the summer months; and circular houses built with wood, cane, and clay chinking, for winter use (Flores 1977:61). The latter houses may be those Madero deemed of poor construction. Both types of houses are likely present at the Carl Matthews site.

Open plazas or yards were probably present between the various groups of houses and the arbors and granaries, with trash middens downwind. Recent archaeological excavations at Koasati sites on the Red River in northwest Louisiana have also indicated that large earth ovens, trash pits, and corncob fire pits occur in or adjacent to the houses (McCrocklin 1990).

In compiling the 1831 census, Madero tabulated numbers of livestock among the Koasati and Alibamu. Between them, they had 1,100 cattle, several hundred hogs and horses, as well as yokes of oxen. *Mico* Long King alone owned more than a hundred head of cattle. By Texas statehood in 1846 almost all the livestock had been taken from the Koasati by Texan settlers (Williams and Barker 1938–1943, 4:55–56, 87; Winfrey and Day 1966, 1:72–74).

Both the Alibamu and Koasati were described in the mid-19th century as skilled agriculturists, growing corn, potatoes, melons, and beans that they supplied to "the main market at Nacogdoches, where they also come to sell their flocks," according to Jean Louis Berlandier in 1828 (Ewers 1969:47). Corn, beans, and peach seeds have been found on Koasati archaeological sites in northwest Louisiana (McCrocklin 1990).

They were also proficient hunters of deer, bear, and small fur-bearing animals, and the pelts, tallow, and oil were exchanged in American, Mexican, and Texan trading posts for a variety of goods (Williams and Barker 1938–1943, 3:349; Winfrey and Day 1966, 2:165; National Archives 1809–1821:ff. 22–23). Such goods included: blankets, wool hats, needles, calico shawls, vermillion, iron pots, tin cups, ribbon, flax thread, stitching thread, combs, iron knives, gunflints, silver gorgets, corn hoes, hatchets, shears, plates/saucers, brass, silk calico, rifles, cow bells, gloves, powder, lead, scissors, blue stroud, gun locks, butcher knives, linen shirts, wood axes, garters, beads, and tobacco. Many of these goods have been recovered in archaeological contexts on Koasati, Alibamu, and other 19th-century immigrant Native American sites (McCrocklin 1990, 1992).

The Carl Matthews Site

One of the more important Alibamu-Koasati archaeological sites presently known in Texas was discovered on the Carl Matthews farm by a local farmer in 1929 (Perttula 1993a). Flooding along Long King Creek eroded the creek bank and exposed two ceramic vessels that had fallen out of the bank. In 1933, A. T. Jackson, newspaperman-turned-archaeologist for the University of Texas, was taken to the site by a man from Livingston, Texas, who had purchased the vessels from the farmer (Jackson 1933).

Jackson explored the site that August and he described it as an "extensive Indian campsite" on a hillside above Long King Creek. He found quantities of pottery sherds in association with European goods such as hammered copper and brass, bottle glass, and lead musket balls. He collected these materials for the University of Texas, where they remained virtually unstudied until they were examined as part of archaeological research efforts on the historic Native Americans of eastern Texas (Perttula 1992a, 1992b, 1993a).

Jackson also carried out excavations at the Carl Matthews site to find the source of the pottery vessels. He did uncover a large area of charcoal and square nails along the creek bank that may have been from a burned log structure, but he abandoned the effort after encountering two coffin burials near the "campsite." In Jackson's (1933) opinion, these burials were most likely not Indian individuals, even though one of the burials was accompanied by a glass-beaded necklace of bead types commonly seen on Indian sites of the 19th century in Texas, Louisiana, and Arkansas (Hsu 1969; McCrocklin 1990, 1992). The glass beads have subsequently been misplaced at the University of Texas, and were not available for this study. Jackson did wonder whether "Catholic priests might have interred deceased Indians in wooden boxes. If so, this could possibly have been an Indian" (Jackson 1933:11). Research since Jackson's time has shown that Southeastern Indians such as the Creeks used coffins for burials as early as the 1760s (Gregory 1978; Brain 1988).

European Trade Goods

A wide variety of European and American goods have been found at the Carl Matthews site. Although few of the goods can be securely dated, their overall character suggests that these remains may date between ca. 1800 and 1830.

Wheel-thrown European Ceramics

Only eight small wheel-thrown European ceramic sherds were collected by A. T. Jackson at the Carl Matthews farm. These include a body sherd from a pearlware plate (as defined by Majewski and O'Brien 1987:119), one salt-glazed stoneware body sherd, and six coarse earthenware sherds from large jars.

Pearlware was a popular ware in North America between ca. 1780 and 1830. The distinctly blue tint of the Carl Matthews pearlware sherd suggests that its manufacture dates prior to the 1820s (cf. Miller 1980:18).

Salt-glaze was one of the most commonly used glazes for utilitarian stonewares during the late 18th and most of the 19th century in England and North America (Greer 1981). The glazing of the stoneware was done through the vaporization of common table salt that produced a transparent sodium silicate glaze after repeated exposure to the heated kiln during firing. The Carl Matthews salt-glazed sherd appears to be from a jug or crock, and has an unglazed or dry interior with a brown exterior salt-glaze.

The wheel-thrown coarse earthenware sherds are unevenly fired unglazed ceramics from two different vessels, both with orange to light brown cores, interiors, and exterior colors. Three of the sherds from the first vessel are weathered in appearance, and have relatively thin ($X = 5.17$ mm) vessel walls. The other coarse earthenware vessel is represented by three sherds from a large jar; the body sherds from the vessel average 14.0 mm in thickness.

Koasati sites with occupations dating after ca. 1830 in the Red River and east Texas areas tend to have large quantities of English- and American-made whiteware and porcelain saucers, plates, and cups, along with stoneware jugs and crocks, but English and American ceramics are rare on Koasati sites dating ca. 1800–1830 in the Trans-Mississippi South (Hsu 1969; McCrocklin 1990; David H. Jurney 1992, pers. comm.). The use of these English- and American-made ceramics, and the popularity of cast-iron kettles for cooking, led to the eventual replacement of native-made ceramics as culinary vessels by the 1850s.

Bottle Glass

Seventy sherds of mouth-blown bottle glass containers (cf. Jones and Sullivan 1985) are included in the European goods at the site. About 36 percent of the bottle glass sherds are patinated, but among the remainder black or dark green glass is most frequent (45.7 percent), followed by amber (11.4 percent), olive green (5.7 percent), and light bluish-green (1.4 percent). Air bubbles are common in each glass color, along with spiraling striations. There are two hand-molded and sheared lip finishes from wine containers in the bottle glass sample, and a third sherd of olive green glass has an unidentifiable molded pattern on the body. Container bodies of dark green, olive green, and amber color originally held wine and liquor, including ales or brandies.

Seven dark green bottle glass bases have bare iron pontil marks, and kick-up bases are present. The use of the bare iron pontil rod to hold the bottle while its manufacture was completed was common in manufacturing to about 1840; thus, at least part of the bottle glass assemblage predates 1840. Jones and Sullivan (1985:14) also note that until about 1820 dark green or ''black'' glass liquor bottles were the predominant type of container used in the liquor and mineral water trades. Dark green hand-blown bottle glass is common in the Red River Coushatta site material culture assemblages in northwest Louisiana (McCrocklin 1990), and at ca. 1810s–1820s immigrant Indian (Cherokee and Delaware) and Anglo-American sites in southwest Arkansas (McCrocklin 1992).

Four of the dark green bottle glass sherds have been chipped and worn to form handy sharp cutting and scraping tools (Figure 2). At least two of the chipped bottle glass tools have multiple worn, steep edges (Figure 2c–d) with morphologies and edge angles analogous to stone scrapers. Similar dark green chipped bottle glass tools have been reported by McCrocklin (1992:Figure 17) from an early 19th-century Delaware village (3LA185) in southwest Arkansas and on a possible 1838 Koasati site on Caddo Lake in Marion County, Texas (Claude McCrocklin 1992, pers. comm.).

Copper and Brass Artifacts

The most common cuprous artifacts from Carl Matthews are 11 cut sheet copper strips (Figure 3a–d, k). These are flat to rounded pieces 0.5–1.0 mm in thickness; one had a hole punched through it with a metal tool. The cut copper strips are probably scraps from making such artifacts as tinklers and rolled copper arrowheads (McCrocklin 1990: 132).

Figure 3e is a small piece from a brass musket side plate. The specimen has thin engraved lines cut along the border of the side plate.

One rounded piece of copper rod stock (4.5 mm in thickness) has been formed into an awl with a well-fashioned bifacial bit (Figure 3h). Another copper rod stock has been pounded and hammered to shape, but was broken at both ends (Figure 3i).

A brass button is also in the collection (Figure 3f). It is a flat brass disk (12 mm in diameter) with a plain back and face, and a wire eye has been soldered to the button's back. Similar plain brass button types have been recovered from two early 19th-century Coushatta sites in northwest Louisiana (McCrocklin 1990:Figure 4), and from possibly contemporaneous Cherokee and Delaware sites on the Red River in southwest Arkansas (McCrocklin 1992:36, Figure 15). Another brass button was reported from the site surface by Jackson (1933:7), but is no longer in the Carl Matthews collection.

The other cuprous artifacts include an unidentified copper pin (?) and a possible musket rifle sight (Figure 3g, j). The possible rifle sight has a brass cross-bar and a vertical pin of silver.

Gunflints

Six extensively battered English gunflints, dating after 1800, are in the Carl Matthews collection (Figure 2e–j). They conform to English blade gunflints in having their shortest dimensions from side to side, single edges with untrimmed heels, little chipping on the sides, and demicones of percussion (Figure 2d; cf. Hamilton and Emery 1988:13–14). They are of gray, dark gray, and dark brown flint with an off-white chalk cortex (Figure 2e, g).

In general, the gunflints are well-worn through use, with side-to-side measurements of 15.0 mm (σ = 1.67 mm). Hamilton and Emery (1988:21) note that flints for tradeguns typically were 20–28 mm in size from side to side; those less than 20 mm are from either tradeguns or pistols. It is of interest to note that no native-made gunflints are present in the sample; these must all have been obtained from a U.S. trade factory. A larger gunflint assemblage from 19th-century Coushatta sites in Louisiana is also dominated by British blade gunflints (Mc-

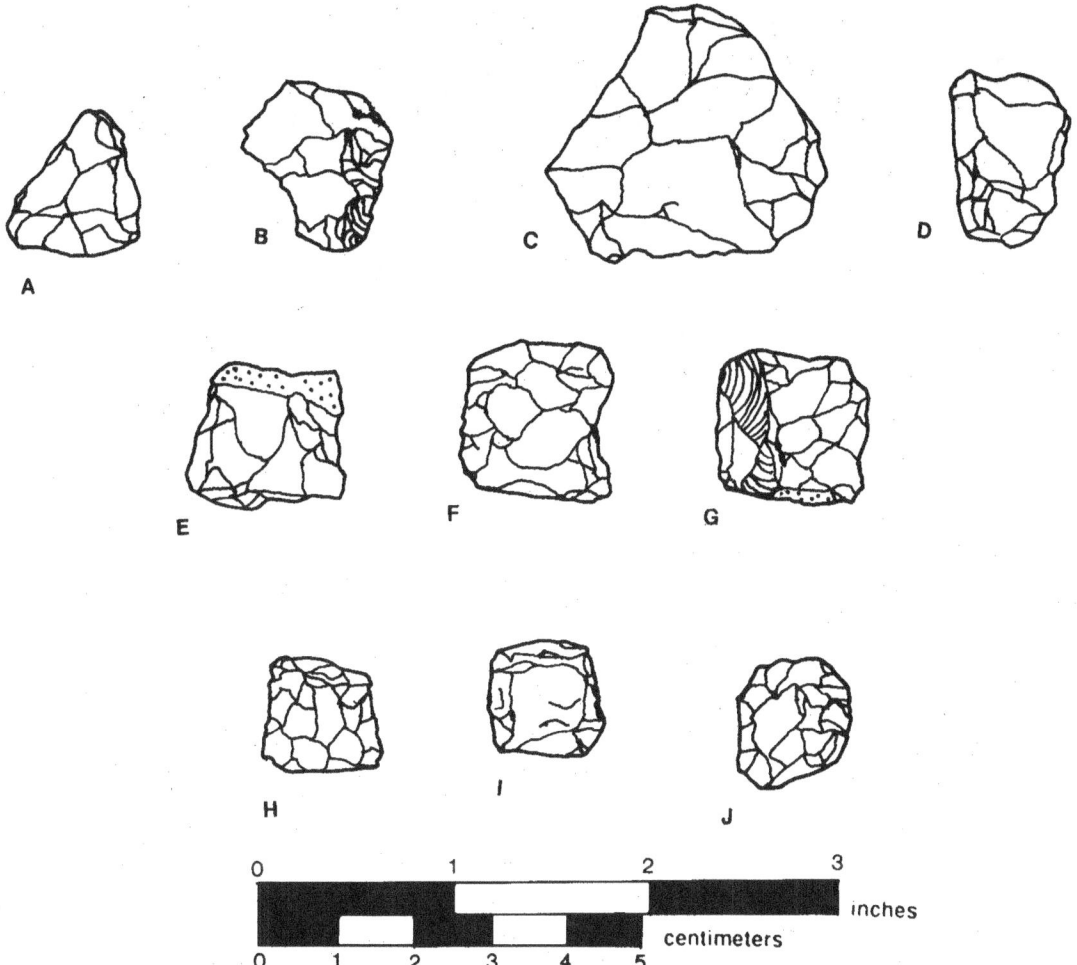

FIGURE 2. Chipped bottle glass (*a–d*) and gunflints (*e–j*).

Crocklin 1990). On earlier 18th-century Native American sites in Texas, however, native-made gunflints are well represented. For example, at the ca. 1760–1790 Vinson site in north-central Texas, thought to have been occupied by Wichita-speakers, native-made (or possible native-made) gunflints account for 57 percent (n = 47) of the gunflint assemblage (Blaine 1993).

Lead Balls

Two different calibers of lead musket balls are present at Carl Matthews—.38 and .54 caliber.

These sizes of lead balls would have been used in English rifles and muskets. Thirteen pieces of lead sprue and three musket ball masses, one spent and two partially cut, at Carl Matthews indicate that the Koasati manufactured their own lead balls at the site.

Iron Tools and Containers

Iron tools and metal containers were relatively common at the Carl Matthews site. With the exception of one iron hook and weight found at a depth of 8 in. (21 cm) and five square nails found

FIGURE 3. Cuprous artifacts (a–k) and iron arrow points (l, m).

in association with a large area of charcoal at 24 in. (62 cm) along the cutbank (Jackson 1933:7, 9), the remainder of these items were recovered from the surface of the site.

Two of the iron tools are iron arrow points made from 2.5-mm-thick barrel hoop scrap (Figure 3l–m). Both iron arrow points have filed edges, and one is also beveled (Figure 3m); this specimen also has a cut and serrated stem. Similar types of arrow points, commonly called Benton metal points (Perino 1985:33), have been found on late 18th-century Wichita or Caddoan sites in northeast Texas (Jelks 1967:Figure 25b) and early 19th-century Coushatta sites in northwest Louisiana (McCrocklin 1990:Figure 2).

Other iron tools at Carl Matthews include a 60-mm-long hook and weight, a chisel and awl from iron rod stock, possible horse trappings, and three knife blades. The awl is on a piece of square iron

rod stock that has been honed to a rounded point, and then subsequently bent through use. A fragment of a possible horse trapping is a thin semi-circular piece of iron with a raised edge above an opening for attachment. The knife blades are from case and clasp knives. These types of knives are quite common at a number of 19th-century Coushatta sites in northwest Louisiana (McCrocklin 1990:Figure 8).

Eight iron kettle fragments were found in the Carl Matthews surface collection. These include three kettle bail ears from kettles of different sizes, four body fragments, and one fluted tripodal leg. The fluted leg is 48 mm in height.

This type of iron container is quite common at 19th-century Coushatta sites on the Red River (McCrocklin 1990:Figure 14), as it is on other contemporaneous Native American and Anglo-American sites. McCrocklin (1990) calls these ''French kettles'' (and they are sometimes referred to as ''French'' kettles in U.S. factory trade lists), and it does appear to be the case that iron kettles were occasionally traded by the French to Native Americans in the 18th century (Brain 1979:134–139, 1988:327). Nevertheless, these heavy and bulky iron kettles are much more common on historic Indian sites dating after 1800, as they were transported from the American trading posts in Natchitoches, Sulphur Fork, and Nacogdoches to the sedentary Native American communities whose people frequented the posts (Gregory 1978; Brain 1988).

Coffin Nails

The 79 coffin nails (51 with head and shank, and 28 shanks) are poorly preserved, and it was impossible to determine if the nails were hand-wrought or machine cut. The shape and size of the heads are about the same as a box nail, and the lengths of the nails indicate they are 6d (penny-weight).

Burial 1 had 50 nails ''found at regular intervals, with the points inward and heads about one inch from grave wall. This seems to show the use of a box only slightly smaller than the grave hole'' (Jackson 1933:10). The coffin, about 47 in. (122 cm) in length and 18 in. (47 cm) in width, appeared to have been for a child. The other coffin nails were found at the edge of the burial fill for Burial 2 (Jackson 1933:13).

Native-made Goods

Although not the main topic of this article, one of the most distinctive aspects of the Alibamu and Koasati archaeological materials from the Carl Matthews site is the native-made ceramics. Over 1,770 rim and body sherds of Koasati ceramics were collected from the site in the 1930s, along with two vessels (Table 1). Eighteenth- and early 19th-century ceramics from Upper Creek sites in Alabama and Georgia (e.g., Knight 1985, 1990), and Seminole sites in Florida (Weisman 1989), are virtually identical with Alibamu and Koasati ceramics from their 19th-century sites on the Red

TABLE 1
CREEK AND COUSHATTA MATERIAL
CULTURE, CA. 1780–1836

Artifacts	ca. 1780–1836 Tukabatchee	ca. 1790–1820 16BO207, Coushatta	ca. 1820–1835 Carl Matthews
ABORIGINAL			
Ceramics	403	242	1,778
NON-ABORIGINAL			
Glass Beads	6	28	26
Copper	0	3	15
Brass	2	1	0
Silver	1	17	0
Flat Glass	0	2	2
Container Glass[a]	47	1	70
Ceramics	20	0	8
Iron Arrow Points	0	2	2
Iron Nails[b]	1	4	5
Horse Parts	0	1	1
Iron Tools	0	4	14
Gun Parts	0	1	2
Gunflints	1	2	6
Lead Balls	0	11	19

[a]The container glass from Carl Matthews includes four pieces of chipped bottle glass.
[b]The iron nail total for Carl Matthews does not include the 79 coffin nails from Burials 1 and 2.
Sources: Knight 1985; McCrocklin 1990; this article.

River and in east Texas (McCrocklin 1990; David H. Jurney 1992, pers. comm.; Perttula [1993b]).

The Creek sites in Alabama and Georgia developed from the Lamar culture, which encompasses a variety of South Appalachian Native American cultures that evolved in this area about 700 years ago (Williams and Shapiro 1990). Historic Upper Creek ceramics from the Tallapoosa River of eastern Alabama (Knight 1990:50–51), and Alibamu-Koasati ceramics from Texas and Louisiana, include flared-rim Chattahoochee Brushed jars with decorated clay strip fillets below the rim and brushed bodies (McCrocklin 1990; Jurney 1992; Perttula 1992a).

At Carl Matthews, these types of large jars had a coarse sandy paste, with crushed bone or shell occasionally added to the paste. Other types of shared vessel forms in Alibamu-Koasati and Upper Creek sites are carinated bowls or cazuelas and flared-rim bowls. Both forms were typically burnished or smoothed by hand, and narrow incised lines were commonly placed below the rim; appliqué fillets and red slips were also used as forms of decoration on the bowls. The two whole vessels from Carl Matthews include a flared-rim jar and a cazuela.

Koasati native-made ceramics are considerably more common at the Carl Matthews site (n = 1,778 sherds) than the European-made ceramics (n = 8 sherds). This suggests that European ceramic wares were not preferred for use by the Koasati in Long King's Village, were probably not easily obtained in trading posts and factories, and that Koasati native-made ceramics were still considered most suitable for the cooking, processing, and storage of foodstuffs. The large Chattahoochee Brushed jars were likely still being used in the preparation of important corn foods, particularly *sofkee*, a hominy stew flavored with venison (Braund 1993:19).

Local Comparisons

The Arthur Patterson site (41SJ67) in San Jacinto County also has provided much information on the material culture of the Alibamu and Koasati groups living in southeast Texas in the 19th century (Hsu 1969). The site, thought to date ca. 1850–1870, had been found and disturbed by looters, but in the late 1960s it was investigated by a professional archaeologist. His work exposed six disturbed burial pits with the types and arrangements of goods seen in many other 19th-century southeastern Indian burials (cf. Gregory 1978; Brain 1988). The predominance of ornaments and items of personal apparel in the Arthur Patterson interments is in concordance with ca. 1830 Creek burial practices in Alabama and Georgia (Waselkov 1993:129).

Clothing in the burial was decorated with glass beads sewn on the collars, arms, and legs; silver conchos; and silver pendants. One individual was wearing a red hat made of hemp or palmetto, with glass beads, silver, and feathers sewn onto it. These types of material culture items found in the 19th-century Koasati archaeological record in Texas and Louisiana are quite similar to the clothing styles shown in 1828 drawings of Koasati men in Texas by Lino Sanchez y Tapia (Ewers 1969:Plate 11) and to 19th-century drawings of Alibamu men in the National Archives (Swanton 1946:Plate 17). Jean Louis Berlandier, a member of the same Mexican boundary commission as Sanchez y Tapia, commented that the Koasati "do not look like a native people. To see them you would say they were a gathering of settlers" (Ewers 1969:52).

The principal artifactual materials recovered at the Arthur Patterson site were the +25,000 glass beads (99 percent white, black, and blue seed beads) in the burials. Five whiteware, stoneware, and porcelain saucers, plates, and cups, along with a few metal tools, and 37 silver ornaments (worn as pendants, conchos, and danglers) were also included as grave goods. Hsu (1969) does mention that "Indian-made" pottery was recovered at the Arthur Patterson site, but he did not describe it in the report since it was assumed that it was not in apparent association with the Alabama-Coushatta cemetery.

Other possible Alabama-Coushatta archaeological sites have been reported in the Trinity, San Jacinto, and Neches river basins in east Texas (Perttula 1993a:Table 2.6.3). These include house sites and probable village locations, remnants of a ball game site, and burials. In most cases, these sites remain poorly studied, but in at least two instances, aboriginally manufactured ceramic vessels, silver conchos, silver bow guards, gun parts, and glass beads have been found at sites being eroded by water fluctuations at Lake Livingston in the central Trinity River basin. The Carl Matthews site is about 10 km east of Lake Livingston.

In summary, a wide variety of European and American goods have been found at both the Carl Matthews and Arthur Patterson sites, and between them these date ca. 1820–1870. They include glass beads, silver ornaments (pendants, rings, and earrings), cut brass/copper strips from making jewelry, and metal tools such as iron knives, arrow points, and awls. No aboriginally manufactured artifacts have been recovered among the goods found with the burials, although many of the silver and iron pieces had been modified by the Koasati to make ornaments and bracelets.

Concluding Comments

Waselkov's (1989) analysis of 17th-century trade in the colonial Southeast indicates that the interior southeastern Muskogean tribes engaged in trade beginning as early as ca. 1580 with the Spanish colonists and mission Indians of northern Florida. Through this trade, these peoples obtained brass ornaments, glass beads, iron hoes, guns, and other types of trade goods for deerskins and other products:

> These goods increase in abundance, variety, and importance following the introduction of the Carolina trade in deer skins and slaves at ca. 1692. By the late eighteenth century, changes in Creek material culture had extended to such presumably more fundamental domains as forms of housing and the economy of food production—most notably, in the archaeological record, the adoption of animal husbandry (Knight 1985:169).

From the emergence of "an economics of ostentation" among the Creeks in the early 1600s (Knight 1985:183), European trade goods were part of a prestige goods economy that served as symbols of rank and political-religious privileges. Through time, these luxuries became incorporated into the relatively conservative domestic spheres of Creek culture, due in part to the ready availability of European trade goods, and to an intensification in the procurement of luxury commodities by Creek merchants, traders, and animal husbandrymen (Knight 1985:178, 181).

Thus, by the end of the 18th century, the Creeks in Alabama and Georgia were experienced consumers of European trade goods (Waselkov 1992). In fact, Waselkov (1993:125) has argued that the essence of historic Creek culture was "a synthetic one incorporating both European trade goods and traditional artifacts, values, and activities in a new, distinctive, stable cultural format." These European trade goods either represented new cultural forms and elements (such as wine bottles or earthenware ceramics), goods that were initially made from unfamiliar materials (iron tools), or goods made from imported or new techniques that duplicated traditional (glass tools or iron arrow points) artifact forms (after Farnsworth 1992:Tables 3, 4).

The archaeological evidence from Creek and Coushatta sites in Alabama and Louisiana, and from the Carl Matthews site in southeast Texas (Table 1) indicates the range and diversity in the types of European goods being used by these Native Americans in the late 18th and early 19th centuries—including ornaments, containers, guns, tools, dishes, and other items. It also shows the continued importance in the domestic context (until the 1840s) of native culinary traditions, as reflected in the aboriginal ceramics, among the Creek and Koasati cattle herders of the Southeast and Texas.

ACKNOWLEDGMENTS

I would like to thank Dr. Darrell Creel and Dr. Thomas R. Hester of the Texas Archeological Research Laboratory in Austin, Texas, for permission to study the archaeological collections from the Carl Matthews site, and for generous access to their records and files. Dr. Frank Schambach of the Arkansas Archeological Survey facilitated my research on Koasati archaeology by allowing me to take on loan collections under his stewardship from Koasati sites on the Red River. Sergio Iruegas prepared the artifact illustrations for this article. My research was greatly facilitated by Claude McCrocklin, who shared his considerable knowledge of Koasati archaeology with me, along with copies of his excellent artifact slides; Dr. H. F. Gregory, Dr. Gregory A. Waselkov, and David H. Jurney, for information on the Koasati and Upper Creeks; and Dr. James E. Bruseth and Nancy A. Kenmotsu for their support during this research effort.

REFERENCES

ABEL, ANNE H. (EDITOR)
1907   *A Report from Natchitoches in 1807 by Dr. John Sibley.* Indian Notes and Monographs. Museum of the American Indian, Heye Foundation, New York.

BEXAR ARCHIVES
1831   Letter of Jose Francisco y Madero on Conchate and Alibamo Indians petitioning for land in Texas. *Mi-*

crofilm Roll 142:267–269. Bexar Archives, Barker Texas History Center, University of Texas at Austin, Austin.

BLAINE, JAY C.
1993   Firearms and Related Artifacts from the Vinson Site. *Bulletin of the Texas Archaeological Society* 63:163–186.

BRAIN, JEFFREY P.
1979   Tunica Treasure. *Papers of the Peabody Museum of Archaeology and Ethnology,* Vol. 71. Peabody Museum, Harvard University, Cambridge, and the Peabody Museum of Salem, Salem, Massachusetts.
1988   Tunica Archaeology. *Papers of the Peabody Museum of Archaeology and Ethnology,* Vol. 78. Peabody Museum, Harvard University, Cambridge, Massachusetts.

BRAUND, KATHRYN E. HOLLAND
1993   *Deerskins and Duffels: Creek Indian Trade with Anglo-America, 1685–1815.* University of Nebraska Press, Lincoln.

EWERS, JOHN C. (EDITOR)
1969   *The Indians of Texas in 1830 by Jean Louis Berlandier.* Smithsonian Institution Press, Washington, D.C.

FARNSWORTH, PAUL
1992   Missions, Indians, and Cultural Continuity. In The Archaeology of the Spanish Colonial and Mexican Republic Periods (Special Issue), edited by Paul Farnsworth and Jack S. Williams. *Historical Archaeology* 26(1):22–36.

FLORES, DAN L.
1977   The Red River Branch of the Alabama-Coushatta Indians: An Ethnohistory. *Southern Studies* 16:55–72.

GELO, DANIEL J., AND TAMMY J. MORALES (COMPILERS)
1992   The Alabama-Coushatta Indians: A Research Guide and Bibliography. *Recent Research from the Institute of Texan Cultures, Department of Research and Collections* 2(2):1–35. Institute of Texan Cultures, San Antonio.

GREEN, MICHAEL D.
1982   *The Politics of Indian Removal: Creek Government and Society in Crisis.* University of Nebraska Press, Lincoln and London.

GREER, GEORGEANNA
1981   *American Stonewares, the Art and Craft of the Utility Potter.* Schiffer, Exton, Pennsylvania.

GREGORY, HIRAM F.
1978   A Historic Tunica Burial at the Coulee des Grues Site in Avoyelles Parish, Louisiana. In *Texas Archeology: Essays in Honor of R. King Harris,* edited by Kurt D. House, pp. 146–164. Southern Methodist University Press, Dallas, Texas.

HAMILTON, T. M., AND KENNETH O. EMERY
1988   Eighteenth-Century Gunflints from Fort Michilimackinac and Other Colonial Sites. *Archaeological Completion Report Series* No. 13. Mackinac Island State Park Commission, Mackinac Island, Michigan.

HAWKINS, BENJAMIN
1916   Letters of Benjamin Hawkins, 1796–1806. *Collections of the Georgia Historical Society* 9. Georgia Historical Society, Atlanta.

HSU, DICK PING
1969   The Arthur Patterson Site: A Mid-Nineteenth-Century Site, San Jacinto County, Texas. *Survey Report* No. 5. Office of the State Archeologist, Texas Historical Commission, Austin.

JACKSON, A. T.
1933   Excavation on Carl Matthews Farm, 7 Miles W. of S. of Livingston, Polk County, Texas, Excavated August 21, to August 24, 1933. Manuscript on file, Texas Archeological Research Laboratory, University of Texas at Austin, Austin.

JELKS, EDWARD B. (EDITOR)
1967   The Gilbert Site: A Norteño Focus Site in Northeastern Texas. *Bulletin of the Texas Archeological Society* 37:1–248.

JONES, OLIVE, AND CATHERINE SULLIVAN
1985   *The Parks Canada Glass Glossary for the Description of Containers, Tableware, Flat Glass, and Closures.* Studies in Archaeology, Architecture and History. National Historic Parks and Sites Branch, Parks Canada, Environment Canada, Ottawa, Ontario.

JURNEY, DAVID H.
1992   Native American Mobility. Paper presented at the Southeastern Archaeological Conference, 30 October–1 November 1992, Little Rock, Arkansas.

KNIFFEN, FRED B., HIRAM F. GREGORY, AND GEORGE A. STOKES
1987   *The Historic Indian Tribes of Louisiana: From 1542 to the Present.* Louisiana State University Press, Baton Rouge and London.

KNIGHT, VERNON J.
1985   Tukabatchee: Archaeological Investigations at an Historic Creek Town, Elmore County, Alabama, 1984. *Report of Investigations* No. 45. Office of Archaeological Research, Alabama State Museum of Natural History, University of Alabama, Tuscaloosa.
1990   Phase Characteristics: Upper Tallapoosa River and Lower Tallapoosa River. In *Lamar Archaeology:*

Mississippian Chiefdoms in the Deep South, edited by Mark Williams and Gary Shapiro, pp. 49–51. University of Alabama Press, Tuscaloosa and London.

MAJEWSKI, TERESITA, AND MICHAEL O'BRIEN
1987 The Use and Misuse of Nineteenth-Century English and American Ceramics in Archaeological Analysis. *Advances in Archaeological Methods and Theory* 11: 97–209. Michael B. Schiffer, editor. Academic Press, Orlando, Florida.

MARTIN, HOWARD N.
1967 Tales of the Alabama-Coushatta Indians. In *Tales from the Big Thicket,* edited by Francis E. Abernathy, pp. 33–57. University of Texas Press, Austin.
1974 Ethnohistorical Analysis of Documents Relating to the Alabama and Coushatta Tribes of the State of Texas. In *Alabama-Coushatta (Creek) Indians,* edited by David A. Horr, pp. 179–256. Garland, New York.

McCROCKLIN, CLAUDE
1990 The Red River Coushatta Indian Villages of Northwest Louisiana, 1790–1835. *Louisiana Archaeology* 12:129–178.
1992 Three Historic Sites on Red River. *Arkansas Archeologist* 31:31–63.

MILLER, GEORGE L.
1980 Classification and Economic Scaling of 19th Century Ceramics. *Historical Archaeology* 14:1–40.

MURRY, ELLEN N.
1992 *"Sorrow Whispers in the Wind": Native Americans and the Republic.* Star of the Republic Museum, Washington, Texas.

NATIONAL ARCHIVES
1809– Natchitoches-Sulphur Fork Agency Ledgers. *Record*
1821 *Group* T1029. National Archives, Washington, D.C.

PERINO, GREGORY
1985 *Selected Preforms, Points and Knives of the North American Indians,* Vol. 1. Points and Barbs Press, Idabel, Oklahoma.

PERTTULA, TIMOTHY K.
1992a The Early 19th-Century Archaeology of the Alibamu (Alabama) and Koasati (Coushatta) in Texas. *Heritage* 10(2):20–24. Texas Historical Foundation, Austin.
1992b *"The Caddo Nation": Archaeological and Ethnohistoric Perspectives.* University of Texas Press, Austin.
1993a Effects of European Contact on Native and Immigrant Indians in Northeast Texas. In Archeology in the Eastern Planning Region, Texas: A Planning Document, edited by Nancy Adele Kenmotsu and Timothy K. Perttula. *Cultural Resource Management Report* 3. Department of Antiquities Protection, Texas Historical Commission, Austin.
[1993b] The Material Culture of Native Americans in the Early Nineteenth Century in Eastern Texas and the

Red River of Arkansas and Louisiana: An Inventory and Analysis of Caddo, Koasati, Cherokee, and Delaware Collections. Manuscript, in preparation.

SMITHER, HARRIET
1932 The Alabama Indians of Texas. *Southwestern Historical Quarterly* 36(2):83–108.

SMITHER, HARRIET (EDITOR)
1931 *Journal of the Fourth Congress of the Republic of Texas, 1839–1840.* Three volumes. Von Boeckmann-Jones, Austin, Texas.

SWANTON, JOHN R.
1946 The Indians of the Southeastern United States. *Bureau of American Ethnology, Bulletin* 137. U.S. Government Printing Office, Washington, D.C.

WASELKOV, GREGORY A.
1989 Seventeenth-Century Trade in the Colonial Southeast. *Southeastern Archaeology* 8(2):117–133.
1992 French Colonial Trade in the Upper Creek Country. In *Calumet and Fleur-de-Lys: Archaeology of Indian and French Contact in the Midcontinent,* edited by John A. Walthall and Thomas E. Emerson, pp. 35–53. Smithsonian Institution Press, Washington, D.C.
1993 Historic Creek Indian Responses to European Trade and the Rise of Political Factions. In *Ethnohistory and Archaeology: Approaches to Postcontact Change in the Americas,* edited by J. Daniel Rogers and Samuel M. Wilson, pp. 123–131. Plenum Press, New York.

WEISMAN, BRENT RICHARDS
1989 *Like Beads on a String: A Culture History of the Seminole Indians in North Peninsular Florida.* University of Alabama Press, Tuscaloosa and London.

WILLIAMS, AMELIA, AND EUGENE C. BARKER (EDITORS)
1938– *The Writings of Sam Houston.* Eight volumes.
1943 University of Texas Press, Austin.

WILLIAMS, MARK, AND GARY SHAPIRO (EDITORS)
1990 *Lamar Archaeology: Mississippian Chiefdoms in the Deep South.* University of Alabama Press, Tuscaloosa and London.

WINFREY, DORMAN H., AND JAMES M. DAY (EDITORS)
1966 *The Indian Papers of Texas and the Southwest, 1825–1916.* Five volumes. Pemberton Press, Austin.

WRIGHT, J. LEITCH
1990 *Creeks and Seminoles: The Destruction and Regeneration of the Muscogulge People.* University of Nebraska Press, Lincoln and London.

TIMOTHY K. PERTTULA
DEPARTMENT OF ANTIQUITIES PROTECTION
TEXAS HISTORICAL COMMISSION
P.O. BOX 12276
AUSTIN, TEXAS 78711

SUMMER ISLAND III:

An Early Historic Site in the Upper Great Lakes

DAVID S. BROSE

INTRODUCTION

The Summer Island site lies on a series of meadow-covered sand dunes rising about twenty feet above the level of Summer Harbor on the northwest side of the island. Summer Island is located about three miles south of Point Detour and is northernmost in the island chain between Michigan's Garden Peninsula and Wisconsin's Door Peninsula, separating Green Bay and Bay de Noc from Lake Michigan (Figure 1).

Topographically, the island consists of a two-tiered outcrop of the Silurian dolomites which forms the western edge of the Niagara Escarpment. Pro-glacial lakes have cut a number of terraces above the current lake level in the bedrock and the thin Pleistocene sedimentary mantle (Brose, n.d.a). Above and within these deposits some thin soils have formed sporadically in the interior level areas of the island. But the bedrock outcrops are ubiquitous and with the exception of the Summer Harbor area itself, meadow soils are rare (Brose, 1970a).

Offshore, the lake bottom consists of broken and jumbled bedrock and large blocks of weathered dolomite. The bottoms shoal outward from the island at shallow depths for several hundred feet. The coastline of the island presents a formidable appearance with blocks of dolomite dropping a sheer 10-12 feet onto the more level rock shelves which form the shoals. There are two exceptions to this picture. At the extreme northwestern point of Summer Island is a low, gravelly bar extending to the north and gently dipping to about four feet below the water midway between the Summer Islands. Toward the foot of Summer Harbor, where the bottom is less than eight feet in depth, it is composed of a rather clean sand which extends shoreward to the beach. Nonetheless, scattered blocks of dolomite often lie inches below the surface of the water and along the sand beach. The beach itself runs along the southwestern shore of Summer Harbor for about nine hundred to a thousand feet. To either side the limestone rises directly from the water to heights of from four to seven feet. Behind the sand beach and twenty-six foot wide sand and gravel shingle the land slopes steeply upward in a high sand bank reaching a rather sudden plateau about twenty feet above the lake. This sandy plain forms a clearing, erratically covered with thin vegetation. The clearing runs along the harbor for about 650 feet north and south and is about 250 feet wide at the center. It is crescentic, following the shoreline, each tapered end meeting a limestone ledge, and, immediately beyond, the forest. It is within this clearing that the Summer Island Site (Figure 4) is located.

The island lies in the northern portion of the "lake forest biotome" (Dice 1938) and is characterized by a forest cover of mixed deciduous and coniferous trees such as Hemlock, Balsam Fir, Sugar Maple, Quaking Aspen, and Birch. The fauna is rather Canadian and Black Bear, Moose, and Beaver are the principal mammalian species present, although the offshore shoal waters support a rich and varied fish fauna.

During the months of July and August 1967 I directed a field crew of five at excavations on the Summer Island site (20DE4) for the University of Michigan Museum of Anthropology. The crew consisted of Bert Barnard (Wayne State University), Kenneth Carstens (Central Michigan University), James Driskell (University of Arkansas), Paul Fellows (University of Arizona) and Victor Fitting (Michigan State University).

160   Perspectives from *Historical Archaeology:*

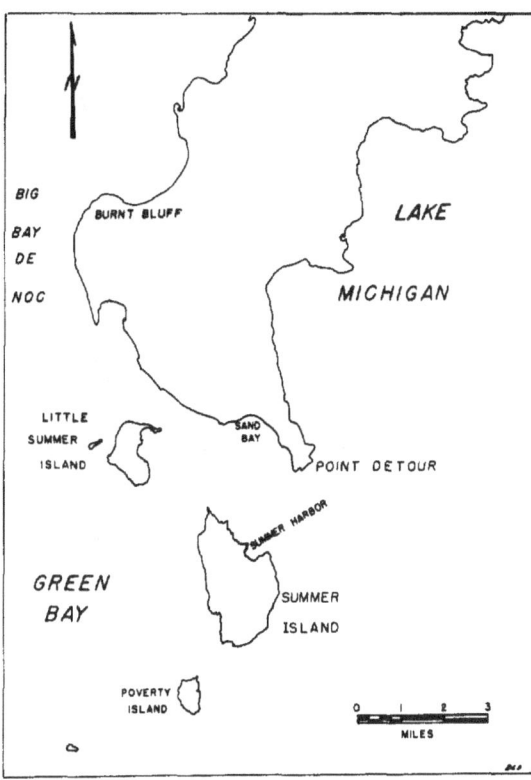

FIGURE 1. *Southern Delta County, Michigan*

THE EXCAVATIONS

Excavations revealed that the site consisted of three distinct components separated by sterile aeolian sands.

The earliest occupation occurred during the latter part of the Middle Woodland period and has been dated at A.D. 250 + 100 (M-1985). This component of the site appears to have been occupied for three or four years from April through September by between twenty-five and forty inhabitants representing six families of a small exogamous, patrilocal band (Brose, 1970b). The site at this time seems to have been primarily a fishing station where the spring-spawning sturgeon were taken by netting and spearing. During the later part of the summer, bear and beaver were hunted or trapped and some line fishing was practiced. The seasonal abandonment of the site coincides with the availability of wild rice, and it has been suggested that this was the reason for the departure of the inhabitants.

During this Middle Woodland occupation the prevalent styles of ceramic decoration demonstrate the participation of these people in what has been called the Northern Tier Middle Woodland tradition (Mason, 1967:338) which extended across the ecologically similar Lake Forest Biotic Province from Lake Winnepeg to the St. Lawrence estuary. The regional cultures of this wide area, described at Nutimik-Anderson, Laurel, North Bay, and Point Peninsula, all share rather distinctive techniques of ceramic decoration characterized by banked and dragged stamping, linear stamping, and various dentate impressions on conoidal smooth-surfaced vessels.

The chipped-stone industry seen in this component is characterized by the use of a bipolar core technique in addition to block and pebble core utilization. These varied manufacturing processes are interpreted to be primarily a result of the extensive utilization of the locally available chert which occurs as glacially eroded and redeposited nodules of varying sizes and shapes. The projectile points ranged in shape from stemmed through side-notched, and little standardization of shape was evident. Scrapers were predominantly the small unifacial "thumbnail" variety (55 percent) although other types occurred. The production of chipped-stone tools appears to have been an individual male activity and all phases of the processing were carried out on the site.

Copper-working was of some importance during this occupation and all post-extractive phases of production appear to have been performed as group activity by several related males. Ceremonial, ornamental, and utilitarian artifacts were made of copper and the effects of annealing on the ductility of the metal were appreciated.

Some use was made of available scrap bone for the production of needles, awls, and net-shuttles, while antler was modified for use as harpoon-heads and drifts. Ground-stone artifacts were rare although beach pebbles were slightly modified for use as net-sinkers, hammers, anvils, and mortars.

The second occupation of the site occurred during the Late Woodland period and dates to A.D. 1290 (M-2070). This component of the site apparently represents a number of short-term mid-summer occupations by small family groups. No population estimates are available for these groups, and their social organization is unknown. The site at this time appears to have been utilized as a

FIGURE 2. *View across Summer Harbor from Area B, looking NE Delta County's Garden Peninsula across channel. Note limestone shoals characteristic of entire coastline of Island with the exception of Summer Harbor.*

temporary base camp sustained by collecting mollusks from the gravel shoal to the north and fish from the weedy shallows of the harbor to the east of the site, while deer and small mammals could be hunted either on the island or on the nearby Garden Peninsula.

The ceramics from this component clearly indicate that the inhabitants were related to other Oneota peoples of the Green Bay region whose culture was incorporating the ceramics of the resident early Late Woodland tradition and the intrusive Mississippian tradition. The Point Sauble site might be typical of the more permanent villages of such people.

In terms of technology the chipped stone industry of this component is quite similar to the earlier Middle Woodland occupation. Bipolar, block, and pebble cores were all worked from the local chert nodules. Projectile points were all triangular in shape and most were quite poorly finished. While one projectile point could be characterized as a side-notched Cahokia point, the others were all classified as Late Woodland Madison points. The predominant scraper type (77 percent) was the unifacial "thumbnail" scraper although most of the other types noted in the earlier component were present. All phases

of lithic production occurred at the site, apparently all performed by individual males. Different areas of the site appear to have been utilized for different phases of the production. Bone tools, while not as requent as earlier, were well represented. Copper-working seems to have suffered a great decline and no copper artifacts can be securely assigned to this component (Brose, 1970a).

THE PROTOHISTORIC COMPONENT

The final aboriginal occupation of Summer Island appears to have been centered in Area "B" (Figure 4) on the surface of a partially vegetation-stabilized aeolian sand dune about 20 feet above the level of Summer Harbor. Much of the component had been severely disturbed by subsequent plowing. While artifacts could be assigned to the proper strata, within this level horizontal associations had been totally destroyed except for materials in pits and post-moulds. Throughout this deposit materials derived from the previous Middle Woodland and Upper Mississippian occupations of the site were common. A total of 247 sherds from twenty-seven Middle Woodland vessels and at least four Oneota vessels were recovered.

Perspectives from *Historical Archaeology:*

FIGURE 3. *Excavation in progress. Victor Fitting and James Driskell, two of five man crew.*

To a great extent the aboriginal artifacts described in this section (with the exception of ceramics) assigned to the protohistoric component were recovered from this depositional unit or from features originating at that level. Over 50 percent of all ceramics recovered from this component could clearly be assigned to the earlier occupations and no reliable inferences can be made from the ratios of chipped stone, copper, or worked bone artifacts.

DESCRIPTION OF COMPONENT STRATA

Within the protohistoric component a thin sheet midden seems to have been deposited upon the surface of the rather flat plateau to the west of the ridge rising from the beach at Summer Harbor. This midden appeared to be quite discontinuous but this may well be a factor of the subsequent plowing during the historic occupation of the site which in many areas truncated the upper portion of the earlier component. The region of Area "B" (Figure 4) to the north of the large blowout area preserved the best sample of these deposits which

were highly sporadic otherwise. Within this area excavation revealed a thin dark brown stratum clearly indicating human occupation. This stratum rested conformably upon the underlying grayish brown sands which here exhibited their greatest thickness. These reached a maximum of 2.05 feet and overlay mixed gravel and sterile reddish-tan sands just above the Valders till. Within these grayish brown sands materials attributable to the Middle Woodland and Upper Mississippian occupations were scattered.

Mixed within the dark brown stratum were several distinctive types of ceramics as well as a large amount of European-manufactured trade material in association with the aboriginal material. This situation occurred in several areas of the site in pits intruding into earlier deposits. Only in Area "B", however, was the area of continuous midden large enough so that post-moulds originating in that level could be followed to infer some structural pattern, or could features be correlated with this structure. After trowelling through this level the floor was shovel-shaved flat and

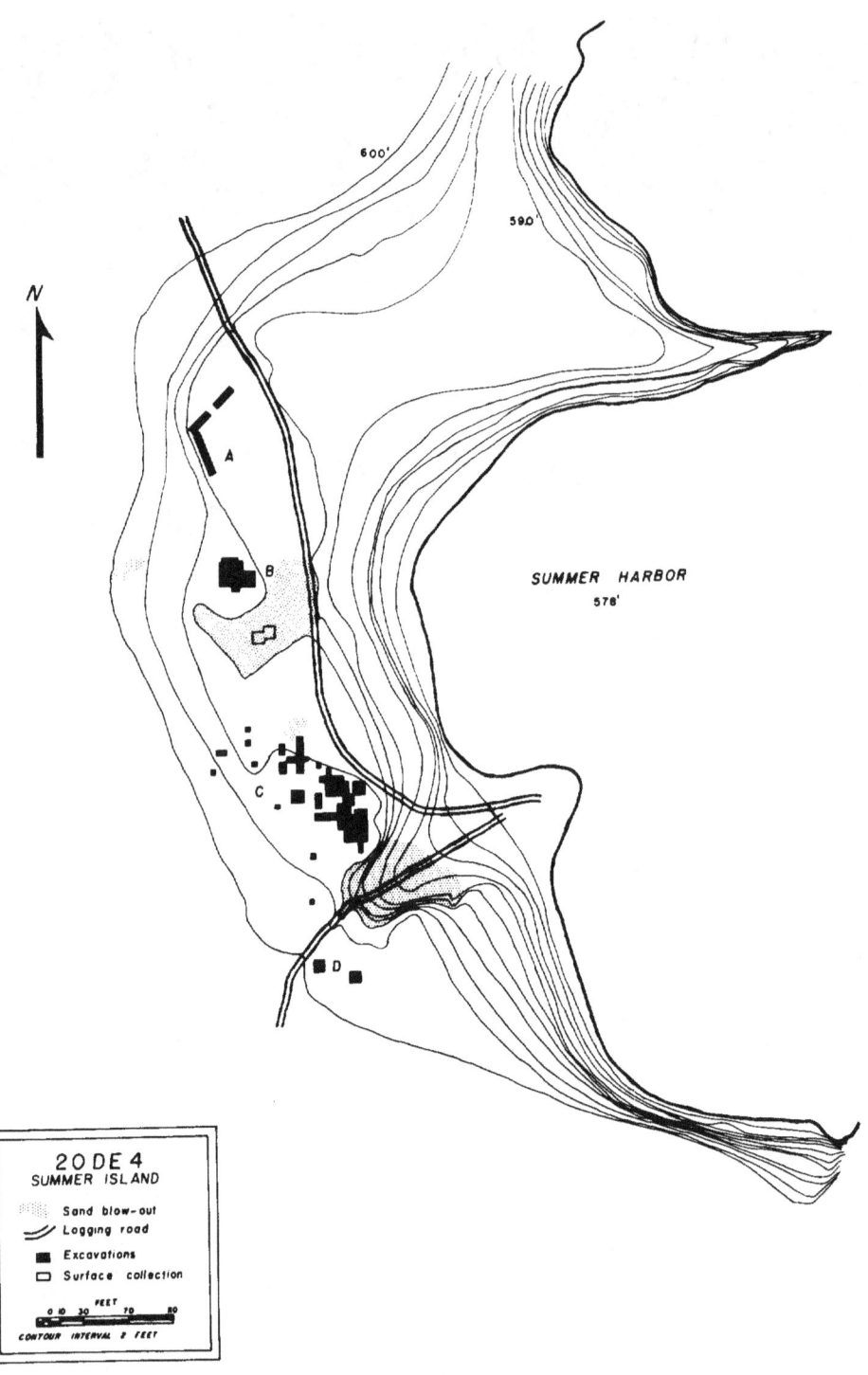

600'

590'

N

SUMMER HARBOR
576'

A

B

C

D

20 DE 4
SUMMER ISLAND

Sand blow-out
Logging road
Excavations
Surface collection

FEET
0 10 30   70   80
CONTOUR INTERVAL 2 FEET

FIGURE 4. *The Summer Island site*

Perspectives from *Historical Archaeology:*

20DE 4

AREA "B"

N

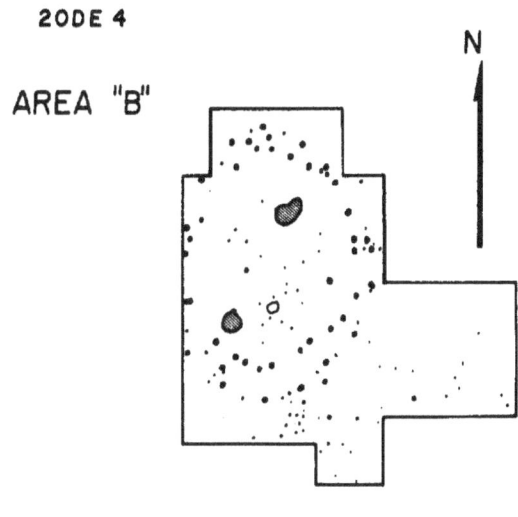

☐ LIMIT OF EXCAVATIONS
◔ HEARTH
○ PIT
•. POST-MOULD over 0.45 feet in dia. & depth
.· POST-MOULD under 0.45 feet in dia. & depth

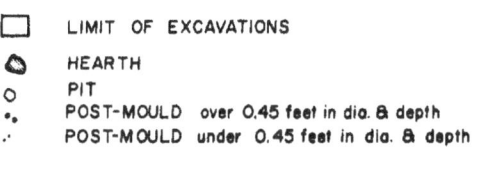

0   5   10
FEET

FIGURE 5. *Archaeological evidence for structure*

features such as pits and post-moulds could clearly be seen as very fine textured dark brown circles on the medium grayish brown sands below.

STRUCTURES

The pattern taken by the post-moulds which originated at the protohistoric level was followed in a rough circle, after which the central area was excavated. The post-mould pattern seen in Figure 5 shows evidence for a structure about eighteen feet north-south by about twelve feet east-west. There is some suggestion of an entrance in the center of the eastern wall. Two large internal support posts are each located about a third of the distance along a line running across the center of the house, rather than along its length. The north wall of the structure has undergone a fair amount of post for post replacement, and there probably has been one complete rebuilding of the south wall about 2.5 feet further south than it originally had been. It is assumed that such reconstruction took place only when needed because of the decay of the original wall posts.

Several small interior posts were noted in the structure. In general one could say the only pattern they seemed to follow was one of avoiding the areas around each of the two hearths and in the entranceway. A correlation coefficient computed between the number of small interior posts and the distance from the center of either hearth had an r value of .814, significant to the .01 level of probability (t = 10.015; n = 53) thus indicating that the observed distribution is probably not random. Those posts forming a semi-circle around the northern hearth (Feature #40) may have been a wind screen of some sort. A majority of the other interior posts seem to cluster around the refuse pit (Feature #34) just northeast of the smaller hearth (Feature #33), but no functional reason for such a pattern suggests itself. Alternately, the posts could be viewed as a number of replacements along a line running northwest-southeast which separated the structure into two more or less equal areas, each with a centrally located hearth. On this view the structure may have housed an extended family or possibly two related nuclear families.

Numerous small and large post-moulds were noted outside the structure at this level. With the exception of the small rectangular pattern directly to the south no functional interpretation is offered for these. This small ancillary structure can probably best be interpreted as

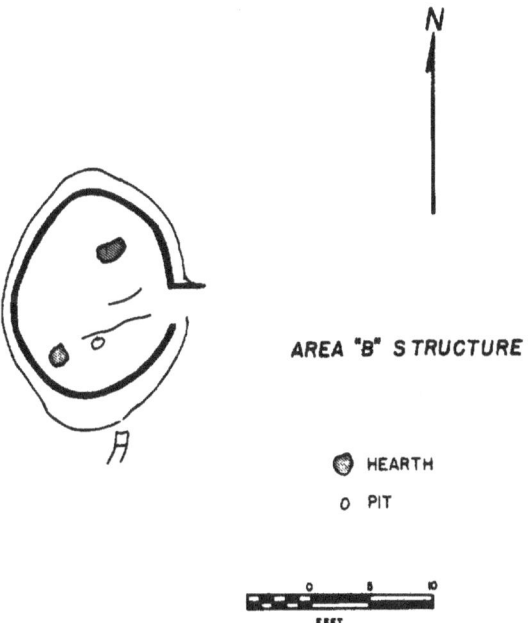

N

AREA "B" STRUCTURE

◉ HEARTH
○ PIT

0   5   10
FEET

FIGURE 6. *Area "B" structure*

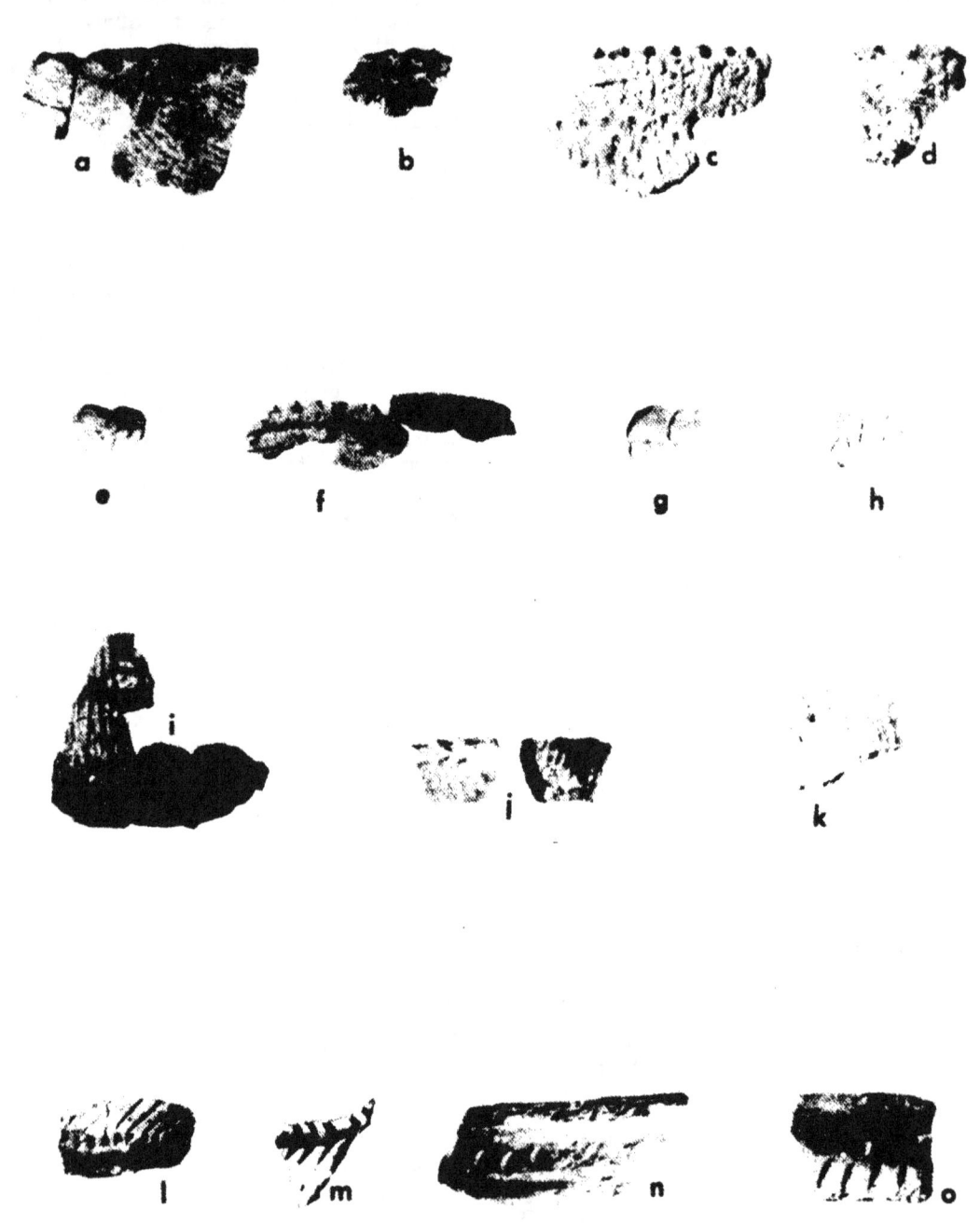

FIGURE 7. *Aboriginal ceramics from the protohistoric component of Summer Island (a-e) Bay de Noc Notched Lip (f-h) Garden Incised (i-k) Summer Island Cordmarked (l-m) Iroquoian Ceramics (n-o) Lake Winnebago Trailed.*

Perspectives from *Historical Archaeology:*

a storage or drying rack used by the occupants of the lodge at some time. There is no evidence for post replacement and the rack is assumed to have been rather temporary.

Features

Nine features were assigned to this component. All originated in the dark brown sands below the plow zone. No evidence of intrusion into this thin stratum from the overlying unit was noted on any of them. The data for these features is presented in Table I. While most of the data is self-explanatory several of the features require further discussion. The squash seeds from Feature #34 were identified by Mr. Volney Jones of the Ethnobotanical Laboratory, Museum of Anthropology, The University of Michigan. The charred mammal bone from Feature #47 was identified by Dr. William Burt of the Museum of Zoology, The University of Michigan. Feature #47 was one of the most stratigraphically intact features on the site, lying outside the areas where most of Middle Woodland, Mississippian, or Historic occupation was recovered.

A sample of the charred bone was submitted to The University of Michigan Radiocarbon Laboratory. The date on this sample was B.P. 330 $\pm$ 100, or A.D. 1620 $\pm$ 100 (M-2014). However, utilizing the most current research on radiocarbon dates and their deviations from true ages of specimens due to fluctuations in the production of atmospheric production of C^{14}, the date of B.P. 330 $\pm$ 100 (M-2014) can be reinterpreted. Based upon an estimated half-life of 5730 years (U.S. Bureau of Standards: 1963) and employing the 1969 Suess correction chart the sample from the Protohistoric component at Summer Island may represent a true age of either A.D. 1499; A.D. 1642, or A.D. 1677.

Ceramic sherds which could be fitted together to represent a single vessel were recovered from Features 17 and 47; from Features 13, 17, and 41; from Features 13 and 47; and from Features 34 and 41 indicating that this was probably a single contemporaneous occupation.

ABORIGINAL ARTIFACTS

Ceramics

From the Protohistoric component at Summer Island 66 sherds representing 13 vessels were recovered. All but four of these vessels seemed to be constructed of the same paste. This was a slightly sandy clay tempered with crushed granitic grit ranging in size from 0.5

mm to 2.5 mm ($\bar{x}$ = 1.2 mm) which seemed to represent about 25 to 30 percent aplastic by volume. The texture ranged from rather laminar to somewhat compact. No coil breaks were observed and manufacture is assumed to have been by a paddle and anvil technique. Vessel surfaces ranged in color from buff to dark grayish brown with interiors considerably darker. Hardness as indicated by a scratch test ranged from 2.5 to 3.0 on the Mohs scale. All nine of these vessels seemed to display the same form having a medium high slightly flaring rim, a slightly constricted neck gradually rounded below the shoulder, probably to a globular base.

Of this group, 13 rimsherds and 31 bodysherds representing four vessels could be assigned to the type Bay de Noc Notched Lip (Figure 7, a-e). Bodysherds on these vessels ranged in thickness from 3.5 mm to 7.0 mm ($\bar{x}$ - 6.3 mm). On the three vessels with a thickened rounded lip (Figure 8, a) rim thickness 1 cm below the lip ranged from 4.9 mm to 5.5 mm ($\bar{x}$ - 5.1 mm) and at the lip maximum thickness ranged from 6.0 mm to 7.5 mm ($\bar{x}$ - 6.5 mm). The one vessel having (in places) evidence of a slight exterior folded rim and a more flattened lip (Figure 8, b) had a mean rim thickness of 5.5 mm and a mean lip thickness of 6.8 mm.

All of these vessels had a surface treatment consisting of malleation with a loosely cordwrapped paddle which obliterated clear impressions of the twining. Where this can be seen it seems to be an $\S$Z twisted cord about 1.5 mm to 2.0 mm in diameter. Where these impressions overlap at an angle they resemble fabric impressing. These impressions extend from the base of the vessel up to the lip, although on several sherds there is evidence of subsequent smoothing just below the neck (Figure 7, c-e). Rim decoration seems to be confined to carelessly done finger-crimping or alternate-edge tool notching of the lip, although one sherd (Figure 7, c,d) seems to show tool notching with a rather squared implement about 3.1 mm in width and 4.5 mm in length. These notches average 7.5 mm apart and this vessel showed an intermittent band of decoration 2.5 cm wide just below the smoothed rim. This decoration seems to consist of impressing a tool into the clay and rotating it to produce an annular punctate. However, this design may also have been created by impressing the cut rounded end of a stick into the clay.

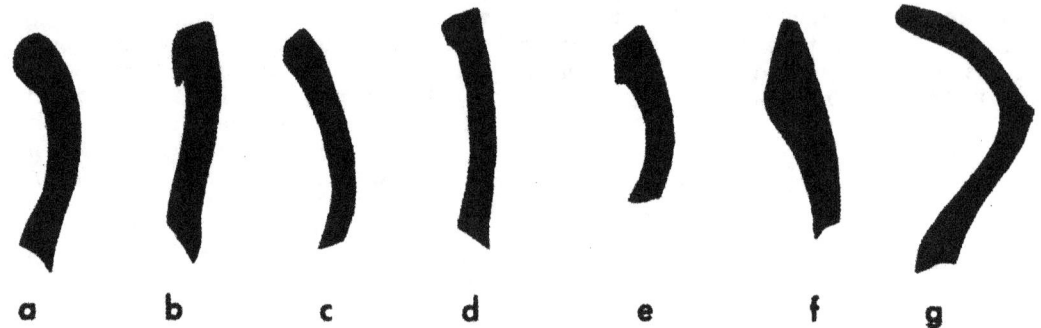

FIGURE 8. *Rim profiles of aboriginal ceramics (interiors to right)*

In general all of these vessels seem to show quite close resemblances to illustrations of the Type II pottery recovered from the Bell site just south of Big Lake Butte des Morts, Winnebago County, Wisconsin (Wittry, 1963: 25-26; Figs. 13B, 16) as well as to some of the pottery from the Dumaw Creek site, Oceana County, Michigan (Quimby, 1966b: 64-72; Fig. 31, upper left, lower right). It is also similar to ceramics from the surface collections at the Juntunen site (McPherron, 1967: Plate XXIII, h, j).

Sixteen bodysherds and ten rimsherds representing three vessels were classified as *Garden Incised* (Figure 7, f-h). All of these vessels had a smoothed band just below the lip decorated with a double incised line. On two of these vessels with a rounded thickened lip (Figure 8, a) these parallel lines were continuous and horizontal. They were 1.5 mm wide and from 3.0 mm to 4.2 mm apart. The uppermost line was 6.0 mm below the edge of the lip. The other vessel with a more squared lip (Figure 8, c), was represented only by a single rimsherd. This sherd displayed two very sloppy double horizontal lines of zig-zag incising or trailing forming a continuous chevron motif. These lines were 3.5 mm to 5.2 mm apart. The peaks of the upper line often came all the way up to the lip. All of these vessels displayed an encircling row of exterior lip notches created by the shallowly impressed edge of a stick. These impressions were 3.2 mm to 5.5 mm long, 2.5 mm to 3.8 mm wide, and averaged 10.1 mm apart on the two vessels with a horizontal line and 5.0 mm apart on the third vessel. These ceramics are vaguely reminiscent of some of the Bell site Type I ceramics in technique (Wittry, 1963: 22-25; Fig. 13, c), although the decorative motif is not very close

and seems to resemble some of the late Upper Mississippian motifs from the area such as Lake Winnebago Trailed and Perrot Punctate (Hall, 1962, I: 171-174, 175-177; II: Plate 74-76, 41, 61-62). The lip treatment of these vessels is identical to that described for many of the Dumaw Creek rimsherds (Quimby, 1966b: 67, 70, 71-72). There are also vague similarities to the Langford Trailed ceramics from Starved Rock, Illinois (Brown, 1961: 31-35; Fig. 9, c-e).

The last group of three vessels made on the previously described paste were represented by 17 bodysherds and five rimsherds. All three of these vessels were classed as *Summer Island Cordmarked*. These were characterized by the strong, clear, predominantly vertical cordwrapped-paddle impressions which extended from the globular base to the outflaring thickened lip (Figure 8, d). This lip thickening was apparently the result of impressing the top and/or outer edge of the lip with an angular tool (Figure 7, j) or with the tip of the finger (Figure 7, i,k). On the latter sherds the fingernail impression is quite evident along the interior portion of the lip. The only other decoration on these ceramics occurred on a single sherd. It consists of a vertical row of three short horizontal twisted cord impressions made with the same 1.5 mm diameter §Z cord which was used to wrap the malleating paddle. These three impressions are 9.0 mm long and 1.5 mm wide. They begin 4.7 mm below the lip and are 5.3 mm and 6.2 mm apart. These ceramics are virtually identical to sherds in the collections in The University of Michigan Museum of Anthropology from both Dumaw Creek and the surface collections from the Moccasin Bluff site overlooking the St. Joseph River in Berrien County, Michigan. These ceramics also correspond to the printed descriptions of much of the excavated Dumaw Creek material (Quimby, 1966b: 67-72). Furthermore, these vessels are somewhat similar to sherds of the terminal Late Woodland Swanson Cordmarked from Starved Rock (Brown, 1961: 39-41). All of the vessels described have a rim diameter which is estimated to be about 20 cm.

Two vessels assigned to the protohistoric component were also grittempered although the paste was different, being very compact and having a somewhat higher amount of temper (about 25 to 40 percent aplastic by volume). Tempering particles were somewhat larger ranging from 1.5 mm to 4.0 mm in diameter ($\bar{X}$ - 2.2 mm). As on the other vessels, no coil breaks were observed and manufacturing technique is assumed to have been with paddle and anvil. Both vessels were represented by one rimsherd each, and no attempt to determine rim diameter was made. Both had (or seemed to have) well-smoothed over surfaces so it cannot be determined whether the malleating paddle had been wrapped at all and if so what with.

The first vessel is quite similar to illustrations of *Huron Incised* (MacNeish, 1952: 34; Plate X, fig. 4) as well as some variants of Lawson Incised (MacNeish, 1952: 14; Plate I, fig. 6-9 [esp. 5]). Decoration of the rim consists of oblique incisions with vertical incision below what appears to have been a pointed castellation (Figure 7, i). These castellations are approximately 25 mm apart and 5 mm high. The oblique incisions run from the rounded lip down the short outflaring collar (Figure 8, f). These incised lines are 1.4 mm to 1.6 mm wide, 0.6 mm deep, 15.0 mm long and 5.7 mm apart. Below these incisions is a single encircling row of squared tool-end impressions which have been put in from the top. These impressions are 3 mm deep at their bases, 4.0 mm high, and 2.3 mm wide and lie just on the upper margin of the collar. Below the collar the vessel seems plain. Similar ceramics have been reported from the Lawson Prehistoric Village site, Middlesex County, Ontario (Wintember, 1939: Pl. V) and the nearby Clearville site (Jury, 1941). These ceramics seem to be the dominant type at the Seed site, the Warminster site (MacNeish, 1952: 29-31) and the Sidey-Mackay village (Wintemberg, 1946: 162-180) further to the west in southern Ontario. Bastian (1963) has also noted similar ceramics from Isle Royale.

The other vessel, represented by a single rimsherd (Figure 7, m), is quite similar to the named type *Sidney Notched* as illustrated by Wintemberg (1946: *loc. cit.*). This type is also illustrated in MacNeish (1952: 33; Plate IX,

figs. 5-8). The vessel from the Protohistoric component at Summer Island displayed a somewhat squared high castellation with a trough to crest height of approximately 8.2 mm and a trough to trough distance of at least 24.8 mm. The rim is outflaring with a short rather thick outflaring collar and a flattened transversely notched lip (Figure 8, e). Below the lip decoration consists of a single horizontal row of parallel oblique incisions 6.5 mm long, 2.1 mm wide and 0.7 mm to 1.2 mm deep. These incisions are 3.0 mm to 4.5 mm apart. Not enough rimsherd is present to determine whether these oblique incisions would be in opposed plats on oppostie sides of the castellation. Below these incisions the vessel is plain-surfaced. Similar ceramics have been reported from numerous late sites between Toronto and Lake Simcoe in Ontario (MacNeish, 1952; Wintemberg, 1939, 1946; Channen and Clarke, 1965, Plate II, fig. 2), as well as from surface collections on Isle Royale (Bastian, 1963: Plate 15). Both of these vessels are presumed to represent early historic Huron or Neutral ceramics.

At least one vessel of *Lake Winnebago Trailed* (Figure 7, n,o) is represented by eleven bodysherds and four rimsherds from the protohistoric component. The shall-tempered vessel has a bodysherd thickness of 3.5 mm to 6.0 m ($\bar{x}$ - 4.1 m) a thickness of up to 6.8 mm at the shoulder and a mean lip thickness of 7.4 mm. The exterior surface is quite smooth. The vessel probably has a squat globular body with a constricted neck, sharply everted rim, and rounded lip (Figure 8, g). The lip is decorated with shallow finger impressions creating a scalloped look with each crest approximately 16.4 mm apart. Below this the rim is undecorated to the constricted neck. The neck has a single horizontal row of rather carelessly executed oval to rectangular punctations 4.2 mm to 6.5 mm long, 3.5 mm to 4.8 mm wide, 1.0 mm to 1.7 mm deep, and 3.5 mm to 5.7 mm apart. Below this decoration there are at least two parallel horizontal trailed lines 4.5 mm to 5.6 mm wide, 0.7 mm to 11.6 mm deep and 14.3 mm apart. These horizontal lines appear to be continuous. No drilled holes were noted. In all respects this vessel be considered as conforming to the type Lake Winnebago Trailed as defined by Hall (1962: I, 171-174, Plates 74-76). Similar ceramics have been reported from numerous sites along the western shore of Lake Michigan as far south as the Anker site in Cook County, Illinois (Griffin, 1943: 284-286), but most examples seemed to occur along the Fox River drainage.

In general the ceramic assemblage represents a considerable mixture of styles and geographical areas. The unifying element is that of temporal position. The Bay de Noc Notched Lip and Summer Island Cordmarked ceramics can be closely associated with the Bell site Type II ceramics presumed to date A.D. 1680-1730 (Wittry, 1963: 56) and with the Dumaw Creek ceramics which have a radiocarbon date of A.D. 1680 + 75 (M-1070) which Quimby (1966b: 80) feels are probably pre-1620. The Iroquoian ceramics are similar to those types having their highest frequencies in post-contact or immediately pre-contact Huron village sites in Ontario (Wintemberg, 1946; Mac-Neish, 1952). The only Upper Mississippian vessel represented is a type which ". . . must have reached its peak of popularity late in the protohistoric period." (Hall, 1962: 155). These ceramic data agree with the radiocarbon date and seventeenth century European artifacts from Summer Island.

Chipped Stone

Because of the disturbed nature of this component (with the exception of features) areal associations have been seen to be non-significant. To the extent that the horizontal distribution of chipped stone exhibited any functional clustering the discussion of feature contents has noted these. Some problem exists in that materials pertaining to earlier occupations have become incorporated into these protohistoric levels through the agency of pits, postholes, and general kicking up of the loose sands. White within categories of artifacts such as pottery the protohistoric material can reasonably be separated from the extrusive earlier occupations, this is emphatically not so when dealing with the categories of chippage: a Laurel flat flake looks just like an Upper Mississippian or protohistoric flat flake. In spite of this mixing of the upper components, if their lithic technologies were radically divergent this should manifest itself in strikingly different frequencies of debitage categories. Since this does not seem to be the case only the counts and weights for the debitage from the protohistoric component are presented in Table II. It should be noted, however, that this certainly represents a mixture rather than the lithic material of a single group of people. For this reason some caution must be exercised in the interpretation of this material. The descriptive categories used are those previously defined for the Middle Woodland component of the site (Brose, 1970a). In general the debitage tends to indicate a good deal of primary and secondary knapping with

a seemingly large amount of block core utilization. This may however, merely be an indication that the larger heavier fragments have resisted disturbance more than other categories. Beyond these qualifications the chippage shows quite similar trends, toward utilization of locally available raw material and a rather generalized tool assemblage, much like the earlier components at the site.

Of the 131 bipolar cores recovered 46 were of the opposed ridge variety. Twenty-three of these were examined for signs of use. Fourteen showed no evidence of any use that could be demonstrated not to be a result of the manufacturing processes. All nine remaining cores showed evidence of limited use as wedges or heavy scrapers. All nine bifacial scrapers showed transverse striations indicating their function. Four of these had been made on opposed ridge bipolar cores (Figure 9, k) while the remaining five were rather amorphous (e.g., Figure 9, o). The bifacial blades (Figure 9, f) all showed evidence of use in the form of minute pressure flakes driven off along one face on both edges with occasional longitudinal striae and some degree of gloss. These are interpreted as signs of use as "meat knives" (see Semenov, 1964; Brose, 1970a). Of the six bifacial blanks two each were convex, concave, and straight based (Figure 9, g-i). These had a mean length of 4.25 cm, a mean maximum width of 2.95 cm, and a mean maximum thickness of 1.1 cm. No signs of use were observed on these artifacts. These seem rather large to have been made into projectile points.

The metric data for the seventeen projectile points recovered from this component is presented in Table III, and a representative sample are illustrated in Figure 9, a-e. In general these points can be classified as rather carelessly made. Seven of these points show primary flaking only on one surface, the other face having only slight marginal retouching. The points are generally concave based but this seems only true of the better made points and may be a function of final finishing for hafting. These points are similar to those illustrated from Dumaw Creek (Quimby, 1966b: 20-27, figs, 5-7) and with a length to width ratio of .61 seem similar to the major type of point from the Bell site (Wittry, 1963: 28-29). These points all fall within the range of Ritchie's Madison type (1961: 33-34, 88), which seem to attain their greatest popularity in New York after A.D. 1350 (idem: 31). This type is widespread in eastern North America in the late prehistoric period.

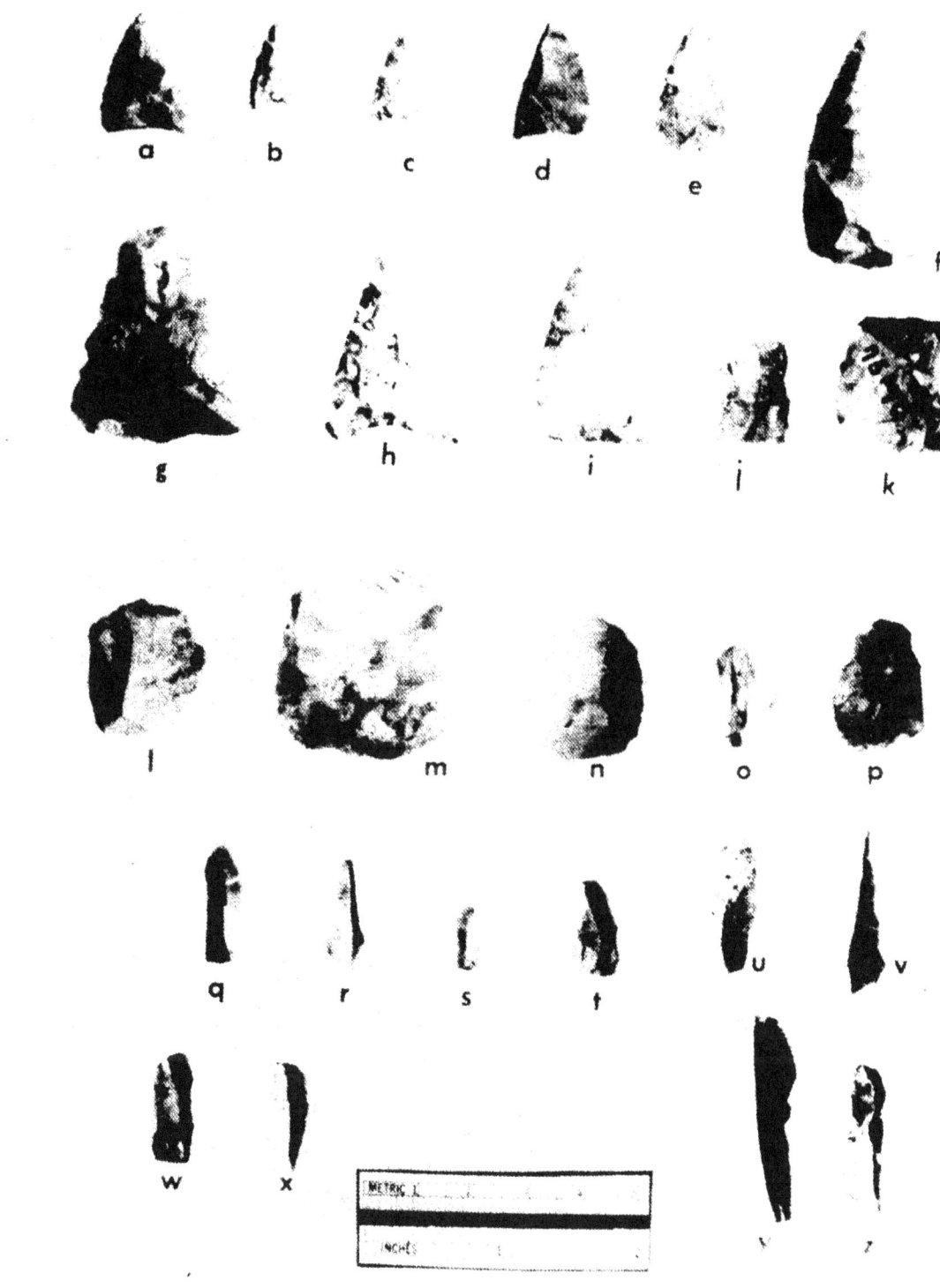

FIGURE 9. *Chipped stone artifacts from the protohistoric component of Summer Island*

The metric data for the twenty-six unifacial scrapers recovered from the protohistoric component is presented in Table IV and a number of these are illustrated in Figure 9j, l-n. The thirteen scrapers analyzed all had evidence of scraper use although the notched scraper did not show the results heavy pressure noted on these artifacts in earlier components, and the side scraper seemed to have been very little used. The bladelets from this component (Figure 9, q-z) showed the same mechanical association between shape, use, and material as did those of earlier components. Only seven (20%) of the thirty-five bladelets showed any signs of use, this in the form of small striations parallel to the long axis of the blade along one face with minute pressure flakes driven off the other face. Four of these seven bladelets showing use (57%) were made on nonlocally derived flints.

Forty of the eight-two utilized flakes were carefully examined to determine what type of use could be inferred from the wear patterns. Fifty percent had been employed as "meat knives," twenty percent as side scrapers, and thirty percent showed so little sign of use that accurate functional interpretation was not possible. One utilized flake (Figure 9p) showed very intensive wear on all edges indicating function as a "meat knife," end scraper, side scraper, notched scraper and ultimately, as a wedge. This degree of utilization was most unusual both for the component and the site as a whole. Some fifty of the utilized flakes were decortication flakes, twenty-four were flat flakes, and eight were block flakes.

Ground Stone

Only five pieces of rough ground and pecked stone could be assigned to this protohistoric component. From Feature 13 a flat polished fragment of very compact state was recovered (Figure 10 a). This item was 3.7 to 4.2 mm thick and relatively flat. There was evidence of a unifacially drilled hole 2.5 mm wide at the base, with a "countersinking" of 4.0 mm. The object bore no other signs of deliberate alteration. This looks as if it might once have been part of a drilled slate gorget. Such artifacts have been present in the upper Great Lakes at least since middle Archaic times (Griffin, 1967), but it is unusual to find one in so late a context. There is, of course, no evidence that such an artifact was actually made by the protohistoric inhabitants of Summer Island. It may have been picked up elsewhere and subsequently lost on the site whence it became incorporated in the refuse pit from which it was excavated.

From Feature 47 a small fragment of a slate abrading stone was recovered (Figure 10, b). This artifact had several more or less parallel striations 0.3 mm to 0.5 mm deep and 0.2 mm wide. Because of the narrow width of these grooves it is inferred that this piece may have been used for sharpening copper awls or points.

Two ground stone celts were recovered from the stratum assigned to the protohistoric component (Figure 10, c, d). The larger of these, composed of felsite, was about 83 mm wide across the bit, and was 133.6 mm long and 47.2 mm wide in the center. This celt was ungrooved. It had been subjected to heavy use and both edges of the bit were broken and heavily battered. The second celt, composed of diabase, was 52.3 mm wide across the bit, 114.1 mm long, and 27.2 mm thick in the center. Both edges of this ungrooved celt were broken and battered also. Unlike the large celt, this smaller celt showed no evidence of use after these fractures had occurred. On the larger celt the broken edges along the bit showed considerable small transverse striations. These occurred only on the small unbroken portion of the original bit of the small celt. Both celts were oblate in cross-section although the smaller one approximated a circular cross-section as the poll was approached. Both celts had a rounded poll although on the smaller one it was much more pointed. The larger of these celts is somewhat similar to the smaller celt reported for Dumaw Creek (Quimby, 1966b: 34, fig. 10, left). Two fragments of specualr hematite were also recovered from this component. These weighed 5.7 and 11.2 grams respectively.

Copper

Ten aboriginal artifacts of native copper were recovered from features and excavation units pertaining to this component. Three of these artifacts were rolled copper beads quite similar to those from the Middle Woodland component of the site (Figure 10, e). Two of these, (recovered from Features #13 and #34 respectively) were the wide rolled strip type like the majority of the Middle Woodland copper beads. The third bead from the protohistoric component was similar to the narrower, thicker, minority type. All three beads could be described as somewhat ductile. The first two beads had been formed from a copper strip 0.5 mm to 0.7 mm thick, 7.1 mm to 11.2 mm wide and 14.3 to 17.9 mm long. The finished beads had an external diameter of about 6.7 mm with an internal diameter of 5.2 mm. The third bead had been formed of

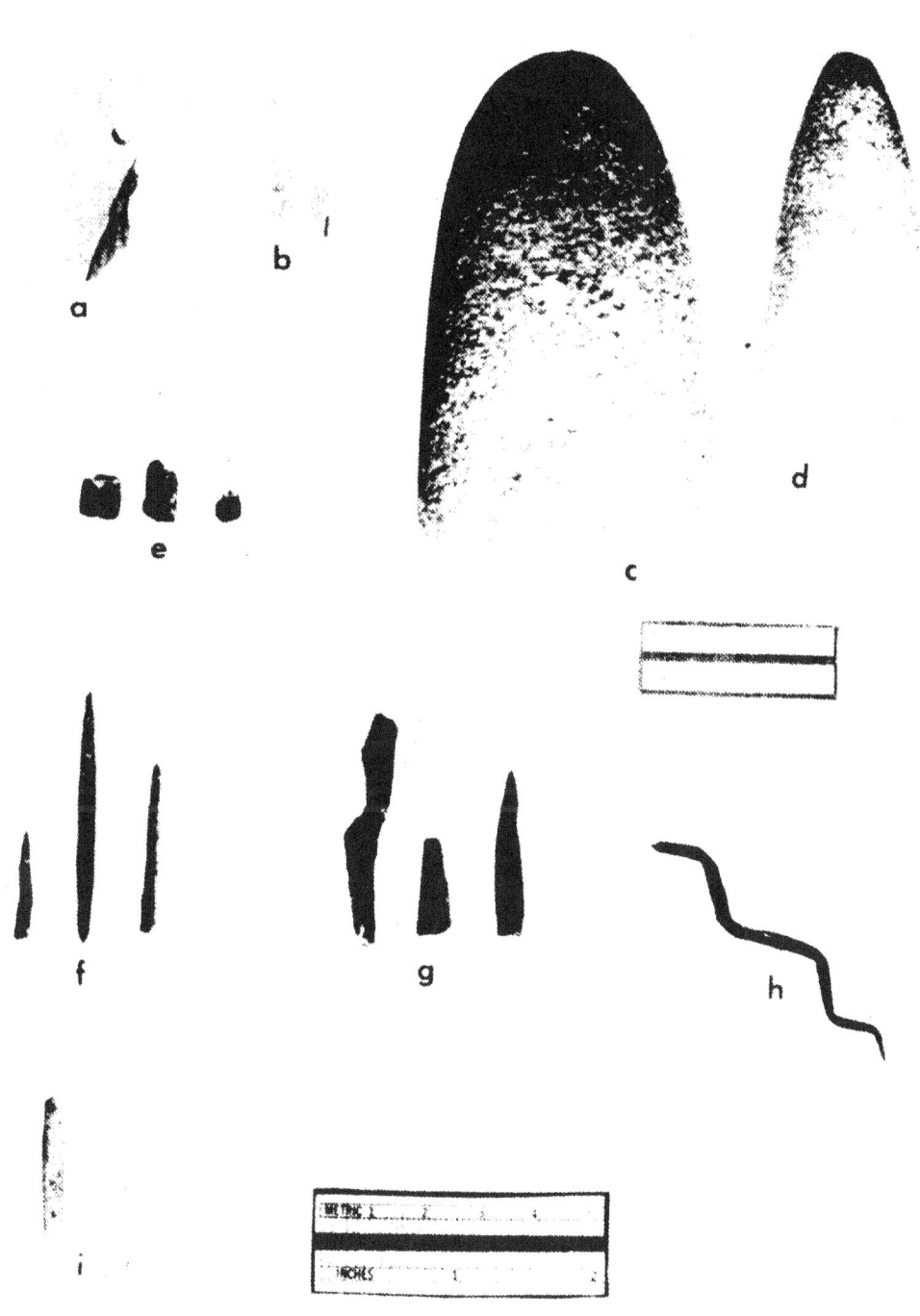

FIGURE 10. *Bone, copper, and ground stone artifacts from the protohistory component at Summer Island*

a copper strip 1.7 mm to 2.5 mm thick, 2.5 to 3.0 mm wide and about 16.5 mm long. The external diameter of the finished bead was 5.9 mm with an internal diameter of 3.1 mm. Both types of beads are similar to some of the small beads recovered from the Late Woodland Juntunen site (McPherron, 1967: 171; Plate XXXIII). They are also similar to the beads recovered from the burials at Dumaw Creek (Quimby, 1966b: 39-40; Fig. 13, 15). They could also be placed easily within the sample of rolled copper beads from the Middle Woodland component and in fact may actually have been derived from that component.

This may also be the case with the three copper awls (Figure 10, f) only one of which was recovered from a feature. All had been constructed with the fold-and-hammer technique noted for the Middle Woodland copper awls. Two of the protohistoric component awls were broken and resulting lengths were 22.1 mm and 27.8 mm. The intact awl was 41.6 mm long. All appear to have been bi-pointed and rectangular in cross-section. The mean maximum width of these artifacts was 2.7 mm and the mean thickness was 2.1 mm. The two broken awls were somewhat bent and twisted which may have occurred during that operation which broke them. All three awls bore some signs of use as awls and/or reamers (see Brose, 1970a). Copper awls similar to these have been reported for virtually all sites in the upper Great Lakes from Late Archaic through the historic period.

Four rolled copper points (Figure 10, g) from this component were at first thought to be recut and rolled brass kettle fragments. Specific gravity analysis indicated that they were the same material as the awls from the Middle Woodland component, presumably constructed out of the Lake Superior copper. Two of these copper points were wrapped around a single highly oxidized fragment of iron. All four of the copper points appeared to be similar in size and shape having a mean length of 28.5 mm, a mean basal diameter of 4.9 mm and having all been rolled of a single sheet of copper with a mean thickness of 1.6 mm. Quimby (1966b: 42) has reported similar artifacts from Dumaw Creek as tinkling cones; they are not particularly common in the Great Lakes area.

The last aboriginal copper artifact from the protohistoric component (Figure 10, h) is interpreted as an effigy snake. This artifact was composed of a copper sheet folded and hammered into a squared bar at least 63.2 mm

long and 3.5 mm square in cross-section. This bar was pointed on one end where it was also somewhat rounded. There were several striations at this parallel to the long axis of the implement and extending from the tip for about 25 mm. Some time after these wear patterns were made the implement was bent at five alternating 60 degree angles located 7, 16, 27, 43, and 54 mm from the rounded point. The other end of this artifact is broken. While the original implement seems to have been an awl (and could easily fit within the range of Middle Woodland awls from the site), in its final form it resembles the snake effigies reported from Dumaw Creek (Quimby, 1966b: 42, Fig. 16), from the terminal Woodland-Upper Mississippian Anker site in the Chicago area (Bluhm and Liss, 1961: 126; fig. 66, a), and from a late component of the Fort Ancient Aspect at the Madisonville site just northeast of Cincinnati, Ohio (Griffin, 1943: 128). These artifacts are well-represented in northeastern Iowa (Mildred Mott Wedel, 1959: 72) and in Wisconsin at Upper Mississippian sites of late appearance (McKern, 1945).

Only two bone artifacts were recovered from this component. Both seem to represent the broken tips of flat splinter awls (Figure 10, i). Use marks confirm this interpretation. The soil acidity is not significantly different in this stratum than in those pertaining to earlier components and there is some reason to expect that bone artifacts from earlier components would have been incorporated into this protohistoric component. The almost total absence of bone artifacts, then, must be more than a factor of sampling error and should reflect the cultural preferences of the inhabitants of the protohistoric component at Summer Island.

EUROPEAN ARTIFACTS
Trade Beads

From features and excavation units of the protohistoric component forty-nine glass beads and eight shell beads were recovered. Four of the glass beads (Figure 11, a) were long tubular beads of an opaque, brick red glass. One was 3.2 mm in outside diameter with an internal diameter of 1.6 mm. Two were 2.4 mm in outside diameter with an internal diameter of 1.2 mm. All were broken at both ends. Similar beads have been recovered from the excavations at the Site of Sainte Marie I, a Jesuit mission located in what was Huron territory near Midland Ontario. The mission was established in A.D. 1639 and occupied until its deliberate abandonment and destruc-

FIGURE 11. *European glass beads from the protohistoric component at Summer Island*

tion in late A.D. 1650 (Kidd, 1949: 3, 5, 142). Similar beads have been reported from the Neutral ossuary at Beverly, near Sundas, Ontario. These burials should antedate A.D. 1650 (Quimby, 1966a: 188). On Oneida Iroquois sites in New York these beads are assigned to the A.D. 1625 to A.D. 1710 period (Pratt, 1961: 10-14, figure 52). In western New York similar beads were reported from the Seneca Dutch Hollow site estimated to date around A.D. 1630 (Ritchie, 1954: 43, 69-70) and the Erie/Wenro/Neutral Kleis site in the Niagara region (White, 1967: 21) of about the same period.

Two dark blue opaque and one white opaque glass bead (Figure 11, b) having the same dimensions as the smaller red bead described above, were recovered from the component. Blue tubular or stick beads are reported from the Beverly ossuary (Quimby,

Two dark blue opaque and one white opaque glass bead (Figure 11, b) having the same dimensions as the smaller red bead described above, were recovered from the component. Blue tubular or stick beads are reported from the Beverly ossuary (Quimby, *loc. cit.*) the Dutch Hollow site (Ritchie, *loc. cit.*), the Kleis site (White, *loc. cit.*), and Oneida sites of the A.D. 1640-A.D. 1710 period (Pratt, *op. cit.*, figure 70). They are also reported from the Bell site (Wittry, 1963: 31) and the Zimmerman site (Brown, 1961: 60-62) where they indicate a late seventeenth or early eighteenth century period. The white opaque tubular bead is reported from the Beverly ossuary (Quimby, *loc. cit.*). Such beads were recovered from the earliest levels of Fort Michilimackinac dated at 1715 (Maxwell and Binford, 1961: 60), and from the late seventeenth century Lassanen site in St. Ignace, Michigan (Charles Cleland: personal communication). On the Oneida Iroquois sites this type is assigned only to the period A.D. 1660—A.D. 1677 (Pratt, 1961: 12, figure 74) which seems somewhat too restricted a time span.

Two round tubular polychrome beads (Figure 11 c) both had a number of parallel longitudinal narrow bright red stripes on an opaque dark cobalt blue or black bead. The larger bead was 13.2 mm long, 3.5 mm in outside diameter and 1.8 mm in internal diameter. The smaller bead had a length of 9.3 mm, an exterior diameter of 2.4 mm and an internal diameter of 1.4 mm. Both beads showed evidence of hot-tumbled squaring of the ends. These are apparently quite a rare type in the upper Great Lakes being reported only at the Bell site (Wittry, 1963: 31; fig. 21, J), and at

the lower levels of Michilimackinac (Maxwell and Binford, *loc. cit.*; Pl. I, q). In New York Pratt (*op. cit:* 13) has assigned this type to the period A.D. 1660-1677.

The only other polychrome glass bead from the protohistoric component at Summer Island (Figure 11, d), was a spheroidal bead 10.2 mm in length with an external diameter of 13.7 mm and an internal diameter of 2.9 mm. This bead has alternating opaque white and very dark opaque blue spiralled stripes of equal width. Similar beads have been reported from the Beverly ossuary (Quimby, 1966a: 189), the Plum Island site (Fenner, *op. cit.*: 89), and from New York Oneida sites dated A.D. 1642-1677 (Pratt, 1961: 11).

Two small "melon" beads (Figure 11, e) of a solid dark opaque blue color have a mean length of 5.3 mm, an external diameter of 3.0 mm and an internal diameter of 1.9 mm. Similar beads have been recovered from Ste. Marie I (Kidd, 1949: 141-142), the Dutch Hollow Site (Ritchie, *loc. cit.*), the Kleis site (White, *loc. cit.*), and from Oneida sites assigned to the period A.D. 1625-1677 (Pratt, 1961: 8-14).

Nine barrel-shaped opaque to translucent blue glass beads had a mean length of 6.3 mm, a mean outside diameter of 5.8 mm, and a mean internal diameter of 1.7 mm (Figure 11, g). Beads of this type had been reported from Ste. Marie I (Kidd, *loc. cit.*), the Bell site (Wittry, 1963: 31, fig. 21, G), the Kleis site (White, *loc. cit.*: Pl. VI, VII), the Dutch Hollow site (Ritchie, 1954: 43), the Old Birch Island Cemetery in Georgian Bay, which is thought to date to the period around A.D. 1700 (Greenman, 1951: 49-56), and from the earliest level at Michilimackinac (Lyle Stone: personal communication). Pratt has assigned these beads to the A.D. 1660-1677 Oneida sites in New York (1961: *loc. cit.*, 68).

Four similar barrel-shaped beads from the Summer Island component were very dark blue and opaque (Figure 11, h). Beads of this type have been reported from Ste. Marie I (Kidd, 1949: *loc. cit.*), Ossossane (Kidd, 1953: *loc. cit.*), the Kleis site (White, *loc. cit.*), the Dutch Hollow site (Ritchie, 1954; *loc. cit.*), the Old Birch Island Cemetery (Greenman, *loc. cit.*), and the Zimmerman site (Brown, 1961: 60-63). They occur on Oneida sites assigned to the period A.D. 1637-1710 (Pratt, *loc. cit.*).

There was a single oblate spheroidal transparent amber bead (Figure 11, i) 4.5 mm in length, 6.8 mm in outside diameter and 1.8 mm in internal diameter. This type of bead is also quite uncommon in the Great Lakes area, only being reported from the earliest levels of Fort Michilimackinac (Lyle Stone: personal communication; Maxwell and Binford, *loc. cit.*).

Also recovered was a single large translucent amber colored spun glass bead (Figure 11, j), 12.2 mm long, 14.3 mm in external diameter, and 2.8 mm in internal diameter. This bead appeared to have been made of a quickly spun low temperature glass for fusing was not complete and the finished bead is quite grainy, as if it had been weathered wood. A single bead quite similar to this has been reported from the Dutch Hollow site (Ritchie, 1954: *loc. cit.*) and several are noted from the Bell site (Wittry, 1963: *loc. cit.*), as well as the earliest level of Fort Michilimackinac (Maxwell and Binford, *loc. cit.*). In general this style seems most popular in the early eighteenth century.

Three opaque white glass elliptical beads were also recovered from this Summer Island component (Figure 11, k). These were somewhat ragged-edged as if they had been broken at the tapered extruded ends. In length these beads averaged 13.1 mm and had an average outside diameter of 7.3 mm and an internal diameter averaging 1.9 mm. Similar beads have been reported from the Ossossane ossuary (Kidd, 1953: Fig. 123), the Frank Bay site on Lake Nipissing, Ontario (Ridley, 1954: 49), the Bell site (Wittry, 1953: *loc. cit.*), the Old Birch Island Cemetery (Greenman, 1951: *loc. cit.*), and the lowest level of Fort Michilimackinac (Maxwell and Binford, 1961: Pl. I, i). This type of bead is not reported for any of the New York sites which may indicate a distribution via French sources.

Two faceted octahedral beads, one white and one blue, were recovered from the protohistoric component at Summer Island (Figure 11, l). Both were rather opaque. Both white and blue faceted beads of this type have also been reported from the Old Birch Island Cemetery (Greenman, *loc. cit.*), the Bell site (Wittry, 1963: 31, fig. 21f) and the lowest levels at Michilimackinac (Maxwell and Binford, 1961: Pl. I, d). They occur in Oneida territory and are assigned to the period around A.D. 1710 although no good provenience data exists for them (Pratt, 1961: 16).

Of the sixteen small seed beads six were dark opaque blue (Figure 11, m) while ten were opaque white (Figure 11, n). Both colors of this type bead were squared by hot-tumbling. These beads were about 2.0 mm in length and external diameter. This was probably the

most popular type of glass trade bead in North America and is thus almost useless for dating purposes. It has been reported from Ste. Marie I (Kidd, *loc. cit.*), Ossossane (Kidd, *loc. cit.*), the Beverly ossuary (Quimby, *loc. cit.*), the Dutch Hollow site (Ritchie, 1954: 43-44), the Kleis site (White, *loc. cit.*), the Zimmerman site (Brown, 1961: Fig. 20, d), the Old Birch Island Cemetery (Greenman, *loc. cit.*), the Lassanen site (Charles Cleland: personal communication) from all levels of Fort Michilimackinac (Maxwell and Binford, 1961: Pl. I, r) and from numerous late historic sites in Michigan (Quimby, 1966a; Brose, 1966). In New York Pratt has reported this type on Oneida sites dated from A.D. 1625 through A.D. 1745 (1961: 9-17, 34, 65, 110).

Ten wampum beads (Figure 11, o) were also recovered from this level of Summer Island. These were made of Quahog (*Venus mercenaria*) or "hard clam" shell. The uniform outside diameter of 2.8 mm and the even, centered drilling of the internal hole (diameter= 1.5 mm) probably indicates that these beads are of European manufacture. Wampum of this type was being manufactured in large amounts in North America at least as early as 1650 (Orchard, 1929: 61-70). It is reported from every site previously mentioned with the exception of the Bell site, Plum Island and the Zimmerman site. Like the small cane or seed beads the drilled wampum is too widespread in space and time to be of much value for dating the components in which it occurs.

Iron Artifacts

The nine iron artifacts of European manufacture recovered from the protohistoric competent at Summer Island consisted of two rectangular and one rounded awl (Figure 12, a-c), one barbed fish hook (Figure 12, d), two clasp-knives blades (Figure 12, g), a needle (Figure 12, h), and a hinge fragment (Figure 12, i). Awls similar to those recovered from Summer Island are also reported from the Bell site (Wittry, 1963: 34, Fig. 24, M-Z), the Frank Bay site (Ridley, 1954: 43), the Ossossane ossuary (Kidd, 1953: 369), the Kleis site (White, 1967: 17) the Dutch Hollow site (Ritchie, 1954: 25-26), the Old Birch Island Cemetery (Greenman, 1951: Pl. XIX, Fig. le), the Zimmerman site (Brown, 1961: Fig. 20, n), and from all levels of Fort Michilimackinac (Maxwell and Binford, 1961: 88, Pl. XIII, h).

Eyeless barbed fish hooks similar to the Summer Island specimen are reported from Ste. Marie I (Kidd, 1949: 125-126; Plate XLIX, g), the Frank Bay site (Ridley, 1954: 43), and

FIGURE 12. *European trade goods from the protohistoric component at Summer Island*

Perspectives from *Historical Archaeology:*

from Fort Michilimackinac (Maxwell and Binford, 1961: 96). All of these hooks have a flattened end which may have been set into a handle thus conforming more to a modern gaff hook. In size however, all are somewhat smaller than modern gaffs and correspond to what is currently a number two or three fish hook.

The smallest knife blade fragment seems to have been the tip of a "hawk-billed" clasp knife. Such knives have been reported from the Kleis site (White, 1967: 16-19), the Frank Bay site (Ridley, 1954: 45), the Bell site (Wittry, 1963: 35; Fig. 25, b, g-j), the Plum Island site (Fenner, 1963: 89; Fig. 39, d), the Ossossane ossuary (Kidd, 1953: 367) and from Fort Michilimackinac in the earliest levels (Maxwell and Binford, 1961: 105-106). The other clasp-knife blade is described as "sword-shaped." It had a small horizontal flange along the upper proximal portion of the blade. Stamped horizontally along the blade were letters interpreted as LR while above this was an L followed by three Maltese crosses and the numeral 0. Knife blades of this type have been reported from Ossossane (Kidd, 1953: 367-369), Ste. Marie I (Kidd, 1949: 113-114; Plate XLIII), the Zimmerman site (Brown, 1961: Fig. 20, h), the Bell site (Wittry, 1963: 35; Fig. 25, a, c-f), and the earliest levels of Fort Michilimackinac (Maxwell and Binford, 1961: 105-106). While marks were common, the only site yielding the three Maltese crosses was Ste. Marie I (Kidd, 1949: 114; Fig. 19).

The iron needle from the Summer Island protohistoric component was 53.9 mm long and about 1 mm in diameter. It had broken at the eye leaving two short prongs. Similar needles are reported from Ste. Marie I (Kidd, 1949: 118; Plate XLI, e), the Bell site (Wittry, 1963: 34) and from later levels of Fort Michilimackinac (Maxwell and Binford, 1961: 107).

The iron wire bale is assumed to have been part of a brass kettle. Iron wire has been found on most of the sites named above.

The small hinged iron rod from Summer Island was very well made. The rod itself was threaded at one end and burred, as if riveted at the other. While this may have been a sear element in a flintlock of snaphaunce, it is too fragmentary to identify with certainty.

Brass Artifacts

Fourteen brass artifacts of European origin were excavated from the Summer Island protohistoric component. A brass hawk-bell or morris bell 15 mm in diameter (Figure 12, j) is similar to others reported from the Dutch Hollow site (Ritchie, 1954: 45; Plate 12, fig. 12), Ste. Marie I (Kidd, 1949: 127), all levels of Fort Michilimackinac (Maxwell and Binford, 1961: 90) and appropriately, the Bell site (Wittry, 1963: 17; Fig. 11, c).

Four brass tinkling cones probably cut from bass kettles were recovered from Summer Island (Figure 12, k). These ranged from 28.4 to 35.3 mm in length and from 7.0 mm to 11.5 mm in basal diameter. Similar ornaments are reported from the Dutch Hollow site (Ritchie, 1954: 44; Pl. XII, fig. 7, 13-15), the ossuary at Ossossane (Kidd, 1953: 370), the Frank Bay site (Ridley, 1954: 47), the Plum Island site (Fenner, 1963: 89; Fig. 39, a), the Zimmerman site (Brown, 1961: 60-61; Fig. 20, b), the Bell site (Wittry, 1963: 19; Fig. 10, a-m), the Old Birch Island Cemetery (Greenman, 1951: 45; Pl. XX, fig. 1, c, d), and from all levels of Fort Michilimackinac (Maxwell and Binford, 1961: 111).

The brass thimble from Summer Island was 23 mm high with an upper diameter of 10 mm and a basal diameter estimated at 14.5 mm. Similar artifacts have been reported from Ste. Marie I (Kidd, 1949: 118), the Bell site (Wittry, 1963: 21; Fig. 11a) and from the Franch occupation of Fort Michilimackinac (Maxwell and Binford, 1961: 110).

The fragment of a brass kettle with a rim rolled over an iron hoop is a common artifact on early historic sites. The only sites referred to above which did *not* yield at least one similar artifact were the Plum Island and Zimmerman sites in northern Illinois. This near universal occurrence is also true of the cut strips of brass which were no doubt obtained from such kettles once they had become unserviceable. All sites described above had at least two such fragments, and many had considerably more than the five pieces recovered at Summer Island.

The last brass artifact from Summer Island consisted of the two fragments of a small brass ring presumed to have been a "Jesuit" ring. Similar rings and ring fragments are reported from the Ossossane ossuary (Kidd, 1953: 369; Fig. 125, c-f), Ste. Marie I (Kidd, 1949: 128), the Bell site (Wittry, 1963: 18; Fig. 11, d-k), and from all levels of Fort Michilimackinac (Maxwell and Binford, 1961: 105; Pl. IX). The Dutch and English-oriented Iroquoian Dutch Hollow and Kleis sites, predictably, have yielded no Jesuit rings. The lack of these artifacts from the Illinois country is not as easily explained. While both LaSalle and Cadillac were apparently somewhat Anti-clerical (Parkman, 1879; 1885), Marquette and

Joliet were necessarily not. While regional differences in their distribution may well be due to sampling error, further study may indicate that these artifacts are a good indication of the extent of those areas in which greater or lesser influence was exercised by the various religious orders of New France.

Miscellaneous Artifacts

A single gunflint was recovered from Area "B" in those deposits attributable to the protohistoric component (Figure 12, p). This was a wedge-shaped flake of somewhat mottled opaque dark gray to light gray to tan flint having a waxy surface and an excellent conchoidal fracture. There are tiny white inclusions of an unknown chalky nature in this flint matrix. One face of this flake (illustrated) is unmodified showing the inner surface of the flake with a thinned positive bulb of percussion, and slight marginal retouching. The dorsal surface of the flake shows somewhat more intensive finishing having several long flakes driven off along the edges. The entire flake is rather thin having a striking edge with about a ten to fifteen degree angle. The striking edge shows heavy battering from use. The flake has broken vertically to approximately two-thirds of its original width. This is the type of gunflint Hamilton has characterized as "gun-spall" (1960: 76) which he feels attained their popularity in Europe at about A.D. 1675. Witthoft has indicated that these may have been gunflints of Dutch manufacture which were predominant during the period A.D. 1650-1700. Gunspalls similar to the Summer Island specimen are reported from the Kleis site (White, 1967: 14) and from the Lassanen Cemetery (Charles Cleland: personal communication). A single similar gunspall was recovered from the surface of a village site at Chippewa Harbor on Isle Royale (Bastian, 1963: 309).

The last three artifacts of European origin from the Summer Island protohistoric component were three lead balls, all clearly made in a clamp or pliers-type mold (Figure 12, q). Two of these had an average diameter of 12.2 mm, while the third had an average diameter of 10.4 mm. It is assumed that these were lead shot for a musket or pistol. Due to the variable nature of lead shot little precision is possible in attempting to infer bore diameter (and thus probable firearm) from a sample of three. The great difference between the diameter of the single small ball and that of the two larger ones does make it clear however that at least two different firearms are represented in this component.

In terms of the trade goods recovered from the protohistoric component, the last aboriginal occupation of Summer Island seems to have taken place some time during the last half of the seventeenth century A.D. If the presence of the Lawson Opposed or Lawson Oblique, and the Sidey Notched rimsherds are taken as evidence of refugee Huron potters living among the Bay de Noc Lip potters, a date after the dispersal of the Huron-Neutral confederacy in 1650 may be postulated for this occupation. G. Wright (1967: 187) has adduced evidence indicating that while foodstuffs and tobacco were the major items of aboriginal trade, active trade in ceramics did occur at least in A.D. 1658. Somewhat analogous to Greek Amphorae, one might also reasonably expect to find a movement of ceramic containers wherever shelled corn or similar foodstuffs are traded. Under these conditions the presence of Huron or Neutral pottery may be an indication of trade rather than of forced migration.

Although some of the diagnostic European-manufactured artifacts from this component have been reported in sites in the Great Lakes area as early as A.D. 1625 or as late as A.D. 1730 this in no way detracts from the more limited dates of occupation proposed here. Of the sixty-nine such artifacts, fifty-five, or nearly eight percent, can be classified as articles of personal adornment or jewelry. These beads, bells, and rings seem to have complimented the aboriginal artifacts. The remaining articles, which here occur in such a low frequency, are those items which eventually replaced the native manufactures completely. At this point in time and space chipped flint projectile points still occur in much higher frequency than gun parts, aboriginal ceramics are much more evident than brass kettles, and iron knives and scraping tools have not yet replaced the native stone tools. The greatest change in the native tool kit is probably the replacement of bone awls and needles by their iron counterparts. If any conclusion as to the nature of acculturation can be drawn from these observations it may be that those native tools most directly connected with subsistence activities were among those most governed by tradition and therefore least amenable to rapid change. Whether this can be taken to indicate that the women were more conscious of the new fashions, or more desirous of them, is a moot point. It is clear, however, that the protohistoric component at Summer Island represents a group whose aboriginal material culture had not been too greatly altered by the contact with European trade.

ECONOMIC ADAPTATION

Subsistence

From the protohistoric component of the site 13,273.0 grams of mammal bone, 196.0 grams of bird bone, 832.9 grams of fish bone, and 289.0 grams of other bone were recovered. A faunal analysis by species was undertaken by Barbara (Bird) Luxenberg, Research Assistant at The University of Michigan Museum of Anthropology. While the final report is not yet completed, the preliminary analysis clearly shows that the major food resources during the protohistoric occupation were whitetail deer, elk, black bear, cottontail rabbit, and beaver. Fish, bird, and turtle apparently provided only secondary roles in the subsistence of the group. Among the identified fish remains bass (*Microptirus sp.*), sturgeon, and northern pike were the most frequent species recovered.

It should be noted that most of the large fish present in this region were not extensively exploited. The fishing industry evidenced by the faunal remains seems to have been confined to the shallow weedy shoal water which during summers was considerably warmer than the waters below five feet in depth, and which still today supports large summer populations of bass and pike. These fish could be taken by hook and line angling equally well as by spearing (Rostlund, 1952: 115-119). The sturgeon, inhabiting these shallow shoal waters year-round, would be most easily obtainable by spearing in the late spring or early summer when they spawn (Scott, 1954: 7).

The mammalian fauna recovered is noteworthy because of the presence of elk and the absence of moose. Given the aboriginal environment of Summer Island moose should have been the major large herbivore present (see Dice, 1938: 504; map 2), and elk would not be expected much nearer than the southern edge of the Canadian Biotic Province in northeastern Wisconsin (Dice, 1938: 511; Cleland, 1966: 6). The presence of charred elk bone in association with the Lake Winnebago Trailed and Summer Island Cordmarked ceramics (Feature 47) may indicate that the protohistoric group spent some part of their seasonal round in that part of Wisconsin, probably the fall or winter seasons. According to Lalemant, in the seventeenth century the inhabitants of this biotic transition zone comprised ". . . more wandering than settled people. They seem to have as many abodes as the year has seasons." (J. R., XXI: 239).

The faunal remains from this component confirm the hypothesis that the occupation was primarily a summer one. The botanical remains recovered from the protohistoric features were identified by Mssrs. Volney Jones and Daniel Caister, of The University of Michigan, Ethnobotanical Laboratory. They consisted of eight charred fragments of hazelnut shell (*Corylus sp.*), two chokecherry seeds (*Prunus virginiana*) and twenty-eight charred squash seeds (*Cucurbita pepo*). The fruit of the hazelnut and chokecherry both ripen in late August to early September (Yarnell, 1964: 59, 63). The squash from this component is the most northern archaeologically recovered in North America (Yarnell, 1964: 109, Map 2). While there is no climatic reason why squash could not have been grown on Summer Island (*idem:* 149-151) it may also have been obtained in trade from other groups further to the south. This would be increasingly likely if the Neo-Boreal episode of climate cooler than present which existed from about A.D. 1550 to A.D. 1880 can be shown to have had as much effect on the cultivation of squash as it seems to have had on maize (*idem:* 34-36).

Regardless of the origin of the squash seeds, the subsistence economy of the protohistoric occupation of Summer Island seems to have centered about the hunting of deer, rabbit, and beaver, supplemented by black bear and shallow water fishing with both hook and line and spear. Agricultural products played a minor role if, in fact, they were not imported onto the site by members of this same ethnic group from the agricultural site of the previous season or by outsiders in trade for furs or meat. The view of a minor role for agriculture is reinforced by the diffuse nature of the economy (Cleland, 1966: 44-75) as seen in the large numbers of quite different animal species utilized as food.

Seasonal Cycle

One could hypothesize that the protohistoric occupation of Summer Island represents a group who arrived from the Wisconsin mainland in early spring probably carrying with them some foodstuffs such as dried meat or shelled corn. While on the island some crops such as squash were probably planted, ". . . more for pleasure and that they might have fresh food to eat than for their support." (Lalemant, *loc. cit.*). The major resources were apparently deer, bear, and beaver which were probably hunted on the Garden Peninsula by small male parties which absented themselves from the village on Summer Island for a few days at a time. On the island some fishing was practiced, and beaver, rabbits, and other small mammals were trapped or hunted throughout the summer. Toward the end of summer the fishing was gradually abandoned in favor of hunting deer, and the harvesting of nuts probably occupied most of the remaining time. With the first frost the entire group left the island for the more open ground to the immediate southwest of Green Bay where they would engage in hunting elk or bison, or where a larger "parent" agricultural village (such as the Bell site) composed of a number of similar small family groups might be located. With the coming of winter either the entire group would fractionate into separate nuclear families which would head into the interior forests for hunting, or elders, children, and women might remain in the "parent" village while the men went off on hunting expeditions which would last several weeks.

It can be seen that a wide range of possibilities exist in the interpretation of the seasonal pattern of the Summer Island protohistoric occupants. On one hand they are seen, via the faunal remains, to have a diffuse economy such as is characteristic of the historic Chippewa. In this model large summer fishing settlements split into small nuclear families for winter hunting (Alexander Henry, cited in Quimby, 1966a). On the other hand the model outlined above seems to allow an adaptation much like the historic Miami (Kinietz, 1940: 171) where large permanent agricultural villages are supplemented by male and female hunting parties in the winter, and male trading and/or hunting parties in the summer (G. Wright, 1967), with the entire village taking part in autumn hunts on the prairie. A similar situation, with an economy lying between that of the Chippewa and that of the Miami, was the case for the historic Ottawa (Kinietz, 1940:236-238) but the Ottawa summer parties leaving the main village were practicing a type of economic exploitation relying on a very limited number of animal species. The summer villages of such an economic pattern would appear to exhibit a quite polarized focal economy.

Sexual Composition

No doubt much of the problem could be solved if some idea of the sexual composition of the group at Summer Island could be determined. Because of the disturbed nature of much of the deposit pertaining to this component areal distribution of artifacts cannot be used to infer "fragile patterns" of behavior. If one ignores the variations certain to occur in any human group one can assume that the presence of both lithic debitage and ceramics implies the presence of both male and female members of the group. In attempting to go beyond this one might, like Fitting (1968: 69-70), assume that the relative frequencies of these artifacts to some extent reflect the ratio of men to women at any particular site. This, of course, entails the further assumption that on a site such as Summer Island intermittent occupation was by similar groups. Granted these assumptions the ratio (as expressed by a ratio of finished artifacts of chipped stone to ceramic vessels of about 3 to 1) indicates a predominantly male group but with some number of females accompanying them.

There are several factors which argue against the acceptance of this ratio as meaningful. There is no reason to suppose that a group of males planning to stay at a hunting site for several weeks would not have brought with them foodstuffs in a ceramic vessel, or would not require one for cooking. There is no adequate ethnographic data, even for the late groups referred to in the models above, to indicate whether the relative ratios of artifacts will remain the same if the size of the group varies. If a family group with three men and three women need, say, three pots will six women need six pots? More pertinent still is the lack of data which would allow one to state with any degree of certainty that the ratio of artifacts will not vary principally as a result of functional or mechanical factors. Perhaps more ceramic vessels will occur where clays are sandier or where vessels are larger and thus have less structural strength. Perhaps the number of scrapers can be correlated more with the type of flint than the type of family.

As a further consideration one might note that in this component European materials have replaced several aboriginally made artifacts. This replacement was seen to have been quite selective with artifacts directly related to subsistence seemingly less amenable to such replacement. Unless some correction can be made for these factors of differential artifact replacement by trade goods the ratios arrived at will be of little value. One would like to know whether a brass kettle should be considered as a male status symbol or as a female implement.

Acculturation

It is not surprising that the Summer Island occupation of the mid-seventeenth century does not conform to models derived from late eighteenth or nineteenth century ethnohistory. The Summer Island protohistoric component represents a period of major, even catastrophic change in the upper Great Lakes. Ethnic groups had been unaccustomed to the accumulation of material surplus beyond what aboriginal channels of trade could immediately accommodate. The introduction of the European into what aboriginal fur trade there may have been, wrought major changes. Whether aboriginal trade ever had the significance it later assumed throughout the Great Lakes area is a doubtful, though unanswered question. Ethnohistorians who cite early and mid-seventeenth century reports of Indians trading furs for corn or tobacco as evidence for an aboriginal fur trade are indeed begging the question (cf., G. Wright, 1967; Hickerson, 1960). What would the Iroquois and Huron want with thousands of peltries prior to the arrival of the Dutch and French with whom they could exchange them for European goods? What evidence can be cited for such trade prior to A.D. 1600? The type of trade postulated by McPherron (1967: 288-295) for the precontact population of the Juntunen site is not of sufficient magnitude to cause the major alterations in cultural ecology which accompanied the European trade goods.

In a good season any upper Great Lakes hunter could probably accumulate more fur (in the form of food packaging) than would be needed for his own family. That such surplus furs entered some aboriginal exchange network is expectable. This trade is far from the classic fur trade with its debtor-creditor relationship and intendant loss of economic freedom. To create the latter, European trade goods were essential. In its later stages the acculturation process has been extensively reported for the Indians of upper Great Lakes (Eggan, 1966; Fenton, 1940; Hickerson, 1960, 1962; Hoffman, 1893; Innis, 1962; Radin, 1923; Trigger, 1962). Ethnohistory and ethnography have not dealt with the initial stages of the acculturative processes for the good reason that European accounts are anywhere from twenty to a hundred years later than European trade goods in this area (Brose, n.d. b).

With the arrival of European outlets for the accumulation of surplus furs and hides, these items took on a value which the aboriginal populations could not have placed upon them. In the competition for fur those Indian groups whose focal economic adaptation was based on agriculture or fishing were in a less advantageous position than those groups with a diffuse economy or a focal economy based on hunting. No aboriginal group in the upper Great Lakes seems to have had an economic adaptation focused so narrowly that hunting was entirely precluded. The highly diffuse

economies such as that practiced by the historic (eighteenth century) Chippewa, however, incorporated both extreme mobility and a utilization of the fur-bearing mammals for at least a third of the year. Of the early economic adaptations reported by Europeans in the area of the upper lakes, this "aboriginal" Chippewa pattern could accommodate itself to the acquisition of surplus pelts with the least changes. Rather than viewing this Chippewa economic pattern as one where winter hunting supplemented the winter-curtailed fishing industry, it can be seen as one where summer fishing annually avoided hunting while pelts were in the poorest condition. European troops subsequently garrisoned where Chippewa summer fishing villages existed were often able to sustain themselves year-round without resorting to extended hunting trips into the interior forests (Parkman, 1885; Hickerson, 1962).

For the aboriginal groups whose economy provided less opportunity for the acquisition of peltries, two routes existed whereby a share of the European trade goods might be obtained. Groups such as the Huron and Iroquois located nearest the European settlements acted as middlemen, obtaining furs from the more distant Indians (perhaps along precontact exchange networks as suggested by Hunt (1940) and G. Wright (1967).) In return for these furs the European trade goods entered the network through these eastern aboriginal groups. Those aboriginal groups favored by more beaver and less Europeans would have been forced to readjust their economic adaptation. At first simply to meet the increased demands of their "trade-partners" and later, dependent on European goods, in competition with similar aboriginal groups. By the mid-seventeenth century the eastern Iroquoian groups were being bypassed both by unlicensed Europeans and by the more acculturated western Indians. In this view the interjection of European trade goods leads to a total collapse of precontact exchange networks rather than to their intensification.

The machinations of the eastern Indians have been explored at some length by Hunt (1940), Trigger (1962), and others. The exact processes of acculturation which the western Indians underwent is more poorly understood (e.g., Quimby, 1966a). I would offer the hypothesis that the major change was the readjustment of the aboriginal economic pattern to one more closely approximating that of the historic northern Chippewa in order to maximize the opportunities for hunting or trapping the fur-bearing mammals.

With the exhaustion of the faunal resources in the upper Great Lakes the center of European-based fur trade moved to the upper Mississippian and Saskatchewan drainage basins. By the time the British entered the Great Lakes the local Indian had either been forced into a role as middlemen for Indians further to the west (Innis, 1962) or had, like some Chippewa, themselves moved further west following the fur trade (Hickerson, 1962), or had begun to readapt their economy away from a focus on hunting or trapping fur-bearing mammals. If this view is correct the economic patterns exhibited by the Indians of the Great Lakes in A.D. 1800 may be closer to those of the period before A.D. 1600, than they are to those of the early seventeenth through mid-eighteenth century. Models derived from the ethnographic accounts of the late eighteenth and nineteenth century would thus be quite inapplicable to the period when the fur trade was paramount. The economic pattern practiced by the protohistoric inhabitants of Summer Island during the period of initial readaptation to the fur trade, then, cannot be determined by reference to either the early historic Chippewa, the contemporary Ottawa, or the later Miami. It must be understood strictly in terms of the transitional position it occupies, its geographical location, and the nature of the material recovered.

Social Organization

Taking into consideration the above qualifications I would view the Summer Island protohistoric component as representing several extended families, each containing from five to ten people, and each occupying a single structure at the site. While there is no way to determine the original descent reckonings of this group I would expect the emphasis which the fur trade placed upon small, quite mobile, predominantly male hunting groups to be exerting strong selection for patrilocality (see Service, 1962: 50-54; Murdock, 1949: 530). If the presently known distribution of culturally similar sites of this time period can be taken as a reflection of the population density some form of cross-cousin marriage may have been practiced (see Eggan, 1966: 89-91). The entire population of the group, assuming there were at least three simultaneously inhabited structures, would have been about fifteen to thirty people. Assuming the group had been subjected to the same type of acculturative processes as the Chippewa of the Sault Saint Marie region, one could postulate a situation where the social organization was transitional from a patrilocal band to a

composite one (Hickerson, 1960: 101; Service, 1962: 85). Therefore the interrelationship of the several families cannot be inferred with any degree or accuracy.

Adaptation to the Fur Trade

In general, the best interpretation of the protohistoric component at Summer Island would seem to be that the occupation consisted of a small number of patrilocal and probably patrilineal families most of which may have been patrilineally related but who were beginning to be identified more by territory than by family (Hickerson, 1960). The occupation took place over several years during the late spring to early fall period of the year. While on the island the major subsistence activity was the hunting of deer and fur-bearing mammals on the nearby islands and mainland. These hunting parties were probably composed of a few related males. Some fishing and possibly some limited agriculture was practiced by the members of the group remaining on the island. Since the major faunal resource of the island, fish, was under-exploited, one might assume that the economy had to some extent been readapted to meet the demands of the growing fur trade, stimulated by European trade goods from the east. In this respect Summer Island with its central location and well-protected harbor would be an ideal point from which eastern trade could move into Bay de Noc, Green Bay, and western Lake Michigan. With the onset of winter the island was probably abandoned.

Certainly the European fur trade is the only reasonable explanation for Summer Island to have been occupied as a non-fishing village. In that respect it is so ideally suited for a rendezvous point that prior to the excavation of the site Quimby (1966a: 55-57) had decided that it must be the "Island of the Poutouatamis" to which LaSalle sailed the *Griffin* late in the summer of A.D. 1679. Quimby (1966a: 45-62) had chosen Summer Island after an analysis of the voyage of the *Griffin* (as reported by Hennepin) and a journey by sailboat from Saint Ignace (old Michilimackinac) Michigan: taking into consideration the probable size and shape of the vessel, and inferring from Hennepin the rigging, Quimby attempted to duplicate the last leg of the *Griffin's* voyage. By sailing just offshore and sounding frequently (as the *Griffin* presumably did in uncharted waters) Quimby found that Summer Island lay about 110 miles from St. Ignace thus corresponding to Hennepin's statements. Due, however, to the variability in the concepts of just what distance a league represented (G. Wright, 1967: 182n) and the inaccuracies inherent in estimating distances travelled over water with a home-made log (if any), any one of the seven islands in the mouth of Green Bay could be considered forty leagues west of the straits. Several of them have harbors which could match the description of that of the "Island of Poutouatamis" (Hennepin, 1938: 38-39). The type of storm Hennepin described (*ibid.*) does not rule out Washington Island as Quimby implies (166a: 56-57). Furthermore, if one accepts Hennepin's estimates of forty leagues from Michilimackinac to the "Island of the Poutouatamis" one should not ignore his statement that this island was only a good four leagues from the southern mainland (Hennepin, *op. cit.*: 41). Using Quimby's own unverified estimate of 2.765 miles per league the distance between the tip of the Door Peninsula of Wisconsin the the "Isle" should be from eleven to thir-

teen miles. This corresponds more closely to the northwest bay of Washington Island than to Summer Harbor which, by Quimby's formula, is over ten leagues from the southern mainland. G. Richard Peske of the University of Wisconsin, Milwaukee is currently conducting archaeological excavations of the aboriginal village site of the northwestern harbor on Washington Island. The results of these investigations may add to the solution of this problem.

It is clear in any event that the protohistoric component at Summer Island could have been the site visited by LaSalle in A.D. 1679. That site was one to which LaSalle had sent his men the previous spring to barter for furs (Hennepin 1938: 38) with the small group of Indians living there. If that village is not represented by the protohistoric component at Summer Island it will be represented by one very much like it.

Table I

Features of the Protohistoric Component

F.#	Definition	Ex. Unit	Location	Size	Shape	Contents
13	Refuse Pit	480E 510-515	No association with known structures	4.3' x 2.7' x 1.7'	Asymmetrical pit with 2 steep walls uneven flat bottom	12 flat flakes; 2 decortication flakes; 1 pebble core; 1 notched triangular point; 47 grams mammal bone; 1 human incisor; 4 sherds Summer Island Cordmarked; 1 sherd Garden Incised; 1 Iroquoian shers; 2 glass beads; 1 iron fish hook; 1 copper bead; 2 Oneota sherds; 1 Middle Woodland sherd
17	Refuse Pit	460E545	No association with known structures	3.6' x 1.9' x 1.1'	Asymmetrical pit with 2 steep walls, uneven flat bottom	7 decortication flakes; 8 flat flakes, 2 bipolar cores; 1 end scraper, 1 bifacial blade; 6 bladelets; 20 grams fish bone; 40 grams mammal bone; 1 iron needle; 1 brass thimble; 4 glass beads; 4 sherds Summer Island Cordmarked 1 sherd Grand River Plain; 3 Middle Woodland sherds
18	Storage Pit	460E550	No association with known structures	2.8' x 2.2' x 0.8'	Asymmetrical pit with 1 steep, 1 gently curved wall, flat bottom	12 flat flakes; 49 grams fish bone; 0.75 kg. fire-cracked rock
30	Hearth	685E430	North hearth in structure, 8.0' from entrance	3.4' x 2.7' x 0.9'	Symmetrical gently rounded walls flat bottom	26 decortication flakes; 37 block flakes; 89 flat flakes; 1 bifacial blade; 4 bladelets; 1 triangular point; 1 copper bead; 2 brass kettle fragments; 1 clasp-knife blade; 20 grams fish bone; 30 grams mammal bone; 4.25 kg. firecracked rock

Table I
(Continued)

33	Hearth	685E435	South hearth in structure, 12.3' from entrance	2.9' x 2.3' x 0.9'	Symmetrical gently rounded walls, flat bottom	13 decortication flakes; 67 flat flakes; 3 bipolar cores; 1 bifacial blank; 2 lead balls; 1 gunflint; 40 grams mammal bone; 5.0 kg. firecracked rock
34	Refuse Pit	609E435	In S-center of structure, between F.#33 and entrance	1.2' x 1.1' x 0.7'	Asymmetrical pit with 2 steep curved walls	17 decortication flakes; 35 flat flakes; 17 block flakes; 1 bifacial blank; 2 triangular points; 2 block cores; 1 bipolar core; 3 sherds Bay de Noc Notched Lip; 1 sherd Summer Island Cordmarked; 1 sherd Garden Incised; 1 copper bead; 1 lead ball; 28 charred squash seeds (Curcurbita pepo.), small variety
41	Storage Pit	545E495	No association with known structures	2.7' x 2.2' x 1.4'	Bell-shaped pit with gently rounded walls and floor	4 decortication flakes; 10 flat flakes; 1 block flake; 1 end scraper; 27 grams mammal bone; 10 grams bird bone; 3 sherds Garden Incised; 3 sherds Bay de Noc Notched Lip; 1 sherd Lake Winnebago Trailed; 2 glass beads; 1 iron awl
47	Hearth	510E550	On far SE edge of component No association with known structures	2.2' x 2.1' x 0.7'	Symmetrical gently rounded walls, flat bottomed pit	3 flat flakes; 1 decortication flake; 1 bipolar core; 1 end scraper; 1 slate abrader; 278 grams charred mammal bone; (Bear [Ursus americanus] and Elk [Cervus canadensis]); small flecks of charcoal; 1 sherd Summer Island Cordmarked; 5 sherds Bay de Noc Notched Lip; 3 sherds Lake Winnebago Trailed; 7.05 kg. firecracked rock

Table II

Chipped Stone Distribution from Protohistoric Component

Category	Number	Percent of Total Number	Weight (in grams)	Percent of Total Weight	Percent of non-local cherts
Flakes:					
Decortication	1042	6.45	7184	29.37	12.4
Block	3981	24.28	6182	25.08	9.1
Flat	9877	60.45	4215	17.08	7.3
Cores:					
Pebble	295	1.80	1881	7.65	9.8
Block	874	5.30	2837	11.48	9.0
Bipolar	131	0.81	1141	4.63	8.3
Bifaces:					
Scraper	9	0.05	138	0.56	0
Blade	4	0.02	53	0.21	25.0
Bank	6	0.04	236	0.96	16.5
Projectile					
Point	17	0.10	201	0.81	6.0

Unifaces:					
End Scraper	16	0.09	157	0.64	6.3
Side Scraper	5	0.03	69	0.28	0
Notched Scraper	4	0.02	29	0.12	0
Bladelet	35	0.24	68	0.27	20.0
Utilized Flake	82	0.50	284	1.15	7.4
Total	16378	100.18	24675	100.29	
		216		116	28

Table III
Late Woodland Projectile Points

Catalog Number	Length	Width	Thickness
74170	2.90	0.61	0.40
74140	1.96	1.43	0.39
74325			0.34
74325			0.36
74325	2.33	1.12	0.43
74325	1.64	1.05	0.33
74175	4.90	2.97	0.49
74294	3.60	2.89	1.59
74294	3.43	3.46	1.03
75138	5.62	3.33	0.73
75138		1.38	0.30
75130		1.37	0.37
75136	4.46	2.23	1.18
74428	5.56	2.89	1.44
75190	3.67	2.75	1.06
75190		2.00	0.99
75178	1.62	1.08	0.34
MEAN	3.47	2.10	0.69
	0.78	0.46	0.22

Table IV
Late Woodland Scrapers

Umma Cat. Number	Max. Length (cm)	Max. Width (cm)	Thickness at Scraping Edge (cm)	Length of Scraping Edge (cm)	Degree of Arc on Working Edge	Cortex Present
74878	2.36	1.81	0.70	1.81	50	No
74656	3.70	3.05	0.72	3.05	0	No
74903	1.84	2.12	0.50	1.85	-40	No
74857	2.69	2.49	0.60	2.49	75	No
74858	2.85	2.97	0.80	2.77	60	Yes
74503	2.80	1.81	0.54	1.22	-20	No
74571	2.79	2.80	0.51	2.54	-10	No
74478	3.88	2.14	0.73	1.87	30	No
74437	3.04	1.92	0.81	1.92	40	No
74607	2.22	1.85	0.26	2.22	-35	No
74004	1.42	2.07	0.32	1.91	70	No
74428	3.18	1.75	0.76	2.29	60	No
74428	3.15	2.41	0.57	2.98	90	No
74428	2.38	2.46	0.60	2.63	90	No
74444	2.10	1.48	0.38	1.91	140	No
74325	1.83	1.96	0.33	1.53	50	No
74209	4.13	2.49	0.96	2.99	70	Yes
74230	2.56	2.23	0.69	2.10	0	No

74252	2.77	3.32	0.42	1.54	30	No
75129	2.76	2.59	0.66	2.59	0	No
75258		2.35	0.48	2.25	0	No
75189	3.44	2.90	0.65	2.90	105	No
75190	1.85	1.80	0.59	1.77	60	No
75148	3.51	2.79	0.71	1.43	20	Yes
75187	3.33	2.41	0.40	2.41	0	No
75187	4.78	3.63	0.75	2.42	0	No
MEAN	2.86	2.36	0.60	2.24	67	
	.56	.29	.10	.30	24	

REFERENCES

BASTIAN, TYLER
1963 *The Archaeology of Isle Royale.* National Park Service Report (ms), Ann Arbor.

BLUHM, ELAINE A. AND ALLEN LISS
1961 "The Anker Site, Chicago Area Archaeology." *Bulletin Illinois Archaeology Survey, No. 3.* Urbana.

BROSE, DAVID S.
1966a "The Valley Sweets Site, Saginaw Co., Michigan." *The Michigan Archaeologist,* Vol. 12, No. 1, pp. 1-24. Ann Arbor.

1966b "Excavations in Fort Mackinac: 1965." *The Michigan Archaeologist,* Vol. 12, No. 2, pp. 88-102. Ann Arbor.

1970a "The Archaeology of Summer Island: Changing Settlement Systems in Northern Lake Michigan." *Anthropological Papers, University of Michigan Museum of Anthropology, Number 41.* Ann Arbor.

1970b *Middle Woodland Culture Ecology and Social Organization in Northern Lake Michigan.* CWRU Papers in Anthro., No. 1. Cleveland.

n.d. a "Geological Analyses of Beach and Dune sands in Northern Lake Michigan." *The Ohio Journal of Science.* In press.

n.d. b "The Direct Historic Approach to Michigan Archaeology." *Ethnohistory.* Vol. 17, No. 4, Tucson. In press.

BROWN, JAMES A.
1961 *The Zimmerman Site Report of Investigations No. 9.* Illinois State Museum, Springfield.

CLELAND, CHARLES E.
1966 "The Prehistoric Animal Ecology and Ethnozoology of the Upper Great Lakes Region." *Anthropological Papers, Museum of Anthropology, University of Michigan, No. 29.* Ann Arbor.

CHANNEN, E. R. AND N. D. CLARKE
1965 "The Copeland Site: A Precontact Huron Site in Simcoe County, Ontario." *Anthropological Papers, National Museum of Canada, No. 8.* The Queens Printer, Ottawa.

DICE, LEE R.
1938 "The Canadian Biotic Province with special Reference to the Mammals." *Ecology,* Vol. 19, No. 4, pp. 503-514. Urbana.

FENNER, GLORIA J.
1963 "The Plum Island Site, La Salle County, Illinois." *Reports on Illinois Prehistory: I,* Bulletin No. 4. Illinois Archaeology Survey, Urbana.

FENTON, WILLIAM
1940 "Problems Relating to the Historic Position of the Iroquois." *Smithsonian Miscellaneous Collection, Vol. 100.* G.P.O. Washington, D.C.

FITTING, JAMES E.
1968 "The Spring Creek Site." *Anthropological Papers, Museum of Anthropology, University of Michigan, No. 32,* pp. 1-78, Ann Arbor.

GREENMAN, EMERSON
1951 "Old Birch Island Cemetery." *Occ. Pap. Univ. Mich. Museum of Anthrop., No. 11.* Ann Arbor.

GRIFFIN, JAMES B.
1943 *The Fort Ancient Aspect.* University of Michigan, Ann Arbor.

1967 "Eastern American Archaeology: A Summary." *Science,* Vol. 156, No. 3772, pp. 175-191. Washington, D.C.

HALL, ROBERT L.
1962 *The Archaeology of Carcajour Point.* 2 Vols. University of Wisconsin Press, Madison.

Perspectives from *Historical Archaeology:*

EGGAN, FRED
1966 *The American Indian.* Aldine, Chicago.

HAMILTON, T. M.
1960 "Additional Comments on Gunflints." *The Missouri Archaeologist*, Vol. 22, pp. 73-79. Columbia.

HENNEPIN, FR. LOUIS
1938 *Description of Louisiana Newly Discovered to the Southwest of New France by Order of the King.* Trans. by M. E. Cross, University of Minnesota Press, Minneapolis.

HICKERSON, HAROLD
1960 "The Feast of the Dead Among the 17th Century Algonkians of the Upper Great Lakes." *American Anthropologist*, Vol. 62, No. 1, pp. 81-107. Menasha.

1962 "The Southwestern Chippewa." *Mem. American Anthropological Association*, No. 92. Salt Lake City.

HOFFMAN, W. J.
1893 "The Menominee." *14th Annual Report of the Bureau of American Ethnology.* Washington, D.C.

HUNT, GEORGE
1940 *The Wars of the Iroquois.* University of Wisconsin Press, Madison

INNIS, HAROLD
1962 *The Fur Trade in Canada.* Yale, New Haven.

J. R.
see Thwaites, R. G.

JURY, WILFRID
1941 *Clearville Prehistoric Village Site in Oxford Township, Kent County, Ontario.* Bulletin of the Museum No. 2, University of Western Ontario. London, Ontario.

KIDD, KENNETH E.
1949 *The Excavation of Ste. Marie I.* University of Toronto Press, Toronto.

1953 "The Excavation and Identification of a Huron Ossuary." *American Antiquity*, Vol. 18, No. 4, pp. 359-79. Menasha.

KINIETZ, VERNON
1940 "The Indians of the Western Great Lakes." *Occasional Contributions Museum of Anthropology, University of Michigan, No. 10*, Ann Arbor.

MACNEISH, RICHARD S.
1952 "Iroquois Pottery Types." *Bulletin No. 124, National Museum of Canada.* Ottawa.

McKERN, W. C.
1945 "Preliminary Report of the Upper Mississippian Phase in Wisconsin." *Bulletin, Public Museum of Milwaukee*, Vol. XVI, No. 3. Milwaukee.

McPHERRON, ALAN L.
1967 "The Juntunen Site and the Late Woodland Prehistory of the Upper Great Lakes Area." *Anthropological Papers, Museum of Anthropology, University of Michigan, No. 30.* Ann Arbor.

MASON, RONALD J.
1967 "The North Bay Component at Porte Des Morts Site." *The Winconsin Archaeologist*, Vol. 48, No. 4, pp. 267-344. Lake Mills.

MAXWELL, MOREAU S. AND LEWIS R. BINFORD
1961 *Excavation at Fort Michilimackinac/ 1959 Season.* Pub. Museum, Cultural Ser., Michigan State University, Vol. I (1). East Lansing.

MURDOCK, GEORGE P.
1949 *Social Structure.* The Free Press, Collier-MacMillan. New York.

ORCHARD, WILLIAM C.
1929 *Beads and Beadwork of the American Indian.* Heye Foundation Publication Contributions, Vol. XI, New York.

PARKMAN, FRANCIS
1879 *LaSalle and the Discovery of the Great West.* Little Brown and Co., Boston.

PARKMAN, FRANCIS
1885 *The Conspiracy of Pontiac.* Little, Brown and Co., Boston.

PRATT, PETER P.
1961 *Oneida Iroquois Glass Trade Bead Sequence/1585-1745.* Color Guide Series No. 1, Fort Stanwix Museum, Onondaga Printing Co., Syracuse.

QUIMBY, GEORGE I.
1966a *Indian Culture and European Trade Goods.* University of Wisconsin Press, Madison.

1966b *The Dumaw Creek Site.* Fieldiana: Anthropology, Vol. 56, No. 1, Field Museum of National History. Chicago.

RADIN, PAUL
1916 "The Winnebago." *Thirty-seventh Annual Report, Bureau of American Ethnology.* Washington, D.C.

RIDLEY, FRANK
1954 "The Frank Bay Site, Lake Nipissing, Ontario." *American Antiquity*, Vol. 20, No. 1, pp. 40-50. Salt Lake City.

Ritchie, William A.
1954 "Dutch Hollow, An Early Historic Period Seneca Site in Livingston County, New York." *Researches and Transactions of the New York State Archaeological Association*, Vol. 13, No. 1. Albany.

1961 *A Typology and Nomenclature for New York Projectile Points*. New York State Museum and Science Suc. Bulletin 384. Albany.

Rostlund, Erhard
1952 *Freshwater Fish and Fishing in Native North America*. University of California Geographical Publication No. 9. University of California Press, Berkeley.

Semenov, S. A.
1964 *Prehistoric Technology*. Trans. by M. W. Thompson, Barnes and Noble, New York City.

Service, Elamn R.
1962 *Primitive Social Organization*. Random House, New York.

Thwaites, Ruben G., Editor
1959 *The Jesuit Relations and Allied Documents, 1610-1791*. 73 Vols. Burroughs Bros., New York City.

Trigger, Bruce G.
1962 "Trade and Tribal Warfare on the St. Lawrence in the Sixteenth Century." *Ethnohistory*, Vol. 9, No. 3, pp. 240-255. Bloomington.

Wedel, Mildred Mott
1959 "Oneota Sites on the Upper Iowa River." *The Missouri Archaeologist*, Vol. 12, No. 2-4, pp. 1-181. Columbia.

White, Marian E.
1967 *An Early Historic Niagara Frontier Iroquois Cemetery in Erie County, New York*. New York State Archaeological Association, Research and Transactions, Vol. XVI, No. 1. Rochester.

Wintemberg, W. J.
1939 "The Lawson Prehistoric Village Site, Middlesex County, Ontario." *Bulletin 94, National Museum of Canada*. The Queens Printer, Ottawa.

1946 "The Sidey-Mackay Village Site." *American Antiquity*, No. 11, pp. 154-184. Menasha.

Witthoft, John
1967 "A History of Gunflints." *The Pennsylvania Archaeologist*, Vol. 36, No. 1-2, pp. 12-49, 1966 (Printed Oct. 1967), Gettysburg.

Wittry, Warren L.
1963 "The Bell Site." *The Wisconsin Archaeologist*, Vol. 44 No. 1, pp. 1-57. Lake Mills.

Wright, Gary A.
1967 "Some Aspects of Early and Mid-17th Century Exchange Networks in the Western Great Lakes." *The Michigan Archaeologist*, Vol. 13, No. 4, pp. 181-197. Ann Arbor.

Yarnell, Richard A.
1964 "Aboriginal Relationships between Culture and Plant Life in the Upper Great Lakes Region." *Anthropological Papers, Museum of Anthropology, University of Michigan*, No. 23. Ann Arbor

* * *

Rob Mann

"True Portraitures of the Indians, and of Their Own Peculiar Conceits of Dress": Discourses of Dress and Identity in the Great Lakes, 1830–1850

ABSTRACT

During the 1830s and 1840s frontier artist George Winter painted the Potawatomi and Miami Indians of the Wabash Valley. Winter's paintings existed at the intersection of competing colonial discourses. Like many "Indian painters" of his time, Winter believed he was capturing the final images of a vanishing race. At the same time, Winter's work runs counters to the imagery of "nakedness" and "savagery" that characterize many Anglo-American paintings of Native Americans during this period. By holding these visual sources in "productive tension" (Stahl 2001:15–16) with documentary and archaeological sources, the role dress played in the construction of identity by members of Great Lakes fur trade society during the 19th century can be unraveled.

Introduction: The Wabash Valley in the 1830s

In 1837, an English painter named George Winter closed his portrait studio in Cincinnati, Ohio, and, upon hearing of the impending removal of the Potawatomi from their villages in the Wabash Valley, was struck with "the enthusiasm of adventure and love of the romantic." He determined to visit this spectacle "for the purpose of seeing and learning something of the Indians and exercising the pencil in this direction" (Feest 1993:2).

Winter arrived in the Wabash Valley at a time of great chaos and uncertainty. Unbeknownst to him, it was the nadir of Great Lakes fur trade society. Over the course of the previous century European traders, primarily Canadiens (French Canadians), had created a pluralistic society with the Potawatomi, Miami, and other native groups of the Great Lakes region. The ethnogenesis of this society was rooted in the social, sexual, political, and economic relations that resulted from the fur trade (Peterson 1978, 1982, 1985; Van Kirk 1980; Boureault 1983). These relations were so fluid and complex that Anglo-American colonial officials and settlers, obsessed with "whiteness" and fixing race, were often baffled and generally dismayed by this multiethnic society (Paynter 2001; Sleeper-Smith 2001).

Like Anglo colonial officials and settlers, Winter also tried to fix the fluidity (Leavelle 2001) of fur trade society, transforming Canadiens and métis into "Indians," in his effort to capture on canvas the "Indian of reality, rather than the one of *fiction* I had often read of [emphasis in original]" (Cooke and Ramadhyani 1993:41; Sleeper-Smith 2001). Because of this conflation, Winter's paintings existed at the intersection of competing colonial discourses. Like many "Indian painters" of his time, Winter believed he was capturing the final images of a "vanishing race" (Flavin 2002). Yet, as he was determined to avoid what he called "poetic fiction," Winter's sketches and paintings run counter to the imagery of "nakedness" and "savagery" characteristically found in the writings and images of this period. By placing Winter's images in what Ann Stahl (2001:15–16) refers to as "productive tension" with other documentary sources (including Winter's own writings) and the archaeological record, it can be seen that he was actually capturing something much more complex. The tensions within and between these sources are explored here in order to discover and expose the silences, tropes, and discourses surrounding the role of dress in the construction of Great Lakes fur trade society.

Envisioning Capitalist Futures: Anglo Discourses on Manifest Destiny

As Anglo-Americans began pouring into the western Great Lakes region during the late-18th and early-19th centuries, they imagined that they were coming to a savage and untamed wilderness (Vibert 1997:84–118; Sleeper-Smith 2001). With what Mary Louise Pratt (1992:61) called the "gaze of the European improving eye" intently focused on agrarian "capitalist futures," travelers and settlers repeatedly described the agricultural potential of the Wabash country. They also found, however, thriving multiethnic communities at places such as Miamies Town (Kekionga) at the headwaters of the Maumee River and Vincennes on the lower Wabash River. Here and at countless other villages and trading hamlets Canadiens, Native Americans, and their métis offspring had created a unique social formation, fur trade society. Anglo-American discourses clearly mark fur trade society as an impediment to settlement and the development of agrarian capitalism.

As such, Canadiens and métis were often conflated with Native Americans in discourses of savagery, thereby precluding them from any legitimate claim to the lands they occupied. As Susan Sleeper-Smith (2001:56) notes, "Fur trade communities were linked by kin networks, relationships so complex that they baffled outsiders and transformed Frenchmen into Indians." She quotes one British officer as remarking that the Canadiens had "adopted the very principles and ideas of Indians, differ little from them only a little in colour." Canadien and métis dress were particular targets of scrutiny (Edmunds 1985). At Vincennes in 1792, Moravian missionary John Heckewelder claimed, "there is hardly *one* Frenchman in 5 who dresses decently. If you know the Indian costume, you know theirs [emphasis in original]" (Wallace 1958:282). Later at Vincennes in 1811, a U.S. soldier encountered the local Canadien militia and noted that while they spoke French, their dress "was a short frock of deer-skin, a belt around their bodies, with a tomahawk and a scalping knife attached to it" (Edmunds 1985:190). Finally, at Fort Wayne in 1820, American John Keating wrote:

> To see a being whom, from his complexion and features, we should expect to find the same feelings which swell in the bosom of every refined man, throwing off his civilized habits to assume the garb of the savage, has something which partakes of the ridiculous, as well as the disgusting (Edmunds 1985:190).

By emphasizing only certain aspects of Canadien and métis dress such as breechcloths or animal hides and certain accoutrements like the tomahawk and scalping knife, these accounts conjure up images of violence, nakedness, and filthiness, well-worn colonialist tropes of the savagery discourse (Comaroff 1996:22). Conflating Canadien, Native American, and métis dress allowed Anglos to categorize Canadiens and métis as "uncivilized." In colonialist discourse, their fate was sealed; they had shunned the "laws of civilized society," and, like the savages they lived among, they would vanish, assimilate, or be forcibly removed (Edmunds 1985). This discursive ploy reinforced and legitimated the U.S. government's efforts to remove the Potawatomi from their villages in the Wabash country, already underway when Winter arrived in Logansport, Indiana, in 1837.

Winter's sketches and paintings provide a visual record of the people of the Wabash Valley that constitutes an independent line of evidence, which can be juxtaposed with the documentary record created by Anglo settlers. Like all documentary sources, Winter's images were the products of the cultural and ideological semantics of particular historical moments and, as such, must be used critically (Stoler and Cooper 1997:18).

Source Criticism: Winter's Art as "Ethnographic Documents"

Winter produced more than 200 graphite, ink, and watercolor sketches and watercolor paintings of the native and métis inhabitants of the Wabash Valley. The imagery for these works, many of which were rendered at a later date, stem primarily from Winter's days in Logansport, Indiana, between 1837 and 1849. Winter interacted with Canadien, native, and métis people at formal councils, in their camps and villages, at trading posts, and in the streets of Logansport and Peru, Indiana. He also took extensive notes, kept journals of his visits to Kee-wau-nay village and Deaf Man's village, and corresponded frequently with his brother and sisters (Winter 1948).

Christian F. Feest (1993:15–18) assesses the ethnographic value of Winter's art, relying primarily on standard historical method, which stresses authenticity—of both the sources themselves (external criticism) and the information contained within the sources (internal criticism) (Wood 1990). Because Winter definitely produced these images, Feest (1993:16) focuses on the authenticity of the ethnographic information depicted in Winter's sketches and paintings. He notes that Winter's paintings "show that their documentary contents, while generally based on original sketches, were subject to certain modifications caused by compositional needs." For instance, Feest cautions against placing too much confidence in the accuracy of the colors of the clothing depicted, "although their overall appearance seems to be largely appropriate." Feest (1993:17) contends that Winter's images are a "reliable visual record of selected aspects of the lifeways of the Potawatomis and Miamis of northern Indiana." As "ethnographic documents," Winter's paintings and sketches are "exceptional in their depiction" of certain aspects of Potawatomi and Miami life. In particular, Feest (1993:17–18) notes that Winter's images shed light on some activities of women, certain ceremonial and cultural practices, and aspects of material culture only poorly known from other sources.

Cultural Production of Historical Images

The ethnographic reliability of Winter's "pictorial documents" undoubtedly makes them invaluable primary sources for understanding the Potawatomi and Miami people of the Great Lakes region (Edmunds 1993; Wagner 1998, 2003; Sleeper-Smith 2001:125–131). Feest's (1993) emphasis on "authenticity," however, leads him to privilege the "facts" contained within Winter's images over the cultural production of those images. This "one-sided historicity" artificially separates past sociohistorical processes (what happened) from the processes and conditions of historical production (what is said to have happened), effectively silencing the power inherent in both historical sources and historical narratives based on those sources (Trouillot 1995:2,23–29). Feest (1993) fails to adequately consider that Winter's sketches and paintings are themselves products of power-laden sociohistorical processes. For example, in his analysis of George Catlin's Mandan paintings, Mark Miller (2000:302–303) suggests that Catlin's images are "defective." They are not "disinterested, objective purveyors of truth." Like all historical documents, Catlin's paintings are "artifacts, fashioned and used by human agents for various purposes." As such, the paintings are situated within the colonialist discourses that both conveyed and created the ideological and cultural semantics of the period (Stoler and Cooper 1997:18; Vibert 1997:5).

Revealing the discursive source of the silences, tensions, ambiguities, and contradictions within all colonial documents, including historical images, requires retooled methods of source criticism. This means avoiding what Patricia Galloway (2002) refers to as the "a la carte" method of ethnohistorical analysis, that is, picking and choosing from among and within sources for specific references without regard for the totality they represent. As Diana DiPaolo Loren (1999, this volume) notes, this analysis leads to "simple analogy and a functional view of culture found in the direct historical method." The emphasis is on coherence, and differences are often elided. Images, the persons and objects within them, as well as the text that often accompanies them should be examined for disjunctures as well as conformity. A retooled historical method also entails a broader understanding of what is generally included under the rubric of "historical sources" and the construction of "alternative archives," including the archaeological record (Comaroff and Comaroff 1992:34; Loren 1999, 2001; Stahl 2001; Mann 2003). These various lines of evidence must be brought into productive tension with one another, exposing the incompatibilities within and among sources. Once highlighted, these incompatibilities become entry points into complex colonial situations, such as the one Winter found in the Wabash Valley.

Discourses of Savagery and Vanishing Primitives in Winter's Work

Winter's art and writings were part of competing colonialist discourses that were both shaping and being shaped by the events unfolding in the Wabash Valley. On the frontiers, where Native Americans, Canadiens, and métis were impediments to the "Manifest Destiny" of Anglo-America, colonial elites propagated the notion of the "savage savage," naked, vile, and treacherous (Edmunds 1985, 1993; McGuire 1992). Among the "urbane gentlemen" of Europe and the East Coast, Enlightenment thought held sway, and they debated the character of Native Americans safely removed from the struggles between settlers and Indians in places like the

Wabash Valley (McGuire 1992). For these liberal Enlightenment thinkers, Native Americans were "noble savages," pure, uncorrupted children of the forests. Whether noble or ignoble, Native Americans were universally viewed as primitives who were destined to vanish under the corrupting influences of civilization (McGuire 1992:817–818).

Until he ventured west in 1835, Winter spent most of his life in the art circles of London and New York and was undoubtedly aware of these debates. When he arrived in the Wabash Valley, he struggled to reconcile these competing discourses. On the one hand, he flatly rejected the "nakedness" and "war-like" tropes so characteristic of the "savage savage" discourse. He wrote that the "more 'poetic Indian,' that is represented always in nudity, with a fine roman nose, shaven head—with the scalp lock decorated with tufts of feathers ... has never come within my observations" (Cooke and Ramadhyani 1993:50). On the other hand, they were no longer noble savages either, "alas! since they have come into contact with the 'pale faces,' they have become degenerate—lost much of their national character—and their number has fearfully decreased. They are an ill-fated race" (Winter 1948:96). Fallen noble savages could not survive, for they remained primitives ill prepared for the "evils of civilization, which only the learned man could endure" (McGuire 1992:819). In Winter's view, the Potawatomi and Miami were primitives who would soon vanish, not only from the Wabash Valley, where removal seemed immanent, but also from existence as well. "The time is fast coming," he wrote, "when the Indian will cease to be numbered among the human family—when they will be remembered only as a departed and persecuted part of it" (Winter 1948:111).

The contradictions and tensions within and among these discourses shaped how Winter depicted and wrote about the people he met in the Wabash Valley. For example, although he was convinced they were rapidly vanishing, Winter saw Indians everywhere he went (Cooke and Ramadhyani 1993:42). Indians were not "frontier exotics"; they were part of the daily, face-to-face world of the Wabash country (Sleeper-Smith 2001:149). Winter noted he had "daily opportunities" to observe "the Indian character" and that "indians were always visible on the streets," constantly coming and going from the Ewing and Walker trading house in Logansport, next door to his studio (Cooke and Ramadhyani 1993:42–45). Winter's sketches and paintings, though, never show Indians in town or among Europeans, except in formal colonial settings such as the Lake Kee-wau-nay Council. As shown in Figure 1, a composition Winter entitled *Pottawattamie Indian Logansport June 1837*, they remained, as primitives, part of nature (Cooke and Ramadhyani 1993:plate 16).

"True Portraitures of the Indians": Dress and Identity in the Wabash Valley

Figure 1 is characteristic of the detailed attention Winter paid to dress, both in his writings and in his sketches and paintings. Winter "recorded the details of each subject's dress. He relied on his journal entries to transpose his notebook sketches to canvas accurately" (Sleeper-Smith 2001:127). In his writings, Winter also linked the importance of dress as a key to identity to the competing discourses of savagery and vanishing primitives (Cooke and Ramadhyani 1993:42):

> The costumes of the Indians are faithfully followed, and no attempt has been made to make subjects fanciful or in any way objects of "poetic fiction" (i.e., Noble or Savage Savages). These are true portraitures of the Indians, and of their own peculiar conceits of dress ... Fidelity to the subject must give real value to all efforts of the artist, as contributions to the history of this unfortunate race who are rapidly disappearing from earthly existence.

Like most Anglos, Winter essentialized "these peculiar conceits" of dress as "Indian" and subsequent researchers have accepted this characterization (Edmunds 1993:26–29; Sleeper-Smith 2001:127). When juxtaposed against his notes and journals, however, key silences and tensions are exposed.

Take, for example, his portrait of Maurie, the daughter of Mas-saw. Winter's painting, based on a sketch he made in 1837, depicts Maurie as an Indian woman (Figure 2). He wrote that she was adorned "with the silver ornamentations which are very conductive to the happiness and worldly vanity of an Indian woman" (Cooke and Ramadhyani 1993:62). According to Winter, Maurie was initially reluctant to sit for a portrait. Following up on this tension begins to

FIGURE 1. *Pottawattamie Indian Logansport June 1837*. (Courtesy of Tippecanoe County Historical Association, Lafayette, Indiana. Gift of Mrs. Cable G. Ball.)

Plate 22. DAUGHTER OF MAS-SAW. MAURIE *(Cat. #78)*

FIGURE 2. *Daughter of Mas-saw. Maurie.* (Courtesy of Tippecanoe County Historical Association, Lafayette, Indiana. Gift of Mrs. Cable G. Ball.)

reveal the complexities of dress and identity in the Wabash Valley silenced in Winter's "Indian paintings." Maurie's mother, who Winter calls "the Chieftess Mas-saw," eventually convinced her to sit and even directed her to put on a string of beads and her most ornate outfit, heavily adorned with trade silver (Cooke and Ramadhyani 1993: 62). When Maurie returned, she also carried with her a parasol and a large pocket-handkerchief. In Winter's essentialized vision of identity in the Wabash Valley, the trade silver and beads were "authentic" aspects of native dress, but the parasol and handkerchief were affectations. Maurie, he said in his journal, carried the parasol "in imitation of white people whom she had noticed used parasols" and "thought it would be an adornment to have one in her hand" (Cooke and Ramadhyani 1993:62).

It seems likely that Maurie was trying to communicate something much more complex. Here it is necessary to look at the contradictions in Winter's own writings. In his journal he repeatedly refers to her as the "young Indian girl." He notes, however, that Maurie's father was Andrew Goshlieu (Cooke and Ramadhyani 1993:62). Goshlieu (Gosselin) was, according to Winter, "a French Canadian, and was of that class so often found identified by intermarriage with the Indian people" (Cooke and Ramadhyani 1993:77). That is, he was a fur trader. Furthermore, Winter's journals indicate that Maurie was herself married to a fur trader, following by that time a well-established pattern (Van Kirk 1980). Her husband, Henry Taylor (Yo-ca-top-kone), was a trader in the employ of one of the most influential fur trade companies in the Wabash Valley (Cooke and Ramadhyani 1993:62).

Maurie, then, was not simply an "Indian girl," she was métis and, along with her multiethnic kin, was a member of Great Lakes fur trade society. Women's dress in Great Lakes fur trade society was characterized by ankle-length broadcloth skirts, brightly colored blouses, trade cloth shawls that also served as head coverings, leggings, and moccasins (Edmunds 1993:28). Women often carried red or black "mantles," trade blankets made of "superfine broad cloth" (Edmunds 1993:28). On their feet were center-seam leather moccasins. Skirts, blouses, shawls, leggings, and mantles were almost invariably decorated with colored ribbons and trade silver. Moccasins were elaborately adorned with colored

ribbons, glass trade beads, and porcupine quills. Additional adornments included multiple strands of glass trade beads worn around the neck and trade silver earbobs in bunches. Mas-sa's outfit (Figure 3), as painted and described by Winter, exemplifies this mode of dress (Cooke and Ramadhyani 1993:77, plate 28):

> She had her cape covered with circular silver ornaments … . Several strings of small blue beads hung around her neck. She wore a ke-chep-so-win or belt—pendent from it were several steel chains with *watch keys* attached, falling as low as the knee over a mich-a-ko-the or petticoat handsomely ornamented with silver rings … her petticoat was handsomely bordered by rows of ribbons of the primitive colors, an occasional row of a secondary color. These ribbons were about two inches wide, cut into points and vandykes—very neatly sewed. Her cloth blanket too was bordered by ribbons and silver rings … . Her blanket and petticoat were of a good dark blue broad cloth … her moccasins … were neatly made and handsomely checkered on the laps with ribbons of the primitive colors … . Red leggings … completed the handsome costume … [emphasis in original].

Clearly, the dress of Maurie and Mas-sa *was* typical of native and métis women in fur trade society, but as Maurie tried to convey to Winter, it was not merely "Indian."

Likewise, Winter struggled to fix the identity of the men he met, eliding the messy and fluid reality of social boundaries within Great Lakes fur trade society. As with Maurie, they are portrayed as "Indians," even as his journals both contradict and affirm such a portrayal. For instance, both Noaquet (Luther Rice) and Joseph Napoleon Bourassa were métis men who served as interpreters for the U.S. in its dealings with the Potawatomi. Winter wrote that they were "*aboriginal men*—intelligent and had a good knowledge of English [emphasis in original]" (Cooke and Ramadhyani 1993:67). He went on to note that Bourassa was an "Educated half-breed" and noted on his sketch of Rice that he was "a half-breed Indian." Bourassa, Rice, and many other native, Canadien, and métis men are shown in Winter's sketches and paintings wearing frock coats over waistcoats and ruffled shirts, aspects of dress silenced in the discourses of Anglo settlers.

As with Maurie, the tensions surrounding dress and identity are illustrated in Winter's sketches, painting, and journal descriptions of Jean Baptist Brouillette (Figure 4). Brouillette

FIGURE 3. *Mas-sa*. (Courtesy of Tippecanoe County Historical Association, Lafayette, Indiana. Gift of Mrs. Cable G. Ball.)

Perspectives from *Historical Archaeology:*

FIGURE 4. *Bouriette-Indian Interpreter*. (Courtesy of Tippecanoe County Historical Association, Lafayette, Indiana. Gift of Mrs. Cable G. Ball.)

was métis, his father was Canadien, and his mother was Miami. Winter sketched Brouillette in 1837 when the two happened to meet on the road outside of Peru, Indiana. Although he titled his sketch "Beau-ri-ette—Miami Indian," in his journal Winter always refers to him as a French "half breed" (Cooke and Ramadhyani 1993:112–113). Winter described Brouillette's dress in detail:

> His tout en semble was unique, as his aboriginal costume was expensively shewey [sic]. He wore around his head a rich figured crimson shawl *a la turban*, with long and flowing ends gracefully falling over the shoulders. Silver ornaments—or clusters of ear-bobs testified their weight by a partial elongation of the ears … . He wore a fine frock coat of the latest fashion. (When the indian assumes the white man's garb, he always chooses a frock coat. It is an object of beauty to his eye.) His "pes-mo-kin," or shirt was white, spotted with a small red figure, overhanging very handsome blue leggings, "winged" with very rich silk ribbons of prismatic hues, exhibiting the squaw's skillful needlework. A handsome red silk sash was thrown gracefully over his left shoulder, and passing over the breast and under the right arm, with clusters of knots, and fringed masses, gave point and style to Brouillette's tall and majestic figure (Cooke and Ramadhyani 1993: 112).

Brouillette's outfit was, in fact, characteristic of male dress in Great Lakes fur trade society. Men typically wore well-tailored, broadcloth frock coats with wide, fashionable lapels and unpadded shoulders (Edmunds 1993:27). These were often worn over waistcoats or vests and ornate ruffled shirts, which were worn loose and very long (Figures 1, 4) (Edmunds 1993). Breechcloths, held in place by a belt, were preferred over trousers or breeches and were worn under the long shirts. Leggings were highly ornate, decorated with fringe, multicolored ribbons, and embroidery. Men also preferred moccasins, which like leggings were often very ornate. Winter depicts some men wearing woven sashes, worn over the shoulder or around the waist. Many men wore colorful silk scarves wrapped around their heads to form turbans and most wore trade silver earrings (Edmunds 1993: 27–28).

Maurie, Mas-saw, Noaquet, Bourassa, Brouillette, and many others sketched and painted by Winter were not the vanishing primitives he imagined them to be. They were members of Great Lakes fur trade society, and their mode of dress was a constitutive component of this identity system. This does not mean that there were not different styles of dress *within* fur trade society. Certainly, there were aspects of fur trade dress that were distinctively Miami, Potawatomi, Canadien, and métis. Moreover, factions within each of these groups may have used dress to express class, political, or ideological distinctions. During the War of 1812, for example, conservative Miami may have eschewed certain types of clothing associated with assimilationist factions of the tribe (Mann 1999b). Still, when the tensions, ambiguities, and silences within and between Winter's sketches, paintings, and journals are examined, the creation of something new, something definitively associated with fur trade society can be discerned.

Once it is understood that the "ethnographic reliability" of Winter's images must be situated within the contexts of their cultural production, they can be a powerful comparative source in an attempt to understand the nature of identity in fur trade society. Winter's images captured on paper and canvas reveal that the members of fur trade society combined European cloths and garments with applied ornamentation such as colored ribbons, beads, and trade silver to create a unique mode of dress.

Material Archive: Dress Artifacts at the Cicott Trading Post

The archaeological record is also instructive, for it represents yet another independent line of evidence to be brought to bear upon these issues. The Cicott Trading Post is a ca. 1816–1850 trading post in north-central Indiana. The post belonged to Zachariah Cicott, a Canadien trader from Detroit. By his own recollection, Cicott arrived on the Wabash in 1792 (Goodspeed 1883:36–37). As he plied the waters of the Wabash, Cicott made a number of contacts among the native groups living there. Particularly important was a band of Potawatomi led by a métis *okama* or *wkama* (clan leader), Pierre Moran—known variously as Parish, Peerish, Perig, or the Stutterer (Whicker 1927; Robertson and Riker 1942:371). Among Moran's band was his sister, Pe-say-quot. Zachariah and Pe-say-quot were married sometime early in the 19th century. Taking a native or métis bride meant the formation of kin ties that formalized trading relations and gave some measure of stability to independent traders such as Cicott. He and Pe-say-quot had four children, a son and three daughters.

Evidence from trading licenses granted to Cicott in the 1820s indicates that he was trading with the Piankashaw, Wea, Kickapoo, and Miami in addition to his kin among the Potawatomi (United States Congress 1826, 1827; Anson 1953:83–84). Pe-say-quot disappears from the historic record sometime around 1825, and it is presumed that she died. Cicott's second wife, Elizabeth, was a member of the Brotherton Indians, a remnant band of Native Americans made up of Mahicans, Wappingers, Pequots, and Narragansetts (Hodge 1912: 166; Henry 1982; Tanner 1987:75). Cicott and Elizabeth had two daughters. Elizabeth died in 1838. Cicott lived until 1850, at which time the trading post was abandoned.

The Cicott Trading Post site (Indiana state site number 12WA59) is situated atop a precipitous bluff overlooking the Wabash River in present day Warren County, Indiana. In 1990, the Warren County Park Board (WCPB) purchased the property containing the site of Cicott's trading post and began making plans to convert the property into an historical and recreational park. The Cicott Trading Post Project, initiated in 1990, is a long-term archaeological and ethnohistorical investigation of the material conditions of daily life at a Canadien trading post during the late fur-trade era in the Wabash Valley (Mann 1994, 1999a, 2003; Stahl et al. 2004). Archaeological investigations in 1990, 1991, 1992, and 1997 were undertaken in support of the WCPB's park development and interpretation needs. Only materials excavated during the 1997 field season have been completely analyzed and reported (Mann 1999a). These materials are used in the present study. At this site inhabited by Canadien, Native American, and métis individuals, a wide variety of dress-related artifacts typically thought to be indicative of a "European" mode of dress are found intermingled with an equally wide variety of adornment artifacts often associated with a Native American mode of dress. (Tables 1, 2).

The glass beads recovered during the 1997 excavations were classified using the system developed by Kenneth Kidd and Martha Kidd

(1970) and elaborated by many subsequent researchers (Mason 1986; Fogelman 1991; Lorenzini 1996). The majority are white, Type IIa seed and pony beads, which were commonly used in detailed embroidery work. Necklace beads were also recovered; the majority were Type If faceted beads. Silver and cupreous ornaments were highly desired by the native,

TABLE 1
ADORNMENT ARTIFACTS,
CICOTT TRADING POST

Artifact	Material	Count
Beads	Glass	249
Brooches	Silver	10
Cross	Silver	1
Thimble	Silver	1
Earbobs	Silver	2
Coil	Silver	1
Miscellaneous ornaments	Silver	12
Tinkling cones	Cupreous metal	3
Tinkling cones	Tinned sheet iron	2
Hawk bell	Cupreous metal	1
Ring	Ferrous metal	1
Ring	Composite	1
Total		284

TABLE 2
CLOTHING ARTIFACTS,
CICOTT TRADING POST

Artifact	Material	
Buttons	Cupreous metal	17
Buttons	Ceramic	21
Buttons	Bone	8
Buttons	Ferrous metal	5
Buttons	Shell	3
Buttons/cuff links	Composite	4
Button eye loops	Cupreous metal	5
Hooks and eyes	Cupreous metal	27
Grommets	Cupreous metal	2
Buckles	Cupreous metal	2
Total		94

European, and métis members of Great Lakes fur trade society. Winter noted the importance of trade silver. He said of his painting of D-mouche-kee-kee-awh, a "full-blooded" Potawatomi woman, that she was "as her likeness indicates—'*plated*' with silver broaches, the very ne plus ultra of an Indian woman's toilette [emphasis in original]" (Cooke and Ramadhyani 1993:76, plate 27). She was also wearing several strands of necklace beads. The small round silver brooches Winter referred to in his description of D-mouche-kee-kee-awh were the most common silver adornment item found on the site. All were small ring brooches with one exception. It was a type of heart-shaped brooch sometimes referred to as a "drooping heart" brooch (Fredrickson and Gibb 1980:52).

Other silver ornaments recovered include two pieces of a silver cross, earbob fragments, a silver coil, and a silver thimble fragment. Although thimbles obviously had functional uses for both European Americans and Native Americans, the fact that this thimble is made from silver leads to the conclusion that it was likely used as personal ornamentation. Thimbles were used as decoration for drums, as ear ornaments, as hair ornaments, sewn onto jackets and leggings, and suspended from belts (Karklins 1992:11–97). The silver coil is a thin strip of trade silver that was cut from a larger finished silver object, such as an armband or gorget, and tightly wound to produce a spiraled effect. Similar silver coils have been recovered from the site in the past. Although the function of these artifacts is still not completely clear, it is likely that they were ear or hair ornaments.

Tinkling cones were usually attached in large numbers to the fringes of clothing, pouches, and moccasins; worn in the hair; or dangled in bunches from the earlobes in order to produce a pleasant tinkling sound whenever the cones moved. Of the two finger rings, one was made from a ferrous metal, while the second was a cupreous band and face (or set mount) with a rectangular, red cut glass set. The cupreous bell is of the type commonly referred to as hawk bells. Like thimbles, hawk bells were commonly used as personal adornment (Karklins 1992). Finally, the 12 miscellaneous silver scraps were cut from trade silver ornaments.

Artifacts typically related to a European American style of dress include buttons, cufflinks, hooks and eyes, clothing grommets, and brass clothing buckles. Hook-and-eye sets were used to fasten sections of clothing (Stone 1974:81). The buttons and cufflinks were classified using Stanley South's (1964) button typology and Richard Polhemus's (1977) elaboration of that typology. A total of 63 buttons or button fragments representing 11 different button types were recovered from the site. The buttons are typical of many articles of European-style clothing, including blouses and shirts, vests or waistcoats, frock and great coats, breeches, and trousers. The majority of the buttons recovered were Type 23 ceramic four-hole and three-hole buttons that would have been used on the ruffled shirts and blouses commonly worn by men and women in fur trade society.

Older brands of archaeology and ethnohistory might suggest that these artifacts indicate that the Cicott Trading Post was a "mixed" household in which the inhabitants were "acculturating" toward the prescriptive norms of the newly dominant Anglo-American society. In these models, artifacts would be classified as either "European" or "Indian," and a group's "degree of acculturation" would be based upon the relative percentages of "European" and "Indian" artifacts recovered at the site (Jones 1988; Lightfoot 1995:206–207; Loren 1999: 22–25; Mann 1999b:403).

This is also how Edmunds (1993) would have us view Winter's images—as a "mirror of acculturation." He contends that Winter's subjects are "arrayed in clothing that ... indicated their degree of acculturation" (Edmunds 1993:27). Both approaches decontextualize fur trade dress, isolating different aspects of dress and then ranking them along an artificial continuum between "native" (less Western) and Western (less "native"). Instead of seeing fur trade dress as a whole, Edmunds (1993:27) tends to separate and characterize different aspects of dress as either European or Indian, "Most of the Potawatomi and Miami men portrayed in Winter's paintings are dressed in frock coats similar to those worn by prosperous white settlers ... Yet other parts of the men's clothing indicate the ties to their Indian heritage." From this perspective, both the archaeological record and Winter's images are direct reflections of an unambiguous past in which colonized people naturally and inevitably adopted the norms and practices of the colonizers, rather than being partial and power-laden glimpses into a much more complex past in which daily practices are part and parcel of negotiated colonial processes (Comaroff and Comaroff 1992).

Conclusion

By remaining attuned to the tensions, contradictions, and ambiguities within and between the documentary, visual, and archaeological records, it becomes apparent that the members of Great Lakes fur trade society had indeed created something new. In this view, the seemingly endless combinations of European cloths, garments, applied adornments, and buckskins coupled with native styles of ornamentation offered a "host of imaginative possibilities" to Canadiens, Native Americans, and métis as they forged a new society on the Great Lakes frontier (Comaroff 1996:27; Sleeper-Smith 2001:125). Mode of dress is only one of many mundane pursuits of daily life, such as house construction and repair and cross-cultural exchange, that provide keen insights into the processes of Great Lakes fur trade society identity formation, often elided or silenced in the documentary record (Mann 2003). Because identities are made and remade through these quotidian practices, this new style of attire and personal ornamentation played an active role in the ongoing process of fur trade society ethnogenesis.

Because this mode of dress was made from materials that inexorably drew the members of fur trade society ever deeper into the Anglo-American market economy, it was also "iconic of the predicament of its wearers" (Comaroff 1996:38). Canadiens, Native Americans, and métis used Anglo-American commodities to make and remake local identities through the inventive elaboration of their garb, even as they attempted to avoid being removed from the Great Lakes area and stem the tide of Anglo-American colonization. When used comparatively and in conjunction with documentary and material archives, it becomes clear that Winter's images captured not a vanishing, ill-fated race but, rather, a vibrant, colorful, multiethnic society of individuals attempting to reproduce themselves in a social environment increasingly hostile to their unique lifestyle.

Acknowledgments

My thanks go to Diana DiPaolo Loren and Uzi Baram for inviting me to participate in the symposium that has resulted in this volume. My thanks also go to the anonymous reviewers; each has substantively increased the quality of my arguments and their presentation. The ultimate responsibility for both, however, belongs solely to me. This article is dedicated to the memory of Mrs. Judy Henry. My work at the Cicott Trading Post site has long been encouraged and facilitated by John and Judy Henry and could never have come to fruition without their support.

References

ANSON, BERT
1953 *The Fur Traders of Northern Indiana, 1796–1850.* Doctoral dissertation, Department of History, Indiana University, Bloomington. University Microfilms International, Ann Arbor, MI.

BOUREAULT, RON G.
1983 The Indian, the Métis, and the Fur Trade: Class, Sexism, and Racism in the Transition from "Communism" to Capitalism. *Studies in Political Economy: A Socialist Review* 12(Fall):45–86.

COMAROFF, JEAN
1996 The Empire's Old Clothes: Fashioning the Colonial Subject. In *Cross-Cultural Consumption: Global Markets, Local Realities*, David Howes, editor, pp. 19–38. Routledge Press, New York, NY.

COMAROFF, JOHN L., AND JEAN COMAROFF
1992 *Ethnography and the Historical Imagination.* Westview Press, Boulder, CO.

COOKE, SARAH E., AND RACHEL B. RAMADHYANI (COMPILERS)
1993 *Indians and a Changing Frontier: The Art of George Winter.* Indiana Historical Society in Cooperation with the Tippecanoe County Historical Association, Indianapolis, IN.

EDMUNDS, R. DAVID
1985 "Unacquainted with the Laws of the Civilized World": American Attitudes towards the Métis Communities in the Old Northwest. In *The New Peoples: Being and Becoming Métis in North America*, Jacqueline Peterson and Jennifer S. H. Brown, editors, pp. 185–193. University of Manitoba Press, Winnipeg, Canada.
1993 George Winter: Mirror of Acculturation. In *Indians and a Changing Frontier: The Art of George Winter*, Sarah E. Cooke and Rachel B. Ramadhyani, compilers, pp. 23–39. Indiana Historical Society in Cooperation with the Tippecanoe County Historical Association, Indianapolis, IN.

FEEST, CHRISTIAN F.
  1993 G. Winter, Artist. In *Indians and a Changing Frontier: The Art of George Winter*, Sarah E. Cooke and Rachel B. Ramadhyani, compilers, pp. 1–21. Indiana Historical Society in Cooperation with the Tippecanoe County Historical Association, Indianapolis, IN.

FLAVIN, FRANCIS
  2002 The Adventurer-Artists of the Nineteenth Century and the Image of the American Indian. *Indiana Magazine of History* 98(1):1–29.

FOGELMAN, GARY L.
  1991 Glass Trade Beads of the Northeast. *The Pennsylvania Artifact Series*, Booklet No. 70. Fogelman Publishing, Turbotville, PA.

FREDRICKSON, N. JAYE, AND SANDRA GIBB
  1980 The Covenant Chain. In *The Covenant Chain: Indian Ceremonial and Trade Silver*. The National Museum of Man, National Museums of Canada, Ottawa.

GALLOWAY, PATRICIA K.
  2002 Comments on Session Papers: Bridging the Great Divide. Presented at the 35th Annual Meeting on Historical and Underwater Archaeology, Mobile, AL.

GOODSPEED, WESTON A.
  1883 *Counties of Warren, Benton, Jasper, and Newton, Indiana*. F. A. Battey and Company, Chicago, IL.

HENRY, JOHN
  1982 Zachariah Cicott. In *The Independence Sesquicentennial*, pp. 27–33. Warren County Historical Society, Williamsport, IN.

HODGE, FREDERICK WEBB (EDITOR)
  1912 Handbook of American Indians North of Mexico, Part 1. *Bureau of American Ethnology, Bulletin* No. 30, Washington, DC.

JONES, JAMES R. III
  1988 *Degrees of Acculturation at Two Eighteenth-Century Aboriginal Villages near Lafayette, Tippecanoe County, Indiana: Ethnohistoric and Archaeological Perspectives*. Doctoral dissertation, Department of Anthropology, Indiana University. University Microfilms International, Ann Arbor, MI.

KARKLINS, KARLIS
  1992 *Trade Ornament Usage among the Native Peoples of Canada: A Source Book*. Studies in Archaeology, Architecture, and History, Parks Canada, Ottawa.

KIDD, KENNETH E., AND MARTHA A. KIDD
  1970 A Classification System for Glass Beads for the Use of Field Archaeologists. *Canadian Historic Sites: Occasional Papers in Archaeology and History* 1: 45–89. Parks Canada, Ottawa, Ontario.

LEAVELLE, TRACY N.
  2001 *Religion, Encounter, and Community in French and Indian North America*. Doctoral dissertation, Department of History, Arizona State University. University Microfilms International, Ann Arbor, MI.

LIGHTFOOT, KENT G.
  1995 Culture Contact Studies: Redefining the Relationship between Prehistoric and Historic Archaeology. *American Antiquity* 60(2):199–217.

LOREN, DIANA DIPAOLO
  1999 *Creating Social Distinction: Articulating Colonial Policies and Practices along the Eighteenth-Century Louisiana/Texas Frontier*. Doctoral dissertation, Department of Anthropology, State University of New York, Binghamton. University Microfilms International, Ann Arbor, MI.
  2001 Manipulating Bodies and Emerging Traditions at the Los Adaes Presidio. In *The Archaeology of Traditions: Agency and History before and after Columbus*, Timothy R. Pauketat, editor, pp. 58–76. University Press of Florida, Gainesville.

LORENZINI, MICHELE A.
  1996 A Classification of the Glass Trade Beads from the Bell Site (47-Wn-9), Winnebago County, Wisconsin. Archaeology Laboratory, *Reports of Investigation*, No. 8, University of Wisconsin, Oshkosh.

MANN, ROB
  1994 Zachariah Cicott, Nineteenth-Century French Canadian Fur Trader: Ethnohistoric and Archaeological Perspectives of Ethnic Identity in the Wabash Valley. Master's thesis, Department of Anthropology, Ball State University, Muncie, IN.
  1999a The 1997 Archaeological Excavations at the Cicott Trading Post Site (12WA59). IMA Consulting, Inc., *Report of Investigations* No. 520, Minneapolis, MN.
  1999b The Silenced Miami: Archaeological and Ethnohistorical Evidence for Miami-British Relations, 1795–1812. *Ethnohistory* 46(3):399–427.
  2003 *Colonizing the Colonizers: Canadien Fur Traders and Fur Trade Society in the Great Lakes Region, 1763–1850*. Doctoral dissertation, Department of Anthropology, State University of New York, Binghamton. University Microfilms International, Ann Arbor, MI.

MASON, RONALD J.
  1986 Rock Island: Historical Indian Archaeology in the Northern Lake Michigan Basin. *Midcontinential Journal of Archaeology, Special Paper* No. 6. Kent State University Press, Kent, OH.

McGUIRE, RANDALL H.
  1992 Archaeology and the First Americans. *American Anthropologist* 94(4):816–836.

MILLER, MARK S. PARKER
2000 Obtaining Information via Defective Documents: A Search for the Mandan in George Catlin's Paintings. In *Interpretations of Native North American Life: Material Contributions to Ethnohistory*, Michael S. Nassaney and Eric S. Johnson, editors, pp. 296–318. University Press of Florida, Gainesville.

PAYNTER, ROBERT
2001 The Cult of Whiteness in Western New England. In *Race and the Archaeology of Identity*, Charles E. Orser, Jr., editor, pp. 125–142. University of Utah Press, Salt Lake City.

PETERSON, JACQUELINE
1978 Prelude to Red River: A Social Portrait of the Great Lakes Métis. *Ethnohistory* 25(1):41–67.
1982 Ethnogenesis: The Settlement and Growth of a "New People" in the Great Lakes Region, 1702–1815. *American Indian Culture and Research Journal* 6(2):23–64.
1985 Many Roads to Red River: Métis Genesis in the Great Lakes Region, 1680–1815. In *The New Peoples: Being and Becoming Métis in North America*, Jacqueline Peterson and Jennifer S. H. Brown, editors, pp. 37–71. University of Manitoba Press, Winnipeg, Canada.

POLHEMUS, RICHARD R.
1977 Archaeological Investigations of the Tellico Blockhouse Site. The University of Tennessee, Department of Anthropology, *Report of Investigations*, No. 26, and *Tennessee Valley Authority Reports in Anthropology*, No. 16, Knoxville.

PRATT, MARY LOUISE
1992 *Imperial Eyes: Travel Writing and Transculturation*. Routledge Press, London, England.

ROBERTSON, NELLIE ARMSTRONG, AND DOROTHY RIKER (EDITORS)
1942 *The John Tipton Papers*, Vol. 1. Indiana Historical Bureau, Indianapolis.

SLEEPER-SMITH, SUSAN
2001 *Indian Women and French Men: Rethinking Cultural Encounter in the Western Great Lakes*. University of Massachusetts Press, Amherst.

SOUTH, STANLEY
1964 Analysis of the Buttons from Brunswick Town and Fort Fisher. *Florida Anthropologist* 17(2):113–133.

STAHL, ANN B.
2001 *Making History in Banda: Anthropological Visions of Africa's Past*. Cambridge University Press, Cambridge, England.

STAHL, ANN B., ROB MANN, AND DIANA DIPAOLO LOREN
2004 Writing for Many: Interdisciplinary Communication, Constructionism, and the Practices of Writing. *Historical Archaeology* 38(2):83–102.

STOLER, ANN LAURA, AND FREDERICK COOPER
1997 Between Metropole and Colony: Rethinking a Research Agenda. In *Tensions of Empire: Colonial Cultures in a Bourgeois World*, Frederick Cooper and Ann Laura Stoler, editors, pp. 1–56. University of California Press, Berkeley.

STONE, LYLE M.
1974 *Fort Michilimackinac 1715–1781: An Archaeological Perspective on the Revolutionary Frontier*. Publications of the Museum, Michigan State University, East Lansing.

TANNER, HELEN H.
1987 *Atlas of Great Lakes Indian History*. University of Oklahoma Press, Norman.

TROUILLOT, MICHEL-ROLPH
1995 *Silencing the Past: Power and the Production of History*. Beacon Press, Boston, MA.

UNITED STATES CONGRESS
1826 Abstract of Licenses Granted to Citizens of the United States to Trade with the Indians. 19th Congress, 1st Session, *House Document 118*, (Serial Set No. 136). Washington, DC.
1827 Abstract of Licenses Granted to Trade with the Indians. 20th Congress, 1st Session, *House Document 140*, (Serial Set No. 172). Washington, DC.

VAN KIRK, SYLVIA
1980 *"Many Tender Ties": Women in Fur Trade Society, 1670–1870*. University of Oklahoma Press, Norman.

VIBERT, ELIZABETH
1997 *Trader's Tales: Narratives of Cultural Encounters in the Columbia Plateau, 1807–1846*. University of Oklahoma Press, Norman.

WAGNER, MARK J.
1998 Some Think It Impossible to Civilize Them at All: Cultural Change and Continuity among the Early-Nineteenth-Century Potawatomi. In *Studies in Culture Contact: Interaction, Culture Change, and Archaeology*, James G. Cusick, editor, pp. 430–456. Center for Archaeological Investigations, Southern Illinois University, Carbondale.
2003 In All the Solemnity of Profound Smoking: Tobacco Smoking and Pipe Manufacture and Use among the Potawatomi of Illinois. In *Stone Tool Traditions in the Contact Era*, Charles R. Cobb, editor, pp. 109–126. University of Alabama Press, Tuscaloosa.

WALLACE, PAUL A.
1958 *The Travels of John Heckewelder in Frontier America*. University of Pittsburg Press, Pittsburg, PA.

WHICKER, J. WESLEY
1927 Pierre Moran or Chief Parish of the Potawatomi Indians. *Indiana Magazine of History* 23(2):229–236.

WINTER, GEORGE
1948 *The Journals and Indian Paintings of George Winter, 1837–1839*. Indiana Historical Society, Indianapolis.

WOOD, W. RAYMOND
1990 Ethnohistory and Historical Method. In *Archaeological Method and Theory*, Vol. 2, Michael B. Schiffer, editor, pp. 81–109. University of Arizona Press, Tucson.

ROB MANN
REGIONAL ARCHAEOLOGY PROGRAM
MUSEUM OF NATURAL SCIENCE
LOUISIANA STATE UNIVERSITY
BATON ROUGE, LA 70803

PAUL FARNSWORTH

Missions, Indians, and Cultural Continuity

ABSTRACT

A technique has been devised for measuring the rate and degree of culture change represented in archaeological assemblages from the California Missions. Using this technique on data from excavations at the missions of Soledad, San Antonio, and La Purisima, shows that while there are differences between these missions, the most important result is that the California Indians maintained a high degree of traditional cultural continuity at all three missions. Using a sequence of assemblages from Mission Soledad, changes through the Mission period are evaluated and interpreted in relation to changes in the economic structure of Spanish and Mexican California.

Introduction

Spanish colonial archaeology has been in the forefront of studies of culture change in contact situations (i.e., acculturation studies) for some time. Spanish colonial policy in the New World attempted to incorporate indigenous populations into the social hierarchy, albeit at the lowest levels, in contrast to British colonial policy which largely excluded indigenous populations. Consequently, Spanish colonial archaeologists have a major role to play in understanding both the development of New World cultures and the processes of culture change in human societies.

Archaeological Classification and Culture Change Studies

A classification system designed specifically for the study of culture change and material culture was produced by Quimby and Spoehr (1951) for the analysis of museum collections (Table 1). Although not designed for archaeological assemblages, this approach has considerable utility in

archaeological analyses of contact situations. Cheek (1974:26) attempted to systematize this classification and then to apply it to archaeological assemblages from San Xavier del Bac, Arizona.

Cheek (1974:24) points out that the Quimby and Spoehr (1951) classification uses two artifact "states" (Indian or European) and four "attributes" (form, material, technique of manufacture, and manufacturer), although not all possible permutations of these states and attributes are present in their system. In order to produce "a more systematic and logically complete typology," Cheek (1974:26) used the same two states (Indian or European) and three of the attributes (form, material, and technique of manufacture). The result was eight categories of Indian-manufactured artifacts (Table 2). Cheek (1974:26) eliminated the fourth attribute, manufacturer, by arguing that because her "emphasis is on the changes in the Indian culture, it seemed reasonable to limit consideration of European-made items" (Cheek 1974:26). However, she noted that:

> One class (out of a possible total of eight, using the three other attributes) of European-made items must be considered. European-made items that were European in form, material, and technique were significant in the process of Indian acculturation (Cheek 1974:26).

Consequently, a ninth category was added to her classification for this one class of European-made artifacts (Table 2). The remaining seven classes of European-made items were only considered to be relevant for studies of European cultural reactions to Indian culture, but of no interest in her study (Cheek 1974:26).

This decision suggests a major flaw in Cheek's understanding of acculturation processes, that is her assumption that Indians did not use European-made artifacts unless they were also of European form, material, and technique of manufacture. She is not alone in making this kind of assumption. For example, Di Peso (1974:916–919) divides his artifacts into "Iberian" and "indigenous" types, and clearly considers the "native inventory" to be the "indigenous" artifacts. The direct implication is that any European-made artifact is only used by Europeans.

TABLE 1
CATEGORIES OF CULTURE CHANGE USED BY QUIMBY AND SPOEHR (1951)

New Types of Artifacts Introduced through Contact	Native Types of Artifacts Modified by Contact
A1. Objects imported through trade or other contact channels	B1. Native artifacts modified by the substitution of an imported material for a local material that is inferior in physical properties or lacking in prestige
A2. Forms copied from introduced models, but reproduced locally of native materials	B2. Native artifacts modified by the substitution of an imported material whose use involves a different technological principle, although the same end is achieved
A3. Introduced forms manufactured or decorated locally, partly from native materials and partly from imported trade materials	B3. Native types of artifacts modified by the introduction of a new element of subject matter
A4. Introduced forms manufactured locally from imported materials through the use of an introduced technique or a native technique similar to the introduced one	

TABLE 2
CHEEK'S (1974:27) CLASSIFICATION FOR HISTORIC ABORIGINAL CONTACT ARTIFACTS

Indian-Made Artifacts	European-Made Artifacts
A. European Form, European Material, European Technique	I. European Form, European Material, European Technique
B. European Form, European Material, Indian Technique	
C. European Form, Native Material, European Technique	
D. European Form, Native Material, Indian Technique	
E. Indian Form, European Material, European Technique	
F. Indian Form, European Material, Indian Technique	
G. Indian Form, Native Material, European Technique	
H. Indian Form, Native Material, Indian Technique	

Di Peso also clearly regards acculturation as a one-way process, terming Iberian culture as the "donor" and the Indian culture "recipient." From this perspective, only Indian culture could change, not Iberian. This view is a second major flaw in his model, as it is generally recognized today that acculturation is a two-way process in which both cultures coming into contact are subject to some degree of change.

Cheek (1974:12–16, 26) clearly understands this, but states she is not studying European culture change and is therefore justified in not including European-manufactured artifacts in her classification (Cheek 1974:26). This position is an error: Indians did use European-manufactured items of all types. No reason exists to suppose that this usage was restricted to items of European form, material, or method of manufacture as Cheek suggests. Europeans manufactured items specifically for trade to, or use by, Indians (e.g., glass beads) and copied Indian forms (e.g., canoes, hammocks, moccasins, smoking pipes, etc.). Equally, European use of New World materials (e.g., gold, silver, furs, stone, wood, etc.) or Indian methods of manufacture (e.g., adobe construction) is far from unknown. As a result, in constructing a systematic classification system, it would seem inadvisable automatically to rule out seven classes of artifacts, even if they might not fit one's preconceived notions of who should be using them.

Who was using the artifacts is, of course, the crux of the matter. Quimby and Spoehr (1951) studied museum collections of ethnographic artifacts which were, presumably, all used by Indians. Cheek (1974), Di Peso (1974), and many other archaeologists deal with sites where both Europeans and Indians were present, and it is not possible to assume that any object was used by one culture or the other based solely on the attributes of the artifact itself. However, this is not to say that archaeologists cannot study culture change in this way, because they are not dealing with isolated artifacts, but with assemblages and subassemblages of artifacts which have provenience and context. Based on the overall combination of artifacts, their provenience and context, specific groups of artifacts can be assigned to use by Europeans or Indians. These groups should be the basis for culture change analysis, not total site artifact inventories or even temporal groups that cut across contextual subassemblages.

Unfortunately, this realization presents a major practical problem. Cheek (1974:187–188) attempted to apply her nine-category classification to the assemblage from San Xavier del Bac divided into two stratigraphic/chronological groups. The results showed that seven of the nine categories were not represented by sufficient numbers of artifacts to justify the use of the classification. A classification which results in many categories containing only one or two artifacts is of little use for quantitative analysis, as the statistical validity of the variations between categories is likely to be meaningless. The usefulness of such a complex classification for purely descriptive purposes is also likely to be extremely limited, especially if the categories do not have a specific interpretive meaning. The interpretation of the meaning of Quimby and Spoehr's categories has long been discussed, and although Cheek (1974:187–188) had positive expectations that she had hoped would be met by the categories in her analysis, these remain untested. As a result, Cheek (1974:189) was forced to abandon this approach in her analysis, although still suggesting it to be of potential value for other sites.

As an alternative approach, Cheek (1974:189–198) adopted a less divisive classification with only three categories: aboriginal, European, and European-influenced. This approach was then used very effectively to compare cultural change at different time periods at San Xavier del Bac and then to compare these data with those from other sites in the Southwest. Unfortunately, Cheek (1974:252–253) took this success to mean that her original classification is also a useful one, clearly not the conclusion suggested by her study. With the benefit of hindsight, it becomes increasingly clear that if researchers are to base culture change analysis on anything less than total site artifact inventories, then classifications cannot be too complex, if they are to retain any semblance of validity when applied to archaeological subassemblages. Cheek has shown that a simple classification could be used to study culture change and compare the cultural changes occurring over time at one site and between sites.

As stated above, this conclusion is based on hindsight, and was not immediately apparent when analysis of the collections excavated from Mission Soledad was attempted. Cheek's (1974) conclusion that her systematic classification could work on other sites was seductive, although the additional seven categories of European-manufactured objects would also have to be considered. Study of Quimby and Spoehr's original categories revealed that although Cheek's systematic version considered the same attributes, it did not encompass all of their categories. In essence, working with ethnographic collections, Quimby and Spoehr had identified artifacts that did not fit into Cheek's classification. The reason was that the two "states" identified by Cheek—Indian or European—are not mutually exclusive. Ethnographic artifacts include examples that contain both Indian and European materials and/or techniques and/or forms. If one were to be entirely systematic, therefore, the 16 categories identified by Cheek are only the beginning of a rapidly growing number of possibilities. If Cheek's nine categories were too complex, then a completely systematic classification would be entirely useless, no matter how seductive their appeal to the scientific archaeologist.

As a result, the initial classification system used

for the collections from Mission Soledad (Farnsworth 1987, 1989) went back to that developed by Quimby and Spoehr (1951), because these were categories that were known to occur ethnographically. In addition, three categories of artifacts which occurred in the Soledad collections were added to the seven they described. They included artifacts not present in the ethnographic collections, or not considered significant.

The first change was to make the critical distinction between European objects which represented new cultural elements and those that directly replaced traditional Indian ones. This resulted in subdividing the one category of European-made objects that appears in both Cheek's nine-category classification and her three-category classification, a vital modification for the analysis of archaeological assemblages. Archaeologists are concerned primarily with material culture, because that is the nature of the data. However, as researchers, archaeologists are really interested in behavior, which may be extrapolated from the data. Viewed from the perspective of behavior, the presence of a European object that is used in precisely the same way as a traditional Indian object does not represent any change in behavior. However, the presence of a European object that has no role in traditional Indian culture indicates a change in behavior, and therefore, of cultural change. If historical archaeologists are to analyze cultural change through the archaeological record, they must attempt to separate those European artifacts that functioned as direct replacements for traditional Indian artifacts and those that required cultural change to occur for them to play a role in Indian culture. The converse is also true. If one were studying European cultural changes in the New World, Indian artifacts in the assemblage would have to be divided in this same fashion.

This division is not an easy task. It requires a considerable degree of knowledge of the cultures in question, but fortunately in historical archaeology, researchers have historical and ethnographic data on which to base such decisions. In a prehistoric culture change study, archaeologists would not be as fortunate.

The second addition to Quimby and Spoehr's (1951) classification was a category for traditional objects which continued in use with no modification at all. Because their study focused on museum objects that individually showed cultural change, these artifacts were not included in their study. Such objects represent complete continuity of traditional Indian culture, or lack of Indian cultural change.

The third addition was of a category for traditional Indian objects made from local (i.e., Indian) materials, but using an imported or modified (i.e., European) technique. This category was added for purely descriptive purposes, as there were a number of artifacts that fit this description such as shell beads with holes drilled with a piece of iron wire. None of the categories in Quimby and Spoehr's classification encompassed these artifacts.

The resulting classification has 10 categories (Table 3) which adequately describe the assemblage from Mission Soledad, although not all of Quimby and Spoehr's original categories are represented in the collection. The percentages that resulted from the use of this classification were termed the "acculturation profile" (Farnsworth 1987, 1989). There are a number of ways to examine the "acculturation profile" which results from this analysis. The first is to compare the total percentage of new elements to traditional elements. It could be argued that this approach provides a measure of the degree of influence of the two cultures in the resultant combination. However, it is not a true measure of the continuity of traditional cultural practices, for those imported artifacts which directly replace traditional elements also represent continuity of traditional practices.

The most accurate measure of continuity of traditional Indian activities is the combined total of imported artifacts which directly replace traditional Indian ones and the total of traditional forms. This method is the measure used in this study. The problem here is the previously mentioned interpretation of which artifacts directly replaced traditional ones. Thus, in the following analysis, only clear direct replacements have been included. The percentage of traditional continuity is, therefore, almost certainly underestimated, because there are almost certainly imported artifacts

TABLE 3
CATEGORIES USED IN ACCULTURATION PROFILE ANALYSIS[a]

Category Number	Description	Examples from the California Missions[b]
1	New artifact forms, imported, representing new cultural elements	Earthenware plates Wine bottles Buttons
2	New artifact forms, imported, directly replacing traditional cultural elements	Glass beads Tobacco pipes
3	New artifact forms, made from local materials	Tiles Mission ceramics
4	New artifact forms, locally made from both local and imported materials	Imported iron tools with wood or bone handles made at the mission
5	New artifact forms, locally made from imported materials	Iron tools made at the mission
6	Traditional artifact forms, unmodified by contact	Stone tools Bone awls Manos and metates
7	Traditional artifact forms, made from imported materials	Glass projectile points
8	Traditional artifact forms, made from local materials using imported or modified techniques	Wire-drilled shell beads Tile gaming pieces
9	Traditional artifact forms, made from imported materials and imported or modified techniques	Mission-made ceramic bowls modeled after traditional baskets
10	Traditional artifact forms, incorporating new elements that change their meaning	Baskets incorporating Spanish designs

[a]Farnsworth (1987:479, 1989:239)

[b]Depending upon the traditional culture of the Native American groups being brought to a particular mission, the examples might fall into different categories than suggested here.

that directly replaced traditional ones but have not been identified as such and have thus been grouped with the new elements.

It would also be possible to measure the degree of continuity of the new, Spanish culture in the acculturation situation by taking the comparable index, that is the total of new forms to the area plus those traditional Indian forms that function unchanged in Spanish culture. This study, however, will focus on assemblages associated with Indian neophytes in the California Missions, not the Spanish padres. Consequently, this measure will not be applied.

The ratio of imported artifacts that directly replace traditional elements to imported artifacts that do not may indicate to what degree the agents of the new culture are attempting to change the basics of the traditional culture, or merely supply goods which function within it. The converse situation with traditional artifacts that function unchanged within Spanish culture does not necessarily imply the same interpretation, because the traditional culture did not usually initiate the culture contact and was not bringing specific cultural elements into the arena where culture contact was occurring. This ratio could provide a measure of the degree to which the members of the traditional culture could be accepted within the new culture without any cultural change.

Many authors have debated the degree of acculturation exhibited by the presence and quantity of the different categories which represent modifications of objects resulting from contact, with no consensus being reached. This author believes that the total percentage of these "hybrid" artifacts is a measure of the intensity of the exchange between

TABLE 4
CATEGORIES AND INDICES USED IN CULTURE CHANGE ANALYSIS

Category Number	Description	Examples from the California Missions[a]
1	Imported artifacts to the area with no traditional counterparts	Earthenware plates Wine bottles Buttons
2	Imported artifacts to the area which fit directly into the traditional culture	Glass beads Tobacco pipes
3	Hybrid artifacts, new forms, local manufacture or materials or both	Tiles Mission ceramics Iron tools made or modified at the mission
4	Hybrid artifacts, traditional forms, local manufacture, imported materials or techniques or both	Glass projectile points Wire-drilled shell beads Tile gaming pieces
5	Traditional artifacts which fit into the new culture in the area	Manos and metates Basketry
6	Traditional artifacts which do not fit into the new culture in the area	Stone tools Bone awls

Index Name	Categories Used to Calculate Index
Continuity of Traditional Culture	$\dfrac{2+4+5+6}{1+2+3+4+5+6} \times 100\%$
Continuity of New Culture	$\dfrac{1+2+3+5}{1+2+3+4+5+6} \times 100\%$
Intensity of Cultural Exchange	$\dfrac{3+4}{1+2+3+4+5+6} \times 100\%$
Availability of Imported Goods	$\dfrac{1+2}{1+2+3+4+5+6} \times 100\%$
Degree to which New Culture Is Supplying Unchanged Traditional Culture	$\dfrac{2}{1+2} \times 100\%$

[a]Depending upon the traditional culture of the Native American groups being brought to a particular mission, the examples might fall into different categories than suggested here.

the two cultures, for the higher the intensity of exchange, the more of these "hybrid" forms would result. Conversely, if there was little intensity of exchange and more coexistence of the two cultures, then fewer of these "hybrids" are likely to be produced. This total percentage of "hybrid" artifacts is the second index used in this study.

Given these measures, it becomes apparent that, excluding any purely descriptive purposes that may be served, it is not necessary to divide an archaeological assemblage into the 10 categories initially used for the Mission Soledad analysis, the nine categories used by Cheek (1974), or the mul-

titude of categories that could be produced by a completely systematic classification. Six broad categories are all that are needed to perform this analysis (Table 4). By combining these in the ways discussed above, the five different indices can be calculated. In most studies, it is not necessary to divide both the imported category and the traditional category into the two groups possible, because it is unlikely that one subassemblage could be both a Spanish and an Indian context.

Before turning to the archaeological subassemblages, it must be noted that, as an analysis of archaeological data, there is an interpretive leap which must be made from the data to the reality which they represent. The analysis is, by necessity, biased toward material culture—the area which often undergoes the most rapid and radical changes, while ideas and beliefs are often slow to follow.

Even material culture is not uniformly represented, due to differential survival in the archaeological record. In the case of the California Indians, differential preservation is especially important to consider, as their traditional culture relied heavily on such perishable items as basketry, wood, and animal skins. Meanwhile, many of the Spanish items which replaced them such as ceramics, glass, and metal survive in the archaeological record. As a result, this analysis underestimates the continuity of traditional Indian culture. The analysis also underestimates the degree to which the Spanish may have adopted Indian traits. For example, the Spanish are known to have admired the California Indians' baskets. They were used extensively in the missions, and a number of basketry impressions in asphaltum were found by Deetz (1963) at Mission La Purisima, some in European/*mestizo* rooms. The Spanish are even known to have commissioned special presentation baskets to be made for them (Dawson and Deetz 1965:208, Plate 14). However, only under special circumstances will any evidence of basketry survive in the archaeological record.

Another specific problem with the analysis of all the assemblages from the California Missions is the categorization of iron artifacts. All iron was imported, mostly as tools, but all the missions also had their own Indian blacksmiths who modified, maintained, and recycled iron objects. This complexity means that any particular iron object could be imported or made locally from imported materials, with no consistent, practical means available of telling which was the case. However, the availability of imported iron was the major factor controlling the quantity of iron objects, and the products of a mission smithy were Spanish in form and method of manufacture. Therefore, it was decided to treat all iron artifacts as imported, rather than locally-made and, hence, "hybrid" ones, even though most of the iron objects recovered from

Mission Soledad could have been made by the mission's smithy.

This classification system is designed to examine changes in material culture due to the operation of processes of culture change. However, the method is also subject to other potential sources of variability, principally, the availability of imported goods and materials, and differences in socio-economic status. If imported artifacts or imported materials were not available, most categories would be affected, boosting those which involve only local materials. Similarly, if many traditional artifacts were made from materials obtained through trade and exchange networks which were broken by the impact of contact, then these would rapidly disappear.

The abundant availability of imported goods or materials is less likely to have such a direct impact on this analysis. However, if this occurred, then economic factors must also come into play, for at some point cultural preference and economic necessity were likely to have come into conflict. If imported goods became much cheaper than locally-made ones, then this might override cultural considerations, although the reverse situation, with local goods being cheaper than imported, is more likely to occur. Therefore, socio-economic status may have some impact on this analysis. The total percentage of imported goods, whether representing new elements or not, provides a measure of the availability of imported goods, allowing for these factors to be considered in the interpretation of the analysis.

Three California Mission Excavations

Archaeological research by the author at Mission Soledad (Figure 1) started in 1983 and continued to 1989. Considerable effort was devoted to documentary research, but each summer was spent in excavations at Mission Soledad. In total, an area of approximately 500 m^2 was excavated. Most of this area was in and around the mission's west wing which was completely excavated, but the Indian neophytes' barracks were also tested and a

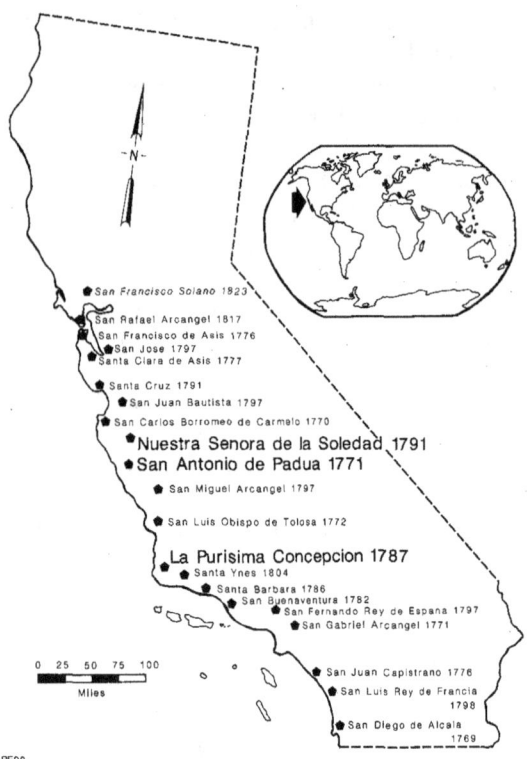

FIGURE 1. The locations and dates of founding of the Franciscan missions in Alta California.

TABLE 5
SELECTED SUBASSEMBLAGES FROM
CALIFORNIA MISSIONS

Context (Approximate Date)	No. of Artifacts N	Continuity of Traditional Cultural Elements %	Intensity of Cultural Exchange %
Mission Soledad Neophytes' Barracks (1800)	161	67.1	9.3
Mission San Antonio Neophytes' Barracks (1810)	155	54.9	20.0
Mission La Purisima Neophytes' Barracks (1820)	90	54.4	15.5
Mission San Antonio Higher-Status Room (1810)	61	57.4	8.2
Mission La Purisima Higher-Status Rooms (1820)	100	32.0	4.0
Mission Soledad Missionaries' Garbage Pit (1809)	69	14.5	4.3

portion of the mission's aqueduct system explored (Farnsworth 1987).

Mission San Antonio de Padua (Figure 1) has been the site of excavations by Dr. Robert L. Hoover since 1976. These excavations, which continue today, have explored part of the Indian neophytes' barracks, the soldiers' barracks, the orchardist's house, and are currently focused on the neophytes' kitchen. Of these excavations, only the neophytes' barracks have been fully published to date (Hoover and Costello 1985).

James Deetz excavated at Mission La Purisima Concepcion (Figure 1) in 1962 and investigated four major features: a tanning vat and accompanying pipeline, the blacksmith shop, a midden area, and a segment of the Indian neophytes' barracks (Deetz 1963).

This paper draws on data from these three ex-

cavations to explore the cultural changes occurring in the California Missions. Because the analysis has been limited to subassemblages from specific features and contexts with known associations, the total number of artifacts in each subassemblage is not sufficiently large to justify complex statistical comparisons. Consequently, the study will be based on simple inspection of percentages of artifacts in the different classes discussed above and will focus on the major changes and trends reflected in the data.

Analysis of Archaeological Assemblages

Table 5 shows the subassemblage recovered from a midden deposit associated with the neophytes' barracks at Mission Soledad. This subassemblage dates to ca. 1800, and 67 percent of the artifacts represent continuity of Indian traditional culture, while the artifacts representing the intensity of cultural exchange represent 9 percent of the subassemblage. Table 5 also shows the subassemblage from the neophytes' barracks at Mission San Antonio de Padua, which dates from around the end of the first decade of the 19th century. The combined total of artifacts representing Indian cultural continuity is 54 percent of the assemblage, suggesting considerable continuity of traditional culture, although not as much as at Soledad. This difference would be expected as Mission Soledad (founded 1791) had only been in existence for a decade by the time represented by its assemblage (1800), while San Antonio (founded 1771) had been in existence for approximately 40 years by the time of its assemblage (1810).

The total of artifacts representing cultural exchange at San Antonio is 20 percent of the assemblage, suggesting that there was considerable exchange and culture change occurring, and far more than at Soledad. This difference is probably due to the period ca. 1800 being that of most dramatic population growth at Soledad, while San Antonio was well past this phase by 1810. As a result, Soledad had a large population of Indians with only relatively brief contact with the Spanish, while the Indians at San Antonio had been in contact with the Spanish for a comparatively long period of time.

Comparison with the assemblage from Mission La Purisima Concepcion's neophytes' barracks (Table 5), dating to ca. 1820, shows a similar pattern to San Antonio. The total of artifacts representing continuity of traditional Indian culture is the same as at San Antonio, just over 54 percent. The total of artifacts representing intensity of cultural exchange is slightly lower than at San Antonio, about 15 percent of the assemblage, but still considerably higher than at Soledad. By the time of this assemblage (1820), La Purisima (founded 1787) had been in existence for over 30 years and was also beyond its peak of population growth.

These results appear to confirm traditional expectations of culture change over time in the missions. The longer the Indians were in the missions, the more acculturated to Spanish culture they became. Thus the Indians at Mission Soledad—with only 10 years at the mission—retain a far higher percentage of their traditional culture that those at either Mission La Purisima after 30 years or Mission San Antonio after 40 years.

Although the subassemblages from the neophytes' barracks at the three missions have been discussed as a chronological series, the fact that each is from a different mission recruiting different groups of Indians, located in different environments, and so forth, introduces a whole set of variables that cannot be easily controlled. As a result, the changes observed may not be due to the factors suggested.

Equally, this analysis is based on a small sample of data from one, albeit the major, segment of mission society. At present, it is impossible to assess how representative these samples are of that segment. Further, it is not to be expected that these results are representative of every segment of the mission's society. Table 5 shows the assemblage from what was interpreted by the excavators (Hoover and Costello 1985) as a higher-status room at Mission San Antonio. The total of artifacts representing continuity of traditional Indian culture is over 50 percent of the assemblage, comparable to the neophytes' rooms discussed above, but the percentage of artifacts representing intensity of cultural exchange totals under 10 percent of the assemblage. This contrast suggests reduced intensity of exchange, with a retention of a high percentage of traditional material culture.

Two rooms at La Purisima were interpreted by the excavator (Deetz 1963:183, 189) as being occupied by a higher-status individual, either a European or a *mestizo*. The subassemblage from these rooms (Table 5) has only 32 percent of the artifacts representing continuity of traditional Indian cultural elements. Meanwhile, the total percentage of artifacts representing intensity of cultural exchange is dramatically less than in the San Antonio assemblage, under 5 percent, suggesting minimal cultural exchange.

Thus, unlike the higher-status individual at Mission San Antonio, who appears to have maintained a high percentage of traditional Indian culture, the higher-status individual at La Purisima maintained more Spanish cultural elements. This contrast may be due to the chronological difference between these assemblages, 1810 for San Antonio versus 1820 for La Purisima, but more likely indicates that the San Antonio individual was a California Indian, whereas the individual at La Purisima was indeed a European or a *mestizo* with dual cultural heritage, as suggested by Deetz (1963:183, 189).

Table 5 also shows a subassemblage from a garbage pit at Mission Soledad which has been interpreted as resulting from the activities of Spanish padres in ca. 1810 (Farnsworth 1987). With only 14 percent of the artifacts representing Indian cultural continuity and 4 percent of the artifacts indicating intensity of cultural exchange in this European subassemblage, these data suggest that the percentages in the higher-status subassemblage from La Purisima, 32 percent and 4 percent respectively, most likely represent the presence of a *mestizo* with a dual cultural heritage, rather than a European.

Each subassemblage discussed above represents one point in time in each mission's existence. Although the changes examined in the neophytes' assemblages were explained in terms of the length of occupation time of the Indians in the mission, the effects of a wide variety of other factors could also be responsible. Each mission was recruiting a different cultural group, was operating in a different environmental setting, was controlled by different padres, and recruited its population at different times. Thus, the interpretation of the differences between the missions solely on the basis of length of time since the mission was founded may not be valid. To understand fully the changes in cultural continuity of a mission population, as many as possible of these external factors must be held constant. To achieve this control requires using subassemblages that are representative of a mission's existence as a whole. While no such sequence of subassemblages exists from neophytes' barracks of a mission, there is a sequence of subassemblages from the central quadrangle at Mission Soledad. Since these come from the area where many of the Indians worked under Spanish supervision, the results are not directly comparable

TABLE 6
SUBASSEMBLAGES FROM THE CENTRAL
QUADRANGLE AT MISSION SOLEDAD

Context (Approximate Date)	No. of Artifacts N	Continuity of Traditional Cultural Elements %	Intensity of Cultural Exchange %
Pit A (1795)	62	29.1	9.7
Pit B (1796)	50	26.0	4.0
Early-Period Kitchen Floor (1798)	214	39.2	7.5
Pit C (1802)	144	46.5	23.0
Middle-Period Kitchen Floor (1809)	210	30.5	2.8
Late-Period Floor Deposit (1822)	505	39.4	3.2

to those from the neophytes' dwellings, but they should reflect the same trends in Indian cultural continuity or change, if to a different degree.

The sequence of subassemblages from Mission Soledad (Table 6) shows that the degree of continuity of Indian traditional activities changed significantly during the Mission period. During the last decade of the 18th century, the mission's first decade, the percentage of artifacts which represented continuity of traditional Indian activities increased from under 30 percent around the middle of the decade to approximately 45 percent of the subassemblage by the early part of the 19th century.

During this period of increased continuity of traditional Indian culture, the number of Indians at Mission Soledad increased rapidly, tripling from 240 in 1795 to 725 in 1805. In contrast, during the first four years (1791–1794), the population had grown more slowly. Therefore, it seems that with a lower ratio of Indians to Spanish and fewer "pagan" Indians being baptized, the missionaries were able to influence the Indians more during the mission's early years than during the following years of rapid population growth which resulted in greater continuity of traditional Indian activities in the population.

This is not to say that the missionaries had decreased their efforts, rather that the overall intensity of cultural exchange had increased. In the middle of the last decade of the 18th century, artifacts representing the intensity of cultural exchange totalled under 10 percent of the subassemblage, while by the turn of the century, they had increased to well over 20 percent of the subassemblage.

At this point, one can also compare the Indians' behavior in the central quadrangle with their dwellings (Table 5). Not surprisingly, the degree of cultural continuity is far higher in the neophytes' barracks at Mission Soledad than in the central quadrangle, an interpretation which holds true whether one takes the evidence of garbage pit C, which is the most directly comparable context, or the early-period floor from the mission's kitchen.

The degree of cultural exchange occurring in the neophytes' barracks appears to have been slightly greater than that represented by the early floor deposit, but considerably less than in pit C. Viewed in chronological sequence, this interpretation is consistent with the trend increasing from pit E (4.0%) and the early floor (7.5%) to the neophytes' barracks (9.3%) and then a dramatic jump in pit C (23.0%). The jump between the neophytes' barracks and pit C may be partially a result of sampling error. However, comparison of the garbage deposit from the neophytes' barracks with the garbage deposit in pit C is probably more likely to be valid than with the deposit built up on the floor of a building that was in use. Therefore, the difference between them is more likely to be real than entirely due to sampling problems. If one accepts this interpretation, then the dramatic difference between these functionally and virtually chronologically equivalent assemblages must be explained in other terms. The explanation must lie in the location and origin of the two deposits and suggests, as might have been predicted, that the

degree of cultural exchange was less in the Indian barracks than in the central quadrangle.

Returning to the sequence of subassemblages from the central quadrangle, the first decade of the 19th century saw a new trend. The overall degree of continuity of traditional activities decreased from 40 percent of the subassemblage from the early floor in the kitchen to 30 percent of the subassemblage from the middle-period floor. During the period from 1805 to 1810, the mission's population was gradually declining, and the number of new baptisms was lower than in any previous five-year period. Thus, the ratio of Indians who had been in Mission Soledad for some time to new, "pagan" Indians was considerably lower than before. It appears that the lull gave the missionaries the opportunity to attempt to change the culture of the Indians that had been brought to the mission during the previous decade.

This drop in continuity of traditional culture was coupled with a decrease in elements representing the intensity of cultural exchange from over 7 percent to below 3 percent. The Indians still maintained about 30 percent elements of traditional continuity in their material culture, but by the end of the decade, it appears that the Spanish padres were no longer devoting as much energy to attempting to change the Indians' culture as before.

Given the decrease in intensity of cultural exchange at the end of the first decade of the 19th century, an increase in overall continuity of traditional activities would be predicted to follow with the renewed influx of "pagan" Indians. This possibility is supported by the assemblage from the early 1820s, where the percentage of traditional artifacts had increased to 40 percent of the subassemblage, while the intensity of cultural exchange did not change significantly, remaining low.

During this time, the mission's population had experienced a gradual decline, though shored up by the importation of Indians from the Central Valley. Only in 1822 were the number of new baptisms comparable to the years of heavy recruiting of the local Indians around the turn of the century. As a result, this increase in continuity of traditional activities cannot be adequately explained by a sudden influx of large numbers of "pagan" Indians.

Overall, this analysis has revealed a number of significant trends from the subassemblages in the central quadrangle at Mission Soledad. First, during the years of heaviest recruiting of Indians, the degree of continuity of traditional culture increased because of the increasing ratio of "pagan" Indians to padres, and with only a small pool of neophytes with a longer period of exposure to Spanish culture. After an initial period of little cultural exchange, however, as the ratio of "pagan" Indians to neophytes declined around the turn of the century, the rate of cultural exchange increased considerably. However, by 1809 cultural exchange appears to have virtually ceased, resulting in a "hybrid" culture with approximately 30 percent of the material culture containing elements indicating continuity of traditional Indian activities. These elements of continuity increased from this point to nearer 40 percent by the late Mission period as renewed recruiting brought in more "pagan" Indians from the Central Valley of California. However, this renewed recruiting apparently was not accompanied by renewed efforts to change traditional Indian culture by the Spanish padres, as the degree of cultural exchange remained very low.

Analysis of Spanish padres' views in 1813/1815 (Farnsworth 1987, 1989) suggests that Mission Soledad was not unique. The missionaries in general had accepted that they were not able to make further progress in acculturating the California Indians. They had decided to allow time to produce a mission-born population which would not know traditional Indian patterns and hence, adopt Spanish ones instead. However, the missionaries were not fully aware of the degree to which traditional culture was maintained by the Indians in the missions, and the constant influx of "pagan" Indians further contributed to the increase in continuity of traditional cultural elements. Thus, even if the Indians had not died as a result of European-introduced diseases, the padres' plan to produce a "Spanish" population would not have worked.

Summary and Discussion

This study shows that it is possible to extract information about culture change in contact situations from archaeological subassemblages. Using both archaeological and historical data it has been possible to develop a model of culture change in the California Missions.

Comparison of subassemblages from the neophytes' barracks at the missions of Soledad, San Antonio, and La Purisima shows that the Indians at all three missions were able to maintain a high level of traditional culture while living at the mission. In each case, the neophytes maintained over half of their material culture related to traditional activities, with those at Soledad maintaining as much as two-thirds. Viewed in terms of time from mission founding to the time of the assemblage, the results appear to support the traditional theory that the longer the Indians were in the missions, the more acculturated they became. Even the gradual increase in intensity of cultural exchange appears to support this conclusion.

The analysis has also revealed that the higher-status assemblage at Mission La Purisima differs dramatically from that from Mission San Antonio. This contrast is interpreted as a result of the San Antonio assemblage being from a California Indian, whereas the La Purisima assemblage is from either Europeans or, based on a comparison with a European assemblage from Mission Soledad, the La Purisima assemblage is more likely to have come from *mestizos*.

It appears that in the central complex at Mission Soledad, the Spanish succeeded in imposing a greater degree of Spanish culture than in the neophytes' rooms at Soledad, San Antonio, or La Purisima. However, the neophytes were still able to maintain one-third of their material assemblage as artifacts continuing their own cultural tradition. While initially there was little intensity of cultural exchange, this interaction had increased considerably by the turn of the century. However, by 1809 the intensity of cultural exchange appears to have declined, resulting in a "hybrid" culture with approximately 30 percent of the material culture containing elements indicating continuity of traditional Indian activities. Further, the evidence suggests that these elements of continuity increased from this point to nearer 40 percent by the late Mission period.

The cause of the changes in the continuity of Indian culture and cultural exchange at the missions is found in the change in the economic structure of Spanish California (Farnsworth 1987, 1989). The period from 1800 to 1810 was characterized by a dramatic increase in economic production. Labor was diverted from food production into diversified agricultural production, craft specialization, and the specialized production of livestock, the major source of wealth for trade both within California and internationally.

During this period, the missions changed emphasis from attracting, controlling, and acculturating the California Indians to exploiting their labor for economic production. The missionaries still required a certain degree of Spanish culture, especially in the male population, which composed the prime labor force, for they had to be able to carry out the introduced European agricultural tasks, industrial processes, and crafts needed to produce the missions' wealth. However, in other aspects of their lives—except in religious practices, greater continuity of Indian traditions could be tolerated. As long as the Indians carried out Christian religious activities—not those which the missionaries associated with pagan rituals—and did the tasks assigned to them, the missionaries did not attempt to introduce other aspects of Spanish culture as energetically as before. The result was a decline in the intensity of cultural exchange and increased continuity of traditional culture.

The concrete elements of culture, material items, and explicit behaviors generally are transferred between cultures much more rapidly and easily than symbolic, ideological, and valuational elements (Broom et al. 1954). If the California Indians were able to maintain 50 percent or more of their material culture, even if in modified form, then their retention of the non-material elements was probably far higher. Such a high figure becomes even more significant if allowance is made for perishable items. Therefore, after the change in the missions' main emphasis during the first decade of the 19th century, there cannot have been any appreciable change in these non-material and religious realms of culture, given the rapid decline of the rate of change in material culture.

It appears that an end point in the culture change of the California Indians occurred at an early date, during the first decade of the 19th century, not at the secularization of the missions as is often assumed. Thereafter, there was a measurable return to traditional activities. While this situation may not have been the case for individual Indians, with the constant influx of "pagan" Indians throughout the Mission period at most missions, it was the pattern for the population as a whole. The amount of culture change of the population declined, not necessarily of each individual. On average, the degree of culture change experienced by individuals was less after the missions changed emphasis to economic production than it was before.

This scenario directly contradicts the traditional model of Indian culture change in the missions, which is suggested by the comparison of the assemblages from the neophytes' barracks at the three missions. It would appear at first glance that these differences cannot be reconciled. However, this is not the case.

First, it must be remembered that any comparison between missions introduces a series of variables that cannot be fully controlled. However, if these are ignored, it is possible to explain the apparent contradiction in the data. It has already been shown that the earliest neophytes' barrack assemblage, that from Soledad, is entirely consistent with expectations for an assemblage of this type at that time at Mission Soledad. That is to say that it fits the pattern of the other data from Mission Soledad, in particular from pit C and the early-period floor in the mission kitchen. What has to be reconciled are the differences between this subassemblage and those from San Antonio and La Purisima.

The San Antonio assemblage dates to the end of the first decade of the 19th century, approximately the same time period as the middle-period floor from the mission kitchen. The Soledad assemblages indicate a decline in both the continuity of traditional cultural elements and in the intensity of cultural exchange over this time period. Comparison of the San Antonio neophytes with the Soledad neophytes also indicates a decline in elements representing cultural continuity, but an increase in the intensity of cultural exchange. At Mission San Antonio at this time, as at Soledad, there was a lull in the numbers of "pagan" Indians being recruited, hence the decrease in cultural continuity. However, it would appear that, unlike Soledad, the padres at San Antonio did not relax their efforts at missionization, therefore the increase in cultural exchange.

The neophytes' assemblage from La Purisima, dating to around the beginning of the second decade of the 19th century, is approximately contemporary with the late-Mission-period floor from the kitchen at Mission Soledad. During this decade, the Soledad data suggest that an increase occurred in elements of cultural continuity, with virtually no change in the intensity of cultural exchange, and that an end point to the culture change at the mission had already been reached.

Comparison of the La Purisima neophytes' assemblages with those from Mission San Antonio shows virtually no change in elements of cultural continuity and a decline in cultural exchange over this same period. At this time, the population of Mission La Purisima was steadily declining, with very limited recruitment of "pagan" Indians, unlike Mission Soledad. Hence, there was no influx of traditional Indian culture-bearers as at Mission Soledad. As a result, one does not see an increase in traditional culture as the Soledad data suggest. However, it is also apparent that no further decrease occurs; there is not more culture change occurring, as the traditional model would suggest. Equally, there is a decline in the intensity of cultural exchange compared to Mission San Antonio, again in contradiction to the traditional model and, if anything, more consistent with the new model than the lack of change seen in the Soledad data. Thus, these data also suggest that an end point to Indian culture change in the California Missions has already been reached by the end of the first decade of the 19th century, as suggested by the Soledad data.

Thus, while the data from missions San Antonio and La Purisima at first appear to fit the more traditional model of culture change in the California Missions, it may be seen that these two instants in archaeological time can be explained more sat-

isfactorily by the model proposed here. The culture change experienced by the California Indians in the missions virtually ceased around the end of the first decade of the 19th century as the missions switched their emphasis to economic production. Thereafter, the mission populations maintained or even increased their traditional cultural practices.

ACKNOWLEDGMENTS

I wish to express my appreciation to all the students and volunteers who have participated in the excavations at Mission Soledad. In particular, I thank Douglas V. Armstrong for his contribution as co-instructor of the UCLA Archaeological Field Schools held at the Mission from 1984 to 1987. The Catholic Diocese of Monterey and the Mission Soledad Restoration Committee both granted permission for the excavations at Mission Soledad which form the core of this project. Funding for this research has been provided by: the University Research Expeditions Program (UREP); UCLA Summer Sessions; UCLA Graduate Division; the UCLA Friends of Archaeology; the Mission Soledad Restoration Committee; the Native Daughters of the Golden West; the UCLA Program on Mexico; the Institute of Archaeology, UCLA; the Museum of Cultural History, UCLA; and the Institute of American Cultures and the American Indian Studies Center, both at UCLA. Finally, I should like to thank Laurie Farnsworth for her help in the preparation of this article and Robert L. Hoover, J. W. Joseph, Anita Cohen-Williams, and Jack S. Williams for their comments on earlier versions of this paper.

REFERENCES

BROOM, LEONARD, BERNARD J. SIEGEL, EVON Z. VOGT, AND JAMES B. WATSON
   1954   Acculturation: An Exploratory Formulation. *American Anthropologist* 56:973–1002.

CHEEK, ANNETTA LYMAN
   1974   *The Evidence for Acculturation in Artifacts: Indians and Non-Indians at San Xavier del Bac, Arizona.* Ph.D. dissertation, Department of Anthropology, University of Arizona, Tucson. University Microfilms, Ann Arbor.

DAWSON, LAWRENCE, AND JAMES DEETZ
   1965   A Corpus of Chumash Basketry. *UCLA Archaeological Survey Annual Report* 7:193–276.

DEETZ, JAMES J. F.
  1963 Archaeological Investigations at La Purisima Mission. *UCLA Archaeological Survey Annual Report* 5:163–208.

DI PESO, CHARLES C.
  1974 *Casas Grandes*, Vol. 3. The Amerind Foundation, Dragoon, Arizona.

FARNSWORTH, PAUL
  1987 *The Economics of Acculturation in the California Missions: A Historical and Archaeological Study of Mission Nuestra Senora de la Soledad*. Ph.D. dissertation, Archaeology Program, University of California, Los Angeles. University Microfilms, Ann Arbor.

  1989 The Economics of Acculturation in the Spanish Missions of Alta California. *Research in Economic Anthropology* 11:217–249.

HOOVER, ROBERT L., AND JULIA G. COSTELLO
  1985 Excavations at Mission San Antonio: The First Three Seasons, 1976–1978. *Institute of Archaeology, Monograph 26*. University of California, Los Angeles.

QUIMBY, GEORGE I., AND ALEXANDER SPOEHR
  1951 Acculturation and Material Culture—I. *Fieldiana: Anthropology* 3(6):107–147.

PAUL FARNSWORTH
DEPARTMENT OF GEOGRAPHY AND ANTHROPOLOGY
LOUISIANA STATE UNIVERSITY
BATON ROUGE, LOUISIANA 70803

Lynn H. Gamble
Irma Carmen Zepeda

Social Differentiation and Exchange among the Kumeyaay Indians during the Historic Period in California

ABSTRACT

Long distance exchange between the Kumeyaay Indians and other southern California Indian groups after Spanish colonization is poorly documented and understood. The intensive study of thousands of shell beads from an historic cemetery in the San Diego region indicates that traditional socioeconomic interactions persevered among some California Indians despite missionization, epidemic diseases, and the seizure of California Indian lands. A mortuary analysis of the distribution of beads and other grave associations in the same cemetery further suggests that Kumeyaay sociopolitical organization was more complex than previously noted. It does not appear that this complexity developed as a result of Spanish colonization, but instead continued after at least 80 years of intensive contact. The Kumeyaay example illustrates that often important economic and sociopolitical traditions are maintained despite clear attempts to acculturate colonized societies.

Introduction

After the arrival of the Spanish in 1769, life for the Kumeyaay Indians of the San Diego area changed. Franciscan priests and soldiers were sent to secure the Spanish northwest frontier against the Russians and British by setting up missions and presidios throughout Alta California (Shipek 1987:19). Mission San Diego de Alcalá was the first to be established in 1769. Along with these orders, the Spanish arrived with the idea of civilizing the California Indians, thereby infringing on their hunting and gathering activities, exchange networks, and many other aspects of their daily life. The goals of this work are to examine two poorly documented aspects of Kumeyaay society, long distance exchange and sociopolitical organization during an 81-year period (A.D. 1769–1850) after Spanish colonization.

Prehistoric long distance exchange among southern California Indians has been well-docu-mented since the early period, especially obsidian exchange (Ericson 1977, 1981; Hughes 1994; Jackson and Ericson 1994). In contrast, little is known about long distance exchange in the region after historic contact. Most ethnographic and historic accounts assume that long distance trade among California Indian groups broke down due to the Spanish invasion (Earle and Ericson 1977:9; Bamforth 1993:68). Chartkoff and Chartkoff (1984:264) state that vital trade connections between the California coast and interior were severed after Spanish colonization. This study is focused on exchange between the Chumash Indians who lived along the Santa Barbara Channel Coast and the Kumeyaay Indians who lived to the south in San Diego County. The maintenance of long distance exchange between different California Indian groups is addressed in the context of the manufacture of shell bead money used in traditional economic transactions during a period of time when Indian social systems in southern California were severely impacted by the Spanish.

Very little has been documented indicating that goods were exchanged between the Kumeyaay and Chumash during any time periods. The data presented here suggest that because there is a relative lack of shell bead manufacturing evidence in San Diego County, the presence of *Olivella biplicata* rough disk beads at *Amat Inuk* (C-144) indicates that the beads must have been brought to the site through an historic exchange system. It is well documented that the Chumash manufactured large quantities of shell beads and traded them long distances within and outside of California (Bennyhoff and Hughes 1987; King 1990a). Given this situation and the similarity in the diameters, perforation sizes, and thicknesses of the rough disk beads recovered from *Amat Inuk* with those manufactured by the Chumash, it is hypothesized that the shell beads from *Amat Inuk* were manufactured by the Chumash and traded to the Kumeyaay. In addition, the beads were unevenly distributed in the cemetery where they were recovered, possibly indicating an unequal distribution of wealth or status among the Kumeyaay during the historic period.

Given that the collection of shell beads was found in a mortuary context, it is also possible to address sociopolitical organization during the historic period. No systematic analyses have been completed and published on archaeological examples of Kumeyaay mortuary practices during any time period. Therefore, this aspect of the research is considered an important contribution in understanding Kumeyaay social organization.

Kumeyaay Culture

Kumeyaay is the contemporary term for the Diegueño (both Northern/Western and Southern/Eastern), Kamia (Eastern Kumeyaay), Tipai, and Ipai (Hedges 1975:75; Luomala 1978:592; Shipek 1987:5). The Kumeyaay are Yuman-speakers who occupy southern San Diego County (Figure 1). The variable terrain includes mountain and upland, coastal, and desert climates. Exchange was an important means for acquiring essentials for survival, a variety of food, and valuable items, because of the different resources offered by each environment.

The Kumeyaay were organized into territorial bands, each of which had a central primary village with numerous outlier homesteads (Shipek 1982:297). Bands moved seasonally according to available food resources (Shipek 1982:297, 1987:7). Each band had a captain, who was called *Kwaapaay* and was usually an adult male who inherited his position, but was sometimes appointed by all the *Kwaapaay* from throughout the Kumeyaay area (Shipek 1982:297–298). The *Kwaapaay* instructed the band on economic matters regarding resources, oversaw ceremonies, and resolved disputes. The *Kwaapaay* was paid in food and valuables for these services (Shipek 1987:7–8). Kumeyaay officials, including the *Kwaapaay*, religious specialists, and shamans, had more decision-making powers, more land resources, and more personal valuables, such as shell beads, than other band members (Shipek 1982:299–300).

The Kumeyaay lived in two different villages that were situated near water sources, one for winter and one for summer and fall (Spier 1923:307; Luomala 1978:597). There also may have been subsidiary camps for both winter and summer sites (True 1970:55). Historically, the Imperial Valley Kumeyaay planted maize, beans, teparies, gourds, pumpkins, and melons in the floodplains of the Colorado River. Apparently agriculture was not an essential subsistence

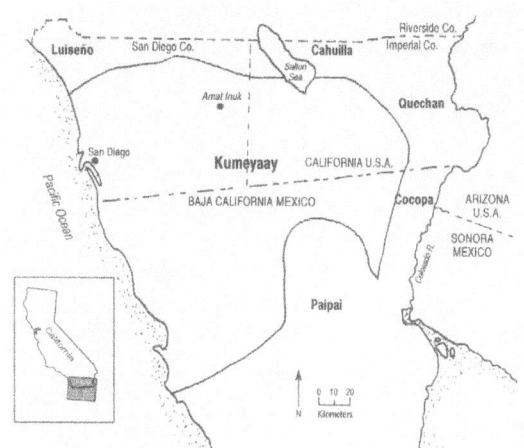

FIGURE 1. Map of Kumeyaay territory.

strategy among the Kumeyaay. If they heard of rich gathering spots elsewhere, they abandoned their crops (Gifford 1931:11; Luomala 1978:600; Shipek 1993:381). Fish and shellfish were important subsistence resources for coastal Kumeyaay (Luomala 1978:601; Gallegos 1992:213; Hildebrand and Hagstrum 1995:90).

The Kumeyaay usually did not bury their dead but cremated them. The body was placed in a pyre over a pit with the head positioned to the south or east towards the afterworld. All of the belongings of the dead were burned to insure the spirit did not return for them (Heye 1919:14–16; Davis 1921:95–97; Luomala 1978:603). Waterman (1910:306) reported that the belongings of the dead were not burned until the mourning ceremony, which occurred about one year after the death of an individual. After cremation, the ashes of the bones and belongings were usually gathered and placed in a pottery jar or mortuary olla and then buried or sometimes hidden in rocks or crevices (Waterman 1910:306; Kroeber 1925:716; Luomala 1978:603). Often specific cremation areas, or defined cemeteries, were designated where cremation ollas or urns were buried (Heye 1919; Davis 1921; True 1970:59). If death occurred in a house, it was burned down (Moriarty 1969:183; Luomala 1978:597). At cremations there was "wailing, speech making, all-night singing of song cycles, and gift exchange with non-relatives from friendly clans. . . . Mourners cut their hair, blackened their faces, and never mentioned the person's name again" (Luomala 1978:603). Kumeyaay cremation burials have been described as being shallower in depth than Cahuilla cremations (Bell 1975:19).

After the founding of the Mission San Diego de Alcalá in 1769, the Kumeyaay's traditional way of life changed dramatically. The Spanish missionaries came in with the idea that "they alone had all the knowledge, civilization, and the only real religion and that they had been designated to control and Christianize the area" (Shipek 1986:15). This was accomplished in part through the Spanish colonial policy of *reducción* in which California Indians were taken into the missions in order to teach them Catholicism, European-style agriculture, leatherwork, and textile production (Jackson and Castillo 1995:3). Mission San Diego de Alcalá, however, did not follow the system of *reducción* because there was a lack of arable land and no easy irrigation system near the mission. Mission San Diego de Alcalá opted for a rotating system in which groups of Kumeyaay were brought into the mission, taught the basics of Christianity, shown European-style agriculture, and then released back to their villages when a new group was brought into the mission. The Kumeyaay were also used as the Spanish labor force in rotating shifts (Shipek 1987:20). Many attempted to resist Spanish control, while some fled east to the mountains where the Kumeyaay were left relatively untouched (Shipek 1986:15).

Mission San Diego de Alcalá was less effective in its goals than other missions throughout California. The Spanish invasion disrupted the Kumeyaay settlement and subsistence patterns, forcing the Kumeyaay to look for new places to gather foods (Shipek 1991:27). The Spanish also introduced epidemic diseases that severely impacted some of the Kumeyaay population (Jackson and Castillo 1995:41). During the Mexican period (1822–1848), Mission San Diego de Alcalá was secularized and the lands were distributed into ranchos among the Mexican *mayordomo*. Many Kumeyaay migrated from the mission to the ranchos, looking for food and employment. Often the Kumeyaay were treated as feudal slaves and dehumanized by this system. Under the United States rule, California Indians were denied land rights, and most of their historic villages were destroyed between 1860 and 1880 by Anglo entrepreneurs and ranchers (Carrico 1987:14–16). The violence against the California Indians continued. Despite these obstacles, the Kumeyaay succeeded in keeping many of their traditions alive.

Exchange in Southern California

Exchange transactions involve complex relationships with social, economic, political, and religious components (Baugh and Ericson 1993:4; Plog 1993:287). Spanish explorers recorded that California Indians often traded many of their possessions, such as baskets and otter skins, for glass beads during the early historic period (A.D. 1542–1769) (Costanso 1910:49). These necessities or desirable items were acquired through organized exchange networks. It has been documented that the Eastern Kumeyaay served as traders between the Yuman and Western Kumeyaay groups (Mohave Tribe of Indians 1958:18). Given the distance between the Chumash and the Kumeyaay, intermediaries or down-the-line trade may have been an important distribution mode between the groups.

California is ideal for the development of exchange networks because of its variable environment that resulted in localized resources and biological communities (Ericson 1977:111). Exchange networks that develop in this type of setting provide assurance of food in times of stress (Brumfiel and Earle 1987:2). Exchange networks in precolonial stateless societies, such as hunting-gathering groups, were vital for individual and group survival because they served as a form of security in times of natural disaster, environmental stress, and warfare (Dalton 1971:90–91).

The Spanish were quick to take advantage of the California Indians' interest in exotic goods once contact was initiated. California Indians exchanged shellfish, fish, acorns, and water with men aboard expedition ships such as Cabrillo's, de Unamuno's, Cermeño's, and Vizcaino's ships. In exchange, the Spanish provided glass beads, silk, and cotton cloth for food and water (Erlandson and Bartoy 1995).

Ethnographic information indicates that the Kumeyaay traded with the Mohave, Yuman, Cocopa, Cahuilla, and Luiseño (Davis 1961; Eidsness et al. 1979; Carrico and Day 1981; Shackley 1981). Exchange items included eagle feathers and salt, for tobacco, acorns, baked mescal roots, yucca fibers, sandals, baskets, carrying nets, gourd seeds, dried greens, tule roots, bulbs, cattail sprouts, yucca leaves, mescal, pine nuts, manzanita fruit, berries, chokecherries, dried sea food, and mesquite beans (Davis 1961; Shipek 1991:33).

Exotic materials in the archaeological record are another indication of trade or movements of people in the region. Obsidian from Obsidian Butte and Coso in southern California and Baja is well documented at many sites in southern California (Ericson 1977, 1981; Eidsness et al. 1979:96; Carrico and Day 1981:90; Hughes 1994; Jackson and Ericson 1994; Shackley 1995). Chert and Palomar Brown ceramic sherds from the Luiseño territory are documented at the village of *Ystagua* in the Sorrento Valley (Eidsness et al. 1979:96). Ceramics from the Lower Colorado River and the Salton Sea area also have been found in numerous mountain and coastal sites (Hildebrand and Hagstrum 1995).

Little is known about the frequency of exchange or the quantity of goods that were exchanged. Most trading among the Kumeyaay probably occurred through a barter system, although Shipek (1987:6) describes food being traded for shell beads. Another report mentions that the Kumeyaay used *Olivella* shell beads as a mainstay in their widespread trade and barter system (Carrico and Day 1981:75). The Kumeyaay may have used shell beads as a form of money, but this is not clear.

In contrast, it is well documented that the Chumash used *Olivella* shell beads as a form of money (Arnold 1987, 1991, 1992; Arnold and Munns 1994; King 1976, 1978, 1990a). Probably the best known historic account of Chumash use of shell beads as money was made by Longinos Martinez in 1792. "When they trade for profit, beads circulated among them as if they were money, being strung on long threads, according to the greater or smaller wealth of each one" (Simpson 1939:45–46). The Chumash had an intricate trade network that involved three different environmental regions: island, coastal mainland, and inland (King 1976). The Island Chumash manufactured shell beads to trade for food and other resources from the coastal mainland because they had less than half as many plant species as the coastal mainland and only small mammals as food resources (King 1976). Chumash exchange with groups outside their area is well documented in the ethnographic

and ethnohistoric record. King (1976:304–307) provides several historic accounts of exchange between the Chumash and the Mojave, Yokuts, and other California Indian tribes. The archaeological record demonstrates that Chumash shell beads were traded throughout southern California and some surrounding areas, such as the Great Basin and the Southwest (Bennyhoff and Hughes 1987:156–160; King 1990a:107). Los Angeles, Orange, San Bernardino, and Riverside counties have Early, Middle, and Late period shell beads similar to those from the Chumash area (King 1990a:111, 122, 129). One ethnographic account states that shell beads were taken from the Chumash on the Santa Barbara Channel Islands to the Gabrieleño, and then to the Cahuilla in the Palm Springs area (Strong 1929:95–96). In central California, *Olivella biplicata* beads with their spires removed have been found that are possibly contemporary with Middle period Phase 1 (1400–800 B.C.) (King 1990a:119). Clearly, Chumash goods, including shell beads, had a wide distribution among numerous Indian tribes.

In contrast, exchange to the Kumeyaay has not been clearly documented. In San Diego County, at least two sites have evidence of exchange with the Chumash prior to the historic period. One site (SDI-603) contained a clam disk bead similar to those found in the Santa Barbara Channel Early period Phase Ex (6000–4500 B.C.) or Early period Phase Ey (4500–2400 B.C.) (King 1990a:108) (Figure 2). An *Olivella biplicata* rectangle bead (typical of the Early period) was recovered from Indian Hill Rockshelter, another site in the San Diego area (King 1990a:110; McDonald 1992).

The *Amat Inuk* (C-144) Site

Amat Inuk was located in Mason Valley about 4 mi. (6 km) west of Vallecitos in eastern San Diego County. The site has been identified by various historic names, including *Net Nook, Matnook, Amat Inuk, and Matrink* (True 1966:89; Moriarty 1969:87; Cupples and Ezell 1974:8; Cline 1979). In this work, it will be called by its most common name of *Amat Inuk*. The site was occupied until 1870 and then abandoned due to a smallpox epidemic (Rogers 1929:1). This date is significant because it marks the discovery of a gold mine at Rancho Cuyamaca, just to the east of Mason Valley, which brought

Date	C. King (1990a)	Bennyhoff & Hughes (1987)	Arnold (1992)	Warren (1968)	Rogers (1945)
A.D. 1800	L3a (1804)	Historic			
A.D. 1700	L2b (1782)	Late Protohistoric			
A.D. 1600		Early Protohistoric	Late Period	Undefined	Undefined
	L2a				
A.D. 1500					
A.D. 1400	L1c	Late Phase I			
A.D. 1300	L1b				
A.D. 1200		Middle Phase I	Middle to Late Transition Period	Yuman/ Shoshonean	
	L1a				
A.D. 1100					
	M5c				
A.D. 1000		Early Phase I			Yuman
	M5b				
A.D. 900	M5a				
A.D. 800	M4	Middle/Late Period			
A.D. 700		Transition		Encinitas Tradition	
A.D. 600	M3	Late	Middle Period		
A.D. 500					
A.D. 400		Late			
A.D. 300					La Jollan
A.D. 200	M2b	Intermediate			
A.D. 100					
200 B.C.					
800 B.C.	M2a				
1400 B.C.	M1				
2400 B.C.	Ez		Early Period		
3500 B.C.	Eyb				
4500 B.C.	Eya				
6000 B.C	Ex				
				San Dieguito Tradition	
10,000 B.C.					San Dieguito

FIGURE 2. Chronology for Southern California.

many more people to the region. Brott (1963), who worked at the site in 1963, suggested that the site was abandoned in 1897 and considered it a Yuman III village (Brott 1963:1), as did Rogers (1929). True (1966:89, 1970:56) described the site as one of three large Kumeyaay winter villages with a cremation burial area. Rogers (1929:1) noted that in addition to Yuman III, there were traces of San Dieguito II. Non-native historic artifacts from the cemetery include glass beads, a Spanish spur, two pieces of bronze bridle trappings, metal knives, a Spanish crockery pendant, a brass U.S. Army button, a lump of melted copper, and a piece of willow ware (Rogers 1929). Apparently Pedro Fages described this settlement in his journals when he crossed from the Anza Trail to San Diego in 1782–1783 (Rogers 1929:1). In his 19 April 1782, diary entry, Fages stated that Mason Valley "extended north and south probably two and a half leagues [12 km/7.5 mi.], and east and west about one and a half leagues [7 km/4.5 mi.], on the slope of a range of moderate sized, well grassed mountains, with plenty of springs. Nearby the latter we found a very large village of Camillares Indians (Kumeyaay), who climbed up a hill as we were passing, and came down to talk to the soldiers who were coming behind with the horses" (Rensch 1955:199).

Amat Inuk was excavated by Malcolm Rogers between 1925 and 1929. Rogers (1929:1) found three cemeteries with cremations: a large one, "Cemetery A," and two smaller ones, "Cemetery B" and "Cemetery C," as well as "Isolated Cremations" (Figure 3). He estimated that a total of 100 cremations existed, but because of the repeated looting and other disturbance processes, it was not possible to reconstruct the original number. Rogers (1929:1) remarked in his notes that this was the largest cremation cemetery in the "Yuman territory." Rogers took notes on 46 cremations in Cemetery A (Rogers 1929:1–10), and 10 in Cemetery C (Rogers 1929:11–13), although some of the cremations were excavated by other individuals. The only reference to Cemetery B in Rogers' notes is on his map showing the locations of the three cemeteries (Figure 3). Five isolated cremations (Rogers 1929:14) were also found and recorded, totaling 61 cremations at the site. Data on these cremations include locational information, maps of cremations (Figures 3–7), and relatively detailed notes on grave goods. Nine cremations from Cemetery A lacked detailed notes and exact provenience, as they had previously been excavated in 1924 by John Glenn, who apparently did not take notes (Rogers 1929:1, 8). Nevertheless Rogers (1929) provided approximate information on the location of Glenn's cremations, as well as those conducted by Ben Squires. Squires' excavations included a cremation buried inside a house and a charred log

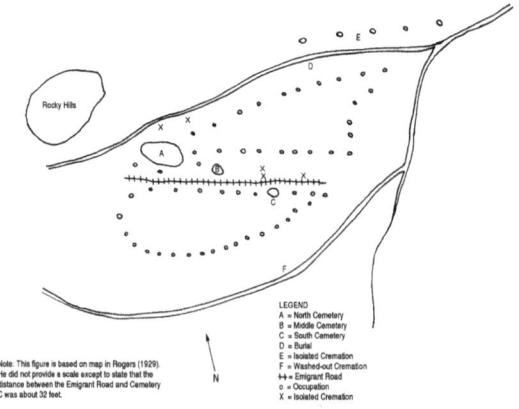

FIGURE 3. Cemeteries and isolated cremations at *Amat Inuk* (based on Rogers 1929).

Perspectives from *Historical Archaeology:*

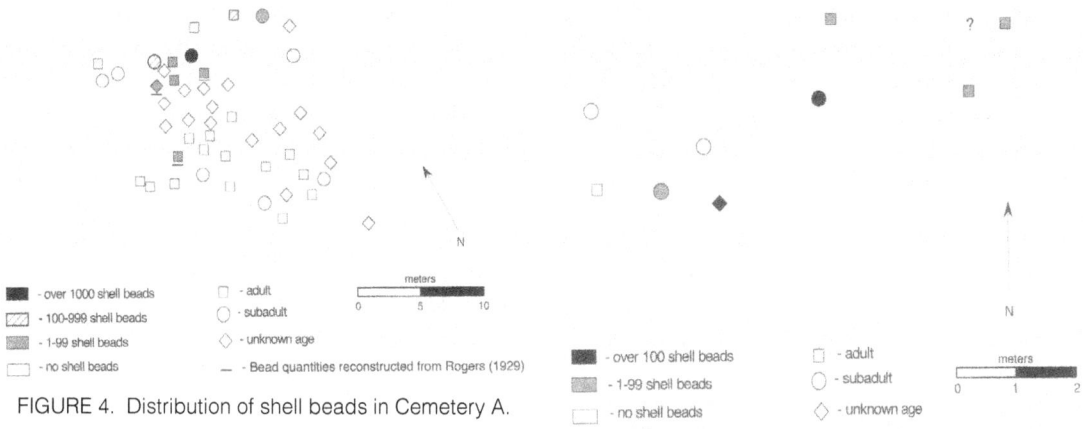

FIGURE 4. Distribution of shell beads in Cemetery A.

FIGURE 6. Distribution of shell beads in Cemetery C.

structure. It is not clear when his work occurred, but it was probably in the late 1920s. Rogers indicated whether the cremations that he excavated were urn-gathered, pit-gathered, or un-gathered and provided a general description of what was found associated with each burial. Urn-gathered cremations were those that contained cremation contents in an urn or olla, pit-gathered were those that contained the cremation contents in a pit that was dug out before the burning took place, and un-gathered ones were types that had no pit and no urn. There were 20 urn-gathered, 10 pit-gathered, and 20 un-gathered types (Rogers 1929). The others were not designated because Rogers did not excavate them, or they were disturbed. He listed the artifacts associated with these cremations, however.

Since Rogers' excavations, a skeleton was discovered by hikers on an eroding bank at *Amat*

Inuk in 1963. The skull was submitted to the sheriff. The human remains were determined a possible Christianized Kumeyaay female (because traditional Kumeyaay did not bury their dead, but cremated them) or a non-Kumeyaay about 35–40 years old. The skeleton was entangled in mesquite tree roots, making excavation difficult.

Shell Beads and Shell Bead Manufacture

Ample archaeological and ethnographic evidence exists to indicate that the Chumash had craft specialization in the form of shell bead manufacturing (King 1976; Arnold 1987), and that their beads were traded extensively (King 1990a:107–157; Gibson 1994, 1995a). In order

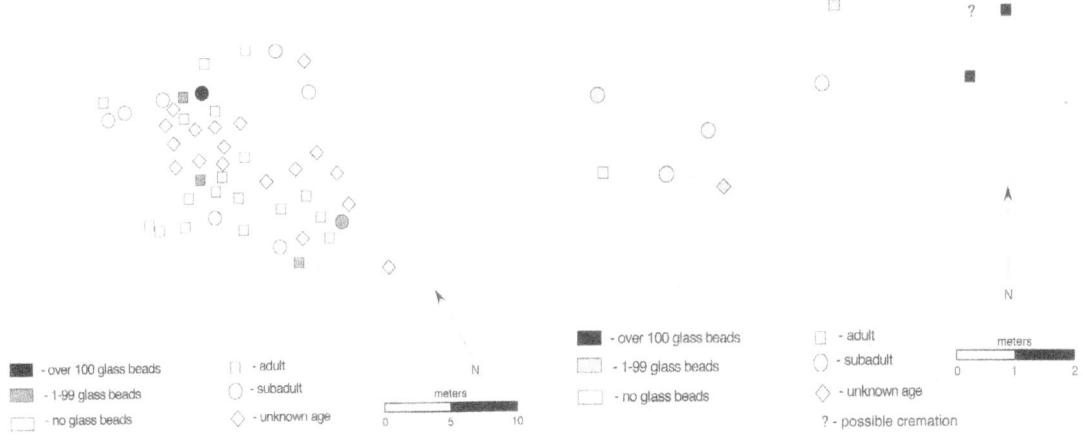

FIGURE 5. Distribution of glass beads in Cemetery A.

FIGURE 7. Distribution of glass beads in Cemetery C.

to address the issue of exchange of shell beads from the Santa Barbara region to San Diego County, the *Amat Inuk* bead collection was chosen because of the large numbers of shell beads that were found at the site.

Olivella biplicata shell was the most commonly used material for beads in California throughout all time periods (King 1990a:103) (Figure 8). *Olivella biplicata* beads are one of many shell bead types that are temporally diagnostic in King's (1990a) bead typology for southern California. *Olivella biplicata* shells can be found along the West Coast from Vancouver, Canada, to Baja California. The maximum body length of *Olivella biplicata* shells is approximately 20 to 38 mm, which is relatively large compared to other *Olivella* species (Rehder 1986:585; Mitchell 1992:49). The *Olivella biplicata* shell is hard and durable, making it an appealing material for bead manufacturing. Different parts of the *Olivella biplicata* shell, including the spire, wall, and callus, were used in bead manufacturing (Figure 8). Beads made from the hardest part, the callus, were considered more valuable because of the difficulty of working the callus during bead manufacturing (King 1981:13).

Other *Olivella* species in southern California are *Olivella dama*, found in the Gulf of California, and *Olivella baetica* found along the West Coast from Alaska to Baja California. The *Olivella dama* and *Olivella baetica* are smaller and more slender than *Olivella biplicata* (Rehder 1986:585–586; Mitchell 1992:46, 49). Some *Olivella biplicata* are nearly white in color, while others are very dark, ranging from bluish-gray to purple (Morris 1966:99). *Olivella baetica* range from blue to brown in color (Morris 1966:98). *Olivella dama* are similar to the latter in color, with the spire sometimes pale gray (Morris 1966:192). Usually the color fades over time, with most beads from archaeological contexts being white. Perhaps the availability, durability, and high value due to the difficulty of working the shell made the *Olivella biplicata* shell the most commonly used material for bead manufacturing in California.

Ethnographic accounts indicate that shell beads were used for decorative, economic, and ceremonial purposes among southern California Indians. According to Gifford (1947:37), the Kamia (Eastern Kumeyaay) women wore necklaces of "blue beads" made from clamshell from the Gulf of California, and the men wore shells or strings of small, white clamshell discs in their nasal septums. Among the Cahuilla, shell bead money was used in ceremonial exchanges. Clan chiefs of each ceremonial group had several strings of shell beads. There were two classes of money that were given at different occasions. The first class, named *witcu* by the Palm Springs Cahuilla, was given to all clan leaders at the close of every image-burning ceremony, thus keeping a perpetual exchange. Some strings came from as far away as Santa Catalina Island from the Gabrieleño (Strong 1929:94–96). The other type, called *napanaa*, was sent by all leaders to the clan leader after a death in the clan (Strong 1929:95). Clearly, shell beads were integrated into the culture of southern California Indians.

Shell beads have been used as chronological markers in California, just as pottery sequences have been used to identify particular time periods in the Southwest. King (1990a) developed a detailed chronology of shell bead use among the Chumash based on burial lot seriation. The focus of this research is on *Olivella* wall disk beads. Wall disk or saucer beads were the most frequently made beads during the Middle period (1400 B.C.–A.D. 1050). Their importance and use decreased as cupped beads increased in significance during the initial part of the Late period (A.D. 1050–1150), but wall disk beads regained their significance at the time of Spanish colonization and became the most common type of bead after colonization. By 1776, wall disk beads had larger diameters and ground edges that

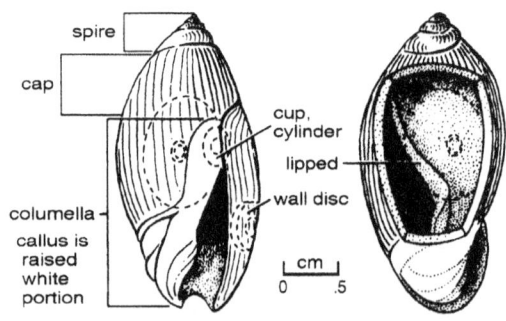

FIGURE 8. Areas of the *Olivella biplicata* shell used to manufacture beads (after King 1978:60).

were less smooth (Figure 9). These are called *Olivella* rough disk beads (King 1990b:8–19, 1996:23). Small stone drills were used to make the perforation until iron needles were introduced by the Spaniards in 1782. Chumash rough disk beads made with stone drills have perforations larger than 1.0 mm. Iron needles rapidly replaced stone drills and resulted in a smaller perforation of about 1.0 mm in diameter (King 1990a:8–19; Gibson 1995b:4). By 1816 the outside diameter of the rough disk beads was between 5.0 and 6.2 mm. Small disks, however, were still in use and had a diameter between 1.6 and 3.0 mm (King 1990a:179–181). With the passing of time, bead edges and diameters became more variable. Some hole diameters increased due to larger needles, and hole shape changed from the earlier circular shape to a triangular shape (King 1990b, 1995).

Shell bead manufacturing required an abundance of shell in addition to tools such as drills. Massive amounts of shell detritus, stone micro-drills or broken drill bits, and bead blanks indicate evidence of shell bead manufacturing. Results from a study of Late period (A.D. 1300–1782) bead manufacturing sites from the Chumash area show that the ratio of finished beads to bead blank and *Olivella* shell fragments is about 200:1400:60000 (or 1:7:300) per cubic meter (Arnold 1992:135–136). Many sites where shell beads were made have been found on Santa Cruz Island. One of the largest of these in the Chumash area is SCRI-330, a Late period site where a density of 150,000 *Olivella* shell debitage pieces per cubic meter were found (Arnold and Munns 1994:479–480). It is clear that at a bead-manufacturing site where hundreds of shell beads were made, thousands of fragments of detritus should exist.

Very little ethnographic evidence of shell bead manufacturing in San Diego County exists. In three ethnographic accounts, informants claimed to have no knowledge of bead manufacturing (Gifford 1931:37; Drucker 1937:25; Shipek 1991:57). When shell beads are mentioned in ethnographies on the Kumeyaay, it is usually in relation to trade. Gifford stated that shell beads in the Imperial Valley were not common due to the distance to the Gulf of California. The clamshells that the Eastern Kumeyaay used evidently were traded from the Cocopa (Gifford

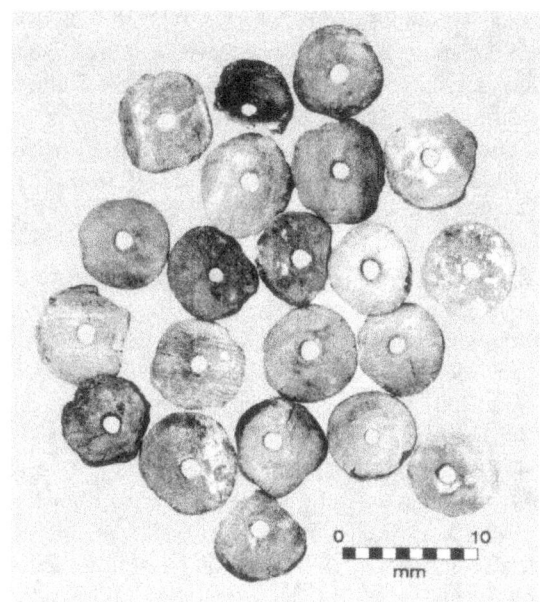

FIGURE 9. A sample of *Olivella* rough disk beads from Cremation 2 at Amat Inuk.

1931:37). Luomala noted that the coastal Kumeyaay traded their abalone shells for inland products (Luomala 1978:601–602). There is no mention of bead manufacturing by any of these ethnographers.

The archaeological record provides even less evidence of shell bead manufacturing in San Diego County. Rogers (1945:172) suggested that Pacific shell possibly was traded from the Chumash or Shoshonean people because of the similarity between shell beads found in the Kumeyaay area and those found in the Chumash area. No evidence of shell bead manufacture has been identified in San Diego County (although it has been identified in Imperial County), and evidence of shell bead use is limited. A thorough discussion of beads found in San Diego County and their locations is provided by Zepeda (1999). Few *Olivella* shell beads tend to be recovered from San Diego County sites when compared to Chumash sites. When they are present, they have been found in limited numbers at sites along the coast, in the mountains, and in the desert. It is difficult to discuss the full extent of the use of *Olivella* rough disk beads because they have not always been identified as such by archaeologists. The most common *Olivella* bead type found in San Diego County is the spire-lopped bead. This type of bead is not chronologically sensitive because it was used during most time periods in San Diego County (Martin D. Rosen 1999, pers. comm.).

The only evidence of bead manufacturing from a Kumeyaay site is from the Elmore site (IMP-5427) in Imperial County (Rosen 1994). This protohistoric site (ca. A.D. 1660) produced 229 pieces of *Olivella* shell. Of these, 60 were either completed beads or bead fragments and 169 pieces were *Olivella* detritus, of which 7 were identified as *Olivella dama*. The other pieces did not have enough diagnostic information to identify by species. Of the 60 beads, 14 were *Olivella dama* spire-removed, 3 were *Olivella biplicata* spire-removed, 2 were *Olivella dama* barrel beads, 30 were *Olivella* sp. barrel beads, and 9 pieces could not be identified to the species level. Of the 169 detritus pieces, 89 were canal pieces and 74 were outer body whorl pieces. Both types of detritus would have resulted from the manufacture of spire-removed and barrel beads (Rosen 1994:4–6, 15–18). There was approximately 1 bead for every 3 pieces of detritus at the site (Rosen 1994:7–8). Rosen (1994:13) suggested that there were stronger ties with the south or Gulf of Mexico than with the west or Pacific Ocean because *Olivella dama* beads were more common than *Olivella biplicata* beads at the site. He (Rosen 1994:14) further suggested that evidence of bead making may have been overlooked in San Diego sites because shell detritus was grouped with unworked shell.

Field notes and other records from the Museum of Man also lack discussion of bead manufacturing. Their records indicate which collections have beads, and if they were associated with cremations. According to the list of 40 cremation sites, only 11 had shell beads; of these 11 cremation sites, only 2 (C-160 and W-263) besides *Amat Inuk* contained what appears to be over 1,000 beads, while most had less than 100 beads (San Diego Museum of Man 1920–1940). Undoubtedly, large quantities of shell beads are not characteristic of San Diego County sites, as they are for many Chumash sites, nor is it common for shell bead manufacturing to be discussed in reports. Perhaps a partial explanation for the small quantities of

shell beads recovered from San Diego County sites is due to screening and recovery practices used in the past.

Given the relative lack of information on shell beads, an analysis of a substantial collection of beads from *Amat Inuk* is critical in assessing the significance of beads in the San Diego region, their role among the Kumeyaay, and if they are present in the region as a result of long distance exchange. It is probable that if historic shell beads from San Diego sites are similar in size and to types in the Chumash area, then the Kumeyaay trade network was more far-reaching during the historic period than previously documented. Strong (1929:95–96) indicated that beads the Cahuilla used were from the Chumash area. It is possible that the Cahuilla then exchanged Chumash beads with the Kumeyaay. There are also other routes that may have been used. Regardless of the route, it is clear that a fairly complex exchange network that has not previously been documented was still intact approximately 80 years after Mission San Diego de Alcalá was established.

Mortuary Analysis

Only a preliminary mortuary analysis was conducted because the primary focus of this research is to examine exchange between the Kumeyaay and the Chumash. The data provided in this analysis were taken from Rogers' (1929) fieldnotes from *Amat Inuk* (C-144) located at the Museum of Man and from the analysis of beads. The other grave associations were not examined in detail. One individual was assumed per cremation, except in two cases (Cremations 9 and 54). Number 9 appeared to be two adults and number 54 was identified as a mother and an infant. Given the lack of knowledge regarding the exact placement of the beads, the dual cremations were considered one cremation when the spatial distribution of grave goods was mapped. The sex of most of the individual cremations was not identified by Rogers, therefore data on sex are not presented in this analysis. Several variables were examined, including cremation type, age of individual at death, presence of grave goods, and spatial distribution of grave goods, especially glass and *Olivella biplicata* rough disk beads. These variables were chosen because of their potential significance in interpreting Kumeyaay social organization.

A few minor problems were encountered during the course of analysis. There were discrepancies between the cremations Rogers designated as containing *Olivella* beads and the cremations in the collection at the Museum of Man that were found to contain *Olivella* beads at the time of the bead analysis. In Cemetery A, Rogers identified eight cremations with *Olivella* beads, however only five in the collection appeared to have beads. One of these cremations only had a few fragile beads and it is likely that they were not taken to the museum or had broken subsequently. In Cemetery C, Rogers indicated seven cremations with *Olivella* beads, but beads were located with only five of the cremations. None of the beads recorded by Rogers in the isolated cremations was located at the time of the bead analysis. Three boxes (identified as Cemetery A/Glenn, Trench 2, and tin can) contained *Olivella* beads that were not labeled as associated with any particular cremation. One of these boxes was labeled as the Glenn cremation, which was assumed to be beads from all nine cremations excavated by John Glenn. These three boxes were not used in the mortuary analysis section of the results because they lacked provenience information. This means that 21% (*n* = 265) of the total bead sample was not used in the mortuary analysis. This percentage of beads, however, was included in the comparative bead analysis of the *Olivella biplicata* rough disk bead measurements (Table 1).

The human remains from the two cemeteries and the isolated cremations at *Amat Inuk* indicate that age at death varied considerably. There were 54 cremated individuals in Cemetery A and C (this number does not include the nine cremations excavated by Glenn, but includes the two dual cremations as four), of which the majority were adults (Tables 2–4). The adult and subadult cremations appear to be inter-mixed within the cemeteries, possibly a result of families being cremated together (Figures 3–7), however almost twice as many adults when compared with subadults were buried in Cemetery A. In Cemetery C, the number of adults to subadults was the same (Table 3).

The total number of beads found in both cemeteries was 884 glass beads and 7,831 shell beads, with the majority being *Olivella biplicata* rough disk beads (*n* = 7,630) (Table 5). The other types of shell beads included spire, spire-lopped, cylinder, and cap beads (Figure 8), all of which were probably made from *Olivella* spp. shell (King 1990a). In addition, abalone beads were in the collection. The glass beads in the collection were not as temporally sensitive as the shell beads, therefore were not a focus of this study.

The preponderance of artifacts of native origin versus non-native origin can also be seen in the rest of the collection. Most of the pots, as described by Rogers (1929), were wares traditionally found in the Kumeyaay area. As listed earlier, there were artifacts of non-native origin, though they occur in much lower frequencies at the site. Cremations buried with objects of Spanish origin always had objects that were of native origin as well (Zepeda 1999:Table 3).

Mortuary goods appear to be unevenly distributed in the cemeteries at the site. Cemeteries A and C contained historic items, while none of the isolated cremations had them. According to the notes by Rogers and the presence of beads in the collection, the majority (*n* = 25, or 75.7%) of the cremations in Cemetery A did not have shell or glass beads. Cemetery A had a total of six cremations with shell beads (16.2%) and five (13.5%) with glass beads, while only two (5.4%) of these cremations had both shell and glass beads (Figures 4, 5; Table 5). Despite the limited distribution of beads in Cemetery A, the majority of cremations had grave goods, such as ceramic ollas, bowls, and jars; only four cremations (10.8%) lacked associated goods. In contrast to Cemetery A, most cremations (*n* = 9, or 81.8%) in Cemetery C had either shell or glass beads. There were eight (72.7%) cremations with shell beads and five (45.5%) with glass beads, while four of these had both shell and glass beads (Figures 6, 7; Table 5). Only two cremations in Cemetery C lacked glass and shell beads.

Certain cremations are distinctive based on their associated funerary goods. Cremation 2 in Cemetery A, a subadult, had the most *Olivella biplicata* rough disk beads (*n* = 3,733, or 48.9%) in the entire site of *Amat Inuk* and was the only

TABLE 1
SAMPLE OF *OLIVELLA BIPLICATA* ROUGH DISK BEADS FOR MEASUREMENT

Cemetery	Cremation	Box	Total	%	Sample
A	2	27-22	26	100	26
A	2	Cem A	3707	5	183
A	4	27-28	86	100	86
A	5	27-32	49	100	49
A	26	3	4	100	4
A	27	22	272	50	136
A	29-37	Glenn	779	15	117
A	Trench 2	27-14b	13	100	13
C	48	13	2	100	2
C	51	17	947	15	141
C	52	18	24	100	24
C	54		64	100	64
C	54	1	9	100	9
C	54	2	19	100	19
C	54	16	273	50	137
C	54	29	448	25	112
C	55	14	11	100	11
Unk,	Unk.	Tin Can	897	15	135
Total			7630		1268

cremation with a significant amount of glass beads (*n* = 155) (Figures 4, 5; Table 5). Aside from the glass beads, there were other historic items found by Rogers associated with Cremation 2, including a Spanish spur, two pieces of bronze bridle trapping, and a knife (Rogers 1929:3). The remaining grave goods included a hair net, parts of a willow basket or cradle, and three ceramic vessels. The abundance of grave goods indicate that this individual was treated in a special manner, as no other cremation had this many items. Another individual with numerous grave goods was identified as Cremation 48 from Cemetery C. This adult had the most glass beads (*n* = 519, 58.7%) found in the entire site; however, only two *Olivella biplicata* rough disk beads and 12 other shell beads were associated with this individual (Figure 6, Table 5).

Numerous other funerary objects were associated with Cremation 48, including a Piñon Brown bowl, miniature jar, a *tinaja* (ceramic water olla or water jar), a Carrizo Buff II olla, four arrow straighteners (three broken), three arrow points, two quartzite hammerstones, two bone awls, part of an antler flaker, burned abalone and cardium shells, part of a burned twined basket, a red paint stone, a cinerary canteen, a bowl, two pieces of white marl, and piñon gum nodules (Rogers 1929). This represents the greatest variety of grave goods at the site. Both Cremations 2 and 48 were urn-gathered.

The cremations with *Olivella biplicata* rough disk beads at *Amat Inuk* appear clustered in certain areas of the cemetery. The majority of shell beads (*n* = 5097, or 65.1%) found at the site were concentrated in Cemetery A, while Cemetery C had most of the glass beads (*n* = 713, or 80.7%) (Table 5). In Cemetery A, all of the individuals with *Olivella biplicata* rough disk beads were concentrated in the northwestern section (Figure 4). Three of the five cremations with *Olivella biplicata* rough disk beads were subadults, and the other two were adults. In contrast to Cemetery A, the cremations with *Olivella biplicata* rough disk beads appeared more evenly distributed throughout Cemetery C (Figure 6). Over half (54.5%) of the cremations

TABLE 2
AGE OF INDIVIDUALS AT DEATH FROM *AMAT INUK* CEMETERY

Age	n	%
Adult	29	53.7
Subadult	17	31.5
Unknown	8	14.8
Total	54	100.0

Cemetery A

Age	Urn-gathered		Pit-gathered		Un-gathered		Unknown		Total	
	n	%	n	%	n	%	n	%	n	%
Adult	9	60.0	3	42.9	9	60.0	1	100.0	22	57.9
Subadult	4	26.7	4	57.1	2	13.3	0	0.0	10	26.3
Unknown	2	13.3	0	0.0	4	26.7	0	0.0	6	15.8
Total	15	100.0	7	100.0	15	100.0	1	100.0	38	100.0

Cemetery C

Age	Urn-gathered		Pit-gathered		Un-gathered		Unknown		Total	
	n	%	n	%	n	%	n	%	n	%
Adult	1	20.0	2	100.0	1	50.0	1	50.0	5	45.4
Subadult	4	80.0	0	0.0	1	50.0	0	0.0	5	45.4
Unknown	0	0.0	0	0.0	0	0.0	1	50.0	1	9.1
Total	5	100.0	2	100.0	2	100.0	2	100.0	11	99.9

from all cemeteries with *Olivella biplicata* beads were urn-gathered, and over half (54.5%) of them also contained historic items, such as glass beads and metal items (Zepeda 1999:Table 11). Of the cremations with *Olivella* beads, only the urn-gathered ones also had historic items.

Data from this preliminary mortuary analysis indicate a number of different patterns. There appears to be a relatively even distribution of adult and subadult cremations throughout *Amat Inuk*, perhaps indicating family groups. If the ratio of subadults to adults is compared between the two cemeteries, however, there were more subadults buried in Cemetery C than Cemetery A. The ratio in Cemetery C is 1:1, indicating as many children were cremated as adults. Obviously, though, the population in Cemetery C is very small, and it is possible that not all of the cremations in this area were recovered by Rogers prior to looting. Nevertheless, grave goods were

distributed unevenly in both cemeteries, with a few individuals buried with the majority of the beads. In particular, Cremations 2 and 48 had an unusual amount of beads when compared to other cremations. *Olivella biplicata* rough disk beads appeared concentrated in the northwestern section of Cemetery A, while glass beads were concentrated in Cemetery C.

Bead Analysis

One of the primary objectives of this research is to compare *Olivella* rough disk beads from the site of *Amat Inuk* with those from the Chumash area during the historic period to see if they are similar. If they are close in appearance and technique of manufacture, the most likely explanation is that they were traded from the Chumash to the Kumeyaay region. Evidence that the Chumash made massive quantities of

Age	Urn-gathered		Pit-gathered		Un-gathered		Unknown		Total	
	n	%	n	%	n	%	n	%	n	%
Adult	0		1	100.0	1	33.3	0	0.0	2	40.0
Subadult	0		0	0.0	1	33.3	1	100.0	2	40.0
Unknown	0		0	0.0	1	33.3	0	0.0	1	20.0
Total	0		1	100.0	3	99.9	1	100.0	5	100.0

TABLE 5
AMAT INUK CREMATIONS WITH GLASS AND SHELL BEADS

Cemetery	Cremation	Glass Beads	*Olivella* Disk	Other Shell
A	2	155	3733	5
A	3	7	0	8
A	4	0	86	79
A	5	0	49	0
A	15	3	0	0
A	16	1	0	0
A	26	0	4	0
A	27	0	272	7
A	44	5	0	0
A	29-37	0	779	0
A	Trench 2	0	13	62
C	47	3	0	0
C	48	519	2	12
C	50	129	0	21
C	51	0	947	2
C	52	56	24	0
C	53	2	0	0
C	54	4	813	3
C	55	0	11	0
Unident	Unk	0	897	2
Total		884	7630	201

beads and traded them throughout southern California and into the Great Basin and Southwest strongly supports this hypothesis. Moreover, there is a virtual absence of bead making detritus in San Diego County. *Olivella biplicata* rough disk beads were chosen for study because these bead types were the most common shell bead type in use after Spanish colonization (King 1990a:179, 1990b:8–19), and therefore an important indicator of traditional exchange systems after contact.

Bead diameters, perforation diameters, and bead thicknesses were measured from a sample of beads from *Amat Inuk* in order to compare to Chumash samples. Methods used to analyze the *Olivella* rough disk beads have been standard-ized by King (1990a) and others (Gibson 1976; Bennyhoff and Hughes 1987). Shell and glass beads from the site were counted, and shell beads were assigned to a type. The only beads that were chosen for measurements were *Olivella biplicata* rough disk beads. A sample of beads was selected for measurements because of the large number of *Olivella biplicata* rough disk beads. The number of beads sampled from each cremation was not always the same. If a cremation had less than 100 beads, all the beads were measured. For cremations with over 100 beads, a percentage of beads was measured so that at least a minimum of 100 beads was measured for each cremation (Table 1). The sample was taken by evenly dispersing the beads on a grid, and then randomly selecting the specified percentage of beads for each cremation box.

A total of 1,268 *Olivella biplicata* rough disk beads was selected for detailed measurements. The maximum diameter, maximum thickness, and minimum perforation diameter were measured for each bead in the sample. All measurements were taken in millimeters with a dial caliper and comparator. Complete measurements were not possible for all beads because

TABLE 6
T-TEST COMPARISONS OF BEADS FROM *AMAT INUK* AND MISSION BUENAVENTURA

Location	p	df	t-value
Ventura S8-W6/ *Amat Inuk*	0.01	1249	4.19
Ventura S12-W62/ *Amat Inuk*	0.01	1510	3.22
Ventura S17-W20/ *Amat Inuk*	0.01	1685	1.53

some were broken or the edges were so eroded that an exact measurement was not possible. The burned state of the beads from *Amat Inuk* resulted in the beads being fragile and subject to erosion. This may have affected the accuracy of the bead measurements, resulting in slightly smaller bead diameters and larger perforation diameters. Of the total sample of 1,268 rough disk beads, the diameters of 120 beads, the hole perforations of 45 beads, and the thickness of 23 beads could not be measured because of erosion or breakage. Finally, each bead was catalogued, and this information was entered into a database (Zepeda 1999:Appendix B).

The results of the bead analysis indicate that the sizes of *Olivella biplicata* rough disk beads from *Amat Inuk* fall within the range of *Olivella biplicata* rough disk beads from the Chumash area. In general, Chumash *Olivella biplicata* rough disk beads have diameters greater than 4.0 mm with straight perforations of 1.0 mm and are on the average 1.0 mm thick (King 1996:8–19). Given the trend for *Olivella biplicata* rough disk beads to increase in overall size between 1780 and 1840 (King 1995:XIII-14, 1996:8–19), beads from *Amat Inuk* fit King's description for historic rough disk beads. Diameters of beads from *Amat Inuk* range between 5.1 and 9.8 mm, with the majority (*n* = 1,116, or 88.0%) ranging between 5.2 and 8.0 mm. (Figure 10). (There were 32 bead diameters from *Amat Inuk* that were considered outliers and were not used in the sample.) The mean diameter is 6.71 ± 0.018 mm. When the diameters of rough disk beads from *Amat Inuk* are compared to those in King's sequence of diameter ranges for *Olivella biplicata* rough disk beads from several Chumash sites, the *Amat Inuk* diameters coincide most closely with diameters of beads dating from around 1822 to 1850 (King 1995:XIII-17). Diameters of Chumash rough disk beads during this time period range between approximately 5.5 and 7.8 mm.

In order to determine the similarity of *Olivella biplicata* rough disk beads from *Amat Inuk* with those from historic Chumash sites, including Mission San Buenaventura, *Talepop*, Mescalitan Island, Malibu, and Medea Creek, bead diameters were compared (King 1995:XIII-17). Rough disk beads from three midden units (S8-W6, S12-W62, S17-W20) from Mission San Buenaventura provided an ideal comparison because

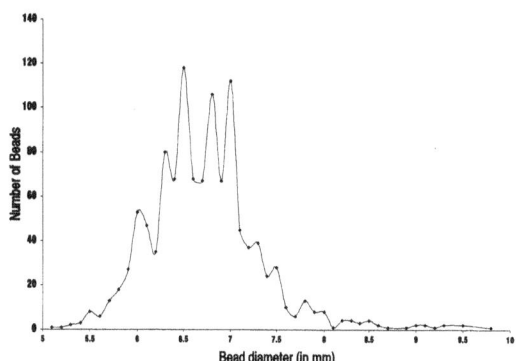

FIGURE 10. Diameter of *Olivella* rough disk beads from *Amat Inuk*.

many beads found after 1815 in southern California may have been made at Mission San Buenaventura (King 1990b:8-8). Bead diameters from *Amat Inuk* are significantly larger than diameters of beads from two units from Mission San Buenaventura (S8-W6 and S12-W62) (Zepeda 1999:Figures 11, 12). T-tests confirm the observation that bead diameters from these two units and *Amat Inuk* are significantly different (Table 6). The t-test comparing bead diameters from *Amat Inuk* and Unit S17-W20 from Mission San Buenaventura indicate no significant differences in diameter sizes (Table 6). King (1995) suggested that Mission San Buenaventura beads were used between 1782 and 1850. Most of the beads from *Amat Inuk* have similar diameters to those at Mission San Buenaventura and are probably from the same time period.

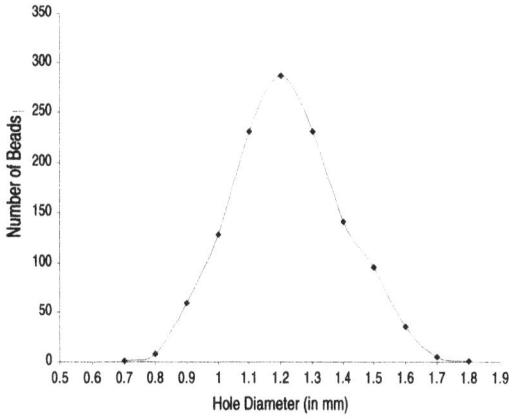

FIGURE 11. Hole Diameters of *Olivella* rough disk beads from *Amat Inuk*.

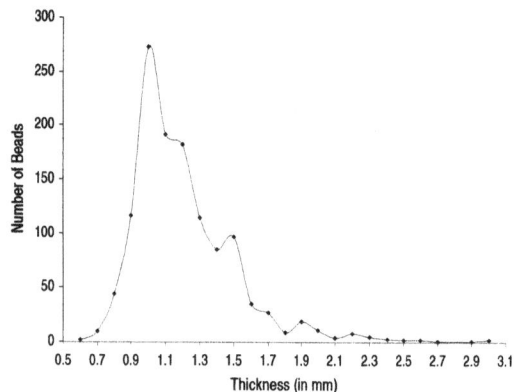

FIGURE 12. Thickness of *Olivella* rough disk beads from *Amat Inuk*.

The measurements of *Olivella* rough disk beads from *Amat Inuk* also were compared to rough disk beads found outside the Chumash area. Beads from Tahquitz Canyon (King 1995), an historic Cahuilla site in Riverside County that has documented evidence of Chumash *Olivella biplicata* rough disk beads, were chosen for this comparison. The diameters of beads from *Amat Inuk* were compared with diameters of beads from three cremation lots and two midden units from Tahquitz Canyon that date to A.D. 1803–1850 (King 1995:XII-77; Schaefer 1995:VI-2). For purposes of this study, each cremation and midden unit was arbitrarily assigned a lot number (Zepeda 1999:Table 7). King (1995:XIII-18) suggested that the *Olivella biplicata* rough disk beads found at Tahquitz Canyon were manufactured by the Chumash, perhaps at the Mission San Buenaventura. The t-tests comparing bead diameters from *Amat Inuk* and bead diameters from Lots 1, 3, and 6 at Tahquitz Canyon indicate a significant difference between the bead diameters from both sites (Table 7). The bead diameters from Tahquitz Canyon Lots 1, 3, and 6 are significantly larger than those from *Amat Inuk*. These may be later than those from *Amat Inuk*. The t-tests comparing bead diameters from *Amat Inuk* and Tahquitz Canyon Lots 4 and 7 indicate no significant difference (Table 7), suggesting they are probably from the same time period during the historic period.

Diameters of perforations of *Olivella biplicata* rough disk beads from *Amat Inuk* range between 0.7 and 1.8 mm, with a mean of 1.22 ± 0.005 mm (Figure 11). The majority of the hole

perforations have parallel sides like historic Chumash *Olivella biplicata* rough disk beads. The mean hole diameter of 1.22 mm coincides with beads from the later historic period. The hole perforations may have been enlarged due to erosion, as many were eroded.

Thickness and edge treatment were also examined. The thickness of the *Amat Inuk Olivella biplicata* rough disk beads range between 0.6 and 3.0 mm with an mean of 1.21 ± 0.009 mm (Figure 12). This mean thickness is close to King's 1.0 mm mean thickness for historic Chumash *Olivella biplicata* rough disk beads (King 1990b:8-20). The edges of the majority (52%) of the beads from Mason Valley are slightly ground, coinciding with the trend of edges becoming rougher and ground less smoothly in the historic period (King 1990b:8-19, 1995:XII-14, 1996:23). The majority (75%) of the beads from *Amat Inuk* were burned, as was expected due to their association with cremations.

This analysis demonstrates that the *Amat Inuk Olivella biplicata* rough disk bead measurements conform to the general measurements for *Olivella biplicata* rough disk beads from

TABLE 7
T-TEST COMPARISONS OF BEADS FROM *AMAT INUK* AND TAHQUITZ CANYON [a]

Location	p	df	t-value
Tahquitz Lot 1[b]/ *Amat Inuk*	0.01	1478	8.85
Tahquitz Lot 3[c]/ *Amat Inuk*	0.01	1632	8.77
Tahquitz Lot 4[d]/ *Amat Inuk*	0.01	1208	1.67
Tahquitz Lot 6[e]/ *Amat Inuk*	0.01	1255	5.58
Tahquitz Lot 7[f]/ *Amat Inuk*	0.01	1262	1.43

[a] Lots 2, 5, and 8 were not used in the statistical analysis due to their limited number of beads [Lot 2 = Locus E, West (cremation Unit 47: 18 *Olivella* rough disk beads; Lot 5 = Locus E, West (cremation) Units 17, 28, and 29: 10 *Olivella* rough disk beads; Lot 8 = Locus E, East Feature, midden deposit: 23 *Olivella* rough disk beads.
[b] Lot 1 = Locus E, East (cremation) Units 136, 137, 145, and 148: 332 *Olivella* rough disk beads.
[c] Lot 3 = Locus E, West (cremation) Units 48 and 49: 484 *Olivella* rough disk beads.
[d] Lot 4 = Locus E, West (cremation) Unit 38: 60 *Olivella* rough disk beads.
[e] Lot 6 = Locus C, Features 1 and 2, midden deposits: 109 *Olivella* rough disk beads.
[f] Lot 7 = Locus E, West Feature, midden deposit: 114 *Olivella* rough disk beads.

historic Chumash sites. The similarities of some bead diameters from Mission San Buenaventura, Tahquitz Canyon, and *Amat Inuk* indicate that these sites were occupied during similar time periods. Nevertheless, because the diameters of some of the beads from *Amat Inuk* are larger than those from Mission San Buenaventura, it is likely that *Amat Inuk* was occupied later in time. Some of the bead diameters from Tahquitz Canyon indicate that this site may have been occupied even later than *Amat Inuk*.

Discussion and Conclusions

Very little archaeological research has been conducted on exchange patterns after historic contact in the Kumeyaay region. Even less is known about status and sociopolitical organization during this time period. The results of the mortuary analysis reveal a pattern of uneven distribution of grave goods. This pattern is most apparent in Cemetery A, where over 65% of the shell beads from the site were found. Most of these beads were clustered with individuals in the northwestern section of Cemetery A. One individual in this area (Cremation 2), a subadult, had almost half of the beads ($n = 3,893$) found at the site. This individual also had a wealth of other grave associations, including Spanish metal goods, ceramic vessels, and other traditional Kumeyaay items. Given that this was a subadult, it is unlikely that they achieved their wealth, but were buried with these items by relatives or others. Ethnographic evidence indicates that the possessions of the dead were placed with the body at the time of cremation and burned or burned one year later at the mourning ceremony (Waterman 1910:306; Kroeber 1925:716; Luomala 1978:603). Based on these accounts, one can assume that the grave goods were the possessions of the dead or close family members. The person (Cremation 2) buried with all these goods had not yet reached adulthood, therefore may have inherited these burial associations. This possibly represents status differentiation among the Kumeyaay that has not previously been documented.

The other individual with an abundance of grave goods (Cremation 48) differed significantly from Cremation 2 in that this person was an adult and was found with numerous glass beads

($n = 519$), but with only 14 shell beads, 2 of which were *Olivella* rough disk beads. The individual was also found with many other artifacts, including arrow points, arrow shaft straighteners, bone awls, and ceramic vessels. It is possible that this adult earned the goods that were buried with him or her. Certainly, in the 1800s during the Hispanic era, followed by the Mexican and American periods, many non-traditional methods of acquiring wealth and material goods existed, including working on ranchos as cowboys or domestic helpers. The closest rancho was Rancho Cuyamaca to the east and the probable location of the summer and fall settlements for the people of Mason Valley.

This preliminary analysis of mortuary practices at *Amat Inuk* clearly indicates a differential distribution of grave goods and is especially apparent in Cemetery A where approximately 76% of the cremations lacked shell and glass beads. Moreover, the relatively even distribution of adult and subadult cremations could be indicative of members of nuclear families having been placed with each other. The clustering of grave goods, especially beads, further suggests that these families may have held the bulk of wealth and status items that were available to members of Kumeyaay society.

Rogers map (Figure 3) shows the location of three cemeteries in addition to isolated burials. The significance of different cemeteries at *Amat Inuk* that were used contemporaneously is not fully understood. Glass beads were much more prominent in Cemetery C than Cemetery A, while Cemetery A had more shell beads. Cemeteries A and C appear to have been in use between 1782 and 1850, and possibly later. No information was available for Cemetery B. It is possible that the different cemeteries at the site represent burial locations for different families or clans. If this is the case, it may be of particular significance that there was one individual in each cemetery (Cemetery A and C) who was cremated with substantial wealth and who stands out as different from the other individuals. These high status individuals may have been *Kwaaypaay*, members of *Kwaaypaay* families, or other high ranking individuals such as religious specialists. It was noted earlier that the *Kwaapaay* and other Kumeyaay officials, such as religious specialists, owned the majority of beads and other wealth items. Obviously more research is needed to substantiate these hypotheses.

The analysis of beads from *Amat Inuk* indicates that long distance exchange networks among California Indian societies continued well into the period after Spanish contact. Moreover, this exchange network involved items traditionally produced by southern California Indians. The diameter, hole size, and thickness of *Olivella biplicata* rough disk beads from *Amat Inuk* are within the parameters of historic *Olivella biplicata* rough disk beads found in the Chumash region as described by King (1990a). *Olivella* rough disk beads are described as increasing in overall size between 1780 and 1840. Given that the *Amat Inuk* sample of beads falls within the continuum of bead diameters from Mission San Buenaventura and Tahquitz Canyon, they apparently fit the trend of increasing size during the historic period. The beads probably were made after 1800 because the diameters and hole perforations from *Amat Inuk* are larger and more variable than those described by King for the early historic period and are more similar to those described from the later historic Chumash sites (King 1990b:8-4). Other data indicate that *Amat Inuk* was not abandoned until 1870 at the earliest (Rogers 1929). The lack of evidence for *Olivella biplicata* shell bead manufacturing outside the Santa Barbara Channel area (King 1995:XIII-18) and the standardized size of beads from *Amat Inuk* strongly suggest that the beads found there were manufactured by the Chumash during the historic period and then traded to the Kumeyaay, either directly or indirectly.

Evidence of exchange between California Indians and Spaniards during the historic period is well established (King 1976). Given that there has been no previous documentation of exchange between the Kumeyaay and the Chumash, this research is of particular importance. It is possible that Chumash shell beads were traded to the Cahuilla, who then, through an established communication network, exchanged these beads with the Kumeyaay. Another scenario may be that the beads arrived on Spanish ships or overland on some of the Spanish expeditions that went up and down the California coast. Often American Indian guides accompanied the Spanish. These individuals could have served as middlemen in intertribal trade between the Chumash and the Kumeyaay after Spanish colonization. An example from the Pomo Indians in northern California serves as an interesting parallel. Manufacture of clam shell and baked magnesite beads was an important industry during the historic period in central California north of San Francisco. In 1875, Hudson (Heizer 1975:9–27) wrote about the Pomo bead makers of the time and suggested that this traditional medium of exchange was more valued than the glass beads offered by the Spanish. Archaeologists and anthropologists have tended to overlook the significance of traditional exchange systems that persist well after historic contact. Acculturation, or the lack thereof, is a subject that can and should be more thoroughly examined after Spanish colonization. Too often archaeologists assume that there was rapid disruption of traditional cultural systems after intensive contact situations. This subject is well worth more thorough examination throughout North America.

As early as 6000 B.C., there is evidence of exchange between the Chumash and Great Basin groups. Exchange during the following 8000 years continues to be documented between the Chumash and Great Basin, Southwestern, and California groups. The research presented in this work suggests that this traditional exchange system continued up to 80 years after Spanish colonization and extended further south than previously documented. The perseverance and maintenance of traditional socioeconomic interactions by the California Indians after Spanish colonization is impressive given the attempt by the Spaniards to destroy the traditional life of California Indians. The dramatic changes brought about by missionization, epidemic diseases, the seizure of California Indian lands, and the use of California Indians as a Spanish labor force did not stop traditional long distance exchange networks from operating. In order to continue this exchange network, communication and organization that existed before contact had to persist. Exchange networks could not have survived without the cooperation and effort of the groups involved. Moreover, the fact that the Eastern Kumeyaay did not come under the control of the missions was significant in that it allowed these Kumeyaay to avoid contact for a much longer time than was possible for the coastal Kumeyaay (Van Wormer 1986). It is apparent from the grave goods in the *Amat Inuk* cemetery and their distribution, that maintenance of traditional social systems persisted despite the efforts of the Spanish to destroy these traditions.

The mortuary analysis provides only hints of Kumeyaay sociopolitical complexity after historic contact. Future research on the timing and development of social differentiation among the Kumeyaay is needed. Given that no other mortuary analyses have been completed in the region, it is difficult to interpret the meaning of all the patterns presented. Further research at this and other Kumeyaay sites is needed to fully understand the nature of Kumeyaay sociopolitical complexity before and during the historic period.

ACKNOWLEDGMENTS

We would like to acknowledge the Kumeyaay people who allowed us to complete this research, particularly Clarence Brown for allowing us to study the collection. Ken Hedges and Cheryl Jeffrey from the San Diego Museum of Man, where the Rogers collection and notes were curated, provided tremendous help and were patient with all of our questions. We are grateful to Chester King, who was instrumental in instructing us on the details of bead measurements and checked some of the measurements and bead identifications. Larry Leach, Alan Kilpatrick, Glenn Russell, and Marty Rosen read Zepeda's thesis and provided very important and constructive comments. Others who helped facilitate this research include Tim Gross, Alex Kirkish, Jerry Schaefer, Richard Carrico, and John Johnson. Finally, we very much appreciate the productive comments of three anonymous reviewers, the journal's associate editor William Turnbaugh, and editor Ronald L. Michael. All these individuals helped make this paper a stronger contribution.

REFERENCES

ARNOLD, JEANNE E.

1987 *Craft Specialization in the Prehistoric Channel Islands.* University of California Press, Berkeley.

1991 Transformation of a Regional Economy: Sociopolitical Evolution and the Production of Valuables in Southern California. *Antiquity,* 65(249):953–962.

1992 Cultural Disruption and the Political Economics in Channel Islands Prehistory. In *Essays on the Prehistory of Maritime California,* Terry L. Jones, editor, pp. 129–144. Center for Archaeological Research at Davis, Davis, CA.

ARNOLD, JEANNE E., AND ANN MUNNS

1994 Independent or Attached Specialization: The Organization of Shell Bead Production in California. *Journal of Field Archaeology,* 21(4):473–489.

BAMFORTH, DOUGLAS B.

1993 Stone Tools, Steel Tools: Contact Period Household Technology at Heló. In *Ethnohistory and Archaeology Approaches to Postcontact Change in the Americas,* J. Daniel Rogers and Samuel M. Wilson, editors, pp. 49–72. Plenum Press, New York, NY.

BAUGH, TIMOTHY G., AND JONATHON E. ERICSON

1993 Trade and Exchange in a Historical Perspective. In *The American Southwest and Mesoamerica Systems of Prehistoric Exchange,* Jonathon E. Ericson and Timothy G. Baugh, editors, pp. 3–20. Plenum Press, New York, NY.

BELL, DANIEL A.

1975 An Archaeological Survey for the Proposed Development of Mason Valley Ranch. Report to Hirsch and Koptionak Consulting Engineering, San Diego, from University of California at Riverside Archaeological Research Unit, Riverside.

BENNYHOFF, JAMES A., AND RICHARD E. HUGHES

1987 Shell Bead and Ornament Exchange Networks between California and the Western Great Basin. *Anthropological Papers of the American Museum of Natural History,* 64(2):79–175.

BROTT, C. W.

1963 Field Report of Salvage Excavation on SDM-W-144. Report to C. C. Evernham, from San Diego Museum of Man, San Diego, CA.

BRUMFIEL, ELIZABETH M., AND TIMOTHY K. EARLE

1987 Specialization, Exchange, and Complex Societies: An Introduction. In *Specialization, Exchange, and Complex Societies,* Elizabeth M. Brumfiel and Timothy K. Earle, editors, pp. 1–9. Cambridge University Press, New York, NY.

CARRICO, RICHARD

1987 *Strangers in a Stolen Land: American Indians in San Diego, 1850–1880.* Sierra Oaks Publishing Company, Sacramento, CA.

CARRICO, RICHARD, AND SANDRA DAY

1981 Archaeological Investigations at Ystagua: A Late Prehistoric Village Complex (The Hallmark Circuits/ Cavanaugh Properties: SDI-5443). Report to Hallmark Circuits and Profits and Revision Sharing Trusts, San Diego, from WESTEC Services, San Diego, CA.

CHARTKOFF, JOSEPH L., AND KERRY KONA CHARTKOFF

1984 *The Archaeology of California.* Stanford University Press, Stanford, CA.

CLINE, LORA L.

1979 The Kwaaymii: Reflections on a Lost Culture. *Imperial Valley College Museum Society, Occasional Paper,* No. 5. El Centro, CA.

COSTANSO, MIGUEL

1910 The Narrative of the Portola Expedition of 1769–1770,

Adolph von Hemert-Engert and Frederick J. Teggart, editors. *University of California Publications of the Academy of Pacific Coast History*, No. 4. Berkeley.

CUPPLES, SUE ANN, AND PAUL H. EZELL
1974 A Report on an Archaeological Survey of Mason Valley Ranch Recreational Trailer Park. Report to Hirsch and Koptionak Consulting Engineering, San Diego, from San Diego State University, San Diego, CA.

DALTON, GEORGE
1971 *Economic Anthropology and Development: Essays on Tribal and Peasant Economies*. Basic Books, New York, NY.

DAVIS, EDWARD H.
1921 Early Cremation Ceremonies of the Luiseño and Diegueño Indians of Southern California. Museum of the American Indian, Heye Foundation, *Indian Notes and Monographs*, 7(1):93–110. New York, NY.

DAVIS, JAMES T.
1961 Trade Routes and Economic Exchange among the Indians. *University of California Archaeological Survey Report*, 54:1–48. Los Angeles.

DRUCKER, PHILIP
1937 Culture Element Distribution V, Southern California. *Anthropological Records*, 1:1–52. Berkeley, CA.

EARLE, TIMOTHY K., AND JONATHON E. ERICSON.
1977 Exchange Systems in Archeological Perspective. In *Exchange Systems in Prehistory*, Timothy K. Earle and Jonathon E. Ericson, editors, pp. 3–12. Academic Press, New York, NY.

EIDSNESS, JANET P., DOUGLAS FLOWER, DARCY IKE, AND LINDA ROTH
1979 Archaeological Investigation of the Sorrento Valley Road Pipeline Project Limited Linear Test. Report to Mike Masanovich Construction Company, Arcadia, CA, by Flower, Ike, and Roth Archaeological Consultants, San Diego, CA.

ERICSON, JONATHON E.
1977 Egalitarian Exchange Systems in California: A Preliminary View. In *Exchange Systems in Prehistory*, Timothy K. Earle and Jonathon E. Ericson, editors, pp. 109–126. Academic Press, New York, NY.
1981 Exchange and Production Systems in California Prehistory: The Results of Hydration Dating and Chemical Characterization of Obsidian Sources. *British Archaeological Reports, International Series*, No. 110. Oxford, England.

ERLANDSON, JON M., AND KEVIN BARTOY
1995 Cabrillo, the Chumash, and Old World Diseases. *Journal of California and Great Basin Anthropology*, 17(2):153–173.

GALLEGOS, DENNIS
1992 Patterns and Implications of Coastal Settlements in

San Diego County: 900 to 1300 Years Ago. In *Essays on the Prehistory of Maritime California*, Terry L. Jones, editor, pp. 205–216. Center for Archaeological Research at Davis, Davis, CA.

GIBSON, R. O.
1976 A Study of Beads and Ornaments from the San Buenaventura Mission Site (Ven-87). In *The Changing Faces of Main Street: Ventura Mission Plaza Project*. Roberta S. Greenwood, editor, pp. 77–166. Redevelopment Agency, Ventura, CA.
1994 Results of Analysis of Shell, Stone, and Bone Artifacts, ORA-378, Orange County, California. Report to Henry C. Koerper, Orange, CA, from R. O. Gibson, Paso Robles, CA.
1995a Analysis of Beads, Ornaments, and Fish Hooks, ORA-106, Orange County, California. Report to Chambers Group, Irvine, CA, from R. O. Gibson, Paso Robles, CA.
1995b Preliminary Analysis of Glass and Shell Beads from an Area of SBA-60, the Village of S'axpilil, Santa Barbara County, California. Report to Southern California Edison Company, Rosemead, CA, from R. O. Gibson, Paso Robles, CA.

GIFFORD, EDWARD WINSLOW
1931 The Kamia of Imperial Valley. *Bureau of American Ethnology, Bulletin* 97:1–94. Washington, DC.
1947 Californian Shell Artifacts. *University of California Anthropological Records*, 9(1):1–132. Berkeley.

HEDGES, KEN
1975 Notes on the Kumeyaay: A Problem of Identification. *Journal of California Anthropology*, 2(1):71–83.

HEIZER, ROBERT F. (EDITOR)
1975 *Seven Early Accounts of the Pomo Indians and their Culture*. Archaeological Research Facility, Department of Anthropology, University of California, Berkeley.

HEYE, GEORGE G.
1919 Certain Aboriginal Pottery from Southern California. Museum of the American Indian, Heye Foundation, *Indian Notes and Monographs*, 7(3). New York, NY.

HILDEBRAND, JOHN A., AND MELISSA B. HAGSTRUM
1995 Observing Subsistence Change in Native Southern California: The Late Prehistoric Kumeyaay. *Research in Economic Anthropology*, 16:85–177.

HUGHES, RICHARD. E.
1994 Mosaic Patterning in Prehistoric California—Great Basin Exchange. In *Prehistoric Exchange Systems in North America*, Timothy G. Baugh and Jonathon E. Ericson, editors, pp. 363–383. Plenum Press, New York, NY.

JACKSON, ROBERT J., AND EDWARD CASTILLO
1995 *Indians, Franciscans, and Spanish Colonization: The Impact of the Mission System on California Indians*. University of New Mexico Press, Albuquerque.

JACKSON, THOMAS L., AND JONATHON E. ERICSON
    1994   Prehistoric Exchange Systems in California. In
           Prehistoric Exchange Systems in North America,
           Timothy G. Baugh and Jonathon E. Ericson, editors,
           pp. 385–415. Plenum Press, New York, NY.

KING, CHESTER D.
    1976   Chumash Intervillage Economic Exchange. In *Native
           Californians: A Theoretical Retrospective,* Lowell J.
           Bean and Thomas C. Blackburn, editors, pp. 289–318.
           Ballena Press, Ramona, CA.
    1978   Protohistoric and Historic Archeology. In *Handbook
           of North American Indians, Vol. 8 California,* Robert
           F. Heizer, editor, pp. 58–68. Smithsonian Institution,
           Washington, DC.
    1981   Prehistoric and Early Historic California Beads.
           Ornament, 5(1):11–17.
    1990a *Evolution of Chumash Society: A Comparative Study
           of Artifacts Used for Social System Maintenance in
           the Santa Barbara Channel Region before A.D. 1804.*
           Garland Publishing, New York, NY.
    1990b Beads from Heló. In Archaeological Investigations
           at Heló on Mescalitan Island, pp. 8-1–8-63. Report
           to the County of Santa Barbara, Santa Barbara, from
           Department of Anthropology, University of California
           at Santa Barbara, Santa Barbara.
    1995   Beads and Ornaments from Excavations at
           Tahquitz Canyon (CA-RIV-45). In Archaeological,
           Ethnographic, and Ethnohistoric Investigations at
           Tahquitz Canyon. Palm Springs, California, pp. XIII-
           1–XIII-77. Report to Riverside County Flood Control
           and Water Conservation District, Riverside, CA, from
           Cultural Systems Research, Menlo Park, CA.
    1996   Beads and Ornaments from Cemetery Excavations at
           Malibu (CA-LAN-264). In Distribution of Wealth
           and Other Items at the Malibu Site, CA-LAN-264.
           Appendix 1, pp. 1–50. Report to California
           Department of Parks and Recreation, Sacramento,
           from American Indian Studies Center and Institute
           of Archaeology University of California at Los
           Angeles, Los Angeles.

KROEBER, A. L.
    1925   Handbook of the Indians of California. *Bureau
           of American Ethnology, Bulletin* 78. Washington,
           DC. Reprinted 1976 by Dover Publications, New
           York, NY.

LUOMALA, KATHERINE
    1978   Tipai-Ipai. In *Handbook of North American Indians,
           Vol. 8 California,* Robert F. Heizer, editor, pp. 592–608.
           Smithsonian Institution, Washington, DC.

McDONALD, ALISON MEG
    1992   *Indian Hill Rockshelter and Aboriginal Cultural
           Adaptation in Anza-Borrego Desert State Park,
           Southeastern California.* Doctoral dissertation,
           Department of Anthropology, University of California
           at Riverside, Riverside.

MITCHELL, LAURA LEE
    1992   Accurate Identification of Olivella Shell Species: A

           Problem Affecting the Interpretation of Prehistoric
           Bead Distributions. *Pacific Coast Archaeological
           Society Quarterly,* 28(3):46–58.

MOHAVE TRIBE OF INDIANS OF ARIZONA, CALIFORNIA, AND
NEVADA
    1958   Mohave Tribe of Indians of Arizona, California, and
           Nevada; and Robert Jenkins, et al. Claimants vs.
           United States of America, Defendant. Claimant's
           Brief on Dockets 31 and 37 Claim of Exclusive Right
           to Recover Compensation for Lands in California.
           Harold Payne, Needles, CA.

MORIARTY, JAMES R.
    1969   The Yuman Indians of Southern California: An
           Interdisciplinary Synthesis. Master's thesis,
           Department of Social Science, San Diego State
           College, San Diego, CA.

MORRIS, PERCY A.
    1966   *A Field Guide to the Pacific Coast Shells.* Houghton
           Mifflin Company, Norwalk, CT.

PLOG, STEPHEN
    1993   Changing Perspective on North and Middle American
           Exchange Systems. In *The American Southwest
           and Mesoamerica Systems of Prehistoric Exchange,*
           Timothy G. Baugh and Jonathon E. Ericson, editors,
           pp. 285–292. Plenum Press, New York, NY.

REHDER, HAROLD A.
    1986   *The Audubon Society Field Guide to North American
           Seashells.* Alfred A. Knopf, New York, NY.

RENSCH, HERO EUGENE
    1955   Fages' Crossing of the Cuyamacas. *California
           Historical Quarterly,* 34(3):193–208.

ROGERS, MALCOLM J.
    1929   C-144, Mason Valley 1925–1929 Period of Excavation
           Notes. Ms., San Diego Museum of Man, San
           Diego, CA.
    1945   An Outline of Yuman Prehistory. *Southwestern
           Journal of Anthropology,* 1(2):167–198.

ROSEN, MARTIN D.
    1994   Analysis of Shell Beads, Ornaments, and Unmodified
           Shell Fragments from CA-IMP-6427. In Phase III
           Data Recovery at the Elmore Site (CA-IMP-6427)
           Imperial County, California, pp. 1–50. Report
           to Federal Highway Administration, Sacramento,
           CA, from California Department of Transportation,
           San Diego.

SAN DIEGO MUSEUM OF MAN
    1920–1940 Archaeological Site Record Files. Ms., San
           Diego Museum of Man, San Diego, CA.

SCHAEFER, JERRY
    1995   Site Descriptions. In Archaeological, Ethnographic,
           and Ethnohistoric Investigations at Tahquitz Canyon.
           Palm Springs, California, pp. VI-1–VI-141. Report
           to Riverside County Flood Control and Water
           Conservation District, Riverside, CA, from Cultural
           Systems Research, Menlo Park, CA.

SHACKLEY, M. STEVEN

 1981 Late Prehistoric Exchange Network Analysis in Carrizo Gorge and the Far Southwest. Master's thesis, Department of Anthropology, San Diego State University, San Diego, CA.

 1995 Sources of Archaeological Obsidian in the Greater American Southwest: An Update and Qualitative Analysis. *American Antiquity*, 60(3):531–551.

SHIPEK, FLORENCE C.

 1982 Kumeyaay Socio-Political Structure. *Journal of California and Great Basin Anthropology*, 4(2):293–303.

 1986 The Impact of Europeans upon Kumeyaay Culture. In *The Impact of European Exploration and Settlement on Local Native Americans*, Cabrillo Festival Historical Seminar, pp. 13–25. Cabrillo Historical Association, San Diego, CA.

 1987 *Pushed into the Rocks: Southern California Indian Land Tenure 1769–1986.* University of Nebraska Press, Lincoln.

 1991 *The Autobiography of Delfina Cuero.* Ballena Press, Menlo Park, CA.

 1993 Kumeyaay Plant Husbandry: Fire, Water, and Erosion Control Systems. In *Before the Wilderness: Environmental Management by Native Californians*, Thomas C. Blackburn and Kat Anderson, editors, pp. 379–388. Ballena Press, Menlo Park, CA.

SIMPSON, LESLEY B. (TRANSLATOR AND EDITOR)

 1939 *California in 1792: The Expedition of Longinos Martinez.* Huntington Library, San Marino, CA.

SPIER, LESLIE

 1923 Southern Diegueño Customs. *University of California Publication in American Archaeology and Ethnology*, 20(16):292–358. Berkeley.

STRONG, WILLIAM D.

 1929 Aboriginal Society in Southern California. *University of California Publication in American Archaeology and Ethnology*, 26(1):1–358. Berkeley.

TRUE, D. L.

 1966 *Archaeological Differences of Shoshonean and Yuman Speaking Groups in Southern California.* Doctoral dissertation, Department of Anthropology, University of California at Los Angeles, Los Angeles.

 1970 *Investigation of a Late Prehistoric Complex in Cuyamaca Rancho State Park, San Diego County, California.* Archaeological Survey, Anthropology Department, University of California at Los Angeles, Los Angeles.

VAN WORMER, STEPHEN

 1986 The Ethnohistory of the Eastern Kumeyaay. In *The Impact of European Exploration and Settlement on Local Native American*, Cabrillo Festival Historical Seminar, pp. 38–76. Cabrillo Historical Association, San Diego, CA.

WARREN, CLAUDE N.

 1968 Cultural Tradition and Ecological Adaptation on the Southern California Coast. *Eastern New Mexico University Contributions to Anthropology*, 1(3):1–14. Portales.

WATERMAN, T. T.

 1910 The Religious Practices of the Diegueño Indians. *University of California Publications in American Archaeology and Ethnology*, 8(6):271–358. Berkeley.

ZEPEDA, IRMA CARMEN

 1999 Exchange Networks, Beads, and Social Status among the Historic Kumeyaay. Master's thesis, Department of Anthropology, San Diego State University, San Diego, CA.

LYNN H. GAMBLE
DEPARTMENT OF ANTHROPOLOGY
SAN DIEGO STATE UNIVERSITY
5500 CAMPANILE DRIVE
SAN DIEGO, CA 92182-4443

IRMA CARMEN ZEPEDA
CALIFORNIA DEPARTMENT OF PARKS AND RECREATION
8885 RIO SAN DIEGO DRIVE
SAN DIEGO, CA 92108-1624

Rick Minor
Laurie E. Burgess

Chinookan Survival and Persistence on the Lower Columbia: The View from the Kathlamet Village

ABSTRACT

Prominently mentioned in the Lewis and Clark journals, the Kathlamet were devastated by infectious diseases and gradually lost their identity as a distinct, local Chinookan group in the historical record. In part because of the alleged abandonment of the Kathlamet village about 1810, the Kathlamet were subsumed under the Lower Chinook in the principal ethnographic account of the Chinookan peoples around the mouth of the Columbia River. Archaeological evidence from the Kathlamet village, as well as historical records, contradicts the alleged date of abandonment, and indicates that occupation of this settlement actually persisted into the mid-19th century. The use of material culture and historical records to examine the Kathlamet's post-contact experience helps reestablish their cultural identity for this time period, and reasserts their position as one of the more important of the many local groups of Chinookan peoples in the Lower Columbia Valley.

Introduction

At the time of historic contact, the Chinookan peoples consisted of at least 28 local groups occupying villages along the shores of the Lower Columbia River from the Pacific Ocean upstream some 195 river miles to the vicinity of The Dalles (Hajda 1984:62–63). As their territory coincided with the main route of trade and travel between the Pacific coast and interior Columbia Plateau, the Chinookans experienced all of the major epidemics introduced by contact with European Americans in the early historic period. A steep decline in the Chinookan population began with the introduction of smallpox in the 1770s and culminated with the "fever and ague" or "intermittent fever" epidemic (most likely malaria) of the 1830s (Boyd 1999:84–115). A study of the effects of infectious diseases on

the native inhabitants of the Pacific Northwest by demographer Robert T. Boyd estimated that epidemics between the 1770s and 1850s resulted in the death of 90% of the native population in the Lower Columbia Valley (Boyd 1999:263).

In many respects, the post-contact experience of the Kathlamet was similar to that of other Chinookan peoples of the Lower Columbia Valley. The Kathlamet, who resided along the upper portion of the Columbia River estuary at the time of historic contact, were prominently mentioned in the Lewis and Clark journals. After the steep decline in population from infectious diseases, the surviving Kathlamet intermarried with native peoples from other groups and amalgamated into fewer settlements. The Kathlamet were later subsumed under the Lower Chinook in the principal ethnographic account of the Chinookan peoples around the mouth of the Columbia River, written by Verne F. Ray (1938).

The Kathlamet's loss of identity as a local group distinguishable from other Chinookans was based in part on the alleged abandonment of the Kathlamet village on the Oregon shore and resettlement with surviving Chinookans on the Washington shore about 1810 (Ray 1938:39). Analysis of historic period artifacts from the Kathlamet village curated at the Smithsonian Institution since the 1960s, as well as a closer examination of the historical record, contradicts the idea that the settlement was abandoned about 1810. Unlike most of the other Chinookan groups in the Lower Columbia Valley, a remnant population of Kathlamet survived the epidemics and persisted as an identifiable local group well into the mid-19th century.

Early Contact History

The Kathlamet are first mentioned in the journals of the Lewis and Clark expedition, when, near the mouth of the Columbia River on 11 November 1805, William Clark referred to Indians "of a nation who reside above and on the opposit [sic] Side who call themselves *Calt-har-ma*" (Moulton 1990:41). The Indians' name for themselves was derived from the name of their principal village, variously spelled *Kahláamat* (Curtis 1911:182), *kala'amat* (Ray 1938:39), or *Kath-la-mat* (Silverstein 1990:534) and often anglicized as Cathlamet (Farrand 1907:216; Swanton 1952:414). This village was located on the south shore of the Columbia River at Kathlamet Point, known today as Aldrich Point in Clatsop County, Oregon (Figure 1).

The territory of the local group known as the Kathlamet extended along the south shore of the Columbia River from the vicinity of Tongue Point upstream to the neighborhood of Puget Island (Farrand 1907:216). The south shore is separated from the main channel by a series of low islands, referred to as "the marshey islands" and also as the "Seal Islands" by Lewis and Clark (Moulton 1983:Maps 82 and 89, 1990:89, 1991:10). In passing through this area on 24 March 1806, Meriwether Lewis noted that "this side of the river is very shallow to the distance of 4 miles from the shore tho' there is a channel sufficient for canoes near S. Side" (Moulton 1991:9).

Only four Kathlamet settlements are specifically identified in historical sources. These include the aforementioned village named *Kahláamat* (Curtis 1911:182) or *kala'amat* (Ray 1938:39) at Aldrich Point, and a second village named *Hlilúsqaẖiẖ* (Curtis 1911:182) or *Tlelas-qua* (Silverstein 1990:534), a short distance downstream on the Columbia near the present town of Knappa, Oregon. It is perhaps worth

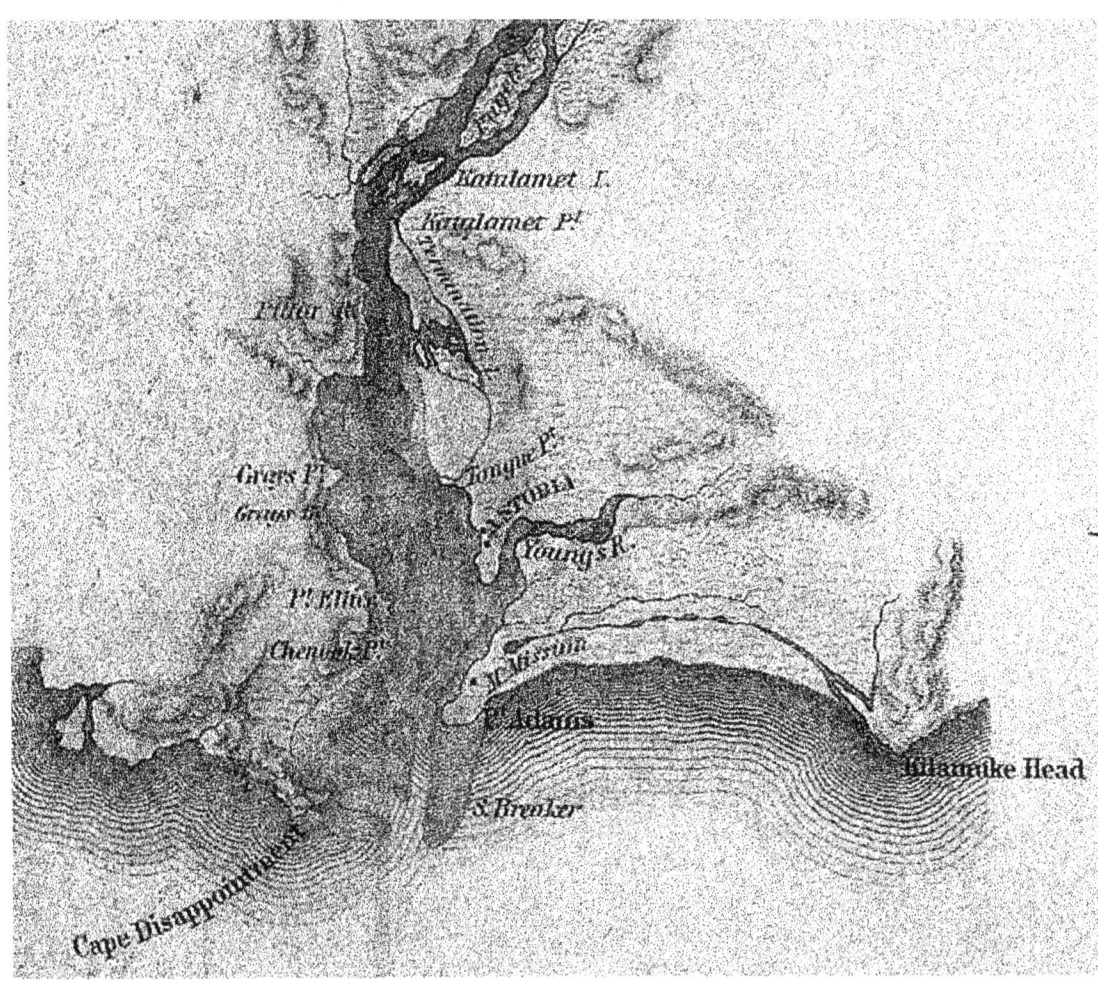

FIGURE 1. Location of Kathlamet Point, site of the Kathlamet village, on a portion of the inset from "Map of the Oregon Territory," drawn by Horatio Hale, ethnologist and philologist for the Wilkes Expedition, 1841 (Wilkes 1849). The map is oriented with north to the left. (Digital image courtesy of the Lane County Historical Society and Museum.)

Perspectives from *Historical Archaeology:*

noting that in the *Handbook of North American Indians* the village identified as *Kath-la-mat* is erroneously placed downstream from Knappa instead of upstream at Aldrich Point (Silverstein 1990:534). The other settlements attributed to the Kathlamet, both noted by Lewis and Clark in their journal entries for 25 March 1806, were described by these explorers as fishing camps.

The name of the local group known as the Kathlamet was derived from the village at Aldrich Point, but most of the information available about these people is from observations recorded by Lewis and Clark at the village of *Hlilúsqaħiħ*. On their way downstream on 26 November 1805, Clark wrote that the expedition crossed over from the north shore to the south side of the Columbia River, passing Aldrich Point, referred to by Clark as Point Samuel, without noting the village there, and:

> proceeded near the South Side leaveing the Seal Islands to our right and a marshey bottom to the left 5 Miles to the *Calt-har-mar* Village of 9 large wood houses on a handsom elivated Situation near the foot of a Spur of the high land behind a large low Island Seperated from the Southerly Shore by a Chanel of about 200 yards Wide, This nation appear to differ verry little either in language, Customs dress or appearance from the *Chin nooks* & *War-ci â cum* live principally on fish and *pappato* they have also other roots, and Some Elk meat.
>
> We purchased Some green fish, & *wap pa to* for which we gave Imoderate pricie's [original spelling and italics] (Moulton 1990:89).

At the end of his journal entry for this day, Clark added that "a Short distance below the *Calt har mer* Village on the Island which is Opposit I observed Several Canoes Scaffold in which Contained their dead, as I did not examine this mode of deposing the dead, must refer it to a discription hereafter [original spelling and italics]" (Moulton 1990:89).

Both Lewis and Clark recorded accounts of their visit to the village of *Hlilúsqaħiħ* during the trip back upstream in their journal entries on 24 March 1806. The account by Lewis again mentions the burials in canoes, and also includes observations of decorative features present on the rectangular plank houses at this settlement:

> at 1 P.M. we arrived at the Cathlahmah village where we halted and purchased some wappetoe, a dog for the sick, and a hat for one of the men. on one of the seal Islands opposite to the village of these people thy

have scaffolded their dead in canoes elivating them above tidewater mark. these people are very fond of sculpture in wood of which they exhibit a variety of specemines about their houses. the broad peices supporting the center of the roof and those through which the doors are cut, seem to be the peices on which they most display their taist. I saw some of these which represented human figures setting and supporting the burthen on their sholders [original spelling] (Moulton 1991:9–10).

Kathlamet houses conformed to the southern variant (with a gable roof) of the rectangular plank house characteristically constructed throughout the Northwest Coast culture area (Suttles 1990:6–7).

Clark's account of the expedition's visit to the village of *Hlilúsqaħiħ* is mainly noteworthy for its description of canoes seen there:

> at this Village I saw two very large elegant Canoes inlaid with Shills, those Shills I took to be teeth at first View, and the nativs informed Several of the men that they the teeth of their enemies which they had killed in War. in examineing of them Closely haveing taken out Several pices, we found that were Sea Shells which yet contained a part of the iner [*blank*] they also deckerate their Smaller wooden vessles with those Shells which have much the appearance of humane teeth [original spelling] (Moulton 1991:10).

The canoes described above were examples of the Nootka canoe, the large seagoing canoe used by coastal peoples from the northern end of Vancouver Island south to Cape Blanco in Oregon, as well as by Chinookan peoples of the Lower Columbia Valley as far upstream as The Dalles (Olson 1927:20). Inlaid shells were apparently a common decorative feature of these large canoes (Swan 1857:82; Gibbs 1877:216). Lewis and Clark also mention smaller canoes "from 16 to 20 feet long and calculated for two or 3 persons" that "are most common among the *Wau-ki-á-cums* and *Cath-lâh-mâhs* among the marshey Islands, near their villages [original spelling and italics]" (Moulton 1990:270).

After departing from the village of *Hlilúsqaħiħ* on the afternoon of 24 March 1806, the expedition proceeded on to camp for the night at site of the village of Kathlamet at Aldrich Point. As described in Clark's account:

> we proceeded on through Some difficult and narrow Channels between the Seal Islands, and the South Side to an old village on the South Side opposit to the lower War ki a com village, and Encamped. to this

old villg. a very considerable deposit of the dead at a Short distance below, in the usial and Customary way of the nativs of this Coast in Canoes raised from the ground as before described [original spelling]. (Moulton 1991:10–11)

The journal entry by Lewis more specifically notes that the expedition "encamped at an old village of 9 houses opposite to the lower Wackkiacum village [original spelling]" on that date (Moulton 1991:10).

It is likely that the settlement and subsistence practices of the Kathlamet were similar to those of the Wahkiakum across the river who followed an annual round that was biseasonal in nature (Martin 1980:41; Minor 1983:74–78). The Kathlamet village on Aldrich Point most likely was occupied during the summer, as suggested by the fact that it was unoccupied when Lewis and Clark camped there in March 1806. The absence of the inhabitants at that time may have been due to the fact that Aldrich Point is exposed to winter storms that blow down the valley from the Columbia River Gorge upstream. With the onset of the summer, Chinook salmon run in May and June, however, and a settlement on Aldrich Point would have been favorably situated for fishing, since the significant narrowing in the width of the river at this point creates a constricted channel through which fish must pass on their migration upstream.

The village of *Hlilúsqaⱨiⱨ*, on the other hand, is more likely to have been a winter settlement, since Lewis and Clark observed it was inhabited in both November and March. This village was located on a narrow channel behind some low islands in a more sheltered location than Aldrich Point. The channel today is noted as a favorable location for spring fishing. Later in the summer, however, it might have been preferable to fish elsewhere, and it seems reasonable to suggest that at least some of the residents of *Hlilúsqaⱨiⱨ* probably moved to the village on Aldrich Point for the summer fishing season.

In their "Estimate of the Western Indians," Lewis and Clark estimated the population of the "*Cath-lâh-mâhs* [who] reside on the S. Side of the Columbia oposit to the Seal Islands" as 300 living in nine houses, and that of the "*Wack-ki-a-cums* [who] reside on the N. Side of the Columbia opposite the Marshey Islands [original spelling and italics]" as 200 living in 11 houses (Moulton 1990:485). These estimates

are the earliest available, but it is now widely recognized that Lewis and Clark arrived in the region after smallpox epidemics in the 1770s and 1801 had ravaged the native population and therefore their estimates are certainly too low (Boyd 1999:28–49). The autumn 1805 and spring 1806 estimates of the Chinookan population by Lewis and Clark also varied widely because of seasonal population movements, with substantially higher populations along the river during the spring-summer fishing season (Boyd and Hajda 1987; Boyd 1999:234–237).

Only a few years after the Lewis and Clark expedition was in the area, Robert Stuart undertook a journey by canoe up the Columbia and on 30 June 1812, noted passing "the Cathlamat village containing 94 warriors" (Rollins 1935:28). Stuart's account refers to the settlement of *Hlilúsqaⱨiⱨ*, since he proceeded on to camp that night some distance upstream. Stuart's description of this campsite as "on a small rising ground" (Rollins 1935:28) suggests it was probably somewhere along the marshy lowlands between *Hlilúsqaⱨiⱨ* and the Kathlamet village on Aldrich Point. Multiplying the 94 "warriors" by a factor of four to reflect family size and dependents, Boyd (1999:Table 16) suggests a Kathlamet population of 376 in 1812. The Kathlamet population was estimated at 600 in 1820, with a decline to 125 by 1824–1825 (Boyd 1999:Table 16). The latter estimate was apparently made after an unidentified infectious disease spread through the Columbia Valley (Boyd 1999:240–241). The Kathlamet population was reported to number 60 in 1851, declining to 41 by 1854-56 (Boyd 1999:Table 17).

Before the reduction of their population from infectious diseases, the Kathlamet served an important role as middlemen in trade along the Columbia River. Lewis and Clark noted that "no Chinnooks come above the marshey islands nor do the Skillutes visit the mouth of the Columbia. the Clatsops, Cathlahmahs and Wackkiacums are the carriers between these nations being in alliance with both [original spelling]" (Moulton 1991:18). Their role in trade along the river was probably enhanced by their skill with canoes. After their first encounter with the Kathlamet near the mouth of the Columbia River on 11 November 1805, William Clark observed "the Indians left us and Crossed the river which is about 5 miles wide through the highest Sees

I ever Saw a Small vestle ride, their Canoe is Small, maney times they were out of Sight before the[y] were 2 miles off Certain it is they are the best canoe navigators I ever Saw [original spelling]" (Moulton 1990:40).

Test Excavation at the Kathlamet Village

Aldrich Point is a prominent headland located approximately 30 river miles upstream from the mouth of the Columbia River. The point is situated near the upstream end of the estuary at the first major constriction, as well as the first major bend, in the Columbia River. The site of the Kathlamet village at Aldrich Point was included in a list of Clatsop County archaeological sites compiled in 1974 by George E. Phebus, Jr., in which the site was described as "Aldrich Pt. site; opposite Quinns Island. Washed away and later buried by earth slide. Probably a Cathlamet site and later a cemetery. 0–12" trade goods and human remains, 12–26" village midden. Tube pipes, phoenix buttons, baked clay, etc., occurred" (Phebus 1974). This location was officially recorded as an archaeological site 35CLT35 in 1978 during a survey in conjunction with small-scale excavations at late prehistoric settlements around the mouth of the Columbia River (Minor 1983).

In 1978, two days were spent by the senior author conducting small-scale testing at the site of the Kathlamet village on Aldrich Point. The site has been severely eroded by the Columbia River, and it was also damaged by landslides and by construction of a railroad along the Oregon shore. According to a local resident who visited during this fieldwork, the railroad tracks were cut across the site about 1900, at which time steam-shovel excavations exposed graves on the hillside above the point. The site was well known among local residents for containing large numbers of blue and white glass beads, as well as bone beads and English pipe and ceramic fragments.

A single test unit (1 × 1 m) was excavated to test the depth and artifact density of the cultural deposit in a narrow strip of ground between the railroad tracks and the river, which appeared to be the only remaining portion of the site. This unit was excavated through 80 cm of disturbed silt clay that rested on large rounded boulders. A mix of objects of European American and Native American manufacture were recovered from the test unit and from a surface collection on the eroded shoreline below the site. Altogether, 86 artifacts of stone were recovered, along with a metal (brass?) bracelet, a tubular copper bead, ceramics, window glass, a glass button, and a glass bead.

Three small corner-notched projectile points found at the site are characteristic of the late prehistoric–early historic period in the Lower Columbia Valley. No evidence of an intact prehistoric cultural deposit was found, as the copper bead was recovered from the bottom of the test unit. This situation, together with the disturbed condition of the cultural deposit along the river bank, led to the decision to conduct further excavations in 1978 and 1979 at other sites around the mouth of the Columbia River (Minor 1983).

The Phebus Collection from the Kathlamet Village

George E. Phebus, Sr., an avocational archaeologist from Astoria, Oregon, assembled a sizable collection of artifacts from the Kathlamet village at Aldrich Point. These were part of a series of collections he gathered from sites in the Lower Columbia Valley that were accessioned by the Smithsonian Institution's Department of Anthropology, National Museum of Natural History, in 1967. His son, George E. Phebus, Jr., worked in the department's collections processing lab. Little is known about the extent of the investigations by George Phebus, Sr., at the Kathlamet village on Aldrich Point. Information accompanying the collection is limited to notes on catalog cards. The following information appears on the first catalog card, under "Remarks:" "The Aldrich Point site consists of a midden accumulation ca. 12"–30" [deep] which is covered by 12" of slide soil or river silt thoroughly mixed with trade goods and some human bone. Probably a hillside cemetery slid into the Columbia River" (Smithsonian Institution catalog card 449,791).

The Phebus collection includes approximately 3,744 objects. Based on the information on the catalog cards, Phebus grouped the artifacts in the collection into three general provenience units: (1) surface collection; (2) test pit: depth 0–30 in.; and (3) burial stratum: 4–12 in. (also listed as burial area: 4–12 in.). Under "Remarks" on the catalog card for the glass beads it was noted that "total collections includes surface collected; Burial area (4-12"); and test pit (0-30")." The implication is that glass beads were recovered from all three of these contexts, but that they later were lumped together (probably for analy-sis) and their original proveniences lost. The 3,327 glass beads are referred to here as from mixed proveniences. The objects in the Phebus collection can be assigned to two broad catego-ries: artifacts of Native American manufacture and artifacts of European American manufacture (Table 1).

TABLE 1
ARTIFACTS IN THE PHEBUS COLLECTION FROM THE KATHLAMET VILLAGE

Artifact Class	Surface Collection	Test Pit 0"–30"	Burial Stratum 4"–12"	Mixed Proveniences	Totals
Artifacts of Native American Manufacture					
Projectile points	44	5			49
Scrapers	29	2			31
Foliate knife		1			1
Bifaces	2	1			3
Drills	3				3
Graver	1				1
Flake knives	2				2
Used flakes	2				2
Maul	1				1
Choppers	4				4
Peripherally flaked cobble	1				1
Girdled netsinkers	5				5
Notched netsinkers	6				6
Palette fragment	1				1
Spherical stones	2				2
Charmstone	1				1
Baked clay problematics	2	1			3
Artifacts of European American Manufacture					
Metal projectile point			1		1
Round lead balls	10				10
Metal pendants	4	1	5		10
Metal bangles	3				3
Metal thimbles			2		2
Metal buttons	6		4		10
Metal bracelets	4		2		6
Metal rings	2		5		7
Metal pin			1		1
Nail fragment	1				1
Steatite pipe (with inlaid lead)	1				1
Clay pipe fragments	11				11
Copper tube beads	111		125		236
Miscellaneous cordage			2		2
Glass beads				3,327	3,327
Totals	259	11	147	3,327	3,744

Perspectives from *Historical Archaeology:*

Most of the artifacts of Native American manufacture in the Phebus collection fall into familiar classes previously defined in the archaeological literature for the Lower Columbia Valley (Pettigrew 1981; Minor 1983). A noteworthy exception is the occurrence of three items identified by Phebus as "baked clay problematics" with incised decoration. These artifacts appear to represent the farthest downstream occurrence of a poorly documented late prehistoric ceramic complex apparently centered upstream in the Portland Basin of the Lower Columbia Valley (Stenger 1991).

The Phebus collection from the Kathlamet village contains many classes of artifacts of European American manufacture characteristically found at Native American settlements occupied during the historic period. Metal artifacts include a projectile point, round lead balls fired from muzzle-loading firearms, pendants and bangles, thimbles (with holes punched in the top

to facilitate suspension), a metal pin or pendant modeled on a stylized scallop shell, bracelets, rings, and buttons, a square nail fragment, and copper tubular beads (Figure 2). Among the 236 copper tubular beads are 82 specimens retaining "a length of cordage within the copper tube" and two pieces of cordage "probably associated with the copper tube beads" (Smithsonian Institution catalog card 449,839).

Among the metal buttons in the Phebus collection are four examples of the distinctive phoenix button, all of which were collected from the surface (Figure 3). Employing the phoenix button typology developed by Strong (1975), three of these specimens can be classified as I1b6, I1b27, I1b29. Unfortunately, the fourth button is not well preserved and therefore must be classified as IIb2 (style unknown). These four specimens are listed in the most recent synthesis of information about phoenix

FIGURE 2. Metal artifacts in the Phebus collection from the Kathlamet Village include (*clockwise from left to right*) pendants, bracelets, buttons, and copper tube beads (Photo by Donald Hurlbert; courtesy of Smithsonian Institution.)

FIGURE 3. Phoenix buttons in the Phebus collection from the Kathlamet Village. (Photo by Donald Hurlbert; courtesy of Smithsonian Institution.)

buttons by Sprague (1998:68–69), who noted that one other phoenix button classified as type IIb28 has also been reported from the Aldrich Point site (Adam 1968). Phoenix buttons are generally thought to have been introduced into the Lower Columbia Valley by trader Nathaniel Wyeth in 1832 or 1834 (Strong 1975:77–79).

Eleven clay pipe fragments in the collection include nine stem fragments of various lengths and two bowl fragments. Two stem fragments exhibit maker's marks (Figure 4). A stem midsection fragment bearing the name

MCDOUGALL/GLASGOW was probably made by Duncan McDougall and Co. of Glasgow, Scotland, in business from 1847 to 1968. At Fort Vancouver, upstream near the confluence of the Willamette with the Columbia River, McDougall pipes for the most part postdate the Hudson's Bay Company's operations and were apparently used after 1849 by U.S. Army soldiers at Vancouver Barracks (Chance and Chance 1976:169,172; Pfeiffer 1982:116–117).

The other marked pipe stem fragment includes the mouth piece and bears the name L. FIOLET/

Perspectives from *Historical Archaeology:*

FIGURE 4. Among the clay pipe fragments in the Phebus collection from the Kathlamet Village are one McDougal pipe (*above*) and one Fiolet pipe (*below*). (Photo by Donald Hurlbert; courtesy of Smithsonian Institution.)

ST OMER/FRANCE. According to Michael A. Pfeiffer, who has examined most of the clay pipes from historic sites in the Pacific Northwest, Fiolet pipes are conspicuously absent in collections from early contact sites on the Lower Columbia River. The only "Fiolet" marked pipe reported in the Pacific Northwest was from the Hudson's Bay Company's Bellevue Farm on San Juan Island dating from 1853 to 1870. Fiolet pipes probably were not imported in large numbers into the Pacific Northwest until the late 1860s through the 1870s (Michael A. Pfeiffer 2006, pers. comm.).

Glass Beads from the Kathlamet Village

The largest class of artifacts of European American manufacture in the Phebus collection from the Kathlamet village contains 3,327 glass beads. These were classified using the Kidd and Kidd (1970) system as expanded by Karklins (1985), and also following Ross (1990, 2000). Drawn beads are the most commonly encountered 19th-century bead type in collections of this time period, usually followed by wound beads and then molded beads. The collection from the Kathlamet village follows that general model, with drawn beads accounting for 97% of the bead assemblage. Altogether, 56 bead varieties are represented in the collection (Table 2).

TABLE 2
GLASS BEADS IN THE PHEBUS COLLECTION FROM THE KATHLAMET VILLAGE

Manufacture	Kidd and Kidd Code	Diaphaneity,[a] Color, and Munsell Value	Shape	Size[b]	Count
Drawn, monochrome, untumbled (n=95)	Ia	op white (R-Y9/5Y)	barrel	S	60
		op white (N9.5/)	disk/barrel	S	35
Drawn, 6 straight sides, 2 row ground facets (n=1)	If	tsl blue (7.5PB3/8)	barrel	L	1
Drawn, monochrome, tumbled (n=542)	IIa	op white (R-Y9/5Y)	barrel	S	506
		op white (N9.5/)	disk/barrel	S	4
		op blue (5B4/8)	barrel	S	1
		op blue (10B3/8)	barrel	S	1
		op blue (10PB4/6)	barrel	S	1
		op blue (5PB3/6)	disk	S	1
		op blue (7.5PB3/6)	disk	S	1
		tsl blue (2.5B3/3)	barrel	S	1
		tsl blue (2.5B4/4)	barrel	S	1
		tsl blue (5B5/6)	barrel	S	7
		tsl blue (10B4/4)	barrel	S	2
		tsl blue (2.5PB3/6)	barrel	S	1
		tsl blue (5BG4/5)	barrel	S	2

TABLE 2 (CONTINUED)

Manufacture	Kidd and Kidd Code	Diaphaneity,[a] Color, and Munsell Value	Shape	Size[b]	Count
		tsl blue (2.5B5/4)	barrel	L	1
		tsl blue (2.5B5/8)	disk	S	1
		tsl blue (10BG4/4)	disk/barrel	S	8
		op black (5RP2/2)	barrel	S	1
		op black (5RP2/2)	disk	M	2
Drawn, monochrome, decorated w/ simple, straight stripes (n=50)	IIb	op white (N9.5/) w/ tsl blue (2.5PB6/4) stripes (4 stripes)	barrel	S	14
		tsp blue (5PB2/8) w/ op white (N9.25/) stripes	barrel	M	1
		op black(5RP2/2) w/ op (N9.5/) white stripes (5 or 6 stripes per bead)	barrel	S	7
		op black (5RP2/2) w/ alternating op red (10R4/8) and op white (N8.75/) stripes (4 stripes)	barrel	M	1
		op black (N1.5/) w/ op white (N8.5/) stripes (4 and 6 stripes)	barrel	S	2
		op white (N9.25/) w/ tsl blue green (10BG7/6) stripes (4 and 6 stripes)	disk/barrel	S	25
Drawn, multi-layer, tumbled (n=2,533)	IVa	op white (R-Y9/5Y) on op white (R-Y9/5Y)	barrel	S	2,344
		op white (N9.5/) on op white (N9.25/)	barrel	L	1
		op white (R-Y9/5Y) on op white (R-Y9/5Y)	disk/barrel	S	179
		op red (7.5R3/10) on tsp green (10GY8/2)	barrel	S	6
		op red (10YR3/10) on tsp green (10GY8/2)	barrel	M	2
		tsl red (5R4/14) on op white (N9.25)	disk	S	1
Mold-pressed, w/ molded facets, straight perforation, zigzag mold seam (n=1)	MPIIa	op black (N1.5/)	spherical	L	1
Wound, barrel (n=5)	WIa	op blue (7.5B5/4)	barrel	M	2
		tsl blue (7.5B4/6)	barrel	M	2
		tsp blue (5B6/8)	barrel	M	1
Wound, spherical (n=98)	WIb	op white (N9.5/)	spherical	L	1
		op blue (5B5/6)	spherical	M	1
		op blue (10B5/6)	spherical	M	1
		op blue (5B6/4)	spherical	L	11
		op blue (5B7/4)	spherical	L	11
		op blue (7.5B6/6)	spherical	L	2

TABLE 2 (CONTINUED)

Manufacture	Kidd and Kidd Code	Diaphaneity,[a] Color, and Munsell Value	Shape	Size[b]	Count
		op blue (7.5B5/4)	spherical	M	5
		tsl blue (5B5/6)	spherical	M	1
		tsl blue (5B5/10)	spherical	M	8
		tsl blue (10B4/6)	spherical	M	2
		tsl blue (2.5PB3/6)	spherical	M	1
		tsl blue (10B3/8)	spherical	VL	1
		tsp blue (5B4/6)	spherical	L	43
		op black (5RP2/2)	spherical	M	1
		op black (5RP2/2)	spherical	VL	1
		op red (7.5R2/4)	spherical	M	1
		tsl red (5R4/10)	spherical	M	7
Wound, oval (n=2)	WIc	op blue (too weathered to obtain Munsell)	oval	S	1
		tsl blue (10B3/6)	oval	L	1

[a] op = opaque; tsl = translucent; tsp = transparent.
[b] S = 2–4 mm; M = 4–6 mm; L = 6–10 mm; VL = 10+ mm.

Within the Kathlamet village collection, 95% of the beads are white and 4% are blue, with the less common red and black beads making up just under 1%. The overall blue and white colors of the Kathlamet village bead collection are consistent with an early 19th-century time period, but some of the specific bead varieties present in the collection provide temporal information that supports the idea of later occupation at the site. In his studies of bead collections from the Plains, Ross (2000) found that blue and white bead collections predominated in the 1830s, with limited inclusions of other bead colors such as red and black. While the Plains and the Plateau are very distinct geographic and cultural regions, general temporal comparisons between the two areas based on bead attributes appear valid. As with other historic period trade materials, different varieties of glass beads seem to appear in different areas of the country at roughly the same time, especially during the 19th century. For example, the bead collection from Fort Vancouver on the Columbia River and the collection from Fort Union in North Dakota, which both operated during much of the 19th century, contain similar, general bead varieties, even though both forts were supplied by different outfits, namely, the Hudson's Bay Company and the American Fur Company, respectively (Ross 1990, 2000).

The drawn, polychrome beads in the collection, the red-on-white and the red-on-green beads (Kidd and Kidd variety IVa), serve as temporal indicators. The red-on-green and red-on-white varieties are often referred to as greenhearts and whitehearts, respectively. While red-on-white beads are sometimes also called *cornaline d'Aleppo*, the term red-on-white is preferred by bead researchers, as is the term red-on-green, and those terms will be used here. The eight drawn red-on-green beads have transparent green cores; one drawn red-on-white bead is present (Figure 5). Based on various Plains collections, Ross (2000:162) found that drawn red-on-white beads first occur in the 1830s, and become "more common than the red-on-green by the 1840s." Both varieties also occur at nearby Fort Vancouver (Ross 1990). Drawn red-on-white beads do not appear in the Leavenworth bead collection, which dates from 1803 to 1832 and contains over 150,000 beads, further suggesting that their appearance postdates 1830 (William Billeck 2005, pers. comm.).

The presence of a particular variety of a mold-pressed bead in this collection suggests a mid-19th century presence at Kathlamet village. The bead from the Kathlamet village is opaque black, with molded facets; a straight, or cylindrical, perforation; and a horizontal, zigzag mold seam (Figure 5). This variety of bead, also in black, apparently has not been found at Fort Vancouver itself, but it does occur at the adjacent Kanaka village site, although there is no mention of mold seam type (Ross 2000). According to Ross (2000), the presence of a straight perforation in this bead variety suggests a *terminus post quem* of mid- to late-19th century. An identical opaque black, mold-pressed bead with facets, a straight perforation, and a zigzag seam was found at Fort Pierre I in South Dakota, which has a firm date range of 1832 to 1857 (William Billeck 2005, pers. comm.).

The Collapse of Local Group Identity

The Kathlamet and the neighboring Wahkiakum who resided across the Columbia River on the Washington shore were situated at the junction of the two branches of the Chinookan language family (Boas 1894:5–6, 1901:6). Immediately downstream to the west were the Chinook proper, sometimes referred to as the Shoalwater Chinook, on the Washington shore and the Clatsop on the Oregon shore, who

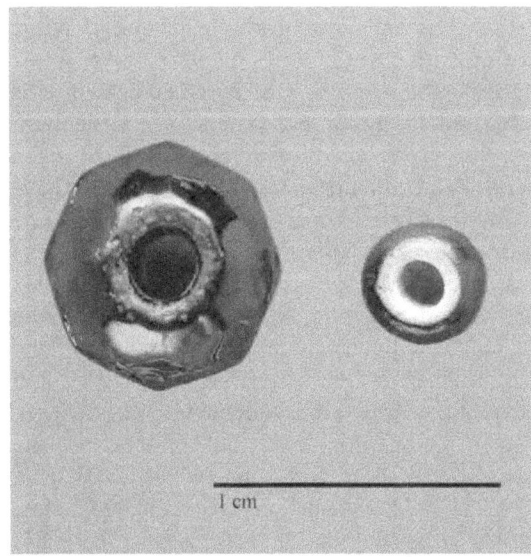

FIGURE 5. Black mold-pressed glass bead with molded facets (*left*) and red-on-white drawn bead (*right*) in the Phebus collection from the Kathlamet Village. (Photo by Donald Hurlbert; courtesy of Smithsonian Institution.)

spoke two dialects that were practically identical and which, together, comprise the Lower Chinookan language. Beginning with the Kathlamet and Wahkiakum, the Chinookan peoples living upstream from the Chinook proper and Clatsop on the Columbia River spoke the Upper Chinookan language.

The Kathlamet and Wahkiakum spoke a dialect of the Upper Chinookan language given the name Kathlamet by Franz Boas (1901:6). The name Kathlamet took on a broader meaning in a linguistic sense when it was applied by Boas to the particular dialect of the Upper Chinookan language spoken by what is now referred to as "a dialect cluster of villages" stretching along the Columbia River from about Grays Bay on the Washington side and Tongue Point on the Oregon side upstream to the vicinity of Kalama on the Washington shore and Rainier on the Oregon shore (Boas 1901:6). Use of the name Kathlamet to refer to both the local group and the linguistic dialect has resulted in some confusion in the literature (Swanton 1952:414). At least two other dialects of the Upper Chinookan language, Multnomah and Kiksht, were spoken by Chinookan groups living farther up the Columbia River (Silverstein 1990:534–535).

The Kathlamet and Wahkiakum began to slip from the historical record with observations in the 1850s by George Gibbs, who viewed the Chinookan population in terms of "two nations–the Upper and the Lower Chinooks; the former extending from the Dalles nearly to the Cowlitz river; the latter from thence to the ocean" (Gibbs 1854:33, 1877:164). Gibbs' division of the Chinookan peoples into "two nations," with the dividing line around the Cowlitz River, was later criticized by Spier (1936:21–22), who observed that "Gibbs appears to have classified Kathlamet incorrectly with Chinook proper," as "this places the Chinook and Kathlamet in one category, Clackamas and the peoples upstream in another. But the Kathlamet spoke an Upper Chinookan tongue quite distinct from Chinook proper."

By the time ethnographic fieldwork took place in the 1930s, few informants were available among the surviving Chinookans around the mouth of the Columbia River. Apparently following Gibbs (1854, 1877), Verne F. Ray (1938) presented a classification of Chinookan groups that crosscut the boundary between the Lower and Upper Chinookan languages when he grouped the Kathlamet (under which the Wahkiakum were subsumed) along with the Clatsop, Chinook, and Shoalwater Chinook into "a single ethnic unit" under the name "Lower Chinook." Ray (1938:38) mistakenly referred to the distinction between the language spoken by the Clatsop and Chinook proper (Lower Chinook) from that spoken by the Kathlamet and Wahkiakum (Upper Chinook) as a difference in dialects rather than languages. He supported his grouping of these peoples into "a single ethnic unit" by referring to the "constant intercourse and intermarriage [that] occurred from one part of the area to another" as reflected in the genealogies of "practically all of the families yet living" at Bay Center "with a marked Chinook component in the ancestry" (Ray 1938:37–38, 63). The high rate of intermarriage among the native groups around the mouth of the Columbia River documented in the genealogies, however, almost certainly reflects the steep decline in the native population from the effects of infectious diseases and the subsequent amalgamation of the survivors in a few settlements (Boyd 1999:238).

Unlike earlier writers such as Lewis and Clark, who had recognized the Wahkiakum as a separate local group, Ray (1938:38–39) subsumed them under the Kathlamet. His justification for doing so was based on an account by pioneer Thomas Nelson Strong (1906:61) who, in describing the devastating effects of infectious diseases on the native population, wrote:

> They fled from their homes and temporarily settled in any place that provided them with the means of livelihood or that promised exemption from the plague that afflicted them. In this way the Cathlamets, whose home was originally upon the Oregon side of the Columbia River, below Puget Island, after wanderings that are not recorded, finally settled upon the present site of Cathlamet and near the place of the ancient Indian town, and from this people the modern town derives its name.

Citing Strong's account, Ray (1938:38–39) stated that the "remnant population" of the village of kala'amat moved across the river to join the residents of the village of wa'qaiya·qam at "their new site" at present-day Cathlamet, Washington. While the pioneer account he relies upon makes no mention of the date of this alleged movement across the river, Ray (1938:39) placed this event "around 1810." Ray's assertion that the Kathlamet

amalgamated into Wahkiakum settlements on the Washington shore, and that they no longer had a presence on the Oregon shore after 1810, has been uncritically accepted by all subsequent writers (Suphan 1974:217–218; Taylor 1974:19; Ruby and Brown 1976:6).

The Last Years of the Kathlamet Village

Ray's (1938:39) statement asserting that the Kathlamet settlement at Aldrich Point was abandoned about 1810 is directly contradicted by archaeological evidence from the site. As discussed above, the recovery of phoenix buttons, McDougall and Fiolet clay pipes, and certain of the glass trade beads indicates continued occupation of the Kathlamet village into the middle decades of the 1800s. The archaeological evidence is consistent with references in the historical record supporting the idea that some Kathlamet survived the epidemics and persisted as a community based at the Kathlamet village into the mid-19th century.

A list of Chinookan settlements along the Lower Columbia River provided in *Indians of North America* by Edward S. Curtis includes information about the villages of the "Cathlamet" and other Chinookan groups around the mouth of the Columbia River. This information was said to have been obtained "from the almost sole survivor of the Cathlamet group, a man of mixed Cathlamet and Chehalis blood, who observed the villages as early as 1845–1850" (Curtis 1911:182). This informant described the village of "Hlilúsqaħiħ" as "four large houses under chief Stuliáħ" and the village of "Kahláamat, on Cathlamet Head," as "seven houses under chief Wákaħohlk" (Curtis 1911:182). Curtis's "Cathlamet" informant was later identified as Samuel Mallett (sometimes spelled Millet), a nephew of the Kathlamet chief To-tili-cum and the father of Emma Millet Luscier, the principal informant for Ray's *Lower Chinook Ethnographic Notes* (Ray 1980:123).

In an account pertaining to the period around 1845, pioneer John Minto described traveling up the Columbia River from Astoria and "approaching Cathelamett Point, the village of the tribe, on the south shore" (Minto 1900:311). Minto's party was "hailed from the shore and found ourselves near the women and girls of the tribe, having a good time gathering the newly risen stems of the common fern and preparing it for food in earth ovens over heated rocks" (Minto 1900:311). The traveling party was invited to visit the village, where a "bountiful meal of fresh salmon and wapatos" was served (Minto 1900:311). Afterwards, Minto (1900:312) commented:

> This was, with perhaps one exception, the cleanest, most self-respecting body of natives left on the Lower Columbia in 1845, where Lewis and Clark had, only forty years before, enumerated, by information from the natives, thirteen thousand eight hundred and thirty below the cascades and between that and the ocean. I do not believe that thirteen hundred could be found within the same limits at the latter date.

One of the inhabitants at the Kathlamet village at Aldrich Point around this time was Charles Cultee, Franz Boas's informant for both *Chinook Texts* (Boas 1894) and *Kathlamet Texts* (Boas 1901). According to Boas, Cultee "lived for a considerable number of years at Cathlamet, *on the south side of Columbia river, a few miles above Astoria* [emphasis added]" (Boas 1901:5). Cultee is thought to have been born around 1830 and to have died in 1897 (Boxberger and Taylor 1986), a lifespan that would seem to place him at the Kathlamet village in the middle decades of the 1800s.

By the 1850s, the surviving Chinookans around the mouth of the Columbia River had intermarried with other native peoples and were concentrated in only a few settlements. George Gibbs (1854:33) observed:

> Of the Lower Chinooks there are six or seven settlements, most of which consist of single families. The one on Chinook beach is the largest, and amounts to 66. Almost all these are, however, intermingled with Chihalis. One of their grounds is upon the south side of the Columbia, opposite the mouth of the Cowlitz, and therefore in Oregon. The total number of this tribe is reduced to about 120. There are four persons who claim to be chiefs: Ske-ma-que-up at Wahkiakum, To-tili-cum at Woody Island, E-la-wah at Chinook, and Toke at Shoalwater bay [original spelling].

While Gibbs does not specifically mention the Kathlamet, Woody Island, where To-tili-cum was listed as chief, is located in the Columbia River directly across from the Kathlamet village at Aldrich Point. In a 1906 census, To-tili-cum was mentioned by two individuals as a chief of the Kathlamet band who had died about 35

years before (c. 1875). To-tili-cum had several children, all of whom had preceded him in death (McChesney 1969).

Perhaps the most telling historical evidence that the Kathlamet maintained a separate identity from the Wahkiakum into the 1850s is found in the fact that in 1851 Anson Dart and other Treaty Commissioners entered into separate treaties (never ratified) with each group. The treaty with Wahkiakum was signed by Ske-ma-que-up and the treaty with the Kathlamet was signed by To-tili-cum (McChesney 1969; Suphan 1974:270). These two individuals were identified as "chiefs" in the passage by Gibbs (1854:33) quoted above.

Under Article 1, the Kathlamet ceded to the United States a huge tract of land on the south shore of the Columbia River that was "intended to include all the land owned or claimed by said Kathlamet band of Indians" (Suphan 1974:270). Under Article 2, the Kathlamet reserved from the cession "two of the islands in the Columbia river, to wit: one called Woody island, and one called by the Indians Sky-lic-la. The said band also reserve the privilege of residing at what is called the old Kathlamet town, and of cutting timber on the land above described for their own fuel and building purposes" (Suphan 1974:270). The phrase "old Kathlamet town" refers to the village of *Hlilúsqaẖiẖ*, as in an account written in 1846 Joel Palmer observed that "from Tongue Point across Gray's Bay to Cathlamet Point is about sixteen miles. Small craft are frequently compelled to run the southern channel, which passes 'old Cathlamet town,' as it is called, a point where once stood an Indian village" (Palmer 1906:203). Considering the information pointing to continued residency by the Kathlamet along the south shore of the Columbia River into the mid-19th century, Palmer's observation of "a point where once stood an Indian village" almost certainly reflects seasonal movement of *Hlilúsqaẖiẖ's* inhabitants, most likely to *Kahláamat,* for the summer fishing season, rather than permanent abandonment of *Hlilúsqaẖiẖ* by that time.

The Kathlamet have not been previously recognized as one of the remnant populations of Chinookans that persisted into the mid-nineteenth century (Boyd 1999:254-255). With the passage of time, the Kathlamet village and its inhabitants gradually faded from the pages of history. By the time of the 1907 publication of the *Handbook of North American Indians North of Mexico*, Livingston Farrand's entry for the Cathlamet reported that "they are now extinct. They seem to have had but one village, also known as Cathlamet" (Farrand 1907:216). Farrand's description of the Kathlamet as "now extinct" is not accurate. Some individuals who trace their heritage to the Kathlamet gained allotments on the Quinault Reservation in northwest Washington, and others are enrolled in the non-federally recognized Chinook Tribe based in Pacific County, Washington. The Kathlamet are almost certainly represented among the "more than 2,000 Chinook, lineally descended from the survivors of the mid-1800s, [who] remain within the general area of their ancestors" (Boyd 1999:256fn).

Summary and Conclusions

The Kathlamet village at Aldrich Point was one of the two main settlements of the Chinookan people of the same name who lived along the south shore of the upper Columbia River estuary at the time of historic contact. Most of the information of an archaeological nature available about this settlement is derived from excavations by avocational archaeologist George Phebus, Sr., whose records indicate the presence of a prehistoric component as well as the more obvious evidence of occupation in the early historic period. Notes accompanying the Phebus collection of artifacts recovered from this site indicate that this settlement included a living area as well as a separate burial area. The temporal information gained from a reanalysis of objects from the Kathlamet village site highlights the value of museum collections, especially when contemporary research advances, like the developments in dating certain beads, can draw new answers from older collections.

Up to a point, the post-contact experience of the Kathlamet was similar to that undergone by other Chinookan peoples of the Lower Columbia Valley. Early accounts, notably by Lewis and Clark, indicate that the Kathlamet were a distinct local group that occupied its own separate territory. The Kathlamet were most closely related to the Wahkiakum directly across the Columbia River who spoke the same dialect of the Upper Chinook language. Following the decimation of the native population by infectious diseases and amalgamation of survivors into a few settlements, local groups like the Kathlamet and Wahkiakum lost their separate identities and were combined by observers into "ethnic units" ("Lower Chinook" and "Upper Chinook") that obscured their earlier distinctions (Gibbs 1854; Ray 1938).

Unlike most of the other Chinookan groups, however, a remnant population of Kathlamet survived the epidemics and persisted as a local group identifiable in the historical record. Artifacts recovered from the site of the Kathlamet village at Aldrich Point, including phoenix buttons, Fiolet and McDougall pipes, and certain types of glass beads, indicate that occupation at Aldrich Point continued well after 1810, the approximate date given by Ray (1938) for the abandonment of the village. As a whole, the assemblage of artifacts of European American manufacture is consistent with the information recorded by Edward S. Curtis, John Minto, and Franz Boas indicating continued occupation of this settlement well into the mid-19th century.

Lewis and Clark's accounts convey the impression that the Kathlamet were one of the more important of the local Chinookan groups in the Lower Columbia Valley, described by these explorers in the same manner as the better known Clatsop and Chinook proper at the mouth of the Columbia River. The Kathlamet were said to play an important role as middlemen in trade along the Columbia River, and William Clark described them as "the best canoe navigators" these explorers had ever seen. Judging from their diminished status in post-epidemic historical and anthropological studies, it seems that little is gained, and much is lost, by lumping distinct local groups of Chinookans like the Kathlamet into "ethnic units" based on their disastrous experiences in the post-contact world.

Acknowledgments

Test excavations in 1978 at the Kathlamet village were carried out as part of a program of archaeological research around the mouth of the Columbia River supported by a doctoral dissertation grant from the National Science Foundation (NSF Grant BNS-77-06028). The opportunity to examine artifacts from the Lower Columbia Valley in the Phebus Collection at the National Museum of Natural History, Smithsonian Institution, was made possible by a National Endowment for the Humanities Travel Grant in 1989. We thank the following who contributed information from their own research about various topics considered in this article: William Billeck (glass beads); Michael A. Pfeiffer (pipes); Roderick Sprague (phoenix buttons); and Stephen Dow Beckham and Irene Martin (historical sources). This article was improved by comments by Kent Lightfoot, R. Michael Stewart, and an anonymous reviewer, as well as those of Associate Editor Grace Zeising. The authors are solely responsible for any errors of fact or interpretation contained in this article.

References

ADAM, CHUCK
    1968   The Phoenix Button. *Central States Archaeological Journal* 15(1):35.

BOAS, FRANZ
    1894   *Chinook Texts*. Bureau of American Ethnology, Bulletin 20. Washington, DC.

    1901   *Kathlamet Texts*. Bureau of American Ethnology, Bulletin 26. Washington, DC.

BOXBERGER, DANIEL L., AND HERBERT C. TAYLOR, JR.
    1986   Charles Cultee and the Father of American Anthropology. *The Sou'wester* 21(1):3–7.

BOYD, ROBERT T.
    1999   *The Coming of the Spirit of Pestilence: Introduced Infectious Diseases and Population Decline Among Northwest Coast Indians, 1774–1874*. University of Washington Press, Seattle.

BOYD, ROBERT T., AND YVONNE P. HAJDA
    1987   Seasonal Population Movement Along the Lower Columbia River: The Social and Ecological Context. *American Ethnologist* 14(2):309–326.

CHANCE, DAVID H., AND JENNIFER V. CHANCE
    1976   *Kanaka Village/Vancouver Barracks 1974*. University of Washington, Office of Public Archaeology, Reports in Highway Archaeology No. 3, Seattle, WA.

CURTIS, EDWARD S.
    1911   *The North American Indian*. Vol. 8. Cambridge University Press, Cambridge, England.

FARRAND, LIVINGSTON
    1907   Cathlamet. In *Handbook of American Indians North of Mexico*, F. W. Hodge, editor, pp. 216–217. Bureau of American Ethnology Bulletin 30(1). Washington, DC.

GIBBS, GEORGE
    1854   Report of Mr. George Gibbs to Captain Mc'Clellan, on the Indian Tribes of the Territory of Washington. In *Reports of Explorations and Surveys, to Ascertain the Most Practical and Economical Route for a Railroad from the Mississippi River to the Pacific Ocean, Made Under the Direction of the Secretary of War, in 1853-4, According to Acts of Congress of March 3, 1853, May 31, and August 5, 1854*. 33rd Congress, 2nd Session. *House Executive Document*, 91. A. O. P. Nicholson, printer, Washington City. Reprinted 1967 by Ye Galleon Press, Fairfield, WA.

    1877   Tribes of Western Washington and Northwestern Oregon. In *Contributions to North American Ethnology*, Vol. I, pp. 157–241. Government Printing Office, Washington, DC.

HAJDA, YVONNE P.
    1984   Regional Social Organization in the Greater Lower Columbia, 1792–1830. Doctoral dissertation, Department of Anthropology, University of Washington, Seattle, WA.

KARKLINS, KARLIS
    1985   Guide to the Description and Classification of Glass Beads. In *Glass Beads*, 2nd edition, pp. 85–118. Parks Canada, Studies in Archaeology, Architecture and History, Ottawa, Ontario, Canada.

KIDD, KENNETH E., AND MARTHA A. KIDD
    1970   A Classification System for Glass Beads for the Use of Field Archaeologists. *Canadian Historic Sites: Occasional Papers in Archaeology and History* 1:45–89. Ottawa, Ontario, Canada.

MARTIN, IRENE
    1980   Ethnohistorical Notes on the Wahkiakum Indians. In *Further Archaeological Testing at the Skamokawa Site (45-WK-5), Wahkiakum County, Washington*, by Rick Minor, pp. 40–52. University of Washington, Office of Public Archaeology, Reconnaissance Report 36, Seattle, WA.

McCHESNEY, CHARLES E.
    1969   *Rolls of Certain Indian Tribes in Oregon and Washington*. Ye Galleon Press, Fairfield, WA. Reprint of 1906 59th Congress, 2nd Session, *House Executive Document*, 133, Washington, DC.

MINOR, RICK
    1983   Aboriginal Settlement and Subsistence at the Mouth of the Columbia River. Doctoral dissertation, University of Oregon, Eugene, OR.

MINTO, JOHN
    1900   Number and Condition of the Native Race in Oregon When First Seen by White Men. *Oregon Historical Quarterly* 1(3):296-315.

MOULTON, GARY E. (EDITOR)
    1983   *Atlas of the Lewis & Clark Expedition*, Vol. 1. University of Nebraska Press, Lincoln, NE.

Perspectives from *Historical Archaeology:*

1990 *The Journals of the Lewis & Clark Expedition, Volume 6: November 2, 1805–March 22, 1806*. University of Nebraska Press, Lincoln, NE.

1991 *The Journals of the Lewis & Clark Expedition, Volume 7: March 23–June 9, 1806*. University of Nebraska Press, Lincoln, NE.

OLSON, RONALD L.
1927 *Adze, Canoe, and House Types of the Northwest Coast*. University of Washington Publications in Anthropology Vol. 2, No. 1. Seattle, WA.

PALMER, JOEL
1906 *Journal of Travels Over the Rocky Mountains to the Mouth of the Columbia River, Made During the Years 1845 and 1846*, Reuben G. Thwaites, editor. The Arthur H. Clark Company, Cleveland, OH.

PETTIGREW, RICHARD M.
1981 *A Prehistoric Culture Sequence in the Portland Basin of the Lower Columbia Valley*. University of Oregon Anthropological Papers No. 22. Eugene, OR.

PFEIFFER, MICHAEL
1982 The Clay Pipes. In *Kanaka Village/Vancouver Barracks 1975*, by David Chance, Jennifer Chance, Caroline Carley, Karl Gurcke, Timothy Jones, George Ling, Michael Pfeiffer, Karl Roenke, Jacqueline Storm, Robert Thomas, and Charles Troup, pp. 113–127. University of Washington, Office of Public Archaeology, Reports in Highway Archaeology 7. Seattle, WA.

PHEBUS, GEORGE
1974 A Survey of Archaeological Sites in Clatsop County, Oregon, with a Brief Description and Evaluation. On file, Museum of Natural and Cultural History, University of Oregon, Eugene, OR.

RAY, VERNE F.
1938 *Lower Chinook Ethnographic Notes*. University of Washington Publications in Anthropology, Vol. 7, No. 2. Seattle, WA.

1980 Deposition of Verne F. Ray, March 27-28. The Wahkiakum Band of Chinook Indians, et al., Plaintiff, v. Mrs. Allen Bateman, et al., Defendants. United States District Court for the District of Oregon Civil Action No. 79-39, Volume II, Exhibit O. Washington, D.C.

ROLLINS, PHILIP A. (EDITOR)
1935 *The Discovery of the Oregon Trail: Robert Stuart's Narratives of His Overland Trip Eastward From Astoria in 1812–1813*. Charles Scribner's Sons, New York, NY.

ROSS, LESTER
1990 Trade Beads from Hudson's Bay Company Fort Vancouver (1829–1860), Vancouver, Washington. *Beads, Journal of the Society of Bead Researchers* 2:29–67.

2000 *Trade Beads from Archeological Excavations at Fort Union Trading Post National Historic Site*. National Park Service, Midwest Archeological Center, and the Fort Union Association, Williston, ND.

RUBY, ROBERT H., AND JOHN A. BROWN
1976 *The Chinook Indians: Traders of the Lower Columbia River*. University of Oklahoma Press, Norman, OK.

SILVERSTEIN, MICHAEL
1990 Chinookans of the Lower Columbia. In *Handbook of North American Indians*, Vol. 17, *Northwest Coast*, Wayne Suttles, editor, pp. 533–546. Smithsonian Institution, Washington, DC.

SPIER, LESLIE
1936 *Tribal Distribution in Washington*. General Series in Anthropology No. 3. George Banta Publishing Company, Menasha, WI.

SPRAGUE, RODERICK
1998 The Literature and Locations of the Phoenix Button. *Historical Archaeology* 32(2):56–77.

STENGER, ALISON T.
1991 Japanese-Influenced Ceramics in Precontact Washington State: A View of the Wares and Their Possible Origin. *The New World Figurine Project* 1:111–122.

STRONG, EMORY
1975 The Enigma of the Phoenix Button. *Historical Archaeology* 9:74–80.

STRONG, THOMAS NELSON
1906 *Cathlamet on the Columbia*. The Holly Press, Portland, OR.

SUPHAN, ROBERT J.
1974 An Ethnological Report on the Identity and Localization of Certain Native Peoples of Northwestern Oregon. In *Oregon Indians I*, David A. Horr, editor, pp. 167–256. Garland Publishing, New York, NY.

SUTTLES, WAYNE
1990 Introduction. In *Handbook of North American Indians*, Vol. 7, *Northwest Coast*, Wayne Suttles, editor, pp. 1–15. Smithsonian Institution, Washington, DC.

SWAN, JAMES G.
1857 *The Northwest Coast; or, Three Years Residence in Washington Territory*. Harper & Brothers, New York, NY. Reprinted 1972 by University of Washington Press, Seattle, WA.

SWANTON, JOHN R.
1952 *The Indian Tribes of North America*. Bureau of American Ethnology Bulletin 145. Washington, DC.

TAYLOR, HERBERT C.
    1974 Anthropological Investigation of the Chinook Indians
         Relative to Tribal Identity and Aboriginal Possession
         of Lands. In *Oregon Indians I*, David A. Horr, editor,
         pp. 103–165. Garland Publishing, New York, NY.

WILKES, CHARLES
    1849 *Narrative of the United States Exploring Expedition,*
         Vol. 5. C. Sherman, printer, Philadelphia, PA.

RICK MINOR
HERITAGE RESEARCH ASSOCIATES, INC.
1997 GARDEN AVENUE
EUGENE, OR 97403

LAURIE E. BURGESS
DEPARTMENT OF ANTHROPOLOGY
NATIONAL MUSEUM OF NATURAL HISTORY
MRC 11
SMITHSONIAN INSTITUTION
PO BOX 37012
WASHINGTON, DC 20013-7012

Paul R. Mullins
Robert Paynter

Representing Colonizers: An Archaeology of Creolization, Ethnogenesis, and Indigenous Material Culture among the Haida

ABSTRACT

Rather than reduce colonial encounters to a universal creolization process, creolization is examined as conflict between various colonial powers and indigenous groups with distinct social and resource organizations. The concept of ethnogenesis focuses analysis of creolization by probing colonial power relations and approaching material culture as the active negotiation of colonization and colonial inequality. The subject of analysis is indigenous objects that depict European colonizers; such material culture should provide a sensitive insight into indigenous perceptions of colonization and illuminate the relations between various colonizers and indigenous peoples throughout the world. This examination of material culture from the Haida of the Pacific Northwest demonstrates how one indigenous group developed distinctive strategies to negotiate colonial power relations.

Introduction

In July 1787, English captain George Dixon made one of the first records of European contact with the Haida, the indigenous peoples of the Queen Charlotte Islands in the Pacific Northwest (Fisher 1977; MacDonald 1989:20; Blackman 1990:255). Upon trading with one Haida chief, Dixon observed that "Of all the Indians we have seen, this chief had the most savage aspect, and his whole appearance sufficiently marked him as a proper person to lead a tribe of cannibals. . . . However, he proved very useful in conducting our traffic with his people, and the intelligence he gave us, and the methods he took to make himself understood, showed him to possess a strong natural capacity" (MacDonald 1989:33). Dixon's depiction of the Haida as both savages and shrewd traders was typical of the contradictory European characterizations of indigenous peoples. He and many subsequent Europeans were hard-pressed to accommodate their preconception of a universal primitive to the reality of diverse indigenous peoples who rapidly adapted to, manipulated, and defied colonization's profound transformations.

The arrival of the King George's Sound Company was indeed a pivotal historical moment, much like similar "contacts" throughout the world over several hundred years. Yet such colonial experiences were each distinctive because they were shaped by unique factors, including pre-existing kinship and social structure, local resources, and specific European interests in diverse regions. Various threads of creolization theory provide a range of ways to analyze the Haida's post-European contact transformations. The rich archaeological literature on cultural change, for instance, includes approaches that systematically model cultural transfiguration (Wilkie 1997), emphasize the persistence of cultural tradition (Patten 1992), or acknowledge assimilation to dominant material consumption patterns (Stewart-Abernathy and Ruff 1989). Given the diverse range of colonial experiences, creolization most often is framed as a generalized and syncretic "multicultural adjustment" (Ferguson 1992:xli), an approach that recognizes non-European peoples' capacity to shape their own cultures and often impact that of colonizers.

Creolization scholarship provides a substantial foundation to study colonial cultural change, but it remains curiously devoid of any sustained analysis of the power relations within which that euphemistic "change" occurs (Howson 1990:82; Orser 1996:21-22). This work examines creolization as indigenous peoples' negotiation, evasion, mediation, confrontation, and resolution of power conflicts resulting from (or heightened by) colonization. Creolizing cultures consistently forge new cultural subjectivities that negotiate and resist colonizers' interests, a process of cultural construction known as ethnogenesis (Gailey and Patterson 1987; Perry and Paynter 1998). The concept of ethnogenesis is not intended to replace creolization; rather, it is used here to situate creolization's somewhat vague cultural syncretism within clear structural power relations in specific colonial political economies. Ethnogenesis frames creolizing contexts within state-structured inequalities, posing indigenous representations of themselves and Europeans as a negotiation of contradictory interests. In any given context, colonization could be expressed in many different material forms: for instance, material goods could be stark expressions of indigenous resistance; they might be subtle and oblique statements about colonial and local relations; or objects could be relatively inchoate and unrecognized comments on colonial life. This reflects the fact that European domination itself took many experienced forms, from masters to merchants to the military, and local groups had a wide variety of responses, from rebellion to willing incorporation. Post-contact change like that among the Haida was not simply routine cultural dynamism, the sort of change expected in any cultural context: it was transformation fueled by agency within and against a colonial political economy. The most salient feature of creolization as it is defined here is the continual mediation of indigenous agency, local cultural practice, and colonial structure in an ever-hybridizing culture which unfolds long after colonial contact (Gilroy 1987; Ferguson 1992:xli-xlii; Lightfoot and Martinez 1995; Singleton 1995:133; Orser 1996:12). Certainly colonizers did not utterly determine the possible forms of indigenous decision-making, but local agency inevitably mirrors both the structural domination of a colonizer and the local material organization and cultural identity of a colonized people.

This approach retains creolization's established focus on cultural syncretism in contact contexts, but highlights the ability of local creolizing cultures to fundamentally negotiate the inequalities cultivated by colonial political economies. Creolizing cultures attempt to appropriate empowering resources and opportunities while also resisting various forms of material, political, and cultural domination Europeans inflicted on or encouraged within indigenous groups. This framing of creolization rejects approaches that neglect local cultural organization or reduce colonization to a universal encounter between dominant Europeans and subordinate indigenous peoples. It is simplistic to expect that any monolithic cultural change models can capture the vast diversity and contradictions in the colonial world.

"Varying sentence upon the white man": Indigenous Material Culture and European Representation

Eric Wolf's (1982) remarkable study of the post-Columbian world emphasizes that indigenous peoples had myriad experiences and visions of their confrontations with European colonizers. One of the most interesting, albeit neglected expressions of such relationships is indigenous material culture that depicts Europeans. Throughout the world, indigenous people produced a vast quantity of objects that depicted European colonizers in a diverse range of guises. Few scholars, though, have devoted sustained attention to such material culture. The earliest and most noteworthy exception is Julius Lips (1966), whose 1937 study *The Savage Hits Back* argued that indigenous material culture depicting Europeans was veiled resistance to European colonization. Lips (1966:10) approached colonization as a confrontation across the color line, arguing that "While the relation of the white to the coloured world down the centuries has been that of exploiter and exploited, the coloured world has, in its different branches and at different periods, pronounced varying sentence upon the white man." Lips' reduction of colonization to a racial encounter between polarized dominators and resisters certainly is flawed, but his monograph remains the most comprehensive study of such objects.

Such material culture seems particularly likely to illuminate how various indigenous and post-colonial subjects perceived Europeans (Jules-Rosetta 1984; Hiller 1991; Malbert 1991; Steiner 1994). Contemporary research projects study these objects within various specific colonial systems, examine local cultures, and probe variation in motifs and forms. Rather than paint a universal creolization process, these studies reflect vast global variation in the ways in which indigenous peoples chose to represent Europeans and, by extension, themselves within and opposing a colonial world.

This study is based on an ongoing inventory of high art objects, trade goods, and archaeological material culture made throughout the world since the 15th century (Paynter and Mullins 1994). These objects today reside in scattered museums and private collections, variously displayed as documents of culture contact, exhibited as exotic oddities, or forgotten in storage. Some are classified as paragons of local culture, others are viewed somewhat disdainfully as proto-tourist art, and some are simply ignored enigmas. Not surprisingly, there is considerable diversity in worldwide representations of Europeans. Far more European representations come from Africa than anywhere else in the world, although there is no pan-African aesthetic style (Ben-Amos and Rubin 1983; Ezra 1992; Kramer 1993; Ben-Amos 1995). North America has a rich history of European representation as well, ranging from the Northwest Coast to Plains peoples (Ewers 1979; Wright 1982, 1985). Highland South America, Mesoamerica, India, Japan, and China also have artistic traditions that depict Europeans (Burland 1969; Gruzinski 1992). For reasons which are not yet evident, the regions with relative absences of European imagery are Oceania and lowland South America.

Typically scholars impose monolithic aesthetic values upon such objects, pigeonhole them within artistic genres, or reduce them to polarized reflections of either cultural tradition or cultural degradation (Steiner 1994:33-36). Instead, they all are approached here as histories of colonization that illuminate a chain of indigenous producers, consumers in local markets and colonial centers, and individual and museum collectors who have projected a variety of social and economic values onto these goods. Creolization in these material goods is an aesthetic expression of political-economic transformation and conflicting colonial and indigenous interests. This approach shares with other creolization studies an emphasis on the moment of production and the maker's distinctive identity (Ferguson 1992:150), focusing on how these material representations of Europeans reflect indigenous agency. This project situates such agency in relation to colonial power structure, neither determined by it nor wholly independent. It demands reflection on Westerners' own fascination, disinterest, and bewilderment over these goods, not simply producers' thoughts at the moment of creation or their subconsciously encoded cultural and aesthetic principles.

Wolf's concept of modes of production provides a systematic mechanism to assess colonial encounters. Wolf argues that interpretation of colonization must evaluate how interacting Europeans and colonized groups mobilized and distributed material resources in different ways which impacted social formations. He uses the notions of kinship, tributary, and capitalist modes of production to describe fundamentally distinct sets of social relations through which labor is organized to acquire and distribute resources (Wolf 1982:75). Wolf notes that within each of these modes of production specific social relations must be constructed in order to reproduce material relations. In the kinship mode, for example, a distinction is constructed between kin and strangers, juniors and elders, and men and women in order to reproduce resource distribution structure and social organization. Similarly, in a tributary mode a distinction must be made between prestigious tribute takers and subordinated tribute producers. In the capitalist mode, the production of workers and owners (and the various classes that mediate between these two) is necessary for its continued existence. Unlike the other modes, in a capitalist, market-based economy social relations do not define insider/outsider or kin/stranger relations, because the market is infinitely open in its inclusive notion of buyers and sellers. Wolf argues that any concrete social situation may be illuminated by any combination of these modes. Examination of encounters between various modes of production reflects that the field of colonial encounters certainly is characterized by the greatest ambiguity, contradiction, and contestation. There is considerable variation within these modes of production, as Wolf himself concedes, but they clearly describe the political economic forces within and against which indigenous material culture assumed meaning.

The Haida colonial encounter has left a rich body of material culture representing Europeans. The Haida immediately began to trade with a variety of Europeans who ventured into the Pacific Northwest beginning in the 1770s (Boxberger 1994:288-289). Europeans initially came for the trade in sea otter pelts, and they had little interest in actually settling the region until the mid-19th century. English, American, Russian, and western European traders met a chiefdom scattered from the Alexander archipelago through the Queen Charlotte Islands with no centralized administration. The Haida shared cultural practices, traded among themselves, and traced their lineage to one of two moieties, but they were divided into a series of communities that did not form a broad polity (Blackman 1990:248-252). After the 1820s, the Haida traded a considerable volume of argillite carvings to Europeans and Americans (Kaufmann 1976; Sheehan 1981; Wright 1985). Europeans and European scenes rapidly became a fundamental feature of Haida trade goods such as pipes and figurines, remaining common motifs until the late-19th century. Today Haida artists still produce argillite carvings and other craft goods for the tourist trade, but the vast majority of these have traditional mythological and symbolic motifs (Stearns 1990:265-266).

The Haida colonial experience is well documented from the European perspective (Murdock and O'Leary 1975; Vaughan 1982). From the indigenous perspective, a vast volume of trade goods and domestic material culture speaks subtly but eloquently to colonization. These objects should be examined as symbolic mediations of conflicting European and Haida social organization and resource distribution. That inquiry will provide an insight into how the Haida encounter was a distinctive cultural negotiation conceived within yet not controlled by colonizing powers.

Creolization among the Haida

Between 1784 and the 1820s, the Haida conducted a thriving European trade in sea otter pelts. The Spanish reached the Haida first in 1774, trading clothes, beads, and knives for Haida pelts and carvings. Captain Cook arrived in the region four years later and acquired several pelts that his crew sold in China for an astounding price of $120 each (Wolf 1982:182; Sahlins 1992). Envisioning massive profits from their Haida trade, George Dixon's purser enthused in 1787 that "In less than half an hour we had purchased three hundred of the finest pelts we had ever seen" (MacDonald 1989:20).

The Europeans were somewhat startled by the Haida's trade acumen. Exchanges were negotiated between Haida chiefs and hundreds of captains during the height of the otter trade (Sheehan 1981; Wolf 1982:185; Macnair and Hoover 1984). Haida had been trading between villages and with mainland indigenous groups such as the Tlingit and Coast Tsimshian for centuries, and they rapidly developed a European reputation for being notoriously firm traders

(Blackman 1990:246). These exchanges created a sphere of social life that facilitated trade with Europeans and empowered Haida chiefs and artisans.

The Haida were divided into two exogamous matrilineal moieties, Raven and Eagle, whose lineages and sub-lineages controlled property, access to some natural resources (such as salmon streams), and symbols, such as crest figures, dances, songs, and names (Swanton 1905; MacDonald 1989:15; Blackman 1990:248). Lineage chiefs orchestrated their lineage's resource management and distribution. Embedded within these relations of kin and tribute production, these Haida chiefs developed additional exchange relationships that in some aspects took on the character of market-based trade. A shrewd trading chief could benefit materially and increase their status from astute exchange, so chiefs pressed for optimal terms and would abandon lengthy negotiations rather than accept a poor trade (Blackman 1990:252).

Similar goals and tactics familiar to European merchants were applied by Haida chiefs in dealing with these new participants in regional trade. Dealing from a position of strength, Haida chiefs would demand that Europeans provide clothing sewn from sailcloth, forge iron hardware to meet their specification, or secure goods from indigenous groups to the south (MacDonald 1989:31). In 1830, a fatigued American concluded that the Haida "expect to have free access to the cabin to eat, drink, and lounge and must have things in style too or they will be highly offended. They make a regular business of bartering–talk till they are weary, take a short nap on deck, or in the cabin–after which they will resume the business with renewed vigor. . . . They exceed all that I have yet seen for keenness in trade" (Van Den Brink 1974:32).

The large multi-lineage villages that Europeans reported on in the 19th century likely were fostered by the maritime fur trade, which presented new socioeconomic opportunities to chiefs who secured resource surpluses and consolidated formerly modest, single-lineage Haida communities. In contrast to late-19th century Haida communities, archaeological evidence indicates that pre-contact Haida settlements were small, single-lineage settlements in which single hereditary chiefs likely could not mobilize a substantial labor base or significantly expand collective resources. Steven Acheson (1995) surveyed 99 pre-contact sites in the southern Queen Charlotte Islands and identified a clear preference for small, widely dispersed, year-round settlements at coastal locations, quite unlike the nucleated, multi-lineage post-contact Haida villages in better-defended inland locations (Fladmark et al. 1990). Acheson argues that ambitious Haida chiefs transformed longstanding social and material organization by calculating trade in European resources–in some cases even attacking European ships–and warfare which extended their authority over lesser chiefs and consolidated scattered communities (Stearns 1981:31-33).

In the 1820s, otter populations rapidly declined, and Europeans shifted their exchange to the mainland in hopes of controlling trade into the hinterland. Hudson's Bay, for instance, established a permanent outpost in Tsimshian territory at Fort Simpson in 1834 (Van Den Brink 1974:28; Stearns 1981:33; MacDonald 1989:35). Goods like flour, clothing, guns, and rum were traded in these posts, much as they had been exchanged in maritime trade before the 1830s. With their most valuable exchange medium fatally depleted, the Haida provided new goods for the European trade, including carvings, dried fish, potatoes, and furs (Kaufmann 1976:58; Blackman 1990:255). Carved ceremonial tobacco pipes were probably the first argillite objects

Haida produced for European trade (Wright 1985). A black shale, argillite was virtually never carved before the 1820s. Carveable argillite is only quarried in the Queen Charlotte Islands, so the Haida enjoyed a monopoly, but it was apparently an insignificant medium before the introduction of steel-bladed tools and the European demand for argillite carvings (Wyatt 1984:60). The first argillite trade pipes were marginally functional, but after about 1830 long flat "panel" pipes began to be produced; many have no bowl or stem hole, plus heated argillite cracks easily, so most pipes likely were consumed as decorative curios.

Initially panel pipes depicted Haida cosmological motifs, but the Haida rapidly developed an aesthetics that featured European elements. Argillite pipes with ship motifs were quite common by 1840. Haida ship pipes combine genuine nautical features with apparently incongruous European architecture (e.g., forts and houses), domesticated animals (e.g., horses and dogs), and other European design elements (e.g., American coin motifs). For instance, a late-19th century example of a panel pipe collected by the Harvard Peabody Museum in 1894 includes a ship's prow and keel alongside a paddle wheel (Figure 1). The ship holds three long-nosed Europeans, one of whom sits behind a rising-sun decorated deckhouse at a cash register.

FIGURE 1. A Haida argillite panel pipe of steamboat scene collected in 1894 showing a prow, keel, and quarter paddlewheel; the European figure to the left appears to be seated at a cash register. (Courtesy Peabody Museum, Harvard University, Cambridge, MA.)

Such motifs probably were objects, activities, and designs Haida witnessed among Europeans aboard ships and in regional forts. There is no evidence for why particular design elements were selected or the pipe form itself was adopted. Art historians traditionally seek a single or predominant origin point for such stylistic innovation (e.g., a particular artist, the introduction of European carving tools, and so on). Rather than resort to such simplification, it is evident that pipe motifs had their origins in a complex mosaic of European consumer demand, Haida aesthetic conventions, technological change, and carvers' idiosyncratic stylistic innovations.

Freestanding argillite and ivory inlaid European figures began to be carved in the early 1840s. These objects departed significantly from Haida art's conventional two-dimensional aesthetic and absence of individual representation. The bodies and clothing of figures like the book-reading European man in Figure 2 tend to be relatively standardized, but the highly individualized detail on many figures' faces suggests some were made-to-order (Drew and Wilson 1980:189). There is no surviving record, however, of such an agreement between a Haida producer and European consumer.

The carvings' style is a complex reflection of shifting cultural subjectivity and market demands, and their symbolic enigma is likely heightened by the distance of time. The rapid transformations in Haida aesthetics could be reduced simply to the "loss of tradition," but this likely overstates the permanence of cultural traditions and underestimates Haida sociocultural flexibility. For instance, Haida conceive of much meaning as fluid and ambiguous: unlike most of the Europeans with whom they traded, the Haida recognized no absolute distinction between sacred and profane realms or the material and symbolic (Boelscher 1988:6-7). Social scientists generally assume a stark division between sacred cultural tradition and profane worldly practice, presuming that material culture representing each uses an exclusive set of material symbols. Typically the assumption is that "sacred" cultural practice will change very slowly, implying that traditional cosmological and religious symbolism is more meaningful than (if not the inverse of) the social symbolism forged in commodity exchange (Miller 1995:25). For example, Carole

FIGURE 2. Haida figurine of a European reading a book, argillite and ivory. This example is undated, but most argillite figures were produced after 1840. (Courtesy Peabody Museum, Harvard University, Cambridge, MA.)

Kaufmann (1976:67-68) argues that "objects, themes, and designs having any sacred relevance to the Haida were not translated into argillite until they had lost their revered significance" (cf. a comparable assessment of shaman figures in Clifford 1991:26). This assumes a dichotomy between meaningful (i.e., sacred) Haida traditional art on one hand and meaningless (i.e., commodified) Haida trade goods on the other. It is unlikely, though, that such an absolute division between spiritual and worldly dimensions actually existed in any time and space.

Perspectives from *Historical Archaeology:*

Haida material culture not produced for trade appears to have focused on symbols that displayed lineage history and status. Monumental architecture such as house poles, house fronts, and masks often used zoomorphic crests or cosmological symbols controlled by a lineage (Blackman 1990:249). Crests were displayed on architecture, portable objects, and bodies, suggesting that kinship and lineage ranking remained at the heart of Haida social organization even after European designs were incorporated into trade goods (cf. examination of mortuary practices in Blackman 1973). Europeans sometimes appeared in 19th-century Haida goods such as house poles, so the Haida apparently did not perceive local and trade motifs as exclusive design sources. It seems likely that the absence of a clear Haida division between the sacred and secular contributed to their rapid embrace of an aesthetics that incorporated elements of pre-existing tradition and colonial experience alike. The lack of a centralized patronage system or chief regulating aesthetics also may have fueled flexible stylistics among Haida crafts people (or at least provided the opportunity for such innovation). For the Haida, meaning was neither inherited in ahistorical tradition nor imposed by kinship structure, European colonizers, or commodities themselves; instead, it was negotiated in a host of social interactions ranging from Hudson's Bay exchanges to public displays of lineage crests in house architecture.

Re-producing Culture

The incorporation of Europeans in Haida material culture suggests the ease with which Europeans were defined in Haida cosmology and material exchange systems. For the Haida, it may not have been a profound cultural disruption to integrate distinctly new representational conventions, such as European motifs. It is critical to avoid romanticizing Haida craft producers' creativity and ignoring the political-economic conditions of exchange (Jules-Rosetta 1984:230). Initially trade was conducted between scattered, maritime-based Europeans and numerous Haida lineage heads, but this seemingly untroubled material accommodation–and European disinterest in settling and regulating the region–changed radically by mid-century. In 1853, the Queen Charlotte Islands became a crown colony, and the gold rush reached the region in 1858, bringing with it thousands of miners, state interest in the lucrative gold trade, and a new wave of epidemics (Blackman 1990:256). From the outset, Europeans had transmitted diseases to the Haida that thinned indigenous populations and contributed to the gradual abandonment of small Haida villages (Acheson 1995). Haida who made the trip to the gold-rush town of Victoria transmitted a devastating smallpox epidemic to the Islands in 1862. Within a decade, most remaining Haida villages were abandoned as the smallpox survivors regrouped in the towns of Skidegate in the south and Masset in the north. In the 1860s, crown administrators also began securing indigenous land rights and regulating everyday life in resettled Haida communities. Missionaries focused on converting the Haida: after their 1873 arrival in Masset missionaries demanded all memorial poles be torn down and communal plank houses abandoned for single-family homes (MacDonald 1989:71). Within a year of missionary George Simpson's 1883 arrival in Skidegate, all traditional plank houses likewise were dismantled or left vacant (MacDonald 1989:37). Skidegate's community was resettled in single-family frame homes, and the village was reorganized into a grid plan centered on the church.

These shifts are reflected in Haida material depictions of Europeans. After about 1870, argillite and wood carvings continued to be produced for trade, but very few depict Europeans. Instead, cosmological motifs and forms that previously were not produced in argillite were marketed to European consumers, including house post models, miniature totem poles, ceremonial chests, and shaman figures (Kaufmann 1976:63). The move to traditional motifs suggests an effort to reaffirm (if not *re*-produce) cultural traditions, but it clearly was an adjustment to shifting market demand as well. Steamships began to haul tourists throughout the Pacific Northwest in the late-19th century, and tour companies published pamphlets that hailed the thrill of purchasing "primitive art" from its maker (Wyatt 1984:22-23; Miller 1991). Genteel East Coast tourists who stepped ashore in the Queen Charlotte Islands expected to purchase an exotic native curio, not an enigmatic representation of themselves, and this consumer demand likely contributed to the disappearance of European design elements.

Among the new consumers was a wave of ethnographers including Franz Boas, who sent anthropologists into the Queen Charlotte Islands in 1900 and 1901 on behalf of the American Museum of Natural History. The express purpose of Boas' team was to obtain "authentic" (i.e., precolonial) Haida material culture or recreations of such objects (Jonaitis 1992:32). Like the tourists wading off steamships, Boas was in search of the "primitive" and uninterested in material goods depicting Europeans. Yet when Boas' emissary John Swanton arrived in the Queen Charlotte Islands in 1900, he found no standing longhouses, few memorial poles, and relatively little of the traditional cultural practice that he and Boas hoped to document and collect (Swanton 1905; Jonaitis 1992:31). In lieu of precolonial material objects, Swanton commissioned Haida craftsman Charles Edenshaw to produce a variety of masks, miniature house posts, scale models, and drawings. Boas' lieutenants elsewhere in the Pacific Northwest recreated cultural tradition through the same relationships with commissioned community artists who produced local material culture (Jonaitis 1992:32). Models were favored because the miniaturization of monumental Haida poles and houses made it possible to view the different aesthetic elements of an enormous object as one small, possessable entity forming a stylistic and narrative whole (Jonaitis 1992:50). A few full-scale Haida poles were displayed complete or in sections in the American Museum of Natural History, but in grand museums even full-scale objects were dwarfed by the monumental size of the museums themselves.

Known to the Haida as Nngkwigetklas (i.e., They Gave Ten Potlatches for Him), Edenshaw was a particularly gifted artist who transformed or originated many aesthetic elements not found in earlier Haida domestic material culture or trade goods (Champagne 1994:1053). Edenshaw reproduced some existing material culture, but he did not simply carve literal duplicates: he provided many objects that interpreted Haida culture and aesthetics but did not actually represent an existing object (Jonaitis 1992:38). In itself, Edenshaw's modifications of Haida aesthetics are not a dramatic violation of traditional style; rather than reduce craft production to mechanical duplications of a template, craft typically reflects individual craftspeoples' interpretations of inherited style (Benjamin 1969:96). Edenshaw's flowing carving style is considered more dynamic than the typically staid lines and designs among his Haida contemporaries (Jonaitis 1992:29). A purely formal stylistic analysis, though, is relatively meaningless without an examination of the power relations within and against which this style was transformed.

Edenshaw produced miniature poles, house models, and masks that Boas and Swanton deemed "authentic." The Field Columbian Museum in Chicago also sent C. F. Newcombe to assemble a collection that would "represent all phases" of Haida culture (Wyatt 1984:24). Like Swanton and Boas' other Northwest Coast intermediaries, Newcombe avoided materials such as silver and goods with European motifs because they did not meet his criteria for "authentic" Haida material culture. As Daniel Miller (1995:25) argues, anthropologists typically define the authentic as practices or objects with roots, which they contrast to transient or recently introduced practices or goods, a definition that Boas, Swanton, and Newcombe apparently favored.

Boas specified that he desired objects that clearly illustrated accompanying traditional narratives (Jonaitis 1992:34). Along with his products, Edenshaw provided accompanying myths and songs for use in museum and ethnographic interpretation of his products. Edenshaw carvings were rendered both sensible and valuable to their European consumers through these indigenous fables and symbolic descriptions that stressed stylistic and cultural difference (Steiner 1994:114-115). Archaeologist Alan Hoover (1983) agrees that Edenshaw likely favored busy aesthetic compositions because they appealed to European consumers like Boas who desired to see carvings as exotic material narratives.

Boas hoped to use Edenshaw's models as a mirror which represented the last traces of Haida cultural traditions. Instead, they were creolizations that captured a distinctive aesthetic confluence of indigenous production and consumption by Europeans. In contrast to the idyllic vision of a primeval Haida, virtually all Haida producers lived in villages planned by Europeans, wore Western clothing, and had been forced to abandon many longstanding customs (e.g., dances). John Swanton is probably the single most influential ethnographic observer of the Haida, and he knew the turn-of-the-century Haida quite well, but their social and material transformation complicated his construction of a mythic Haida. Rather than probe the complex contradictions of the pre-colonial and colonized Haida caricatures, Swanton simply ignored them.

Consuming Tradition? Creolization, Consumption, and Colonization

For observers like Boas, trade goods were deviations from a timeless cultural tradition irrevocably dismantled by European contact (Jonaitis 1992:47). Most European ship captains and collectors likely displayed argillite objects to evoke a distant place and exotic people, not to document colonization or cultural transformation. It would be shortsighted to argue that "tourist art" like Haida argillite is simply a contrived aesthetics with no significant link to cultural tradition or reflection of colonial inequalities. Boas' polarization of, on one hand, bounded traditional culture and, on the other hand, European society, framed material culture's meaning entirely within a dichotomy which assumed that meaning came from either authentic cultural tradition or external European socioeconomic practice. Yet traded objects routinely contained elements of indigenous symbolism and European-influenced aesthetics alike (Jules-Rosetta 1984:18-19). Equally untenable is Julius Lips' implication that trade goods simply carried cryptic native messages that were unintelligible to Europeans. For the Haida, trade goods likely were neither wholesale resistance nor covert cultural tradition; instead, they were a constant production whose stylistic shifts confronted, mediated, or evaded the material and social dynamism of colonization in the Queen Charlotte Islands.

Today Boas' search for the primordial, pre-colonial Haida seems somewhat naive. Yet approaching distinct groups as circumscribed entities–ethnic collectives, cultures, races, and so on–hazards reproducing Boas' own simplification. Like many social scientists to follow him, Boas' dilemma was a focus on an identity in isolation, rather than the relations within which subjectivity and material style are forged. Rather than focus on contrived precolonial homogeneity, the persistence of uniform traditions, a sterile vision of a uniform colonial power structure, or utter "assimilation" of indigenous peoples, an archaeology of creolization more productively would focus on indigenous material culture as an active negotiation of colonial power relations. The Haida negotiated these power relations through material forms that cannot be reduced to either high art or profane commodities, and their meanings do not mirror either revolutionary resistance or assimilation into a "European order." Haida pipes and many other indigenous material styles address colonization in various self-evident and enigmatic forms which can only be understood by examining the relationships within which their meanings were forged. Acknowledging the complexity of creolizing material symbolism and its embeddedness in power relations inevitably can illuminate the tangled sociopolitics of both colonizers and colonized peoples.

ACKNOWLEDGMENTS

Thanks to Shannon Dawdy and an anonymous referee's helpful suggestions on a late draft. Funding for this research was graciously provided by a Getty Foundation grant. Thanks to grant collaborators Rowland Abiodun, Frank Couvares, Judith Fryer, and Jacqueline Urla for their intellectual stimulation. Many museum curators helped us gain access to their holdings and listened to our ideas. These include: Susan Bean and Christina Behrmann (Peabody-Essex); Kathy Skelly (Harvard Peabody); Rob Leopold, Candace Green, and Adrienne Kepler (Museum of Natural History); Rosalyn Walker (Museum of African Art); Enid Schildkrout, Tom Miller, Robert Carneiro, Bill Weinstein, and Stanley Freed (American Museum of Natural History); Kate Ezra and Virginia Webb (Metropolitan Museum of Art); and the librarians at Smith College Art Museum. Colleagues Ralph Faulkingham, Oriol Pi-Sunyer, and Don Proulx passed on images and advice. Ivan Karp, Lynn and Larry Jones, Charles Derby, Peter Gathercole, Deborah Gewertz, Fred Errington, Bob Preucel, Chris Steiner, Helan Page, Tom Patterson, Eric Wolf, Art Keene, and Martin Wobst were among the folks who discussed key ideas in our research. Marlys Pearson read an early version of this paper and helped restructure it. Of course, we are solely responsible for the interpretations here.

REFERENCES

ACHESON, STEVEN R.
1995 In the Wake of the Iron People: A Case for Changing Settlement Strategies Among the Kunghit Haida. *Journal of the Royal Anthropological Institute,* 1(2):273-300.

BEN-AMOS, PAULA GIRSCHICK
1995 *The Art of Benin.* Smithsonian Institution Press, Washington, DC.

BEN-AMOS, PAULA GIRSCHICK, AND A. RUBIN (EDITORS)
1983 The Art of Power, the Power of Art: Studies in Benin Iconography. UCLA Museum of Cultural History, *Monograph Series,* No. 19. Los Angeles, CA.

BENJAMIN, WALTER
1969 The Storyteller: Reflections on the Works of Nikolai Leskov. In *Illuminations,* Hannah Arendt, editor, pp. 83-109. Schocken, New York, NY.

BLACKMAN, MARGARET B.
1973 Totems to Tombstones: Culture Change as Viewed through the Haida Mortuary Complex, 1877-1971. *Ethnology,* 12(1):47-56.
1990 Haida: Traditional Culture. In *Handbook of North American Indians,* Vol. 7, *Northwest Coast,* Wayne Suttles, editor, pp. 240-260. Smithsonian Institution, Washington, DC.

BOELSCHER, MARIANNE
1988 *The Curtain Within: Haida Social and Mythical Discourse.* University of British Columbia, Press, Vancouver.

BOXBERGER, DANIEL
1994 Northwest Coast Indians. In *The Native North American Almanac,* Duane Champagne, editor, pp. 285-293. Gale Research, Detroit, MI.

BURLAND, C.A.
1969 *The Exotic White Man: An Alien in Asian and African Art.* McGraw Hill, New York, NY.

CHAMPAGNE, DUANE (EDITOR)
1994 *The Native North American Almanac.* Gale Research, Detroit, MI.

CLIFFORD, JAMES
1991 Four Northwest Coast Museums: Travel Reflections. In *Exhibiting Cultures: The Poetics and Politics of Museum Display,* Ivan Karp and Steven D. Lavine, editors, pp. 212-254. Smithsonian Institution, Washington, DC.

DREW, LESLIE, AND DOUGLAS WILSON
1980 *Argillite: Art of the Haida.* Hancock House, Surrey, BC.

EWERS, JOHN C.
1979 Images of the White Man in Nineteenth-Century Plains Indian Art. In *World Anthropology,* Justin Cordwell, editor, pp. 411-430. Mouton, New York, NY.

EZRA, KATE
1992 *Royal Art of Benin: The Perls Collection in the Metropolitan Museum of Art.* Metropolitan Museum of Art, New York, NY.

FERGUSON, LELAND
1992 *Uncommon Ground: Archaeology and Early African America, 1650-1800.* Smithsonian Institution Press, Washington, DC.

FISHER, ROBIN
1977 *Contact and Conflict: Indian-European Relations in British Columbia, 1774-1890.* University of British Columbia Press, Vancouver.

FLADMARK, KNUT R., KENNETH M. AMES, AND PATRICIA SUTHERLAND
1990 Prehistory of the Northern Coast of British Columbia. In *Handbook of North American Indians,* Vol. 7, *Northwest Coast,* Wayne Suttles, editor, pp. 229-239. Smithsonian Institution, Washington, DC.

GAILEY, CHRISTINE WARD, AND THOMAS PATTERSON
1987 Power Relations and State Formation. In *Power Relations and State Formation,* Thomas Patterson and Christine Ward Gailey, editors, pp. 1-26. American Anthropological Association, Washington, DC.

GILROY, PAUL
1987 *"There Ain't No Black in the Union Jack": The Cultural Politics of Race and Nation.* University of Chicago Press, Chicago, IL.

GRUZINSKI, SERGE
1992 *Painting the Conquest: The Mexican Indians and the European Renaissance.* Flammarion, Paris, France.

HILLER, SUSAN (EDITOR)
1991 *The Myth of Primitivism: Perspectives on Art.* Routledge, New York, NY.

HOOVER, ALAN
1983 Charles Edenshaw and the Creation of Human Beings. *American Indian Art Magazine,* 8:62-67, 90.

HOWSON, JEAN E.
1990 Social Relations and Material Culture: A Critique of the Archaeology of Plantation Slavery. In Historical Archaeology on Southern Plantations and Farms, Charles E. Orser, Jr., editor, pp. 78-91. The Society for Historical Archaeology, *Special Publications Series,* No. 4. California, PA.

JONAITIS, ALDONA
  1992 Franz Boas, John Swanton, and the New Haida
        Sculpture at the American Museum of Natural History.
        In *The Early Years of Native American Art History*,
        Janet Catherine Berlo, editor, pp. 22-61. University
        of Washington, Press, Seattle.

JULES-ROSETTA, BENETTA
  1984 *The Messages of Tourist Art: An African Semiotic
        Perspective.* Plenum Press, New York, NY.

KAUFMANN, CAROLE N.
  1976 Functional Aspects of Haida Argillite Carvings. In
        *Ethnic and Tourist Arts: Cultural Expressions from
        the Fourth World*, Nelson H. H. Graburn, editors, pp.
        56-69. University of California Press, Berkeley.

KRAMER, FRITZ W.
  1993 *The Red Fez: Art and Spirit Possession in Africa.*
        Verso, New York, NY.

LIGHTFOOT, KENT G., AND ANTOINETTE MARTINEZ
  1995 Frontiers and Boundaries in Archaeological
        Perspective. *Annual Reviews of Anthropology,*
        24:471-492

LIPS, JULIUS E.
  1966 *The Savage Hits Back,* reprint of 1937 edition.
        University Books, New Hyde, NY.

MACDONALD, GEORGE F.
  1989 *Chiefs of the Sea and Sky: Haida Heritage Sites of
        the Queen Charlotte Islands.* University of British
        Columbia Press, Vancouver.

MACNAIR, PETER, AND ALAN HOOVER
  1984 *The Magic Leaves: A History of Argillite Carving.*
        Royal British Columbia Provincial Museum,
        Victoria.

MALBERT, ROGER (EDITOR)
  1991 *Exotic Europeans.* South Bank Centre, London,
        England.

MILLER, DANIEL
  1991 Primitive Art and the Necessity of Primitivism to
        Art. In *The Myth of Primitivism: Perspectives on
        Art*, Susan Hiller, editor, pp. 50-71. Routledge,
        New York, NY.
  1995 Consumption as the Vanguard of History: A Polemic
        by Way of an Introduction. In *Acknowledging
        Consumption: A Review of New Studies*, Daniel Miller,
        editor, pp. 1-57. Routledge, New York, NY.

MURDOCK, GEORGE PETER, AND TIMOTHY J. O'LEARY
  1975 *Ethnographic Bibliography of North America,* Vol.
        3, *Far West and Pacific Coast*, 4th edition. Human
        Relations Area Files Press, New Haven, CT.

ORSER, CHARLES E. JR.
  1996 *A Historical Archaeology of the Modern World.*
        Plenum, New York, NY.

PATTEN, M. DRAKE
  1992 Mankala and Minkisis: Possible Evidence of African-
        American Folk Beliefs and Practices. *African-
        American Archaeology,* 6:5-7.

PAYNTER, ROBERT, AND PAUL R. MULLINS
  1994 Spirits, Soldiers, Saints: Representations of Europeans
        by Colonized Peoples. Paper presented at American
        Anthropology Association Annual Meeting, Atlanta,
        GA.

PERRY, WARREN, AND ROBERT PAYNTER
  1998 Epilogue: Artifacts, Ethnicity and the Archaeology of
        African Americans. In *I, too, am American*, Theresa
        Singleton, editor, pp. 299-310. University of Virginia,
        Charlottesville.

SAHLINS, MARSHALL
  1992 *Anahulu: The Anthropology of History in the Kingdom
        of Hawaii*, Vol. 1, *Historical Ethnography*. University
        of Chicago, Chicago, IL.

SHEEHAN, CAROL
  1981 *Pipes That Won't Smoke; Coal That Won't Burn.*
        Glenbow Museum, Calgary, Alberta.

SINGLETON, THERESA A.
  1995 The Archaeology of Slavery in North America. *Annual
        Reviews of Anthropology,* 24:119-140.

STEARNS, MARY LEE
  1981 *Haida Culture in Custody: The Masset Band.*
        University of Washington Press, Seattle.
  1990 Haida Since 1960. In *Handbook of North American
        Indians*, Vol. 7, *Northwest Coast*, Wayne Suttles,
        editor, pp. 261-266. Smithsonian Institution,
        Washington, DC.

STEINER, CHRISTOPHER B.
  1994 *African Art in Transit.* Cambridge University Press,
        Cambridge, England.

STEWART-ABERNATHY, LESLIE C., AND BARBARA L. RUFF
  1989 A Good Man in Israel: Zooarchaeology and
        Assimilation in Antebellum Washington, Arkansas.
        Historical Archaeology, 23(2):96-112.

SWANTON, JOHN R.
  1905 Contributions to the Ethnology of the Haida. *Memoir
        of the American Museum of Natural History* 5(1).
        New York, NY.

VAN DEN BRINK, J. H.
  1974 *The Haida Indians: Cultural Change Between
        1876-1970.* E. J. Brill, Leiden, Netherlands.

VAUGHAN, THOMAS
  1982 *Soft Gold: The Fur Trade and Cultural Exchange on
        the Northwest Coast of America.* Oregon Historical
        Society, Portland.

WILKIE, LAURIE A.
1997 Secret and Sacred: Contextualizing the Artifacts of African-American Magic and Religion. *Historical Archaeology,* 31(4):81-106.

WOLF, ERIC
1982 *Europe and the People without History.* University of California Press, Berkeley.

WRIGHT, ROBIN K.
1982 Haida Argillite: Carved for Sale. *American Indian Art Journal,* 8(1):48-55.
1985 *Nineteenth Century Haida Argillite Pipe Carvers: Stylistic Attributions.* Ph.D. dissertation, University of Washington, Seattle, WA. University Microfilms International, Ann Arbor, MI.

WYATT, VICTORIA
1984 *Shapes of Their Thoughts: Reflections of Culture Contact in Northwest Coast Indian Art.* University of Oklahoma Press, Norman.

PAUL R. MULLINS
DEPARTMENT OF ANTHROPOLOGY
INDIANA UNIVERSITY-PURDUE UNIVERSITY INDIANAPOLIS
413 CAVANAUGH HALL
INDIANAPOLIS, IN 46202

ROBERT PAYNTER
DEPARTMENT OF ANTHROPOLOGY
UNIVERSITY OF MASSACHUSETTS
AMHERST, MA 01003

Perspectives from *Historical Archaeology:*

Kent G. Lightfoot

Russian Colonization: The Implications of Mercantile Colonial Practices in the North Pacific

ABSTRACT

The maritime fur trade propelled Russian expansion into the North Pacific in the 18th and 19th centuries. The mercantile legacy of Russian colonization is evident in the rapid founding of settlements across an immense region, the corporate hierarchy of the colonial administration, and the policies and practices for the treatment of indigenous peoples. Russian fur merchants transported to North America colonial practices that originated in Siberia. In contrast to American and British merchants on the Northwest Coast who relied on commodity exchange with autonomous native hunters for furs, Russians forced native hunters to work directly for their companies, initially by military force and the taking of hostages to insure tribute payments and later by mandatory conscription. While relatively few Europeans immigrated to

Russian America, colonial administrators relocated scores of native and "mixed blood" workers to new colonies. What emerged was a different twist to the colonial encounters that unfolded among indigenous populations and "colonists." Rather than confronting successive waves of European immigrants, local peoples interacted primarily with other natives from homelands dispersed across the North Pacific. Historical archaeology has much to contribute to understanding the long-term impacts of "native-to-native" interactions in pluralistic colonial communities.

Introduction

Russian exploration and settlement in the North Pacific was driven primarily by the commercial incentives of the maritime fur trade, specifically the intensive harvesting of sea otters and, to a lesser extent, fur seals. A network of Russian colonies extended eastward from Siberia, including outposts on Kamchatka and the Kurile Islands, into what would become known as "Russian America," a vast region extending across the Aleutian, Kodiak, and Pribilof archipelagos, southern Alaska, northern California, and even Hawaii (Figure 1). While the Tsarist government

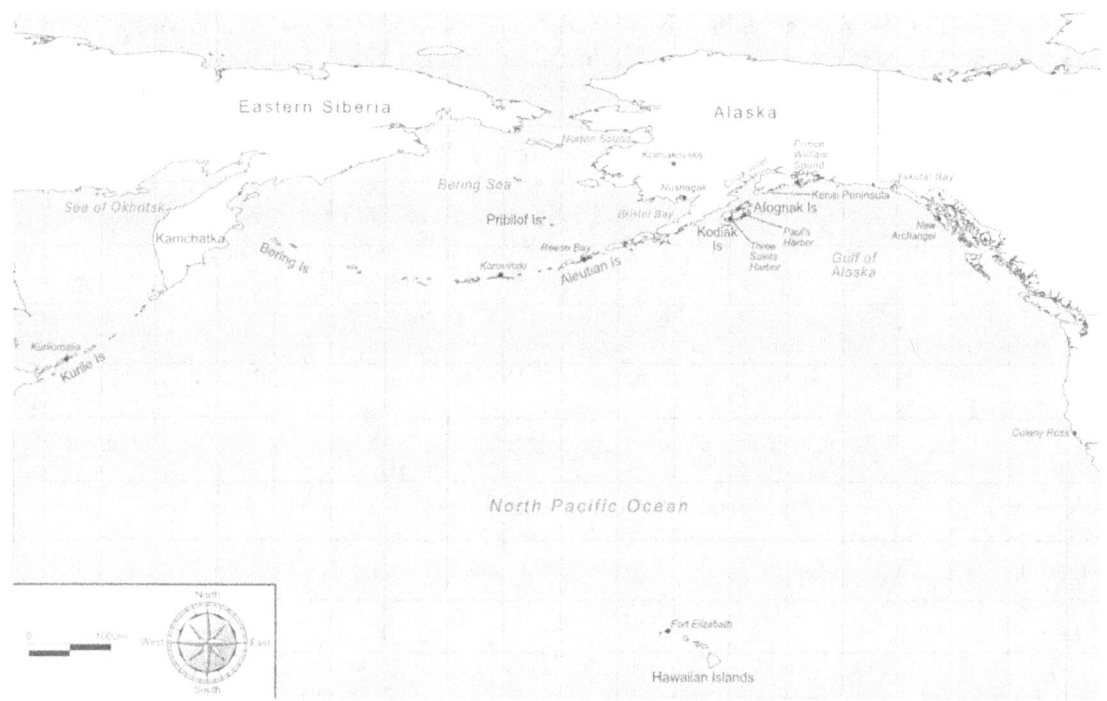

FIGURE 1. Eastern Siberia and Russian America, showing selected place names and archaeological sites. (Map by Lisa Holm.)

was concerned with the North Pacific for geopolitical reasons and the Russian Orthodox Church founded missions among native populations, Russian presence in North America focused on the exploitation of commercially viable resources. The mercantile roots of Russian colonization had long-term implications for how the colonies were administered, who controlled access to economic resources, how the colonial hierarchy was organized, and ultimately how native peoples were treated.

In presenting a brief overview on Russian colonization in North America, the early history of Russian movement into the North Pacific and the formation of the Russian-American Company are outlined. Three salient characteristics of the Russian colonial program are discussed: its extensive scale, its administration by a corporate hierarchy, and its reliance on native hunters in order to compete in the maritime fur trade. The resettlement of scores of native and "mixed blood" workers into Russian colonies had significant consequences for the composition of multiethnic communities and the kinds of colonial encounters that took place with indigenous communities. The study of these "native-to-native" encounters in Russian settlements is crucial for understanding how social processes unfolded in these pluralistic colonial contexts and how native identities were both transformed and perpetuated in the North Pacific.

Maritime Fur Trade

Peter the Great initiated the early exploration of the cold and mysterious waters of the North Pacific by drafting orders for the first official reconnaissance east of Siberia shortly before his death. In 1728, Vitus Bering, a Dane serving in the Imperial Russian Navy, directed the small coastal ship, *St. Gabriel*, on its voyage of discovery to determine whether Siberia was connected to the American coastline (north of the Kamchatka coast) and to report on any signs of European settlements (Fisher 1990:17–19; Smith 2000:9). While the first voyage failed to "discover" America, it led to another, more elaborate program of exploration known as the Second Kamchatka Expedition. The celebrated Pacific crossing of Vitus Bering and Alexeii Chirikov in 1741–1742, on board the *St. Peter* and *St. Paul* not only made landfalls along the northern

and southern ends of the Alaskan panhandle but also stops at Shumagin Islands and several of the Aleutian Islands (Fisher 1990:25–28). Bering and his crew also wintered on what would be known as Bering Island, where many of the men, including the captain, died from scurvy.

The Bering and Chirikov voyage of 1741–1742 brought back to Russia eyewitness accounts of rich waters and verdant lands teaming with fur-bearing mammals—stories that were backed up with the procurement of 900 pelts of sea otter, fur seal, and blue Arctic fox during the winter encampment on Bering Island (Fisher 1990:28). The resulting "fur rush" to the North Pacific was precipitated by Russian traders who knew that Chinese merchants would pay very dearly for sea otter pelts. The dense, luxuriant fur served as a distinctive trim for the clothes of the Manchu upper class and produced exceptionally soft, warm, and attractive robes for any Asian or European elite experiencing a cold winter. Sea otter, the royal fur of the Middle Kingdom in China, opened the door to the hugely profitable but closely guarded traffic of Asian goods (Gibson 1987:34–35). The Tsarist government initiated treaties with the Chinese to grant Russian commercial houses the privilege of trading their pelts at Kiakhta (or Kyakhta) on the Russian-Mongolian border south of Lake Baikal and Tsurukhaitui (Gibson 1992a:12–18). Here pelts were exchanged for tea, spices, silk, nankeen, porcelain, sugar candy, and other goods that were then readied for export to European and American consumers (Tikhmenev 1978:162). In addition to the lucrative sea otter trade, there was also a strong market in Europe and Asia for fur seal pelts (Fedorova 1973:188).

Beginning in 1743, a plethora of Russian fur companies competed with one another in the extensive exploitation of fur-bearing mammals from North Pacific waters. Financed by Russian investors and merchants, these companies typically existed for only a single voyage, with the sea otter and fur seal catch being divided by shares among the financiers, captain, crew, and Russian fur trade workers or *promyshlenniki* (Fisher 1990:28–30). During the first 12 years (1743–1755), about 22 companies harvested sea mammals off the coast of Kamchatka to the Near Aleutian Islands (Fedorova 1973:104–105). As sea otter populations near the Siberian coast were exterminated, fur traders were forced to voyage ever farther eastward. Between 1756 to 1780, 48 fur hunting expeditions took place along the Aleutian Islands, Kodiak Island, and the Alaskan Peninsula and contacts were made with local Unangan (Aleut) and Alutiiq-speaking peoples (Fedorova 1973:105).

By 1780, many of the smaller companies had become obsolete as the fur trade voyages became more capital intensive, involving bigger ships, more extensive provisions, larger crews, and bases for wintering workers. Among the earliest Russian settlements in Alaskan waters were Illiuliuk and Eguchshak, established on Unalaska Island in 1772–1775 (Senkevitch 1987:149–153). But it was not until two of the most successful merchants, Grigorii Shelikhov and Ivan Golikov, merged their holdings that formal plans could be implemented for establishing permanent, self-sustaining settlements in Russian America (Fedorova 1973:15, 106; Fisher 1990:30). Beginning with the founding of Three Saints Harbor on Kodiak Island in 1784, these settlements served as bases on Pacific islands and the Alaskan coastline for harvesting fur pelts. The consolidation of fur trade companies continued with the creation of the Russian-American Company in 1799. In granting the company its first charter, Tsar Paul I conferred upon this commercial venture an exclusive Russian monopoly over the exploitation of resources in North America, as well as the rights to be the sole Russian agency for founding and administrating colonies in the Americas.

The Russian-American Company

Russian colonization in the Americas was directed and administered by the Russian-American Company from 1799 to 1867, at which time Alaska was purchased by the United States. The company was modeled after other commercial monopolies of the day (e.g., Hudson's Bay Company, East India Company), as it was run as a quasi-private mercantile corporation financed primarily by private capital from stockholders. However, the company was closely monitored by the Tsar and various departments of the Russian Imperial government, and the Tsar's family owned stock in the fur trade conglomerate (Fedorova 1973:130–134; Gibson 1976:10; Tikhmenev 1978:56).

Some scholars stress that the Russian-American Company served as a "de facto agency of the Imperial Russian government" in North America (Dmytryshyn et al. 1989:li). Nonetheless, the company was a mercantile venture that had to answer to stockholders and produce dividends. Profits had to be generated in order to operate its fur trade enterprise, and it appears that the Tsarist government subsidized very little of the commercial activities of the company. Following the Bering expeditions, the Russian government did send naval ships to the North Pacific to explore and map the region, to make scientific observations, as well as to raise the imperial flag. Catherine II dispatched voyages in 1768–1769 (Krenitsyn-Levashov voyage) and 1785–1792 (the renowned Billings-Sarychev expedition). In 1803 the government initiated the first of 40 round-the-world voyages from Kronstadt, its navy base on the Baltic (Wheeler 1987:49–50; Fisher 1990:30–31; Smith 2000). In their circumnavigation, Russian naval vessels probed much of the North Pacific, visited Russian-American Company settlements, explored uncharted coastlines, and kept a watchful eye on foreign intruders. However, the Russian-American Company had to pay high prices for any freight transported to its colonies, and it reimbursed the government for most of the salaries of military personnel stationed in Russian America (Fedorova 1973:157–158; Gibson 1976:87).

The commercial underpinnings of the company become clear when one considers three salient characteristics of the Russian colonial program: its extensive scale, its corporate hierarchy, and its treatment of native workers.

Extensive Scale

Compared to the French, British, and Spanish colonial programs in the Americas, the Russians are often portrayed as a rather marginal colonial enterprise. The former superintendent of the Sitka National Historical Park estimates that up to 90% of United States citizens are unaware of Russian colonial efforts in North America (Suazo et al. 1990:454; see also Smith and Barnett 1990: 9). While working at the Fort Ross State Historic Park in northern California, it was noted that most Californians are pretty well versed about nearby Franciscan missions, Spanish *presidios*, and Mexican *ranchos*, but they know very little about Russia's settlements outside Alaska, even those in their own backyard. It is apropos that the organizers of a recent museum exhibition and publication on Russian colonization entitled their project "Russian America: The Forgotten Frontier" (Smith and Barnett 1990).

The relative obscurity of the Russian enterprise makes little sense when one considers that the commercial empire of the Russian-American Company spanned the entire North Pacific (Figure 1). More than 60 Russian settlements were founded in a vast region from the Kurile Islands, the Aleutian and Kodiak archipelagos, coastal and interior Alaska, as well as northern California and Hawaii (Fedorova 1973:272; Mills 2002). While geopolitical aspirations of the Russian Imperial government most certainly played a role in this expansionary colonial program, it was the profit-making motive of commercial enterprise that drove it. The overhunting of sea otter and fur seal populations continually forced the Russians to search for untapped marine habitats where fur-bearing sea mammals could still be harvested. Company administrators also advocated the exploration of new regions that might contain commercially viable resources, such as minerals, timber, fish, and terrestrial fur mammals.

The Russian-American Company's expansion into southeastern Alaska and northern California in the early 1800s followed the overexploitation of sea otters in the Aleutian and Kodiak archipelagos, the Alaskan Peninsula, and Prince William Sound and the need to build new posts where sea mammal hunting could still be undertaken. When Colony Ross was founded in northern California in 1812, it not only served as a base for hunting sea otters but also as a settlement where agricultural and mercantile production could take place (Farris 1989; Lightfoot et al. 1991). The aborted attempt to establish Fort Elisabeth and two smaller forts on Kaua'i Island, Hawaii, in 1816–1817 was entwined with both geopolitical aspirations and commercial incentives (Pierce 1965; Mills 2002). The company recognized Hawaii's potential for producing sandalwood, sugarcane, and food crops as well as serving as a convenient mid-Pacific stop between Kamchatka and Russian American colonies (Barratt 1990). After about 1818, when yields of sea otter and fur seal decreased markedly along coastal Alaska and northern California due to overharvesting, the managers of the Russian-American Company turned their attention to the northern latitudes, "into the heart of Alaska" (Fedorova 1973:107). Small trade outposts, *redoubts*, were established at the mouths and along the interior drainages of the Copper, Nushagak, Kuskokwim, and Kvikhpak (Yukon) rivers as well as on Bristol Bay and Norton Sound. These served as trading posts for procuring beaver, river otters, fox, marten, bear, lynx, and walrus tusks as well as bases to explore the interior for minerals and other resources (VanStone 1972; Oswalt 1980; Arndt 1990; Dumond and VanStone 1995).

Archaeological research provides an excellent window for viewing the extensive scale and diversity of Russian America. Outside of a few vodka-drinking circles, it is a little-known fact that archaeological studies of Russian settlements and associated native villages span the entire North Pacific and that a sizeable corpus of information exists for undertaking comparative work on the Russian colonial program through time and space. Archaeological investigations along the northern Pacific Rim include the Kurile Islands, with emphasis on the Kurilorossiia outpost on Urup Island (Shubin 1990, 1994); Atka Island, where field work focused on Korovinski, an important company base in the central Aleutian Islands (Veltre 1979, 2001); Reese Bay, Unalaska Island (Veltre and McCartney 2001a); Kodiak Island, including Three Saints Harbor (Clark 1985; Crowell 1997a), St. Paul's Harbor (the first administrative center of the company in Russian America) (Dilliplane 1990a:138–139; Smith and Peterson 1990) and Nunakakhnak village (Knecht and Jordan 1985); Afognak Island (Woodhouse-Beyer 2001); and the Sitka region, location of St. Archangel Michael (Old Sitka) and New Archangel (the second administrative center) (Blee 1985, 1990; Dilliplane 1990b; Suazo et al. 1990; Petruzelli and Hanson 1998; Thompson 1999; Grover 2000). In addition, a comprehensive archaeological investigation of Russian-period settlements on the Pribilof Islands (focusing on St. Paul Island) was initiated in 2000 by Douglas Veltre and Allen McCartney (2000, 2001b).

A significant program of survey and excavation has focused on interior Alaskan trade posts (e.g., Nushagak [Aleksandrovskiy Redoubt], Kolmakovskiy Redoubt) and nearby native villages (e.g., Paugvik, Akulivikchuk, Tikchik, and Crow Village) along the Copper, Nushagak,

Kuskokwim, and Naknek rivers (VanStone 1955, 1968, 1970a, b, 1972; Oswalt and VanStone 1967; Oswalt 1980; Dumond 1981; Dumond and VanStone 1995). Considerable archaeological research has also been undertaken at Colony Ross in northern California, including studies of the Ross settlement, adjacent residential neighborhoods of the multiethnic workers, nearby native communities, the Ross cemetery, outlying ranches, and the Russian hunting camp or *artel* on the Farallon Islands (Treganza 1954; Riddell 1955; Farris 1989, 1990, 1993, 1997; Lightfoot et al. 1991, 1997; Goldstein 1992, 1995; Osborn 1992, 1997; Wake 1995, 1997a, b; Parkman 1996/1997; Allan 1997, 2001; Ballard 1997; Martinez 1997, 1998; Selverston 1999; Parrish et al. 2000). Finally, recent survey and excavation work has been directed at the study of Fort Elisabeth on Kaua'i Island, Hawaii (Mills 1997, 2002).

Corporate Hierarchy

A rather unique characteristic of Russian colonization was the administration of the far-flung colonies by a corporate hierarchy. The Russian-American Company was directed by a four-member board of directors, elected by the stockholders who worked out of the main administration offices in St. Petersburg, Russia. The directors were responsible for maintaining capital assets, for increasing profit margins, and for developing economic strategies for fur hunting and world trade (Dmytryshyn et al. 1989:xxxvii). The directors reported directly to the Tsar and various governmental department heads on critical issues concerning the company and Russian American colonies. The company's operations in Russian America were directed by the chief manager (or chief administrator) who served in the capacity of governor for the Russian American colonies. His duties involved managing the different administrative *counters* or districts, enforcing Russian laws, negotiating with foreign traders, entertaining important visitors, and hiring much of the workforce (Dmytryshyn et al. 1989: xxxviii–xl). The chief manager reported directly to the board of directors, and he was headquartered in the commercial and administrative capital of Russian America, which moved from St. Paul's Harbor, Kodiak Island, to New Archangel in Sitka, Alaska, in 1804. The first chief manager was Aleksandr Baranov, a pragmatic and seasoned merchant with many years of service in commercial initiatives in Siberia and the North Pacific. However, after Baranov's retirement in 1818, government officials and military officers became more influential in the administration of the company, and future chief managers were selected from among senior Russian Imperial Navy officers.

The corporate hierarchy below the chief manager included the individual managers of the Russian colonies. The immense colonial territory was divided into seven separate counters, which included (1) Kurile (Kurile Islands), (2) Atkhinsk (the Western Aleutian, Near, and Komandorskie islands), (3) Unalaska (the eastern Aleutian and Pribilof islands), (4) Kodiak (Kodiak archipelago and Alaskan Peninsula), (5) Sitka (Northwest Pacific Coast), (6) Mikhailovsk Redoubt (Norton Sound area), and (7) Ross (Dmytryshyn et al. 1989:xl). The chief manager appointed a manager for each of the seven counters, as well as other key personnel who reported directly to his office in New Archangel.

As Glenn Farris (1997:190) notes, administrative centers for the counters such as the Ross settlement and other sizeable Russian settlements retained the character of company towns. They consisted of the residences of the elite managers and other staff members, Russian Orthodox churches and chapels, as well as impressive buildings that served as company stores and storage space for pelts. Nearby were industrial sectors where assorted equipment and trade goods were manufactured and repaired. Here were found forges, metal shops, carpenter shops, cooperages, and even shipyards (in a few colonies). Outside the administrative and mercantile centers or cores were the residences of the pluralistic workforce that typically was located in outlying neighborhoods or villages.

Historical archaeology has contributed much to understanding of the spatial structure of these colonial communities. Some studies have focused on the industrial/mercantile spaces, including the brick kilns on Kodiak Island and Sitka Island (Dilliplane 1990a, b), the shipyard and ancillary shops that comprised the industrial sector at Colony Ross (Allan 2001), and the black smithy and forges associated with the Kurilorossiia settlement on Urup Island (Shubin 1990: 433). Recent excavations (1995, 1997, 1998) at Castle Hill in Sitka unearthed the foundations of at least four structures, a metal workers' smithy (kiln), a profusion of copper slag and waste, iron bar stock, associated metal-working tools as well as textiles, ceramics, faunal remains, and other artifacts. While the archaeological materials are still being analyzed, this project promises many new insights on the industrial sector of New Archangel and the daily lifeways of Russian, Creole, and native workers in Russian America (see Petruzelli and Hanson 1998; Thompson 1999; Grover 2000). These archaeological investigations stress how craftspeople in Russian colonies came up with innovative solutions to technological problems on the distant frontier. For example, James Allan describes the resourceful solution for constructing a steaming oven for shaping wood in the construction of ships at Colony Ross (Allan 2001).

Other archaeological projects have examined the spatial organization of colonial communities where the ethnically heterogeneous workforce of Russians, Creoles, and native laborers resided. The corporate ethos of the company was evident in the colonial hierarchy that defined the status, work, pay, and residential arrangement of all its employees. While several factors were employed in defining an employee's position in the company (e.g., level of education, job skills, and overall motivation), ethnicity was the primary variable employed for defining three major "estates" or classes: (1) Russians, (2) Creoles, (3) Indigenous Peoples (Wrangell 1969: 210–211; Fedorova 1975:11–15; Khlebnikov 1990:188–194).

Russian workers were divided into three groups (Fedorova 1975:15). At the apex of the hierarchy were the "honorable ones" who served as company administrators and military officers. "Semi-honorable ones" (men of lower rank) comprised the next step as clerks, soldiers, navigators, and laborers. The third group, "colonial citizens," was made up of Russian laborers who remained in Russian America after they retired from service in the company. Creoles, the offspring produced from Russian men and native women, were classified as a separate estate. They were typically not accepted by either the Russian or Native-American communities (Fedorova 1975: 13–14). Some Creole men were educated at the expense of the Russian-American Company, and they often served in important positions as officers on company ships and as middle-level managers, clerks, and skilled craftsmen (Black 1990; Spencer Pritchard 1991:43).

Archaeological research on the lifeways and daily practices of the Russian and Creole estates focuses on the investigation of the managers' houses and honorable and semi-honorable residential zones in company towns. Aron Crowell's investigation of Shelikhov's Log House at Three Saints Harbor provides insights on the material trappings and foodways of elite Russians in this early trade outpost founded on Kodiak Island in 1784 (Crowell 1997a:108–127, 1997b). He also excavated a *promyshlennik* barracks or *barabara*, where Russian workers probably lived, which consisted of a three-roomed semisubterranean dwelling built of driftwood poles and probably thatched with grass. The integration of European material culture with native architectural features and artifacts indicates the workers adopted many indigenous practices and/or that local native peoples, most likely Qikertarmiut women, worked in or occupied the barrack structure (Crowell 1997a: 127–152). Valery Shubin's excavations at Kurilorossiia in the Kurile Islands unearthed the well-preserved remains of a tripartite log structure (with a house-foreroom-storage room floor plan), probably postdating 1827. Shubin notes that this type of architectural structure was commonly built in contemporaneous Russian Siberian villages (Shubin 1990:431–432). Detailed observations have also been made of the architectural structures associated with the managers' houses, fur warehouse, and palisade walls associated with the elite stockade compound at the Ross settlement, built between 1812 and 1841 (Treganza 1954; Farris 1989, 1990).

Other work has focused on the elite architecture of New Archangel, where archaeologists and other specialists have been involved in the restoration of the Bishop's House (built 1841–1843) and testing archaeological deposits (ca. 1860) associated with the Russian hospital (Blee 1985, 1990; Suazo et al. 1990). Veltre provides information on the spatial layout of the Russian administrative center of Korovinski on Atka Island (ca. 1820s and later), including sod-walled enclosures, the area of the church and Russian Orthodox cemetery, garden plots, and boat slips (Veltre 1979, 2001). Wendell Oswalt details the spatial arrangement, architectural foundations, and associated artifacts of the interior Alaskan redoubt of Kolmakovskiy on the

Kuskokwim River, including various buildings constructed between 1841 and 1866: the block-house, store, Creole barracks, priest's house, and prayer house as well as the "Eskimo barracks" and *kashim* (native men's house) (Oswalt 1980). Peter Mills describes recent mapping and excavations of the impressive star-shaped fort at Fort Elisabeth, Hawaii, built out of basalt stones with the help of Kaumuali'i, a high-ranking Hawaiian chief in 1816–1817. This settlement differs in layout, building material, and organization from anything found in the rest of Russian America (Mills 2002).

Russian Treatment of Native Peoples

A third characteristic of the Russian colonial program is the company's treatment of the third estate or indigenous peoples. The explicit commercial agenda of Russian colonization permeated the policies and practices of its colonists and very much structured their encounters with local populations. However, colonial interactions with native peoples were not always tied to mercantile pursuits. Similar to other colonial programs in the Americas, missionaries worked with native peoples in Russian America. The Russian-American Company was required to support the missionary efforts of the Russian Orthodox Church (Osborn 1997:5–6). But it is important to note that the company's commercial policies often clashed with the objectives of the priests, especially during the early years of the fur trade (Kan 1988:507; Dmytryshyn et al. 1989:xli–xlii; Gibson 1992b:20). In reality, there were very few Russian Orthodox priests in Russian America until the middle of the 19th century (Rathburn 1981:12). For example, in 1816 there was only a single priest serving the entire Russian American territory, and by 1825 the number had only increased to five (Gibson 1992b:20). Some Russian colonies never had a permanent priest assigned to them. Until 1840, the intensity of missionary activities among native peoples and the establishment of schools varied greatly across Russian America. Some Unangan, Alutiiq, and Tlingit peoples received considerable attention from missionaries, while others were largely ignored (Rathburn 1981:13–15; Kan 1988:506–509; Veltre 1990:180–182; Black 2001). The Russian Orthodox Church expanded its missionary enterprise greatly in 1840 when the energetic Ivan Veniaminov was appointed to the rank of Bishop of Alaska, and the number of clergy, missions, and native schools increased significantly across Russian America (Kan 1988; Dmytryshyn et al. 1989:xlii).

The Russian-American Company, especially for the years prior to 1840, paid mostly lip service to saving native souls. Its primary interest in local natives was their exploitation as cheap laborers. The company depended on Creole and native peoples as the economic lifeblood of its colonies. There were two primary reasons for this.

First, the company experienced difficulties recruiting ethnic Russians to populate its colonies. Company recruiters were said to be among the loneliest people in all of Russia. Few ethnic Russians signed up to work in Russian America, no doubt put off by the harsh and often dangerous conditions in the colonies, the mediocre pay, and the isolated nature of the frontier. As was true for other European colonies in the Americas, Russian-American Company settlements were isolated from Mother Russia by tremendous distances and treacherous waters.

The Russians enticed to work for the company were primarily single men or married men who left their families at home (Fedorova 1975:11). Svetlana Fedorova (1973:150–151) estimates that from the period 1799 to 1867, there were only between 225 and 823 Russians (a mean of about 550) in all of Russian America. Thus, unlike some other European colonial programs, Russian colonization did not involve the massive emigration of European families to American soil (Farris 1997:188, 191). Rather, those Europeans who populated Russian settlements were primarily company employees who typically did not put down roots for long (Fedorova 1973:154). The company tended to rotate employees from one colony to another across the North Pacific, depending upon ever changing managerial and labor demands in the different counters. More importantly, unless they were in debt to the company, the *promyshlenniks* and managers typically left Russian America at the end of their five- to seven-year contracts. Thus, a constant turnover took place in the European labor force in Russian colonies (Gibson 1976:48–50, 108).

The second reason the Russian managers depended on non-Europeans as their primary workforce was the particular mode of mercantile practices the company employed in the North Pacific. Most fur trade companies were dependent on native producers to provide them with pelts. British and American merchants, who competed with the Russians for furs in the North Pacific, instituted what is known as the "commodity peonage" system. Using their ships as floating emporiums, the merchants enticed native hunters to exchange their furs for manufactured goods, such as cloth, metal hatchets, glass beads, blankets, and knives. Russian merchants employed a different method for extracting furs from native peoples. Based on their experiences in the earlier Siberian fur trade, the Russians brought to North America the practice of subjugating native peoples and forcing them to pay a tax or tribute (*iasak*) in furs (see discussions of the North Pacific fur trade in Wolf 1982: 182–194; Gibson 1988; Crowell 1997a:7, 10–16, 233, 1997b:14–15, 2002).

The early exploitation of sea otters on the Aleutian Islands and Kodiak Island involved using military force against native communities and taking women and children hostages to insure that local native leaders paid their *iasak* (Veltre 1979:64–67; Crowell 1997a:11–16, 40–53; Crowell and Lührmann 2001). Catherine II banned this form of tribute taking in 1788, but it was replaced by the mandatory conscription of native peoples to hunt for Russian companies. When the Russian-American Company was granted its imperial monopoly in 1799, it continued the practice of drafting men between the ages of 18 and 50 from the Aleutian Islands and Kodiak Island for three years of service (Fedorova 1975:16). Native hunters conscripted by the Russians were among the most sophisticated and effective sea otter hunters in the world. Trained from childhood to become skilled hunters, they employed lightweight *baidarkas* (skin kayaks) to pursue sea otters in kelp beds and along shallow, rocky intertidal waters. Using lethal barbed-bone projectile points attached to darts, which were fired with great accuracy from bows or throwing sticks, thousands of sea otters and other commercially valued sea mammals were systematically harvested in coastal Pacific waters (Ogden 1941:11–14).

The mandatory service of Native-Alaskan hunters was critical to the success of the Russian-American Company. Russian merchants could not compete directly with American and British

traders by exchanging manufactured goods for pelts harvested by independent native hunters. True, some goods were produced in the industrial sectors of company administrative centers. But most manufactured goods had to be imported into the colonies. It was actually cheaper and more efficient for the Russian-American Company to obtain merchandise from British and American merchants, the company's major competitors in the North Pacific fur trade (Gibson 1976: 83–87, 172–174). From the founding of the Russian-American Company until 1840, many of the manufactured goods imported into company settlements were acquired from American merchants. In the late 1830s an agreement was reached with the Hudson's Bay Company, which began to supply food and merchandise to the Russian colonies. Therefore, in undertaking archaeological work on company settlements, it can be rather perplexing to find little evidence of diagnostic Russian material culture per se (Van-Stone 1972:81; Farris 1989:492). One discovers that much of the assemblage of manufactured goods, such as glass and ceramic vessels, originated from the United States, Britain, or Asia. Nonetheless, archaeological research indicates the percentage of Russian imports did vary among the colonies. For example, recent work at Castle Hill in New Archangel discovered a relatively large quantity (10.7% of the ceramic assemblage) of Russian lead-glaze earthenware, which is fairly rare in excavations at other Russian settlements (Thompson 1999).

The company classified native peoples into different colonial categories, which had significant implications for how they were treated, the kinds of jobs they performed, and how they were compensated. Sea mammal hunters from the Aleutian Islands and Kodiak Island were classified as "Islanders" (also referred to as "Settled Aliens" or "Dependents") along with native peoples from the Kurile Islands and the Kenai Peninsula of Alaska (Fedorova 1975:15–16; Dmytryshyn et al. 1989:xliii). In addition to commercial hunting, they also served the company as porters, fishermen, and skilled craftsmen. While they were obligated to work for the company, they were paid for their labors. The Islanders worked on commission (paid per sea otter pelt) or received daily or yearly salaries in scrip, a parchment token that could be exchanged for goods in company stores (Tikhmenev 1978:144).

Other natives employed by the company were defined as "Semi-Dependent" peoples (Fedorova 1975:17). At the Ross counter in northern California, the local Pomo- and Miwok-speaking communities fell into this category. Identified as "Indians," they were recruited to serve as general laborers and seasonal agricultural workers. They were paid through barter or in-kind for their services, usually receiving food, tobacco, beads, and clothing (Wrangell 1969:211; Khlebnikov 1990: 193–194).

In describing the colonial hierarchy and treatment of native workers, it is emphasized that the boundaries between the different colonial estates and native categories were not rigid or impermeable. In reality, the imposed colonial estates were composites of diverse groups of people who often hailed from different homelands, spoke diverse languages, and maintained distinctive ideologies and worldviews. Since these broad ethnic categories existed primarily in the minds of company managers, the cultural practices associated with each of the different estates in the colonial hierarchy were somewhat ambiguous. Latitude certainly existed for the creation of "invented traditions" in these colonial contexts (Upton 1996:5). In order to be recognized as a member of the Russian, Creole, Islander, or Indian categories, "it was imperative that you 'talk the talk' and 'walk the walk' in the eyes of the Ross managers" (Lightfoot et al. 1998:205).

Sannie Osborn (1997:172) makes this point in describing how native peoples could be reclassified as Creole, and Creole workers as Russian.

> In practice, not all persons designated as Creoles were of mixed ancestry. Some individuals of entirely native descent were designated as Creole because of their occupations or positions within the Company hierarchy. After 1821, Native Alaskans who became naturalized citizens by pledging allegiance to the tsar could be also considered Creoles (Oleksa 1990:185). And, others who were Creole by definition, were listed as Russian on the basis of the social position of their father (Black 1990: 152). Perhaps more importantly, being a Creole was "more a matter of the spirit, a state of mind, a question of self-identity" (Oleksa 1990:185).

Furthermore, it was very common for sexual unions to take place between men and women of different estates. The general policy of the upper administration of the Russian-American Company was to support interethnic unions between company employees and local native peoples so as to increase the population of Creole people who would eventually enter the service of the company (Fedorova 1973: 206–207, 1975:11–13). In some Russian counters, such as Colony Ross in California, the most common households containing two or more people were interethnic households of men and women from different ethnic estates (see the Kuskov [1820–1821] and Veniaminov [1836, 1838] censuses published in Istomin 1992; Osborn 1997). At Colony Ross "Indian" women were a significant component of the interethnic households involving Islander, Creole, and Russian men, although their participation in pluralistic residences decreased substantially by the 1830s. By this time an increasing number of the households were comprised of Creole and Native-Alaskan women.

Historical archaeology is examining the long-term impacts that Russian colonization had on local native peoples. There is a long tradition of undertaking holistic, diachronic studies of Pacific peoples caught within the Russian colonial world, with researchers employing multiple data sources drawn from archaeology, ethnography, native narratives, and historical texts to examine the dynamics of native cultures that transcend prehistory and history. Frederica De Laguna pioneered this approach in her 1949–1954 study of northern Tlingit peoples in Angoon and Yakutat Bay, southeastern Alaska. Her research team's collaborative work with local Tlingit communities generated "ancient" and recent histories of the regions as well as rich descriptions of Tlingit material culture derived from native informants, European sources, and archaeological findings (Laguna 1960; Laguna et al. 1964). Beginning in the late 1950s and 1960s, James VanStone, Wendell Oswalt, Don Dumond, and others maintained a focus on long-term native cultural dynamics by examining changes in subsistence, settlement patterns, house types, and artifacts in the late-prehistoric, Russian, and American periods, even though stratigraphic separation of the latter two proved difficult in some sites (Oswalt and VanStone 1967; VanStone 1968, 1970b; Oswalt 1980; Dumond and VanStone 1995). This tradition of emphasizing the *longue durée* in Russian America as well as working closely with local tribes and native organizations in community partnerships has continued with field work on Atka Island (Veltre 1979); Unalaska Island (Veltre and McCartney 2001a); Pribilof Islands (Veltre and McCartney 2000, 2001b); Kodiak Island (Knecht and Jordan 1985; Crowell 1997a); Afognak Island (Woodhouse-Beyer 2001); the outer Kenai Peninsula (Crowell and Mann 1998); Kaua'i Island, Hawaii (Mills 2002); and Colony Ross, California (Lightfoot et al. 1991, 1998; Lightfoot 1995; Wake 1995, 1997a; Martinez 1997, 1998; Parrish et al. 2000).

In tracing indigenous life ways from late prehistory to post-Russian times, the above studies are attempting to evaluate the degree to which native foodways, artifacts, architectural forms, sociopolitical relations, and ideological constructs underwent change or persistence and how native identities were constructed and transformed over time. One of the most significant characteristics of Russian colonialism stems from the fact that the Russian-American Company would deploy an international, multiethnic workforce to any of its coastal colonies. Here we get a different twist on the traditional perspective of European immigration to the Americas. Rather than Europeans carving out new lives in frontier settlements, the Russian colonial system involved the relocation of scores of native and Creole workers to distant settlements across the North Pacific. The "core" population of most of the coastal counters involved in the maritime fur trade were the indispensable Islander sea mammal hunters—primarily Unangan (or Aleut) people from the Aleutian Islands, Alutiiq people from Kodiak Island, as well as Chugach hunters from Prince William Sound. They were dispatched in large numbers throughout coastal Russian America, from the Kurile Islands to Sitka, and Hawaii to northern California. In most cases, the transplanted Islander and Creole workers were relocated to populated areas where they encountered local peoples, although they did colonize some uninhabited places, such as the Pribilof Islands (Veltre 1990:177).

The interior redoubts established along Alaskan rivers after 1818 were organized differently. They maintained small resident populations of native, Creole, and Russian traders who bartered with indigenous hunters for land mammal pelts of beaver, river otter, fox, and other species (Arndt 1990). Some interior hunting and trapping was done by groups of company hunters (Creoles and Islanders), especially after the outbreak of smallpox among local native populations (Oswalt 1980:79–84; Dumond and VanStone 1995:99). However, the majority of the terrestrial furs were obtained by trading tobacco, glass beads, textiles, copper, and iron utensils with local native populations (Dumond and VanStone 1995:7–8). Archaeological work at redoubts and nearby native villages indicates that the Russian traders were "not lavish" in their exchange of trade goods for furs (Oswalt 1980: 96–97; Dumond and VanStone 1995:99).

In examining colonial encounters with native peoples in Russian colonies, especially the coastal counters involved in the maritime fur trade, it is important to consider the implications of native-to-native interactions. Indigenous contacts with the colonists probably did not focus on the Russian managers or *promyshlenniks* per se who made up a small percentage of the overall workforce. The daily encounters and close bonds that transpired were primarily with Creole and Islander workers. The formation of many of the interethnic households, whether they were on the Kurile Islands or at Colony Ross, involved local native women and Creole or Islander men. This presents a very different kind of social arena for examining the complexities of colonial relationships than that envisioned for most other European colonies in the Americas.

A recurrent theme that is emerging from archaeological studies of Russian colonies is the evidence for the strong persistence of native cultural beliefs and practices, despite dramatic disruptions that unfolded over time. The history of Russian colonization is a legacy of significant impacts to local native populations, beginning with the brutal taking of hostages to ensure that fur tributes were paid in the North Pacific. After the Russian-American Company received its charter, successive onslaughts to the fabric of native culture continued. The Russians exposed native peoples to lethal epidemics, enforced excessive labor demands, implemented massive relocations of native villages in some counters, and took young men away from their communities to work in distant colonies. The Russian period also witnessed the creation of innovative marriage patterns and social networks as well as the introduction of new kinds of material culture, foodways, and cultural practices (Veltre 1990; Lightfoot and Martinez 1997; Crowell and Lührmann 2001).

Despite these enormous transformations, several studies highlight how people continually re-created strong native identities that involved the active selection of new cultural traits that were modified or molded to fit local cultural perceptions and practices. How much this cultural persistence is linked to the nature of native-to-native interactions in Russian colonies remains to be seen. However, it is interesting that this active construction of native identities appears to have taken place among native groups in coastal counters involved in the maritime fur trade as well as with indigenous communities associated with the redoubts along interior Alaskan drainages (Oswalt and VanStone 1967; VanStone 1968, 1970a, b, 1971; Oswalt 1980; Knecht and Jordan 1985; Lightfoot et al. 1997, 1998; Woodhouse-Beyer 2001; Mills 2002).

Conclusion

The investigation of Russian expansion into the Pacific Ocean presents an exceptional opportunity to examine the processes and implications of mercantile colonialism in North America. The salient characteristics of the Russian colonial program are its broad-scale spatial distribution across the North Pacific and its administration by a mercantile conglomerate. Russian colonies were essentially company towns that supported few Europeans but many Creoles and native workers. The study of Russian colonization provides the potential to examine the kinds of social dynamics that transpired when local indigenous populations were confronted with other native peoples and mixed bloods from across the North Pacific. The ramifications this had on the cultural practices, belief systems, and worldviews of indigenous communities are just now being investigated. Many questions remain to be answered. Did the Russian colonial system facilitate the spread of pan-Pacific native practices during the late-18th and 19th centuries? How did the missionary activities of the Russian Orthodox Church impact native cultural practices, especially after 1840? How did native and colonist relationships differ in the coastal colonies and interior redoubts? And did native-to-native encounters in coastal Russian colonies produce a colonial legacy fundamentally different from that found in other European colonies in North America?

Clearly, historical archaeology in the North Pacific has much to contribute in developing a broader understanding of European colonization in the Americas.

ACKNOWLEDGMENTS

I an indebted to Aron Crowell, Glenn Farris, Roberta Jewett, Breck Parkman, and Douglas Veltre for their advice and assistance in writing this paper. I very much appreciate the kind invitation of Bonnie McEwan and Gregory Waselkov to participate in the 2002 SHA Plenary Session and their encouragement and help in publishing the papers. My sincere thanks to Lisa Holm for assistance with Figure 1.

REFERENCES

ALLAN, JAMES M.
1997 Searching for California's First Shipyard: Remote Sensing Surveys at Fort Ross. In *The Archaeology of Russian Colonialism in the North and Tropical Pacific*, Peter R. Mills and Antoinette Martinez, editors, pp. 50–83. Kroeber Anthropological Society Papers, 81. Berkeley, CA.
2001 *Forge and Falseworks: An Archaeological Investigation of the Russian-American Company's Industrial Complex at Colony Ross.* Doctoral dissertation, Department of Anthropology, University of California, Berkeley. University Microfilms International, Ann Arbor, MI.

ARNDT, KATHERINE L.
1990 Russian Exploration and Trade in Alaska's Interior. In *Russian America: The Forgotten Frontier*, Barbara S. Smith and Redmond J. Barnett, editors, pp. 95–108. Washington State Historical Society, Tacoma.

BALLARD, HANNAH S.
1997 Ethnicity and Chronology at Metini, Fort Ross State Historic Park, California. In *The Archaeology of Russian Colonialism in the North and Tropical Pacific*, Peter R. Mills and Antoinette Martinez, editors, pp. 116–140. Kroeber Anthropological Society Papers, 81. Berkeley, CA.

BARRATT, GLYNN
1990 A Note on Trade between Oahu and the Russian Northwest Coast: 1806–1826. In *Russia in North America: Proceedings of the 2nd International Conference on Russian America*, Richard A. Pierce, editor, pp. 144–156. Limestone Press, Kingston, ON.

BLACK, LYDIA T.
1990 Creoles in Russian America. *Pacifica*, 2:142–155.
2001 Forgotten Literacy. In *Looking Both Ways: Heritage and Identity of the Alutiiq People*, Aron L. Crowell, Amy F. Steffian, and Gordon L. Pullar, editors, pp. 60–61. University of Alaska Press, Fairbanks.

BLEE, CATHERINE H.

1985 *Archaeological Investigations at the Russian Bishop's House 1981, Sitka National Historical Park, Sitka, Alaska.* Denver Service Center, National Park Service, CO.

1990 The Archeology of a Russian Hospital Trash Pit. In *Russia in North America: Proceedings of the 2nd International Conference on Russian America*, Richard A. Pierce, editor, pp. 407–412. Limestone Press, Kingston, ON.

CLARK, DONALD W.

1985 Archaeological Test at the Russian Three Saints Bay Colony. *Historical Archaeology*, 19(2):114–121.

CROWELL, ARON L.

1997a *Archaeology and the Capitalist World System: A Study from Russian America.* Plenum Press, New York.

1997b Russians in Alaska, 1784: Foundations of Colonial Society at Three Saints Harbor, Kodiak Island. In *The Archaeology of Russian Colonialism in the North and Tropical Pacific*, Peter R. Mills and Antoinette Martinez, editors, pp. 10–41. Kroeber Anthropological Society Papers, 81. Berkeley, CA.

2002 Russian Colonialism. In *Encyclopedia of Historical Archaeology*, Charles E. Orser, Jr., editor, pp. 486–489. Routledge, London, UK.

CROWELL, ARON L., AND SONJA LÜHRMANN

2001 Russian Conquest and Colonial Rule. In *Looking Both Ways: Heritage and Identity of the Alutiiq People*, Aron L. Crowell, Amy F. Steffian, and Gordon L. Pullar, editors, pp. 54–61. University of Alaska Press, Fairbanks.

CROWELL, ARON L., AND DANIEL H. MANN

1998 *Archaeology and Coastal Dynamics of Kenai Fjords National Park, Alaska.* Department of Interior, National Park Service, Alaska Support Office, Anchorage.

DILLIPLANE, TIMOTHY L.

1990a Industries in Russian America. In *Russian America: The Forgotten Frontier*, Barbara S. Smith and Redmond J. Barnett, editors, pp. 131–143. Washington State Historical Society, Tacoma.

1990b Material Culture and the Frontier in Russian America. In *Russia in North America: Proceedings of the 2nd International Conference on Russian America*, Richard A. Pierce, editor, pp. 398–406. Limestone Press, Kingston, ON.

DMYTRYSHYN, BASIL, E. A. P. CROWNHART-VAUGHAN, AND THOMAS VAUGHAN

1989 *The Russian American Colonies, 1798–1867: Three Centuries of Russian Eastward Expansion*, 3 Vols. Oregon Historical Society, Portland.

DUMOND, DON E.

1981 Archaeology on the Alaska Peninsula: The Naknek Region, 1960–1975. *Anthropological Papers of the University of Oregon*, 21. Eugene.

DUMOND, DON E., AND JAMES W. VANSTONE

1995 Paugvik: A Nineteenth-Century Native Village on Bristol Bay, Alaska. *Fieldiana: Anthropology*, 24 (New Series):1–109.

FARRIS, GLENN J.

1989 The Russian Imprint on the Colonization of California. In *Columbian Consequences, Volume 1, Archaeological and Historical Perspectives on the Spanish Borderlands West*, David H. Thomas, editor, pp. 481–498. Smithsonian Institution Press, Washington, DC.

1990 Fort Ross, California: Archaeology of the Old Magazin. In *Russia in North America: Proceedings of the 2nd International Conference on Russian America*, Richard A. Pierce, editor, pp. 475–505. Limestone, Press, Kingston, ON.

1993 Life in the Sloboda: A View of the Village at Fort Ross, California. Paper presented at the Annual Meeting of The Society for Historical Archaeology, Kansas City, MO.

1997 The Age of Russian Imperialism in the North Pacific. In *The Archaeology of Russian Colonialism in the North and Tropical Pacific*, Peter R. Mills and Antoinette Martinez, editors, pp. 187–194. Kroeber Anthropological Society Papers, 81. Berkeley, CA.

FEDOROVA, SVETLANA G.

1973 *The Russian Population in Alaska and California, Late 18th Century–1867*, Richard A. Pierce and A. S. Donnelly, translators. Limestone Press, Kingston, ON.

1975 *Ethnic Processes in Russian America.* Translated by Antoinette Shalkop. Occasional Papers No. 1. Anchorage Historical and Fine Arts Museum, Anchorage, AL.

FISHER, RAYMOND H.

1990 Finding America. In *Russian America: The Forgotten Frontier*, Barbara S. Smith and Redmond J. Barnett, editors, pp. 17–32. Washington State Historical Society, Tacoma.

GIBSON, JAMES R.

1976 *Imperial Russia in Frontier America: The Changing Geography of Supply of Russian America, 1784–1867.* Oxford University Press, New York.

1987 Russian Expansion in Siberia and America: Critical Contrasts. In *Russia's American Colony*, S. Frederick Starr, editor, pp. 32–40. Duke University Press, Durham, NC.

1988 The Maritime Trade of the North Pacific Coast. In *Handbook of North American Indians: History of Indian-White Relations, Vol. 4*, Wilcomb E. Washburn, editor, pp. 375–390. Smithsonian Institution, Washington, DC.

1992a *Otter Skins, Boston Ships, and China Goods: The Maritime Fur Trade of the Northwest Coast, 1785–1841.* University of Washington Press, Seattle.

1992b A Russian Orthodox Priest in Mexican California. *The Californians*, 9(6):20–27.

GOLDSTEIN, LYNNE

    1992 Spatial Organization and Frontier Cemeteries: An Example from a Russian Colonial Settlement. Paper presented at the 25th Annual Meeting of The Society for Historical Archaeology, Kingston, Jamaica.

    1995 Politics, Law, Pragmatics, and Human Burial Excavations: An Example from Northern California. In *Bodies of Evidence*, A. L. Grauer, editor, pp. 3–17. John Wiley & Sons, Inc., New York.

GROVER, MARGAN

    2000 *Textiles, Buttons, and Beads: An Analysis of Castle Hill Clothing*. Alaska Department of Natural Resources, Division of Parks and Outdoor Recreation, Office of History and Archaeology, Castle Hill Archaeological Project. <http://www.dnr.state,ak.us/parks/oha_web/castle~1.htm>.

ISTOMIN, ALEXEI A.

    1992 *The Indians at the Ross Settlement According to the Censuses by Kuskov, 1820–1821*. Fort Ross Interpretive Association, Fort Ross, CA.

KAN, SERGEI

    1988 The Russian Orthodox Church in Alaska. In *Handbook of North American Indians: History of Indian-White Relations, Vol. 4*, Wilcomb E. Washburn, editor, pp. 506–521. Smithsonian Institution Press, Washington, DC.

KHLEBNIKOV, KIRILL

    1990 *The Khlebnikov Archive: Unpublished Journal (1800–1837) and Travel Notes (1820, 1822, and 1824)*, J. Bisk, translator. University of Alaska Press, Fairbanks.

KNECHT, RICHARD A., AND RICHARD A. JORDAN

    1985 Nunakakhnak: An Historic Period Koniag Village in Karluk, Kodiak Island, Alaska. *Arctic Anthropology*, 22(2):17–35.

LAGUNA, FREDERICA DE

    1960 *The Story of a Tlingit Community: A Problem in the Relationship between Archeological, Ethnological, and Historical Methods*. Bureau of American Ethnology Bulletin, 172. Smithsonian Institution, Washington, DC.

LAGUNA, FREDERICA DE, FRANCIS A. RIDDELL, DONALD F. MCGEEIN, KENNETH S. LANE, J. ARTHUR FREED, AND CAROLYN OSBORNE

    1964 *Archeology of the Yakutat Bay Area, Alaska*. Bureau of American Ethnology Bulletin, 192. Smithsonian Institution, Washington, DC.

LIGHTFOOT, KENT G.

    1995 Culture Contact Studies: Redefining the Relationship between Prehistoric and Historical Archaeology. *American Antiquity*, 60(2):199–217.

LIGHTFOOT, KENT G., AND ANTOINETTE MARTINEZ

    1997 Interethnic Relationships in the Native Alaskan Neighborhood: Consumption Practices, Cultural Innovations, and the Construction of Household Identities. In *The Archaeology and Ethnohistory of Fort Ross, California, Volume 2, The Native Alaskan Neighborhood: A Multiethnic Community at Colony Ross*, Kent G. Lightfoot, Ann M. Schiff, and Thomas A. Wake, editors, pp. 1–22. Contributions of the University of California Archaeological Research Facility, No. 55. Archaeological Research Facility, Berkeley, CA.

LIGHTFOOT, KENT G., ANTOINETTE MARTINEZ, AND ANN SCHIFF

    1998 Daily Practice and Material Culture in Pluralistic Social Settings: An Archaeological Study of Culture Change and Persistence from Fort Ross, California. *American Antiquity*, 63(2):199–222.

LIGHTFOOT, KENT G., ANN M. SCHIFF, AND THOMAS A. WAKE (EDITORS)

    1997 *The Archaeology and Ethnohistory of Fort Ross, California, Volume 2, The Native Alaskan Neighborhood: A Multiethnic Community at Colony Ross*. Contributions of the University of California Archaeological Facility, No. 55. Archaeological Research Facility, Berkeley, CA.

LIGHTFOOT, KENT G., THOMAS A. WAKE, AND ANN M. SCHIFF

    1991 *The Archaeology and Ethnohistory of Fort Ross, California, Volume 1, Introduction*. Contributions of the University of California Archaeological Research Facility, No. 49. Archaeological Research Facility, Berkeley, CA.

MARTINEZ, ANTOINETTE

    1997 View from the Ridge: The Kashaya Pomo in a Russian-American Company Context. In *The Archaeology of Russian Colonialism in the North and Tropical Pacific*, Peter R. Mills and Antoinette Martinez, editors, pp. 141–156. Kroeber Anthropological Society Papers, 81. Berkeley, CA.

    1998 *An Archaeological Study of Change and Continuity in the Material Remains, Practices, and Cultural Identities of Native California Women in a Nineteenth-Century Pluralistic Context*. Doctoral dissertation, Department of Anthropology, University of California, Berkeley. University Microfilms International, Ann Arbor, MI.

MILLS, PETER R.

    1997 Historical Ethnography and Archaeology of Russian Fort Elisabeth State Historical Park, Waimea, Kaua'i. In *The Archaeology of Russian Colonialism in the North and Tropical Pacific*, Peter R. Mills and Antoinette Martinez, editors, pp. 157–186. Kroeber Anthropological Society Papers, 81. Berkeley, CA.

    2002 *Hawai'i's Russian Adventure: A New Look at Old History*. University of Hawai'i Press, Honolulu.

OGDEN, ADELE
    1941   *The California Sea Otter Trade, 1784–1848.* University of California Press, Berkeley.

OLEKSA, MICHAEL J.
    1990   The Creoles and Their Contributions to the Development of Alaska. In *Russian America: The Forgotten Frontier*, Barbara S. Smith and Redmond J. Barnett, editors, pp. 185–196. Washington State Historical Society, Tacoma.

OSBORN, SANNIE K.
    1992   Demographics of the Russian Colony at Fort Ross, California, Derived from a Study of the Russian Cemetery. Paper presented at The 25th Annual Meeting of the Society for Historical Archaeology, Kingston, Jamaica.
    1997   *Death in the Daily Life of the Ross Colony: Mortuary Behavior in Frontier Russian America.* Doctoral dissertation, Department of Anthropology, University of Wisconsin, Milwaukee. University Microfilms International, Ann Arbor, MI.

OSWALT, WENDELL H.
    1980   *Kolmakovskiy Redoubt: The Ethnoarchaeology of a Russian Fort in Alaska.* Monumenta Archaeologica, Vol. 8. Institute of Archaeology, UCLA, Los Angeles.

OSWALT, WENDELL H., AND JAMES W. VANSTONE
    1967   *The Ethnoarchaeology of Crow Village, Alaska.* Bureau of American Ethnology Bulletin, 199. Smithsonian Institution, Washington, DC.

PARKMAN, E. BRECK
    1996/1997   Fort and Settlement: Interpreting the Past at Fort Ross State Historic Park. *California History*, 75(4):354–369.

PARRISH, OTIS, DANIEL F. MURLEY, ROBERTA A. JEWETT, AND KENT G. LIGHTFOOT
    2000   The Science of Archaeology and the Response from within Native California: The Archaeology and Ethnohistory of Me?tini Village in the Fort Ross State Historic Park. *Proceedings of the Society for California Archaeology*, 13:84–87.

PETRUZELLI, RENEE, AND DIANE K. HANSON
    1998   *Fauna from Mid-Nineteenth-Century Structures at Castle Hill State Park, Sitka, Alaska.* Alaska Department of Natural Resources, Division of Parks and Outdoor Recreation, Office of History and Archaeology, Castle Hill Archaeological Project. <http://www.dnr.state,ak.us/parks/oha_web/castle~1.htm>.

PIERCE, RICHARD A.
    1965   *Russia's Hawaiian Adventure, 1815–1817.* University of California Press, Berkeley.

RATHBURN, ROBERT R.
    1981   The Russian Orthodox Church As a Native Institution among the Koniag Eskimo of Kodiak Island, Alaska. *Arctic Anthropology*, 18(1):12–22.

RIDDELL, FRANCIS A.
    1955   Archaeological Excavation on the Farallon Islands, California. *Reports of the University of California Archaeological Survey*, 32:1–18.

SELVERSTON, MARK D.
    1999   An Introduction to the Vasili Khlebnikov Ranch. Paper presented at the 33rd Annual Meeting of the Society for California Archaeology, Sacramento.

SENKEVITCH, ANATOLE
    1987   The Early Architecture and Settlements of Russian America. In *Russia's American Colony*, S. Frederick Starr, editor, pp. 147–195. Duke University Press, Durham, NC.

SHUBIN, VALERY O.
    1990   Russian Settlements in the Kurile Islands in the 18th and 19th Centuries. In *Russia in North America: Proceedings of the 2nd International Conference on Russian America*, Richard A. Pierce, editor, pp. 425–450. Limestone Press, Kingston, ON.
    1994   Aleut in the Kurile Islands: 1820–1870. In *Anthropology of the North Pacific Rim*, William W. Fitzhugh and Valerie Chaussonnet, editors, pp. 337–346. Smithsonian Institution Press, Washington, DC.

SMITH, BARBARA S.
    2000   *Science under Sail: Russia's Great Voyages to America 1728–1867.* Anchorage Museum of History and Art, Anchorage, AK.

SMITH, BARBARA S., AND REDMOND J. BARNETT
    1990   Introduction. In *Russian America: The Forgotten Frontier*, Barbara S. Smith and Redmond J. Barnett, editors, pp. 9–15. Washington State Historical Society, Tacoma.

SMITH, BARBARA S., AND STEVEN M. PETERSON
    1990   Russian Cultural Heritage: A Resource at Risk. In *Russia in North America: Proceedings of the 2nd International Conference on Russian America*, Richard A. Pierce, editor, pp. 379–390. Limestone Press, Kingston, ON.

SPENCER PRITCHARD, DIANE
    1991   The Good, the Bad and the Ugly: Russian-American Company Employees of Fort Ross. *The Californians*, 8(6):42–49.

SUAZO, ERNEST J., ROBERT L. CARPER, AND GARY J. CANDELARIA
    1990   The Russian Bishop's House. In *Russia in North America: Proceedings of the 2nd International Conference on Russian America*, Richard A. Pierce, editor, pp. 451–474. Limestone Press, Kingston, ON.

THOMPSON, DANIEL R.

1999 *Russian Earthenware on Russian Sites: A New Look.* Alaska Department of Natural Resources, Division of Parks and Outdoor Recreation, Office of History and Archaeology, Castle Hill Archaeological Project. <http://www.dnr.state,ak.us/parks/oha_web/castle~1.htm>.

TIKHMENEV, P. A.

1978 *A History of the Russian-American Company,* Richard A. Pierce and Alton S. Donnelly, translators and editors. University of Washington Press, Seattle.

TREGANZA, ADAN E.

1954 Fort Ross: A Study in Historical Archaeology. *Reports of the University of California Archaeological Survey,* 23:1–26.

UPTON, DELL

1996 Ethnicity, Authenticity, and Invented Tradition. *Historical Archaeology,* 30(2):1–7.

VANSTONE, JAMES W.

1955 Exploring the Copper River Country. *Pacific Northwest Quarterly,* 46(4):115–123.

1968 Tikchik Village: A Nineteenth-Century Riverine Community in Southwestern Alaska. *Fieldiana: Anthropology,* 56(3):215–368.

1970a Akulivikchuk: A Nineteenth-Century Eskimo Village in the Nushagak River, Alaska. *Fieldiana: Anthropology,* 60:1–123.

1970b Ethnohistorical Research in Southwestern Alaska: A Methodological Perspective. In *Ethnohistory in Southwestern Alaska and the Southern Yukon: Method and Content,* Margaret Lantis, editor, pp. 49–69. University Press of Kentucky, Lexington.

1971 Historic Settlement Patterns in the Nushagak River Region, Alaska. *Fieldiana: Anthropology,* 61: 1–149.

1972 Nushagak: An Historic Trading Center in Southwestern Alaska. *Fieldiana: Anthropology,* 62:1–93.

VELTRE, DOUGLAS W.

1979 *Korovinski: The Ethnohistorical Archaeology of an Aleut Russian Settlement on Atka Island, Alaska.* Doctoral dissertation, Department of Anthropology, University of Connecticut, Storrs. University Microfilms International, Ann Arbor, MI.

1990 Perspectives on Aleut Culture Change during the Russian Period. In *Russian America: The Forgotten Frontier,* Barbara S. Smith and Redmond J. Barnett, editors, pp. 175–183. Washington State Historical Society, Tacoma.

2001 Korovinski: Archaeological and Ethnohistorical Investigations of a Pre- and Post-Contact Aleut and Russian Settlement on Atka Island. In *Archaeology in the Aleut Zone of Alaska: Some Recent Research,* Don E. Dumond, editor, pp. 187–213. University of Oregon Anthropological Papers, 58. Eugene.

VELTRE, DOUGLAS W., AND ALLEN P. MCCARTNEY

2000 The St. Paul History and Archaeology Project: Overview of 2000 Field Operations. Manuscript, Department of Anthropology, University of Alaska, Anchorage.

2001a Ethnohistorical Archaeology at the Reese Bay Site, Unalaska Island. In *Archaeology in the Aleut Zone of Alaska: Some Recent Research,* Don E. Dumond, editor, pp. 87–104. University of Oregon Anthropological Papers, 58. Eugene.

2001b The St. Paul History and Archaeology Project: Overview of 2001 Field Operations. Manuscript, Department of Anthropology, University of Alaska, Anchorage.

WAKE, THOMAS A.

1995 *Mammal Remains from Fort Ross: A Study in Ethnicity and Culture Change.* Doctoral dissertation, Department of Anthropology, University of California, Berkeley. University Microfilms International, Ann Arbor, MI.

1997a Bone Artifacts and Tool Production in the Native Alaskan Neighborhood. In *The Archaeology and Ethnohistory of Fort Ross, California, Volume 2, The Native Alaskan Neighborhood: A Multiethnic Community at Colony Ross,* Kent G. Lightfoot, Ann M. Schiff, and Thomas A. Wake, editors, pp. 248–278. Contributions of the University of California Archaeological Research Facility, No. 55. Archaeological Research Facility, Berkeley, CA.

1997b Mammal Remains from the Native Alaskan Neighborhood. In *The Archaeology and Ethnohistory of Fort Ross, California, Volume 2, The Native Alaskan Neighborhood: A Multiethnic Community at Colony Ross,* Kent G. Lightfoot, Ann M. Schiff, and Thomas A. Wake, editors, pp. 279–309. Contributions of the University of California Archaeological Research Facility, No. 55. Archaeological Research Facility, Berkeley, CA.

WHEELER, MARY E.

1987 The Russian-American Company and the Imperial Government: Early Phase. In *Russia's American Colony,* S. Frederick Starr, editor, pp. 43–62. Duke University Press, Durham, NC.

WOLF, ERIC

1982 *Europe and the People Without History.* University of California Press, Berkeley.

WOODHOUSE-BEYER, KATHARINE

2001 Historical Archaeology at the Afognak Artel. *In Looking Both Ways: Heritage and Identity of the Alutiiq People,* Aron L. Crowell, Amy F. Steffian, and Gordon L. Pullar, editors, pp. 130–131. University of Alaska Press, Fairbanks.

WRANGELL, F. P. VON

1969 Russia in California, 1833, Report of Governor Wrangell. Translation and editing of original 1833 report by James R. Gibson. *Pacific Northwest Quarterly,* 60:205–215.

KENT G. LIGHTFOOT
ARCHAEOLOGICAL RESEARCH FACILITY
DEPARTMENT OF ANTHROPOLOGY
232 KROEBER HALL
UNIVERSITY OF CALIFORNIA, BERKELEY
BERKELEY, CA 94720-3710

Douglas W. Veltre
Allen P. McCartney

Russian Exploitation of Aleuts and Fur Seals: The Archaeology of Eighteenth- and Early-Nineteenth-Century Settlements in the Pribilof Islands, Alaska

ABSTRACT

Shortly after Russian fur hunters found the uninhabited Pribilof Islands of St. Paul and St. George in the late 1780s, they began forcing Aleut men from the Aleutian Islands and Alaska Peninsula to travel there seasonally to provide labor for the profitable commercial harvest of northern fur seals. Recent archaeological surveys of the earliest Aleut and Russian work camps that were established on the islands show them to be unusual in many respects when compared to contemporary sites in the Aleutian Islands region. These include the absence of precontact site components, their relatively narrow period of occupation, their occupancy by an exclusively or nearly exclusively male population, and their potential as multiethnic settlements to reveal differences between the lives of Russian overseers and Aleut laborers.

Introduction

This paper presents the results of initial historical and archaeological investigations of Russian and Aleut settlements in the Pribilof Islands, Alaska, and begins with a review of the cultural and historical background leading up to the discovery of these islands in the late-18th century. What is known of the early settlement of the Pribilofs from historical documents, oral traditions, and archaeological surveys is outlined. Finally, the unique potential of the Pribilof Islands for contributing to an understanding of Alaska Native cultural change generally and of multiethnic work camps and settlements specifically is discussed.

Precontact Background

For at least 4,000 (and as many as 8,000) years prior to the arrival of foreigners to Alaska in the mid-1700s, Aleut people were the sole occupants of the 1,600-km-long Aleutian Islands chain, the western end of the Alaska Peninsula, and the small Shumagin Islands group south of the Alaska Peninsula (Figure 1). Numbering some 12,000–15,000 prior to contact, Aleuts were culturally and linguistically related to, yet distinct from, neighboring Eskimo groups to the east. Aleut culture was focused on the rich marine ecosystem of the North Pacific Ocean and the Bering Sea as the direct or indirect provider of most of its food and raw materials for manufacturing (McCartney and Veltre 1999). Major sources of food included marine mammals, marine invertebrates, fish, birds, and eggs. Of relatively minor importance were plant foods, such as wild rice, berries, and wild celery. Due to the isolation of the Aleutian Islands, land animals were largely absent from most Aleut territory.

Because of their marine focus, Aleuts established all of their settlements along the coast. Villages, varying from a few small families to perhaps 200 or more people, might have been occupied by some individuals for the entire year, while smaller subsistence camps were occupied seasonally. Semisubterranean Aleut houses, *barabaras*, were home to large extended families, tied to each other very likely through matrilineal kinship.

Aboriginal Aleut society was ranked, with the highest rank going to those individuals having the greatest wealth, the largest families, the most local kin support, and the closest proximity to important subsistence resources. Villages composed the basic political units, although regional political affiliations apparently were important in times of warfare. While relatively little is known about the details of precontact Aleut religious beliefs, they were fundamentally animistic, with spirits of humans, animals, and natural entities requiring placation and with shamans acting as intermediaries between the everyday and supernatural worlds.

Contact Period

Foreign contact in Alaska began in 1741. In that year, Vitus Bering and Alexei Chirikov sailed from Kamchatka to the waters of south-central Alaska and the Aleutian Islands and

FIGURE 1. Southwest Alaska, the eastern Aleutian Islands, and the Pribilof Islands.

made the first reported contact with Aleuts. Within the three decades that followed, several dozen fur hunting expeditions were made to the Aleutians, the Russian fur hunters continually pushing eastward in pursuit of an ever-dwindling sea otter population. During these voyages, the Russian hunters demanded *iasak*, or tribute, from the Aleuts, usually in the form of sea otter skins, and, to insure their own safety, the fur hunters took hostages from among the Aleuts to be held until the required skins were procured. The Russian fur hunting companies also compelled Aleut men to work for them, often taking them away from their families and villages for long periods.

Most areas of Aleut life changed drastically during the early decades of the Russian period. Aleut population decline from diseases and atrocities was profound. Though accurate Russian censuses were not taken until substantial population loss had occurred, it appears (Lantis 1970) that approximately 80% of the precontact Aleut population was lost during the first half of the Russian period, until about 1800, by which time roughly 2,500 Aleuts remained. Other significant changes occurred in village and household settlement patterning, religion, and social organization (Lantis 1970; Veltre 1990). In short, by the end of the 1700s, Aleuts were to a large extent no longer in control of their own lives. Their precontact adaptive mechanisms for coping with changing conditions were wholly inadequate for handling the kind and magnitude of changes forced upon them by the Russian fur hunters. As forced laborers, the Aleuts became

a part of the expanding world economic system of the time.

Settlement of the Pribilof Islands

Although Aleut oral tradition holds that at least one Aleut man had ventured to the Pribilof Islands in the precontact past (Veniaminov 1984:134–135), no ethnohistoric or archaeological evidence points to the use or occupation of the Pribilof Islands, north of the Aleutian archipelago, by any native people prior to the Russian period in Alaska. Had it been otherwise, it must have been on a sporadic basis at most, since even a small coastal settlement of semisubterranean houses and associated midden debris, typical of most Aleutian Island sites, would have left obvious traces today. This absence of precontact occupation is likely due in part to the isolation of the Pribilofs: they lie well out of sight of any other islands or the Alaska mainland, some 400 km north of the eastern Aleutian archipelago and 500 km west-southwest of the Alaska mainland.

By the 1780s, it had become clear to the Russians, as it must already have been known to Aleuts for millennia, that northern fur seals (*Callorhinus ursinus*) swam northward through the passes of the Aleutian Islands in the spring and southward—with their recently born pups—in the fall. Fur hunting companies began searching the waters of the Bering Sea, north of the Aleutians, for the islands that they and Aleuts knew must exist to serve as the breeding grounds for these animals.

In 1786, the navigator Gerasim Pribylov culminated a three-year concerted effort to locate the breeding grounds of the northern fur seal by discovering St. George Island (Elliott 1881:19; Veniaminov 1984:134). He worked in the service of the Lebedev-Lastochkin company, one of the fur trading enterprises competing for control of Russian-American trade (Fedorova 1973:118ff). Pribylov left some of his men on the island to hunt fur seals, sea lions, and sea otters, and it was these men who eventually sighted St. Paul Island, 65 km distant, the following year.

St. Paul and St. George islands are the two largest of the five-island Pribilof Islands group in the central Bering Sea. The islands, which during the last ice age would have been unglaciated high hill tops on the now-submerged Bering Land Bridge (Barth 1956; Hopkins and Einarsson 1966:343), are of volcanic origin with small cinder cones (on St. Paul), gently rolling hills, and precipitous coastal cliffs. For the most part, the land is rocky and thinly vegetated.

Weather conditions in the Pribilofs are typically maritime; annual temperatures commonly range from -5°C to 10°C, and wind, overcast, drizzle, and fog are common. The Pribilof Islands lie near the southern limit of sea ice in most years; only once in every several years will ice surround the island. Marine fauna dominate the animal resources of the area, with arctic fox being the only indigenous large terrestrial species on the islands. Several species of whales and seals are found in Pribilof waters, although the most important is the northern fur seal, which is discussed below. Other resources include marine invertebrates, fish, and vast numbers of marine birds.

Because it was the commercially valuable pelts of fur seals that drew the Russians to the Pribilof Islands, a brief examination of this resource is essential to understanding the subsequent settlement history of the islands. Northern fur seals breed only on a small number of isolated islands in the North Pacific region, which includes the Pribilof Islands and several locations to the west of the Aleutians and off the coast of southern California. At Russian discovery, there may have been some 3–4 million fur seals in the Pribilofs. By 1950 the fur seal population had been reduced to nearly 2 million and by the mid-1980s to about 1.2 million (Fowler 1985), somewhat less than three-quarters of which (about 800,000) bred on the Pribilof Islands (U.S. Federal Register 1986:47158).

Fur seals spend the winter months entirely at sea, returning in late May and early June to several locations around the coasts of St. Paul and St. George. The large (181–272 kg [U.S. Department of Commerce 1977:4]), 10- to 17-year-old breeding males arrive first, establishing and defending territories on the beaches within which subsequently arriving females (which are one-quarter the size of males) find themselves resident. Females give birth at these rookeries in late June and July, during which time nonbreeding adolescent seals continue to arrive on the islands. By October, fur seals begin leaving the islands, a process that continues until December.

Fur seal pelts are quite different from those of other sea mammals, the latter having only a single layer of hair. Seal pelts, instead, have fur composed of both longer and shorter layers of fibers, very tightly packed at about 57,000 hairs/cm^2 (Fiscus 1978:154). The shorter hairs, in particular, are extremely soft, and they give the pelts their high commercial value.

To the Russians, the Pribilof Islands represented a "gold mine" of furs, since harvesting the fur seals could be done much more easily and quickly on land than at sea—and with fewer losses and less damage to pelts. The seal harvesting methods employed by the first Russians and Aleuts in the Pribilofs were essentially the same as those that continue to be used today. During the summer months, seals are driven from their haulouts to nearby grassy areas, where men with long wooden clubs strike them on their heads to stun them. Immediately following this, other men kill the animals by cutting through the heart and then make cuts in the skin to facilitate removing the pelt from the carcass. Until the cessation of commercial harvesting in 1984, the pelts were processed and tanned, eventually being sold to international furriers. The carcasses were available for consumption by Aleuts and for use as fishing bait and other purposes. Since 1984, only a subsistence harvest, utilizing the same procurement methods, continues (Veltre and Veltre 1987).

Intense exploitation of the animals began immediately after discovery of the Pribilofs. A 1789 letter mentions that 20 Russians and 20 Aleuts "remained to hunt on these islands" for two years, presumably 1786 and 1787 (Tikhmenev 1979:19). Soon thereafter, Russians brought Aleuts, primarily from villages on Unalaska and Atka islands in the Aleutian chain, to the Pribilofs seasonally to provide the bulk of the manpower for the large-scale sealing operations that had begun.

Documentary material dealing with the history of settlements on St. Paul and St. George islands is quite limited. The works of the naturalist Henry W. Elliott (1881, 1886) stand as the leading published historical works pertaining to the early Russian period occupation of the islands. In 1872, following the 1867 sale of Alaska to the United States (which was motivated to a large degree by the economic value of the commercial Pribilof fur seal industry), Elliott was sent to the Pribilof Islands as Special Agent of the U.S. Treasury Department, which administered the federal government's sealing lease to the Alaska Commercial Company. Elliott's job was to assure that provisions of the lease were being performed properly, but he was also given the somewhat less formal task of studying the fur seals and other animals of the islands (Gay 1973:211–212). Elliott, who married a young Aleut woman from the Pribilofs shortly after his arrival, took his observations of the fur seals seriously, and he became a champion for protection of the herd from overharvesting.

Shortly after initial Russian discovery, "more men [Aleuts] were brought up from Atkha [Atka] and taken over [from St. George] to St. Paul, where five or six rival traders posted themselves on the north shore, near and at 'Maroonitch,' and [at Vesolia Mista] at the head of Big [L]ake, among the sand dunes there . . ." (Elliott 1881:19). Prior to 1796, other villages were founded at Polovina, Zapadni, and Webster Lake. By the mid-1790s, early Russian period settlement (seasonal and year-round) took place at several island locations, although the precise timing and, in some cases, the exact locations of settlements are currently unknown (Figure 2).

Conditions at these earliest work camps were almost certainly bleak (Torrey 1978:47–48). Living quarters were built partially into the ground and must have been damp, cool, and crowded. Work at the fur seal harvest, likewise, was arduous. In the absence of roads and means of land transport, workers hiked daily on foot trails to the various seal hauling areas during the sealing season. Instead of killing the seals on the spot, the animals were often driven overland to killing grounds close to the settlements, thereby saving the Aleuts the heavy work of hauling the pelts themselves (Figure 3).

Once animals were clubbed and skinned, the skins were processed by laboriously scraping any remaining blubber from them and then drying them. After some weeks, the dried pelts were rolled and bundled, eventually to be loaded into skin-covered boats and taken to ships lying offshore. The amount of work involved in this entire enterprise was enormous, especially when one considers that Elliott (1881:70) estimated an

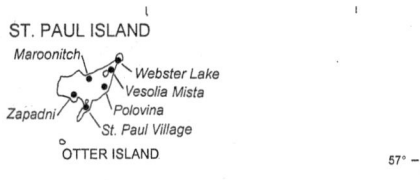

FIGURE 2. Past and present settlements in the Pribilof Islands.

average of nearly 50,000 fur seals killed each year from 1797 to 1821.

In 1799, the Russian-American Company was formed, having been granted monopolistic rights to all hunting activities north of 50° north latitude by the Russian government (Tikhmenev 1979). As with earlier fur hunting enterprises, the Russian-American Company's success was based on the availability of Aleut labor (and other indigenous labor elsewhere in Alaska). Because there were usually fewer than 600 Russians in the whole of Alaska at any one time, there was a chronic shortage of Russians to undertake hunting pursuits. Moreover, Aleut hunting skills were unsurpassed.

It was sometime after the establishment of the Russian-American Company that the St. Paul settlements were consolidated at Polovina, northeast of today's community of St. Paul. This location was occupied until 1825, when the village was resettled at its present location to take advantage of the harbor there (Elliott 1881:20). At about the same time, the Russian-American Company began to keep its Aleut workers on the islands year-round along with their families, who were brought from their home villages in the Aleutian Islands, bringing to an end the less efficient earlier system of seasonal labor recruitment.

Thus, by the 1820s, seasonal, male-only (or predominantly male) work camps transformed into full fledged, family-based Aleut communities. Their populations, however, fluctuated, presumably as Russian managers transported some Aleuts back and forth to the Aleutian

Islands as the labor requirements of the fur seal harvest dictated. In 1820, for example, 225 Aleuts were on St. Paul and 165 were on St. George (Fedorova 1973:202). However, in the following decade (some unspecified time between 1824–1834), the St. Paul population was reduced to only 137 Aleuts, Creoles (offspring of Aleut women and Russian men), and Russians combined (Veniaminov 1984:140). This number was divided between two villages: one at Gavanskoe (in Russian, harbor), the principal and current village of St. Paul; and the second, probably the Webster Lake site, at Stoshnoe or Novastashnah, (in Russian, of recent growth), so named "because this locality in pioneer days was an island to itself; and it has been annexed recently to the main land of St. Paul" (Elliott 1881:note). During the later 1820s, Frederic Litke (1987:110) reports the St. Paul population at 11 Russians and 150 Aleuts (including women and children).

According to Elliott (1881:20), Aleuts lived in semisubterranean sod-covered houses until the Pribilofs came under the jurisdiction of the Alaska Commercial (A-C) Company in 1870, this following the sale of Alaska to the United States in 1867. The A-C Company built frame houses for the native population during the 1870s.

Presumably, however, some Aleuts continued to live in the sod *barabaras*, at least seasonally, since Elliott (1881:Plate II) captioned one of his drawings of a *barabara* "1787–1874," and showed another in good condition near Webster Lake at the northeastern end of the island (1881:Plate XIX).

Previous Archaeological Research and the Present Survey

The archaeological surveys conducted on St. George in 1986 (Veltre and Veltre 1986) and on St. Paul in 1994 (Veltre and McCartney 1994) were preceded by only a few investigations. These include a 1966 survey by Alan Bryan, whose express purpose was to search "for evidence of early man at the time when the islands are [were] high hills on the Beringian plains" (Bryan 1966:6). Although he located no prehistoric sites, Bryan recognized the potential significance of the early Russian period sites for investigating aspects of Aleut culture change (Bryan 1966:6). His report, while it lacks detailed site maps, is the only archaeological summary for the islands prior to our work.

In addition, brief reports of archaeological materials were made by former schoolteacher

FIGURE 3. Aleuts driving fur seals on St. Paul Island in 1872. (Drawing by Henry Wood Elliott 1881:Plate XIII.)

William Browne (1970), by archaeologist Donald Clark (1981), and by archaeologist Michael Yarborough (1986), who examined possible construction areas on St. George. Finally in 1994, a brief archaeological examination of a construction site on the east side of the current village of St. Paul revealed no archaeological remains (Veltre 1994).

The 1986 and 1994 archaeological surveys, completed at the request of the Pribilof communities, were directed at visiting the known early Russian period sites on St. Paul and St. George, that is, those occupied prior to the consolidation of settlements in the early 1800s. The goals were to supplement information from previous efforts, to assess current site conditions, and to define avenues for future archaeological inquiries. Altogether, seven sites were surveyed. Two additional sites could not be located: in one case (Vesolia Mista on St. Paul), migrating sand dunes had presumably covered a former settlement area; in another case (Zapadni on St. George), human activity subsequent to the site's occupation had rendered identification of the site location from surface features imprecise. Field findings are summarized below.

As would be expected, the seven sites are located close to fur seal hauling areas, often situated on hillsides or sandy rises near small drainages or ponds. Cultural features visible on the surface are heavily vegetated and are mostly of two types. The larger features are rectangular depressions surrounded by raised sod walls; they are generally about 3 x 5 m in size and 0.5 m deep. In some cases, internal walls are evident as are breaks, or discontinuities, in the outer walls themselves. Whale bones, especially mandibles and vertebrae, occur in the walls of many of these features and presumably functioned as roof supports. The second type of feature includes distinctly smaller depressions, sometimes only 1–2 m across, lacking a surrounding raised wall. The first type of feature was interpreted to be houses, workshops, or warehouses, and the second type to be small storage structures, privies, and outbuildings.

Earlier research on precontact and postcontact Aleut sites in the Aleutian Islands has shown a very distinct change in house form following contact. Most earlier Aleut dwellings were quite large semisubterranean structures, with entry and exit accomplished through holes in the wood, bone, and sod roofs. Throughout the Aleut region, houses of this type left characteristic depressions as surface features on archaeological sites, usually oval or rounded rectangular in shape. Russian period buildings, on the other hand, had floors only slightly below ground level and walls, including those for internal rooms, created from blocks of sod with support from long whale bones and/or driftwood. Side windows and doors were also present as were roofs made from dried grass, held in place with netting. Houses of this type (from Unalaska in the 1820s and from St. Paul during the Russian period) were illustrated by Kittlitz (Litke 1987:216) and Elliott (Figure 4; Elliott 1881:Plate II), respectively. Archaeologically, this type of construction is easily distinguished from the earlier form.

Most of the sites found on St. Paul and St. George had 3 to 9 of the Russian period sod-walled features, although the largest site, the Zapadni site on St. Paul, had approximately 20 features. The remains of whale bone and/or wood wall supports, which were found at several of the St. Paul sites, parallel the observation from 1803 to 1807 by Georg Langsdorff (1993:II, 4), who described "several abandoned earthen huts" made with whale bones (probably at Webster Lake near the northeastern point) that he and his crew observed. In addition to sod-walled features, all of the sites surveyed had smaller depressions, as described above.

Discussion

Based on the findings, the following assessment of the significance of these Pribilof Island sites can be made. First, unlike typical Aleutian Island sites, where vaguely dated historic-period layers and materials rest atop dense precontact midden and where substantial mixing of materials from those two periods has undoubtedly occurred, the Pribilof sites have rather narrowly defined beginning and ending dates. For example, historical documents suggest that two sites, Maroonitch and Vesolia Mista, were occupied for about 12 or 13 years, between 1787 and 1799, and two others, Polovina and St. Paul Zapadni, were occupied for up to only 25 or 26 years, between 1799 and 1825.

These sites, then, are important because they may well contain early-contact artifact materials and styles from known source areas (Atka and/or Unalaska) that could be used to cross-date recent (upper) midden deposits in the Aleutian Islands. From residents of St. Paul and St. George who have found artifacts over the years, it is known that the initial Pribilof Aleuts were using a combination of native and traded materials (stone projectile points, whale bone harpoon socket pieces and foreshafts, trade beads, metal, etc.; see Bryan's list of excavated artifacts in Veltre and Veltre 1986:13–14). This combination of artifacts made of native and traded materials had its direct roots in the mid-1700s sites of the central and eastern Aleutians (McCartney et al. 1990, 1991 [examples of 1760s–1780s Unalaskan Island artifacts]). Very few late prehistoric or early historic Aleutian Island sites have been precisely dated, and the Pribilof materials could be of great value in establishing the stylistic artifact sequence for them.

Second, Pribilof archaeology would add significantly to what is known about the 18th-century Russian colonial activities in southwestern Alaska. Very few archaeological projects have dealt with this topic (Reese Bay on northern Unalaska Island [ca. 1759–late 1700s, McCartney et al. 1990, 1991], Korovinski on Atka Island [ca. 1820–1870, Veltre 1979], and Three Saints Harbor on Kodiak Island [ca. 1784–early-19th century, Crowell 1997]). Because of their pristine nature, the Pribilof sites, as outlined above, offer excellent potential for understanding early colonial-period Alaska Native acculturation, particularly in light of the paucity of associated documentary materials. In this regard, the fact that multiple contemporaneous Russian and Aleut sites exist in the Pribilofs would add a unique dimension to such work.

Related to this is the difficulty Alaskan archaeologists have had in distinguishing Russian and American period deposits from one another (Oswalt and VanStone 1967). Because the early Pribilof sites were occupied for such short time spans entirely within the Russian period, information from them may assist in dating and interpreting materials from sites throughout the area of Russian occupation in Alaska.

Third, the movement of Aleuts to the Pribilofs in the late 1780s was the first major movement by Russians of these excellent sea mammal hunters outside of their precontact territory. Comparative settings against which to evaluate

FIGURE 4. An Aleut *barabara* on St. Paul of the kind used throughout the Russian period. (Drawing by Henry Wood Elliott 1881:Plate II.)

this exist at Fort Ross, north of San Francisco, which was operated between 1812 and 1841 as a Russian-American Company post (Rokitiansky 1990; Lightfoot et al. 1991), and on Urup Island in the Kurile Islands, south of Kamchatka, where Aleuts (and/or possibly Koniag from Kodiak) were taken by Russians in the 18th and 19th centuries (Shubin 1990). With the study of these outlier hunting settlements over the past decade, it is now possible to begin to understand the archaeology as well as the documentary history of Aleut dispersion during the Russian colonial administration of Alaska. While each of these three instances (the Pribilofs, Fort Ross, and the Kurile Islands) is unique in some ways, these sites collectively reflect the common Russian pattern of scattering Aleuts in far-flung Pacific locales for the effective hunting of sea otters and similar sea mammals.

Fourth, although the Russian colonization of the Aleutian Islands had early and severe effects upon the native population (such as warfare, introduction of diseases, forced sea mammal hunting/fur production, etc.), the nature of such colonization has not been studied through the archaeological record other than to ascertain the degree of Russian trade materials introduced into Aleut society (Veltre 1979; McCartney et al. 1990, 1991). The restricted nature of the Russian-Aleut colonization of the Pribilofs later in the 18th century makes these islands ideal for the study of isolated male laborers. As noted above, few, if any, women and children were included in the earliest occupation of St. George or St. Paul. It can be hypothesized that the Russian fur hunters and overseers left on the

Perspectives from Historical Archaeology:

islands to supervise fur seal hunting lived in separate houses from the Aleut laborers and that such a housing distinction should be noted archaeologically through architectural styles, differential deposits of indigenous and Russian-derived goods, and differing faunal and other food remains. Also, the Pribilof Island sites should contrast markedly with contemporary sites in the Aleutian chain, from which men (and their artifacts) were probably missing for long periods, since they were taken on extensive sea mammal hunts away from their villages by Russian fur hunters in the 18th century and by Russian-American Company officials during the 19th century.

Finally, several other interesting archaeological questions could be addressed in the Pribilof Islands. The small Pribilof dwellings stand in dramatic contrast to the houses found at some precontact and early postcontact sites in the eastern Aleutian Islands, which were extremely large (up to 45 m long) and had complex floor plans. These differences might reflect changing social systems and subjugation under Russian rule. Also, at some point in the early 1800s, women and children were brought to St. Paul and St. George, something that may have occurred at certain Pribilof settlements before others. How this is reflected archaeologically would be fundamental to understanding the settlement history of the islands.

Summary

The earliest known archaeological record of the Pribilof Islands is confined to the postcontact period, from 1786 to the 1820s. Except for the continued use of some locales as recreational and hunting camps, most of the first settlements on the islands have been disturbed little since their abandonment in the early 1800s. Our surveys have shown that there is substantial potential for continued historical archaeological research in the Pribilofs, including associated documentary and oral tradition investigations. Such efforts can address important anthropological questions concerning culture contact and change in general and, more specifically, the nature of fur sealing work camps, political developments in the Pribilof Islands (Jones 1980), and the history of the Aleut subsistence economy (Veltre and Veltre 1981). Further, these questions are of interest not only to archaeologists, but also to the Aleut people of today's Pribilof communities, and future site investigations could be integrated with other historical programs to add a further dimension in promoting local cultural heritage.

ACKNOWLEDGMENTS

We would like to thank the TDX Corporation of St. Paul, especially Ron Philemonoff, CEO, for its support of our research on St. Paul in 1994. Several individuals in St. Paul helped make our stay there especially enjoyable; they include Rena Kudrin, Victor Merculief, and Debbie Bourdukovsky. David Cormany of the National Marine Fisheries Service authorized access to the village site at Zapadni, currently located on federal land. Thanks go, too, to the St. George Tanaq Corporation and the St. George Bicentennial Committee cochairpersons, Iliodor Philemonof and Sarah S. Merculief, who generously supported the 1986 research. Finally, we appreciate the field assistance of Kathryn Veltre and Erin McCartney in 1994 and Mary Flanigin in 1986.

REFERENCES

BARTH, TOM F. W.
   1956 Geology and Petrology of the Pribilof Islands, Alaska. *U.S. Geological Survey, Bulletin 1028-F.* Washington, DC.

BROWNE, WILLIAM R.
   1970 Site Survey: Pre-American Village Sites Located on St. Paul and St. George Islands, Alaska. Paper to the Department of Anthropology, University of Alaska, Fairbanks.

BRYAN, ALAN L.
   1966 An Archaeological Reconnaissance of the Pribilof Islands. Manuscript, Office of History and Archaeology, Anchorage, AK.

CLARK, DONALD W.
   1981 Notes, State of Alaska, Office of History and Archaeology, Anchorage.

CROWELL, ARON L.
   1997 *Archaeology and the Capitalist World System: A Study from Russian America.* Plenum, New York, NY.

ELLIOTT, HENRY WOOD
   1881 *The Seal-Islands of Alaska.* Washington, DC.
   1886 *Our Arctic Province, Alaska and the Seal Islands.* C. Scribner's Sons, New York, NY.

FEDOROVA, SVETLANA
  1973 *The Russian Population in Alaska and California, Late 18th Century–1867.* Materials for the Study of Alaska History, No. 4, Richard A. Pierce and Alton S. Donnelly, translators and editors. Limestone Press, Kingston, Ontario, Canada.

FISCUS, CLIFFORD H.
  1978 Northern Fur Seal. In *Marine Mammals of Eastern North Pacific and Arctic Waters*, Delphine Haley, editor, pp. 152–159. Pacific Search Press, Seattle, WA.

FOWLER, CHARLES W.
  1985 Status Review: Northern Fur Seals (*Callorhinus ursinus*) of the Pribilof Islands, Alaska. Manuscript, National Marine Mammal Laboratory, National Marine Fisheries Service, Seattle, WA.

GAY, JAMES THOMAS
  1973 Henry W. Elliott: Crusading Conservationist. *Alaska Journal* 3(4):211–213.

HOPKINS, DAVID M., AND THORNLEIFUR EINARSSON
  1966 Pleistocene Glaciation on St. George, Pribilof Islands. *Science* 152:343–345.

JONES, DOROTHY K.
  1980 A Century of Servitude: Pribilof Aleuts Under U.S. Rule. University Press of America, Lanham.

LANGSDORFF, GEORG HEINRICH VON
  1993 *A Voyage Around the World, 1803–1807.* Alaska History No. 41, Richard A. Pierce, editor; Victoria J. Moessner, translator and annotator. Limestone Press, Kingston, Ontario, Canada.

LANTIS, MARGARET
  1970 The Aleut Social System 1750 to 1810, from Early Historical Sources. In *Ethnohistory in Southwestern Alaska and the Southern Yukon: Method and Content.* Margaret Lantis, editor, pp. 139–301. University of Kentucky Press, Lexington.

LIGHTFOOT, KENT G., THOMAS A. WAKE, AND ANN M. SCHIFF
  1991 The Archaeology and Ethnohistory of Fort Ross, California. *Contributions of the University of California Archaeological Research Facility* No. 49. Archaeological Research Facility, University of California at Berkeley.

LITKE, FREDERIC
  1987 *Voyage Around the World, 1826–1829, Vol. I: To Russian America and Siberia.* Alaska History No. 29, Richard A. Pierce, editor. Limestone Press Kingston, Ontario, Canada.

MCCARTNEY, ALLEN P., AND DOUGLAS W. VELTRE
  1999 Aleutian Island Prehistory: Living in Insular Extremes. *World Archaeology* 30(3):503–515.

MCCARTNEY, ALLEN P., DOUGLAS W. VELTRE, LYDIA T. BLACK, AND JEAN S. AIGNER
  1990 Unalaska Archaeology and History Project: Preliminary Report of Operations, 1989, to the National Science Foundation, the National Endowment for the Humanities, and the National Geographic Society.
  1991 Unalaska Archaeology and History Project: Report of Operations, 1990, to the National Science Foundation, the National Endowment for the Humanities, and the National Geographic Society.

OSWALT, WENDELL H., AND JAMES W. VANSTONE
  1967 *The Ethnoarchaeology of Crow Village, Alaska.* Smithsonian Institution Bureau of American Ethnology Bulletin 199. Washington, DC.

ROKITIANSKY, NICHOLAS I.
  1990 The Reconstruction of Fort Ross, A Unique Russian-American Historic Monument in California. In *Russia in North America*, Richard A. Pierce, editor, pp. 506–518. Limestone Press, Kingston, Ontario, Canada.

SHUBIN, VALERY O.
  1990 Russian Settlements in the Kurile Islands in the 18th and 19th Centuries. In *Russia in North America*, Richard A. Pierce, editor, pp. 425–450. Limestone Press, Kingston, Ontario, Canada.

TIKHMENEV, P. A.
  1979 *A History of the Russian-American Company, Vol. 2: Documents.* Materials for the Study of Alaska History, Richard A. Pierce and Alton S. Donnelly, editors. Limestone Press, Kingston, Ontario, Canada.

TORREY, BARBARA BOYLE
  1978 *Slaves of the Harvest.* TDX Corporation, Anchorage, AK.

U.S. DEPARTMENT OF COMMERCE
  1977 *The Story of the Pribilof Fur Seals.* Washington, DC.

U.S. FEDERAL REGISTER
  1986 *Department of Commerce, North Pacific Fur Seal-Pribilof Island Population; Designation as Depleted.* 51(249):47156–47161.

VELTRE, DOUGLAS W.
  1979 Korovinski: Ethnohistorical Archaeology of an Aleut and Russian Settlement on Atka Island, Alaska. Doctoral Dissertation, Department of Anthropology, University of Connecticut, Storrs.
  1990 Perspectives on Aleut Culture Change During the Russian Period. In *Russian America: The Forgotten Frontier*, B. S. Smith and R. J. Barnett, editors, pp. 175–183. Washington State Historical Society, Tacoma, WA.
  1994 Archaeological Investigation of a Possible Grave Site on St. Paul Island, Alaska. Report to the City of St. Paul, AK.

VELTRE, DOUGLAS W., AND ALLEN P. MCCARTNEY

1994 An Archaeological Survey of the Early Russian and Aleut Settlements of St. Paul Island, Pribilof Islands, Alaska. Report to TDX Corporation, St. Paul, AK.

VELTRE, DOUGLAS W., AND MARY J. VELTRE

1981 A Preliminary Baseline Study of Subsistence Resource Utilization in the Pribilof Islands. Technical Paper No. 57, Alaska Department of Fish and Game, Division of Subsistence.

1986 Early Settlements on St. George Island: An Archaeological Survey of Three Russian Period Sites in the Pribilof Islands, Alaska. Report to Alaska Division of Parks and Outdoor Recreation, Anchorage.

1987 The Northern Fur Seal: A Subsistence and Commercial Resource for Aleuts of the Aleutian and Pribilof Islands, Alaska. *Études/Inuit/Studies* 11(2):51–72.

VENIAMINOV, IVAN

1984 Notes on the Islands of the Unalaska District. L. T. Black and R. H. Geoghegan, translators. Limestone Press, Kingston, Ontario, Canada. Originally published in Russian in 1840.

YARBOROUGH, MICHAEL R.

1986 Archaeological Survey of a Proposed New Runway and an Expansion of the Existing Runway on St. George Island, Alaska. Report to the Alaska Department of Transportation and Public Facilities, Project 56124.

DOUGLAS W. VELTRE
DEPARTMENT OF ANTHROPOLOGY
UNIVERSITY OF ALASKA ANCHORAGE
3211 PROVIDENCE DRIVE
ANCHORAGE, AK 99508

ALLEN P. MCCARTNEY
DEPARTMENT OF ANTHROPOLOGY
UNIVERSITY OF ARKANSAS
330 OLD MAIN
FAYETTEVILLE, AR 72701

www.ingramcontent.com/pod-product-compliance
Lightning Source LLC
Chambersburg PA
CBHW080952120626
46546CB00010B/2868

* 9 7 8 1 9 5 7 4 0 2 5 3 6 *